Preface

I never aspired to write or perform music—I didn't get past fourth grade classical piano, although I do play a mean tambourine—but for as long as I can remember I've been singing along to the songs that have formed the soundtrack to my life. I'm not sure when I first made the distinction between songs from overseas and homegrown music, but I do recall the first time an Australian song transported me to another realm. It was "Cassandra" by Sherbet, and it stood out like an exquisite jewel on my favourite K-Tel album of 1973, *Rock Explosion*. I was eleven years old, and music had become the centre of my world.

Australian songs were already playing in the wider world by then. Slim Dusty, Rolf Harris, The Seekers, The Easybeats and The Bee Gees had made their mark, Olivia Newton-John was a rising star, and soon Sherbet, John Paul Young, Little River Band, AC/DC and Air Supply would hit the international charts. Many have since followed, and this volume is full of songwriters whose music has been successful for some of the above-mentioned acts as well as Men At Work, INXS, Midnight Oil, Icehouse, Crowded House, Silverchair and Savage Garden.

It's impressive to note just how global the stories of our songwriters are. Those who speak here have written for performers as diverse as Cliff Richard, Tina Turner, Michael Jackson, Robert Palmer and Christina Aguilera. And throughout this book the passing parade of co-writers, producers, friends and admirers includes Bob Dylan, Paul Simon, Albert King, David Bowie, Richard Thompson, Elvis Costello, John Oates, Van Dyke Parks and Bono.

But this is not essentially a book about the international success of Australian music. It is a collection of in-depth conversations with songwriters whose work has left an indelible imprint on Australia's cultural landscape. It is an insight into the hearts and minds of some of our greatest musical poets. The forty-five songwriters interviewed here were not all born in Australia and a number of them have chosen to base themselves overseas for most of their careers. Some speak with foreign accents and less than half have made a deliberate effort to write songs that are overtly identified with this great southern land. But something unmistakable connects the writers in this book to each other, an indefinable but palpable creative sensibility that has to do with growing up or settling in a unique and faraway country.

New Zealand songwriters are here, too; all had their greatest successes while based in Australia, and each has created music that is linked in some way to his or her homeland. Sense of place is one of the key points of interest I focused on in my interviews, along with family and peer influences, education, religion, musical inspirations, band politics, collaboration, lyrical subject matter, conceptual ideas of how song ideas arrive and where they arrive from, and pure songwriting mechanics—how a song takes physical shape.

Some songwriters describe intricately how they put music together note by note, some speak of the trigger of inspiration, and others discuss relationships and circumstances that created the environment from which a song could take shape. Most songwriters don't "write" per se. There is hardly any composition in the traditional sense of notation, even for the classically trained. Rolf Harris was a rare exception, and I've now added to my mementos a hastily scribbled sheet of notation for "Tie Me Kangaroo Down, Sport", which he gave me after a demonstration of his own method. Most songwriters use notebooks; some use recording devices to capture their moments of inspiration—although most seem to lose them. Many begin organically, strumming a guitar or playing a chord on the piano; several use no instrument at all. For many the digital age has transformed the writing process, and especially for those songwriters who create songs for other artists to perform, that process involves the ability to create a fully produced studio demo. Steve Kipner calls himself a "record writer" rather than a songwriter. Even those who began in their earliest days simply singing out ideas to their bandmates and bringing a song to life in rehearsal are now engrossed by the possibilities of Pro Tools. Fortunately, whatever the method, the songs continue to come.

A great array of songwriters are interviewed here, but there will always be gaps in such a collection. *Songwriters Speak* is mainly and unashamedly historical in focus. I had been mulling over the idea for some years but it was Ted Mulry's death in early 2001 that gave me the impetus to put it together sooner rather than later. I had already missed out on talking to Peter Allen, Paul Hewson, Marc Hunter, Michael Hutchence and now Mulry; I felt an imperative to record the thoughts, inspirations and anecdotes of our greatest songwriting legends before we lost any more. Sadly, as the book progressed, the health of Slim Dusty deteriorated. I spoke to his wife, Joy McKean, on the telephone one day in September 2003 and she told me, "You're too late, Debbie. You've missed Slim. He won't get better." Slim Dusty passed away the following day. My interview with McKean, a pivotal songwriter in her own right, took place three months later and is imbued with love and longing for her husband, soul mate and musical partner.

But nothing can make up for missing out on talking to Slim. And so the shortage of young, contemporary songwriters here is not out of disrespect for their contributions, but out of a pressing need to record the stories of those who came before them. There are many more stories to be told, and perhaps other volumes like this will follow. It was gratifying to find a publisher who believed in a project of this immensity and trusted that one person with a lifelong passion for song could conduct so many interviews in a relatively short period and elicit such frank and heartfelt responses from some of the most respected musical luminaries of our time.

At the end of four years of interviewing, I was intrigued and at the same time content that no one songwriter could offer the key to songwriting success. Many recognised when one or more of their songs had hit a certain benchmark, and then admitted that they had no idea how they did it but wished they could bottle it. "The best songs are the ones that surprise you. Astonish you," Paul Kelly said. Neil Finn is often baffled by where the initial spark comes from. "I still haven't figured out the smallest aspect of what brings inspiration," he admitted. Part of the allure of speaking to great songwriters is that no matter how many wonderful stories I hear, the enigma of how songs come to be remains unsolved. It means that every new song I listen to contains an enchantment of its own, keeping me enthralled and eager for the next one. I hope that these interviews offer some enlightenment and at the same time help to keep the mystery and the magic in the music alive.

DEBBIE KRUGER
Sydney, April 2005

SONGWRITERS
SPEAK

DEBBIE KRUGER

SONGWRITERS SPEAK

conversations about creating music

Bouley Bay
BOOKS

ISBN: 978-0-6457859-0-6 (paperback)
ISBN: 978-0-6457859-1-3 (ebook)

National Library of Australia Cataloguing-in-Publication data:

Kruger, Debbie.
        Songwriters Speak: conversations about creating music.
        Includes index.
        ISBN 0 9757080 3 1 (previous)
        ISBN 978-0-6457859-0-6 (current)
        1.   Composers – Australian – Interviews.
        2.   Composers – New Zealand – Interviews.
        1.   Title.
        780.922

Published by Bouley Bay Books, Sydney & Jersey (2023)
ABN: 7814 9606 225
www.bouleybaybooks.com

First published by Limelight Press (2005)
Original ISBN: 0 9757080 3 1
Designed by Melanie Feddersen, i2i design
Author photo by Bob King

To my father, Lou Kruger, 1924–2004,
who sang to me the first songs I ever heard.

Foreword

When this book was originally published in 2005, it was the first in-depth study of Australasian songwriters, and the first time several of the people I interviewed felt they had been taken seriously, considered as more than just rock or pop stars whose spotlights had faded. The book arrived in an era between some artists' hit-making years and their later resurgence on the "legacy" touring scene. Before certain bands reunited, before some went on to stage farewell tours. And, for others, before their lives took unexpected turns, glorious or tragic, that elevated their songwriting to new heights. In light of those evolutions, as well as the subsequent deaths of six of the songwriters here, I believe these interviews stand as meaningful historical testaments to the times they were conducted and unique perspectives on what came before and what was to come later.

For this reason – that it is a work of historical worth – I have chosen to retain the chapter on one songwriter who has since been found guilty of abhorrent crimes, incarcerated and discredited. For some readers his inclusion in a new printing might be offensive, and to them I say, please just skip that chapter. He wrote songs that were and arguably still are a significant part of Australia's cultural landscape, and the interview was illuminating. I stand by his work and my work as the interviewer in the context of this book.

Many times over the past 18 years I was asked if I would do a second volume of *Songwriters Speak*, featuring younger, newer talents. I was always more interested in filling the gaps in this volume, speaking to other iconic songwriters with decades of work in their catalogues, who were not included in the first publication for reasons beyond my control. An enlarged edition nearly happened a few times, but mostly my own life just got in the way. People who missed out on reading the book contacted me throughout those years asking if it could at least be republished as it was. So for finally getting *Songwriters Speak* back into circulation, I thank my friend of nearly 40 years, Mick Le Moignan, who has revived the title through his publishing company, Bouley Bay Books and, with the assistance of Roger Haubrich at Image DTO, retained the format, design and spirit of my original publisher, Limelight Press.

When Limelight's founders dissolved their company and moved on to other endeavours two years after *Songwriters Speak* was published, there were 500 copies left from the original print run ready for potential readers. Sadly those books were mistakenly destroyed by the distributor, putting the title prematurely out of print. The copy you have in your hand is one of a limited edition printing to replace those 500 copies, and if you are reading the eBook, I am glad that this work has at last caught up with the ways of the 21st century. Either way, thank you for getting yourself a copy!

DEBBIE KRUGER
Sydney, April 2023

Contents

Acknowledgements

It took many years of loving and living music to understand that the point of it all to me was the way the music was composed. It then took several years of interviewing songwriters overseas to realise that my calling was to look closely at the work of the great popular music composers of my home country. Once I committed myself to doing this book, it took four years of networking, researching, interviewing and writing. While I had no research assistant, transcribed the hundreds of hours of tapes myself, and spent way too much time ignoring my dog, Morgan, while hidden away in my home office, there were also many people without whose support I could not have brought this project to life.

First, to my warm, wise, wonderful agent Rachel Skinner, and to the great Rick Raftos for putting Rachel and me together, a thousand thanks. My appreciation also goes to Jayne Denshire and Helen Bateman at Limelight Press for their commitment to publishing this book and the care they have taken with every aspect of it.

To my sagacious soul mate and sometime sparring partner, Paul Zollo, for changing my life with his incredible book, *Songwriters on Songwriting*, and for always being there to explain, guide, debate and commiserate—thankyou with all my heart Paul, it's been quite a journey.

I am deeply indebted to Norm Lurie for being the first to encourage me and urge me to take my concept to reality, and for being a most ardent advocate throughout.

To all the songwriters who took the time to share their stories with me, welcoming me into their homes and studios, I am eternally grateful. I am especially beholden to those songwriters whose support and actions tangibly furthered the progress of this book through endorsements and referrals, namely Graeme Connors, John Farrar, Andrew Farriss, Graeham Goble and Glenn Shorrock.

Jo Shorrock championed my cause with great gusto and I thank her for her munificent spirit and invaluable help in making things happen. Special thanks also to Lyn Connors and family for tropical hospitality and use of the ute.

I humbly thank my generous and brilliant friends Henry Diltz, John Elliott, Bob King, Andrew Murray and Keith Saunders for their photography. It is an honour to have their pictures in the same book as my words.

Thanks to my trusty gang of Killara High friends, who lived the music with me in the early years, shared their old vinyl collections with me for research purposes in later years, who know me too well and stick with me anyway, most especially Peter Dixon, James Fulton and Andrew Stutchbury.

Thanks to other close friends and allies who listened, advised and helped in different and important ways, especially Jon "Ando" Anderson, Michael Bald, Lynden Barber, Jeffrey Bartolomei, Gina Block, Tania Buffin, Tracy Cahn, Ricky Dukes, Justin Fleming, Adrian Franulovich, Les Fremder, Wayne Harrison, Wayne McCardell, Mandy Maier, Blake Murdoch, Amber Rees, Gill Robert, Bill Townsend, Barbi Von, Gerry Williams and Karena and Peter Wynn-Moylan.

In Melbourne: Richard Conrad, Kaori Hamamoto, Vanessa Brown and Bob Evans—thanks for looking after me during all those interview trips down south.

In England: Cyndy, Michael, Ginny and Nicola Bloom, Ros and Paul Davis, Robert Sedar and Danielle Lockwood—thanks for making the long haul such a joy.

In California: Eric Alatorre, Melissa Algaze, Ned Doheny, Paul Fischer, Tim Krol, Sharon Larisey, Stefanie Michaels, June Mikrut, Russ and Julie Paris, Erin Warner, Paul Zollo and especially the inimitable Henry Diltz—thanks for housing me, feeding me, sharing music with me, and always welcoming me back to the fold.

Thanks to the music publishers, record company people, artist managers, publicists, personal assistants, industry executives, journalists and music buffs who helped me with contacts, lyrics permissions, recordings, information and encouragement. In particular the following organisations: ABC Music, J Albert & Son, BMG Music Publishing, Canetoad Records, EMI Music Australia, EMI Music Publishing Australia, Festival Music, Festival Mushroom Records, Hal Leonard Australia, Jacobsen Entertainment, Matthews Music, Liberation Music, Mushroom Music, Music Sales, Mute Records, Origin Music, Rough Cut Music, Shock, Sony Music Australia, Sony/ATV Music Publishing, The Sound Vault, Undercover Music, Universal Music Publishing, W Minc Productions, Warner Music, Warner Chappell and Westside Talent. And these individuals: Bob Aird, Amanda Alexander, John Anderson, Glenn A Baker, Skip Beaumont-Edmonds, Arlene Brookes, Catherine Burgess, Emmanuel Candi, Nash Chambers, Arif Chowdry, Natalie Corkill, Janet Dawes, David Edwards, Christie Eliezer, Bernadette Faddoul, Peter Green, Karen Hamilton, Thomas Heymann, Peter Hebbes, Ruby Hunter, Ian James, Peter Karpin, Joe Kimpton, Sue Konon, Judy Kopperman, Pat Lake-Smith, Valerie McIver, Dean McLachlan, Phil Manning, Philip Mortlock, David Nichols, Annie Phillips, Julie Reilly, Fifa Riccobono, Michael Roberts, Petra Sitsky, Grant Thomas, Phil Tripp, Keith Welsh, Rachel Willis and Bernard Zuel.

And the final thankyou goes to my mother and sister, Lisa Kruger and Paula Kruger.

JOY McKEAN

SYDNEY, AUSTRALIA, DECEMBER 2003

It's a long way from Nulla Nulla Creek, the Hunter Valley or the countless outback towns travelled to over the years by Slim Dusty and his wife Joy McKean. In a leafy, exclusive suburb of Sydney, in a quiet neighbourhood street, the couple's home was a hive of activity on the day I visited. The gardens were being tended to, Dusty's producer, Rod Coe, was dashing in and out of the house and adjacent studio to discuss and work on production for Slim's new album, and the phone never stopped ringing. Something was missing, of course. Slim himself. It was less than three months since his funeral, since the deluge of tributes had been spoken and written on the passing of Australia's greatest bush poet since Henry Lawson and Banjo Paterson. McKean, as always, was getting on with business, and business for many years, particularly since co-writing her husband's autobiography, was talking about Slim. Talking about herself was more unusual; spending several hours in such talk was remarkable.

While Slim Dusty was best known for novelty songs like "A Pub with No Beer" and "Duncan", and most lauded for writing and singing ballads about the landscape he loved and the ordinary Australians whose characters moved him, at the hub of his career success was the stream of songs provided for him by McKean. Songs that heralded the start of a successful vocation singing trucking songs, such as "Lights on the Hill". Songs that got to the heart of Slim's spirit in the way even he could not have revealed, such as "The Biggest Disappointment". Sometimes Slim was so busy representing the other ordinary Australians out there that it was left up to Joy to represent Slim in song.

Joy McKean was born on 14 January 1930 in Singleton, New South Wales. Her schoolteacher father moved the family around the Hunter Valley for some years, but just before turning five, McKean was afflicted with polio. She spent long periods in a Sydney hospital, separated from her family, until they moved to the city to be closer to her. When she went home with them, it was to a house full of music; her parents were learning Hawaiian guitar, had also bought a ukulele, and Joy's mother showed her eldest daughter "how to strum on the piano". By 1940 the family was back in the country, this time in Yanderra, near Mittagong. Influenced by the records of Jimmie Rodgers, the Carter Family and yodeller Harry Torrani, McKean started playing steel guitar, singing, yodelling and writing songs. Sister Heather followed in her path, playing, singing and yodelling, but Joy was the only McKean to take to songwriting.

In the early to mid-1940s, the McKean family lived in the Murwillumbah area of northern New South Wales, and there Joy got the inspiration to write her Tweed Valley songs, recorded by the McKean Sisters when they moved back to Sydney, based in Granville. From their first local talent quest to top billing at dances and concerts, the duo were in great demand. Joy abandoned university studies for a full-time career in music and radio, and then in 1950 she met Slim.

Dusty was born David Gordon Kirkpatrick on 13 June 1927 in Kempsey, New South Wales and grew up on his family farm in Nulla Nulla Creek. On the death of his father he took over the running of the farm, and although he had been writing songs since the age of ten, he was almost resigned to a pastoral life. But from his first recording contract in 1946, to his death while recording his 107th album in 2003, Slim Dusty was first and foremost a song man. And an Australian legend, beside whom, for more than half a century, stood McKean.

McKean's history in music is so closely tied to her family history that sitting in her kitchen eating Aunty Una's butter cake, just before Christmas in 2003, was like connecting with a time in the 1930s. Back then, the young Joy, recovering from polio, would spend her weekends with Una and her two sisters, their big radio, their fashionable friends and their flashy cars. Her endurance during her illness's recurrence, and her resilience as she moved in and out of hospitals and new family homes, gave her a strength and courage that she carried with her during the decades of touring remote regional areas with Slim Dusty's travelling show, driving trucks and caravans on dark, wet, winding roads, raising and educating their children Anne and David, co-founding the Country Music Association of Australia and its associated College, and writing songs that a male Australian icon could proudly sing. That resilience also brought her to this day in the kitchen, shortly after Slim's death, recounting their years as songwriters and performers with tenderness, inescapable grief and endless distractions, as the business of running Slim Dusty Enterprises never once came to a pause.

McKean is not one to stop and reflect on her standing as Australia's first woman songwriter of note. She has spent most of her life building, managing and reflecting on Slim's career. As this interview was originally intended to be with both Dusty and McKean, I asked questions about both, but the biggest joy from Joy was to hear her personal stories and that hearty laugh, which punctuated nearly every recollection of a truly happy life in music.

It's well known that the first song Slim wrote was "The Way the Cowboy Dies" when he was ten. Do you remember the first song that you wrote?
I only remember about one line from it and it sounds dreadful. Something like, "Dear mother, standing at the door." That's about all I can remember.

Did you write it on the steel guitar or the ukulele?
Steel guitar probably. I don't remember it vividly. I may have even just composed it without an instrument.

Were you writing down your songs on paper?
That very first song I wrote when I was about nine, I didn't write that one down. By the time we moved up to Cudgera near Murwillumbah, I know I wrote down the words of the songs I wrote up there. I remember that. And I would have used the guitar then because at that time we did a lot of singing. Heather and I together sang at the church socials and the school dances and things like that. And wartime fundraising.

Was being a young girl writing songs an unusual thing? Did you know other girls your age who were writing songs?
No, but it was just something I did. I began writing a bit more then, but we were singing mostly popular country songs and yodelling. Dad went into the army, and we came back to Sydney and shared the aunties' home. It was a big, old, double-storey house at Granville, one of the first houses built there. And I was still writing songs. Many of them were based on where we were living up in the Tweed Valley.

You were missing it? It's very lush up there in the Tweed.
Mmm, beautiful. One was "The Gymkhana Yodel" because from where we lived on Church Hill you could look straight down on the showground, and we used to watch all the gymkhanas down there. And also for the shows or anything, Heather and I discovered we could go through the cemetery, down through a fence and to the showground.

Songs like "The Valley Where the Frangipanis Grow" were gentle, picturesque, feminine kind of songs.

Yes. And then I had yodelling ones like "Yodel Down the Valley". Most of them were very cowboy-oriented, as well as being like the Tweed Valley.

You were writing these from a situation in Granville. Was it that you had to look outwards and back to where you'd come from?
Outwards and back, but also to what you're listening to at the time in music as it influences you, and using your imagination. You're not writing about situations from real life then. If you listen to the Tweed Valley ones, it's about the Tweed Valley, about being there or travelling to it or from it, that sort of thing, the life you had there. In Sydney, after I'd left high school and when we were recording, there was a huge amount of activity with country music concerts. There was a huge boom. Tim McNamara had this really big radio show, we had ours, there was something else going on 2CH, and there were a lot of country music artists. You could go to a country music concert in some suburb of Sydney every week.

You went to university for a while; did Slim ever lament the lack of an extensive formal education?
He regretted it.

Did he feel it ever limited his lyric writing?
I don't know, because Slim wrote from real life. Situations, what he knew, what he saw. Although he had a very limited formal education, he started reading a lot of Lawson and Paterson, although he wasn't a reader as such. But so far as music and poetry was concerned, he would read more poetry than I would. And I think that his music was always very direct. He didn't feel the need for a huge vocabulary or an educated vocabulary. He used words that just said it.

He would also take an existing lyric, whether it was Lawson or a contemporary lyricist, and put his music to it. Did the music side come more easily to Slim than the words?
It wasn't a case of that so much, as Slim used to write nearly all of his own songs up to a certain stage. Then when we started travelling the outback and also when we started finding these lyrics from other people, once he did a couple of them it started a flood of these lyrics coming in. So actually it short-circuited a lot of Slim's writing. He used to think, "Now that is a lyric that's really telling a person's life—I'll set that to music". He concentrated on finding the stuff and setting it to music rather than writing it himself. And I think we probably missed out on quite a bit that way.

But he was open. Rather than being a blinkered songwriter who said, "No I will only write about what I see and it has to be my experience", he wanted to take in it all.
He wanted everything. He said, "Those words are coming from people that are living the lives that they're writing about". And they were so genuine, so gritty. Someone said—I've forgotten who wrote it—that sometimes you'd think that a lot of these rough poets and balladeers were just waiting for someone like Slim to come along and find them, and sing their songs.

When you and Slim first got to know each other, did you have discussions about songwriting, putting songs together? Or was it an unspoken understanding that it was simply something you both knew how to do?
We didn't discuss it as a big deal. It's just that we would sing each other a song. We all did. In those days it was very open. Often people used to come in on a night during the week. Heather might be there, or some of our other friends. All were singing each other the songs we'd just written. So Slim and I knew what the other one was writing and what we were doing. It was never a discussion about techniques of songwriting. This is what I find very different now. Everybody says, "Right, now there's a hook, and we're going to write a song about that." To me, that is totally foreign. And to me and to Slim, we would never ever discuss techniques or how we should write it or what you did about lyrics or what you did about a song. It was a natural thing that you did if you were going to write a song.

So for you, songwriting is a very unselfconscious, natural thing. You don't analyse it.
You don't analyse it, but I have gone in specifically to write a particular song. I did that with "Walk a Country Mile". They wanted to do an album to come out the same time as the book, and I thought, we really need to have a song of that title, "Walk a Country Mile". It was a saying we'd always heard. But it's a natural thing, I can't analyse it. "Kelly's Offsider", I know I woke up at two o'clock in the morning and I had the first verse or the first two verses and the tune in my head. Because I'd been thinking about it for a long time. And it generally is that I'm thinking about things for a while.

What did you like about Slim's songs when you first heard them?
They were fresh, they were different, like "Stay Away from Me". I hadn't heard "Rain Tumbles" when I first met him. The first time I ever heard a Slim Dusty song, we were doing a concert, we were out at either Penrith or Windsor, somewhere like that, and there was a girl there called Pauline Cowper, she was a tall sort of a rough girl, long, fair hair, she had a black hat, dressed all in black with black leather chaps and she stands up there, she plays guitar, she's just like a man. And I said, "What's that song? Where did you get that?" She said, "It's a Slim Dusty song." I said, "Who's he?"

And what was the song?
I think it was either "Stay Away from Me" or "Why Worry Now".

Was Slim as serious about his songwriting when you first met as you were?
He was, because he'd been writing since he was a kid. That was one of the things that, more so than the performing, we had in common, that we were both so keen on.

You don't analyse songwriting, but you must have an idea of what the important ingredients are in a song. So when you sit down to write, what are the essentials?
Well, I look for a hook. And the idea, if I've got an idea for a song. But it doesn't always

happen that way. I started writing a truck song and it ended up as "The Biggest Disappointment". A song will sometimes just take over and go in a different direction to what you've planned.

So you'll always follow the way the song is going rather than try and consciously guide it?
Yeah, because you may start on some lyrics, and there might be something in there which catches your interest or fits better, and that'll take you off on a totally different tangent.

Does the lyric usually guide you?
I try and get a bit of a lyric to begin with but I like also to get just a first line of music. If the words and the music fit together then I can go on from there. And then once I've got a melody set, too, I can fit the lyrics in as well. I generally try and write the two together.

On the guitar?
Piano. Only vamping, I'm not a good pianist. Banging out the chords to sing to. Otherwise on guitar.

How important is rhyming?
I think it's important.

Have you written anything that doesn't rhyme?
I've only used a tag, like in "Ringer from the Top End"—that doesn't rhyme—at the end of a verse. But that is just a style of a song. That last line, "I'm a ringer from the Top End", doesn't rhyme with anything. But it's a statement that goes right through the song.

But you always felt lyrically that rhyming would move a song forward?
I prefer rhyming. Even if you do it a different way, like the internal rhyming sometimes.

"When the Rain Tumbles Down in July" was a classic case of Slim writing down what he saw, and his songs were usually simple yarns or descriptive scenarios, often standing on the outside, observing. But were all of Slim's songs personal to him?
He could put himself in the place, or in that person's shoes. There's one he wrote called "Gum Trees by the Roadway, Willows by the Creek". Now that is a description really of the Nulla, and a story about a soldier returning from war, although he wrote that sitting on a stump in the moonlight outside our caravan at a little place called Marlborough near Rockhampton in Queensland. I think he would have looked back at all the farm boys coming back from the war, and that probably was a personal issue.

Did a song need to have a personal resonance for him to sing it convincingly, or was he just happy to sing a good song even if he felt the subject matter wasn't a part of him?
It depends on what he thought was a good song and why he thought it was a good song. He'd been in all those situations or he had known people like that, so you could say he had a personal relationship to it in one way. Coming from the farm and from the country, and travelling in the country with us so close to people, talking to them after the shows, talking to them in the small towns, so that no matter what lyrics there were, it was something he would know about.

So something like "Pub with No Beer"—
He just thought that was funny. He didn't get emotional at all about being in a situation of a song. He could understand what that song was about and he could project that, that was one of his strengths. "The Pub" he thought was the funniest thing he'd ever heard.

What did you think of it?
I laughed. [*Laughs*] I thought it was funny, too.

Could you ever have imagined that it would become the biggest song of his career?
No, because it was impossible for us to think, during a rock 'n' roll era, that any country song would even pierce the veneer of the city radio stations. So no, we had no idea.

Can you tell me about the writing of "Lights on the Hill"? For a woman to write Australia's first trucking song, to write a song about dying at the wheel of a truck, it's pretty bizarre.
Yeah, but you see, I'd been travelling in the big truck very often and I'd been driving a caravan in the most horrific conditions you can imagine. We had to. And with caravans they can slither and slide and they can pull you into the gutter of the dirt roads and all that sort of thing.
   The first trip that Aunty Una came on with me, she came up and joined me at Nyngan. I was trying to teach David correspondence school as well, and we were moving every day. If I was working at night, I couldn't leave him in a caravan park. Aunty Una came to help me out. She ended up staying for eight years. But that first trip we went from Nyngan, we were going out through Hillston, Ivanhoe, we were heading for Wilcannia. And wet greasy roads. The first trip she's in the car with me, and David's in the back, pouring rain, and the road was, as we say, greasy as a pork chop. And we're sliding around. She hopped out, pulled some branches off things, shoved them under wheels. We got out of there, we kept going and got up over the next little tiny bit of a rise, and there were the blokes all bogged! [*Laughs*]

So "Lights on the Hill", then, it was literally a dark, rainy night?
Yes. We were to pick up the rest of the show in Queensland. I was driving the car and caravan on my own. Between Armidale and Guyra, there's a stretch of road called the Devil's Pinch. And it is a dreadful drop down this side, very nasty. I had to keep myself awake to start with, because it was dark and raining. It was raining as I went up the

Moonbi Range above Tamworth. Slim and Barry were ahead of me and I couldn't even see them. So anyway, I started writing the song; I think it was the rhythm of the windscreen wipers, and the engine, and everything, and I've always been interested in the marriage of words and music. I always feel the two have to really fit together if they're going to tell the story. And that's how I began writing it. By the time I got into the Devil's Pinch I thought, "Gee whiz, if I went over there I wonder how long it'd be before anybody found me." It was really quite scary.

Now, the main problem for me is I can't use a clutch with that leg. [*Shows polio-affected leg in caliper.*] I can only drive an automatic. And this was in 1970 or '71. I used the accelerator, the brake, and then the dimmer switch was on the floor. It was not on the column. So every time you're going up over mountains, up and down, you've got your brights on, because it's a dark, rainy night, and I see lights coming at me, I've got to take my foot off the accelerator, off the brake and use the dimmer switch, and then get back over onto the accelerator. And I'm pulling a heavy caravan, as well, on the small car. When the trucks came over, they'd come over that bit of a rise. I couldn't really see, and I tried to get back onto the dimmer switch so that I could see again.

I got up to Warwick at about ten o'clock at night, Slim was unhooking the big van, and I said to him, "I wrote a song on the way." He said, "Oh good, do you want to just put it down on a cassette?" I got inside, that's just what I did, I pulled out the cassette and I sang the song onto this little cassette. So that was that, I thought no more about it. We did the tour, and six months later we came back down to Metung, to our little house there, for Christmas. I'd invited some of the Hamilton County Bluegrass Band to come and spend a few days with us. And that included Colleen Trenwith, the fiddle player. I said to Slim, "Where's that cassette?" If Slim wanted a cassette for something, he'd just pull it out, use it, fine! You know? So in amongst his cassettes I pulled it out, and I said, "You've wiped it off!" "Oh," he said, "Oh, you can write it again." So they all went fishing, and I got down on Mum's old piano, which I've got down at Metung, and I rewrote the bridge and the last part of it.

But you remembered the verses?
Yes. The first verse, I think, and the second part of the verse, that was still on there.

Did that teach you a lesson about writing down the lyrics or putting the tapes away?
It taught me a lesson about never letting Slim get his hands on any cassette of anything that I had written and which I didn't want to lose or have wrecked! It taught me a lifelong lesson. [*Laughs*] And he laughed about it.

You were talking about the marriage between the lyrics and the music. It was certainly unusual to have such a bright, happy melody, all major chords, telling a story of someone dying behind the wheel of a truck on a rainy night.
I didn't look at it as being a happy melody. I looked at it totally as a rhythm thing. And it was the rhythm of the words being the rhythm of the engine and the motor and the windscreen wipers. That's what the words were supposed to exemplify. Not the actual melody.

20

Until the end, when the accident does happen, the listener doesn't know that that's the direction it's going in. So it has this twist, but it still stays happy.
Too right!

That was quite a turning point for both of you, wasn't it?
Mmm. He took notice of my writing well and truly after that.

Was it a song that you thought deserved to be a bigger hit than other songs you'd written to that point? Were you surprised by its success?
I hadn't thought in terms of hits. There were songs that were popular with audiences. I had written "Ghosts of the Golden Mile" and things like that that were very popular and played a lot. This one was just another surprise. But I did want him to try singing that song, because Slim was capable of a lot more than what he thought he was. He had a remarkable voice. He could sing bass; if Anne was singing some bluegrass or something, Slim would sing the bass line. And then, when he was singing something like "Cattle Camp Crooner", he was singing really high tenor on some of the notes. If he wanted to, he had this remarkable range. And I used to write songs knowing he had that range from there on. Like "Biggest Disappointment". Also, I wanted him to record "Lights on the Hill" because I thought it was good. I like Cajun music, I like the rhythms. I could hear Colleen playing Cajun rhythm behind that, and that's what really drove me to try and push him into it. And it was Colleen and the rest of the band that talked him into it.

There was some resistance on his part because it had too many words. What was your point in writing the lyrics that way?
The words had to go with that rhythm. If you tried to use that rhythm without that number of words, you'd lose the feel of it altogether. Because you bend the note as you're singing it to fit with the rhythm. And that did herald a big change for Slim, because after that he was more open to trying things differently. It also opened a field in trucking songs for him. There had been a trucking scene in the States apparently. And then John Minson said to me, "You realise you've written the first successful Australian trucking song. You must have known there was a big trucking scene." And I said, "Well I didn't." Because we were very isolated.

But you'd been driving past trucks for years.
Yeah. But we didn't know there was a big truck music scene. Because when you're on tour like that ten months of the year, you're very isolated. Also in earlier days, it wasn't usual to have radios in the car where you could tune in when you're travelling in the outback to try and get hold of radio stations that might play country music. You wouldn't know where they were or anything else as you were trying to move around. So you didn't hear a lot that was going on. That's why we developed in our own way. And then I come back and I'm told I've written the song to fit into the trucking scene that I didn't know existed.

You said "The Biggest Disappointment" started as a trucking song. What was the original concept for it?

A boy hitching a ride in a truck. And it absolutely changed from there.

It turned into Slim's life story?

Mmm. [*Nods*]

Why did Slim think that was your best song?

I think he felt that the melody and the style of it were good. He did say to me once, "I think that's the best song," but he never told me why.

But did he think that he was a disappointment in his family?

Mmm.

All the time? Even until he grew old?

Not till he grew old. I think his mother finally realised that he was doing what he wanted and he was happy. And I think in her own way she became proud of him. I know his remaining sister, Kathleen, is very proud of him. But when he was growing up, it was that kid from up the Nulla tearing around the countryside doing this and doing that, not settling down to life on the farm. Though he'd been left the farm to run at the age of seventeen, which is a bit rough for any kid.

And I guess he felt that losing his father was like losing his greatest supporter. Did he feel that had his father lived, he might not have felt like a disappointment because he had that support?

That support, yes. He felt he was doing the wrong thing by his mother and all the rest of it, but he was just so single-minded. Music was Slim's reason for living, really. He had a strange background, a hard background in that way, and his father was his supporter because his father loved music.

Did you make a deliberate decision to put your own career and profile on the backburner and concentrate on Slim's career, writing specifically for him?

It happened of its own accord because marrying Slim, we did concerts together in Sydney where Heather and I performed together, but when we went on tour that broke up the partnership, because Heather stayed in Sydney and she kept running the radio program, we kept sending tapes back on our big old Ferrograph, sent them back to the radio show. But then when Heather married later, she and Reg, her husband, also went on tour. So for many years we were never in the same town together. It was the end of the McKean Sisters performing or recording for years.

Did you miss it?

Oh I did, yes. I missed that. But I think it did slew me a lot more towards songwriting.

Solo performing, I never felt confident enough to sing my own songs on stage most of the time. Not until recent years, and I have become more confident about that and now it's expected of me.

Some of the songs you had been writing for the McKean Sisters had titles with a feminine slant, like "Ribbons on My Guitar", "Prairie Love Knot" and "My Darling White Rose". Did you miss that connection with the female side of songwriting when you started writing primarily for Slim?
No. In later years, in the seventies, there's one song, "Old Aunt Eliza". And then there was "Wind Up Gramophone". They were more feminine-style songs. Slim always meant to record "Old Aunt Eliza". Anne did it, and then a singer from Victoria did it, someone else has too, I think. And he always said, "That's a good song, I should record that. I will one day." And never did.

Nope, I didn't miss any of that. See, those were more feminine songs I suppose because that was the style of the song and I was writing for Heather and me. Later, I began writing some songs I didn't know who was going to record them, and then I wrote consciously for Slim. You have to remember, too, that I was living a lifestyle where I was mostly working with men. My father always treated me like an elder son more than a daughter. I was generally with Slim when he was with all his mates, and so I picked up the masculine side of language and outlook. I was living the same hard life as he was or anyone else, and it toughens you up in that respect.

Did it then come naturally for you to put yourself in the place of a male protagonist in the songs you were writing?
Not always. Some of those songs are quite general, like "Who Wants Moss?". "Top Springs" is about that brawl at Top Springs; that was just factual. No, it meant that I could understand a lot of the male outlook on things, more so than perhaps some women could. And yet for some years in the show we had families travelling with us as well but I had to learn to try and keep all those people together and off each other's throats if they were with you for ten months. You've got to do all those things and it doesn't make always for a soft feminine style.

You were definitely the first important female songwriter in Australia and you weren't writing typical female songs. You were just writing about your life.
Yes. I just wrote. And if something upset you, sometimes I'd have a say like "Clean Up Your Own Backyard" and that sort of thing. I've written a lot of very different styles of songs. Different things need different treatments, and I enjoy that. I wrote one, "I've Been Seen and Done That", when I thought I might be losing my sight. I didn't know very much about glaucoma, and they had discovered a blind spot here. At the time they were just doing investigations to make sure it wasn't a tumour or anything like that, so it was all rather scary. And that's when I wrote that particular song. About all the beautiful things there are that I've seen, I was glad I'd seen them. And I am. I've seen some wonderful,

beautiful things around this country. Australia's a beautiful country. I wish that more people would write about it and about the people, actually, and then sing it with an Australian accent.

I'd like to run past you a few comments people have made about Slim and his music, and get your response, both from your point of view and how Slim would have seen himself. He's been called "a modern day Banjo Paterson or modern day Henry Lawson" – a bard.
No. He admired Paterson, he loved Lawson's poetry, and he never ever thought of himself in that category.

"He will be equally as important a historian as any Manning Clark."
I think that is probably fairly accurate because when you listen to his body of work or a selection of it, it traces the development of country music in Australia over all those years, but also it does trace the change in people's attitudes, the change in culture, in people's ideas and everything like that. It is. It's a musical history of Australia.

Your songs are a part of that history.
Yes, and I did a lot of the collecting and the finding of stuff for him.

"A unique conveyor of the Australian idiom."
[*Chuckles*] Yes. You should hear him in full flow sometimes; you could get quite a good flow of it too. Because he was just an everyday Australian. He was a lot quieter in some ways than many people would have thought that he would be, but he knew how an ordinary Australian talked because he was one.

As the years went on and other songwriters were writing for Slim, and you got very busy in industry business, what compelled you to keep writing?
Slim's gentle boot in the backside! He used to get on my back and say, "You've got to get out of that office and get back onto your writing!" And it was true. I did mostly keep writing because of Slim's encouragement. A lot of people have said to me now, "I hope you're going to keep on writing." So many people have said that. Possibly I will but I don't know when. I really don't know when.

As you grew older and weren't travelling as far and wide, did that make it harder to come up with ideas for songs, because you were stuck in an office a lot of the time and more based in the city? Was inspiration more elusive?
I suppose it would have been. Mostly because it's difficult to switch off from a heavy morning in the office and the computer and then try and be creative. For a while I tried to stay out of the office on a Friday and do a bit of writing. There seemed to be so many other things that had to be done then, so that went by the wayside after a while. After we did the trip across the Nullarbor in the big trucks, I said, "Look, if you want some songs out of this I need to go away for a few days." So I did, I went right up to

Currumbin Palms, where we stay when we're working at Twin Towns, and I just took the guitar and a little cassette recorder and I wrote three songs. Because I had the material and I had come straight back from this trip which was real inspiration. But it is harder here. I don't know why I wrote the story of Top Springs, for instance. We used to go out to a lot of things and that's why I wrote "Ringer from the Top End", being up at Carlton Hill Station. Then "Who Wants Moss?" came from something a friend said to me years ago. There's still a lot of things to write about. A lot of things to think about. I'm not so much into writing love songs. I'd rather write something that says something or is just a real good song to sing.

You've preferred to mainly write on your own, separately from Slim, haven't you?
Yes. I prefer to write on my own, and funnily enough, we both usually used to not talk too much about the song until we had it just about finished.

Did the process of writing a song change for you at all over the years? Is it still a very organic process of sitting at the piano or picking up the guitar?
It's still a very disorganised, impulsive sort of thing, except if Slim had to have a song for an album or something, then that's the only time I'd really say, okay. He did encourage me. In the early days he did not, he didn't want to know about my writing that much. And yet he recorded quite a lot of them over the years. After "Lights on the Hill" and a lot of people started talking about my writing, Father took another look, I suppose.

Did Slim have favourite songs that he had written?
"Rain Tumbles" was his favourite.

Did he have a favourite written for him by someone else?
I think he liked "Looking Forward Looking Back" by Don Walker. He liked "Camooweal"—the old Mack Cormack wrote the lyrics and Slim set them to music. There were a lot of good songs. One bush balladeer wrote "When the Currawongs Come Down", Ernie Constance. There was Tony Brooks, Tom Oliver, Joe Daly, all of them have written such good lyrics.

What about you? Do you have a favourite song that you've written?
Some of the not so well-known ones possibly. "Sweet Rain" and "Nulla Creek". "Lights on the Hill" I'm always happy with. "Old Aunt Eliza" and "Wind Up Gramophone", they're special to me because they're childhood memories, they're pictures, both of them. "Aunt Eliza" is a picture of my grandfather's sister. And "Wind Up Gramophone" is really the story of building my great-grandfather's farm—he and his family of girls and boys built their slab farmhouse—and the way it is with all those old farmhouses, they're modernised and forgotten.

Do you believe songwriting is a gift, a god-given talent, or do you think anyone can write a song?
Anyone can write a song but whether it's a good one or not is the difference. And whether a song has enough heart in it, that's a different thing too. There are books on songwriting

and so you can craft a song, I suppose. I have never read or used them. Neither had Slim. I have always steered clear of invitations to hold songwriting workshops, simply because I do not feel qualified to tell other people "how to write a song". I don't know myself! That is the truth. I am always intimidated by the factual approach to songwriting; it just doesn't work for me.

I think most of the really good songs or great songs are a given thing. A gift. And if, as some people have done, you can marry that with the craft and the songwriting techniques, then you come up with the great ones.

ROLF HARRIS

BRAY, ENGLAND, MAY 2004

There is a yearning, a hunger even, that one might think Rolf Harris sated many years ago. At the age of 74, he could be resting on his laurels. Just resting on anything, the nearest couch perhaps, after a long, productive life in showbusiness. But having celebrated his career golden jubilee with a concert at London's Albert Hall in 2003, Harris was as busy as ever the following year. Two television series kept his schedule full enough—one on animals, the other on art—and music remained at the heart of his existence, songwriting still a compelling pursuit. Even though, to his constant dismay, the kinds of songs he enjoyed writing the most were least likely, in his view, to find an audience, he was full of ideas that inevitably ended up being set to music.

The songs closest to Harris's heart, those that he feels most emotionally aligned to, are patriotic hymns to his homeland or odes to people who influenced and touched him. One song, an Irish folk ballad for his friend and mentor Jack Neary, was never recorded because those close to Harris responded with, "Oh rubbish, nobody wants that sort of thing." They want, evidently, endless performances of "Tie Me Kangaroo Down, Sport", "Jake the Peg" and "Sun Arise"—which, certainly, Harris is immensely proud of—or novel cover versions of songs that are so far from what is normally associated with Rolf Harris that he has uncanny hits with them, such as Led Zeppelin's "Stairway to Heaven."

The success of "Stairway" inspired Rolf's rock phase in the 1990s, with an album (*Rolf Rules, OK?*) of covers featuring the likes of "Walk on the Wild Side", "Satisfaction" and "I Feel Good" and then, after a succession of triumphant appearances at the hard-core Glastonbury Festival, a witty version of Queen's "Bohemian Rhapsody" just for good measure. This and other unexpected chapters in Harris's career are often instigated by Bruce Harris, Rolf's brother and manager, who has a knack for identifying where the perennial star can find new outlets for his talents. Nostalgia with a Rolf flavour works.

But Rolf is a man who works hard in the present and plans way into the future. He was born in Perth on 30 March 1930 and as a junior swimming champion and aspiring artist and musician, his career might have taken any direction. Art led him to London, where he studied painting and entertained rowdy audiences at the Down Under Club to support himself. "Tie Me Kangaroo Down, Sport" was the result of needing new material to satisfy the relentlessly ravenous audiences who loved good choruses and funny verses, and the song changed Harris's life forever. Juggling his music career with television programs (children's entertainment, wildlife, variety), pantomime, world touring and families in England and Australia, Harris became a living legend, a persona both mocked (as evidenced in a famous episode of *The Goodies*) and revered. As old as Rolf gets, he will always be the homely, ingenuous fellow with the wobble board singing songs that are at once reminiscent and timeless.

Meanwhile, his love for art never waned, and wherever possible painting or drawing was incorporated into his television and stage entertainment. To his own amazement—and Rolf is often amazed by the twists, turns and good fortune in his life—he is now showing his paintings in major exhibitions and his works are sold for small fortunes.

I visited the Harris residence, on the Thames River in picturesque Bray, just a week after Rolf had been in Amsterdam filming an episode of *Rolf on Art* that had him painting a self-portrait in the style of Rembrandt. He was tired; away from the spotlight in the privacy of his home, it seemed age could indeed weary him. But the unmistakable sparkle in his eyes was there, and the unstoppable performer in him entertained throughout the interview. He would break out into song, slapping his knee, clicking his fingers, delivering entire songs to illustrate a small point. He cried occasionally, laughed a lot, was passionate, angry, joyous and generous with his memories.

I began by commenting on the influence his work has had on some of Australia's songwriters, mentioning that INXS's Andrew Farriss had referred to Harris as having made a major impression on him in his childhood. Harris related a charming story about an encounter he'd had with another of the Farriss brothers.

"I met Tim on a plane. I was sitting there and he came up and crouched down beside me. He said, 'You won't know me but my name's Tim Farriss.' I said, 'Oh, from INXS? You're kidding!' He said, 'Yes.' I said, 'Good grief, how exciting.'

"And he said, 'Well, I just saw you sitting there and I had to talk to you because you've been my hero all my life. So much so that when our son was born I wanted to call him Rol Farriss. And my wife point-blank refused. She wouldn't do it.' And he said, 'Thank goodness she did talk me out of it because it would have been a terrible weight on the poor kid's life.'

"But isn't that incredible? And he said, 'I just had to get your autograph.' He crouched in the aisle alongside my seat and I can't believe it even now," recounted Harris, self-effacing as always.

Have you thought of yourself as a songwriter, or have you considered yourself more generically, as an entertainer?
The songwriting's a huge part. I must have written about a thousand songs, most of which hardly ever see the light of day because they're so weird and off the wall in most directions. I wrote one called "Come to the Sydney Opera House", which I thought was going to be a dramatic, huge thing with big orchestra and trumpets. [*Sings*] "Come to the Sydney Opera House, it's unique in the world ..." Dum dum, talking about the roof, "Like sails unfurled ..." Put it out on record and sold one copy, I think, to me. It was a disaster.

I did the first concert there in the Concert Hall, and I had worked towards that with my mentor in the showbusiness field in Australia, a wonderful man named Jack Neary. I wrote that song especially for that opening concert. I don't think anybody in Australia is interested in songs like, for example, "New York, New York" or "Chicago". It's like, how embarrassing to sing about Sydney or the Opera House!

And yet if it's patriotically nationalistic like "I Still Call Australia Home", then it's huge.
That was wonderful, yeah. But that's not exactly the same thing. Like the Americans would love to write a song about Chattanooga or a song about Kalamazoo. We were happy to sing "On the road to Gundagai" way back when, but since then I don't think Australians care.

I wrote a song called "Back to WA", a really nice one; it was a very nostalgic and very personal song about my home. It goes [*Sings*]:

> I wanna go back to WA, back to WA
> That's the only place for me
> I've been to Indonesia and I've seen Hong Kong
> Took the tourist bus to Europe and I sort of tagged along
> But all those fancy places, well they're hardly worth a song
> When you could live in WA.
>
> The tiny little town that I was born in
> Hardly changed a scrap through the years
> One main street coming and going out
> And in the pub they still serve ice-cold beers
> And old Mr Meacham runs the corner shop

> If anything happened to him well the world would sort of stop
> He smokes this big old pipe and everybody calls him Pop
> I want to go back to WA
>
> I want to go back to WA, back to WA ...

And would anybody play it? They wouldn't play it anywhere except in Perth. Nobody in Sydney would play it, nobody in Melbourne. But they would play "Surf City USA" or they would play "Ohio Mama" or some thing which has got nothing to do with Australia. But would they play my song? "It's too parochial," they said. Too parochial! What's that supposed to mean?

I've written another one which everybody I talk to about it, they say, "Oh God, nobody wants songs like that." It was a song about Jack Neary. He was telling me that he had gone to Ireland for the first time when he was in his late sixties. He and his wife went because his granddad was from Ireland, and he used to sit with his granddad up in Lismore where he grew up, and the old man used to sing him all these songs about Ireland. And the song went [*Sings*]:

> All of my childhood I'd sit with my granddad
> He told me such tales of the land of his birth
> And as I grew older I'd sing the songs with him
> His songs full of old memories of Ireland.
>
> And when he went from us I made him a promise
> I swore in my heart I would go back one day
> And now as I fly o'er the seven wide seas
> I pray I may love it as he did.
>
> He'd say, "Go back home Neary. Go back home
> See my green fields of Ireland
> You take my dream John, I'll never have the chance, John
> You make the trip for me back home."
>
> Now as I stand in the hut he was born in
> I picture his feet on that bare earthen floor
> I hear such a clamour of brothers and sisters
> All striving to grow tall here in Ireland.
>
> I've picked up one stone from the path by the thorn tree
> And I'll keep it close till the day that I die
> I've kept you my promise my dear, dear old man
> But I've other voices that call me. That call me ...

They say, "Come back home, Neary, come back home
Home is here in Australia
Fulfil your dreams John and not someone else's dreams John
Come to the place you love, come home."

"Come back home Neary, come back home
Home lies here in Australia
Here where our fathers started to build a new life
Come to the land you love, come home."

Then that last bit repeats in a new key with huge orchestral and choir build-up to a marvellous monumental ending. Everybody says, "Oh Jesus, nobody wants sentimental crap like that." And it upsets me because I think that could be as important to people in a similar way as "I Still Call Australia Home", because every second person in Australia has a grandparent who came from Poland or from Germany or from Malta. It will ring such a bell to people.

But if you don't record it, how can you know that it won't affect a lot of people?
Well I'm fighting opinion, really. I will do it one day. I want to do it with Eulean pipes, the wonderful Irish pipes, at the beginning and I want maybe a ghostly voice talking in Gaelic at the very beginning. "I have this dream, John. I pass it on to you, John. You make the trip for me back home."

Are you still writing now?
Yeah! I'll think, "Oh, that's a good idea, why don't we do that?" The only reason I write the songs is so that I can perform them. I write them with the end view in mind of me on stage doing it.

Writing songs was originally a means to an end when you were entertaining cabaret audiences in London, supporting yourself as an art student.
Well, that's how "Tie Me Kangaroo Down" started really, but everything else I sang at that club was like "Wild Colonial Boy", all the songs that everybody remembered. "Waltzing Matilda" and songs from Aussie.

At that time art was really your main passion. Did the two art forms—painting and writing songs—infuse each other? Do they to this day?
When I'm painting I cannot bear to have any music anywhere in my surroundings 'cause I want to concentrate. Music while I'm painting is a definite no.

But can you come up with a musical idea or an idea for a song when you're painting?
No. You're so engrossed in the painting.

When you're working on a song, do you ever see it as a picture?
[*Laughs*] No, no, no. Wait a minute, that's not quite true. You sometimes get ideas of how you would illustrate it if you had to do an illustration for the cover of the sheet music book. That gives you an idea of how far back in the past I'm still running, when I talk about an illustration for the cover of the sheet music. Does that exist any more, sheet music? First one I ever got was "In the Mood". Glen Miller.

The wobble board is a tangible manifestation of the two vocations merging for you—art and music intrinsically linked. Every time you use the wobble board you remember that it all started from a painting.
Yes, that's right.

Your classic line when you are creating an artwork for an audience is, "Can you tell what it is yet?" Can that also apply to writing a song for you? Do you discover what the song is as you go, or is the subject and structure always determined when you embark on it?
I'm a very literal sort of a guy, I don't do free-thinking lines where I just let them roll and the ideas come out and I put down the words. I plan it as a poem first and it's all rhyming patterns and I see it as a very ordered structure.

So the subject matter is already set. A song about the Opera House. A song about Jack Neary.
Yes.

Do you write the lyrics first?
They quite often develop at the same time, tune and words.

Do you write the tune on an instrument? Are you playing around on the piano or guitar?
I just write it on paper. I've got a special method of writing music, which is sort of a shorthand. I'll get a bit of paper and show you. I write everything in my mind in the key of C; then you don't have to have any sharps and flats in it. Let's use "Kangaroo" for example. [*Starts writing notation*] So it's [*Sings*] "G C E D C A D". So I write that down and put the time values on it. "G C E"—and that's tied over to another E there. "G"—and those are quavers—"G C E D C"—and a bar line—"A" as a half note—"D" another half note—"G B D F A"—so it's a quarter note, eighth note, two eighth notes tied together, another eighth note, a quarter note there.

I had this idea together with a schoolteacher in Canada, who sadly called it "Instant Music", and so I took up the title and I published a book about Instant Music when I came back to England. And of course to the musical establishment the word "instant" is a total anathema. So they really jumped on it and destroyed it.

When you write your Instant Music do you then give it to your musical director and he'll actually chart it?
No, it's just for notation when I'm travelling. Then I write it all out properly.

Do all your songs, including your new songs, get written out like this? First in the Instant Music and then properly notated?
Yep. I had a very good training as a kid; when I was nine I started learning piano at a convent in my home town of Bassendean. I learned from Sister Mary Magdalene and I really learned well, learned all my notation, and I was really good at theory and musical perception and all that.

Has that helped you with your songwriting?
Tremendously, yeah. I see guys that I'm working with sometimes that come into it without any background and they're really hard-pressed to know what you're talking about.

How do you feel about the term "novelty song"?
I think it's a put-down for a start. I think all songs work or they don't work, and to classify them one way or another, it's crazy. I dislike the term.

It's always used to describe a kind of song that isn't perceived as a serious work, yet often it's the novelty songs in our popular music history, whether it's "Tie Me Kangaroo Down, Sport" or "The Pub with No Beer," or "Shaddap You Face", that have been the biggest hits.
Unusual songs, coming from a different viewpoint, coming from a different direction, coming from a different angle. The interesting story about the recording of "Kangaroo" is that the guys who were doing the backing for it when I first recorded it were singing it with broad American accents. And I said, "Oh jeepers, why would you say 'sporrrrt' with a big 'r' in the middle of it?" They said, "Well, that's the way everybody sings." And I said, "Well, not with this one, this is an Australian song." And they said, "Well, you'll never sell any records if you don't have an American accent on it." I said, "Look, just sing it the way you talk. Four Western Australian blokes, just sing it the way you actually speak. Don't try and be somebody else, don't do a false, phoney accent." And they said, "Well, it's your mistake. You'll never sell any records."

I have vivid memories of seeing you actively involved in debates on TV, on *Sound Unlimited* industry forums, about singing accents, fighting for the preservation of an Australian sound.
Well, just being yourself. I remember the guy said, "Okay, what do you want to sing—'bonza beauty Bluey'?" And I said, "Well, no, you don't have to be stupid, but just say the words in your own accent. Why do we have to pretend to be Yanks with everything we write?"

Do you think, then, that Australian songwriters who sing their songs with American accents are writing American songs?
Why would you write songs about something that you know nothing about? Why would you pretend to be Americans? There's a million real Americans over there.

What if they're writing love songs, which are universal, but they just happen to sing with that American twang?
Yeah, but isn't it sad? And yet I think the reason they do it, and I can understand this,

the reason they do an American accent is because the Australian ethos says, you wouldn't say "I love you, I honestly love you" to a girl. You'd rather have your head boiled in oil, because the blokes might think you're a weirdo or something. You'd rather be seen to say, "Listen desert head, I'll be home at twenty past seven, have the meal ready otherwise you're in bloody trouble. I'm gonna stay with the guys and have a few more beers."

I had been afraid to cry all my life, embarrassed to cry, until I was in my sixties. And I suddenly thought, it's the greatest release of tension in the world and I've been saddled with this thing, this "Australian men don't cry" rubbish. Gene Pitney was in a television program that I was on, singing a song where he was saying, "I cried over you" or something. And I was acutely and physically and personally embarrassed to have this grown man sitting next to me on the couch talking about this song and actually confessing that he cried over a girl. I was in my thirties then, I suppose, and it embarrassed the living daylights out of me. And this is what we are stuck with in Australia and this is why we cannot sing a love song in our own accent, because we would feel so stupid.

There are exceptions to that. John Williamson, whose ballads and bush songs, like "Cootamundra Wattle"—
John Williamson, yes. "Cootamundra Wattle" is an amazing song! But I went to see John doing cabaret in Kings Cross when he had this huge hit with "Old Man Emu". I was in Sydney and I found out he was performing, I'd never met him. He did "Old Man Emu" because that was his big hit, and then every other song he sang was with a broad American accent. I went up to him afterwards and said, "Why are you doing it in American?" He said, "Because everybody expects it." And I said, "But there's your hit! This is the thing that you killed them with! And is there any American accent in 'Old Man Emu'? There isn't. And you killed the whole of Australia with it; they were clamouring over themselves to buy it. Why would you do American accent stuff?" I really had a go at him. But I'm happy to say he went on to do all his own stuff in his own way, in his own voice. And it was brilliant.

Can you recount the process of transforming the traditional Jamaican song "Hold 'Em Joe" into "Tie Me Kangaroo Down, Sport"?
I was working at the Down Under Club in London looking for songs that I could use with a chorus that everybody could sing and would know. Like "Waltzing Matilda", "Botany Bay" and "The Wild Colonial Boy", everything that I could possibly think of that was Australian, I would do. My cousin was out from Sydney, cousin Halcyon, Pixie O'Harris's daughter. I went round to her place and there was an album on the turntable, brand new album, in the mid-fifties this was. Harry Belafonte. And going through there's one, "Hold 'Em Joe" [Sings] "Hold 'em Joe, hold 'em Joe, hold 'em Joe but don't let 'em go/ Me donkey want water, hold 'em Joe, me donkey want water/ Don't tie me donkey down there, let 'im bray, let 'im bray/ Don't tie me donkey down there, let 'im bray, let 'im bray."

And I thought, wow, what a great rhythm. And what a great song for the club! We'll get everybody singing the chorus, we'll make it Australian—instead of donkey I'll put kangaroo.

And I tried it and of course there's one syllable too many. [*Sings*] "Tie me kangaroo down there"—oh, damn. Doesn't fit. But I couldn't get it out of my mind. So I worked out what the rhythm of that was and the tune just jumped out of mid-air; it was handed to me on a plate from some powers that be up in the sky. And then I thought the word "there" was so gutless for such a strong beat, so we could make it [*Sings*] "Tie me kangaroo down, mate." No. [*Sings*] "Tie me kangaroo down, sport." That'll do. It took that long. Then I started thinking of all the names of all the animals, and all the comedy fellas' names. And Bluey and Curly jumped into my mind straightaway from the comic strip.

So I just kept writing verses and there were about a dozen verses when I first started. Like [*Sings*] "Brush me bunyip's back teeth, Keith, brush me bunyip's back teeth/ Or I'll call for the police Keith"—you know, it had things like that, police sung with a lisp as in poleith to rhyme with Keith. [*Sings*] "Let me grey dingo go, Dig, Let me grey Dingo go/ He can't stand all this snow, Dig." And a voice from the background says, "Poor old coot's gone delirious. That's not snow, that's his dandruff!" [*Sings*] "All together now, Tie me kangaroo down, sport ..."

My brother was over on business in London for a year. He came down to the club, and I gave him a lift home in the car afterwards, and he said, "You know, you need some structure in that. Come upstairs and we'll get a bit of paper." So I went up to his room in the hotel, and he said, "Look, why don't you start it off like the old stockman lay dying ... [*Sings*] 'A saddle supporting his head/ Around him the blowflies were flying/ And these were the last words he said.' Something like that. So you have a picture in your mind as to what it's all about."

And it also gives a legend sort of feel to it.
Yeah. So that's where "There's an old Australian stockman, lying, dying" came from, it came from that song, "The Dying Stockman". And then he said, "You need a joke ending, you need some sort of a tag at the end." "So we tanned his hide when he died, Clyde/ And that's it hanging on the shed"—like it was a wonderful joke. It was his idea. And a macabre joke, which is the essence of what Australian outback life is like. You work for ten years to build up a flock of sheep and then there's a drought for three years and they all die. Now unless you can laugh at this, you go and blow your brains out. And that's the sort of comedy that I was trying to get. The acceptance of the disaster as matter-of-fact. Make a joke out of it and get through somehow.

Do you ever reflect on the impact and the legacy of "Tie Me Kangaroo Down, Sport" on Australian culture and on the world?
I don't really think about it too much, I just take it for granted in a way. It's interesting that when it first came out, everybody's reaction in Australia was, "We don't talk like that at all! Good lord!" And the next day they knew all the words. It just fell out of their mouths and they didn't know how they knew them, but they knew every word of the songs. Because it was exactly how they spoke.

The wobble board is your trademark sound. Has it ever guided you through the writing of a song, with a rhythm perhaps suggesting an idea, a melody, even a lyric?

I have it in my head as a very strong rhythmic sound. I think in advance, "The wobble board would go very well there." I certainly construct songs with that in my head, really. But I don't stand there with the board playing it.

The "deedle eedle eedle um" in "Jake the Peg" sounds like it might have been a verbalisation of the wobble board. Or was it already in Frank Roosen's version of the song?

Yeah, that was his. He sang it to me and I was just trying to imitate his Dutch accent. I've had people say, "What a dreadful Jewish accent. Why would you do a fake Jewish accent like that?" And I try to explain it, "No wonder it's dreadful, it's supposed to be Dutch."

How did you come to write "Sun Arise" with Harry Butler?

When I went back to Perth in 1960 when I had the big hit with "Tie Me Kangaroo Down, Sport", I met up with Harry again, and he'd been a friend from the time I was about sixteen. All of a sudden here I was producing children's programs and being the presenter five days a week, half an hour a day, and I enrolled him as a naturalist, talking about different things, snakes, spiders, this, that and the other. He was wonderful. He was fascinated with Aboriginal things and was playing these tape recordings that he'd made out in the desert country, and I heard the didgeridoo for the first time on a tape recording. Bowled me over, I just loved it, and I loved the flatness of the Aboriginal voice and the sound of the beating sticks. There were three elements. One really low [*Imitates didgeridoo*] and then the voice somewhere [*Imitates Aboriginal singing*], very flat and nasal that said Australia to me, and then another element right up there, which is the beating sticks going *bing bing bing*. And not one of them fought with the other sound. You could hear all three because they were so disparate, so far apart.

I said, "What would these songs be about?" And he said, "Well, they're songs about for example, the sun, they're singing to the sun and they imagine the sun as a young goddess getting up in the morning and donning the skirts of light." And I said, "Oh Christ, that's marvellous." So that's how it all started. Got the didgeridoo going in my mind with the wonderful 12/8 rhythm.

The thing was, I first recorded it exactly as the Aboriginals would have sung it. Which was repetitious, over and over again forever and ever and a day, going through the same tune. I got a professor of music, a guy called Trevor Jones, to record the didgeridoo for me on it. And we put it out in Australia and sold nothing at all. Not a copy. Terrible. Disaster. But when I came back to England I took this along with all the other recordings that I'd done in Australia, took it straight to EMI, they said, "We'll send you along to see George Martin." Never heard of George Martin. But I discovered later that he was the one they sent any weirdies to. Anybody odd, not the run-of-the-mill singer that sings ordinary songs, the off-the-wall type blokes.

So I went to George Martin and he heard "Sun Arise" and he said, "Yeah, it's boring." My hackles went up and I said, "But that's authentic. That's exactly how they sing, the

repetition becomes mesmerising and they get into a trance-like state singing the song."
And he said, "Yeah, I know. Tell me about it. It's boring. Let me put it this way. You could take 'An Eriskay Love Lilt' from the Outer Hebrides and you could record it in the original Gaelic, and you might sell 107 copies to enthusiasts. Or you could write English lyrics to it and call it 'A Scottish Soldier' and you could sell over a million copies with the same tune. What do you want to do? Do you want to sell 107 copies or would you like to sell a few more?"

He said, "Why don't you go home, have a listen to it, see if you can write a middle bit that takes you away from that boring section which you now know backwards." A middle-eight, it's called a release, which is exactly what it does, it releases you from the boredom of the repetitious first bit, and then you can come back to that first bit and then everybody knows it and loves it, it's like an old friend, you know it. Ahh, we're back to a bit we know. "And see if you can write a special ending to it. But keep the same feel." So I went back and I thought, he might bloody be right, you know. So that's when I wrote [*Sings*]:

> Sun arise, come with the dawning,
> Sun arise, she come every day.
> Sun arise, bring in the morning,
> Sun arise, every, every, every, every, day

Back to the bit they know—

> She drive away the darkness, every day
> Every day, drive away the darkness,
> Bringing back the warmth to the ground

And then the final bit—

> Sun arise, oh, oh,
> Sun arise, oh, oh,
> Spreading all the light all around

"Sun Arise" has had a few covers, including Alice Cooper. What did you make of that?
I loved it. He turned the rhythm round and did it in a different way. It was wonderful. It was very flattering.

Did George Martin influence you in any other ways with your writing?
No, I don't think he did. I would come up with things and he would be stunned and amazed and say, "Okay, we'll try that."

So then you were good preparation for him with the Beatles.
Yes, well, I was working with him from 1962 roughly, and suddenly in '64 he had no time. 'Cause those guys came along.

Are you still in touch with him?

Yeah. He's a lovely man. And he made a wonderful speech at my seventieth birthday; he was very complimentary.

"Fijian Girl" was more complex musically than many of your previous songs, particularly with the time changes.

"Fijian Girl" had a disastrous recording history. Because it was written for a little extended play record, to be handed out to people on the inaugural BOAC flight, which gives you an idea how long ago that was. It was taking in a whole lot of new places—Fiji and Hawaii and San Francisco and London. So I had to write a song for each of those things. I'd heard a Russian song called "Bells across the Meadow" with a great Russian choir. And that melody just resonated with me. So I borrowed that initial few bars and built on that. It was a very complex rhythmic thing that I created, because it was in 4/4 to start with, and then in the next verse it goes into a 6/8 feel. But the quavers, the eighth notes, are exactly the same length as the eighth notes in the 4/4 verse. So instead of being in 4/4 they go into 12/8.

I wrote the poem bit, "Fijian girl undulating by, how could you improve a Suva mover", I thought it was a great line, and then I thought, how am I going to get that into the rhythm? And then that will change the rhythm. A fellow called Philip Green was doing the orchestrations for all the songs that I had written for this little extended play, and I'd written it all out accurately, I'd written quaver equals quaver throughout. Eighth note equals eighth note. Against the metronome it's exactly the same length, even in the 6/8 bits and the 4/4 bits, the eighth notes are identical lengths. Because it was so tricky to explain to anybody. I handed him my perfectly written out manuscript music, and I said, "Now it's important that—" And he said, "Listen, young man!" He said it from a great height, looking down his nose at me, old experienced bloke to young upstart whippersnapper. "I've been writing orchestrations for music all my life and I know what I'm doing, so don't try and tell me my job." And I backed off.

So when he turned up with the recording it was all wrong. He'd written it all in 4/4 and he'd changed the length of the quavers. A total botch. And I said, "I can't record it." He said, "You have to record it. It's got to go in to be pressed this week." I did it with very bad grace and it was awful. So at my first available opportunity I re-recorded it with somebody else who could play it right. A man called Ronnie Hazelhurst, who was a BBC composer/conductor who'd worked on a lot of my shows. And he did an absolutely amazing recording.

The Islander influence is also there in "Hurry Home", a song where you wrote English lyrics for an existing Maori song. Did you have any input into the orchestration arrangements on that, even with some sketchy ideas?

No, I didn't. Somebody else did that for me, and I've often thought I could have done that better. There's a young girl, Hayley Westenra, who's done "Pōkarekare Ana" just recently, she had a huge hit with it here in this country. And I thought, I must get my lyrics over to her and perhaps she could record my lyrics for it some time. The reason I wrote English lyrics was I was working in the Blue Angel in New York and I had a bunch of guys from

Epic Records come along on opening night. I'd just had the big hit for them with "Tie Me Kangaroo Down, Sport". Somebody shouted out, "Sing a New Zealand song!" and I went, "Well the only one I know is ..." So on the accordion on my own, I just went [*Sings*]: "Pōkarekare ana/ ngā wai o Waiapu/ Whiti atu koe hine ..." which I'd sung at the Down Under Club. "Marino ana e/ E hine e/ hoki mai ra/ Ka mate ahau/ I te aroha e." They all went "Yeah!" and one of the guys from Epic Records said, "That is beautiful. Why don't you write some English words to that and record that?" So I got in touch with the New Zealand embassy, or whatever it is there, and said, "What's it all about?" They said it was from Rotorua, the lake of troubled waters and that whole thing. I constructed all the English words to that.

I liked the fact that you wanted to be very authentic. You could have written any lyrics to that melody if you'd chosen to. But you actually went to the trouble to find out what's the essence of this song.
Yes. Talking about authenticity, there was an interesting thing about "Fijian Girl". I was going to call it "Hawaiian Girl" originally. I had no lyrics; I just had the tune going in my mind. I was in Vancouver doing cabaret, and I met an Australian guy who came backstage to see me afterwards. I had a drink with him. "What do you do?" And he said, "Oh, I've just come back from Fiji, I've been school teaching there for three years." And I said, "Oh really? Tell me some things, 'cause I'm writing a song, and it was going to be about Hawaii, but Fiji would fit rhythmically as well. Tell me, I need some facts." So he told me about the sulus, the garment the girls wear which is wrapped around them. And he told me about the Kandavu bird, which is like a parakeet. The best line in that is [*Sings*]: "Kandavu birds fly, a million waterfalls high." Isn't that lovely? It's just a lovely line. But he gave me all the facts and things about Fiji. And I started writing the lyrics then and there.

Arranging existing songs has always been a great strength of yours. What makes an existing song or lyric appealing for you?
How can you ever say? Either the song grabs you or it doesn't. Something like "Pub with No Beer", it was just perfect, it was the first Australian song to hit England and have success here, even before "Tie Me Kangaroo Down, Sport" did. And it was just so basic, you know. It was just perfect, it was totally at ease and it just told a story.

I read a great article about rock festivals in London's *The Telegraph* newspaper, where the journalist said his favourite Glastonbury moment was when you came on one year and did "Two Little Boys" and left not a dry eye in the audience. That to me spoke volumes about the power of a great song. Does it matter to you that a song you are well known and loved for is one that somebody else wrote?
No. I knew from the moment I heard it that it was going to be stunning and sensational. When Ted Egan was singing it to me I was thinking, what an awful song this is, how embarrassing, what am I going to say to him? Because he's such a nice bloke. And this dreadful namby-pamby thing, [*Sings*] "Two little boys had two little toys/ Each had a wooden horse ..." And

where it got to the bit where it's almost the same as the original words but not quite—[*Sings*] "Did you think I would leave you dying ..." The back of my neck and my scalp went, like somebody walked over my grave. And I thought, oh! The other little boy, grown up, saying it to the previous one, who'd said, "Did you think I would leave you crying?" Now it's the other kid saying, "Did you think I would leave you dying?" Ohhhh! Tears. Wonderful. Powerful song.

Do you get quite emotional each time you sing it?
Yes, I do still. Sure. Can't quite sing sometimes. Get the huge closing of the throat.

I found it amazing that when you agreed to record a version of "Stairway to Heaven" you didn't want to hear the original Led Zeppelin song.
I'd never heard *of* it.

What do you think has made Led Zeppelin's "Stairway" the ultimate classic that it is?
I don't know, it's just a piece of brilliant music and it's so gently done. It's not blasting your head off. It's gently performed and it's a great melody. I changed the melody for mine. But what they said to me was, "We want to get the definitive Rolf Harris version. We want wobble board, didgeridoo, 'altogether now' chorus, whatever you think says 'Rolf Harris', do it." So that's what I did. I did it to order.

Did you ever get any feedback from Robert Plant and Jimmy Page?
No, but they came along to one of my shows when I was working at Dingwalls in Camden Town, a huge gig, and someone told me afterwards that Plant and Page had been in the audience and they enjoyed the song, which was the second-last song on the gig anyway. And then they went. And I wish they'd stayed and said hello 'cause I'd love to have met them.

After your success with "Stairway", you recorded a bunch of Rolf-style covers of classic rock songs on your *Rolf Rules OK!* album. Were you aware of any of them before the project?
Not really, no. "Smoke on the Water" I didn't have a clue. And I actually got the lyrics wrong. Because they were all in Geneva doing a recording, and this big fire broke out, which is what the song was all about. And they say, "Swiss time was running out." I couldn't hear it, so I recorded "switch time" 'cause I thought it was some musical recording term that I didn't know about. "Switch time was running out." And it was "Swiss time" because they're in Geneva, of course. You find that out years later.

I thought your version of "I Feel Good" was quite inspired.
I was so scared of that one. They were all hard work to get an angle, to get my own handle on it, to make it mine, to impress it with something to do with me.

Did you feel you succeeded in all cases?
In a lot of them, yeah. Things like [*Sings to melody of "Walk on the Wild Side"*] "Doo doo doo doo doo, Didgeridoo doo doo doo doo ..."

Do you have a favourite song of your own?

I'd be hard-pressed to choose between them. I'll tell you what's a good song, have a listen to it some time if you can. It goes [*Sings*]: "Yarrabangee, Yarrabangee, everybody needs Yarrabangee/ Yarrabangee, Yarrabangee, everybody's gone to Yarrabangee." Yeah, "Yarrabangee" was a great song.

What has music, and particularly writing your own songs, given you that you know life as a visual artist alone could not have provided?

It's just a constant accompaniment in my head for everything I do. I can wander along and sing songs and do bits and pieces of songs as I go. I'm forever whistling stuff, walking around the place singing. Without whistling, I would be lost.

BRUCE WOODLEY

MELBOURNE, AUSTRALIA, FEBRUARY 2004

He's best known as a member of Australia's renowned and beloved folk-pop quartet, The Seekers. But he knows himself best as the author of one of Australia's most loved anthems, a catchy song of patriotic fervour that is taught to schoolchildren and used in television advertising campaigns. Life for Bruce Woodley is divided into two distinct phases—before "I Am Australian" and after "I Am Australian".

Before was phenomenal international success with The Seekers, some remarkable co-writing adventures with the likes of Paul Simon and Tom Paxton, and explorations into Australian folk music, both traditional and original. After was a journey that Woodley has described as "obsessive", trying to comprehend the power of the song he had written and find new and innovative commercial applications for it. All the while The Seekers re-formed for reunion tours and albums, new songs would be written and non-musical ventures would be embarked on. But Woodley's life was forever changed by the song he sent off into the world in 1987 without expectations, and all these years later, in his cosy Melbourne home, he seemed both blessed and unsettled by its conquests.

Woodley was born in Melbourne on 25 July 1942. Growing up on a musical diet of Rodgers and Hammerstein, Lerner and Loewe and their ilk, he then soaked up the pop songs of the day from the radio and started frequenting Melbourne's folk clubs. He met Athol Guy, Keith Potger and Judith Durham, who shared an interest in folk and gospel singing, and they started The Seekers. They recorded an album containing songs as traditional as "Waltzing Matilda" and in 1964 took a working holiday on a Sitmar cruise ship. Their planned short visit to the UK turned into a four-year whirlwind of pop stardom, once songwriter and producer Tom Springfield teamed up with them and gave them songs like "I'll Never Find Another You", "A World of Our Own", "The Carnival Is Over" and the infectious "Georgy Girl". Their fame also spread to the US, where they performed on the *Ed Sullivan Show*.

Not content with merely performing other writers' songs or rearranging traditionals, Woodley started honing his own songwriting skills. It didn't hurt that Paul Simon took an interest in him; their co-written "Red Rubber Ball" was recorded by The Seekers but had even more exposure when recorded by US group The Cyrkle in 1966. Woodley spent much of his time in London and New York immersing himself in the constantly evolving, thriving music scene, sitting in on a mixing session of Simon & Garfunkel's *Bridge Over Troubled Water*, hearing Joni Mitchell preview "Chelsea Morning" and "Both Sides Now" on the piano in a friend's living room in Holland Park, befriending Graham Nash while he was still in The Hollies. "I guess over my life so far it's been a rich tapestry of people. As distinct from purely being an Australian songwriter, I've definitely spread myself around," Woodley said with a measure of understatement.

After The Seekers split up in 1968, he returned to Australia and began composing songs for himself and other artists, co-writing with Hans Poulsen on hits like "Boom Sha La La Lo" and "Monte and Me". He worked in advertising, devising campaigns and writing jingles, and then The Seekers re-formed with a new lead singer, Louisa Wisseling. Woodley penned the group's 1975 hit "The Sparrow Song" to relaunch them. In the midst of glam rock, bubble gum, pop and disco, Australia fell in love with a song that began, "Fly little sparrow high above the clouds/ Looking for a place to lay your weary body down."

The song foreshadowed greater things to come. A line such as "I seek a land of far horizons/ Of gentle winds and summer rain" was just a wingspan away from the sweeping topography of "I Am Australian" and its description of hot desert winds, droughts and floods. Childhood innocence, voices from the past, the environment, reconciliation and celebration of diverse cultures—quite a melange of ideas in one song. While he had help on the lyrics from Dobe Newton of The Bushwackers, Woodley proudly wears "I Am Australian" as his personal badge of honour.

As the song took on an iconic life of its own, it was back to business with The Seekers. Durham returned to the fold and in 1993 the Silver Jubilee tour and compilation album were great triumphs. But as the twentieth century came to a close, Woodley became preoccupied with where "I Am Australian" might still take him. "It was much more than a song to me," he confessed. He worked on a book, *I Am Australian—The Illustrated Song*, for schools.

No publisher has yet taken it on. He recorded a concept album that has yet to be released. "The whole basis of it is a complete stage event. From first song to last it's meant to be a sequence of music with narration and audio-visual that would be an 'I Am Australian' event." He has also rewritten the song's lyrics for a version especially to be sung on ANZAC Day.

"I spent four years with a group of people trying to develop some ideas along these lines and it fell in a heap because it was just too hard. It obsessed me for a while, but I always knew the idea behind it was far bigger than the song."

So he backed off, poured his finances, time and energy into building a plush resort in Bali, and took some time out from songwriting. But while the desire may have receded, the seeds of new songs are growing still. Woodley believes songwriters are born, not made, in which case he will never shake off the mantle.

When did you first pick up a guitar?
When I was twelve or thirteen. I'm left-handed, but I couldn't get a left-handed guitar, so I had to learn to play right-handed, which has never really suited me. I've never been able to play particularly fast, right-handed, because all the speed's in the left arm. That's why I gravitated to playing more finger-style guitar.

Did you have any lessons?
A few, just some early days with some chords and things like that, but no, basically, whatever I know, I've taught myself.

So you never learned music theory?
Did some. But it all seemed too logical for me. I was never all that interested in playing other people's music, and written music always bored me to tears. Even though I spent a lot of years in recording studios. I use chord charts. If I need something really fancy played off a written part, I hire someone to do it. That's not what I was ever good at; I was never going to be an instrumentalist and I never wanted to be.

When did you start making up your own tunes?
It would have been fifteen, sixteen, just messing around. I had nothing in mind, really. I can remember thinking of tunes that came into my head, but I never did anything with them.

When did you write your first real song?
It would have been when I went to England with The Seekers. We recorded some albums before we went to England, but it was all traditional stuff, there was no thought of doing anything original.

And yet you hadn't been interested in playing other people's songs.
I was talking about written music. Whatever I am, either left or right brain, I'm not into logical things at all. Or anything that's remotely mathematical.

Which is why, in The Seekers, you started doing your own arrangements of traditional songs pretty much straightaway?
Correct. I used to sing in restaurants to make a few extra dollars from my pathetic income at the time, where I was working for Clemenger Advertising. I was the mailroom guy; I struggled. I played in a jug band for a while for fun with some friends in Melbourne, and I got to know some people in that folk scene, which was very vibrant then. I became very friendly with Trevor Lucas; he married a girl called Sandy Denny in England and he was part of the Fairport Convention for many years. He also produced Redgum's "I Was Only 19". Tragically died fairly young, unfortunately. But he was one of the guys, for example, that was influenced by Pete Seeger, and started playing twelve-string guitar. I remember seeing Seeger at the Melbourne Town Hall with this long-necked banjo and I got hold of one and started playing it as best I could, so that was certainly a very big part of my influence. But it's always been a mixture of more popular music and folk blended together. And not country, interesting enough, I'd never really gotten into that.

Australian country music is such a hybrid. People like John Williamson are not really country music writers, they're folk writers.
That's exactly how I would see it. I was encouraged the other day; I listened to The Waifs' record. The girl was singing in an Australian accent, even though the style was decidedly country, and I thought, great. Absolutely great. I can't say the same for myself, when we started. Although, if I listen to some of those records, it doesn't even remotely sound like anything other than what we are, Australians.

We would listen to gospel groups, the Swan Silvertone Singers, and God knows who, that's where a lot of those early Seekers songs came from, 'cause we liked that white gospel, and I still love that sort of music. Then to go over to London with no expectations, to be thrust into a melting pot of what really was a music revolution in England, it was just an amazing thing to be there when that happened. And to be in the middle of a whole lot of white R&B music, essentially, and an explosion of songwriting talent the world's never seen since. Not even come close to it. The strength of a lot of those songs, even though we listen to them and hear all the dud technology from the day, you can't hide a good song.

But with all those outside influences, the group wasn't diverted from wanting to be a pure folk outfit?
I don't know whether that's quite true, I just think that's what we were capable of doing. The group saw itself as essentially a folk group. But that certainly was changed to some degree by the writing style of Tom Springfield. He had this Latin base to what he did; the songs always had this "Bion" beat to it. So when we combined what we do, that unique vocal sound, with some of that very basic rhythm, it changed the feel a bit, and people didn't know what to make of it. It wasn't a folk group but it sounded like one, but it had twelve-string guitar licks in it and became distinctively synonymous with The Seekers.

That then gave me the opportunity to write some songs, because we had to do an album and we had no material. So I started to attempt to write songs. And I've listened to them, they're not very good, but at least it was an honest effort to try and write something. I cringe when I listen to them.

Which songs particularly make you cringe?
I don't even know where I got these pathetic ideas, but I didn't know what I was doing. There's a song called "Don't Tell Me My Mind", there was another one called "Two Summers". I think they were the first two early efforts. And they were not good. But they certainly sounded okay when you heard the group do them. And by the way, it's important to note, I've never been a prolific songwriter. I've never written a lot of songs. I've never believed in it. People say to me, "I've written 200 songs." I say, "Well, terrific. How many of them have been recorded?" To me, that is the ultimate challenge for any writer, to get their work out to as many people as you can. You can do a lot of performing, but obviously recording's the main game, and you get people to hopefully record the songs.

Was the dynamic in the group such that if you wrote something that they didn't like and didn't want to perform, they would have told you so?
Yeah, sure. Absolutely.

So the songs must have been considered good enough.
Well, that's true. I'm sure you've heard this many times, but if you've got two or more people in a group, musicians that fancy themselves as songwriters, it creates all sorts of interesting problems. I've faced that a few times, particularly with The Seekers, where there are other members that like to think they're songwriters. So that can create a bit of tension. And I'm not really into that. Either the song's good enough or it isn't.

Was writing lyrics together as a group an easy process?
That was a very rare occurrence. A few years ago we collaborated on a song called "The Shores of Avalon". And that was not easy. I've found writing in a group situation quite painful. I don't find it easy, I don't find it pleasant. I'd much rather work on my own, or one on one with someone else.

What about when you and the group worked on arrangements of existing songs? How did that work and what are the skills needed to create a new arrangement of a song?
I just think that you need some approach that's different enough to have warranted doing it in the first place. That you can come up with some musical motifs or melodic lines that make it sufficiently different. And I must give full credit to Keith Potger in the group, 'cause his main skill is in vocal arranging. And arranging those songs so that they suit the sound of that group of people. They wouldn't mess around with little guitar lines. They're very, very simple, there's nothing particularly challenging about what was done musically, but the skill was in the vocal arranging.

Tom Springfield's songs catapulted The Seekers to great heights. How much did he influence you as a songwriter?
I would say a reasonable amount, because the songs are very melodic, which is the way I write. I've always tried to write songs that have memorable tunes. And he used rhythm and in a way that I liked. That's why I enjoyed doing those songs with the group because at least it was a bit different from stepping up and singing yet another traditional ballad.

Was your early songwriting guided by the range and quality of Judith Durham's voice?
Yes, I saw my role to try and help create songs for the group, for the albums. By the time I'd started really taking it seriously, the major hits had already been and gone. So that just awakened my interest in it and I did the best I could to write things that she could sing. On some of the early albums I used to sing some of the lead vocal parts because I wrote a couple that suited my voice and they liked the songs enough to want to record them.

When writing alone, would you usually come up with a melody first or a lyrical idea?
There's no rhyme or reason to it, it can be either. But probably more often than not I'll have some sort of melodic idea in my head.

From picking around on the guitar?
Yeah, sometimes I just hear it.

Away from the instrument?
Yeah. I remember Paul Simon and I talking about that, the fact that if you can create a melody without going near an instrument, without worrying about what the chords are, and let the harmonising of it take its course later on, it's not a bad way to go. I know he'd used that approach.

Is it difficult to find a balance that keeps both elements, the melody and lyrics, interesting and working together?
Yes. Some people are naturally gifted lyric writers. I've worked with a few where the words and phrases seem to come a lot easier to them than perhaps they do to me. But most songwriters that I know really labour over lyrics.

One of your biggest songs for The Seekers, in Australia at least, was in its mid-seventies incarnation with "Sparrow Song".
In fact, would you believe that's the only number one hit The Seekers ever had in Australia? But that wasn't with Judith; that was with Louisa.

Do you remember coming up with the idea?
I hadn't written a minor key song in quite a while, in fact I'd hardly ever, just 'cause they sound a bit mournful to me. But this one worked well. I just like the rhythmic feeling to it.

I don't even know where it came from; it was just something I was thinking about at the time. I was here in Melbourne. And that came out of a need to write for a particular reason. I said, "Oh God, I must come up with something, we've re-formed this group." That is really an approach I've taken many times in my work, when I was writing commercials. I write to deadlines and for a reason. I like to have a project to write for and that was one of them. And I liked her voice, I thought she was a very good singer and I thought this style of song would suit her. And it did.

Did the rest of the group like "The Sparrow Song"?
Yeah. It was a good song to perform, a very strong song, and in fact it's not all that long ago that it was suggested, when we were redoing some stuff when Judith rejoined us, that we revisit that song. She didn't want to do that. But it was a strong song and a good radio hit and a lot of people grew up with that one.

I'd like to ask you about some of the interesting songwriting collaborators you had outside of The Seekers and perhaps you could tell me what you remember of the experiences. First, Hans Poulsen. He had a strong pop sensibility, didn't he?
Yes. I liked what Hans did; he was a quirky little character. That was through the studio complex as it was then in Albert Road, Bill Armstrong Studios, and that was a real little centre, because there was the building next door where people like me used to hang out and write, and John Farrar used to be in and out of the studio all the time, they were all around that little precinct there, it was tiny. Someone said, "Hans is in, you know." And I said, "Oh well, let's get together." It was as simple as that.

We used to go in there late at night and write some things and record them on one of the lesser machines in one of the little rooms. He played mandolin, which I've always liked, he used it as a rhythmic instrument. He was a very good instrumentalist and a very melodic writer.

What do you remember about writing "Boom Sha La La Lo", which Hans had a hit with?
If anyone remembered Hans that would be the song that they'd know him for. I don't think at the time he thought of it as something that he might do. 'Cause he'd had "Rose Coloured Glasses", written by him for John Farnham, so when I started writing with him he was already starting to make some headway as a songwriter. But by the time it was finished he saw that it was something that would be good for him. I can't even remember how successful that was. I'm not really remembering what it sold. The fact is it got a lot of airplay, it was a successful song, and it was good for him. And then we wrote stuff for The Strangers, when John Farrar was there. "Lady Scorpio", that was a hit for them.

Do you remember writing "Lady Scorpio"?
I think we were talking about star signs and stuff like that, and females that were around us at the time. I don't know whether it was from my end or his, but we always felt that the Scorpios were a little bit erratic and changeable and you never knew where you were from one minute to the next. That was simply the basis of the song, to try and follow that train

of thought through. That was a successful song; that had some great John Farrar guitar playing on it that made it very distinctive at the time.

Where did the idea come from for "Monte and Me"? Was that written especially for Zoot?
It was just another song. And to be truthful, I don't remember a hell of a lot about that song, it was not one of my favourites. It was fun, you know. Everything I did with Hans was fun; it was quite easy to write with him, 'cause I don't know whether I was taking it all that seriously at the time. The songs kept churning out and people liked them, they heard them and said, "Oh we'll record that." It wasn't that hard to get the songs recorded if they were halfway decent and if they were a bit quirky.

It didn't hurt to get a song recorded by Zoot. They were huge back then.
That's true. That was a very formative time for me, because I wasn't doing it for any financial reason, I just did it because that's what I did and I liked doing it. I made my living at the time writing commercials.

How about writing with John Farrar?
We wrote in London in the mid-seventies. John was very easy to work with. He's such a great musician; good melodic lines would come out quite easily. He worked very hard on lyrics; I don't think John was a naturally gifted lyric writer. He worked hard at it and he did it well. And for me, unless you're a Randy Newman or a Paul Simon, one of those that come out of that background of almost regarding themselves as poets, the bulk of us songwriters generally have to labour very hard over crafting the lyrics. After all, that's what to me songwriting is. It's a craft, it's not an art form. I do believe songwriting sometimes approaches art, but I think more often than not it's a hard slog. To have to labour for hours or days over one or two lines is not an easy thing to do.

The number of people John has collaborated with is very few. So I thought it was interesting that he had done some work with you.
Yes, and we were doing that for a reason at the time, because we were doing an album with Louisa, it was the second one with her, when we were in London, and I asked him if he would do that, because I admired John's skills immensely. We did a couple of things that, when I listen, it's unmistakably John. The guitar arrangements were just fabulous. And even when I hear some of the songs on that album today, there are some absolute pearlers on that. There's a thing called "Standing on Shaky Ground" that Louisa couldn't sing, it was too hard for her. The melodic range was too great. I finished up having to attempt to sing it; we'd recorded the music, and it was either throw the song away or I have a go at it. So I'm singing in a key that's too low for me.

What about writing with Tom Paxton? "Angeline Is Always Friday" is an intriguing title.
That was more Tom's lyrical influence than mine. I wrote all the melody and Tom came up with this little story. He's a great storyteller, comes from that tradition. I'm a huge admirer

of Tom, and meeting him in New York City and meeting a lot of people in that New York folk scene over there was fantastic. That's actually quite important for me, because it goes back to when Paul Simon was trotted into the publisher's office one day to meet us. He had "Someday, Oneday" submitting to The Seekers. He played it to us. That's when he was doing folk clubs in England on his own. From there I got to know him a bit over the course of another year and used to go to a folk club and watch him and think, "This guy's amazing!" And that's when "Red Rubber Ball" was written in England with him. That's another one where I had that melody completed virtually and he wrote probably 80 per cent of the lyrics on that, and then we demoed the song in New York. Then I went over there on two other occasions and we got involved in songs called "I Wish You Could Be Here" and "Cloudy".

"Red Rubber Ball" has a bittersweet tone. "I Wish You Could Be Here" has a real yearning to it. Were Simon's ideas usually of a melancholy bent?
If you listen to the stuff that he wrote, even from *Sounds of Silence*, they're all very introspective songs. People described "Red Rubber Ball" as the quintessential summer pop song at the time. I never really thought of it that way. He did write in that fashion, no question about it. And most of his life there's this underlying sadness in what he's writing about. But that's the way he did it at the time; that was more in that folk tradition I suppose. By the way, that "Red Rubber Ball" has now done two million performances in America. Not many songs have ever done that.

So the Tom Paxton meeting came via Paul Simon?
Yeah, I met a lot of those people around there, the guy that I stayed with was a fellow called Barry Kornfeld who started out with Paul and was his music publisher in the early days. Once Paul became successful he quickly ditched Barry. Paul's a very ruthless man. Extremely ambitious and ruthless when it came to the business side of things and he cast people aside like old sweaters.

Do you remember first hearing "Bridge Over Troubled Water"?
I was in New York and Paul and Art were doing this album; I didn't know what it was, didn't know anything about it. I was invited into the CBS studios, and they were in this huge room with Roy Halee, the engineer. They must have just mixed it. And they played "Bridge Over Troubled Water" on these massive speakers and you can imagine the effect of it, hearing it like that. I asked how they got this exploding drum sound on it, because that technology didn't exist. And they'd put a drummer at the bottom of the lift well in the building and recorded him hitting this drum. So they were very inventive, very creative.

As a songwriter that's one of those seminal moments in your life when you run across people that you know are that distinctive and unique and talented. I didn't find it an easy experience because Paul's not an easy guy to be around. But nonetheless we got on well.

And you said you did have some discussions together about songwriting?
Yes. There was a song he wrote called "A Most Peculiar Man". It's a very bleak song about a guy topping himself in an apartment building. Not a very happy subject. But one of the things I asked him was about a line in the song that said, "That's what Mrs Reardon says and she should know she lives downstairs from him." I asked, "Why would you put her name in there?" He said the image of a fat Irish landlady conjures up a whole mental picture of the building, everything. And what he's been saying is, if you can crystallise a big thought in very few words, that's the essence of songwriting. Word pictures that work at that level. And I agree with him. That's one of the things I remembered out of that. It's an important one because it's too easy to fling words around that are fairly innocuous or meaningless or shouldn't be there. I've tended to try and write things that conjure up word pictures. I try and create mental pictures if I can, but my style is different to his, and different to a Tom Paxton, who is a pure storyteller. Mine are using phrases that evoke emotion or report some images. I've tried to use that technique as best as I can.

But I didn't get into any really in-depth discussions with him other than asking him specific questions, because he didn't offer the information. He wouldn't talk about it; I had to ask. In some ways it was like, well, here we are, we're sitting in a room, let's get on with it. It was a very professional "What have you got?" "Well, I've got this chord here, and this melody" and he would start scribbling on some paper and what did I think of that? From that point of view it was good because I was certainly smart enough to hear things that were working and I'd say, well that works, and that doesn't. Collaborating is difficult. It's hard, and people that tell you any different are lying because you've got to check your egos in at the door. You've got to be not afraid to make mistakes or say something stupid or to get the process going. I've done a bit of it and I've quite enjoyed it, 'cause I get on well with people. And you will know fairly early on in the piece if it's going to work or not. If you're struggling and labouring over something and you know it's crap, I just say, "Let's go have a drink. Forget it."

If you're struggling and labouring over something with a songwriter like Paul Simon, however, are you more likely to persevere than if you're writing with somebody who's not a genius?
A struggle's a struggle. If it ain't happening, it ain't happening. It wouldn't matter to me who it was.

Did you get to know Art very well?
No, not so much. A very nice man, very lovely guy. He's a mathematician actually. He was continually being shoved in the background by Paul and humiliated on a lot of occasions. And not given credit, really, for his contributions. They've had a very fiery relationship, there was some not good stuff going down there. I think Paul almost forced him to sell out his interests in all the copyrights. He paid him a lot of money. Paul wanted to own everything. Absolutely wanted to own everything.

He never tried to do you out of your copyrights, did he?
I got shafted on "Red Rubber Ball", the way the contract was framed out of England, and

for years I only ever got 25 per cent instead of 50. I continually wrote to him and said, "This is not right, this is totally unfair." It was only six or seven years ago that I finally got him to agree to give me 50 per cent of the song I wrote with him. It was like getting blood out of a stone.

Let's talk about one more collaborator, Dobe Newton.
That was when I was putting together an album of songs that were a mixture of some traditional Australian pieces. More to do with the Lawson and Paterson poems; I always thought those guys were great lyric writers. They wrote things that to me translated into songs very well. I had this stuff from an album I did called *The Roaring Days* and I thought, "There's something inherently very good here." So I started writing original songs and mixed them in. I didn't have a title song for the new album, and then I came up with "I Am Australian", which obviously has become very famous. And I needed some help with some of the verse lines. So I asked Dobe if he would have a look at it, which he did, and he came up with some of the verse lyrics on it. I think he wrote one other song on that album, "Pride of the Murray". That was a good song.

Why did you go to Dobe?
I had The Bushwackers playing on some new songs. I loved being around those sort of players, they're very good, and I got them to sing choruses of songs with me, more unison stuff. Dobe was there and I said, "I need a song about a Murray River paddle-steamer", 'cause I liked the idea of it. So we worked on that one and certainly on "I Am Australian". Which was done at a distance from me. I didn't sit down with him, I just said, "There's some gaps, see what you can do with it."

So who came up with the verse where you personify the physical elements of the land—the hot wind, the black soil, the mountains, valleys and so on?
That was Dobe. And full marks to him, it's a great verse. The total effect of the song is quite amazing. The chorus of the song was really the key part of it, because it's a global concept.

What brought this idea to you?
I just wanted a song that was an overarching theme for that album.

Were you at the time trying to write an anthem, as it became?
No, when you're trying to write something like that you've got to be very careful because Australians are not really into anthemic things particularly. You can certainly get your head kicked in very quickly doing things like that around this neck of the woods.

And yet isn't it interesting that "I Am Australian" and "True Blue" are so big and popular?
I wouldn't put the two songs in the same category.

In terms of the recognition factor and that they've both been used in advertising campaigns.
That's true, and I'm not putting John's song down at all. It's a good song. I don't think

it's a great song. And I have to say "I Am Australian" is a great song. Because people have drawn it to themselves since 1987, and particularly children. That song is sung in every single school in Australia, probably, these days. It's part of the fabric. It's one of those things that I would never attempt again, and yet I'm immensely proud I've done it, because it encapsulates the mood of a country at a particular point in time. It leaves a footprint in the sand.

I had some research done on the song, because I wanted to know where it was, what people thought of it. That was in 2001. And the research quite clearly showed that in a particular age group of children, four to twelve, every single child in the country knew it. Then it turns out that almost the same percentage of their parents knew it and were aware of it and what it was saying. So it's just never ceased to amaze me that this thing's taken on a life of its own. I've put a lot of time into trying to understand why it works. Geoffrey Blainey said it must be allowed to succeed because we won't see its like again probably in our lifetime. And it has to do with contemporary language. It's a very personal song, it's what I believe, and some of the lines in it have to do with personal issues, it has family references in it for me. And I think Dobe's sympathetic contribution rounded it out to create the greater whole. So if I had to choose any one thing I've ever written, that would be the most important contribution I'll ever make.

Out of what you've written, is it your favourite song?
I've heard it hundreds and hundreds of times so I tend to get a bit sick of it. But yeah, probably. There are some other things that I would listen to on my own occasionally that I think are better written songs. But nothing will ever come close to that. It has the ability to create a feeling amongst Australian people that is good and positive. It's like a big pot of glue. It doesn't exclude anybody. I've got up and sung this song with Mandawuy Yunupingu in Canberra at a big international event and that was very meaningful to me, that he would do that, and saw absolutely that it was a good thing to do, that it said what it needed to say on behalf of indigenous people. It's very much accepted by them as totally inclusive.

I heard from a journalist that for the last three years they play this song at Gallipoli on Anzac Day with 15,000 people singing along. I couldn't believe it. That's what I mean. I didn't mean to be disrespectful with "True Blue" but this is at a totally different level of consciousness. It's universal. I've sung this song in Carnegie Hall with the Australian Youth Choir with an American audience, and they were just blown away with it.

Do you feel it should be the national anthem?
No I don't. People often ask that question. I don't think so. The song is what it is, people draw it to themselves. It will be around a long time after I'm not here.

"Keep a Dream in Your Pocket" is the ultimate song of optimism. Has it always been important to write songs that are mainly uplifting with positive messages?
Absolutely. I think there's enough difficulty in people's lives, there's enough things that can drag us down without songwriters contributing to it. I don't think that's my role in life. If I'm going to write a song, I want to write something that can be uplifting, that makes us feel

better than bad. That song is the absolute epitome. Friends of mine that have struggled in life, that have had bad things happen, several of them told me that song kept them going. One of my dear friends, a lady called Jane Harold who died about five years ago, when she was really ill she used to play that song every day to keep herself going. It doesn't get any better than that. If you can help somebody or contribute something by creating a song like that, it's done its job. It doesn't matter whether only ten people in that case or ten million hear it, if it works.

Is there an ideal situation where inspiration comes to you?
It can happen anywhere at any time. I've been out of the loop for about a year or so with songwriting. I've chosen to be. And I've known many songwriters that do that. They walk away from it for years at a time, 'cause it just gets too much for them. Those ones that really care about what they do and approach it that this is going to be the best song they've ever written, take that view, and get terribly distressed when they come up with something they think is crap. They'd sooner not do it.

Or when they come up with something they think is wonderful and nobody else does.
It's very solitary and, like any writing exercise, you've got to sit down there on your own mostly and do it. That's why if you can get a collaboration that's fun and get on well with someone like that, it's an absolute joy to do it. Because depending on who I'm working with, I come up with different styles. If I played you some things that I've done you would never pick that I would do something like that. I've worked with a guy purely as a lyric writer, he writes dance-oriented stuff. Okay, nothing happened with it, but I love the fact that he just said, "Look, there's a tune". Sam Panetta is his name. That was so enjoyable for me, 'cause I just rode around for days with the music in the car, writing.

Do you use a little tape recorder in those cases?
No, pen and paper.

As you're driving? You're dangerous!
No, I stop the car.

So the car is an inspirational place for you to write.
Recently I wrote in a car on the way to one of the most beautiful parts of Australia, up near Bright in Victoria, going up towards Mount Beauty, Falls Creek. It's the most heavenly country, and I stopped on one road and I looked around me and I was just totally in heaven, there was only me, nothing around for miles. I had the tune, turned it on, sat there by the side of the road and I finished it. So I thought, yeah, there's still the desire to do it.

HARRY VANDA

GEORGE YOUNG

HARRY VANDA & GEORGE YOUNG

SYDNEY, AUSTRALIA, JULY 2003
DINARD, FRANCE, NOVEMBER 2003

Most Australians are intimately acquainted with at least one Vanda and Young song. For the baby boomers it's "Friday on My Mind", the working class anthem that long ago transcended any notion of class, a shining example of the most exhilarating of sixties Australian rock music— notwithstanding the song having been written and recorded in England—and to this day (and with apologies to Banjo Paterson fans) still topping most polls as the best Australian song of all time.

For the children of the seventies and generations that followed, it's "Love Is in the Air", the synth disco pop tune that John Paul Young sang to the top of charts at home and internationally, making it a pop standard even before Baz Luhrmann cannily used it for the soundtrack of his 1992 film *Strictly Ballroom*. In 1978, when "Love Is in the Air" first breezed its way around the world, it was riding on the crest of a Vanda and Young wave. The duo's songwriting, production and artist development achievements have remained unparalleled by any other songwriter or team of songwriters Australia has produced.

Given the fairly reserved nature of the pair, however, it's usually only the older generations of Australian music fans who stand to attention as soon as the names Vanda and Young are mentioned. Those who recall the hysteria of "Easyfever"—the Beatles-like mania surrounding their band, The Easybeats, in the mid-sixties—or the duo's return to the spotlight as Flash and the Pan in the late seventies. Celebrity was never their motivation, but they weren't averse to commercial success. It was all about business, not art, and they refrain from any kind of deep analysis of their work. Personal matters, happy or sad, were left out of the songwriting as a rule, and attempts to connect certain songs with known incidents in their lives are shrugged off. Harry Vanda's young first wife took her own life during The Easybeats' heyday and he was left with a baby, but he won't be drawn into a discussion about whether "Evie", the three-part epic about a man losing his wife during childbirth, was inspired in any way by his own experiences. The songs are what they are—exuberant pieces of rock or pop, effectively executed and eminently entertaining.

Like so many musical success stories in Australia, the players in this one started their lives on the other side of the world. Harry Vanda was born Johannes Vandenberg on 22 March 1946 in The Hague, the Netherlands. He grew up an only child, a tall, blonde, shy boy, with no English language skills and a wildly expressive face. His first band in Holland was The Starfighters, a mainly instrumental outfit influenced by The Shadows. Uprooted at seventeen when his parents joined the surge of European migration to Australia, he landed in Sydney and lived at the Villawood Migrant Hostel. There, as he gradually picked up the language, he befriended another Dutch boy, Dick Diamonde, and they in turn met the younger English boy Stevie Wright. When they all befriended the recently arrived Scot, George Young, at the hostel, The Easybeats' destiny was set.

Young was born on 6 November 1948 in Glasgow, the sixth child of eight siblings. While his two younger brothers, Malcolm and Angus, looked up to George for inspiration and later formed their own hard rock band, AC/DC, with his guidance, George himself looked for inspiration to his sister, Margaret, and four elder brothers. It was the song and dance of family life that gave him the passion for music, rather than external influences. With a guitar prowess that more than compensated for his diminutive size, he instantly became the musical leader of the group that formed at Villawood. Promptly signed to young music publisher and aspiring record label manager Ted Albert's new company, George began writing with Stevie, who had an aptitude for catchy lyrics. "She's So Fine" shot to number one and their string of British Beat-influenced hits began.

Accessible, well-structured songs were their trademark, and by 1965 Vanda was writing regularly with Young. When they got to London in 1966, the Shel Talmy-produced "Friday on My Mind" made an impact. After that the profusion of influences around them changed their songwriting direction at every turn; one moment they would write a psychedelia-infused opus like "Heaven and Hell", next a full-blown ballad such as "Hello How Are You", and then a pure rock party song like "Good Times". As Vanda recalled, "I suppose all this ocean of influences was very good for us from a development point of view, but it made it awfully difficult to let people know what we were all about. They couldn't pinpoint us from one album to the other. And that wasn't very good for the band."

So The Easybeats disintegrated, and the next phase of Vanda and Young's career began, as writers and producers for other artists, although for a while in the early seventies when they could not find singers for their songs, they invented various pseudonyms and recorded the songs themselves. They struggled in London, writing sentimental songs they hoped the rigidly programmed BBC Radio would play, and then Ted Albert, back in Sydney, started asking them for material. He was building a stable of performers, most of whom (Ted Mulry a notable exception) were not songwriters. After initial success with songs such as "Falling in Love Again" and "Superman", Vanda and Young decided to move home and work in-house for Albert. "To us it really was a wonderful opportunity to get into an environment where we could actually take charge of our destinies instead of living from day to day surviving," Vanda said.

A wealth of Australian talent benefited from the Vanda and Young machine. As well as John Paul Young, who had the greatest number of hits written and produced by the pair, the stable also included Ted Mulry, Alison McCallum, Ray Burgess, William Shakespeare, Cheetah, The Angels, Rose Tattoo, and former Easybeats lead singer, Stevie Wright, whose chart-topping eleven-minute single of "Evie" still rates among the most riveting performances ever recorded by an Australian singer.

Internationally, there have been numerous covers of Vanda and Young songs. "Love Is in the Air" alone, at last count, had forty cuts, including Tom Jones and James Last; "Friday on My Mind" has been recorded by sixteen artists including David Bowie, Peter Frampton and Gary Moore; and Grace Jones and Rod Stewart have wrapped their tonsils around "Walking in the Rain" and "Hard Road" respectively.

In more recent years, Young has all but retired from the music industry. "Apart from a brief couple of months dabbling with some ideas with Harry, I haven't written a song for the past twelve years or so," he said. Vanda, the more outgoing of the pair, still misses their partnership. "George is not much into music now, he's more into football," he said, resigned, but not despondent. His inner-Sydney studio complex, Flashpoint, is one of the largest privately owned state-of-the-art recording facilities in Australia, and from there Vanda works developing new artists, writing and producing with passion, energy and a business acumen refined over four decades.

They miss each other, they are still close friends, but they rarely get together. Young is elusive and hard to find, even for Vanda. At any time he could be in England, Portugal or France, where he granted the rare interview for this book and gave answers both similar and contrary to his former partner.

PART I: Harry Vanda

When did you first pick up a guitar?
When I was about seven. I had some lessons for a couple of years with a guy that used to come around to the flat. But I lost interest, I got into other things like soccer and sport.

When I was little bit older, twelve or thirteen, all of a sudden I got interested in pop music and I thought, yeah, I can do that. So I picked up the guitar again and started bashing away.

Did you start writing while you were in Holland, doodling around, coming up with your own melodies?
I used to just piss around with chords and improvise. Get nice chord shapes and put them together. I didn't think of it as songwriting. I didn't think that I was actually making up a song. I wasn't thinking in terms of lyrics, I just wanted to express myself with beautiful-sounding noises. But I suppose those must have been my very first attempts at coming up with something that's original, something that you do yourself. Of course I knew that there were songs, I knew people must have written them, but to me it appeared that a songwriter was like an architect or a doctor.

A strange, mysterious being.
A bit like jokes—they come from somewhere, but you never know where.

When you came to Australia, the music scene, with everyone thrashing about in the hostel, must have been quite new for you.
For me it was a traumatic thing. I thought it was a bloody disaster! So I'd take it on under protest. I took my guitar and my amplifier along. It was an old Dynacord amplifier, it was quite a good little machine, I shouldn't have gotten rid of it. And I had an old Hoffner electric guitar.

Did you start listening to the radio when you got here?
Yes. The first thing I heard on a little radio was Johnny O'Keefe. [*Sings*] "Move baby move, you're in the groove." It didn't appeal to me very much 'cause coming from an instrumental background, I thought, "This guy can't sing!" And when I became aware of other things that were out at the time. The Searchers, The Springfields. Just a completely different music scene than Holland where it was a bit like socialist music, it was very controlled.

Did you discover The Strangers and what they were doing?
That became apparent later on when we had started The Easybeats, we became aware of The Strangers, because they were the resident band on *The Go!! Show*. That's when I first saw John Farrar and he really struck me as a bloody shit-hot guitarist. When I finally got to meet him he showed me a few tricks, and I thought, "I've got to brush up on my act, this guy is seriously good."

So at that stage you were just keen on being a guitarist and the idea of being a songwriter or producer—
Didn't really strike me the same way. But in Villawood Hostel I'd started this band with Dick Diamonde, and then we ran into Steve, who was called Chris Langdon at the time. And he had a manager. We started to hang out and piss about. Then we heard about this

shit-hot little bloody guitarist by the name of George Young. And that's when I first became aware of music like Chuck Berry and Little Richard; George was far more interested in real rocky stuff. So George joined the band. He said we should be a vocal band and I was far from sure of that. It went against the grain of me wanting to be the best guitarist in the world. But I didn't fight it. And then George also suggested, "Why shouldn't we write our own songs?" Well it's a bloody good idea, old son, but how do you do that? How do you write songs?

And you were still learning English at that time?
I was picking it up as I went. It took me about six months to pick up the language. But obviously I was making all sorts of clangers. Everybody was having a good old giggle. But having said all that, George and I did write a couple songs together in the beginning. The B-side of "For My Woman", the first song The Easybeats ever wrote, was called "Say that You're Mine", which we wrote together.

How did you both throw that together lyrically? You were both really guitar guys.
Yes. But George also writes a mean lyric. We just had a hook line. That's basically how we approach songs. What I do is I get sayings, lines, expressions, and if I see one I like the look of, or something that seems to have something behind it that can be explored, I just write it down and then piss around and try to get a melody to that line. That leads to a chain reaction. To me it's a logical progression musically. But lyrically, I can sum up the main angles, but I can't put things the way a guy like Bon Scott could. Three lines, he can sum it all up. It would take me thirty. That's the difference.

Do you think the migrant experience was reflected at all in the early songwriting that you and George were doing?
Not so much me, but George was very much a product of the environment. Guys were dressing snappy, fashionable haircuts mattered. Looking sharp and with it. And the expression musically was on the cutting edge. He was very much into that sort of thing. And that really rubbed off on me, who came from a completely different environment. I started to see the sense in it, especially being in a band. To have a crash course in something that I wasn't brought up with, took me a while. To understand the music, to understand the feel of Chuck Berry and Little Richard, Jerry Lee Lewis, all those guys, and the mentality that was behind it, was quite a difficult thing to do. It was tough. I had a lot of learning to do.

Did the emotion of being a displaced person come through in your early writing? You were all newcomers in a new land.
It probably would have, it was a bit of an "us and them" mentality. And I think a lot of the way we expressed ourselves—talking, looking, the attitude—would also have been very much a part of the music. But maybe not from an intellectual point of view, just from an attitude point of view.

In the early days when Stevie was doing most of the writing with George, did you find yourself itching to be more involved in songwriting?

No, I didn't. Because I was very much into guitar playing, that was important to me. The other thing was that the amount of rehearsing we did, the contributions that you make to those songs were of the nature that nowadays people would claim writing credits. [*Laughs*] But not then. As far as I was concerned I was just doing my bit, but I hadn't written the bloody thing. The guys come in with an idea, so you work on it, you work on your parts and you throw in suggestions yourself, how about this and that. Without expecting anything for it because you were part of the band.

As you became more of a songwriter, was there any room for writing about personal experiences? You suffered a tragedy when your wife passed away; did you ever want to write about stuff like that?

No. To me it was a private thing. If it's come out in some songs, it's come out from sheer carelessness. Look, I'm a believer in the fact that you cannot escape what happens to you every day. And it's going to come out in your attitude, in what you say, in what you do. So if I write songs for a living, then obviously all these experiences are going to be part of that expression somewhere along the line. Not necessarily on a conscious level, but quite often on a subconscious level. Which I find more interesting rather than to sit down and say, "Look, I've had this incredible moving experience and I'm going to bore the world shitless with my pain." A songwriter is also an entertainer. You can't bore people to death. And a lot of them do, because they think that what happens to them is the central part of the universe. I can't take that attitude.

Have you ever poured your heart out in a song that you don't necessarily want anyone to hear but it's just another way of expressing things for you?

Yes, it's happened once or twice. They come out at different times when the reason that they were written, the way I felt about it at the time, is not apparent. Nobody can put two and two together and say, "Well, you wrote that because of that." Because when you're a songwriter it's like saying, "I'm a plumber". It has to make business sense. The plumber doesn't get up in the middle of the night and study his bleedin' toilet pipes out of an emotional experience.

For a lot of successful songwriters it's all been out of emotional experience.

Those guys never say that. It's the people that sell them that say that. It's the guy that lacks a lot of paint on a canvas and then somebody else will come along and interpret. And the whole intellectual establishment rocks along with it. There's a big difference there. You'll find most people that do these things will never explain. Other people will explain it for him. We had that experience with Flash and the Pan. That was one of the biggest reasons why Flash and the Pan worked very nicely, thank you, because people were interpreting what we were saying. We were saying bugger all! [*Laughs*]

But those songs were a lot more wordy.
They were crafted along the lines of realising that attitude, you see. We were just being commercial songwriters. Other people were putting all the intellect and emotion into it.

Back in 1966 were you feeling stymied by the success in Australia? Was the move to England as much about opening yourselves up creatively as it was about having some chart success over there?
That's a good question. We probably got a hit too early. It seemed too easy almost. We weren't experienced enough, like other songwriters, who know how to take advantage, somebody who understands the marketplace. We did realise, and so did our manager, that at some stage or other we were going to overstay our welcome. Because with five major venues and so many major country towns, how often can you do it? You get to a point where, "Oh shit, not them again!" So we felt, leave on a high note and let's see if we can duplicate the whole experience over there. That's really all it was.

When you got to the UK, did you feel like Europeans who had come home or Australians who were overseas? You hadn't been here very long.
More like Australians that were overseas, funnily enough. We always wanted to relate to Australia; we called ourselves an Australian band, although there were no Australians in it to speak of. But yeah, we felt Australian by that time already. Maybe because of the acceptance we'd had here, all the help, all the people on our side. To us this was an absolutely wonderful country. The alternative to pumping petrol in Glasgow or The Hague. So we were Australians and we remained Australians ever since.

Are your personalities quite opposite and was that helpful or difficult when you started writing together constantly?
We are very similar in many aspects but we are also opposites in many others. George is a very volatile person. In those days I was a lot more mellow. We helped each other along; he gave me a bit of fire and I gave him a bit of peace. And it worked out excellent. The good thing with George is that there is no holding back, no inhibition, no shame. We can make the biggest arses of ourselves in front of each other and it wouldn't matter. We'd laugh at each other. I think in any relationship you start off very cautiously at first, but it became so natural. You know how things just slot in? That's what happened with us. And the reason we had such good results is because there was never any holding back, there was never any, "Well, if I say that, he's gonna laugh his bloody head off." He would, or so would I, but it would not be vicious or malicious.

Can you recount the story of how "Friday on My Mind" came to be written?
We were noticed by Shel Talmy; he showed interest in producing us but it had to be the right one. So we were banging away, and just to get a bit of relief, we all went to see a film. In those days they used to have a pre-feature film, and it was about the Canadian swingle singers. We were taking the piss all the way back to the house, singing, "do do di di di di di

di di di di di." Funnily enough it stuck, so we got back to work and all of a sudden we got this [*Sings*] "Ding a ding a ding a ding a ding a ding."

So that actually started with a guitar riff.
Yeah.

It didn't start with "Friday on My Mind", the line?
No, that was something that came later. The lyrics actually came later. It was a bloody hard song to write.

Did you write the lyrics together?
George had the lion part of the lyrics. The funny thing was that our manager also tried to get a set of lyrics in. He probably thought, "Hey, this is a good one." So he came up with this verse and the first line was, "For a chick doll, you're a drag." George went white, 'cause we had this great little melody going. The way to get into the chorus was incredibly difficult. We didn't know how we were going to get to "Gonna have fun"—a completely different chord. So we had the melody and then we had to contend with "For a chick doll, you're a drag." George disappeared into the back room and came up with a set of lyrics that were on the button. And then we got together and a few suggestions I made, this and that. But we didn't have the title until we had the lyrics.

You didn't all have day jobs in London, it's not like you were hanging out for the weekend. The whole notion of the working class anthem, for all the people who work Monday to Friday—you guys weren't living that way.
No, but the thought over that song, the working class anthem of that particular path, was [*Sings*] "Well, it's Saturday night and I just got paid ..." The Little Richard tune. But people didn't get paid any more on Saturday night, that's what George said, "Well, people get paid on Friday night, you know what I mean?" And that's where it came from. But it was a hard one. It was agony, that tune.

What did you think of David Bowie's cover of the song?
His version is the only cover I ever liked of "Friday on My Mind". Which is not surprising, because David Bowie must be one of best pop brains in the world ever. He would know what he's doing.

I haven't heard the versions by people like Peter Frampton and Gary Moore.
They're okay. But it doesn't quite catch what the tune is all about. I still think we were the only ones who really hit it on the nail. There's always something about the original.

Did you feel pressured in writing the follow-up?
Yeah, very much so. We got paranoid for the first time, and we, for lack of a better word,

dried up. It didn't come. The best we could do was some ditty called "Who'll Be the One". We tried everything with that tune, and so did Shel. It just didn't capture it.

Being in London must have opened you up to not just the psychedelic movement, which showed in subsequent writing, but other styles around you like reggae. What were you being moved and inspired by?
Just about every bit of music that came along. Reggae was called ska at the time. We listened to that. A guy called Roy Head. Lots of soul music. Motown. The Four Tops. That Levi Stubbs is one of my favourite singers of all time. The feels of these things, we started to study all that. I suppose we were learning our craft, instead of letting things just happen almost spontaneously. We were becoming musicians; we were starting to understand music.

Did that study and absorption of everything around you unblock you?
Very much so. But at the same time it also made us a hell of a lot more complicated. Because it was like an overload of information that we had to pick up on. We had so much to learn. So we started to cram it into everything. We even came up with Wagnerian types of pop tunes.

George has referred to "Heaven and Hell" as complicated self-indulgence.
In retrospect. At the time it seemed that's what a band should be—inventive. And the thing was, we couldn't relate to this going to San Francisco with bleedin' flowers in the hair. That was not us at all. But at the same time we did some token lip service to it. I suppose all this ocean of influences was very good for us from a development point of view, but it made it awfully difficult to let people know what we were all about. They couldn't pinpoint us from one album to the other. And that wasn't very good for the band.

Did you feel validated when the BBC banned you? Or did it piss you off because you wanted to have hits?
Of course we wanted to have hits. The problem was the BBC was the other influence on us, which very much contributed to our all-round knowledge, trying to get on radio, getting through to all the old aunties. That was incredibly hard. So that's why we came up with tunes like "Hello How Are You" and real maudlin shit, because we were trying to get onto the radio. We tried to be simple and I honestly don't think we were capable at that time of being simple. We couldn't see the tree from the wood. There were too many bloody trees. Too much wood. It took us a long time to sort that out and put it in perspective so that we could actually use it all. When we did, shit, we did alright. All those experiences set us up for what happened afterwards. And what was really important, we found the outlets here in Australia for all the things we'd learned, when we came back. Because this place was like a goldmine for talent, but they didn't have the experience we had. So we had the edge. I think that combination was a winner. Whether Ted Albert had realised it, I don't know. I wouldn't put it past him, you know.

The strides you were making in terms of your creativity in the late sixties were on par with the strides the Beatles, Beach Boys, The Who and other groups were making, moving from simple two- and three-minute pop songs to songs that twisted that formula and turned it on its head. How difficult was it to be different in an environment where everyone was trying to be different?

It's easy to be different, but it's hard to be good different. We can all be different and do something ridiculous. But to be different and have the commercial acceptability at the same time so that it all works and all makes sense, that's very difficult. And of course it's easier to be acceptable if you're an established band of the stature of the Beatles etcetera. If you listen to all the Beatles stuff, they put out a pile of shit. That's not to speak ill of the incredible gems, I'm not taking that away from them, but there was also a hell of a lot of polyfiller there. With most bands. But they were commercially established.

And yet "Good Times" was pure rocking fun like the early Easybeats.

That's what we wanted, just to have a good time for a change instead of all this, "Oh, my art!" Everybody was walking around with this artistic frock. Don't forget dope was a big thing at the time, so after a few joints everybody was very complicated.

Any of the more complicated stuff that you're quite fond of now?

"Falling Off the Edge of the World" was really highly regarded by the American in-crowd. As an "in" band we were very in with people that later on moved on and became big-time acts themselves, like Lou Reed. But commercially, still you have to sum it up in the end, it's all well and good being an in-joke but you still have to make a buck.

One of the later Easybeats songs, "The Shame Just Drained", has a distinctive intro that's repeated later in "Down Among the Dead Men". That melody is also hinted at in "The Love Game". Were there other instances where you recycled your own work in later songs?

No. On my honour, you're the first one who's picked that up. That totally escapes me. It's totally accidental. We never cannibalised our own songs consciously. Obviously we must have done it at some stage. We put different songs together. We had a song, couldn't finish it, and then it becomes apparent that it could work elsewhere. "Hard Road" was one of those tunes. But obviously from a songwriting point of view you can't escape your own influences, and you probably revisit certain melodies under different guises without even thinking about it.

Do you think there's a finite number of melodies out there?

No. Mind you, in every song you have instant cognitive access to every melody that's ever been written, and you probably find that's the same, that's the same, that's the same. But the differences in the overall picture loom.

What was the fascination with places other than where you were—St Louis, Pasadena, Birmingham?

They sang well. "Show Me the Way to St Louis"—it just sounds good, that's all. I wouldn't know what bloody St Louis was like; I've never been there. Never been to Pasadena either, but the lyrics to that were written by David Hemmings, the actor. In London a guy that did some stuff from Chappell Music let us have an office and he was very well connected with all the cool actresses at the time, and they all wanted to be singers of course. We recorded a couple just for fun, and that's how we ran into David Hemmings, who said, "Hey man, I've got some lyrics, you wanna put some songs to this?" He came up with the lyrics to "Pasadena", which were heavily vetted by George, by the way.

"Falling in Love Again" was a left turn from "Good Times" and songs of that ilk.
That was very much our BBC period. It was with people in mind that would be played on the BBC.

You didn't expect it to be sent back to a rock 'n' roll guy like Ted Mulry in Sydney.
No. But we were writing some strange shit.

Did you like it?
I like what Ted did with it. But then again, I like Ted's voice, I liked Ted. Ted could have recorded "Happy Birthday" and I would have liked it.

Given your earlier comments about how real life can seep into your work, was there any reality based in "Evie"?
Maybe [*Laughs*]. Maybe not.

It's an absolute epic. Guy meets girl, takes her out, falls in love with her, marries her, she has a baby, she dies.
It's one of those situations where subconsciously things work out that way. But it becomes a little bit enhanced in other people's views of it because of what they know about you, so they naturally assume that you are applying that. It's not quite as romantic as all that. But yeah, there are touches of truth in it. It's an emotional piece, especially the second part.

Did you have the idea for a three-part song or were they different songs?
No. There were three different songs. But then it became quite obvious.

Why?
Because they were all about Evie. [*Laughs*]

The emotional heart of those songs was not really about Evie, but about the guy who was in love with her. You don't get to know Evie through these songs.
Again it can be interpreted in many ways. The most effective lyrics are the ones that do not really explain, that leave room for you to interpret it yourself. If there's one thing I learned about lyrics, that's don't sit there and sum it up because you'll spoil it for too many people.

So therefore the language has to be poetic. A song like that is vague but also very specific as well. You make certain definite statements and then leave it open to interpretation. That's why it's so obvious that they did fit together.

I still have a sneaking suspicion that the emotion for the radio play had very little to do with it. I think they just liked the idea that, "It's time for a fuckin' smoko. Eleven minutes for a smoke!" [*Laughs*]

Is that a song you're particularly proud of?
Ah, it's a good song. Yeah.

When the Vanda and Young hit machine took up residence in the mid- to late seventies, were the songs tailored to specific artists? Were Stevie's songs, like "Evie" and "Black Eyed Bruiser" specifically for him and his voice, and were songs like "Yesterday's Hero" and "I Hate the Music" specifically for John Paul Young's voice and persona?
Yes. Absolutely. Having written with Steven in mind for so long, I think he could have done anything we did. But once we became aware of John's style, it became rather apparent what was for John, and we actually tailored the songs to John's acceptance level at the time: a pop singer. And John's so quick, so professional, so easy to work with. Lovely guy, not an ounce of pretence. Just our kind of guy. So we loved working with him. We had all these incredibly commercial ditties, and he'd pick them up so well.

Was "I Hate the Music" a title first?
Yes.

It's a great title. Who came up with that one?
George. 'Cause he generally was hating it! [*Laughs*] He hated the music industry. He'd go, "This fuckin' job's a health hazard!"

It's an audacious title.
I really like the twist in it. Because every time they play that bloody song I keep thinking of, "Gee, piss off!" So that's why you hate it. It worked out really well. But we almost blew it. Before we put the synth on it, the opening, we put a banjo on it. It sounded shite! Once we threw caution to the wind, let's put a bit of excitement in this, it worked out fine.

"Can't Stop Myself from Loving You" and "My Little Angel" might have sounded good also recorded by JPY. Were they specially written for the William Shakespeare project and tailored for John Cave's higher voice?
"Can't Stop Myself from Loving You" was already written in England. When we came back here we were looking for vocalists, and there was John, and he had that very distinct pop voice. "My Little Angel" was written afterwards, for him.

And was "Love Fever" specifically tailored to Ray Burgess and his sensual macho image? There's a hint of Gary Glitter in that song. Somebody with a hairy chest had to sing that song.
It was very much an image type song and it was written as such. Yes, you could see the shark tooth on the hairy chest.

What was extra special about "Love Is in the Air"?
It was just something. We were living in Eastwood at the time. Finally the penny had dropped, we put the song together, and we came into the city. The thing that was always missing was the steps up to [*Sings*] "Love Is in the air, love is in the air ..." The chorus was never there, you see, we were always stuck up to that bit in that song. But when it did, we put down the demo in the studio and something happened that very seldom happened. We played the bloody thing twenty times on the way home, over and over and over and over, and didn't get sick of it. We were actually going to put words where it goes "Whoa, whoa, whoa, whoa, whoa". That only came about because we didn't have the lyrics. It was emotional. John sang, "whoa, whoa, whoa, whoa, whoa" and we said, "That's good enough, leave it."

We played it to Ted Albert, and he never took his eye off us for three weeks. "Have you mixed it yet? What's happening with 'Love Is in the Air'?" So we thought this was a good one. And then it hit the streets and just went kaboom everywhere.

Any reason why the focus had shifted from guitar-based songs to piano-driven songs?
That just made more sense. They were written on the keyboard and made more sense on the keyboard. It very much became John's signature.

But then you employed that in Flash and the Pan, and considering you're both guitar players it's interesting that much of that stuff was piano-based as well.
Flash and The Pan was important keyboard-wise because it gave us a hell of a lot more scope to be spooky. Curtains of sound that sustain, that you can't get on guitar. We were using the Omni synthesiser.

You'd dabbled in spoken word lyrics with "My Little Angel". Why did you go for it en masse on most of the Flash and the Pan songs?
We were stuck for a style. These were songs that weren't really suited to anyone. But Ted again got out his whip and said, "That 'Hey St Peter' is a hit." We said, "Well, who's going to do it?" "Well, try it with John." "No, John won't do that, there's a huge bloody instrumental bit in the middle, what's he going to do—scratch his arse while that's going on?" [*Laughs*] So he said, "Well why don't you guys do it?" "Us? We haven't got the time for that!" "Do it! I love that track! It's a hit!" This is Ted giving us a hammering. So I had a go and sang it. It wasn't doing much for me. So then George had a go at it, and I thought, "That sounds alright." That's how we got to the idea that there's a difference if we sort of sing-talk. It's really rap, I suppose.

It was also a precursor to M's "Pop Musik". Robin Scott, what he was doing.
It was just something that made sense for that particular project. Then we got a vocal sound that was grossly exaggerated. The compression of the voice, like a spitting sound, which really sounds very commanding. And that's how it became a style. We still didn't have a name. I said I thought it would be "a flash in the pan". George went, "Flash and the Pan! That's a good name, Harry. We'll use that!" One of my lyrical genius contributions.

The thing that we liked about "Hey St Peter" was the way that the whole bit in the middle sprang off and became a nice musical of its own. It was something that you did for fun, but you couldn't give it to anyone because it was in the way. No self-respecting singer is going to stand there for three minutes.

Great video, too.
It was great fun. You know that video cost all of $900. And the next one blew out the budget. It was $1,200.

How did "Down Among the Dead Men" come about? Were you both into the Titanic story?
George is a very well-read man. He reads so many books, biographies, every subject matter under the sun. That was something he was really interested in, so that's how that story ended up in a song.

Do you have a favourite song that you've written?
There's a couple of things that are a bit obscure. "Rock 'n' Roll Boogie" and "Woman You're on My Mind". I really like those two songs.

Have there been favourite keys that you've worked in?
I've always been a bit partial to E, A, G, keys like that. Then there are keys that I can't relate to, like E flats and all that bullshit. That's good if you play in groups, if you play with a capo. But it's a different thing. I like full tones in the chords. A is a great chord; you get the ring of the open strings as well, the way that you position the chords. Which you don't get if you play, say, a G sharp.

When you were writing for particular artists, like John Paul Young, were there certain keys that you would always resort to because you knew that's where he was comfortable?
Yeah, John has certain keys where he's very comfortable. Depending on the range. He's a C and a G man. Or A minor.

In your writing with George, how were each of your personalities reflected?
Put it this way. The best songs we've written, we've written together. The ones we've written by ourselves might be good, but ...

Were there many written alone?
Oh, yes, every now and then you finish up writing songs by yourself. I've got 200 songs that

I've written by myself. But to me it always lacks that part that's lacking in me. I think that's why you have a partnership. People that are totally self-sufficient don't need anyone. Why would you if you're completely happy with the songs that you write and it's totally your individual expression, the lot—and there are people like that—then what do you need a partner for? You need a partner to bring something to the equation that you haven't got yourself.

So do you miss George and the full-time partnership?
Sometimes, yes, but I just miss him as a guy. I like having him around. He's an interesting man. He's a smart man. He's my best friend, so what can I say?

After all these years of writing, is it easy for you to connect with your creative source and get inspired?
Yes, I find it very easy to write music. Maybe I should be smart and just concentrate on bloody film music and not worry about lyrics because lyrics are still my bane. I write okay lyrics but if I came to see me, for instance, for advice I would say, "Not bad, Harry, but do yourself a favour, find yourself a lyricist."

And you haven't wanted to do that, find another songwriting partner?
No. It's a bit like being unfaithful to your wife. [*Laughs*]

Do you feel that there is a mystery to songwriting and to where songs come from?
Yes there is, and I have no idea. I know they come. It's like opening a door. You can't really pinpoint it. I think everyone is a songwriter. You just have to believe you are and you can be one. You have to have some understanding of music, so you can be the transmitter. Or whatever all the influences are that go through you and come out in a certain way. You have to be able to channel that with some sort of skill, otherwise it's nothing. I think anyone can do it. Unless you have a problem like you're tone deaf. That must be a highly unfortunate thing.

PART II: George Young

Was music a part of home life in the early days?
Large family gatherings were regular events when I was a kid, and singing and dancing always took place. The music was usually supplied by my older brothers on a variety of instruments like guitars and accordions, and they played a mixture of early rock 'n' roll, country and western, and old Scots songs with a passion and feel that I've rarely heard since. Whatever musical ability I might have, I learned from them and my sister.

Did you do any formal music study?
I never had any musical training.

When did you decide you wanted to be writing songs and not just doing covers? Had you already been experimenting with writing before you left for Australia?
I had never written a song before arriving in Australia. I began writing when The Easybeats were formed, simply because we wanted to be judged as a band on our own terms rather than an imitation of someone else.

Did you already have clear ideas about song structure or did that come once you were playing in Sydney?
I never heard the term "song structure" used in those days. We spoke of arrangements, which to us meant various verse-chorus routines. The main parameter was to try and keep the song under three minutes.

How did you view the Australian music scene and what you heard on radio when you arrived here?
I thought that there were some good musicians and singers around but that they were too heavily influenced by light American pop. But that was the radio format at the time and I can't knock them for being influenced by it.

How was the migrant experience, being a foreigner in a strange place, reflected in your early songwriting work?
It had no bearing.

What brought you and Stevie Wright together initially in a songwriting partnership?
He was the only one of the others in the band with some aptitude for lyrics.

Do you remember how "She's So Fine" came to be written?
I recall thinking that our first release was probably too mid-paced, and because of that, deciding to write a song that was more upfront, having a strong hook and solid rock beat.

Those earliest songs you wrote with Stevie, like "She's So Fine", "Sorry", "Wedding Ring" and "I'll Make You Happy", were very much hooked on the title, repeating the same word or line. Did you or Stevie tend to come up with a title and then write lyrics around, or did you hit on those catch phrases more by accident?
The lyrics were initially music phrases and the words we looked for had to match the energy of those phrases. They also had to roll off the tongue easily. They rarely came about by accident.

Was Stevie mainly contributing the lyrics or was it an even contribution between you both?
I did the music. We co-worked the lyrics.

As you were often writing quickly and to demand, was there any room for writing about private experiences or emotions?
I never gave a thought or felt any need to make a personal statement in an Easybeats' song.

It would've been alien to what we were as a band. I would've been thumped had I even hinted at it.

But have you ever written a song in a cathartic way, for your own personal fulfilment, either in the early days or more lately?
Yes, but only at the tail end of my writing years and only on rare occasions. But no-one's heard them and I'm happy to keep it that way.

What were the noticeable differences between the way you worked with Stevie and the way you worked with Harry?
Being a musician, Harry had more musical input. Stevie, being a singer and performer, had more input on the all-round dynamics of a song.

Would you usually come up with a melody and the chords spring from that, or would you generate melodies by playing chord changes?
Sometimes one, sometimes the other, sometimes a bit of both. But we used many other ways of sparking a song, such as titles, stories, moods.

When you moved to England in 1966, did you feel like Europeans who had come home or Australians who were overseas?
Musically, I felt Australian. I did not feel European, nor that I was coming home. I was brought up in Scotland. England was as alien to me as it was to the Dutch guys.

With "Friday on My Mind" it's interesting that a song written by a Dutchman and a Scot, recorded in London and produced by an American, has gone down as the greatest Australian song of all time. Did it feel like an Australian song to you?
The song felt neither Australian, Scots or Dutch. Nor did I give it any thought. If I had I would have probably said it felt international, in the sense that it was all about the big night out at the end of the working week, and you didn't need a diploma to know that the big night out crossed all borders. I knew from experience that the average Aussie looked forward to it, as did the Scots, English and Dutch, as well as every other nationality I'd ever met. I never thought "nationality" when I wrote. It's too narrow a focus.

Harry explained how the musical idea for the song came from seeing a film about swingle singers, which set you off on a melodic tangent. Do you remember how the lyrical idea came to you? Did you consciously decide that the song was to be an "ode to the working class"?
The lyrical theme was obvious after we came up with the opening line—"Monday morning feel so bad". It's understandable why it can be seen as an ode to the working class given the weekly grind of the average punter. But it had more to do with their outlook on the world than any class statement.

Harry says that the song was a hard one to write. Do you feel the same way?
Can't say that I do. I remember it as being fairly straightforward musically; I don't think it took more than half an hour to put together. The lyrics took around a couple of weeks to knock into shape. Even so, I don't remember them being particularly difficult.

Everyone who worked with Shel Talmy seemed to have a story about him. His work with Axiom broke them up. Did you write "Have You Got a Soul" about him?
It wasn't about Talmy, nor about anybody I care to remember. Talmy himself was a professional, with a good ear for a song. I can't recall any major disagreements with him.

You once referred to "Heaven and Hell" as "complicated self-indulgence". Was it a deliberate move towards more cerebral lyrics? Did the BBC's ban of it validate that move?
It was a deliberate move to darker lyrics. The only lasting memory I have of the ban is that it dismayed the management, not surprising given the power of the BBC, who had become very influential in dictating musical tastes. I can't remember why they banned it but not long before, their political patsies had killed off pirate radio and a lot of people felt that they were out to castrate rock music.

In a period and place of musical eclecticism, was being different important and a challenge?
I don't think we were trying to be different for its own sake. We wrote as we felt. Looking back, I think we found it easier and more enjoyable because the musical shackles were off and we could let our imaginations rip.

"The Music Goes Round My Head" was another shift for you both musically and lyrically. Do you remember writing that one?
Yes. We tried to combine ska, pop and psychedelia in one song. It's been years since I heard it and I'm not sure whether we pulled it off.

There were many songs from that so-called psychedelic period of your work that barely saw the light of day on record. What were some of your favourites from that time?
I have no favourites except, perhaps, the ones that were never released. They were just too far out.

Where did something as straight and hard rocking as "Good Times" come from in the midst of all that quirkiness and innovation?
I like to think that it was a reminder that, musically speaking, we were a long way from home.

The intro in "The Shame Just Drained" is repeated later on in "Down Among the Dead Men" and it's also hinted at in "The Love Game". Harry told me he wasn't aware of that. Were you? Were there other instances where you recycled your own work in later songs?
I'm not aware of that either. It's been years since I heard them and I couldn't say if I agree with you or not. I've never consciously set out to recycle old work.

Why did it become important to start producing yourselves?
It wasn't so much the importance; it was more the realising that, once you had the song, the arrangement and a competent engineer, producing was no big deal.

Was there a conscious decision when you returned to Australia to return to the pop hit-making formula, albeit one tailored more for the seventies market?
Yes. The music business had become too pseudo-intellectual. The average punter hadn't. We wanted to reach that audience again.

"Falling in Love Again" was very schmaltzy for you two, and yet it's one of the most endearing love songs of its time, not the least because of Ted Mulry's tender performance. It sounds almost Bacharach/David-inspired. What is the story behind writing that song?
It was one of a bunch we wrote at a time when we were broke, in the hope of getting covers by other artists. It was deliberately schmaltzy. Those types of songs tend to get covers more easily.

Was "Superman" something that you wrote especially for Alison McCallum or was it one of a number of songs you were sending back from the UK for Alberts to listen to? Was writing for a female vocal any different for you at that stage?
It was one of a bunch sent to Ted Albert. It was not written especially for Alison though she did a good job with it. It was no more difficult to write for a female as it was for a male.

Being that you were in London trying to be international songwriters, how did you feel that your songs ended up back at Alberts being released in Australia, which was quite a small market?
No market is small when you're broke.

What is the genesis of "Evie"? Did anyone or anything in your real lives inspire it?
The lyric is an amalgam of a number of events, some real, some imagined. It started out as five separate musical ideas, and the thought of linking them together occurred after each idea started spawning identical snatches of lyrics. It was reinforced during rehearsals when we found that each musical change flowed smoothly into the next. The changes felt natural and it would have been crass to spoil the mood. So we went with it. We knew it was a gamble, but sometimes a song is what it is, and should not be hacked to bits to fit a radio format.

Were you making a statement by writing and producing an eleven-minute epic? Were you amazed that it went to number one at that length?
No statement. I didn't give much thought to it being a long song and a number one. There had been other long-song hits before and I didn't think it was that unusual. But credit to the radio stations. They took a gamble in playing it, and that they did was mostly down to Rod Muir, the then boss of 2SM. He had the balls to kick it all off.

Is that a song you're particularly proud of?
No, but I was happy that it put Stevie back on the radar.

Was "Yesterday's Hero" about the post-Easybeats experience for yourselves or Stevie? Was it something you suggested Stevie sing before giving it to JPY?
It was not about Stevie or The Easybeats. It was about all those who hit the headlines for one reason or another, and then fade back into obscurity. It was written specifically with JPY's voice in mind.

Harry said that "I Hate the Music" was a title first, and that you came up with it because of frustrations with the music industry. Can you elaborate?
It was because of frustration with a particular song, not the industry. We were pissed off because a song we were working on was not coming together naturally. This kind of logjam can niggle away at you for weeks, months, years. But it came with the territory. It wasn't unusual.

What was at the heart of the formula you were employing in that mid-seventies peak of pop success?
Energy and excitement, and not being highbrow.

Did "Love Is in the Air" feel special to you at the time you wrote it, any more than "Standing in the Rain" or "Keep on Smiling"? Did it feel like it was a cut above the rest?
It did feel a cut above some of the others that we'd recently written, probably because it came together naturally and there were no logjams to get around. But I can't say it felt particularly special, though my sister did. That was a good sign.

Both in JPY's extensive repertoire and in the Flash and the Pan repertoire, there was a focus on piano-driven songs rather than the guitar-driven songs of the Easybeats and Stevie Wright. Was this a conscious move?
Yes, but not because of any anti-guitar sentiment. JPY had a pop/MOR appeal and too much guitar work can grate to that audience. Flash and the Pan was deliberately more electronic. It enabled us to experiment with more edgy ideas. That appealed.

And the spoken-word vocals?
It began with the "St Peter" song. We had each tried singing it with results that were toe-curling. So we either had to bin the song or trying something radical. Talking a song hadn't been done for ages—rap wasn't around then—so we gave that a try. It captured the mood far better than singing so we went with it. It also gave the act an identity. No bad thing to have.

Where did the idea for "Hey St Peter" come from?
Life in the big city.

Had you always been fascinated by the Titanic legend or did "Down Among the Dead Men" spring from seeing a movie or reading a book?
I have a casual interest in history and I had been interested, not fascinated, in the Titanic since I first saw the movie *A Night to Remember* as a kid. I had read a few books on it by the time the song came along. When we first laid down the track we had no lyrical theme in mind, but on hearing the playbacks we began to sense there was a mood of doom in the music. At that point the theme became obvious.

How has each of your personalities been reflected in your songs?
There is a touch of the gambler in both our make-ups. That might be reflected in more than a few of the songs.

Have there been favourite keys that you've worked in?
B major, minus the E flat note.

When you and Harry write together today, has the process changed at all from the early days?
When we knocked around some ideas recently, the routine hadn't changed.

What kind of work are you doing today?
I dabble in a lot of areas that I'm interested in, too varied to go into, enough to say that they keep my brain ticking over.

Do you miss Harry and the full-time partnership?
I miss Harry personally. But full-time partnership? No.

After all these years of writing, is it easy for you to connect with your creative source and get inspired?
What you call creative source I call motivation, and reconnecting with it I would find difficult. But if my life depended on it, I know I can knock out a song or two. Whether they'd be any good or not is another matter.

Do you feel that there is a mystery to songwriting and to where songs come from?
I've heard a lot of psychobabble about this down through the years, some of it vaguely plausible. But in general terms, I don't believe there is any mystery. Songs come from using your imagination and drawing on your own experience of life.

TERRY BRITTEN

RICHMOND, ENGLAND, MAY 2004

On a warm English spring day, Terry Britten met me at Richmond train station in his station wagon and took me for a brief meander around the neighbourhood on the way to his home. "That's Mick Jagger's house," he said, waving his hand in one direction. "And that's Pete Townsend's." It's a casual, laid-back, very British musical enclave. "You see them in the garden centre," Britten said, "or just walking around."

Britten might not be as famous as some of his neighbours, nor as recognisable, for which he is mightily thankful. But on his mantelpiece are various plaques and statues, including Grammy awards and British Academy of Songwriters and Composers Ivor Novello awards. The careers, and subsequent fortunes, of artists like Cliff Richard and Tina Turner were turned around because of his songwriting and producing talents, and the week we met he had been working on a new song for Lenny Kravitz. In fact, he is so far removed, professionally speaking, from his musical beginnings in Australia that he has difficulty recalling how and when songs were written in the 1960s. But it was his foray into songwriting four decades ago that has made him such an integral part of Australia's popular music history.

"I been out on the road with a rock 'n' roll band/ Terry Britten, old Stockley, now Beeb." So sang Glenn Shorrock in his Little River Band song "Sweet Old Fashioned Man" in 1976. Back then I was singing along to those lyrics without fully appreciating the importance of Britten's legacy. At around the same time I was singing along with Cliff Richard to "Devil Woman". It's a connection I didn't make at the time, but one that Britten might refer to as "magic".

Terry Britten was born in Manchester on 17 July 1947. Like fellow Mancunians, the Brothers Gibb, Britten only spent a relatively short time in Australia—he arrived at age twelve and moved back to England ten years later—but to this day he considers himself an Aussie. For one thing, his parents are still in Adelaide. And for another, he barracks for the Australian cricket team.

There is also the matter of his having been a pivotal member of Australia's most successful sixties pop group, The Twilights, renowned for their immaculate cover versions of Beatles songs and their peerless standards of live performance. From The Twilights' early single, "I'll Be Where You Are", written with lead singer Glenn Shorrock, until their demise in 1969, Britten was the band's main contributor of original material.

The Twilights' biggest hits were covers of "Needle in a Haystack" and "What's Wrong with the Way I Live" and Britten felt unenthused about recording songs that did not necessarily reflect his growing creativity. His own songs "If She Finds Out" and "Cathy Come Home" charted well, although some of his most critically acclaimed works from that period, like "9.50" and "Time and Motion Study Man", were relegated to B-sides or album cuts. Britten didn't mind, because he never actually thought of himself as a real songwriter, and at the time of this interview, was still unprepared to assume the mantle. "I have no pretensions, even now, about being a songwriter," he said.

Like so many guitar-driven songwriters of that era, Britten's major influence was The Shadows. The Beatles were his watershed, but Cliff Richard and The Shadows were his first calling; they were what made him pick up a guitar, and as did his contemporary, John Farrar, also a Shadows devotee, he eventually made music with his heroes.

Britten played guitar in Richard's band in the 1970s, but it was when he started writing for him that the stars aligned. "Devil Woman" made the fading idol cool again, and was his breakthrough song in America. Britten was from then on Richard's chief writer and eventually his producer, but in 1983, when a song he co-wrote with Graham Lyle was recorded by Tina Turner—much to Richard's chagrin—Britten's attentions turned to R&B and rock acts. Since "What's Love Got to Do with It", which won Song of the Year and Record of the Year Grammy awards in 1984, Britten's association with Turner has been continuous. Meanwhile, his songs, co-written with Lyle or other collaborators, have been recorded by the likes of Kravitz, Michael Jackson and Bonnie Raitt.

While he visits Australia regularly to see family and friends, Britten could not see himself back for good. His work, his studio, family, dogs and sprawling villa on the Devon coast keep him contentedly in Britain.

I began by asking Britten his birth date. He told me, and then exclaimed, "Oh wow!", as though he did not ordinarily contemplate his vintage.

"The weird thing is, quite often you're working with eighteen-, twenty-year-olds, and you don't think about it, because you're just working on a piece of music. You say, 'When were you born?' And they say, '1984' and you go, 'Oh my God! That's when I had a huge hit with Tina, in '84.' It's the strangest feeling. You're up there doing all that and someone's just coming into the world. But there you are working together. I think that's magic."

Do you remember first hearing the Beatles?
Oh yeah! I was going home from work on the bus when I was about fifteen or sixteen, and I was already playing surf music and Shadows, all sorts of stuff. That was the good thing about Australia, they had a lot of surf music, which we didn't really have in the UK. I remember being on the bus and hearing this record [*sings intro to "Please Please Me"*], "Last night I said ..."—with the harmony holding. And I thought, is that The Everly Brothers? It's The Everly Brothers, but it's not. And of course, it was nicked from The Everly Brothers, it's the same as "Cathy's Clown". But it just had this extra little something. I thought, wow! I was so excited. I remember buying it when the album came out and that was it, I was sold.

Was there a moment when you knew that you were going to work in music and write songs?
No, I just followed it. I think you're mesmerised by it, it's just a pull. When I took up the guitar I played it day and night.

Did you take lessons?
No, I was totally self-taught. My first guitar cost three pounds seventeen and sixpence. It was terrible, so hard to play, but that also is good. I got the guitar just before I left England. I was actually playing on the boat. We went to that hostel in Adelaide, lived there for a year. They had a band already, some Aussies and some Brits in it, and they let me sit in. I was only fourteen, and I was up there in a band. I went in and out of groups when I was very young, and I was playing in even more than one band. When I was in Adelaide recently, I was staying in a hotel right opposite the Glenelg Town Hall, where I used to play with a girl called Carol Sturtzel. Had the most amazing Brenda Lee voice. I was out playing country music; I never knew what country music was and I'm doing "Jambalaya". It was all great experience.

So the thing about that sort of background, Beatles to Beach Boys to R&B, is even now at this time, 2004, you can draw on any of those musical styles, mix them up. You can be doing an R&B song and suddenly you hear yourself doing Beatle chords in the middle of it.

Do you think your style of playing initially influenced your writing? Are the two related?
Not really. The whole thing of writing a song never entered my head until the guy from EMI came and said, "Hey, you guys are good, do you want to make a record?" And we said, "Oh yeah! Can we do a Beatles song?" "No, no, no," he said. "You've got to do original material.

You've got to write your own." And we all looked at each other and went, "Oh shit." And I said, "I'll give it a go." So the first song I ever wrote was recorded. It was called "I'll Be Where You Are". It was a Beatle-copy ballad. [*Sings*] "I don't know where love leads us/ Whether near or afar/ Just as long as you love me/ I'll be where you are."

We recorded it on a two-track in Adelaide. And to me that's still a thrill now, because I recently got a cheque for two dollars for that. Now that's cool. Forget everything else, that is a wonderful thing. Obviously it still gets played somewhere in Australia. And I think that's magic. So it was an accident, really. I was never brought up with that sort of confidence.

Could you conceive of developing a style of music that went beyond the Beatles, or was that all you could aspire to?
You slowly became aware that you had to depart from it somewhere, even in a small way. It's like guitar playing, you listen to Hank Marvin, you listen to Dwayne Eddy, you listen to all these different people, and you're an accumulation of all you've heard. But at some point somewhere something happens where there's a little twist. You get all those ingredients and then you put your own little stamp on it. A friend of mine in Adelaide has got these demos I gave him, and he said, "There's a real style, you can hear it all through the songs." I don't know how it develops. Most of the songwriting thing is unconscious and I don't think you do very much actually, to be honest.

So do songs come from outside yourself? Do you think that you're just a receiver?
Oh yeah, absolutely. I think it's an expression. Anybody who says, "I wrote that," really from the beginning to the end he's just not being truthful at all. I think that initial spark that you get is nothing to do with you whatsoever. You're just in a frame of mind, you can be up, down, and you're just vacant. You sit there and you're just twiddling, you might even be doing scales, and suddenly the melody comes, and that initial thing, nobody has control over that. Nobody. Then you employ all your knowledge and know-how in order to get that into a three- or four-minute idea that works. That builds and the craft then comes in, and that's where the accumulation of all your influences comes in.

"If She Finds Out" was probably your first taste of songwriting success, albeit on a small scale. Do you remember how that came together with Peter Brideoake?
It took about ten minutes by the sounds of it. Probably someone had the initial idea, and then someone says, "Oh, what about this for a bridge?" That's usually how it goes. But that's too far back. You're not even aware at that age, that's the lovely thing about it; you're not thinking.

"Needle In A Haystack" was just an obscure Motown song when The Twilights recorded it. Did you see that song as being right for the group?
No. I didn't like it. To me that was a bit weird because you're trying to develop a direction and then suddenly you're taken in another direction because somebody thinks, "Oh, this could be a hit."

And it was a hit.
Yes it was. But that's not to do with The Twilights. That's just to do with it's just a great catchy little tune. It's really weird, because at that point I was so totally Beatle-y, and here I am now writing R&B music. Since the eighties I've been writing mostly R&B pop. I don't know how that happened. I think it was "Heard It through the Grapevine". When I first heard it, it was like first hearing Cliff and The Shadows or something. A light went on in my head and I went, "Oh my God." I seem to have found where I am comfortable. 'Cause all the Tina stuff has an R&B slant to it. But I can still use all the chords and the little riffs.

The intro to "Devil Woman"—I got that idea from "Heard It through the Grapevine". Without a doubt. 'Cause I was so fascinated with the mystery of [*Sings intro melody to "Grapevine"*] and the atmosphere it created straightaway. When you listen to "Devil Woman" at the start it's got the real mystery to it. You don't know quite what's going to happen.

I heard the same atmosphere in "Goosebumps". It almost seemed to me like a follow-on from "Devil Woman".
Yes, it is. It's a bit of a riff, yeah. I like riffs. I can use it a few times. "Carrie" was another one. Actually, it was quite involved, that one, but it still had that mystery. I love creating the atmosphere, it's really important.

And does that usually come from a riff?
Yeah, or a chord. Like on "What's Love", just the opening chord itself. It's got these funny notes in it and it creates the atmosphere straightaway.

Does that atmosphere always come from the music? Can it come from the lyrics?
I think that a great lyric is icing on the cake. But you can create that atmosphere just by feeling a song. And I think you're trying to get something inside you out there. It's probably partly personality as well, that you tune into.

Do you have a favourite song of your own from the Twilights era?
I do, actually, and it's only because of the chords that I discovered. Sometimes, especially if you're not a great player, you suddenly find you've done something melodically and you think, wow, that's new! It was a little song called "Always". It had quite an involved chord structure to it, and I thought, "Wow, that's incredible." I surprised myself with that.

I like "What a Silly Thing to Do!"
Yeah, there's a few weird, wacky things.

Do you have any recollection of writing "One Times, Two Times, Three Times, Four"?
Darryl Cotton said, "Have you got a song for us?"

Was it especially written for Zoot or had you had it up your sleeve for The Twilights?
I wrote it for Zoot. They said, "We're going to be a bubblegum group" or something like

that. And I went, "So you want something really light?" "One times, two times …"—there you go. I was really just trying stuff. Believe me, I have no pretensions, even now, about being a songwriter.

You win a Grammy for Song of the Year and you don't see yourself as a songwriter?
I know, I know. I don't have that image, no. I think it would be a burden if I did.

Was the transition from band member to songwriter-for-hire an easy one for you?
No. It was very difficult. I decided to put myself in the deep end. I could have stayed in Australia, kept writing songs, maybe, developing. But I thought I'd go to London. You're coming from this little backwater, with a band and all the people around you, and suddenly you find yourself sitting there in a basement trying to write songs. Bruce Welch from The Shadows was very keen to nurture me; he'd come down every week and say, "Okay, what have you written?" I'd have my little tape machine in a broom cupboard. And he went, "It's good, but where's the hook?" He kept saying, "Where's the hook?" I hated him by the end of it. He'd be saying, "Where's the hook? Where's the bit? Where is it?" So I'd be thinking about the hook, the hook. It took a long time to sink in. He was a great help to me. Because even when I was in The Twilights, he came to Australia with The Shadows, came to Armstrong Studios looking for songs. And he took a bunch of my songs back then to Cliff. Cliff recorded them. I've never heard them. But someone gave me a 45, which I think I've got upstairs, which I haven't played yet, of Cliff singing one of those Twilights songs.

All the work you did with Cliff over the years, you never said, "Oh by the way, I'd like to hear those songs you recorded"?
No, never occurred to me.

Has your writing process always been basically you and a guitar?
Yeah. Still the same now, and I think I will always stick to that way of doing things because it's organic. I could go and sit in a pub in Silverton or wherever and just sing a song with a guitar. Actually, I need a backing track. I think I was the first person, through John Farrar, to have a LinnDrum in England. It was a Linn and Oberheim Drum Machine, and when I did Tina's stuff that's what I used. I tried real drums, it didn't work. I still use a drum machine to get a feel. But you'll use guitar, even if you're going to eventually use a keyboard player.

After The Twilights, your songwriting was mostly collaborating with other people. Do you prefer having a co-writer to writing alone?
Both really. I usually initially write by myself. And then I'll get a stack of ideas, or I'll get something before I play it to somebody. Other times I'll sit in a room and we've got nothing, we'll start from scratch. That's a bit daunting, especially when you've first met somebody. Sometimes it works, sometimes you end up funnily enough working with

someone that's chalk and cheese, someone who's just not like you in any way, you're so opposite, but it works. You can never say what works. And then you can get with, like John Farrar and myself, the best of mates, both guitar players, and it never quite happens.

What draws you to collaborate when you are totally competent and capable of writing on your own?
Usually the lyric. Because it's craft, and if you feel a bit insecure in that direction or a bit lightweight, it's good to work with other people. I think some people have a particular talent for a lyric or music. I'm much more geared to music. I don't have a lot to say lyrically, to be honest. But musically I could just come out with ideas all day.

You also learn a lot, too. The way they put it together, the way they think out things. I'm lucky that I've got the pop sensibility to sing a hook but you then get someone who really knows what they're doing to give you the verses and the build to make it really strong.

What's the most important quality in a co-writer?
If they really care about what they're doing as much as you do, that's all you can ask. And I've always said the same thing, if you sit down and write a song with somebody and they write 10 per cent, and you write 90, it's still 50–50 split. I've always stuck to that, no matter what. Because I figure if they were not there, that song would never have got written. And yet there are people who argue over splits. I've never done it. Unless it's a specific thing agreed beforehand.

"Devil Woman" was quite a radical departure for Cliff Richard in 1976. Do you remember how it came about?
Yeah, I had that riff for quite a while and at sound checks I'd just work on it. And then I got together with somebody who did a few lyrics and I don't know how that came about, we've only ever written the one song together. But these odd things happen in your life, which are fantastic. You suddenly find yourself in a flat in Kensington, co-writing. You think, "Why the hell am I doing this? I don't want to work with this person." And then you find yourself there.

I said, "Well, let's write a song for Cliff. I've got this riff." And she came up with a title, and I thought, well it's not a very original title, it's been done. There had already been a song called "Devil Woman", a country song. Marty Robbins. But it worked. And it was commercial. Christine Holmes, her name was. She was a TV presenter at one time.

Did Cliff like it straight away?
Oh yeah, Bruce Welch went crazy. We had a great time recording it at Abbey Road. It was fantastic. And then it all went horribly wrong. 'Cause Cliff had this "Honky Tonk Angel" song out and somebody said, "Oh, Cliff obviously doesn't know what a honky tonk angel is, a prostitute, and here is Cliff Richard, the Christian, singing about a prostitute." And poor old naive Cliff, as soon as he realised, he pulled the record. Killed it off. And of course what's the next thing you're going to do after that?

"Devil Woman".
Well you can't do that, you see. So it sat on the shelf for a year. We recorded it in '74 at Abbey Road, Allan Clarke from The Hollies was walking down the corridor, came in, put his head around and went, "That's a hit." And the engineer went, "America. This is going to be a hit in America." And Cliff's never had a hit in America, so I'm going, "Ah, people, what do they know?" Mr Confidence, you know. But when they brought it out, I remember I was in Epsom in the kitchen, I was making my breakfast, it was eight o'clock in the morning, and it came on and he said, "Listen to this! You're never going to guess who this is!" He said, "I'll play it again! I'll tell you what, let's have a competition. You ring in and tell me who you think this is singing this song." And I don't believe this—twice he's played it. Then he played it three times in a row, and I'm going, "Wow!" It sounded fantastic on the radio. And there was this buzz. It was huge in America. Even now, it gets played in America.

After that was your first worldwide hit did that help your confidence levels?
Not really, I was still low on confidence. It bought me a grand piano and all sorts of things, first house. It was a big thrill, I must say. I was touring Russia with Cliff. We were stuck in Leningrad and Moscow and it was miserable as sin. And we'd wait for every Thursday, for chart day in America. It was so exciting.

When you were asked to write songs for Christie Allen, were you conscious that you were using your "Devil Woman" technique on the songs?
Oh yes. I was limited, and you work with your limitations. I thought, yeah, it works. I'm learning. The Christie Allen thing was when Mushroom said, "Will you do this album in London for her and write and produce it?" A mate of mine was managing her, Geoff Skewes from The Vibrants. So he talked me into it. I thought, well, it's good experience. I'm not a producer and I had to do it very quickly and very cheaply. So I learned a lot through doing that.

Christie Allen won at the Countdown Awards because of "Goosebumps".
I know. She was a sweet girl. She wasn't cut out to be a pop star.

Did you like that song?
It's fun. A funny lyric. "Cardiac arresting stare." I think it's hysterical. That's written with another guy I produced at the same time, BA Robertson. We had four or five big hits here with him.

Did "Devil Woman" open things up so you could write anything for Cliff or were you still working within limitations in terms of his image?
I would have liked to do more like that, but Cliff being the beast that he is has got this thing about always trying something different. Which is accepted here, but in America you had "Devil Woman" out and in America if that's what you do, that's what you do. But he came out next with this falsetto, funny, lightweight track, and I thought, why on earth are they wasting this opportunity by not following through with a similar vibe?

I guess vocally he could go just about anywhere.
Cliff's an incredible singer, amazing. People can say what they like but anyone who actually worked with him will tell you the same thing, his vocal quality and delivery are fantastic.

Were there subjects and themes you couldn't touch lyrically?
Yeah, anything slightly smutty might not go down well. But overall, it was all kept pretty straight.

Were there ideas that he had that he asked you to integrate into songs?
No. Not at all. I had written Christian songs for him when he did a gospel album. One song called "Yes He Lives", which he just was knocked out with.

Are you a Christian?
Absolutely not.

So how did you get yourself into that mode?
You just substitute Jesus for whatever you feel within you. So it doesn't matter. If you're talking about something that's true, it's not limited to that one thing. Actually, I have Christians coming up to me saying, "That sums up everything about Christianity today." And I'm going, "Oh, really?" [*Laughs*] I can see why someone would believe that, follow that. And I could put my own feelings about what might be true into a song.

Can you talk about Graham Lyle and how that co-writing relationship worked?
I'd say of all the people I've worked with, he's been the biggest influence on me. I was put together with Graham by a mutual friend of ours, a wonderful keyboard player, Billy Livsey, who used to play with Graham's band, Gallagher and Lyle. I had a studio at home then. And Graham was very much an acoustic man, a folky type. "Heart on My Sleeve" was Graham's song. Beautiful song. But he wasn't really a lyricist. Benny [Gallagher] was the lyricist on most of their stuff. So a funny pairing.

    Anyway, we got together this day, and I thought, "Oh, you've brought acoustic, better go on acoustic." But it was boring. I'm sitting there playing away, wandering around the perimeter, thinking, what are we doing here? And then I said, "Graham, have you ever worked with a drum machine?" "No, no, no." I said, "It's really good fun, because you get the groove, you know. Let's just try something." So I got my electric out and the drum machine. And I started playing a chord. And he went, "Oh, this feels great!" He was really excited, you could tell. So I just started a melody.

    He said, "I had a lyric idea this morning on the way here—'What's love got to do with it?' But it's not anti-love, it's about someone who can't admit to being totally in love." A few lines came out and I thought, "Oh, this is really good." So we're messing around with it, and I went on and musically finished it, more or less. And he said, "Look, can I go away and just play with this? 'Cause I just need to be by myself." So he went home and next week came back and we put it all down, got it into shape and turned around and went, "It's finished."

Who wrote the verses?
Graham did. He wasn't primarily a lyricist, he was music, so it was a departure for him, too. He'd found something about himself. And we both said, "Well, that was nice, wasn't it? Good meeting you, and maybe see you again." "Yeah, it was good." And never thought any more about the song. Never thought about anything, whether it was a hit. If you heard the demo you'd probably know why, 'cause it's not particularly good. It was too high.

Was it something Cliff could have sung?
Oh, Cliff never forgave me for it. Never forgave me for not giving it to him.

It's all part of Tina Turner's story, isn't it?
That was a fluke as well. It was actually recorded by Buck's Fizz. I heard it and it was absolutely terrible. I said to the publisher, "How could you?" At the same time they'd sent it to Tina, 'cause they heard she was doing a comeback. So [Turner's manager] Roger Davies heard it, and he knew me from The Twilights, because when he was a kid he used to sit in the front row and watch us. He heard the song and said, "We want to do it."

Anyway, very unlike me, I went and saw Buck's Fizz's manager, and I said, "Do you think you're going to use this record because honestly, it's pretty awful. And I've got a chance to do it with Tina. I've been asked to produce it; this is a great opportunity." And she said, "We'll drop it then." So the road was clear.

The whole story of that song, if you were there in the studio, was just such an amazing thing. She hated the song. And when I sat in that room and she came in the studio, miserable February day, she was so depressed, meeting all these producers. She was fed up. Came in with a big fur coat and she looked like death. She said, "I've told Roger I really don't like this song."

Were you a fan of hers?
Oh God. "River Deep". Like, oh my God! I was terrified working with this woman. Big person and big personality.

She told you she didn't like it. How did that make you feel?
I said, "Well, put it this way, if we do it and it doesn't work out, we won't use it. There's nothing to lose." So I said, "Why don't we try the other one first?" There was a more up-tempo one I'd done called "Show Some Respect". She was very cold about it. And as soon as I put the drum machine on and it started playing, she said, "Oh, this is good." She took the coat off. We did that and rehearsed the other one, and she said, "No, I just don't see it." It doesn't matter how big the artist is, if you take them out of what they are good at, the insecurity comes in. We had a wonderful simple track and when she came in to do the vocal, she couldn't get it.

I let her go for a couple of times, and she was singing it in the Tina way. I said, "Quieter, quieter." She couldn't get the rhythm, because she'd never done anything like it. It wasn't going particularly well until I went out to the studio and I said, "Tina, look, do me a favour. Jog. Slow jog. Now sing."

She said, "I got it! I got it! I got it!" Great. Did the vocal, played it back. She went, "Oh my God, people are going to say I can sing." I said, "Tina, you're one of the best singers on the planet." She said, "No, I'm a dancer, I'm a rock 'n' roller." I said, "Not any more. Now you've done that song, you can do any song. You can do anything."

She said, "Instead of 'Oh Tina, you did a great version of an Al Green song', people are going to say, 'That's a Tina Turner song.'" She was in love with the record. Because she'd found something about herself that had never been there before. It was a new idea; she'd never sung that quietly. More or less in the end she whispered it. And of course because it was Tina Turner, first up, no Ike, it was a magic moment. I couldn't stop playing it. When I did that recording, I was playing it down the phone to people.

That song turned around the fortunes of one of the greatest female rock artists of all time. Do you see yourself as having played a role in history?
I do now. It was such a story. I definitely feel very much part of that.

Did you then feel that you had to live up to that song, in your writing?
I've been lucky in that I've not made that a hurdle for myself. When I had "Devil Woman", everyone said, "You've got to write another one." I never put myself under that pressure, consciously, and raised the bar. I just said, I still say it now, I don't see myself as a professional songwriter. And I don't need the bar to do it, to say I've got to jump over the bar. I know it sounds weird. I'm not being pretentious, I'm actually serious.

What do you see yourself as? A professional producer who happens to write songs?
No, I'm definitely not a producer. I'm a part-time producer, really. When I did the Tina thing, I had record companies saying, "Here's our roster. Who'd you like to produce?" And I went, "Gladys Knight". They went, "Gladys Knight?" I said, "Yeah." They said, "Well, she hasn't even got a record deal." I said, "But Gladys Knight is my favourite singer."

You could have done a Tina on Gladys.
I could have done. Even today, if someone said, "Do you want to do it tomorrow?" I'd do it. But I never put myself forward like that. Tina's been very good like that. Even when we're doing albums. I say, "I really want to get Eric Clapton to play this". She says, "You want Eric Clapton? I'll give him a ring. But I'll tell you now, Terry, this is your time. You do it." You've got to think about things like that. I got to work with Stevie Winwood. He came in and did a keyboard on "Afterglow" on the *Break Every Rule* album. Oh, Stevie Winwood played on one of my tracks!

What was he like?
Wonderful. Very quiet. And he said, "The track's really good. Who played the guitar?" I did. He liked my guitar. Even Eric said, "Tight track!" We did a 12-inch mix and managed to get him to come in and play on it.

When you and Graham Lyle wrote "We Don't Need Another Hero", was it a commission specifically for Tina, or was the brief more about it being a song for the *Mad Max Beyond Thunderdome* film?

It was both; it was write something for the film, which Tina will sing. We'd just seen a script, no film had been made. And again, atmosphere. It's got to have atmosphere. It's got to have a spookiness about it.

Did Tina like it immediately?

Tina did. The demo was very simple, incredibly under-produced. It was all up here [*points to head*], how you're going to produce the thing. We actually did it as a seven-and-a-half minute song. And cut it down to three and a half minutes. When George Miller heard the track, he said, "Man, you could have done the music score for the film."

Is that something you've wanted to do?

I've thought about it. And he's right; there were lots of elements in the long mix that could have fitted in. They said they'd already commissioned the guy to do the music. But I had a great time doing that.

Did Tina ever talk to you about the kind of songs she wanted you to write for her, subjects she wanted to sing about?

Yeah, she might say, "I like the feel of this thing." The feel of a record. A tempo thing. Or she might suggest a big ballad. We've done things with funny lyrics that you know you need a person larger than life. Like "What You Get Is What You See". When you listen to the story, it's so much fun, and she can carry it off. We did write a song with a very good lyric, which fitted with a lot of her beliefs, the Buddhist thing, called "Something Beautiful Remains".

Did she ever reject something that you had thought would be perfect?

Oh yeah. You learn to deal with those things. I learned very early on. I remember when I first started writing I would play a song for somebody, and if there was a bit that I was particularly embarrassed about, as the bit came up I'd say something like, "Would you like a cup of tea?" And they'd go, "Oh yeah, one sugar, thanks." I'd say, "Okay." Ah, the bit's gone now, they didn't hear it. And it shows you all these silly things go through your head if something's bugging you and you don't know how to fix it. But that's why demos are important. Spend the time on the demo, you make your mistakes, if something needs correcting, a line you're not happy with, you've got a chance to do it then.

How did Michael Jackson come to record "Just Good Friends"?

We were in Rod Temperton's house, a lovely guy from Hull. He was playing some of the demos he'd done for *Bad*. And I said, "They feel so good, they've got a great groove. How do you do that?" He said, "You guys should try and write something, because there's no guarantee, even though I've written 'Off the Wall' and 'Thriller' and everything, that they're going to use these songs. Give it a try."

So we came up with the idea and were very happy with the demo, and a weird thing happened, because we sent it over there and Rod Temperton rang back and said, "Guys, it's a wonderful song, but it's really strange, it's very spooky. On the demo, whoever's singing it, some lines sound like Michael, and there's some lines that sound like Stevie Wonder. And we've just decided yesterday that he's going to do a duet with Stevie Wonder. And this song is absolutely perfect."

But I'll tell you the downside of that. I was at the HMV shop at nine o'clock in the morning the day it came out, to buy it. I ran back to the studio to play it. And I was so disappointed. It just wasn't good. It didn't work. It didn't have heart. To me it was like homogenised. It was like, Michael didn't write it so he wasn't interested in getting involved somehow. But hey, 35 million albums later, I ain't going to complain about it. But you learn. If you want to be a professional songwriter, that's going to happen. Unless you get involved in it every time and take responsibility, you've got to accept that.

Whereas "What's Love Got to Do with It" feels like a child to you that you nurtured from birth.
Right from the beginning to when you're cutting it and it's being pressed.

How did Lenny Kravitz get hold of "Heaven Help"?
Gerry Deveaux is his cousin. I'd never worked with Gerry before, and it was one of those days where we tried a few things, we had a few things on tape, he said, "I'll go away and think about this." And then literally he was about to leave, and I just played the chords and he went, "What's that? What's that?" And I went [*Sings*], "Heaven help the fool ..." And he went, "I love that! I love that! Keep going!" It was frenetic. Five minutes later the tune was done and we actually had the chorus. So he finished the lyric and then he had to go to New York.

When he was there he rang and said, "If you don't mind I'll do the demo." I said, "I'd be delighted for you to do the demo." 'Cause I always get stuck with the demos, having a studio. So he did the demo over there, using the little studio Lenny works at. The engineer Henry Hirsch played the piano and the bass, they had a drummer, and Lenny heard the song and went crazy. He just said, "I've got to do this song." And that was it. Then I did one called "Circus" for him. And I've just done the title track on this one, "Baptism". Wrote it in Sydney, played it to him over the phone, he went, "I just love it." And he recorded it two days later in New York. It's bizarre.

In these cases—Michael Jackson, Lenny Kravitz—you have had fine songwriters in their own right recording your songs.
People say to me, "How do you get your songs on there?" because Lenny writes his own songs. But for some reason he hears something that maybe is not his particular forte or something that he gets off on. I think the Michael Jackson thing was definitely a one-off. Although I did have another song in the running, for *Thriller*, a little demo I wrote with Sue Shifrin, but they asked for all the publishing.

That was before your Tina Turner success.
Yes. I was nobody and I was asked for all the publishing. And I said, "I can't give it to you because it's not mine." "Oh well, we ain't doing the song." But they never asked me about the publishing on *Bad*. Because you've got a couple of cheap trinkets on your mantelpiece, it makes a difference.

"Storm Warning" is a special song.
I love that little tune. That was written with a girl from New Zealand. Again, one of those songs where you only write one song with somebody. I met her here and she suggested maybe we could try and write something. I was intrigued by her name actually, Lea Maalfrid. We fiddled around that day and nothing really happened. She had this lovely way with the piano, this delivery, really nice. And she's very sweet, a bit out there. It wasn't working that day and I said to her, "I'll drive you home." We got in the car, turned on the news and it said, "This is a storm warning." And I went, "Now *there's* a good title!" So that night she got some ideas together and we got together again, and we had a song. We sent it to Bonnie Raitt and they turned it down. Anyway, next year, the publisher said to me, "You know, I just loved that song. I'm going to try it again." So they sent it again, and they did it that time.

So do you think songs have their special time?
Absolutely.

Like "Devil Woman" had sat on the shelf; perhaps if it had been released a year earlier it wouldn't have made its mark.
I've had lots of songs that have sat there for years waiting. I remember one song I did, I was demoing it for Tina and I thought, no, this is not working. And I suddenly thought, Anita Baker. What a voice she has, a beautiful voice. Suddenly it was all change of direction in the middle of the demo. So it worked, and she did it, which was great. She's a wonderful artist.

Do you have any system for staying in shape creatively? Is it playing the guitar every day?
No, it's not, that's something I stopped doing. I had this thing where you have to keep everything oiled, you have to go in every day and do something. And I thought, hang on, no you don't. That's just a fear-based thing. I realised there is no security at all with songs or anything else in life. So let go of it. I don't want to sit there and worry about it. That's the worst thing you can do with any block, is sit and think about it. I down tools and for two or three days, I garden, I walk, I paint, I do anything at all but music. Until that thing inside goes, "Oh, I want to write music." You've got to wait for it.

JOHNNY YOUNG

MELBOURNE, AUSTRALIA, MARCH 2003

If he wasn't so easygoing, Johnny Young might be justified in feeling underrated. While his small-screen persona became a reliable fixture in Australia's popular culture milieu during the 1970s and 1980s, any achievements he had had prior to being the affable host of children's talent show *Young Talent Time* were overlooked or forgotten. The fact that he had been a pop idol himself in the 1960s, that The Easybeats songwriters, George Young (no relation) and Stevie Wright, wrote their first non-Easybeats song, "Step Back", especially for him, was not general knowledge. That he went on to become a worthy songwriter in his own right, his compositions including the landmark "The Real Thing"—a watershed in the careers of producer Ian Meldrum, singer Russell Morris, and many players of significance in the Melbourne music scene at the time, from omnipresent guitarist John Farrar to keyboardist and songwriter Brian Cadd—is still unknown to the larger population to this day. Many Australians grew up believing Young's sole purpose in life was to discover and promote the likes of Debbie Byrne, Jamie Redfern, Tina Arena and Danii Minogue.

Not that Young would ever denigrate the importance of *Young Talent Time* in the nurturing of such talent. But for a songwriter whose output also encompassed the subtle but potent anti-Vietnam song "Smiley", recorded by Ronnie Burns, and the first hit for a boxing champion, "Thank You", recorded by Lionel Rose, Young's place in Australia's songwriting canon deserves to be extolled.

Born John De Jong in Rotterdam, the Netherlands in 12 March 1947, his entry into the world was the stuff of drama and intrigue. While his father was serving in the Netherlands armed services in Indonesia during and after World War II, his mother had a relationship with another man, a young Dutch singer, who was Young's biological father. It wasn't until later in life that Young could appreciate the significance and joy of the union that produced him; for a long time he told people he had been born in Indonesia, so as to avoid suspicion and embarrassment over his father's absence before and after his birth.

It's one of many interesting facets to a man whose jovial face graced Australian television screens for decades. In all the years of closing *Young Talent Time* with weekly renditions of the Beatles' "All My Loving", if there was ever a dark mood, an ill wind in his path, the Australian public never saw a hint of it. There was personal tragedy in the years immediately following the demise of *Young Talent Time*, but Young's response was to write a humorous musical play, and then put a band together and start playing his own music again. To remind people of what had come before and what was still to come.

Young's parents had migrated to Western Australia in 1951 and he grew up around the suburbs of Perth. At thirteen he was selling newspapers outside the Regal Theatre in Subiaco, and by sixteen he was hosting his own television show. In between he had been singing with some local musicians at the Saturday afternoon Hi Five Club Dance, entered talent quests around Perth and then joined popular group The Nomads, which morphed into Johnny and the Strangers, and later Johnny Young and Kompany. "Because it was isolated over there, I was able to do more in Western Australia than I might have been able to do in Sydney or Melbourne. There wasn't much happening and I was pretty, I wanted to achieve it; I wanted to be a pop star," Young recalled over forty years later. He was greatly influenced by Australian rock 'n' roll pioneer Ray Hoff, who brought his group, the Off Beats, from Sydney to Perth in the early 1960s. An ardent R&B fan, Hoff introduced Perth audiences to Hank Ballard's original version of "The Twist", to Little Richard and John Lee Hooker. "I think if there was any person that was singularly involved in really educating Western Australia in music, it was Ray Hoff because everybody went to see him, we copied him and he was fantastic," Young said. But Young's own fascination with R&B and what he saw as the avant-garde in music was belied by the direction his career took. Based in Melbourne by 1965, he replaced Ian Turpie as host on *The Go!! Show*, that city's popular music television program. From there it was over to England, where his friendship with the Gibb brothers propelled him into the songwriting domain, where he became rapt in the evolutionary, revolutionary psychedelic culture that prevailed in his circle of contacts and which ultimately led him to write "The Real Thing" when he was back in Australia.

While Young never took himself too seriously as a songwriter, after the string of hits he had for Russell Morris, Ronnie Burns, Ross D Wyllie and others, the reputation he assumed during his tenure on *Young Talent Time* was a mixed blessing. He recorded two albums on his own in the early years of the show, to keep his independent profile going. "But the problem was that by that time I was Johnny Young from *Young Talent Time*," he said in reflection. "People weren't interested in buying my indulgences." When the show ended, it was time to rediscover himself musically and personally, with songwriting still a major focus.

"I write my best songs when I don't have my tape recorder on," he told me, sitting on the patio of a cafe in Eltham, on the pastoral outskirts of Melbourne. "I'll sit outside with my guitar and do a song if we've got some people up or something, had a few drinks, and [wife] Rose will say, 'I've got to get the tape, you've got to put that down!' 'Cause it will just come out of my head. I'm a very quick writer. Very quick."

Was songwriting something that you were conscious of in your early career, or was it all about the performance?
I didn't really get interested in songwriting until the advent of the Beatles. I didn't think of myself as a songwriter; I was a television host and pop star. I loved The Easybeats' way of writing songs, so I was aware of the difference between a good song and a bad song, but I had no aspirations at all to become a songwriter. It wasn't until after I'd had my hits and hosted *The Go!! Show* for a couple of years, 'cause in those days a couple of years at the top as a pop star was about all that you had. Writing happened later through necessity for me.

How did the connection with The Easybeats happen?
I had my own TV show and was pretty popular, so we were planning to make some records. I was hosting *Club 17*, and The Easybeats were guests. George was there in the dressing room with his little Hofner guitar, and I said, "George, I'm going in the studio next week, I'd love to do something original. You haven't got a song?" And he said, "Oh, we've been working on this song." He hadn't completed the words but he had the chorus [*Sings*], "Step back a little, you're falling in love/ Step back a little ..."

So he said, "Come around to our hotel Sunday morning"—they were doing a concert that Saturday night—"bring a tape recorder and we'll put it down for you." So I was there at seven-thirty on Sunday morning, and I knocked on their door and there was like half a dozen girls in their room, and George, who was the most sensible of all of them, opened the door and had his eyeballs hanging out of his head, said, "What are you doing here?" I said, "You were going to record that song for me on the tape recorder." And he said, "Oh, Stevie hasn't written the words yet." So Stevie went to the toilet and he actually did his morning ablutions and wrote "Step Back" on the Sunday morning.

Were you observing the Gibb brothers and their songwriting prowess?
When I was hosting *The Go!! Show* and The Bee Gees were still in Australia, I was doing very well and The Bee Gees were very poor. It wasn't until "Spicks and Specks" that they got any legitimate appreciation here in Australia. But I loved them. I loved their songs and I loved them as people. Every time I'd go to Brisbane I'd go and see them somewhere. I just

loved their harmonies, I always loved harmony singing. And they'd been on my show, so I knew them pretty well. One day I was up in Brisbane and Barry said, "I've got to drive down to Sydney, I've got a recording session." A long drive and then a big recording session. And I said, "I'll pay for your ticket, fly down with me. But write me a song." So he did. We got there, he came back to my hotel, put down this song called "Lady". I saw Barry time before last when they were here in Australia and we talked about "Lady" because no-one else has recorded it. It was a fabulous song. And he sang it, he remembered, it was really good. I really loved The Bee Gees' songwriting. I could really appreciate that they were different.

Was it Barry Gibb who encouraged you to start writing?
When I went to England and they'd had "New York Mining Disaster", Barry invited me to stay at his house, with his wife, Maureen. He had a beautiful house in New Cavendish Street. They had a spare room that Pete Townsend had used, that still had an amplifier with a Union Jack on it. I was over there recording, I wasn't writing anything at all. They'd just written a new song called "Craise Finton Kirk" and I said, "I really like that, it's really quirky." So I booked a studio and they came and did the backings. For nothing. Just fantastic. I did "Craise Finton Kirk" and "I Am the World." Moderate success in London, it wasn't a huge hit.

Barry taught me a lot about structure of songs. He gave me an insight, and he liked my songwriting vibe, too. He knew I wasn't stupid, I had some ideas for songs, and he gave me ideas and thoughts. I went to Germany, I worked at the Star Club, had my tape recorder with me and wrote half a dozen songs, came back to London, went in to do a demo, did these first half dozen tracks, and somebody introduced me to EH Morris, the publishing company. Which is now Chappell & Co. They gave me a bit of an advance on these half a dozen songs; they quite liked them. I signed a contract with them there, and I'm still with them.

So I came back to Australia and I had all this inspiration, and I recorded an album called *Surprises*, which is pretty much all original songs. There was nothing really sensational on it, but it was the beginnings. Then when I came back to Melbourne in '68 I got involved with Kevin Lewis again, who was my record boss, and we formed a production company and started to produce this show on Saturday mornings for national television, *Happening 70* and *Happening 71*.

And it was at this time that you wrote "The Real Thing".
Russell Morris had had success with his band Somebody's Image, and they had a song called "Hush", which was a hit for them. Molly Meldrum was managing Russell and he said, "I'm going to make you a solo artist." So I wrote a song called "The Girl that I Love" and I played it to Molly at Channel 10. It's a real pop star's type of song, and because Russell had had a couple of hits that were up tempo, it was appropriate for him to start his solo thing, in my mind, with a ballad. I made a little tape recording for Molly of "The Girl that I Love" and gave it to him and he said, "That's great, we'll record that."

And then about ten minutes later I was sitting with the boys in my band and we'd been naughty boys the night before, we'd been up till two o'clock. It was the sixties and we were doing a bit of naughty stuff as you did, smoking a bit of stuff. I'd written this song, which

I played to the boys, and they had the bass and the drum pad, and it was a twenty-minute rave. We were going to go in the studio and record it.

Anyway, after I'd recorded "The Girl that I Love" for Molly, I was just hanging out with the boys playing this thing called "The Real Thing". And Molly came over and he said, "That's the one I want!" I said, "It doesn't suit you. It's not meant for a solo artist." I had ideas of a "Strawberry Fields" type of approach, very different. Molly came around to my house that night, three o'clock in the morning, belting on the door, "I want that bloody song! Give me the bloody song!" So I gave it to him. I said, "It won't work. Not for Russell." Anyway, he went in the studio and the rest is history.

You mention "Strawberry Fields" and I wondered if you dabbled in any of the psychedelics that were available in the late sixties here or in London, "liberating the consciousness" as a lot of creative people did. I read that you apparently tried to bring a copy of *The Karma Sutra* into Australia. You had a clean-cut image but there was this more experimental side to you, wasn't there?
It's true, yeah. But I was never into crazy things. Wasn't into powders or anything like that. We just smoked a few joints. I was very much affected by England, Carnaby Street, Beatles, all of that stuff. I went to the Speakeasy, I met John Lennon, you could go any night in London, 'cause it was such a wild city, go to any of the clubs and there'd be Eric Clapton or George Harrison or both getting up with the band, Ginger Baker, you know, it was like two o'clock in the morning and everybody would be off their face and really loud. It was fantastic; life was experimental. Yes, there were drugs involved, but everything was new. Clothes, colour, even the way we wrote words. "Come and see the real thing, come and see the real thing, come and see/ There's a meaning there but the meaning there doesn't really mean a thing." That's what it was. It was like John Lennon said, "Nothing is real and nothing to get hung about/ Strawberry Fields forever." Do you know what I mean? It was very anti-establishment; it was very anti-short back and sides. My personality on stage as a performer was butter wouldn't melt in his mouth. And I'm not wild, I'm not crazy in that regard. But I loved the whole experiment of the sixties. I came from pretty straight parents, so the sixties affected me as a total thing. And "The Real Thing" still is like an anthem, one of the anthems of the sixties. I'm still amazed that I'm still earning money out of the song thirty years later.

Were you influenced by the Coca-Cola slogan? Was that part of the whole rave?
Well it was funny, because I'd always remembered that the intent of "The Real Thing" was basically everything out there is telling you that it's real, whether it's religion, whether it's lifestyle or whatever, people say, "This is real" and "That's not real" and everything holding itself up as the right way to look at things. And I thought that was bullshit. "There's a meaning there, but the meaning there doesn't really mean a thing." I've always, since I was very young, recognised that life is what you make it and there aren't any rules, really. Just be honest and don't rip people off, is pretty much my only philosophy. And I'd got it into my head that "The Real Thing" was inspired by the Coca-Cola thing, because I don't believe

in Coca-Cola either. You can't be cool unless you're drinking Coke, you know. I just thought that was really off. Coca-Cola says it's the real thing but it's not, there's so many things out there saying that they're the real thing but they're not.

I got it in my head that it was an inspiration, but it wasn't, 'cause Molly reminded me the other day that in fact Coca-Cola didn't bring the "real thing" jingle out until later, 1971. And why I got it tied up was I had a meeting with the advertising agency that did the Coca-Cola account, they were putting it to America that they wanted to use "The Real Thing" as a song for Coca-Cola. But they had [Sings] "It's the real thing, that's the way it should be ..." So it wasn't in any way inspired by that, even though for a lot of years I thought it might have been.

Your intent with "The Real Thing" was quite a simple one, then.
Yeah. It's all bullshit, basically, is what I was saying. We are the real thing. People are the real thing.

How did you feel about Hitler's Youth Choir and an atomic explosion, and the whole concept that Ian Meldrum came up with?
What Molly did with the film clips and what he did with the actual production was in line with how I intended the song. Because Hitler did say, "I am the real thing. I'm going to save the world." He didn't say, "I'm going to screw the world up." Germany believed in him. He was it, he was the real thing, this was the Messiah come to save Europe. And I talked about it with Molly. He got one line back to front, 'cause remember he came at three o'clock in the morning and whacked on this tape recorder. "Trying hard to understand the meaning that you'll see in me" is the line the way that Russell recorded it. Whereas how it really was, was "You're trying hard to understand but really you're not seeing me." You're not really seeing what I am. "I am the real thing." The whole legitimacy of the song to me is what it's saying is, "You are the real thing, I am the real thing, people are the real thing." It's not money, it's not power, it's not Hitler, it's not the Hitler Youth. We get conned, basically. And it wasn't "Ooo mow ma mow." What I did was "Oh my my my."

He just made it more psychedelic?
No, it was three o'clock in the morning—it probably sounded like that. It could have sounded like "Ooo mow ma mow mow."

And I have to say this, Molly is probably the greatest producer of records that we've ever had in this country. Listen to the precision in this mix, the little tambourine bits and stuff. He hears all of that in his head. The minute he heard my song he heard what it was going to sound like. He knew what he wanted to do with it. Molly's problem is that he finds it really hard to communicate to the people he was working with what he wants. We had Roger Savage, who was one of the Rolling Stones' early engineers, so we had a great engineer. But Molly had spent this enormous amount of money for those days, and Russell was an unknown quantity as a solo artist, so it was a bit edgy, the whole thing. They were going to take him off it and put one of the straight EMI producers on, because they went in to hear what he'd done and it was just a mess. Because Molly had it all in his head and laid down this track. He ended up stealing the master tape in the middle of the night, and he said, "Give me in writing an absolute guarantee I can finish it, otherwise I have a cigarette lighter here and I'm going to burn the master. I'll burn it and you'll get nothing." They freaked. They hated him. But of course it was number one and a gold record before it was even released, because there was so much hype about it. So Molly is a genius, definitely. Mad, can't stand him, hate him [*Chuckles*], but as for his art, he's brilliant.

You obviously never could have envisaged the life of the song, that it would become the monster that it has and still be one of the most recognisable songs in Australia more than thirty years later?
You don't do that, do you? I didn't view it that way. As a matter of fact, I didn't really view myself as a songwriter of any note, 'cause I'd only just started, and I happened to hit one after the other. And who knows? I hear some sensational songs these days that never get an airing.

What did you think of Midnight Oil's recording of it?
I loved it! I'm a big Midnight Oil fan. They called their album *The Real Thing*. It blew me away really. And I love Kylie's version, she did it for a movie, and Russell sang on that as well. Which was more of a sampled type of thing, very different, but it was great.

Were you involved in the writing of "Part 3 Into Paper Walls" or did Russell just take your original track and build on that?
Molly wanted to do another epic for the follow-up. I kept saying, "You've got to do 'The Girl that I Love'. People won't take two 'Real Thing's in a row." He said, "No, no, no, write me something." So I wrote "The Real Thing Part 3", which is [*Sings*] "Now you know that nothing is real/ The only truth are feelings you feel/ Keep seeing a picture in my mind telling me on and on and on and on and on it goes." Which wasn't part of what I'd written originally for "The Real Thing," even though it might have been in that twenty-minute rave that I had. But Russell had started writing, and he wrote a song called "Paper Walls", which wasn't strong enough, and Part 3 of "The Real Thing" wasn't strong enough, so Molly combined the two. "Part 3 Into Paper Walls."

Are you happy with it?
No, because I felt really strongly about "The Girl that I Love", and I mixed it; Molly wouldn't even mix it. He'd go, "Oh yeah, that'll do, it's only a B-side, bugger it, it's only a B-side." But I knew that "The Real Thing" had been so big that they didn't want more of that. And this wasn't as strong. If you're going to do "MacArthur Park", you've got to have something a lot bigger than that to reach those same kinds of standards. So the radio stations immediately turned it over to "The Girl that I Love" and it was a gold record and a number one.

Can you tell me about the song "Unconscientious Objector"?
That was one of the songs I wrote and recorded in England. Vietnam was starting to become

an issue in the late sixties. How I write, I always pick a topic. I get the title first. Always. And the title gives me the thrust of it. I like simple titles that are easy to understand and are different. "The Star", "Smiley", "The Real Thing". They're very easy to remember.

Did it become a conscious decision to write for other people rather than for yourself? Most songwriters would like to record their own work.
I didn't. I never considered myself that way. "The Real Thing" came out, that was a hit, everybody wanted my songs. Then I had "The Girl that I Love" as the follow-up, so it wasn't just a flash in the pan, it was a totally different song to "The Real Thing", so people were saying, "This is a legitimate songwriter." Then "Smiley", "Here Comes the Star" for Ross D Wyllie, and then "I Thank You" for Lionel Rose, which was totally different again, 'cause it was a country song. So I had a half a dozen hit songs in the space of two years, gold records and everything, big hits, right up until April 1971. And I probably would have gone on to be a far more important songwriter than I was had I stayed with it. But in March 1971 *Young Talent Time* started and I was back to being lovely little Johnny. [*Laughs*] Butter wouldn't melt in his mouth. So I got married and had kids and went straight.

Is it true that "Smiley" was inspired by the drafting of Normie Rowe?
Yes. Ronnie Burns wanted to record a Vietnam protest song. I used to tour with Normie a lot. I wrote a song for Normie, too, when he came back from Vietnam, a song called "Hello". Before Normie went away to the war he was a real pop star. He was happy-go-lucky, we had a ball. And I was always on his tours with him. We didn't get close or anything, but I noticed when he came back from Vietnam he was pretty angry. He never smiled, he was really serious. It affected him pretty much. So when Ronnie asked me to write a song, I just used Normie as inspiration. The words go, "Yesterday we had laughter and songs to sing/ Yesterday we had lovin' to burn." The song was about the changes that happen to soldiers when they go away to war and they come home. It wasn't so much about the war itself but about the change that happens in people. It was a huge hit for Ronnie Burns and then I wrote a whole album of songs for Ronnie, which John Farrar and Peter Jones did the arrangements for. It was a great album, too. I did some of my best work with John Farrar then. It was quite obvious that John had a real gift. John played on just about every single that was recorded in Melbourne in those days.

That intro to "Smiley" was an amazing opening sequence.
It's a piano with tacks, drawing pins, pushed on the hammers of the piano, and it gave a sort of a harpsichord sound. It was metal on metal hitting the strings.

Did Normie ever respond to "Smiley"? Did you ever have a discussion with him about it?
Well, Normie didn't really know. I told him later. I do shows with Normie now and I sing the songs that I wrote, and I actually tell the story of Normie. I say, "Normie went away to war and he was a really happy-go-lucky kid and we had laughter and songs to sing. And then when he came back he was an angry young man, as you might have noticed when he smacked Ron

Casey on the mouth on the *Midday Show*." So of course he knows it now. But at the time it was purely an inspiration. I was writing a song for Ronnie Burns, that was it.

Tell me about "The Star", which Ross D Wyllie recorded.
Before I'd gone to England I had my own TV show and I had hit records and when I came back I was just a songwriter and doing radio. My pop star image had worn off. I came to a meeting at the offices where they were doing *Uptight,* to see Ross D Wyllie. We were going out to lunch or something. And Ross said, "Look, I've got to have a production meeting. I'll only be half an hour, why don't you write me a song?" Joking. So I was feeling a bit sorry for myself 'cause I was excluded from this meeting and had an ego like everybody else. I was sitting there and [*Sings*] "Look at me now, I'm the loneliest guy in the world ..." And I wrote it and he came out of the meeting and I played it to him.

Were you happy with Herman's Hermits' cover of it?
No. They copied it. A copy's never the same as the original, really.

How did Lionel Rose come to record "I Thank You"?
The daily newspaper had a photo of Lionel playing a guitar. He was the number one boxing champion. He loved country music, he used to go to The Hawking Brothers' gigs and sing along with them. I'd never met Lionel, and there was a photo of him with his guitar, saying how he'd like to make a record. So I rang him and said, "What kind of song do you want to do?" He said, "I want to do some country." And I said, "Well what do you want to say?" And he said, "I don't know, I just want to say thank you, you know." So he gave me the title. A thankyou to his fans and to his girlfriend, who he later married. So we went in the studio and I got The Hawking Brothers in, they did the backing. I sang the song and Lionel sang along with me and we took my voice out of the mix. Because he wasn't a great singer. But I'm very proud of it because it was a double gold record, and it was the first indigenous gold record in Australia.

So you were a great write-to-order songwriter.
That's it. I didn't take it seriously. I made money out of my songs, but it wasn't like today if you have a hit album or you have hit records you make a huge lot of money. In those days you got gigs, that's it. You'd get your 500 bucks and you'd do five shows in a night. They'd have Ronnie Burns, Johnny Young, Normie Rowe, all on the same bill during the night. It wasn't serious. You didn't have lawyers. I never had my contracts checked or any of that sort of stuff done. I was just happy to get the opportunities. It wasn't like, "Oh well, now I'm a songwriter." I was doing radio. I was a radio announcer in Melbourne on 3XY from 1968 to 1972.

When *Young Talent Time* started I used to write a song a show. If we needed an opening I'd write something. *Young Talent Time* was *huge*. We planned a bit of a theme for each show, and if we had a circus show I'd write a circus song; we did an Olympic show, I wrote "Feel the Fire". I've still got tapes of all of these songs. I'd just sit down with Ross Burton, who was our musical director, and say, "Well what are we going to do for an opening?" "Oh, we can't find the right song." "Okay, I'll write something."

You were still writing to order.

Oh yeah! And in five minutes, too. He'd put the tape recorder on and I'd just tap the table, wouldn't even use a guitar, I'd just sing it, and he'd pick out the chords and write them and we'd do it on the show. It was a fantastic way to do demos, really.

When you had several hard blows in the late 1980s, the end of *Young Talent Time*, losing your father, discovering your birth father, did a new era of songwriting begin for you with new inspiration? Whereas in the past you'd written to order and it wasn't about yourself, did you find you could start writing more about your life and experiences?

Yeah, I think so, but I'm not that deep. [*Laughs*] No angst. When *Young Talent Time* finished I wrote a play, a musical, called *The Real Thing*. Very funny play. It was set in the year 3000 when the earth is completely destroyed and everybody is living in domes. Because you couldn't breathe the air any more. And because everything was restricted you weren't allowed to fall in love, because everybody lived to big ages. So they had this little underground movement that worshipped Russell Morris. Because he was the god at the time when love and peace was allowed. I had the whole thing picked, I could see it. Doug Parkinson was going to be the priest and these two kids fall in love and he sends them back to the sixties to find out what it was all about. And they go on a search for Russell Morris, their god. I wrote a whole bunch of new songs for that. That was the first thing that I did after *Young Talent Time* finished. I went up here to the bush and I just wrote this play.

I took it to Paul Dainty and I went quite a way down the road with it but it was a million and a half investment to put it on. I'd been through twenty years of doing business and it was just too hard. So it didn't come together. It probably could have come together had I been more driving, but I was happy to stay on the farm and just chill out.

And then I thought, well, what am I going to do with my life now? 'Cause it was very hard after twenty years to be seen as anything else other than Johnny Young. So I got a band together, some great players, and we went out and started doing gigs. And I've been doing that. And writing. I recorded a couple of CDs. One was *The Johnny Young Story*, which is my versions of all of the songs that I've written for other people, plus a few new songs as well. It's back to the early days of my songwriting up until now. And then I wrote an album of country songs, which are really good songs. I'm hoping some people will pick it up, the publishers have got it, and even if I get a cover somewhere, it's fine.

BRIAN CADD

SYDNEY, AUSTRALIA, MAY 2003

As a composer, performer, producer and impresario, Brian Cadd's contribution to the Australian repertoire is considerable. But it took a long time for him to want to stay home. For most of his career, in his musical heart and in his psyche, he was elsewhere. He was passionate about Australian talent but abhorred overt patriotism. He loved Buddy Holly, the Beatles and The Band, and wanted not only to succeed in England or America, but also to be a part of the fabric of those countries' musical lives. Yet he was an integral part of two of Australia's most important bands in the 1960s and, through his own record label in the 1970s, fostered Australian talent in a pioneering way. This cultural dichotomy was inherent in Cadd's life and work until the end of last century. And then he came home.

He was born on 29 November 1946 in Perth to parents who encouraged his musical leanings. After adlibbing to "Für Elise" in a piano exam, his teacher suggested he give the classical arena a miss. At eleven he was the pianist in a children's band on a local television show, and he later moved to Melbourne as Beatlemania was sweeping the country and beat bands abounded. In The Groop he fell into songwriting by necessity, co-writing hits such as "Woman You're Breaking Me" and "Such a Lovely Way". The writing partnership that he and Don Mudie forged then continued into Axiom and created enduring songs like "Arkansas Grass" and "A Little Ray of Sunshine".

Both bands spent time in London trying to break through internationally and, like most of the Australian acts that went that way in the late sixties and early seventies, they failed. The Axiom experience was particularly disappointing; essentially a country rock band, they were out of place in England, but when they went to Los Angeles to record an album with famed producer Shel Talmy (the Kinks, The Who and The Easybeats) the whole process was a disaster. "First of all they thought we were a rock band, they found out we were a country rock band, they put us in a studio with a pop producer, and we turned out being Eurovision. It was horrifying! It broke us up," Cadd remembered, still aghast over thirty years later. He was consequently not overly fond of the Cadd–Mudie hit "My Baby's Gone", which Talmy produced.

After Axiom disbanded he found himself alone and unsure of his next move. Like his former Axiom colleague Glenn Shorrock, he spent time honing his writing skills. Unlike Shorrock, he didn't gravitate to another band. Cadd was a leader of the new singer-songwriter movement in Australia that allowed artists such as Russell Morris, Kevin Johnson and Ross Ryan to shine outside of a band mechanism. The difference for Cadd was that he was a piano player in a guitar-centric scene, and the melodic richness of songs like "Show Me the Way" and "Ginger Man" are a testament to his uniqueness.

He was also much more than a songwriter and performer; already a leading figure in producing and arranging, his talents were pivotal in the success of Morris's early seventies career, as well as the careers of Robin Jolley, Hans Poulsen and other artists on Ron Tudor's Fable Records, where Cadd made his home and set up his Bootleg imprint. Inspired by Leon Russell's Shelter label, he assembled a team of regular players around him, known as The Bootleg Family Band. Bootleg became the most successful independent record label in Australia before Mushroom, while Cadd also diversified into film and television themes, soundtracks and radio jingles.

But the failure of The Groop and Axiom to crack the overseas market and his long-time love for America and its music finally lured him to Los Angeles where he settled in for the long haul. In the mid- to late 1970s there was a growing gang of Australians trying to break into the West Coast music scene, and their close friendships led them to be known collectively as the Gum Leaf Mafia. Olivia Newton-John was its most successful member, but it also included Billy Thorpe, Steve Kipner and Cadd, all of whom found success as songwriters. Although Cadd had a record deal and released two albums of his own in the United States, for the most part he was content with writing for and producing other artists in Los Angeles and Nashville. The Pointer Sisters, Joe Cocker, Bonnie Tyler, Ringo Starr and others covered his songs.

Returning to Australia periodically to perform, in 1992 he wrote and recorded an album called *Blazing Salads* with Glenn Shorrock before deciding to move back permanently. Before that he spent some years playing and writing with the Flying Burrito Brothers, fulfilling a long-held dream of being a part of America's country rock family tree.

"I'm writing very much at the moment," Cadd said when we met one afternoon in Sydney. He had been enjoying the wave of nostalgia and renewed attention on the touring circuit that events like the Long Way To The Top tour engendered and had for some time been actively involved in different areas of the music industry, including the Australian Music Foundation and Australian Music Industry Advisory Council. He was also teaching songwriting part-time at Griffith University. From our lengthy conversation it was evident how he would inspire and galvanise a young generation of songwriters.

As a child with a bent for improvising Beethoven's "Für Elise", when did you start churning out little melodies of your own?
I don't think it was any time soon after that. The climate then was very different. Everyone was just totally copying English and American records. Nobody ever thought for one minute about writing an Australian song. There were very few recording deals, very few opportunities to do anything like that. Your whole life centred around being in a band and playing. I landed in Melbourne just when the Beatles broke. And even at that point it was very hard to imagine anyone actually writing songs. They were mystical beings that did that; there wasn't that much originality in Australia at all. When I joined The Groop I went to a band that had already had three huge hits. We were going into the studio almost immediately and everyone was required to write. I'd never written a song in my whole life. I got to write with the drummer, Richard Wright, who came up with this little riffy feel. And I just banged around with him on the piano.

And that's how "Woman You're Breaking Me" came to be?
Yes. And it's a nursery rhyme. All the songs of that era were like little nursery rhymes. They were very simplistic forms and there was absolutely no cerebral cogitation. It was all about "you dance and you look and I want and we will or we won't." It was more that they were vehicles for us to do things. The drummer came up with that because he liked that feel, not because he thought it was going to be a hit. And I just came up with that because it was fun to sing and it was where I wanted to be on the piano. It wasn't like, "Gee, gosh, this will be a number one hit"—which it turned out to be. And that was my first record.

Who were the people you were listening to before then?
The most influential thing I ever did was buy an EP of Jerry Lee Lewis. It had "High School Confidential" and "Great Balls of Fire". I played that until there were no grooves left. That's how I learned. There was a guy that I used to hang with and his mother knew that old-fashioned crawling bass boogie-woogie piano. She taught me how to do it. So I played along with the record until I could do it as he could do it. But my biggest single influence back then was Buddy Holly. "Raining in My Heart" and things like that remain with me today as my favourite songs. And there was a Gene Pitney song, "If I Didn't Have a Dime". And here I am at my age now, and recently I got an email from him saying, "Would you like to write?" And I'm going, "God!" It's amazing how life goes.

Pitney covered "Let Go", didn't he?
He did. But I didn't know him. And then all of a sudden we're going to write together. How amazing. But they were the kind of songs that I liked. I liked really melodic, pretty songs. Then the Beatles happened and of course we all fell in love. And we dissected everything. Not as songwriters, but as bands. As players.

Being that the Beatles were mainly a guitar band, did you ever pick up a guitar and see if you could play, put chords together?
No. One of the greatest disappointments of my life. I've tried about six times in my life to learn guitar, and what is so incredibly difficult on guitar is so easy on piano. I just give up. But because I was a keyboard player in predominantly a guitar world, that affected the way I played and certainly eventually affected the way I wrote. Keyboard players were very much the people that had to fit in with the guitar players. It wasn't like now with Tim Freedman from The Whitlams, where everyone plays behind him. And Elton and Billy Joel and people like that. There was none of that except for Jerry Lee Lewis. It wasn't really until Chris Stainton and Leon Russell played with Cocker that I really understood rock 'n' roll piano. But that was quite some time later, and I'd been writing for a long time. I think I'm very lucky because I don't really write even today like a piano player. Piano players seem to have this tick-a-ling-a-ling-a-ling-a-ling vibe that they tend to write piano player songs. I get thousands of demos from kids and I can always tell the ones that are written by piano players. But because I grew up in my formative years in guitar bands, I don't think I'm as much of a piano player writer as I might have been.

So your introduction to songwriting was putting something together ad hoc for The Groop.
Yeah. But it did morph during that period. When I started with The Groop I wrote with Max Ross. Then the band changed configuration and I started writing with Don Mudie. And he's been my longest writing collaborator; we wrote all through The Groop and all through Axiom. With Max it was always a case of half a dozen bottles of beer in a room, a couple of packs of cigarettes and a tape recorder and bash something out. With Don we were a bit more like Elton and Bernie. We didn't necessarily have to be together lots to do something. He would start something and then we'd get together and finish it. And I would start something and we'd get together and finish it. So I started to learn the value of distance. Of not necessarily just being closeted with the one writer day in and day out. Now when I teach I say, "You really have to give yourself and your subconscious some room to develop and build these ideas as opposed to just being in a room until you finish a song."

At such an early career stage, how did it feel having songs like "When I Was Six Years Old" and "Elevator Driver" covered by your contemporaries? Did it occur to you that you could make money from other people's recordings?
They would come to us and say, "Could you write me a song?" Wow, what a concept! Somebody who's not actually in the band. It was wonderful, fantastic. The money part wasn't part of the equation because back then there wasn't any money. Through absolute

ignorance we gave away a lot of our publishing. But the whole principle of being able to write for Ronnie Burns or the Masters Apprentices, and for them to be hits, was the beginning of the dawning of the age of the songwriter for me, because I started to realise that I could do those things and succeed and fail, without having to succeed and fail within the framework of a group.

Did you go home sometimes and think, "I might write a song tonight"? Did you start dabbling in "serious" songwriting in response to that success?
When The Groop went overseas and when Axiom went overseas there were enormous periods of inactivity. 'Cause it all got down to finding a deal, getting it signed, getting a manager, and months would go by. It was really out of a desire to make me feel in my own self that there was progress, that there was a momentum, that we were actually getting somewhere. And I developed then a sort of a methodology. I would find myself succumbing to the desire to bang around, which is what I call it. I'd go in and bang around on the piano and if I was kidding myself and the feeling wasn't really there, I wouldn't come up with anything. And when it was I would come up with a song. Don was up in his room in the same house, so I could go up and say to him, "I just came up with this, what do you think?" It was a work ethic, if you like, that developed around and outside the band. Which enabled us to probably be a bit saner and more focused than some of the other people in the band who didn't write and just saw themselves going to the pub in the afternoon and there was this long stretch of inactivity when they didn't do anything but cook brown rice. As you did back then. And explore every known religion.

I was gradually changing from being a piano player who sang in a group and by the way wrote a few tunes to a writer who happened to play in a band. A subtle change that took a long time.

How did that first trip to the UK and Europe influence your writing?
In '67 and '68 when we lived in London, we lived off Kings Road—that was the centre of the universe. There was no other musical capital in the world. It was phenomenal. All of the stuff that we'd only basically gotten off the radio in dribs and drabs, there were these fantastic bands that were on, and we'd be able to go! We'd just be there! Jethro Tull would be right there. I think it was with Axiom that we saw Creedence and we saw The Band. That was beyond. And remember, we came from a time in Australia where there was very basic television, it was all miming to film clips on *Kommotion* and stuff like that. I'm not knocking that, because that made all of us, but it wasn't a very high quality in terms of performance. And we'd go over there and watch *Top of the Pops* and one electrifying performance on *Top of the Pops* and the record would be Top 10 the next week. You got to sense the real power of being in an industry that had enough people to drive itself successfully.

It awoke us to the fact that rock 'n' roll rocked. Creativity and taking original things into the studio. That was the time of "Whiter Shade of Pale" and The Who and amazingly original records. Whereas it wasn't in Australia—it was all of these cover bands. The Twilights were our best band by far, but they were a cover band. They did Beatles songs. Better than the Beatles, but they did Beatles songs.

The Band's *Music from Big Pink* was a big influence on you, wasn't it?
It was an epiphany. The Easybeats lived in Earls Court. They'd had their big hit and they still toured around. They had their own PA. And they used to bring their PA into their living room, which was in a basement from memory, and set it up. Can you imagine—all the rest of us had little speakers that big, about a millionth as efficient—and they had the record player and the tape recorder, very sophisticated. They had money. They had a joint roller who sat in the corner. But that then was *de rigueur*. Ronnie Charles and I particularly used to love to go around there, and I got very close to Harry and George, particularly Harry, he was such a funny guy. And this night we were sitting there, just the usual thing. It was fairly late, maybe two o'clock in the morning. There was a knock on the door and Cream's tour manager—which was already a mind boggle—arrived, and they'd just come back from America. This guy was clutching a reel-to-reel copy of *Music from Big Pink*, which had only just started to be talked about and was leaking out in America. Of course nobody in England had ever heard of it. He went, "I've got to play it!" And we sat there and played that tape from two o'clock in the morning, all night until God knows what time the next morning, ten o'clock. Nobody could speak. Not because we were all too stoned, but because nobody could believe the music. It was so unbelievably different. Ronnie and I were absolutely transfixed. It changed my life.

It couldn't have been more different to the music that was going on in the UK and the music that was going on in that very living room that we were sitting in. You can't start with Dave Dee, Dozy, Beaky, Mick & Tich, doing this in England, and then have "Chest Fever" play there. They're not like they're on the same planet. And for me it was particularly relevant because when I was very young, my best friend who lived down the street from me in Perth, his father was a Civil War freak. And I fell in love with that period, not because of the war itself but it was something that I took with me through childhood. Then subsequently I started to become fascinated with Western movies and it's something that I carry around now. I've never been able to turn *High Noon* off. If it comes on I have to watch it. I know all about all the gun fighters and all the Wild West.

Anyway, for me, this music represented rural America. It represented all those stories. And they were like little films. They weren't just like three-minute pop songs. That moment changed the way I thought about what songs can do for you or to you as an audience and I realised the power of painting the picture, rather than telling the words. And if there's a trick that I use, and I have used this from then on, and it's something I teach, it's that a picture speaks louder than the actual words. I learned the power of creating such a strength of characters, such a fabulous array of characters and moving them through the song like you would move them through a movie. It turned my world upside down. From then on I was not the same person.

So after you heard this reel-to-reel several times all night, did you go home and write?
No. It was ages, weeks, months. It wasn't something that inspired me—it floored me. It *floored* me. I'd been writing nursery rhymes, you know. And these people were painting Gainsboroughs.

Did you question, then, your songwriting abilities?
A bit, probably. But more importantly, I tried to figure out how I would begin. How to make that huge leap between when I was six years old and "The Weight". I had no way of doing it. I had no historical structure. Australians didn't have a depth of experience like that.

Other than *Music from Big Pink*, obviously *Sgt Pepper's* must have bowled you over.
I can remember hearing Sgt Pepper's at Terry Britten's. He'd got a copy sent out from England and I went around to Terry's and we were sitting there and he was devastated. And I listened to it and I was devastated. I went home and called everyone in the band and said, "Just go back to the day gigs, guys, 'cause we're never going to do this. no-one's ever going to get close to this album." And the truth was that nobody ever did.

The Groop played on "The Real Thing". It's really interesting the number of people I've spoken to who were involved with that song. You delivered the Hitler speech on that as well. Did you have any idea at all that you were working on something that was going to be bigger than all of you?
Yep. It was so unique. It was so unbelievably different. Even the fact that no-one had a clue what the song was about. We were swept along in the whole thing. It was this great piece and it went for seven minutes and that was as brave as you could be in the studio because anything that went over three minutes was a risk that it wasn't going to get played in those days. None of those who were on the band track sessions and the early sessions realised that Molly was going to put what he put on it. In fact the poor engineers had no clue that everybody just short of God was going to finish up on that record. In the end it became this phenomenon. And the reason why it can't be discounted in any way is that it showed us all that it was okay to be completely individual, to just do whatever it felt was exactly right for that song and that record.

Did the experience of playing on that song also influence your songwriting?
No. But it did influence the sort of freedom thinking that we were starting to fall into. One of the most amazing Australian records of all time was "The Loved One". That was an absolutely astoundingly original record. Even to this day no-one's made a record that unique. I never wanted to write one of those, and I never really wanted to write something like "The Real Thing". But it showed me the power of thinking outside the square. Being able to take the courage to just say, "This song is taking me here and I'm not going to ask why." And to this day I don't. I believe that songs have their own essence and their own energy. The moment you start saying, "Well, I'm going to pitch this to Kenny Rogers so I can't have that kind of a chord in it", you're compromising the idea.

Which a lot of songwriters do.
I spent seven years in Nashville. And they all do it in Nashville. They figure out the title and who they're going to pitch it to, and then they write the song. Which absolutely contravenes everything that we've just talked about. And it contravenes the entire feeling of the sixties and the early seventies. Which was, get in there and take the idea as far as you can take it, where it takes you.

When did you and Don Mudie realise that there was a special creative spark between you?
It just evolved. Like so many things back in those days, they were borne out of a necessity. There was an imperative that we needed to make more records. We needed songs. I had never considered myself anything other than a co-writer and neither had he. So we just fell into it. I've written with a lot of people in my life, and I've never felt as comfortable again as when we wrote. The truth is that if we got together tomorrow we probably couldn't write anything, because that was particular to that time. We were about the same standard together at the same time. We were in the same room and we had the same headset, mindset, so we did great. And he spoilt me, because he did give me a lot of freedom to do things. It was a great relationship.

Did you and Don have songs left over that didn't get recorded by The Groop but were played in Axiom?
There were a few we trotted out and had a couple of goes at, but mostly our first set included songs by The Band and Crosby Stills & Nash.

Was Axiom modelling itself on Crosby Stills & Nash?
Glenn was, I think. I was very focused on what I wanted to do. In other words, although I probably listened to Crosby Stills & Nash endlessly and I listened to Chicago and I listened to all the bands that were coming up and through in that point in time—and loved them all— I didn't ever consciously say, "I want to write a Crosby Stills & Nash song." Now that seems like a little thing to say to you, but in actual fact it's enormous. It was the same with Don. Don never said, "I just heard the new Chicago thing and I think we could rip that line off." We both only ever wrote what came out of us. Which is what made Axiom such a hard band to put together in the beginning. Chris Stockley was much closer to Hank Williams than he was to The Band. And Dougie Lavery was an R&B freak. If you listen, you can't really find it in the albums, but if you had a tape of us when we first started playing around you would hear all those very diverse things.

Your story about your childhood friend and the Civil War explains a lot about "Arkansas Grass". Why was Arkansas chosen rather than Virginia or Kentucky or Georgia?
I don't know where Arkansas came from. It was just a picture song. I suppose by that stage I had arrived pretty much into the picture world. And at that point in time there were an awful lot of songs that were in protest to Vietnam. Too many. Some of them were very good and very effective and there was no need for another one really, but I wanted to say

something about the futility of the Vietnam War. You've got to be so careful when you say things like that, because all the vets are our generation and you tend to say things like that in terms of diminishing it, which we're not. It was a ridiculous war, and as ridiculous in some ways and made me as angry in some ways as the futility of the Civil War, which was just the ultimate to me. I could never get over the whole picture of brother against brother, and I still can't. So I figured that I would use the metaphor of the American Civil War to point out how ridiculous Vietnam was. I had a basic verse and chorus structure, and then Don jumped in and we finished the rest of it together. Generally, some of the songs that I started I would tend to get as far in as I could, in terms of structure but not necessarily word-wise; I wouldn't do all the lyrics because together we were great.

Was there a line that started you off?
In those days I had a lot of songs that started with the first line. In all probability I wrote, "If General McAllister gave up the war." I tended to start lineally and tell the story. And the song evolved out of necessity to tell the story. I certainly didn't come up with "Home, home, going alone, laying on Arkansas grass." I would have been thrown out at the end of the chorus and arrived there.

And "Arkansas Grass" has a poetry to it that "Georgia Grass" wouldn't have had.
Yeah, it just happens. I learned never to argue with that. Whatever it gives me, I'll figure it out.

Was the analogy to the Civil War a little bit lost on an Australian public that didn't know much about American history beyond the War of Independence—because that was about colonisation, something we could relate to? I wouldn't have thought Australians, in the late sixties, early seventies, related to the American Civil War as a moment in history.
It was enormously misunderstood. It was accused of being Australia's first drug song. They absolutely considered Arkansas grass to be dope. I have still to this day to get Australians to move from there [*Points with hand*] to there. Even though they sort of understand it's about war and generals going home and stuff like that, they absolutely believed that "Arkansas Grass" was about dope. And so instead of writing the great Australian metaphor for useless war, I wrote Australia's first drug song! Which was particularly bizarre considering that I didn't smoke dope. I got so sick of being on radio talking about it.

One of the joys of songs is that you can completely miss the point and still love the song. And then you can later on discover what the original point was and love it all over again in a different way.
Or it can break your heart. If there's things that you absolutely think a song means and then the writer says, "Nah, nah, it was really my lawnmower broke down, and I was just so annoyed …" And you're, "That's not what it means! It doesn't mean that at all! It's a tribute to New York." One of the tricks about being a writer is that we have no power; I have no power over what you think I write. I can tell you, but because I won't meet you if you're just an audient out there somewhere, then I have to rely on you taking what I say and making

your own story out of it. I was so self-involved, blinkers on, this is what I wanted to write, this is typical of me, and of course this is what it means. What really happened is that every gig we played, all the dealers would hit me. So I'd be standing there with all these guys going, "These are great heads." And I'm going, "What? What?"

And yet at the same time it was a great pop song with a catchy melody.
Yes. I was very fortunate that it happened to be a sing-along song. Which is the trick, of course. And so people who have no real idea what it's talking about can still sing, "Home, home ..."

There was an interesting clash of cultures in "Arkansas Grass" and on the *Fool's Gold* album where you deliberately tried to craft an Australian sound, yet using American styles, American themes and American place names. You did say at the time that you were an Australian band writing about Australian themes. Yet on face value you were writing American music.
Excepting if you accept the fact that it was a whole metaphor. So in other words I could write about a love affair but I could make it the metaphor of bullfighting. I might be accused of being too Spanish, involved in a blood sport or whatever, where in actual fact all I was trying to talk about would be a love affair. That's the danger of metaphors.

There was a backlash. On that *Fool's Gold* album we wrote a song, which must have been all the stuff that I had left in my head from "Arkansas Grass", which I called "We Can Reach Georgia by Morning". We had done some rough mixes and somebody played some of them to Stan Rofe and Rofe got right off his bike about it and said that it was absolutely unconscionable for us to use Georgia and why couldn't we use an Australian name? So I succumbed to the browbeating of everybody, and we found in the atlas a place in Northern Queensland called Fords Bridge, which had the right meter for the words. So we had to change the song to "We Can Reach Fords Bridge by Morning". I never really got over that. It really hurt me. It annoyed me. It was the beginning of my disenchantment with jingoism. I was over all this, "It has to be Australian" and "What's wrong with meat pies" and "There's only one football code." I'd lived overseas and at that stage there weren't a lot of Australians that had, and I just got very annoyed with the parochialism. When it reached out and touched me and made me change a word in a song, I hated it.

Did you write "A Little Ray of Sunshine" about one of your own children?
No, no. It wasn't about me at all. The idea of the story started because around the band there was a couple and we all knew both of them; they were part of our circle. They were a fabulous couple. Towards the end of their time together they got pregnant. By the time that this kid was born, their relationship was acrimonious, horrifying. Everyone divided up into her camp or his camp and it was dreadful. And in the midst of all this, this *fabulous* little kid was born, and nobody seemed to notice. I hated it. It was terrible. And I thought, "You know, regardless of anything else, you guys made this. She's come into the world, and she's gorgeous. And it's such a shame in a way that you can't be affected by this like most people

when this ray of sunshine comes into their life and changes everything about them ..."
So I wrote the song for her.

Does that child, who's now a thirty-something-year-old woman, know?
No.

Did the parents know?
No.

Was it mostly your lyric?
A fair bit of it. Don wrote the bridge. What happened in that song, as would happen quite
a lot, would be he would come in and really tidy up and rewrite and make it nice. He was
fabulous at that. There are four verses in it and I suppose he probably wrote the majority of
two of them and he wrote the bridge. But that was a song that I got a fair way into before
he got involved. There weren't many like that, but it was a personal song for me; it was
something that I really wanted to say.

**Were you worried when Axiom first performed it that the people would recognise
themselves in it?**
No, because there's nothing in the song that refers to them. In fact it refers to the
antithesis of them. 'Cause it's about a happy event.

**There's one line that I never quite got. "I think that I'd rather her hair was much darker."
It seemed like this one reservation in this otherwise adoring tribute to a being.**
I have no idea where that came from. I don't know why I said it. But do you know, I have
been held to task for that line ever since.

**There's a line in Cat Stevens' "Father and Son" that I've also never understood, which is
"You're still young, that's your fault." Just lines that jar.**
And sometimes they're lines that you wish you'd changed afterwards.

Do you wish that you'd written something different in that line?
Absolutely. But there are a few of those, and every now and again there's a jarring moment
when I think, "God, I wish I had said that better." But I believe that a song is born. I've
never had any truck with people who rewrite and rewrite and rewrite for two years and then
give you the finished song. I think that diminishes its momentum and its purpose. Because
it is governed by the time. All this stuff happens inside, internally, in you, because of where
you're standing in the world at that time and what you think. And six months later you
aren't there. You're somewhere else. It would be very easy for me to go back now and
change almost everything of almost all of the songs. I could probably write them better and
they could fit a bit better. But they don't stand for that. They stand for where they were.
I believe implicitly in the moment.

Given that your inspirations at that stage were mainly American, why did you take Axiom to the UK rather than the US?
There you go. It's a question that we have asked ourselves for thirty years. The Flying Burrito Brothers were there, Poco were starting, Stone Canyon Band was there, the Stone Poneys. You know what it was about—the mindset in the industry at that time which decreed that if you went overseas you went to England. Australian bands had always gone to England. Nobody had ever gone to America. Even Olivia went to England. I'm very close now to the Flying Burrito Brothers and they would listen to things like "Arkansas Grass" and they would say, "We're really glad you didn't come here." We could have changed "Fords Bridge" back to "Georgia" and I would've loved that! So what did we do? We take a country rock band to London and nobody wanted any country rock bands from anywhere in the world in London, much less an Australian one. If we turned right instead of left, God knows what would have happened to us.

Was "Show Me the Way" a leftover from Axiom?
Yes, it was written during that time.

There was a spate of religious rock at the time with "Spirit in the Sky" and "My Sweet Lord", Rick Springfield had "Speak to the Sky", there'd been *Godspell*, and *Jesus Christ Superstar* was happening. Were you coming from that mind space?
This is a story that I've never told. In the sixties it was obligatory to study religion, that's what we all did. You had to question everything; you had to find the true belief. You could only do that by being everything. So we were Muslims and Buddhists, everything. It was really a ridiculous approach to it. This was in London, one of those times when we were all trying to find solutions. Shorrock spent months omming up in his room. We had this fantastic guy that Terry Britten knew who came around and he was a teacher, but it was more about spiritualism and the afterlife. His name's John Pilgrim and he found spirits in the house and stuff like that. They were the sorts of things that we went through.

The reality is that I got disenchanted with traditional Christianity at that point. I wrote the first set-up of "Show Me the Way" and then Don organised it. And it is a protest song. I feel uncomfortable now saying that. But why not? That was then. It was really a protest against traditional religion. I was so far out there looking at these other things that to me the whole concept just seemed such a fairytale. And also the incredible horrors and depravation and troubles and wars that Christianity has caused and at that time things were coming out about how rich the Catholic Church was and all that. It all accumulated in this kind of frenzy inside of me so I wrote the beginning of that song. The irony is that I recorded it. Why did I record it? I certainly at that time wasn't angry any more. And it came out and it became this kind of religious statement. But it was originally exactly the opposite. I do "Show Me the Way" on stage today, it's one of the big numbers, and you can see and hear them. They all go, "Ohhhh ..."

Are you detached from it now?
I'm not very involved in the song, I must admit. I really like it musically. It's a favourite song to sing, to perform it's very dynamic, it goes up and down, bands love it. And the audience obviously loves it. But it always feels just minutely hypocritical to me afterwards when they come up to me. I've never wanted to tell the story because it means other stuff to other people.

But it's not putting anyone else's beliefs down. It's just saying where you were at when you wrote the song, which is exactly what you said before about a song coming from the moment it was created. You can't change that.
That's true, but there are people out there who like that song because of what it says to them religiously, and that's fair enough. To find out that's not what it originally meant is probably a bit of a downer. In the same way that there are people out there who have believed implicitly, all the way along the line, that I wrote "A Little Ray of Sunshine" about my daughter.

I'm interested in the writing of "Ginger Man" and whether you had read JP Donleavy's book quite soon before or whether that was something from your past that just came to you while you were writing.
When I wrote that song it was an attempt by me to write a Western movie in song form. I've always been fascinated by the fact that with the mail in those days, in the same way with early Australia, it could be a year before you got a letter. And the letters chased them around the West. A year after it happened they could find out that they were a father, that they were divorced, that they were wanted for murder or that their parents had died, or they could have won a goldmine. A year is an extraordinary time to place it out of whack. I always loved that mechanism of life. So I use it in the song, and obviously the three verses are about him getting the mail. The first one's about his brother Jess, the second one's about his Dad and the third one's about his girl, who falls in love with somebody else.

It was one of those ones where I was finishing the words as we were doing the record. It happened with quite a few of them. We cut the tracks and on the rough I was singing "Ginger Man" and I didn't worry about it, because sometimes I use filler words and then I find words to replace them, just so that I can get the meter right, so that it all feels right. And every time John Sayers, who's co-producing, says, "We've got to do that song, you know, whatever it is." Because every time he'd brought it up, I'd say, "I've got to rewrite the chorus." And every time I tried, nothing happened, I could not get anything that felt to me like that. So in the end we were there at three o'clock in the morning and he said, "You know, you should just sing that. 'Cause it sounds perfect. Maybe it's because I'm so used to it now but it just sounds like it's meant to be there." So I did. The thing comes out and it's a hit. Who the hell would understand what it meant? I didn't understand what it meant. And it wasn't until ages later, maybe a year later, that I'm playing it on stage one night and it occurs to me that the hero in the movie is exactly the same character as in Donleavy's book. And *The Ginger Man* is my favourite book in the whole world.

Albeit that Donleavy's hero was Irish.

Yeah, but still, it's the same person, the same personality as this guy. Which is why I didn't find it so hard that he kept getting all the rotten news. 'Cause the guy in Donleavy's book is actually not a great guy. But it occurred to me after the fact. So the irony to me is that people come up to me even now and they say, "God I love that song. When that song came out it just knocked me out." And I'm waiting for it. They go, "What's it about?" I'm absolutely amazed that so many people bought it not having a clue what it was about.

So maybe in a sense it becomes kind of an oral postcard, or an oral painting. You sometimes look at paintings and you haven't got a clue what they actually mean but they just do it for you.

At the risk of sounding like Stan Rofe, however, I was going to ask why you chose to set it in the wide open spaces of Texas and Utah rather than the Australian outback.

Because it was my *High Noon*. And people say, "Oh, well, you obviously wrote that because you were assuming that was going to come out in America." Which was so far beyond what I thought at that time. That was my first solo album. I was trying to get my head around the fact that I had to sing it.

Had you and Don thought about going on as a duo after "Show Me the Way"?

No. We just drifted apart after that. I think at the time it had to do with me working with Russell Morris. And I did a whole lot of jingles, radio IDs, all the 3UZ and 3XY things. I was really a studio animal at that point. Ron Tudor had Fable, and I became one of his house producers. Which was a remarkable experience. I got to produce all these amazingly diverse acts, which also really helped me in terms of being a producer. I had a lot of studio time, and I had a pretty decent band that I used to record for everything, so I just started recording my own stuff at the end of sessions. There was a part of me that didn't really acknowledge it being an album; it was just this process I was going through, recording. And it wasn't really until we actually got an album that I became a solo artist. I know that's a strange thing to say. When I was recording "Silver City" I didn't imagine me playing it live. To me it was only a recording exercise; it was making a record. I had no idea what a Brian Cadd would be like on stage.

So you were writing songs just to train yourself in the studio.

I was just writing them because I had an opportunity to record them, which I'd never done in the past. I'd always had to be in a band to do that. Many of them were written in the studio. 'Cause I didn't have Mudie then. Don didn't come along and tidy them up and finish them. I had to do that. So I'd do my starting-off bit, I'd get the basic structure up and running and the first verse and chorus and that's where I normally stopped. That was a big exercise for me to finish all these songs, 'cause I'd never had to before.

You've often told the story about how you wrote "Don't You Know It's Magic" at the last minute for the Yamaha Song Contest. Have you written many other songs very quickly and spontaneously like that?

Most of the really successful ones—not necessarily hits, but the ones that I've thought of as being good songs—have come quickly. "Little Ray of Sunshine" I wrote very quickly. "Baby's Gone" was something that I laboured over a bit, maybe that's one reason why I don't like it as much. I think you get to a point where if you know your craft, it's just a question of taking the idea, and making the idea into three minutes. Your subconscious is way ahead of you; it's throwing you all this stuff. And your trick as a songwriter is to see all the flags and see all the directions and grab them and make them consciously go somewhere. I don't believe we really write songs that consciously, I think we assemble songs. We write songs subconsciously. Very often I will write a bit of something and I might be stuck for a line, and I'll think, "I just cannot get the line that goes here." Or I can't get the last line of the chorus, or the last line of the verse going into the chorus. Nothing fits. So I give it up, and I'm not one of those people who bashes and bashes once it stops happening. It goes into a drawer and then I'll bring it out at some point and play it again and it will happen. But I can tell you, and this has happened to me so many times, I have been in the shower or driving over the Sydney Harbour Bridge or—quite rarely—mowing the lawn or whatever, and the line will come to me. And I know that that's because subconsciously it's still working on it.

Is it coming from within you or is it coming from somewhere else?
It comes from within you. And it's to do with the fact that our minds, our memories, are basically hard drives. They've got millions of things on them, things of the way you look, the way people's voices sound, things that they say and the colours of things. But it's fairly random access. A trigger mechanism will start the subconscious throwing stuff out. The trick of the songwriter is to be able to consciously assemble them into a song. As you write over the years you become able to do it. And I'll tell you another way. My method of writing is that I will get a pang, a gnawing away at me, and I know that something's happening. I'll just come in, by myself, usually in the studio, and I'll turn the piano on, I'll sit down and start to bang. I have trained myself to turn a tape recorder on first. I might go for ten minutes or I might go for two hours. I don't know what's happening to me, I just go. Little bits and pieces. Sometimes I can talk out loud. Sometimes I read things out of books. It's the most amazing process.

Are you in a different place when you're writing?
Absolutely. So much so that on a few occasions it's happened when the phone's rung— I now don't do it with the phones on—in the early days, and all of a sudden somebody would open the door and go, "Oh Brian!" And I would be that cat stuck on the ceiling. I was so not here. I was so wherever that was. I have the feeling that if it happened in the extreme sense I could actually have a heart attack. 'Cause it brings me back here so quickly. It's horrifying actually.

As well as your fascination with Westerns, were you also fascinated with outlaws and the crime world? "Every Mother's Son" would suggest so.
Yes. The two periods in history that I've studied are the Wild West and the Mafia. I've got thousands of books on the Mafia. To me they're very similar periods and are fascinating for

the same kinds of reasons. They're the absolute opposite of what I'm like as a person. I'm very non-violent—and I have this morbid fascination for people who can kill people. It's something that I've had as long as I can remember. I'm fascinated in the folklore that goes around it all, how these things happen, how someone as scumbaggy as Al Capone could get where he got and still remain today a folk hero. I don't know why we glorify these people, but we do. Billy the Kid was a little prick, a horrible little bastard. He wasn't brave or anything; he was shithouse. But Billy the Kid is one of America's folk heroes.

Did someone in particular inspire "Handyman"?
You can have a guess. It was a little bit of a slap at somebody. Just a colourful industry figure at the time. And the only interesting thing about it is that it gives us an insight into how we really honestly think at the time that it's going to make a difference. The chances are that the person it's about has no clue and will never have a clue—I'm never going to tell him—but at the time it was a really passionate thing for me. I sang that song as though he was in front of me. So here's the point. Maybe it's the catharsis about it, so it's irrelevant whether he or anyone else ever knows but rather that I got it out. To have it live as an actual recording is just a bit like a bookmark in my life.

There's a song called "Matilda", which is about my frustrations at the time with parochialism. It's a recurring thing with me. It was about the time I was falling in love with America and attempting to figure out how to go there again. And once you commit to that kind of path, then stuff that's going on here starts to annoy you. We had so much interesting music and so much going on, but the industry itself had not caught up with where the music was. So I wrote a song called "Matilda". I find it very difficult to find what I was talking about now, other than I remember the passion of it. I don't think anyone's ever going to call me and say, "You know that song 'Matilda', I just loved the way you pointed that out about Australia."

Does it frustrate you that the original intent of some songs passes people by?
No, because in the process of writing, it I'm not actually talking to them anyway. It's me talking *about* it. There's a big difference between me talking about it or me telling you about it. If I tell you about it I have to make sure you understand. But if I'm talking about it I just have to know how I feel. People resent being told but they love being asked in. "Come in and think about this with me" is what they love. "You will believe in God" they don't like.

How did the song and music for Tim Burstall's film *Alvin Purple* come about? And how do you feel about that song now?
To me it's one of the most idiomatic songs of anything I've ever written. It was written absolutely for the moment. That was at a time when I was looking to diversify. Up until that time scores were pretty much the realm of arrangers, or the guys who did the Channel 9 orchestras, Tommy Tycho and all those guys. They did have a tendency to say that if it's a score it has to be written out and played by real musicians in real keys and they have to be dressed and they have to do this and it's all union. Tim Burstall said, "I just want him to do

the music." Nobody had a clue as to whether I could do it or not, least of all me. It's one of those ones where I said, "Yes!" And then went, "What is it?" I had this great blank page, and this very funny fun movie that was so idiomatic musically that I couldn't really put a foot wrong. That film broke a lot of rules. That was a glorious time.

Whereas how do you feel about "Class of '74"?
I hate it. It was exactly written for the television show. That's its problem because at that time there was a lot of strange timings being used, a lot of very weird juxtaposed timings. In television themes in particular. They were very arranged and they had lots of 2/4 and strange bars in them. For some reason I thought that this should be the same. So I wrote this little song, which was very much a TV theme as it was back at that time. The problem was that they wanted a three-and-a-half-minute version of it. So I built it out into a real song. They never used the three and a half minutes, obviously. Opening credits back in those days were eighty or ninety seconds.

Unfortunately Tudor released it as a single. So this thing came out and got airplay and sold. It certainly was a very clumsy, ugly song but people loved it. My brief for it was that it had to include "Class of '74". Apart from anything else, how easy is it to sing those words? It's not. And so based on how clumsy the hook was, the whole song just progressively got more and more clumsy. I can't stand it. And people come up to me after every show that I've done and say, "Why didn't you play it? We came to hear it."

"Let Go" was a straight country song. Did you write that here or in America?
When I was about six or seven, in Perth on 6IX on Sunday mornings from nine till twelve, they had a country hour. They played Hank Snow and Hank Williams—all the Hanks. All the Carter Sisters. I fell in love with country music. That was one of those songs that I wrote not for me. Tudor and I were starting to do bits and pieces in the States, I was still here, I actually had a publishing deal at that stage in Los Angeles, and it was one of those naive Australian conversations about America. Tudor said, "Why don't you write a country song and I'll get it to"—I forget who his contact was—"in Nashville." So I went in to demo a bunch of songs for the *Moonshine* album, and that was one of them. And the band sent it up. I said, "Well, let's just do it as a country demo." So I actually wrote it as a publishing song and demoed it.

Of course when you do that everyone immediately falls in love with the demo. They said, "You have to do that yourself." "I can't do that!" I'd just come out of "Keep on Rockin'" and "Silver City" and all those things. "First of all, I could never do it on stage, it would be a parody. Don't even go there." So Tudor said, "Well, just cut a band track on it." And it was one of those songs that despite me, it got away. The arranger that was putting the strings on the album loved it, so he worked extra hard on the arrangement. And then there was a steel player in Bluestone who came in one day and he heard the tracks and he said, "Oh please let me play some steel parts on it." This thing built itself into this record, so I knew it had to be a single at least. I was so worried about it when it came out, thinking I was going to alienate all the rock 'n' roll fans. And it was huge. It's the most covered song of all my songs. Twenty-six versions there are. It's been enormous for me. It was on *Southern Nights*, that huge Glen Campbell album. It's been recorded by Gene Pitney. Mostly country artists. Even Cilla Black did a version of it. And it's been number one in South Africa twice, both times in Swahili. It's been recorded all over the world. It's just one of those songs.

Joining the Flying Burrito Brothers, albeit in a line-up changed from its original version, was a nice symmetry in terms of your influences and musical leanings.
It was the closing of the circle. I started out being a Burritos fan when we took the wrong turn, and I felt that I was cheated then, but maybe I got one last go at it. We toured throughout Europe, there's a whole country rock circuit throughout Europe that's really huge, and I felt really natural doing it. And we made a couple of good albums. We wrote all the songs, and they were really genre correct. They were part and parcel of the history of the band.

JIM KEAYS

MELBOURNE, AUSTRALIA, FEBRUARY 2004

On the living room wall of Jim Keays' comfortable house in one of Melbourne's quiet, leafy, southeast suburbs is a framed album cover of Bob Dylan's *Hard Rain*. It's striking for the autograph on it, personally inscribed "To Jim". Dylan is not known for signing autographs, particularly on his own album covers. This one was acquired during Dylan's 2003 Australian tour, which coincided with the Long Way to the Top tour roaming around the country. The common thread was promoter Michael Chugg, who presented the album cover to Dylan at Keays' request, expecting the usual rebuff. To Chugg's surprise and Keays' elation, Dylan was more than happy to sign when he was told the album belonged to the lead singer of legendary Australian band, the Masters Apprentices. It turned out Dylan himself owned two Masters albums.

Such is the reputation of the group that Keays and his songwriting partner, Doug Ford, took to great heights in the late 1960s and early 1970s, charting a course from lightweight pop to tough irreverent rock 'n' roll, from blues to psychedelia and then progressive rock. Voted

Australia's most popular band three years in a row, the Masters Apprentices emerged from the hotbed of Adelaide talent in the mid- to late sixties that also gave birth to The Twilights and Zoot. Having enjoyed two successful albums at home, the Masters followed the lead of other Australian groups and took the customary sea voyage to England to pursue greater fame and fortune. While they fell the way of all the bands that took that trip—they broke up—they did manage to record two albums in London that attained widespread popularity (*Choice Cuts*) and long-term cult following (*A Toast to Panama Red*).

Like many of his contemporaries, Keays fell into songwriting without premeditation. Born in Glasgow on 9 September 1946, he arrived in Adelaide with his family when he was five, and was perceptive enough to work out the Scottish accent wouldn't get him far in the school playground. He became Australian immediately, but his early musical influences were from far away—Chuck Berry, Bo Diddley, Muddy Waters, Elmore James, Robert Johnson. Dylan was also an influence, along with the Beatles and Rolling Stones, but it was Keays' love of the blues that drove his passion to join a band and, lacking any musical experience, he responded to a notice posted on a music shop board for a singer to join instrumental group The Mustangs.

He would have been quite happy just to sing and play blues harp for the band, which changed its name to Masters Apprentices in deference to the members' blues heroes. But when the Masters' original songwriter, Mick Bower, left in 1967, Keays stepped up to the mark, with guitarist Ford providing the instrumental expertise to fashion ideas into polished songs. "Turn Up Your Radio" and "Because I Love You" were two of the best known songs in a considerable output of work that defined them as an important songwriting team long before they were willing to view themselves in that light.

After the Masters finished, Keays embarked on a solo career that he maintains to this day, with uneven results. The nostalgia performing circuit always beckons, and Keays is happy to play where he is wanted, but he is always writing new songs in the hope that they will somehow find an audience.

"The strange thing is that if you were a carpenter or a plumber or any of those things, if you've been doing it for forty years you would be a brilliant cabinetmaker, you could make the finest furniture now. But in this business, apparently you get worse," he said, bemused. "Because the songs you wrote back then are okay but the songs you're writing now aren't. And that doesn't make sense to me. I think I'm a finer songwriter now than I was back then. I've refined ways of doing things and gotten better at expressing things in lyrics. You would think you'd be a better craftsperson, but it appears that that's not the case, because those songs aren't being played."

Did you do any writing before you were in the Masters Apprentices?
No. Although at school I was totally distracted by music; I hardly did any actual schoolwork. I used to incessantly listen to the radio, listen to songs, make up my own Top 40 charts, whatever. Music took me over and enveloped me completely. I was not actually writing lyrics down, but absorbing it all. So I guess when my chance to be a songwriter came, it all came gushing out from those years of absorbing.

119

When I joined the Masters there was already a songwriter in the band, Mick Bower, who wrote all our early stuff. He brought completed songs to the table, so there was no chance of writing anything in those early days. It wasn't until Mick had his "nervous bread van" that we decided we'd better keep writing within the band, and so Doug Ford and I started writing songs together.

Did you and Doug realise there was a special creative spark between you or was it just force of necessity?
At first it was force of necessity. For the very first time in the band's career, we had to go outside the band to get a song to record, which was "Elevator Driver", Brian Cadd's song. We were voted several years in a row as Australia's most original band, and it was no use getting other people's songs if we were going to be called an original band. But Doug was a great guitarist, probably one of the best in the country at the time, and I knew there was the capability there. So we just started doing it. And the very first song we ever wrote, we recorded.

That was "Brigette"?
Yeah, "Brigette". It was a minor hit, but it was a good start. We knew that something we wrote could get into the charts, albeit not in a high position. And then progressively, as we moved on, each song we wrote attained a higher position on the charts until we were number one. Quite amazing really.

At what point then did you recognise that you were a special songwriting duo?
I don't think we ever realised that. I never sat back and thought, "Wow, we're a special songwriting duo." That's not something you would really do.

Do you now?
I look back and I think, gee, they really did have something, there was definitely something there. At the time you would never have thought that it would evolve into being one of the great songwriting teams. It just didn't seem possible. But in retrospect I think we did break some ground and pioneered some songwriting ideas in a way, yeah.

How did you move from your blues sensibility into writing pop songs?
By working out that we had to be a commercial entity, and seeing other blues bands, like for example, Bay City Union. They were getting nowhere, and it just wasn't commercial enough. Even though we loved that sort of music, we had to write commercial music. Having said that, there are blues elements in our songs.

Some of the early songs that you and Doug wrote were very poppy.
They were. At that stage we were managed by Darryl Sambell, who managed Johnny Farnham and Zoot, both very poppy artists. And I guess we were led astray for a brief period there of about a year, in our early songwriting days, by a management that really wanted us

to be commercial. It was a very teenybopper sort of market in those days. We fell for it for a little while, and we wrote "Linda Linda". Which I hate.

And which Ian McFarlane referred to as "vapid" in his *Encyclopedia of Australian Rock and Pop*.
Yeah. And he's right. Although there was a song in there, "Merry-Go-Round", which was actually quite tough. But after a year of writing this sort of stuff, Doug and I consciously got together and said, "Look, we can't keep doing this, we've got to write some good, credible songs here instead of trying to jump on this bubblegum bandwagon that everybody wants us to be on." 'Cause we were never that, we were a blues band, and a band that we thought had some sort of credibility.

It's been well documented how crazy those days were in the Masters Apprentices. Do you remember much about the actual writing of the songs, how you worked and how ideas came to you?
Because it was so hectic—we were going seven days a week, fifty-two weeks of the year— it was only on rare occasions that we could actually get together and sit down and write something. So when we did we made the most of the opportunities and we'd knock out about five songs in a session. There's so many different ways to write a song. But we found the best way was just sitting in a room with an acoustic guitar and away you go and nut the song out. And then teach it to the other guys and go into the studio.

Obviously Doug would be on guitar; would you be contributing to melodies as well?
Yes. I'd come with a melody and a feel and lyrics. And Doug would fill in the blank spaces. On some occasions. And then on other occasions Doug would have virtually an instrumentally finished song, and I would put the lyrics to it. So there are plenty of different ways of writing a song, and they would vary.

If an idea came to you when you were on the road and you weren't going to get a chance to sit down with Doug for a week or two, what would you do? Would you sing it into a tape recorder?
No. Just try and remember it. You can and you do. In those days there were no cassette recorders, there wasn't anything like that. Doug had an old reel-to-reel, but we never used that very often. We would just write the song in its basic essence and then take it to the boys, and then we'd all play it. Then we'd go to the studio and record it. Or we would play it to the boys *in* the studio and record it all at the same time.

Consequently there are no demos from those days?
No, no demos. Not one demo. And in fact, a lot of bands now find their old out-takes and their songs that didn't quite make it. With the Masters, every single thing we recorded we released.

At what point did you pick up a guitar and start working out chords yourself?
Probably when we got to England. And it was later on when I started writing my own solo album, *The Boy from the Stars*, that I actually wrote songs by myself using the guitar. In the Masters days, hardly at all.

Did the guitar open possibilities for you?
Yeah, of course it did. But having been influenced by early blues guys and Bob Dylan, his chord structures are so simple, and that's what I like. If you listen to the song "The Boy from the Stars", it is Dylanesque in a way. I'm very much of the simple school of writing; I don't get very complicated. You can weave a really nice melody around a simple chord structure. In fact the songs that I like most are songs like that.

Do you write mainly on guitar nowadays?
Yeah, I do. A lot of people use computers now, of course, Pro Tools and those sort of things. But I don't believe in that. They all say computers make things fast, but I actually think they make things slow. I think computers get in the way of creating a song.

Many of the songwriters who use Pro Tools still start with a guitar or a keyboard.
Oh, they do. And Pro Tools is a wonderful tool for getting your song to a really good demo stage. But I don't work that way. I'll get a song up and it will just be on a simple little tape recorder, and then in the studio or in the rehearsal hall I'll teach the band, and then from there going to a studio and put the sucker down. And then enhance it; you can use all the Pro Tools in the world after that. But for the actual construction of that song I think the technology gets in the way. That's my opinion. I know a lot of writers will write on computers and go with drum machines and all those things. But it's not my way.

A few of the earlier Masters' hits borrowed from well-known songs or tunes. Like in "Brigette" you use the refrain from "Here Comes the Bride", "5.10 Man" starts out like "The Great Pretender". What was the thinking behind those references?
And "One, two, three o'clock, four o'clock rock" is in the middle of "Turn Up Your Radio". Which was purposely done, that was harking back to the roots of rock 'n' roll. "Brigette" was about her getting married. "Dixie" is in there, too, which was just an idea borrowed from *Sgt Pepper's*, where they'd segue into a weird ending. "The Great Pretender", I can't remember how that came about now. Sometimes people do things without any real motive behind it. Maybe in this case we just wanted something dynamic to start with. I've always tried to hit them with something attention-grabbing right from the start of the song.

Do you think that it's valuable to be derivative as a developing songwriter, a step to go through before you can be highly original?
Yeah, I do. Because nobody is immediately original. It just doesn't work like that. Even if you look at John Lennon or Jimi Hendrix, or Bob Dylan. They all borrowed from somewhere. Bob Dylan from Woody Guthrie, Jimi Hendrix from Bob Dylan and from other guitarists, and

he worked with Little Richard for a long time. John Lennon from the early rockers. Everybody takes a leaf out of somebody's book. It just keeps going back and back. So that's part of the evolution of a songwriter. But then after a while you find your own niche.

How did "Turn Up Your Radio" originate and did you have a sense when you wrote it that it was quite a leap for you in song crafting?
We didn't have a sense that it was a leap because we'd written "5.10 Man" and "Merry-Go-Round", and "Think About Tomorrow Today" just preceded it. They were all tough rock songs and so was "Turn Up Your Radio". But what had happened was that all through that period with Darryl Sambell we were being pushed and goaded and persuaded to be more commercial and to be more a pop band. And the more that happened the more we rebelled against it happening. So Doug and I consciously went, "Let's write a song that will forever allay any fears that we're a pop band. Let's get something so obnoxious and so gratingly horrible, in your face, that they'll go, hang on, this cannot be bubblegum music." So that's when we wrote "Turn Up Your Radio". We just wanted a full-on riff with a primal scream. I suppose it was a protest song. Not like a Bob Dylan protest song, our very own little protest against being pushed against type. We weren't the type to be pushed.

It had a very long introduction for a hit song.
The intro is long and it's against type again. Which is a rule that you're not supposed to do, because radio won't play it. And as it turned out, radio didn't play it. Because at the time there was the great Australian radio ban, where they didn't play any Australian music. We got caught in that, but the record went to number one despite no airplay. Which said a lot for the song, really.

Did you and Doug both write prolifically together?
Yeah, we wrote a lot of songs. Prolific in as much as the time we had to be prolific. Like I said before, in the mayhem of our working conditions of the time, there wasn't a lot of time *to* write the songs. The first time we really felt that we had proper time to write was on the boat going to England. We wrote a whole album of songs.

"Because I Love You" was another discernible leap in your songwriting, but in that wistful folk pop vein.
It was. The verses were Dylanesque in "Because I Love You". It's a strange song, because it's only got two parts, which in modern day wouldn't be enough; you'd have to have a bridge or a refrain or something. But there's only verses and chorus, that's all there is.

And a very long intro again.
The Doug intro is different from the rest of the song, although it repeats again in the middle. It's a strange song because it hasn't got really a lot of content, but it seems to have something intangible that's just kept it going. At the time it wasn't a big hit. But as the years have gone by, it's got bigger and bigger.

It was used in an advertising campaign.
It was used a few times. It was used for Lee Jeans, then it was used by the Milk Board, then Mazda cars used it. That's the three big ones.

So you're quite happy for the song to be used commercially.
Absolutely. I've had this debate with several people over it. Because I know some writers are very precious and will not let their song be used in anything, and I can understand their philosophy in some respects. But I feel that it has kept that song alive. When it was done in '88 for the Lee Jeans ad, it was so popular that they asked us to re-record it. Which we did, and it became a Top 10 hit. Just through the ad. That proved to me then that it really does have a beneficial effect and not a detrimental effect.

It sounds like it could have been two different songs that you put together, the "Because I love you" part in the verses and the "Do what you want to do" part in the chorus.
It wasn't the case, it was written at the one session. It was written very purposefully on the ship. When we left Australia there were 8,000 kids on that dock and it was a huge thing, we were the number one band in the country, we had legions of fans who all came to see us off. The verses of that song hark back to that, all those people there. It sounds like a love song for one particular person, but it actually isn't. It's thinking about what we were leaving behind. "Not because we're far apart." It was a sort of a sadness, really, that we were leaving all that behind to pursue something that we didn't know what was going to happen. But the chorus part, "Do what you want to do, be what you want to be", juxtaposed that, in that we were saying, "Okay, we've left all that behind, and it is sad, but we're going to go ahead and do this." So there was a definite structure to that song that we pre-planned when we wrote it.

When you look back on the *Choice Cuts* album today, over thirty years later, do you think the songs still hold up well?
Absolutely. It was a giant leap for us. I'm proud of that album. There's young guys like Brad Shepherd from the Hoodoo Gurus who think that album is one of the greatest albums of all time. The greatest prog rock album that's ever been recorded, so he says. It did really have some great musical moments on it, for its time. Things like "Michael", "Easy to Lie" is a great track, "Rio de Camero" is a great track. It's diverse, every song is totally different from the one before it.

When an album like *A Toast to Panama Red* misses out on mass commercial appeal and becomes a cult classic, is that satisfying enough for you in terms of your songs being heard and appreciated?
Yeah. It's always good to have an album like that. If every album's a big hit album it can get a bit boring. And if every album stiffs, well that can get a bit boring too. [*Laughs*] But to have an album that people come to you and go, "Gee that *Toast to Panama Red* is just so different, it's so unique, I love it!" That's great that somebody can say that when hardly

anybody knows about it. It's just great that people can find it. And Bob Dylan obviously found it, too. So I love the idea that *Panama Red* wasn't a huge hit album. Although there was a song on it, "Love Is", I thought should have been a hit. It's just that we'd split up right when it came out, so radio didn't get on to it.

How did you set about finding your own distinctive style when embarking on your solo career?
I decided right from the outset, when the Masters split up and I went out on my own, that I wanted to do something that was totally away from what the Masters represented. I didn't want to just be the singer from Masters coming out trying to do Masters-type songs. I wanted to stamp my own persona on my new career. And so I did that with *The Boy from the Stars*, which was absolutely nothing like anything the Masters ever did.

Is that why you chose to do a science-fiction concept album?
No, it just evolved that way. I started writing and after writing about twenty songs, I found that eight or ten of them had this thread, and I thought maybe I could do something like a concept album. The concept of a concept album hadn't really come up that much at that stage. It was pre-*Man Who Fell to Earth*, the Bowie thing. And there were a lot of things emerging about UFOs and space travel, people becoming aware of that side of things that hadn't really been documented much before then. It became a curiosity thing. So I found that the songs were weaving a thread through that concept of some sort of interplanetary intervention that may or may not be going on. The fact that it wasn't anything like the Masters was the most enjoyable part of it.

How was writing alone after being in a partnership for several years?
That was hard, because it didn't really sit well with me, and it still doesn't. On *The Boy from the Stars* about half of the album's written by me, and the other half's collaborations. I'm the type of writer that likes to collaborate. I like being able to bounce ideas off somebody else, and finding a ground that we're both happy with.

Without the guitar prowess that Doug had, did you find yourself restricted in the way the melodies would come?
No, I already had the melodies going on in my head. But I had another guitarist around me at the time, a close friend, Phil Manning, who forms a big part of *The Boy from the Stars*. He played on most of the tracks, and he was there at the time when those tracks were first put to the band and was instrumental in structuring them for a guitarist that had real ability.

Has there been another collaborator through your career that you feel you've had as fruitful a relationship with as you had with Doug?
No, there hasn't. I've tried lots of other collaborations. I've written some really good songs with other people. Nick Smith, who wrote "Harley and Rose", "The Chosen Ones", "Chained to the Wheel", all those great Black Sorrows songs. Great guy and a great writer. Some good

songs have come out of the Nick collaboration. Another guy, Frank Sablotny, we wrote a song called "Waiting for the Big One", which everybody says is destined to be a hit but it hasn't been and I don't think it'll ever be one now, but it's a great song. I'm still writing with Doug, too, by the way.

Has the dynamic between you changed?
No. We still do it exactly the same way as we always did. The only problem is that Doug lives in Queensland now and to write on any meaningful level is pretty hard to do by correspondence. But on the Long Way to the Top tour we wrote a couple of songs together. And we're actually in the middle of a song at the moment that he sent me down a tape of, and I've done the lyrics for. I'm still looking for other people to write with. But I know in my heart that it's probably Doug and I that will come up with the better songs.

You've talked in interviews about the distinctive Australian rock sound in bands like the Masters Apprentices, Cold Chisel and the Hoodoo Gurus. Is that sound a performance thing or does it begin in the way the songs are written?
It's a performance-based thing. 'Cause you perform first before you write songs, in a band. Glenn A Baker said that The Easybeats and the Masters were the instigators of what then became known as the Australian sound. I grappled with that for a while, and I wondered how that happened. In Australia we had to win over audiences who were a lot harder to please probably than audiences in England or America at the time. So we evolved a tougher, more aggressive, raw sort of sound. And that's come through in what we call pub rock and with people like Chisel, Rose Tattoo, The Angels, I think it just evolved out of the way we had to perform.

How difficult is it as an iconic figure in the history of Australian rock music to establish yourself as a contemporary artist, particularly as a songwriter of relevant new work?
Extremely difficult. Not daunting, but extremely difficult. It'd probably be easy to be bitter and twisted about it. But I'm not; I understand that this is the playing field and I've got to play on it. The big problem is radio. Because there are no stations in this country, and I mean none, that have the demographic area that suits a myriad of Australian artists. There's so many, from Richard Clapton and James Reyne, Joe Camilleri and Stephen Cummings. There's millions of them. The gold stations will play their records till the cows come home, but to play anything new by these people is impossible. So unless you're Snotty and the Nosepickers or some other new band, there's no place for us.

Can you stay inspired in an ageist Australian rock climate?
I do. Because when I was young, maybe I was an angry young man, or maybe I had a platform, or maybe I had a gripe, and I don't have that any more, but I do have opinions and I do have observances and passions and all those things are necessary to write songs. So I'm still inspired, yes I am, and I can still find things to write about.

ROSS WILSON

MELBOURNE, AUSTRALIA, JULY 2003

He's not known as Ross "the Boss" Wilson for nothing. He might not present himself as a domineering and forceful character—he is mild-mannered, affable and quite amenable given his iconic status—but cast an eye over his extensive canon of work and there are few who can match Wilson's contribution to the history of Australian popular music. He is best known for "Eagle Rock", a distinctly American-flavoured ditty from 1970 that has long been considered one of Australia's best ever rock songs and even reportedly inspired Elton John to write "Crocodile Rock". But it barely tells the story of Wilson as a songwriter.

His music styles have ranged from R&B, funk, rural blues and country to progressive rock, retro and slick pop. The subjects and themes he has tackled have been light-heartedly flippant, socially pertinent and intimately personal. "Eagle Rock" is just one facet of a myriad, but he is perfectly comfortable with its legendary status. "There's no other track like it," he told me forthrightly.

Ross Wilson was born on 18 November 1947 in Melbourne. After some rudimentary trumpet lessons, he abandoned the idea of formal musical training. Listening to his father's jazz records and buying his own rock 'n' roll and New Orleans R&B records from an early age, Wilson developed a keen, reverential ear and an ardent passion that led him to join his first group, The Pink Finks, while still at school. There he teamed with Ross Hannaford, with whom he would duel on guitar and co-write for years to come. Their next band, The Party Machine, was adventurous and somewhat notorious; if the Frank Zappa-influenced musical structures and in-your-face subjects weren't enough, the Victorian Vice Squad even saw fit to seize a book of the group's song lyrics due to their "unwholesome" nature.

After a brief stint in England with ex-pat Australian band Procession, Wilson rejoined Hannaford in a new group, Sons of the Vegetal Mother, taking the Zappa influence further. But it was their offshoot band, Daddy Cool, which made their first major commercial splash. Conceived as a fun doo-wop act to provide light relief from their earnest experimentalism, and to pay homage to the music of the 1950s, Daddy Cool became one of the most successful Australian acts of the early seventies. Wilson, never one to rest on his laurels or enjoy repetition, broke up Daddy Cool and formed the heavier rock outfit Mighty Kong, before moving into production, spearheading the ascension of Skyhooks, helping to put together Jo Jo Zep and the Falcons, guiding the career of his first wife, Pat Wilson, as well as founding Oz Records.

An unhurried songwriter, for his next band, Mondo Rock, Wilson enlisted the participation of the more prolific Eric McCusker, who wrote most of the band's hits in the early 1980s. But the songs Wilson penned during that period proved powerfully enduring. While "Cool World" goes down as his personal favourite, it was an overlooked album track, "Touch of Paradise", that became one of his bestsellers when recorded by John Farnham on the momentous *Whispering Jack* album in 1986.

As a solo artist Wilson continues to revisit his roots and explore different musical terrains—recent albums *Go Bongo Go Wild!* and *Country & Wilson* were blues and country excursions respectively—and while audiences always clamour for "Eagle Rock", they also get a broad mix that is the cool world of Ross "the Boss" Wilson, a songwriter who began his career just wanting to sing.

"Early in the piece the vocal thing came to the front, and I was more interested in doing that," he said on a chilly winter afternoon in Melbourne, sitting in the garden while his young children played loudly indoors. "Everything else has been a bit of an adjunct to that. I could probably sing better than the guys in my neighbourhood, so very quickly I became a kind of bandleader, and I've assumed the role of director, where I will get the best people available and have them help perform the songs that I've written."

He went on to describe the mechanics of getting his musical concepts into song form. "As a guitarist myself I'm not all that good. I'm a strummer and an ideas man, who will ask someone else to play certain things, and they will do it straightaway and that will make me happy."

When you're working out chords to get a melody going, do you use a piano, a guitar or do you sing it to somebody and ask them to play it?

These days it's more a guitar. There was a time, particularly in the early days, when I was still living at my parents, and then later on in the early stages of my first marriage, where we had a piano, and the first songs I wrote were on the piano, simply just picking out chords and repeating them and working out some kind of tune over the top of that. That's still pretty much how I work; there's a certain amount of riffing involved. But the rudimentary stuff is stitching some chords together to go with some lyrics, or an idea for a song that I've had for a while and then somehow it all slowly comes together.

Do melodies ever come to you away from an instrument?

No, I'm more in the moment of feeling like you want to do a song, which is something that you have to wait for. And with kids running around I haven't done much writing at the moment, so I have to carve out the time to do it. I might get a friend of mine, Eris O'Brien, that I write with a fair bit, set aside time and just start mucking around. Or I'm entering a period where I know I'm going to be writing songs; I've done this certain amount of work and I've released an album, that takes up your head space for a while, and now that's all over, I'm feeling like I've got to move on to the next stage and I'm going to write some more songs. And rather than stressing out about it, it's something you just have to let happen. 'Cause all the time your subconscious is working on new stuff.

The worst thing is in the early stages of any kind of success when the pressure's on from outside sources. "You must deliver a new album by this time!" Your opportunities are immense but you're not working fast enough and you feel the pressure is on and that can be a real drag. I'm a more slow, steady kind of worker rather than some guy who will go, so and so wants five songs, and you sit down and write five songs for their album. I don't enjoy doing that kind of work. Any songs of mine that have been successes, whether it's by me or by the few other artists that have taken my songs, the songs were already there and they were written by me for me to satisfy myself. About as far as I go with writing to order is if somebody invites me to write with them, and they go, "I'm making an album and I want to write a song." I enter that negotiation then of that space, I'm writing this song for this person.

So when you wrote "It Matters to Me" with Paul Kelly, on your *Country & Wilson* album, was that originally written as something for him?

No, I wanted to write something for me. It was during a period, early to mid-nineties, when I was seeking out other people. It was a time when I didn't have a band but I was looking around for opportunities and my manager was helping me line up co-writing things and so was the publishing company. I did a few overseas trips and wrote with people. I sat on that song for a really long time, because I knew that eventually it would get done, and then I demoed it, and then that sat around, and eventually I worked on the raw recording again and it came out with a few more flourishes as the track that's on *Country & Wilson*. I think that was his title. He came up with quite a bit of the chord change stuff, and I came up with the bridge, which is the surprise in the song.

The whole punch line about "It matters to me, it just don't matter all the time", that really grated him at the time, he couldn't quite get that. I go, "That's what relationships are really like, you know, just having been through one like that." This total love thing is not reality; sometimes it doesn't go that far and you have to make a decision to back off. I remember him sitting there going, "Mmmm." It just didn't seem to sit too well with him. But then he came around, and we were throwing lines around. He got the ball rolling and then we were back and forthing on it.

I find that's pretty typical. If you're coming into a songwriting situation with another experienced writer, quite often the first song you get will be pretty good, and you might only ever get that one song. In fact, I've got a bit of a joke on stage with the song "Mood Swing", the Don Walker collaboration. Before I play it I'd say, "I wrote this one with Don Walker. And this song's so great that we decided we'd never write another song together in case we spoilt it." I think there's a certain amount of truth in that but it's mainly a joke.

Do you remember writing your first song?
Yeah. I was mucking around with early rock 'n' roll and getting into R&B and Louisiana Blues and I would just take some 12-bar thing that had a reasonable melody and change the words. So there's this great old Lazy Lester song, "I'm a Lover Not a Fighter", that a few English R&B groups covered, and I wrote this one called "I'm the World's Greatest Lover" that had exactly the same tune and basic idea, and that was an attempt to write something. And we actually played it on stage.

How old were you?
Sixteen or seventeen.

You *were* the world's greatest lover at sixteen.
Yeah [*Laughs*]. But then I started bashing around on the piano and "The Gentle Art", which was a Party Machine song, I count as the first real stand-alone original song that I wrote without any other influences involved, where I wasn't just taking a bit and changing it around. It's a distinct song in its own right.

"The Gentle Art" was quite advanced melodically and lyrically for an early composition.
That's what I think when I listen to it now. I go, "Why can't I do that now?" [*Laughs*] It was to do with just digging the sounds on the piano. I wrote some quite interesting things on the piano, even the "Virgins" song, I played that when we were launching the *Now Listen!* album recently, I got my band at the time to learn it, and the bass player's going, "Where's this coming from? This is out there!"

Can you tap into where you were coming from at the time?
Yeah, I was coming from digging early Frank Zappa. I didn't like melodic thirds in the chords; I liked discordant chords with fourths in them. When you do that the melody has got a lot more scope. The thirds actually get in the road. You can have a major third or a

130

minor third and that dictates everything around it. But you take the third out and just go fifths and fourths. Heavy metal guys typically will play these rock chords without thirds in them 'cause it gives this real solid base, a foundation to everything. I liked the discordant sound of early twentieth-century serious composers, the Russian guys, where they were trying to emulate the sounds of industry and the modern world at the turn of the century. The sounds of war and metal tanks and the Russian Revolution. Stravinsky and those things. And then it got beyond that into really abstract stuff. I think a lot of jazz appeals to me, too, because it's to do with very thick chord structures, where there's a lot of notes you can sing, you're not just stuck on the ones that are dictated by the simple triads. I don't actually like sticking to the same melody all the time. Even on the really well-known songs, I'll sing it a bit different each night. I'll bend the notes around. Never the same.

This is because of your improvisational tendency?
Yeah, and I think it can be a bit of a drag because sometimes when I'm singing someone else's song, say in the Mondo Rock days, Eric McCusker's songs were very well laid out, but sometimes I would not quite hear the same notes that he did. You've got to give the composer some respect, and I realised then that I had certain things that I do that don't always fit what other people want to have happen. It's just how I hear things.

The Party Machine had two sides, the socially outspoken side and the depraved side. Was that a result of the Frank Zappa influence or were you already in touch with your dark side?
It was definitely there already, and if anything that's why what he was doing appealed to me, in particular the first half dozen or so albums of his. I still love that first album, *Freak Out,* 'cause it's both within and outside the mainstream. On the one hand he works within the mainstream by doing these parodies of established music. And then on the other hand he's doing these experimental things of what he was listening to, like Edgar Varèse.

"You've All Got to Go" wasn't complex lyrically but it did have a definite Zappa influence structurally and melodically. Most people that know you from "Eagle Rock" on wouldn't have a clue.
No, and this has been a bit of a struggle with me to reconcile the two sides. I have the sixties social comment songs, that's always been there and still is, like a song like "No Soul" that's on *Country & Wilson*. And then on the other hand I like to have fun, and music with humour in it has always been attractive to me. That's why I gravitated towards the Skyhooks or The Johnnys or people I've produced, because they were having a good time with music and sending things up and stirring people up. So I like to try and get a reaction but I also like to express what I think. I remember having a songwriting session with a guy in the States who was a big hit writer in the country scene and we were sitting down to write a song and I brought up this word. "I'm trying to express myself." And he's going, "Express yourself? I thought we were here to write a hit song." [*Laughs*] And I went, "Oh, right." 'Cause he's very, very talented, but his whole life was writing songs that would get covered, getting cuts. He didn't look at it that way, even though I could see that he was expressing himself.

"Virgins" was one of a number of exercises in being lyrically controversial. It seems bizarre looking back now that it was controversial to write a song about taking the pill.

It was a godsend that we got our songbook seized, 'cause no-one gave a shit, really. But because some mother complained to the vice squad they stormed into *Go Set*'s offices and seized these books, and we went, "Yeah! That's great!" And the next thing Channel 7 wants to interview us, and we're going, "Beauty!" [*Laughs*]

Did you think at that stage that music might actually create change in society or were you more intent on just shaking people up?

Oh, very rarely can any kind of music create change in society, but what it can do is coagulate things. It can draw people together, so they might come to a gig because they like a certain artist and find people of like mind and make connections that way. Even people who just like to dance, that's what it does, it brings people together, it's a social stimulant. I've been aware of that for ages, and that's my mission, to get people up dancing every night, and I'm pretty good at it. If there's some kind of lyric content that makes them think at the same time that they're groovin' around, it's even better, because by the fact that you're up and dancing and you're letting go, you're allowing things to flow more, then you're allowing yourself to absorb any kind of ideas that are in there lyrically as well. And if they happen to be something that is questioning the status quo of any sort, then the act of movement together with that can maybe help it gain a hold.

"Virgins" sounds like a lyrical idea that you wrote a melody around.

I was just mucking around with these weird chords on the piano and that beat that is in "You've All Got to Go" and "Virgins" eventually became this other kind of twist to the rhythm that is synonymous with Daddy Cool, where I was trying to emulate the left-hand rhythmic thing that they do on the piano on a lot of early rhythm and blues.

Frank Zappa was a Howlin' Wolf fan like you and he was also inspired by fifties rock 'n' roll and doo-wop. He talked about words functioning as texture to the music. What appealed to you about fifties rock 'n' roll music?

I liked the real wild stuff and I'm proud of the fact that one of the very first records I ever bought was "Don't You Just Know It" by Huey "Piano" Smith & The Clowns, which I heard on the radio. That is hard-core New Orleans fun rhythm and blues rock 'n' roll by one of the classic guys and his group. I think it's great that as a ten- or eleven-year-old I was attracted to that, because you don't learn so much as put into practice, it's going back to this expressing thing again, it's a window on how you feel and the things that you're interested in and what attracts you. That's why one man's songs are different from another's. So there I was attracted to real pumpin' and syncopation. The syncopation of that New Orleans-style music that I also heard on my dad's jazz records or Little Richard or Jerry Lee Lewis, "Whole Lotta Shakin' Goin' On", all the wild stuff, I really loved it. And I could see how Jerry Lee Lewis's "Whole Lotta Shakin' Goin' On" was a direct link to my father's boogie-woogie 78s that I used to play.

I've never really had the discipline or the interest to study a musical instrument in depth, and the songs that I write are very simple. I think as time goes by I've become even better at making things concise, and the lyric content's a bit better now. But I still work within that structure basically of a three-and-a-half to four-and-a-half minute getting across an idea and a feeling. A musical feeling with a lyric idea. We're not talking brain surgery here or anything; it's just part of the exercise to keep it as concise as possible. So that's where after a while the Frank Zappa influence wore off.

It was interesting that you had an outfit as progressive and hypnotic as the Sons of the Vegetal Mother and then your doo-wop revival band, Daddy Cool, which to many seemed like a major right turn.

It was about following your interests. I'd been ten or eleven when rock 'n' roll hit Australia in a big way, but before that I discovered there was a whole lot of stuff that existed, really fantastic R&B from all over America, vocal group black stuff with great harmonies and really pumpin' bands behind them. And we never got to hear it. So I was going back and following an interest and educating myself about that and then wanting to try some of it out for myself. At the same time all of the things that I had ever done were coming together, my interests in rhythm and blues and then hard-core Chicago blues, what John Lee Hooker was doing. I used to listen to him a lot, and James Brown and all that. We'd put it all together and you'd get something like "Eagle Rock", which is basically John Lee Hooker Mississippi Blues underneath and then a ragtime New Orleans kind of thing. It's all southern American stuff. For instance, there's hardly been anybody that I can think of who can play "Eagle Rock" outside of Daddy Cool or me with my band. They just can't do it. If you sit down and try to analyse what's in that song, it sounds really simple, but it's got all these counter rhythms in it, the parts change as they go and there's a lot going on. It's not the Australian way to play like that, let me tell you.

"Eagle Rock" is rhythmically the most complex of them, but in that style "Come Back Again" is actually the purest one. It's so country rural blues, I think it's an eight-bar structure, there's no chorus to speak of except, "Come back again, I'm just crazy about you, babe." You play that sequence of chords over and over; we used to jam on it for ages at shows, just to extract every kind of variation out of it we could. I think that says a lot about the song. A commercial song form these days means you've got to have a catchy chorus. Repetition is where it's at, but it didn't always used to be like that. If you listen to *Country & Wilson* there's only a couple of songs out of the twelve that actually have a full-blown chorus. The others have got a line. Like "Some of these Blues", there's no chorus, it goes "Some of these blues this" and "Some of these blues that" and it's got all these workings around working out the meaning of that particular phrase. Then you've got "No Soul". It's got a tiny chorus in the middle but it's all about taking the basic idea and then working it in different ways throughout the song so you're twisting the words around, getting new meaning out of the key phrase. And that's like folk music and pre-war rural blues and country. For some reason that's instinctive, I have that in there somehow, and I don't know how I got it. Before I was in any band I used to sneak out on the weekends and go into folk clubs in Melbourne. "Come Back Again" and some of those other ones all came from that same place.

"Eagle Rock" was a real meeting of cultures. It was sparked by something you saw in the *Sunday Times Magazine* in London in 1969, where you were immersed in British prog rock, and musically influenced by an American rural blues style, which became one of the all-time classic Australian rock hits.
Yeah, it is kind of funny that something like that could become an all-time Aussie classic, in that it's distinctly drawing on those forms from elsewhere. But that's what rock 'n' roll is. All of my influences, or 95 per cent of them, I'd say would come from American music. And then the rest of it is experiences I've had, just living.

So then it probably doesn't matter where you are to be inspired?
No. The thing about seeing that photo in the *Sunday Times* in London, all that was some kind of opening, in the way that quite often I'll start off with a song title, because in the back of my brain there's an idea there already, and that song title appeals to me. Then that'll turn into a chorus idea or a key phrase, and then all of the verse stuff is exploring the idea behind those. That's typical of the way I write and I think a lot of people write. The Eagle Rock has been a dance for years and years. There's references to it in songs going back to the twenties, that's about the earliest I can think of, but it's probably around before that, too, as a country dance somewhere. And that's what the flavour of the song is, too. "Eagle Rock" is drawing on traditional forms. It's an archaic sound, that's why it stood out at the time and that's why it's never been swamped by whatever fad goes around, because it exists in its own little bubble. It's original, but it's not. It's just a song that works, and played by guys that knew how to play it.

It didn't all come at once, did it?
It was a slow thing, 'cause I got interrupted. I had to get back to Australia, it took a few months, and then I finished it when I got back.

Did you have a feeling that you'd written something exceptional at the time?
I did, yeah. But I had no idea people would still be listening to it en masse thirty years later. You just don't know, you can't tell the future.

I read where you said that you couldn't believe you'd come up with such an original riff so you kept checking whether you'd unconsciously stolen it from somewhere.
That's a typical experience, too, when you come up with something really excellent, and you're going, "Wow, this is great." And then you think, "Oh gee, maybe I've pinched it from somewhere." 'Cause it seemed to come out fully blown. I was practising and it was more an exercise in trying to learn how to fingerpick on the guitar. I was getting the base note going and getting these top notes. And that's how the riff formed with that syncopated thing. It's like a soul riff, but all off the beat. That's why that song stands out amongst the crowd of

great Australian records that were made around that time, because it's got funk in it. There's no other track like it.

Was producing other artists a happy relief from writing and playing your own music?
Well, the Skyhooks thing was fantastic and I loved 'em. Mighty Kong was where I first saw Skyhooks. They played a gig with us, and then as time went by we were nurturing that and I was getting involved in rehearsals with them and then the line-up was changing, so over a period of about a year it all gradually came together. I knew their songs intimately and scored the job to produce them, and we came out with that first album. I just loved those songs, they were really funny and they were well played and we came up with lots of good stuff in the studio together, lots of production ideas. It was a great time, I really enjoyed it.

Oz Records started up with Glenn Wheatley and me, and we basically helped form Jo Jo Zep and the Falcons out of the remnants of my then wife Pat's band, The Marvels. And got involved with making that album. But that wasn't a fulfilling experience, that taught me that you have to be careful, that as a producer I could only produce stuff that I was really into in a big way. And then get along with the people at the same time. Otherwise I'd just get irritated and it would just annoy me.

Was it as rewarding for you to have produced such a successful breakthrough album as *Living in the '70s* as it was to have written and performed a breakthrough song like "Eagle Rock"?
In a way it was more rewarding. Because it was a very creative thing to be involved with. I just loved it. As time went on we fell out of love, because by their third album Skyhooks were in disarray and so was I. So you'll get different viewpoints from different members of Skyhooks about what actually went down.

Did you write "Living in the Land of Oz" specifically for the film *Oz*, or did you already have that song?
I already had it. I got the call from Chris Löfvén, who was the director of the "Eagle Rock" clip, and he said, "We've got funding, we're going to do this movie based on *The Wizard of Oz* and we need some music." I said, "Well that's funny you should mention that, I've got this song that I've written called 'Living in the Land of Oz'."

What was the original spark for that song?
I went to visit my folks in Hampton, where I grew up, and I was just sitting in the backyard with my guitar and started coming up with that idea. It was all about, here I am, sitting in my backyard where I grew up, but how did I really get here? And the play on words where "Oz" is the mythical kingdom and to a certain extent with our denial of where we really came from, or what has occurred here, we're all subscribing to that, well it really is the Land of Oz.

I remember I went on this Channel 9 pop show that ran for about five minutes. And somebody dug out all this Aboriginal footage of them sitting around the camp in Todd River in squalor, which I thought was perfect for it, and then the director came out tearing his hair out going, "We can't use that! We can't use that! We'll have to scrap the song if you want to use that." I said, "Well, I didn't bring the footage out anyway, but you don't have to scrap the song, just take it off. I still want to sing the song." But I was just amazed. They couldn't have any of that.

Did it frustrate you that the message might not have been getting through?
Not really. It mattered that it didn't get as much airplay as I wanted, because the whole point about releasing records is that you want someone to buy them, otherwise you might as well just leave them on tape and stick them in your back room. I was getting the message out, because it was in a movie. And it was on the soundtrack that was the first big release on Oz Records. So it did get some attention. It still gets attention now. Black Australians remember me for that and they come up and talk to me about it.

The very upbeat melody almost belies the angry message.
It was also, as far as Australia goes, one of the first, if not the first track to use reggae rhythms. Me and Hannaford were into that back in Daddy Cool, early reggae. And he went totally into it for years and years.

And then you formed Mondo Rock.
Mondo Rock was interesting because we were a serious songwriting band. The whole point was to perform new material, and we hardly ever played any covers. Always writing songs, always rehearsing, and in that time I got a bit overwhelmed by the Eric songs, 'cause I wasn't pumping them out as fast, and lost my way a bit there. But when you go back amongst all our stuff and you realise in the first couple of years how many songs we wrote that didn't get recorded that are actually quite good, it was a full-on exercise in writing. There's one school of thought that goes, "Ah, the eighties wasn't a very good time for Australian music." And there's another thought that I've subscribed to where I go, "Well, I thought it was a fantastic time." Because all the bands and the people in the bands had learned a lot of lessons, and you had Split Enz and Midnight Oil and Mental As Anything and Mondo Rock and you go on and on. They were all writing very skilfully put together pop/rock songs. There was a big burst. And they were all getting played on the radio, so there can't be anything wrong with that.

Did you pick up anything from Eric McCusker's writing that stirred you creatively?
You'll notice we didn't actually write many songs together. We wrote a few, mainly B-sides.

Were you in the same mindset when you were writing together?
No, it was just kind of artistic tug-of-war. [*Laughs*] But on the other hand, the reason that I got him in the group was 'cause I heard these songs that he'd written and I realised that he was a good songwriter. Some of them I enjoyed singing, and others I wouldn't touch, I'd say, "No, I don't want to sing that one." Exercising my right there. And he certainly had plenty of songs to choose from. But I recognised that I needed him. He wrote the majority of our hits.

And yet you wrote classics in "Touch of Paradise" and "We're No Angels".
Mondo Rock started in 1976. The first song I wrote for the band that I then called Mondo Rock, our first performance, we performed "Touch of Paradise". So we were doing that all through there and I think I wrote "We're No Angels" the same night I wrote "The Fugitive Kind". So that would have been about '78.

What inspired "We're No Angels"?
Just another one of those reality checks, like "Living in the Land of Oz". We're no angels. The line about how we strive to be perfect, we strive to get up higher, always knowing that there's a limit to it. Maybe that was more the lack of confidence at the time, but to me it's the same way that "It matters to me, it just don't matter all the time" is a reality check on a relationship. It's just about trying to get people to be real, for me to be real about where I actually am. All this stuff about living legends and rock stars and all that, it's all crap. But we use it because we're in showbiz. The real thing is that that you're down here and you're stuck on the flat surface of the earth that's a very thin piece of dirt with trees growing out of it, and down below it's all rock, and you're spinning around in space and you can't get off the ground 'cause of the force of gravity, and that's the reality. We're grovelling around here in the dirt.

Did "Touch of Paradise" spring from a title, and did you come up with that or did Gulliver Smith?
It was his title. It's 95 per cent his lyrics. It was very unusual at the time, because it was one of the first collaborations outside a group context. You're so caught up with the groups that you're in, you're going around the country, you're flat out, particularly in those days, you'd be working six nights a week and still trying to write songs and cut records and have a career and all of the rest of it. But I had an association with Gulliver that went back quite a long time, back to the sixties. I always liked what he was doing; I loved what he did with Company Caine. I went around to his place in '76 and we wrote this song together. I was just strumming and off we went. I took it home and wrote the bridge, and then we had a song. They're all his lyrics; in fact there's an extra verse. I'd forgotten all about it and I found a really old demo on a cassette from the first time we were demoing it way back with early Mondo Rock, and it's got this other verse. But it was too long so we ended up cutting it out.

Like most songs Farnham has covered, from "Help" and "One" to "You're The Voice", he made "Touch of Paradise" his own. How did it feel for one of your songs, particularly a tender one, to become somebody else's?
The first time I heard it I thought it had too much echo on it. I'm not really big on echo and reverb. But now I listen to it and I feel fine. When you first hear records, even the first time I heard "Eagle Rock", the recording, I wasn't sure if I liked it or not.

Is that something to do with something that you've created, maybe laboured over, to be made permanent?
That's right, it's set in stone then. And you have to accept the defects.

And if another artist does it, like "Touch of Paradise", you've got far less control over how it's going to be set in stone.
I remember we were on a plane to go somewhere with Mondo Rock and the manager gave me a cassette of it and I was listening to it, and I thought, "Oh yeah, pretty good, not bad." Then the album took off, and I went "Great!!"

At the time he recorded it on *Whispering Jack* you had no concept of how successful he would be, whereas when he did "We're No Angels", I suppose you knew it was going to be big.
They came to me and said, "Do you want to submit another song? We're doing another album." I said, "Of course I do." I'm thinking, "Well, what can I give him?" And I thought, well if he liked "Touch of Paradise", maybe he'll like "We're No Angels", 'cause it's got a lot of similarities structurally. I gave him two versions; there was the Mondo Rock recording, which I was never totally happy with, and then I had a tape of us at a sound check where we were mucking around with it and I was changing it and I liked it a lot more, so I gave him both. And I gave a little blurb about the meaning that I put into the lyrics.

They weren't quite sure which direction to take the new album, and then they were out at Gotham Studios and they sat down and he just sang it. I think David Hirschfelder played the piano, just piano and voice. And as soon as they cut it, and they really liked it, it gave them a direction. They knew where to go from there. I think that second album's really good. "Age of Reason", the actual song, is fantastic. His version of it's really great.

Your *Dark Side of the Man* album was very inward-looking. Did the songs for that all come out in a burst of writing at the same time?
No, that was over quite a long period. I started writing with Eris O'Brien and John Pullicino and you'll notice that there's co-writes with them that form at least half of the album, and there's also one that they wrote that I didn't have a hand in, and then there's other things like "Go Bongo Go Wild" and "Dark Side of the Man" that came in from other sources. But over a few years I compiled the songs.

So you were writing the material while Mondo Rock was still happening?
I was starting to. I realised I was feeling stifled by certain constraints of being in a group and so I thought there's no reason why I can't do both things. Mondo Rock wasn't quite sure where they were going so I cut that album and it was the start of where I've gone since.

"Bed of Nails" is a fabulous visual idea—"Lay down on a bed of roses, wake up lying on a bed of nails". Who came up with that?
I had the title and I gave it to Eris and John, when we were first starting to write songs together, and I came back and they said, "We've been working on this idea." I listened to it and I went, "Wow!" There's all this stuff about you sign your name and you pay the price, and I'm going, "Did I tell you all about my bad record deals?" A lot of people

respond to that song. It was a little bit countryish for standard pop, but it got a lot of airplay all over Australia.

"Xmas Card" stands out on *Go Bongo Go Wild!* as a very personal song. When did you write that?
This girlfriend that I had, I lived with for a while in the very early nineties, and it turned into a big disaster and was the source of much inspiration for songwriting [*Laughs*]. I had to have a hard look at myself and go, why the hell were you with that person and why did you put up with that for so long? Gee, it must be something to do with me! But I'd gotten through that successfully, and then she sent me a Christmas card that basically said, "Hey, things are going great with me now, we've got to get together some time." Basically like nothing had happened. And this card just made me really angry. It came at the end of October, and that's why it's got the line about, "I got your Christmas card, first one for the year." It's all totally true, from my perspective. So I picked up the guitar and there it was. Twenty minutes. One of those. And then I honed it for a while, I typed out the lyric and sent it to her. Two days later I got another letter back saying, "You just don't understand. Goodbye." And I was going, yeah, fine. We're not going to be friends, what are you talking about?

One of the songs I liked best on *Country & Wilson* was "Under the Waves". It's got a spooky feel to it.
That's a very interesting song because it's about my father's part in discovering this shipwreck, and it mentions his name in it, Ron Wilson. The first two verses are about the famous story of the Loch Ard going down off the coast of Victoria, and the two survivors. Everyone else died. no-one could find the wreck for years and years until Stan McPhee went off for ten years trying to find it, he lived down that way, and my dad just happened to be on the boat the day they found it. So I wrote the song about that. But it's got the spooky feel because, and I didn't realise this till later, it moves like waves, like this swell, because I'm going from minor to major, minor, major, minor, major all the time. It's like E minor, E minor, E minor, E major, E major, which is an unusual thing to do. And then it goes up to B minor, B minor ... It's a very simple song but it's got that wavy motion. I took that to the nth degree on that song. And I didn't even realise it had that effect. So that's where your subconscious and your intuition do things without you even realising it.

Do you have a favourite song that you've written?
I always think "Cool World" is a landmark for me, because it was the first shift into more insightful writing. Before that, with a couple of exceptions, my writing had tended to be more flippant. "Cool World" was a signpost into more mature lyric writing on a regular basis, and now just about everything I write is coming from the kind of insight that I've gained about who I am and how I relate to the world around me.

BILLY THORPE

SYDNEY, AUSTRALIA, MAY 2003

Sometimes it only takes one song to forge a celebrated career and fashion a persona. History will record that that one song defined that artist for posterity. But it's never the full story, and Billy Thorpe is here to tell you that "Most People I Know Think that I'm Crazy" is but one small part of his story.

When we met he was holed up in his inner city Sydney studio working on an instrumental piece based on his personal and musical experiences during a fantastical time in Morocco in 2001. Thorpe was highly entertained at the prospect of surprising people with a creative endeavour that was far removed from his loud, wild days with the Aztecs. Or even the not-so-loud, crooning days with the Aztecs. There were various incarnations of that legendary band before his twenty-five-year stay in America, shifts from blues rock to science-fiction infused progressive rock, scoring music for television and even a stint as a business tycoon with a toy company. Then there was the return to Australia in a wave of nostalgia that culminated in a tour he helped conceive and produce based on the ABC-TV series *Long Way to the Top*. Listening to Thorpe spin yarn after yarn about his years in show business, it became clear that the many and varied lives of Billy Thorpe could fill a book or two or three. Oh yeah, he's written autobiographies, too.

Songwriting, then, might seem to play but a small part in the life of this self-styled journeyman. And through our discussion, Thorpe was by turns pleased with and dismissive of his songwriting output over more than thirty years. "I've never been a serious songwriter," he said, explaining how effortlessly writing music came to him. But as with so many of the songwriters whose careers took off in the 1960s, that ease—an unselfconscious means-to-an-end kind of approach to making music—ultimately led to more serious deliberation and refining of craft. And as flippant as Thorpe tried to be, it was obvious that authoring work of an enduring quality was something he took pride in.

Born in Manchester on 29 March 1946, Thorpe relocated to Australia as a child and his family settled in Brisbane. He was a seasoned television and concert performer by the time he moved to Sydney at sixteen, when he joined the original version of the Aztecs. With songs like "Poison Ivy", "Mashed Potato" and the powerfully executed cover of "Over the Rainbow" from *The Wizard of Oz*, Thorpe was a teenage sensation topping the charts regularly.

Moving to Melbourne in the late sixties, he formed a new version of the Aztecs, gave full vent to his love of the blues, and the loudest band in Australia began its reign, culminating in the famous 1972 appearance at the Sunbury Pop Festival and the hit "Most People I Know Think that I'm Crazy".

By 1976 Thorpe was in Los Angeles as a result of entering a song competition. With a mix of naivety and savvy, he always found himself in the right place at the right time with the right people standing by. Songwriter and industry executive Billy Mishel kick-started his American career with a lucrative publishing deal, and Thorpe spent some years writing in Los Angeles, New York and Nashville before making *Children of the Sun*, the 1980 album that found him a whole new audience and renown. To this day he is both amused and irked that his success in the US with that album was never appreciated back home. By the end of the eighties he was writing music for *The War of the Worlds* television series and shows such as *Star Trek*, *Columbo* and *Eight Is Enough*. He then teamed with Mick Fleetwood and Bekka Bramlett in the rock band The Zoo, started writing books about his early years in music in Australia, and was eventually lured home with the release of a compilation of Aztecs material, *Lock Up Your Mothers*. And then there was the party for his wife's fiftieth birthday thrown in the King of Morocco's palace, which led to the aforementioned opus. Indefatigable, Billy Thorpe accepts that most people probably do think he is crazy.

"People would think I was crazy if I was a plumber. Because I am. I just have a lot of energy and it manifests itself sometimes in lunacy," he said.

Prior to "Most People I Know Think that I'm Crazy", your career was really performance-based. Were you writing away in the background during the sixties?
I come from a very different era. I came from a pre-singer/songwriter era. I started at the age of ten in television in Brisbane, and it was a very broad education for a young artist,

because I was around writers and painters and vaudeville people like George Wallace Jr, and I played the Theatre Royal and things like that. In those days it was a very different business, where to get a record deal in Sydney was the New York of Australia, or of my world, particularly coming from Brisbane. So it was about getting a record deal and the songwriting thing didn't really come into it.

Tony Barber was the writer in the Aztecs. We did a little bit of co-writing but we mainly recorded the stuff that was very popular on stage. I'm kicking myself now because I had the opportunity of a lifetime; we were the first people signed to Alberts, who were publishers. And then The Easybeats came along and the rest is history with them. But it just wasn't something that I even thought anything about.

Do you remember your first complete song?
No. I wrote a lot of stuff that was never recorded. I didn't really get into writing until I started to play instruments. Although I played rhythm guitar, it was just something I played to do more than anything else. And it wasn't until I actually got into instruments and got down to playing piano and started to get those tones and those harmonics and those things that feed you creatively that I really started to put notes together in a way that you would call writing.

When you took on lead guitar duties in the Aztecs in 1969, did that have any influence on your potential as a songwriter?
Yes, in as much as the stuff that I wrote later, which culminated with "Most People I Know Think that I'm Crazy" and the albums after that, had their roots in that time. I'm not a lead guitarist; I'm more a rhythm guitarist. And I had a style that suited my voice and that became the basis of what I started to write later.

Something must have become compelling to you about performing your own material rather than performing covers. It seems to be a common theme in most artists' development.
I don't know that that's quite true. A very good friend of mine, Jenny Boyd, Patti Boyd's sister, was doing a thesis for a doctorate, and found that it was overwhelmingly evident that you don't write your own songs, or you're not consciously writing your own songs. That you're a channel for some energy from somewhere. It's true. There was no time where I physically sat down and said, "I'm going to be a songwriter." People like Stevie Kipner have always written, his father, Nat, was a writer; Nat goes to the dunny in the morning and takes a book with him and writes one on the way to the toilet, writes one sitting on the toilet and writes one on the way out again. Stevie grew up in that environment and just had that natural thing. John Farrar didn't really start writing until he got with Olivia but he'd been putting together all the tools and the craft through studying music and singing and studying albums by the Beach Boys and the craft to lead up to that. I didn't have any of that. I was just a journeyman rocker. I was quite happy doing what I was doing; a great song's a great song, whether I wrote it or somebody else wrote it, it didn't matter to me, as long as I enjoyed playing it.

Willie Dixon said, "All blues is happy blues." What has it always been about blues music for you that feels so comfortable? Blues is not a natural style for Australians; we don't have the tradition of the slavery where the blues was born.

Well, Dan Aykroyd once on *Saturday Night Live* did a great interview with Ray Charles. And he said, "Mr Charles, exactly what are the blues and how do you get them?" I've never forgotten it 'cause it was a fucking classic. So there's no answer to that. I just found within the blues records that I started to listen to—Howlin' Wolf, Muddy Waters—something in there like an earthiness. What I did find was the roots of the rock stuff that I'd been listening to. Aha, this is where it comes from! And then started to synthesise those elements to fit my inabilities more than anything else. Creating a style is stealing a bit from here and a bit from there and somehow you make it your own. And that becomes a style. I didn't consciously go, "Okay, I'm going to become a blues player." I would stick a blues song after "Somewhere Over the Rainbow" on stage, and it worked. And I thought, well this is great, I'm really enjoying this and the audience is enjoying it, I'll do more of this. Very little of what I've done has been conscious, it's just happened. [*Laughs*]

In that case, how did the writing of "Most People I Know Think that I'm Crazy" come about?

I'd gone to Melbourne for two weeks and stayed eight years. Met my wife and thoroughly enjoyed being in a band playing guitar behind some great guitar players like Lobby Loyde and all different people. This was a whole new thing. I was in a band that was lucky to get fifty bucks a week each. Sleeping on the floor. I'd never had that, you see. I'd started as a child performer, went straight onto television, was signed to Channel 9, was doing shows, making money, came to Sydney, hooked up with a band, a year later we had a string of number ones, my own television shows, it was always very easy to me. I'd never suffered. And out of that came the experiences that I realised I was listening to on some of these blues records and rock records. A lot of the lyrics that just didn't make any sense to me, about going without and trying to raise the rent, all of a sudden were a reality. And so a whole new platform emerged for me.

So is that what you meant when you wrote, "All of my life, I've lived a delusion"?

Yeah. People would say to me, "You're crazy." I would play to 1,000 people and 200 of them would be fighting on stage, trying to get to me, trying to kill us. 'Cause people would come along to hear "Somewhere Over the Rainbow" and "I Told the Brook" and they were getting "Mamma" and stuff like that at 1,000 decibels. And this guy said to me, "You know, mate, most people I know think you're fucking crazy." I went home, and I was living with Warren Morgan, "the Pig", in Toorak. There was a piano in the back and he was down there writing, and he remembers hearing me sitting on the bed in the front going, [*Sings*] "Most people I know think that I'm crazy ..." I wrote that song in two minutes.

Where did the melody come from?

It's a country tune. All the early stuff that I started writing, if you listen to it, and if you play it on an acoustic guitar, they're country songs. I was a country artist first, I bought my first guitar off Reg Lindsay, and I did the tents in Brisbane with the country acts. I can play and sing every Hank Williams song ever written, 'cause I love Hank Williams. If you listen to "Most People I Know Think that I'm Crazy", it's a Hank Williams' song. It's from that genre. But it's a country song played by a completely out of control rock 'n' roll band. We took all of our gear including our PA into the studio to record that song. There's no chorus in that song. There's no verse or chorus.

Well, it's a verse and a chorus.
It's just one melody. It's a weird song. People get very emotional around that song, it's very strange. A friend, who was a very big model here, tracked me down, I hadn't seen her in years, and she was checking herself into Larundel, the mental place, and was sitting in the lobby and that came on. And she just laughed and left. I had a guy here who was building a studio next door, he's a bricklayer, was working on the weekend, and he stopped in his tracks when he saw me and just got very teary. A bloke in his late forties. He said, "I left home and went on the street when I was twelve and a half." And he heard "Most People I Know Think that I'm Crazy", it was the first recognition he has after leaving home. Everybody's had that thought at some stage, and still does.

I occasionally find myself on stage playing this thing and looking at the crowd thinking, "What is this?" I've met people that were conceived at my shows. At Byron I met two people and their families, and they were proud as punch that they were conceived during "Most People I Know Think that I'm Crazy", one at Sunbury, one somewhere else. People that have memories of that and "Over the Rainbow" and different things of mine, where they've played them at funerals, where they've met their husbands and their wives. I think songs are references to a time and place that stick with people.

What was the importance to you of the loudness in your music? Everything that is written about you from that era refers to how loud you were.
Volume is a wonderful tool. Volume is a form of expression. The louder the loud, the quieter the silence. It's a dynamic. It's not just bombast for the sake of being loud. In the hands of the wrong people it's a nightmare. And in the hands of the right people and an expert—and I am an expert—it's a wonderful thing. Sound is electrical energy; it charges the air. It creates different patterns in the air, and different wave patterns in the brain. People used to come to Aztec shows to get a feed of that energy.

Were you writing songs, then, that were deliberately made to be played loud?
No. A lot of the writing took place at rehearsals, where we would sit down and start jamming, and a riff would come out. We used to rehearse a lot. We were fanatical. Stuff like "Time to Live" was written as a result of riffing in the club at rehearsals at Sebastians one day. And when we were at rehearsals we played flat out, that was it.

Was the writing equally spontaneous on the *Thump'n Pig & Puff'n Billy* album that you made with Warren Morgan?
Well, that was originally going to be Warren's album. Living in a house with Warren, he was

always playing, he was always writing, day and night. He asked me would I come and sing on this album that he was going to do, and I said sure. And then one thing led to another and it became a joint record. "Captain Straightman" came out of that, and so did a song called "Early Morning", a ballad which was the first "song" song I think I ever wrote—with a purpose to it other than throwing some lyrics over a great riff that felt good. The song "Mamma" came because Pig's wife's nickname was "Mamma". It was very naive; it was a very narrow world that we lived in.

So Warren would have been quite an influence for you on your way to becoming a more "serious" songwriter?
I've never been a serious songwriter. I don't consider myself a songwriter, like John Farrar's a songwriter or Joni Mitchell's a songwriter or John Lennon was a songwriter. I don't put myself in that class. Can I write songs? Yes, I can. If I had to do it as a living, yes I could. Would I do it as a living? No, I wouldn't. It's not something that I aspire to do or to be. Songwriting for me has always served a purpose.

Your music became more layered and complex than "Most People I Know" later in the seventies. Did the mechanics, the way you actually wrote, start to change?
A really significant album was *More Arse than Class*. It was an attempt to take some of Warren's influences, where I was starting to go. I was getting into things like Pink Floyd and esoteric stuff like Tomita, a master musician from Japan, a classical pianist who developed the JVC synthesiser program and synthesised all of the major works, some of the most wonderful stuff ever recorded. In my own way on *More Arse than Class,* some of those things started to come out, layering harmonies, big production, editing songs down, creating drum loops, doing all of the things that became modern techniques for production in songwriting. So that was really the change for me. And I was very unsatisfied after that album because it didn't work for me. It sounded very square. When I listen to some of the material today, it's a great album, I love that album, but I get to a point in every song where I go, "Oh shit, why didn't I go there?" Or "Why didn't we spend more time editing, to craft the stuff?"

But then you did *Million Dollar Bill*, which was kind of more class than arse, and "It's Almost Summer". What brought on that change in style?
That had always been there, that sort of Brazilian groove. As a guitar player they're the things you sit down and learn to play. I was a big fan of George Harrison, particularly an album of his called *Wonderwall*. I love the use of slide guitar which Eric Clapton played on that particular album, it's a great album which still influences me today. I went to America in '76, and I forgot about "It's Almost Summer". I wrote it in one afternoon because we needed one more song for the record. And went away, and unbeknownst to me it was used by Channel 9 as the national summer theme for a couple of years. And I'd occasionally get a royalty cheque on it amongst my other stuff. I came back, and people started yelling out for the song.

145

"It's Almost Summer" is a song I can never get out of my head. It always creeps back in, particularly when summer comes.
I don't know where the song came from. I'd been playing around with that guitar form, which is open tuning; that was the first time I'd used an E open tuning. It's a kind of classic fifties pop song but it also has elements that go back to the thirties and forties. Cole Porter and people like that were an influence on me, 'cause that was the music I grew up with. If you broke that down and took the offbeat off it, you could do a big band version of that that would sound very thirties and forties. But once again, I needed a song so I wrote one.

It was also a very mellow song, and it's ironic that that's the song you left behind when you went off to the land of the mellow. That song could have been written in LA. What made you stay in America so long?
It was the desire to be amongst that level of creative milieu. It's very hard to define what, but there was just something there that wasn't here. LA in 1976 felt so much like the Northern Beaches of Sydney, that it was just so easy to just slide in there. We only went for a year, and one year grew into two, and three, and then twenty-five. Billy Mishel encouraged me to get into writing, into tunesmithing. It was pre sequencers and synthesisers and the home recording thing. And everywhere you went there was a songwriter. I signed to BMI and I got covers for the Osmonds and Ringo Starr. Stuff of mine is still being covered that I wrote then.

The *Children of the Sun* album could not have been more different to what you'd been doing in Australia for over a decade.
The things that I found myself gravitating towards in America, what I started to listen to, was that Genesis, Ambrosia type of stuff. I also started getting quite heavily into classics. I love Dvořák and Debussy. And I've always been a mad sci-fi buff. That album has two sides. One side was the pop kind of thing that they wanted me to write, and the other side was this idea that I had called "Children of the Sun". When the record came out, the A-side, which had all the pop or rock stuff on it, was totally ignored. And the song "Children of the Sun" just got played to death. The song really started something. Because we experimented with a soundscape. That experience musically is what's driven me since then, for twenty years.

In parts it sounded like the *Sgt Pepper's* Beatles meets Pink Floyd meets ELO.
Yeah. We were experimenting with it, having no idea. It was a punt. The era that we're talking about, disco was king, and out of the middle of it came this six-minute science-fiction piece. The reception to it was phenomenal.

Did you write "Children of the Sun" in the studio with the new equipment you were getting into?
No, I wrote it at home on the guitar.

The storyline had the whole population virtually deserting Earth for somewhere more alluring. Did the idea precede the music or did the music you were writing spark the idea?
I sat down with a guitar and went, [*Sings*] "People of the earth can you hear me?" And it just came out. I have no idea where it came from. I believe that melodies float around. I've had ideas that I haven't bothered to put to paper that I've heard come out as hit records by all kinds of people. I think these ideas are around because I think people coming from the same backgrounds, the same sensibilities, the same socio-political, religious beliefs and experiences, tend to have the same thoughts at the same time based on the same influences that give rise to these thoughts. And I think that affects people creatively. And as with "Most People I Know Think that I'm Crazy", "Children of the Sun", this weird song about a bunch of aliens arriving, struck a chord with people. Particularly in the Midwest and the South. It took off in Texas. People in New York didn't get it. I realise now the reason it took off in Texas is because it was about horizons and open space, a linear experience, a global experience. And in Texas, which is exactly like Queensland or anywhere you want to go in this country, that kind of sensibility was there.

Had you been inspired by the *War of the Worlds* album?
No. I liked the *War of the Worlds* movie, the original movie. But one had nothing to do with the other. There was nothing going on in my life that had anything to do with science fiction or television. As a sci-fi buff I'd read Frank Herbert, Asimov, *Foundation Foundation, Empire, Dune, The Illustrated Man* and very early sci-fi in the late sixties, early seventies. I also got into *Autobiography of a Yogi*, comparative religion and all kinds of stuff at the end of the sixties, as a result of all of the heinous chemicals. So it had been generating and fermenting, but just like with "Most People I Know Think that I'm Crazy", that entire album was a spontaneous work that I wrote in about eight hours. As you hear it.

Did you read the theories on the reverse speech in "Children of the Sun" and the suggestion that it was recorded in the 1980s and sent back in time?
There's a number of websites on "Children of the Sun", and one guy's theory is that I'm from the future, because I wrote things that hadn't existed at that point in time, and the technologies that I used didn't exist.

There's also the theory that you could be a mind control slave.
Or a walk-in. A walk-in is when an alien takes over a human body and walks in and embodies them with all of the knowledge and the talent. So yeah, I'm a walk-in from the future.

Have you listened to the clips on the Internet where they've reversed bits of the album and what you're supposedly saying?
Oh yeah. When I listen to it I can hear it, too!

The only thing you don't say is "Paul is dead".
I know. None of that went on in the record, nothing. There were no mind games played, no backwards recording, none of that. But if you've ever been to a *Star Trek* convention, which I have, you realise how many maniacs there are out there. All of these people that are out there waiting for this stuff to come out that they can hook onto. So that really showed me that it didn't have to be pop music, it didn't have to be rock music. That there was a way to engage people, as a writer, that had nothing to do with popular music. That's what became interesting to me.

***21st Century Man* was obviously more deliberate in that you decided this would be the second part of the story. Did you still write it in the same way, with your acoustic guitar?**
Yes, but it was much more calculated. I had this trilogy in my head but what I would have written is not what I ended up writing. Not enough time elapsed and it was just more of the same. Musically, I thought it was quite sound. My forte is melody. Melodies come to me instantly. The way songs and lyrics come to Barry Gibb, melodies come to me. There were some really great ideas in *21st Century Man*, but they were never allowed to breathe. Things that should have been nothing more than melodic motifs were turned into songs and vice versa. And it just didn't work; it just was a pale shadow of what it came out of. I'm working on a whole thing now with an orchestra that has elements of where this should have gone.

How easy was it for you to move into writing television scores and what were the main disciplines that you had to master for that kind of composing?
I'd never scored anything in my life, and *War of the Worlds* was on 240 stations, four plays a week. It was every music television person's dream. I had no idea; I was really naive. I was working eighteen hours a day; when I wasn't sleeping I was writing. It instilled this sensibility of not dwelling on anything; if something didn't work I got rid of it very quickly, because I didn't have time to fuck around. But what I enjoyed was working on visuals. 'Cause every scene has a tempo. Whether it be a tree blowing or a wheel going round or somebody walking. I found it really easy; it came to me like that.

Writing's a lonely thing. It's like writing books. I'm an only child, and I find there's no freedom like the freedom to be alone. And just left to my own devices I have a great work ethic. Nobody has to stand over me, I stand over myself. Because I just have to get it done.

During your period with The Zoo, you wrote with Delaney Bramlett and with Albert King. What was it like writing with legends, with people that you revere that much?
Well, having the experiences I'd had, I met Jerry Lee Lewis, Little Richard and people like that when I was a child. I met most of my musical heroes by the time I'd gotten to America. But Delaney's the son of a Mississippi sharecropper; he's the real deal. I would go over at least once a week just to write with Delaney. One day I hear this groaning coming out of the living room and I said, "Who's that?" And Mama said, "Oh, it's just Albert, he's crashed." I didn't think any more of it. About two hours later we'd been sitting there smoking cigarettes and drinking beers and in the doorway came this giant

black guy, Albert King. Delaney and I had been sitting at the table with our acoustics. And he said something like, "Are you the dude that I've been listening to?" Albert King's been laying in there listening to me singing and playing! He said, "Let's have a jam." So it's Albert King and Delaney Bramlett and this little white boy in the middle. But that whole experience with Delaney was fantastic, because what a songwriter! What an extraordinary songwriter.

What did you do with those songs?
They're still all on tape. I've got a couple hundred songs that are just sitting on tape that I haven't done anything with.

What was writing with Mick Fleetwood like?
Mick is a very wise old man. Mick is very much a part of the roots of popular music, period. He's a drummer who was never a contributing writer as such to Fleetwood Mac or any of the bands that he was in early on, but his phrasing and his style and his demeanour and who he is brought a lot. It was just very important. Extraordinary drummer. Mick and I wrote in as much as I came up with the ideas and then we'd sit together and he'd say, "Let's work with this" or "Let's work with that." And The Zoo album is a bloody good album, a really good album.

Your career since you came back to Australia has largely been based on a celebration of your celebrity, your past and the whole nostalgia thing. How do you move forward in creating new music?
I'm lucky, I'm in a great position; I can work when I want to and of course I have to play some of that old stuff because that's what people come along to hear. But I'm also playing a lot of new stuff, a lot of recent material, and that really works. And I'm in the middle of something I've been writing for two years since a trip to Morocco for my wife's fiftieth birthday. I wrote this musical piece called "Tangier". With this tuning I'd never used before. It's an hour-and-a-half suite for voice, acoustic guitar and orchestra. And it's fucking great. It's *Children of the Sun* twenty years later. I'll do it here, hopefully with the Sydney Symphony and some Moroccan players and some Arabic players, some dancers. So I've just found that what I enjoy doing is writing musical works. Rather than having to stuff lyrics down the throat of every piece of music that comes along. Rather than having to stuff a back beat and a rhythm section down the throat of every piece of music. Some pieces of music and melodies are meant to stand alone, are meant to be orchestrated, are instrumental.

I've been doing nothing but writing. I'm halfway through a third book as well. What seems to happen is when I sit down to write a book, the musical muse arrives, and when I sit down to write music the book muse arrives. For the first time my creative life is in line with where I've known my life is for a long time, but either I wasn't mature enough or never had the desire to align them. The real me hasn't been seen or heard yet. With this album quite a lot of it will be heard for the very first time.

RUSSELL MORRIS

MELBOURNE, AUSTRALIA, JULY 2003

He's rated as one of the finest vocalists and live performers in Australian popular music history and he sang one of the best known, most groundbreaking songs ever recorded in Australia. Russell Morris did not write "The Real Thing", but behind the enduring legend of that performance is a highly rated and unique songwriter who often doubted his own ability to be the real thing.

Like Johnny Young before him, Morris began his career as a pop singer who sang songs by other people. Young's 1969 opus, produced by Ian Meldrum, catapulted Morris into a stratosphere where he was idolised, but it wasn't always a comfortable place to be for a young man striving for individuality. He took up songwriting as a way to forge his own identity, having been moulded and mollycoddled by Meldrum, who managed as well as produced him. Songwriting was also a stand against bandmates who told Morris his guitar playing was wrong. "If I play my own song to someone else, they're not going to say, 'That's wrong.' Because they can't. It's mine and I wrote it."

Morris's unconventional song structures and seemingly illogical timings frustrated other musicians but these were the trademarks, along with sweeping poetic imagery, of his most memorable songs, such as "Wings of an Eagle" and "Sweet Sweet Love". Yet repeatedly throughout his career he styled his writing in the fashion of what other people thought it should be. One of Morris's biggest struggles in more than thirty years of songwriting has been staying true to his own creative spirit.

Russell Morris was born in Melbourne on 31 July 1948. As his musical tastes developed, the Rolling Stones were his main inspiration; it took a while longer for the Beatles to take hold. "I'd heard them but I thought they were too sweet-sounding," said Morris, whose own best work had a sweet, melodic vivacity.

A teenage lead singer in Somebody's Image, who played many gigs with Brian Cadd's band The Groop, Morris came to the attention of not only budding songwriter Cadd but of music journalist and would-be record producer Meldrum. Both played pivotal roles in Morris's career, Meldrum persuading him to embark on a solo career, and Cadd providing strong musical direction in its early years. "The Real Thing" was the perfect vehicle for catapulting Morris to stardom, and its follow-up, "Part 3 Into Paper Walls", continued the phenomenon, but as he was finding his own songwriting feet, the relationship with Meldrum faltered. A trip to London gave him the space to work alone honing his craft, and back in Australia he recorded his first solo album, with much input from Cadd via his piano playing and inspiration. The highly praised *Bloodstone*, a collection of strong songs, some poignant and uplifting, some melancholy and dour, marked him as a frontrunner in the scarcely populated field of introspective Australian singer-songwriters.

In the mid-1970s Morris moved to Los Angeles, recording two well-received albums but struggling for creative control against forces that were pushing him in commercial directions that now, on reflection, he wonders if he should have followed. His record company wanted him to be the new John Denver; he still wanted to be Mick Jagger. After failing to break into the American market, he returned to Australia in 1978 and, other than one album of original material in 1991, *A Thousand Suns*, has worked as a touring act, either alone or on the revival circuit with Ronnie Burns, Jim Keays and Darryl Cotton.

But Russell Morris continues to write and to explore new ways of tapping into his creative source. I asked him which song he hoped to be remembered for, and he gave one of the songwriters' favouite responses: "The next one I'm going to write."

What was the biggest influence on you as a teenager learning about music?
The Rolling Stones were the first band that really got me interested in rock 'n' roll. Strangely enough the types of music that I like the best I find most difficult to write. The music that I really love is blues, and rhythm and blues. But writing it doesn't come easy to me, so I just write what comes easy to me. I feel when I try to write something like that type of music, it feels forced. I've tried enough times now to know that it's not the right way for me to go as a writer.

Was Dylan an influence?

Not until later. But Bob Dylan is actually an influence now; I'm just about to start writing again and I'm going to attempt to write like he does, which is very bizarre. He just types all the lyrics out. That's why his songs have thirteen bars and eight bars and nine bars and they change all the time, because he makes them fit the words. I've never done that before. Whether I can or not I don't know, but I'm about to get a laptop and a recording situation where I can record on the road, and I'll just write lyrics and see how I go from there.

Until now, have you been coming up with melodies first?

They come at the same time sometimes, lyrics and melody. It's like an abstract painting, the way I write. I'll play guitar, and as I'm playing I'll find chords, and then I'll find a melody and the words almost assert themselves into it. It's like you've got a blank canvas and you're throwing paint at it. You've thrown red and some blue and some green and you look at it and then you turn it round upside down, then you turn it on the side, and then you go, "Ooh, gee, that looks like a pastoral landscape with a man standing on the side of a hill." So you think, that's what I'll work at. So you work at finishing off that landscape and putting the man on the side of the hill, trying to make sense of it without it being too abstract and too vague. That's how I write.

In the first instance when you've got the blank canvas and the colours going on, are you conscious in that?

No. Mostly it's the first or second verse that I write first, and it's almost like searching in the dark with a light looking for a direction to head. These words have come to me and what can they mean? Sometimes you never get any meaning out of it so you never finish the song. Sometimes they all fall into place. Like when I wrote "Wings of an Eagle", I sat down on the porch and picked up the guitar and wrote the first and second verse non-stop without a break. Didn't even stop for breath. And the lyrics all just came at exactly the same time as the chords and the melody.

When that happens, do you think it's coming from somewhere else?

No, I don't think so. I think it's just all the right chemicals falling into place in the brain.

Did you have any formal musical training?

I tried. There's a reason I became a songwriter. I started to play the clarinet and I was going to go into the saxophone, but I had really bad timing. I still have, when it comes to beats. Like reading a dotted minim, what the bloody hell does that mean? Or a dotted crotchet. I can count one, two, three, four. But one and a bit? What does that mean? I couldn't get it together.

So what would happen with bands, I would get my guitar—I was only a very rudimentary player—and I'd learn the song off the record, learn all the chords, and then I'd go to rehearsal and play it to everyone and they'd all fall about the floor laughing. They'd say, "That's a great attempt but there's not even one right chord amongst them." It was so embarrassing. Then they'd play it to me and I'd see how logical it was. So I thought, I can't be humiliated any more. I'd better learn to write my own songs, because if I play my own song to someone else, they're not going to say, "That's wrong." Because they can't. It's mine and I wrote it. So that's one of the main reasons I started to write, because I couldn't learn songs off records.

How old were you when you were trying to do that?
About seventeen. I never played guitar when I was young.

What was the first song that you wrote?
"Paper Walls" was the first one. I was in Somebody's Image, and being determined to write songs, I had a tape recorder and I had the words in my head and melody that I'd sung over and over again. I sang it into a tape recorder and I went to the guitar player and said, "Show me the chords that go with that." So I already had the song. Johnny Young had written "The Real Thing". And then when Ian said we need a follow-up, he said, "Haven't you been looking at trying to write some songs?" So I played him that. He thought about it, and then he said to Johnny, "Have you got anything that will go on the front of that?" So it was two songs tacked together.

And then I wrote lots of little bits. It was just a matter of trying to learn a craft that I had no idea about. There was a snobbery amongst Australian musicians. I wasn't a great musician and I had bad timing. So like some of the old blues singers or Dylan, I would add an extra beat, and I'd be unconscious that I'd added it. And people made me feel like I was an idiot for doing it. They'd go, "Hang on, do you want that extra beat there?" And I wouldn't know what they were talking about. I'd go, "What do you mean?" "Those two beats. You've got a two-four bar." I had no idea. And because I'd get so jittery about playing it again, I'd make it a four-four bar rather than a two-four bar. So they'd go, "Is it two-four or is it a four-four bar? What are you going to do?" I consequently worked really hard to straighten my timing out. Which was probably to the detriment of my writing, because me being that way made it unique.

Players would then say, "No, don't you play guitar." I've always played rhythm guitar, but in the last six years I decided I can play lead guitar. I'm way behind all the other guys who've been playing for twenty-five years but I know now if I'd done it then I would have been a really good lead guitar player by this stage, because I'm learning very quickly.

Does being more proficient on the guitar open up songwriting for you?
It closes it. It's a real drag, a double-edged sword. What happens when you can't play lead guitar and you haven't got a way of expressing yourself, you sit down with your guitar and you write a song. When you can play lead guitar, you sit down and you play solos and you work out parts and your creative expression tends to go in that direction. I believe that's why a lot of really good musicians don't write that well. There's always exceptions to the rule, but people who aren't great musicians tend to be better songwriters. They tend to concentrate lyrically. Whereas really good musicians concentrate on the arrangements and the chord progressions and all the clever bits.

"The Real Thing" involved and affected so many Melbourne-based artists, none more than you. As a songwriter yourself, how does it feel more than thirty years down the track to be best known for a song that was written by someone else?
It doesn't bother me. I would have liked to have written it. It's a nonsensical song. It's almost like an "I Am the Walrus"; it doesn't mean anything but to people at that time, because it was so different, it's become bigger than it maybe should have been. It came out of the time in the psychedelic era when no-one in Australia had done anything like that, ever. And that's what makes it a landmark thing, because it was so different to anything that had preceded it.

How instructive was the song for you in your own early development as a writer? Did you take something away from it?
I probably would have taken things subconsciously. But it's written in fourths, and I've never written a song in fourths, ever. So maybe I didn't take anything from it. I still enjoy playing it. It's one of those songs that I could sit down and play just with an acoustic guitar and people will go, "Shit!" It's one of those songs that works, because of our musical ear, the western ear; a fourth is the strongest interval, and people relate to it really strongly. Johnny never wrote anything close to it again. When you write a hit song, it's like throwing paint at the wall or trying to flick a five-cent coin up onto that ledge up there. If you keep flicking, one day it lands. "The Real Thing" was something that comes along once in a writer's lifetime, I guess.

Did Meldrum allow you any creative input?
I could have done anything I wanted to, but the idea was Ian's. Ian was the captain of that ship and he was phenomenal. I've berated him ever since and I've finally bullied and hassled him back into the studio. I said, "Ian, you could have been one of the best record producers in the world, and you gave it up to become a talking head, a personality. Go back into the studio, for Christ's sake! Do something, make sure you do another great record!" I've been writing songs for a guy called Emmanuel Carella, so he's just produced Emmanuel's second single and the third one will be my song.

Was psychedelia also behind the pretty colours and the paper walls in "Part 3 Into Paper Walls"?
It was about teenage angst. I was probably miserable at the time, and I think it was just a thing of, I want to be happy, so I want to pour colours over myself, because colours seem to bring joy and happiness. That's all it was, an expression: if I'm all different colours, I'll be happy.

Is colour significant in your life?
No, I'm a bit drab when it comes to colour. It was just a thought. Some people, like Brian Cadd, think in colours with music. He'll go, "I want a sort of a purpley sound there with the white." I say, "Hang on, Brian, there are two things, audio and visual. Which one do you want? Do you want me to take a photo of it or do you want me to make it sound like something?"

Was it important that your first original song released after the "Real Thing"/"Paper Walls" phenomenon had your own personal stamp on it?

Yeah, what happened was that Ian and I didn't talk for about eight years. He was just like an old mother hen. He would tell me, "You have to dress like that, you should be doing this, you should be doing that", and in the end I couldn't handle it. I kept saying to him, "Ian, this is ridiculous." When we did the second single, I said to Ian, "I think the next single should be so simple, maybe two acoustic guitars and a cello. And he said, "You're crazy. People expect us to do something bigger." Consequently the next single was overblown. "Part 3 Into Paper Walls" had to be big, and even the B-side, "The Girl that I Love" had orchestras and everything on it. And that was when I thought, no, I've got to take control. Because at that stage people were emerging like Cat Stevens. I have to stand on my own two feet, I have to write everything I record. I made that decision. I said, "If they're not good enough, if they don't sell, so be it, I will just run it into the ground. Plus I need to dress the way I want and I need to do what I want to do." Ian and I parted company and he was really bitter over it for a long time.

Many of your lyrics are quite poetical. Did you write poetry when you were younger?

No.

Do you have any idea where all these lyrical ideas have come from over the years?

Out of desperation to succeed.

They're not simple and shallow lyrics.

Some of them are. Some of them are hideous. Some of my songs I look back and go, how could I have done that? How could I have written that? "Let's Do It", things like that. I don't like those songs. The songs I like the most are the ones that didn't sell, like "A Thousand Suns". That to me was a really epic song. The problem is it didn't relate because it wasn't about anything that anyone wanted to hear about. I read a book called *One Crowded Hour* about an Australian war photographer who got killed in a coup in Bangkok. He had written about all his experiences during Vietnam and I thought, gee, what would it be like to be in a little village with your mum and your dad or your wife and kids, somewhere in South-East Asia, and all of a sudden out of nowhere some guerillas come out of the hills, and say, "You're going to support us, and you're going to feed us. And if these other guys come in and you support them, we'll kill you." Next minute the traditional army of the country comes in, starts executing people for conniving with the guerillas—they've done it out of desperation to survive—and then eventually the army goes, the guerillas come back and punish them and everyone runs into the hills. And that's what it's about. It's about a village being decimated by powers that are manipulating for control of it. That's one of my favourite songs, musically as well as lyrically.

"Wings of an Eagle" I like; I like the lyrics to that and I like the story behind it. Ironically, I never told the story of what it was about for a long time, and people kept coming up to me saying, "I hope you don't mind but my father died just recently and we played 'Wings of an Eagle' at his funeral." That kept happening over and over again. And that's what it's about, it's about death. It's about an Aboriginal man who is dying and he's sitting on top of a hill. There's a legend in Arnhem Land that before you die a sea eagle comes to take your spirit to the Dreamtime. That's what he's waiting for; he's waiting for the eagle. People didn't know the story, but they felt it.

Was it about that for you as you wrote it so spontaneously?
I'd been reading about Red Indian traditions and life, because I loved the Indians in America. And then I found a couple of parallels between them and the Aborigines. I love certain things about the Kooris and the Indians, about their culture. I'd been reading and I sat down and obviously subconsciously it had stuck in my head. The words were ambiguous when I wrote them:

> Well I'm looking out on overcast sky in the morning
> And I can hear the warning as it calls to you
> As the birds migrate and the wind is raised I see the eagle soaring
> Although I'm just a pawn in nature's game ...

And I thought, what the hell? I looked at it and I had the "wahoo wahoo" and I went inside and I thought about it and I thought, I wonder if that's where I'm heading? So then I found the title, which was in the TV guide, John Wayne's movie *Wings of the Eagles*. And I thought, that's it! This is what it's about. So then I went from there and finished the chorus. And then the next verse.

The melody tends to soar like an eagle.
I think that was just an accident. Most things in writing are unconscious with me. Sometimes I'll consciously try to do something, and usually when I do that, it's a mistake and it becomes horrible.

Can you tell me about "Sweet Sweet Love"?
I was still wanting to record all my own stuff and I was a little bit nervous about doing it. I saw Johnny Farnham somewhere and I said, "John, I've got a song, would you like to listen to it? You might want to record it." I played it to him, and he said, "Listen, I love the song, but it just takes so long to get to the chorus." Now, I could have listened to him and thought, right, I'll chop that whole first section off and go straight into the D. It starts off with a whole minor section and then it changes to major. And I thought, no, bugger it, I like it the way it is. I think one of the things that's been in my favour, especially with "Wings of an Eagle" and "Sweet Sweet Love", it takes so bloody long to get to the chorus and takes so many different turns, that over the years of it being played, it still doesn't become monotonous. It's not half a verse, chorus, verse, chorus, verse, chorus, chorus, chorus, finish. It goes somewhere, it's like a journey. I think I should have kept writing like that, but when I went to America I had people going, "Oh no, no, no, you've got to make it verse, chorus, verse, chorus!" And I started to write that way, and it became a habit.

I think of "Sweet Sweet Love" as a bit like Stephen Stills' "Suite Judy Blue Eyes". It's not that it takes so long to get to the chorus; the song just has different movements.
Yeah, it was supposed to be different movements. But I hate the vocal on it. I was too naive. I sing it much better now.

Do you remember writing it?
I wrote the first bit sitting in my bedsitter in England, and there was a photo of my girlfriend on the wall. She was on the beach in a bikini, and that's why the words are, "I can't believe I'm really meeting a girl like you on such a day. Maybe I'm only dreaming"—because it's a photo. "Mr Sun"—which is Australia—"come back to stay. " I was in England and freezing, I hated it. "I am I am I am I am I know I am today"— and I think, where's this leading? It had started in a minor key and then went to a major key, which is like a happier, open sort of key. So that was the lamenting part and then a couple of days later I was sitting there again and I started playing and went from there. It was laborious tacking it all together.

It's fortunate, perhaps, that you weren't in Australia or surrounded by other musicians at the time.
Yeah, they would have discouraged me. There's a bit in it that I'd probably not do now, if I wrote a song, but it works really well. It goes from the D to the F sharp to the G, E, then G, and then it goes to an F, which is really weird. And I'd think gee, musically that won't work. But I didn't know any better, so I just did it, 'cause it felt right.

You mentioned Cat Stevens before. At the beginning of the seventies solo artists who wrote their own material were rare, on the charts at least, in a band-centric Australian music scene. Did that daunt you when you were writing songs for your first solo album, *Bloodstone*?
No, the only thing that daunted me is that I might fail. And the other thing that was really annoying, I rushed the songs. Some of the songs on my very first album were written unbelievably quick. And things that happened in the production, I wasn't really happy about.

Do you remember writing "Alcohol Farm"?
I wrote it about Brian Cadd. Brian was into The Band; he loved anything to do with The Band. And Brian was a drinker. He got me so drunk one night before I went to a gig and I humiliated myself because I just couldn't perform, I was so drunk. I'm not a big drinker. So I tried to marry the two, because to me Brian and The Band were one. The first thing I started with was "My moonlight", 'cause I figured Southern, Brian, he loves all that, and he even sings with a Southern accent. So the first lines were "My moonlight doesn't come from the moon, it comes from the back of my barn/ It keeps me tight on the darkest of nights down on Alcohol Farm." It just rhymed.

Brian's piano is very distinctive on your album. Did you think there was too much of his personality in there?
No, not really, it didn't bother me. Brian had been working with me and I was writing that way a little bit, that honky-tonky sort of thing, almost country.

You weren't writing at the piano, though, were you?
No, I was writing on the guitar.

Does the melody ever come to you away from the guitar?
Yes, melodies do. And recently because I've been spending so much time playing lead guitar I need to get back to writing. I've just been analysing a lot of other writers' styles, and there's a couple of styles that I'd really like to have a go at. Bono, for instance. The first two lines in a lot of his songs will rhyme, and then the next three lines don't rhyme, and then the chorus is just a repetitive line over and over again. Same with Bryan Ferry. The choruses are just one line that repeats over and over. [*Sings*] "Slave to love … Slave to love."
     And also the Bob Dylan style, I love his lyrics, I wish I could write like that. But some of his stuff is weird. For a while there we did "My Back Pages". The lyrics don't make sense whatsoever. I remember reading about John Lennon, when they asked him about "I Am the Walrus", what was he trying to do, and he said, "Well, I tried to write like Bob Dylan. Make no sense at all." Some of Bob's songs are like that, and then others tell an unbelievable story. A precise, fantastic, lyrical story. And then he's got things like "Lay Lady Lay". Exceptional writer.

What was inspiring some of those lyrics and those sad stories and woeful characters on *Bloodstone*? Songs like "O Helley", "Saints and Sinners" and "The Gambler's Lament".
Just angst I guess. "Lay in the Graveyard". I was obsessed with death. People would say, "Why are you writing such miserable songs?" And then in those days you'd smoke some grass and listen to your songs and go, "Oh, that's so miserable. I need to find something happy to write about." And you'd consciously try and steer your mind away.

How was the experience of working in the States?
It's a big pop factory, as I can attest for one of my best friends, Steve Kipner. He is a pop factory. He will get up, go to an appointment, or have someone come round and write from ten o'clock till twelve, have lunch, leave and go somewhere else and write from two o'clock till five. And that's all they do in America. And of course you're going to write hit songs out of that, because it's like as I said before, trying to throw the coin onto the ledge. The more times you write, the more chance of success you're going to have.
     I made some disastrous mistakes in America. Clive Davis from Arista wanted to sign me. But Clive wanted me to do other people's songs. Which I didn't mind at that stage, I thought, to get my foot in the door. But he had the guys that wrote Tony Orlando and Dawn songs come up, and the songs they played me were like vaudeville. I thought, "I can't see

me doing this." So RCA signed me, and I did my own album, my own songs, and it got a great review. But then RCA wanted me to become like a John Denver. And I wanted to be a rock 'n' roller. So I reacted against what they wanted and I did an album which was totally against the grain for me, and the critics didn't like it, and that stuffed my career. I probably should have gone along; it would have been right for me to head in that direction. Not so much a John Denver, but like an Eagles, softer type.

More like a Dan Fogelberg.
Yeah. That's what I should have done.

When you returned to Australia at the end of the 1970s, and particularly working here through the 1980s, how was your writing changing stylistically?
I came back and noticed that the biggest bands here were the loudest and had huge touring rigs and huge semitrailers, and I thought, how in the hell am I going to survive in this market? So I immediately turned all my writing around and wrote really punchy songs that would work live. We toured from 1978 right through till 1982, and I made a lot of money, it was good, we were one of the biggest touring bands around.

Did you find that you had to make the songs more hooky or was that a logical progression for you, especially with songs like "Hot Love"?
I had the pressure to try to come up with a hit. I was just grasping at straws, I think, just trying anything to work. The pressure on you to do it is incredibly enormous. And really to your own detriment.

It's been more than ten years since *A Thousand Suns*. Have you been writing continuously since then?
I've got an album in there that I've done just as demos. I've written heaps. The problem is when you're writing songs, it's almost like you're piling them up in a drawer because no-one ever gets to hear them, until I play live. I'll pick a small section of them and do them live. But there's a hundred songs sitting in there.

How frustrating is that for you?
It's frustrating to the point where I'm working with Darryl and Jim so much that I can't do my own solo shows and do my own songs. That frustrates me. So I've requested next year that I want four months to myself so I can do my own songs. And if Emmanuel's song takes off it will open up a plethora of stuff. It's a great song. "I Want You". It's a love song but a good one. The worst part is—it makes you feel real good about your whole life's work—I'm sitting there playing it and my wife came down and she said, "What's that song?" I said, "It's a song I've written for Emmanuel." She said, "That's the best song you've ever written. It's not like anything else you've ever done." [*Laughs*] Shit, just take the knife out of my back.

JOHN FARRAR

MALIBU, CALIFORNIA, USA, SEPTEMBER 2002

It's definitely advisable to talk to John Farrar about his artistry face to face. While I was writing an in-depth piece on Olivia Newton-John in 1994, I spoke to Farrar over the phone and it was obvious that talking about himself and his work was tough. The long-distance phone line was a convenient way for him to duck the hard questions, and his introversion hindered lively conversation. This didn't daunt me in the slightest when I went to his Malibu home eight years later to do this interview. Because as the writer of two hit songs from one of my generation's most essential soundtracks, *Grease*, this man could do no wrong in my eyes—or ears.

While diffident, Farrar is also warm and funny and his modesty is too heartfelt to ever be misconstrued. "You wrote 'You're the One that I Want'—full stop!" I told him. He seemed surprised that it meant so much to me, let alone willing to contemplate too deeply just how many other millions of people of my vintage were out there stopping in their tracks each time the song came on the radio or on a television repeat of the movie.

At a massive party thrown on the Paramount Studios lot in Hollywood two weeks after our meeting, Olivia Newton-John launched the *Grease* DVD with world-headline performances, singing "Hopelessly Devoted to You" and "You're the One that I Want". Enthralled, I witnessed John Travolta join her in song for the first time in twenty years. The music was being celebrated yet again, and all of Farrar's friends in attendance were keen to slap him on the back. His wife, Pat, who was Newton-John's singing partner in the 1960s and remains one of her closest friends, beamed with pride. But while the party raged, the Farrars slipped away. "I don't like all that fuss," he confessed to me on the phone the next day.

John Farrar was born in Melbourne on 8 November 1945 and grew up in the suburb of Moonee Ponds. Back then, one aspired to perhaps work in a bank, not dream of success in the entertainment business, and although he picked up a guitar fairly early, songwriting only became a vocation much later, when his career in music was already established. His influence was keenly felt across the Melbourne music scene in the 1960s, as his guitar playing or arrangements featured on just about every major record of the era, including Axiom's "A Little Ray of Sunshine" and the Ian Meldrum-produced "The Real Thing". "Before I knew what a producer was, we would just go in and make records, supply the backings for people, and pretty much do all the work, but we were never considered producers," Farrar recounted.

Huge fans of Brian Wilson and the Beach Boys, his group, The Strangers, were renowned for high harmony singing, and Farrar's guitar prowess was also a standout. As the house band on Melbourne television's *The Go!! Show*, they played for everyone from The Bee Gees to Olivia and Pat. They were also fans of Cliff Richard's group, The Shadows, and when Hank Marvin and Bruce Welch of that band invited Farrar to England to join them in a new trio, he had no idea that he would never return to Australia to live, nor that he would become a major force in someone else's career. Although totally unplanned, the teaming of Farrar and Newton-John, who had already moved to England, was far more momentous than either of them could have foreseen; it is hard to ascertain whether either would have enjoyed the worldwide success they have experienced for more than thirty years without that partnership.

Not only a master producer and arranger, Farrar became a consummately meticulous songwriter, from "Have You Never Been Mellow", "Sam" and "A Little More Love" to his work on *Grease*, *Xanadu* and the stage musical *Heathcliff*. More recently, he had been working with Francis Ford Coppola on songs for a musical version of *Gidget* for screen and stage. His assiduousness is a trait that stays with him to this day. He labours over his work. "Probably to the point of being mentally constipated," he said. "I think you get to the point where you try so hard, you never actually hone it to where you want it to be."

How old were you when you started writing songs?
I was about twenty-five. I had a shot at it in Australia, but The Strangers were covering the Beach Boys, and things like that. And when I went over to join up with Hank Marvin and Bruce Welch, they'd pretty much written the whole first album. So I realised that to survive I had to start writing. Because I'd never really thought about it before. And it was the focus of everyone in England, to write. So I guess it was just survival, I knew I had to do it.

But you weren't a thirteen-year-old kid sitting in your bedroom putting songs together?
I think I did one song in Australia; I had an old tape recorder that did sound on sound, where you just bounce one track onto the other, adding a track as you go. I did get a real big buzz out of that, and I thought, this does sound interesting, if I can do it on this, I should be able to come up with a song. So when I got with Bruce and Hank I decided to get into it. I started listening to Crosby Stills & Nash, and all these sort of people. 'Cause we were trying to do a three-part harmony type of group. So that's how it started.

At what age did you start playing guitar?
I was about twelve.

A lot of the writers I talk to, as soon as they started playing guitar, after a couple of years of learning everyone else's songbooks, started finding their own melodies. You weren't interested at that time in being a songwriter?
Where I was brought up, I didn't really think you could become a professional musician. I was going through school to get a job probably in a bank or something. I hate to say this, but I didn't really have big dreams at all. So everything's a total surprise to me. [*Laughs*]

Did you have guitar lessons or were you self-taught?
I had a few classical lessons. My first lessons were at the Victorian Banjo Club, where I learned "Springtime in the Rockies". G and D7 were the chords. The good thing was when you went to the Banjo Club, they gave you the words with the chords over the top, so I learned how to sing and play the guitar. If I hadn't done that I probably wouldn't have tried to sing. It seems like you can't write songs if you don't sing in some kind of manner, so it was a good start. Then I had some lessons off a guy called Stan Vizard at Lou Topano's Music School. And then a couple of classical lessons, and that was it.

So you didn't learn to write and read music?
No.

Who were you listening to musically?
Ricky Nelson I loved. And Elvis. I suppose Cliff Richard and The Shadows were the biggest influence on me. So it's strange that I ended up being involved with them. I had an English kid in my class at school who played me the first Cliff Richard record that came out, and I thought it was unbelievable. When I first joined The Strangers we were playing a lot of Shadows things. So I pretty much knew all their stuff.

Did you think of yourself as a good guitar player at that stage?
No, not really. As I got older I realised I definitely wasn't a very good guitar player.

Were you awestruck when you were invited to go over and join them?
It just seemed like an amazing thing to happen to me. I was writing a lot of arrangements

and making a lot of records with people in Melbourne. At the time I got the offer to go over there, I felt like things were pretty rosy. Although I wasn't confident about my guitar playing, I felt that I was a good group member; I loved singing harmonies and things like that. So I felt like I could do it, but I was scared, because I'd never said a word on stage in my life, and suddenly I had to go over there and start speaking, which was tough for me. I did have high hopes for the Marvin, Welch & Farrar thing that we were doing. I thought we had a shot. But people wouldn't let the Shadows thing go. So we were doomed.

You wanted to become the Crosby Stills & Nash of the UK?
Kind of, yeah. It didn't work out, but I definitely felt really privileged to be part of it, to work at Abbey Road. I worked there all the time. As it turned out, I ended up working with Olivia there. But I met Paul McCartney there, Pink Floyd were always recording there. It just was fantastic for me. In those days they talked about "you go abroad". And "abroad" meant going to England. So it seemed like a healthy transition.

How did your working relationship with Olivia begin?
When I first got to England we were scheduled to start making an album—Hank, Bruce and I—but Hank was involved in a television series with Cliff. Hank was the resident comedian on the show. And so there was a period of thirteen weeks where Bruce and I, apart from making a guest appearance every now and then on the show, really had nothing to do. Peter Gormley, who was managing Olivia, said, "Why don't you and Bruce do a couple of tracks with Olivia?" Peter at the time was running Festival Records there. So we cut a few demos and got a really good reaction to it.

And they weren't songs that you had written at this stage?
No, but I immediately saw the possibility. Bruce had a great ear for potential hit songs and I learned a lot from him in the time we worked together.

The first song you did with her was "Banks of the Ohio", which you actually arranged, didn't you?
Well, obviously it was an old traditional song and if you recorded it your own way you got a credit. But I wanted to write properly. It was really important to me. I think writing is, in my view, the only thing that you feel that is yours. no-one can say, "You didn't do that" or "Someone else did that for you." If you write a song it's yours forever. And that was important to me. I'm not a terribly forceful personality, so it was important for my wellbeing.

You said that growing up, it never occurred to you that you could be a successful songwriter. Then you're in the UK, working with an artist who isn't even known yet, and suddenly you've thought, "I have to be a songwriter." What made that shift?
Because I thought I could do it. Because I was playing guitar and I started to hear sounds. When you first start to write, you play a chord and you accidentally sing a note against that chord, and I started to fall in love with these little sounds. Then I'd hear people like Joni

Mitchell using open tunings, and suddenly it all changed. It became something really mysterious and artistic and wonderful.

Even though you were living in London, you were in fact mostly influenced by the songwriters in California?
I was probably influenced by a lot of Americans—James Taylor, David Gates of Bread. But also Cat Stevens, who's English. He used to play the *Old Grey Whistle Test* on TV. I played Cat Stevens' song "Father and Son" the other night. Oh, that's a fantastic song. It still stands up. It's amazing how some of those things still stand up.

When you first put down those tracks with Olivia, did it all gel?
Not straightaway. I remember a lot of the politics of it all, making records, and working with artists. I had no idea about that stuff. There was a period of learning about what a producer actually does, and learning to take responsibility for it, that was hard. As a producer you learn that if it's a hit you don't get the credit and if it's not a hit you get the blame. So that's what I was trying to say about a song, that it's yours. And I'm not talking about the financial rewards of it. I'm talking about just the satisfaction, that if you've written a song that you're really proud of, you can't beat that.

Was there a point where you and Olivia sat down together and consciously discussed the style and content of songs that would work for her?
No. If we were going to record we'd sit down for days going through tapes that had been sent in of songs, so I figured out where she wanted to go. And what Peter Gormley and everybody felt was the sort of material she should be doing. But I think underneath it all the things that I did write that were successful were things that I really liked myself. You can't really contrive it.

Given that you've said you're not particularly forceful personality-wise, were you then quite comfortable stepping off the performance stage and moving behind the scenes and putting your energies into songs and somebody else's performance?
Oh yes, very much. Although I did really enjoy playing guitar for Olivia when she toured here, when she had enough material; that was a nice feeling to be able to play my own songs in her act and be the guitar player. I felt like I belonged, that I really had a part of that, whereas when I was in The Shadows, it was—"Who's in The Shadows this week?" I don't mean that I wasn't made to feel welcome, but we'd go on stage and we'd start to play our vocal things, and they'd go, "Play 'Apache'!" So it was a losing battle.

Olivia once told me about the recording of Peter Allen and Jeff Barry's "I Honestly Love You" in a rickety studio in London.
The control room was actually built as a little square box hung from the ceiling and you had to climb up a ladder to get into it. And there were violin players crammed in there. But it had a great piano. That was the compensation.

You were very focused on trying to be a songwriter yourself, but did you realise at the time what an amazing song that was?

I thought it was a great song, I didn't realise that it would be the hit that it was. A friend of ours, Alan Hawkshaw, did this fantastic piano thing on it with two piano parts, which I thought was a great approach. But I could never claim to think that that was going to be a big worldwide hit. It just sounded like a really touching song and her vocal on it really affected people.

At that stage were you focusing specifically on writing for Olivia? Did you have hopes that your songs would get out there and other artists would record them as well?

I had hopes, but I was focused on writing for Olivia. We just seemed to be in sync musically. We developed together in the studio in a lot of ways. She would push me to another level, and I guess between the two of us we got crazy, but with recording it became so finicky and picky. She gives everything to what she does, and that's the way I feel about it, too. Sometimes I'd do a track, though, and think I had it where I wanted it and she'd come in and she wouldn't like it and I'd be pissed off. And then I'd try a different approach to it and in the end it always came out better anyway. But I would have loved to have hits with other people.

After "I Honestly Love You", her career took off to such a degree that working with her was probably a full-time job anyway.

It turned out to be that way, yeah. I did the Shadows thing for a while after that—I think the last thing I did was the Eurovision Song Contest—and then I left and went to the States.

Were you writing thinking about Olivia's vocals and the style of production that you would work on with her?

Yeah, and the sort of lyrics were an important part of it, writing the lyrics that were right for her.

Do you remember coming up with "Have You Never Been Mellow"?

The word "mellow" I'd never heard used the way the guys used to use it in the tour bus in the band that we were with. I thought it was a cool word.

But you'd heard Donovan's "Mellow Yellow", hadn't you?

Yeah, I know, you hear things. But I never really got it, I didn't quite understand. But hanging out with Americans, there are words that they use; when I was living in England, I thought I knew what they were but I didn't. So it just cropped up. I remember sitting in this little apartment I used to live in, in England. At that time I liked James Taylor a lot so I was trying to write a James Tayloresque sort of song. He'd probably be horrified to hear that.

But also, it was about being around aggressive people, and it was just another point of view. "Do you really have to be that aggressive with everything?" "Shut up and sit down!"

I'm uncomfortable talking about that one because in an interview I once did in America, the interviewer said to me, "So, 'Have You Never Been Mellow', you wrote that, right?" I said, "Yes." He said, "My friend thinks that's the worst song he's ever heard in his life." Nice of you to mention that to me. I was so depressed.

I did read that neither you nor Olivia actually had a lot of faith in "Mellow" at the time. Looking back now, can you understand why it was a hit?
No, I can't. I went to one of her shows last year somewhere and all the guys in the band came up and said that was their favourite song in the show and I was quite surprised. It didn't seem like the sort of song that musicians would like. Probably because of that one guy, that one smart-arse really killed it for me.

Were you writing on the tour bus? In your apartment, solitary songwriter, guitar on lap? What was the method back then?
Usually just with an acoustic guitar and no toys at all. It was before drum machines and all that sort of stuff started to happen. It was a lot easier then. I don't think I ever wrote anything on tour. We'd be travelling all day and I had to really be focused to write. Sometimes I might find an interesting chord with some sort of special voicing and I'd remember and use it at some later date. I think I wrote one song with Olivia in a tour bus. The guys brought out something called Everclear, some sort of really strong alcohol that they sell in the South. I remember the Everclear and I remember sitting in the bus with a guitar and Olivia and I came up with a song.

Do you remember what the song was?
"Love You Hold the Key" it was called. I had to think about that.

How did the writing of "Sam" come about?
"Sam" started out as an instrumental piece. I had a chorus and Hank Marvin had a verse and they seemed to fit together pretty well. Quite a while later I tried to put lyrics to it for Olivia, but all I came up with were the lines "Sam, Sam you know where I am/ and the door is open wide, come on inside." But at the time I treated them as dummy lines—lines you use just to sing the melody until you get the real lyrics. But I couldn't get any further so after I moved to LA, I asked Don Black to have a shot at it.

What were the particular qualities in Olivia's voice and her style that were guiding you when you were writing? Did you feel that they needed to be soft at that stage? Until *Grease* they were all pretty much soft, melodic.
Soft was easier. Writing up-tempo things for her was harder.

Harder for her or harder for you?
Harder for me. Because her voice really lent itself to the soft sound, lyrics that she communicated to people. Coming up with rock things was really hard. I tried. I think I wrote

a couple that were dreadful. But eventually we did a few that were okay. We had a couple of nice ones on the *Totally Hot* album. That was the turnaround for her.

Had you already started writing the *Totally Hot* songs before you wrote the *Grease* songs?
We went through a really bad period where things just weren't working and I'd started to record an album, I think I'd done three tracks, and they weren't getting much of a reaction at all. And then the *Grease* thing came along, and I had an opportunity through Olivia to write a couple of things for that. At the same time I was still trying to come up with songs for this other album, *Totally Hot*. And I think because the *Grease* things were successful that I got much more confident, and it kicked me into another gear, as far as confidence in writing. I felt like that *Totally Hot* album, apart from *Grease*, was a really important album for us.

Did you know that you had something special with "A Little More Love"?
I thought I did, yeah. It felt really good. I think that was a Barry Gibb influence, that one. Because I've always been a huge fan of Barry, he's just fantastic.

Is that where the really high parts came from?
No, when I was in The Strangers we always did Beach Boys things; we'd been doing that falsetto thing for ages before I went to England. That's why Hank and Bruce wanted me to come over, to do the high parts.

When the opportunity came up to contribute to *Grease*, did you submit both songs at once, or just "Hopelessly Devoted to You" initially? Did you have the script?
Yeah. They accepted "Hopelessly Devoted to You" because she had to have a ballad for this particular spot in the movie. I had to write lyrics that would fit that. I don't think there were any other submissions for it; I was just lucky enough to get that opportunity. Well, there probably were other submissions, but I think I had the inside track because of Olivia. And because that went well, I then got a chance to do the last one.

Had you been given the exact picture of that scene—how she was going to come out of the house in her nightgown, how she was going to look?
Yeah. It was great; really a fun challenge to strike the right lyric idea for it. But it was all there.

And did you have a sense of John Travolta's voice for "You're the One that I Want" to write around it?
He was great. He's got this really high voice. Cool dude.

I do see "You're the One that I Want" as a perfect pop song—short and to the point. Whenever you hear it you just want to get up and dance. And because it's totally tied up in that movie, you cannot listen to it without visualising that climactic scene in the movie, seeing Olivia in that sexy gear.
The weird thing was it was the fastest song I ever wrote. It came so fast, the actual melody

and the feel of it. I did the track first with a drum machine and I had this little cassette player that had one speaker on it. The speaker always sounded fantastic, whatever you played in it. I remember Darryl Cotton was staying with us at the time and I played him the track by the pool. He said, "Geez that sounds good." So I was really into it, and I think from start to finish was about two days. When I was driving in to play it to them I was so jazzed up about it, it just felt great. It was only a crummy old demo, but it had all the excitement in it.

Did you sing both parts on the demo?
Yeah. That wasn't the good part of it.

Had the producers given you a title?
No. She was going to do this transition and arrive as this very slutty-looking woman. It was pretty much laid out.

And "Hopelessly Devoted to You"—was it by virtue of the fact that it was in a movie soundtrack that the orchestration was so lush and magnificent? Because your songs previously had been less elaborate.
Yes, they were always simple.

Was that dramatic, lush quality in your original concept?
Everything except the strings. The strings were added. I actually love what the string guy wrote; I thought it was a really beautiful arrangement. But all the stuff was pretty much in the demo.

Did that song come easily to you as well?
I spent the longest period writing the lyrics of any song I've ever written. Every thesaurus and every rhyming dictionary I had, just trying to really make it work properly.

Like, "Can I rhyme 'head' and 'devot-ed'?"
Yes. I wanted to get all these rhyme schemes in. I felt good about that song.

What was the sense around the making of the film? Did anyone have an idea that it could be so big?
I wasn't really around the set all the time. I probably went to the set twice. So I didn't get a sense of what the feeling was. When I went to the premiere of the movie I wasn't that thrilled. And yet now when I see it I understand why it was accepted so much. It was so much fun.

Why were you uneasy about it?
I was uneasy because I thought it was going to be like the big musicals, like *South Pacific* and *West Side Story* and all those things. And it was such a small-scale movie and unpretentious. I didn't get it till years later. But I do now. John Travolta in particular was wonderful.

When you listen back on your early work—you must at least hear them when you're out and about, particularly the *Grease* songs—do you like what you hear? Are you pleased, satisfied?
I feel pretty good about it. I know I gave it my best shot. I never wrote to what I thought people wanted to hear; I always wrote what I thought was the best thing I could do. And a lot of things that I hear from those times don't embarrass me.

Except "Have You Never Been Mellow" because of what that guy said.
Arsehole. Actually, if he had said it to me now ... I felt like I was a kid then, but if he said it to me now ...

Was that comment made at the time it was a hit?
No, it was probably around when I was doing *Xanadu*.

You already had all the success with *Grease*, and this little song that you did five years earlier—
That's why I'm anti-social.

In case somebody doesn't like one of your songs?
I think a lot of people remember negative things that have been said through their life, don't they?

But by 1979–80 you were one of the most successful songwriters in the world.
I just took it the wrong way.

Was "Magic" written specifically for *Xanadu* or did you already have a start to that song?
"Magic" was written for the movie. The brief came mainly from the co-producer, Joel Silver. On all the songs that I wrote for the movie, he would call me into his office and go over the script with me and tell me what he felt the song needed to achieve. Sometimes he would set up a screening room and have me watch old musicals that he thought might help me. It was always a lot of fun to be around Joel.

Do you remember coming upon those interesting chord sequences or was it an unconscious flow?
The chords for the song came from an open B tuning that was a favourite at the time. A lucky accident.

To me, "Magic" sounded like you'd hit a new level. That didn't necessarily have to be an Olivia song. I've always been surprised that it hasn't been covered because I just think it's like a standard.
I was confident about my writing at that time. They'd give me three weeks and say, "You've got to do that song." And I always felt confident that I could do it in three weeks. But by the end of the movie I was pretty burnt out. There was one thing that I had to do in that

movie called "Dancin", where they wanted me to write two songs—one for forties girls, like a Lennon Sisters thing, and a rock song. And then they had to perform them separately and then perform them at the same time. I remember having an idea of what to do and the following day I had to deliver it and I hadn't recorded it. So I started at eight o'clock that night, finished it at three o'clock the next afternoon, no sleep, then had to take it to the choreographer to teach the dancers at four o'clock. The chord sequence and the melody had to work together. It was crazy. By the end of the movie I was a dead man.

I guess the concept of *Xanadu* was more aligned to your idea of a grand Hollywood musical.
I must admit I didn't like the script and the whole rollerskating disco fantasy thing was not that great. But somebody's doing a production of it now, a live production. I think it's a send-up type of thing. They're going to do it off-Broadway, focus on the camp aspect of it all. It was so cheesy.

Would you consider yourself something of a perfectionist in the way you write?
Probably to the point of being mentally constipated. I think you get the point where you try so hard you never actually hone it to where you want it to be. And lately I've just been throwing things away 'cause I just can't get them to where I want them to be. I think that's the result of writing on my own.

You're obviously comfortable doing it that way. You've never thought about deliberately calling up a songwriter and saying, "Do you want to come and write with me today?"
Well, I wrote a few things with a guy called Tom Snow that I had a pretty reasonable thing happening with. That worked, he was a keyboard player. He's had a lot of success. I wrote a couple of things with Stevie Kipner. And a couple of things with Billy Thorpe. We just laughed all the time.

You did some co-writing early on with Bruce Woodley.
Bruce was the first person to show me an open tuning. He's a very accomplished musician and lyricist and joke teller. Together we wrote a few songs for a Seekers album that was recorded in England.

After *Xanadu* Olivia moved on to her next phase, which was "Physical", and suddenly she had a really big hit by another writer. Were your careers starting to diverge at that point?
Not consciously. I was still working with her but things were starting to change. I don't know how to put my finger on it but things were different. There was a period, with *Grease*, *Totally Hot*, *Xanadu* and *Physical*, and I did a solo album of my own. I did five albums on the trot, and I was fried at the end of it all.

What was the aim of the solo album? Did you have a yearning to get back into the spotlight?
There were a lot of singer-songwriter things happening, and I'd been doing all my demos, and the guy who was managing me got me a deal with CBS, so in my spare time I was doing my album and doing all the other stuff.

You must have been writing very prolifically.
I don't think I was ever prolific. But I was certainly spending all my time doing it and recording it. I didn't really have much social life at all. It probably was my most productive period. And I guess that's when good things happen, when you get totally focused.

Were you at this stage writing with a view to getting cuts from other artists?
That was probably one of the motivations for doing my album, to have another voice doing my songs and see if they mean anything.

Were the songs different lyrically and musically because you were going to be singing them?
I don't think style-wise they were that much different. Probably more guitars. When I hear it now I still feel pretty good about everything that's on it. I spent a year on it. There are still a couple of things on that that I think could be done again.

"Fallin'" is a song that really stands out on your solo album, and one that Olivia performs on stage these days.
That song was something I started and never seemed to get beyond the first few bars of the verse. I'd bring it out every now and then, play it for a while, and then forget about it. It wasn't until I found the introduction that it all started to make sense. I was looking for a way of making the key of the verse feel like a surprise.

Cliff Richard described you once as "a pop music intellectual". Being very careful and meticulous and thorough, that must involve a lot of thinking about it.
There are just times in writing where you feel like you're connected to something.

Do you know what that is? Do you have an idea where the songs come from?
I don't know what it is. I just know that sometimes you get an emotional rush. It hasn't happened much lately but when it happens you think, "Shit, where did that come from?" The emotional rush that you get from it, when everything just feels great, you keep trying to find that all the time. And if you don't find it, you don't think that you've got a song. The way I do it. And I need to get those moments in a song where you just go "Wow!" But then I repeat that phrase so many times, trying to get to the next stage, that that little surprise becomes less of a surprise, and then I start to question it.

But that rush is what it was all about for me, the feeling that you'd stumbled on something that was really ... I mean I'm not a religious person so I'm not going to pretend that I feel that I'm connected to some great power. But there was definitely a feeling; you knew it was right. It seems as I get older that I believe less in magic. And songwriting, when it works, can sometimes convince me that there is something else.

Would you say that your most satisfying compositions gave you that feeling every time?
Yeah, it felt great. I wish I could take back what I just said, it sounds so hokey. What I was

171

trying to explain is, in a song there's this form that you take. You usually have an introduction, a verse, it's like a visual journey, and you reach a point where whether it's the lyric line or whether it's the melody or the chord, some action that happens, it just makes you think this is definitely worth persevering with. But it doesn't come that often for me, that feeling.

Do your songs feel like children to you? Creations that you feel very proud of?
No, I don't see them as children, I just see them as a period of time when I worked really hard and was really focused on a particular idea.

Do you have an awareness of how much pleasure your work has brought to people all over the world? Do you ever think of it in those terms?
I'm probably more conscious of the two songs in *Grease* as being fun things. I always feel like everyone else's songs were fun but mine were a bit … I don't think I wrote many fun songs. I wish I could. Working with Stevie Kipner, he's great. He'll just sit there and throw a million ideas at you and sooner or later, it's "Oh, that's great, Stevie!" I'm lucky if I can come up with one idea. So it's hard. I have to sit there and really work hard on it. Maybe I was never really a writer. Do you know what I mean? Something I forced myself to do.

But you were compelled to do it. You said you got to a point where you knew you had to be a songwriter. You don't write a song like "Hopelessly Devoted to You" or "Magic" if you're not a writer.
I guess what I'm trying to say is it's hard work for me.

It's not easy for all writers. One songwriter once described it to me as swimming through molasses. Sweet but so hard.
But Paul McCartney did sit down at the piano when they were at that period, that really creative time, and just knock out a killer song in ten minutes. He was a killer. He's still one of my absolute heroes. Some of the songs he wrote.

Him more so than John Lennon?
Yeah, I love some of his things, like "Martha My Dear." There was something about what he did that was more musical. I loved John Lennon, I thought the combination was wonderful, but there's something about McCartney's work. I loved the *Ram* album.

How did the *Heathcliff* project come about? Was that a dream you had had, to write a musical?
Yeah. It's funny because when I first went to England I remember seeing that movie, *Wuthering Heights*, and I was really touched by it. So when they asked me to do that, I thought, what a perfect opportunity.

How did the collaboration with Tim Rice work?
Usually Tim would send me a lyric and I'd write to the lyric and then send it over.

Was that hard for you? You were used to doing everything.
It was hard for me because I like the melody to lead the way. Writing to lyrics I found very hard. Not because of the quality of his lyrics, because they were great, I just find it hard to be caught in the structure. And also being totally intimidated by the fact that I'm writing with Tim Rice. I didn't want to change anything. I think when he writes with Elton, Elton probably grabs what he wants. But I tried to pretty much do it as it was written. I think I changed a couple of things. When they did *Heathcliff* they took the less romantic approach, they took the hard-core line. The book of *Wuthering Heights* is hard going, intense, very doomy. You want to kill yourself at the end of it. Whereas the Hollywood version of it I thought was great, with Sir Laurence Olivier and Merle Oberon. It didn't dwell as much on the death and darkness. So a lot of the songs got very doomy and it's hard to work on material like that for a long period of time. But I was happy with what we got; I think we did a reasonable job.

When you write generally with the melody leading the way, does the lyric come after?
Yeah. Or at the same time. I'll sing a line and like the way it fits.

Have you ever come up with a hook line—like "You're the one that I want, ooh ooh ooh"—and think, "Oh wow, I must write a song around that"?
No. That just happened to fit. [*Laughs*]

I think it's pretty profound—"Oooh ooh ooh." I don't think anyone should ever downplay the significance of that.
They wouldn't dare. I remember going to see *Grease* in London, and I was walking outside and this little old lady was standing at the bus stop going, [*Sings*] "Oooh ooh ooh."

Didn't that give you a thrill?
It did actually. I thought that was great. And Hilda Baker did it. Have you ever heard that? Hilda Baker and Arthur Mullard did it. It's hilarious.

Is it imperative that you continue to write? Would you feel that you were cheating yourself if you just said, "I am so successful, I have written songs for the most successful movie musical soundtrack, I can retire, I don't need to write any more"?
I do need to write. For my own sanity I do. I feel good about doing musicals. Musicals do have a wider choice about what sort of song you're going to write. I can't really relate to the pop thing that much any more.

JOHN WILLIAMSON

SYDNEY, AUSTRALIA, JANUARY 2004

Well I've ripped and dug out burrows on a sandy bulloak hill,
Eradicating rabbits doesn't take a lot of skill,
And a boy born in the Mallee doesn't find 'em hard to kill.
But they'll never be as rare as a Quandong tree
My grandma made some jam for my brothers and me
They're like the Mallee Fowl you hardly ever see
But I don't mind at all if you call me a Mallee Boy.
　　from "Mallee Boy"

The directness is what first hits you in John Williamson's songs, but it's the beauty of his images and the poetry he makes out of the ordinary that stays with you for a long time after hearing them. Like a Les Murray verse, a Williamson song is unmistakably Australian, unequivocally heartfelt, unashamedly candid and often poignant to the point of bringing on tears. Frequently they are his own tears, as Williamson admitted during our conversation on a warm summer day when the aromas from the garden surrounding his suburban office filled the room and imbued his recollections.

"A good sentimental song will make me cry first, and then I know I've got something," he said, looking just like the Mallee boy he described in his autobiographical song of 1986. At age fifty-eight, Williamson's inherent boyish charm radiated beyond the backwards cap he wore and the impassioned beliefs he fervently shared. His songs keep him rooted in his past, and in "Mallee Boy" it's all there—boyhood in the country, landscape, vegetation, bird and animal life, family, heritage, humour, pathos. The perfect encapsulation of what has made Williamson's work relevant for generations of Australians. There are also songs that nod to an optimistic future, for families struggling on the land, for native Australians too long marginalised, for kids deserving of a safe world to grow up in. Williamson's intent is, for the most part, earnest.

But his songwriting career began with a comedic splash in 1969, and his vocation as an entertainer, although he might not have first realised it, was destined from an early age. Born on 1 November 1945 in Quambatook, in the Victorian Mallee region, Williamson's life was all mapped out for him as a farmer, so he never took his studies very seriously. He passed one subject—practical tuba—and played the large brass instrument in his Melbourne private boarding school military band before ditching it in favour of the guitar when he went home to the farm. The family relocated to Coppa Creek, a small area between Moree and Goondiwindi in northwest New South Wales, and it was there that Williamson wrote his first song, "Old Man Emu", to entertain audiences at his local pub show each week. He saw himself as strictly amateur, but after his performance of the novelty song helped him win the television talent show *New Faces* in 1970, a professional career beckoned and he abandoned the land. Although, of course, he never truly did, as his songs have always reflected his deep passion for the Australian countryside, nature and the true blue people who committed their lives to it.

If the 1982 composition "True Blue" is his most famous song, Williamson has never been content to rest on its laurels. Anthems are but one of his stock-in-trades in songwriting; protest songs have equal force for him. He has sung about Australia's call for its own flag and about needless woodchipping, just to name two of his causes. Williamson can talk about conservation issues until he is blue in the face. "I call myself a bluey rather than a greenie, put it that way," he said.

He also considers his music folk rather than country, but of course it has been the country music industry where he has made his great successes and sold over two million albums. At the time of our interview he had settled into his role as President of the Country Music Association of Australia, a job he took over from Joy McKean, and before her, Slim Dusty. It's a lineage Williamson is honoured to be a part of, just as he is proud of singing in his conversational Australian drawl and of having his songs identified with national sport teams and events.

I began our conversation by telling Williamson that I found it rewarding to approach his work not chronologically but thematically. And I commented that for all the affecting poetry and deep conviction, a lot of his songs just made me laugh.

"Well, there's a reason for that," he responded. "I became a songwriter because I'm an entertainer. So it's not a matter of writing one style of music, which some songwriters might be known for. I write for the show. You've got to have your love songs, your anthems, and of course I'm basically known for Australian landscapes with people in them. And you've got to have your comedy. It doesn't worry me if I write a silly song. It might take away from someone's belief of me being a really serious writer, but I write because I'm an entertainer."

Was music from established country, folk or pop artists influencing you as a child?
When I was a real child the pop industry didn't exist. There were single 78s, I think we had "How Much Is that Doggy in the Window" and probably songs from *Okalahoma*. If I was ever asked is there one song that I reckon is one of the greatest songs, it's "Oh What a Beautiful Morning" out of *Oklahoma*. I just remember how that made me feel when I was in my little town. I had a really nice childhood and my mum had a great rose garden, and there was something about that song.

But it was the fact, more than anything, that we had a musical family. Dad played banjo, and Uncle played fiddle, Mum bashed the piano and had an aunty that played it properly and they all sang. I taught myself to play harmonica when I was about six, then Dad taught me to play the ukulele, and he taught me a couple of George Formby songs. George Formby was a little Pommy comedian who was an entertainer first, and he wrote little funny songs. So I learned the joy of entertaining people as a kid, rather than seriously regarding myself as a singer or a musician.

The huge thing that happened to me, more than anything, was when I went to school in Melbourne at the age of fourteen. The folk scene was huge, and people like Pete Seeger, Joan Baez, the Kingston Trio in particular, were huge for me. I'd lie down on the floor and listen to those records over and over. Josh White, an old black American who played blues, immediately struck a chord with me. The rock 'n' roll thing was always bodgies and bike chains and widgies and awful people fighting, it seemed, from a country perspective. I didn't like the whole rock 'n' roll scene; it seemed to be very negative and not about nice things. Like "Jailhouse Rock". Whereas folk music was songs about real country people. I think that's the biggest difference between country and rock. One's about grass and the other one's about concrete.

The Bob Dylan era came after that for me. Not only did he make folk rock 'n' roll but he made folk country, as well. That *Nashville Skyline* album was my favourite for years. And of course then there was Johnny Cash. So I guess I'm in that area in Australia, where the words are the main thing and the melody comes afterwards, and it's about who we are. Who we are as a whole nation, not as just cosmopolitan Sydneysiders or Melbourneites.

Did you teach yourself guitar?
Yeah, the ukulele's tuned the same as a guitar so I taught myself the guitar about the age of

twelve. I had the rhythm fairly down pat already. Half the chords were already there, there were just two more strings. But I think my finger style came more from listening to Joan Baez in the early sixties. I was into nylon string, the folk stuff. I really wasn't into country until I started to listen to people like Roger Miller and Tom T Hall and it was later on that I started to discover Slim Dusty and Buddy Williams and those sort of people.

Much of your work is pure poetry set to music. Did you write poems as a kid?
No. I had no idea I was ever going to be a writer; I wasn't particularly into literature. I didn't write a song till I was twenty-three. First thing I ever wrote, full stop, was "Old Man Emu". My mother used to write a bit of poetry. And I wasn't a bookworm. What I did as a kid was play football and collect birds' eggs. I was really into birds, and I played by the rules—you only take one egg out of the nest and leave the rest. You wouldn't have been able to beat me on what birds were in the district, even if a new bird came to the district I would know and I would find out what it was and where it was distributed in the country, and that's still with me now, I get it all around Australia. If I ever write an autobiography, it will be about the birds in my life, because I'll remember where I saw a certain Aussie bird first and that will be a story around it. You'll find that in my show, if you wanted to add them up, there'd probably be thirty birds mentioned.

If "Old Man Emu" literally was the first song you ever wrote, what inspired you to write it?
There's two influences. In "Old Man Emu", if you hear that "doo-da-do-do, doo-doo", Roger Miller used to do that in "Dang Me". That idea came from Roger Miller mimicking a guitar. I was never a lead player so I guess I put those things in. But the other biggest influence was Rolf Harris. He got to me straightaway because I thought his stuff was so Aussie, and Rolf to my mind is an entertainer first and a songwriter second. That got to me before I wrote songs, of course, well back. The jaw harp throughout "Emu" was really my answer to his wobble board. So I wrote "Old Man Emu" purposely as a novelty song with gimmicks and all. I have to admit that I had a commercial head with my very first song. I didn't write it to be clever.

I got a ten-dollar job singing at the local pub in a restaurant, doing folk songs and Aussie songs and Roger Miller and Johnny Cash, anything. And then I all of a sudden came up with this idea to write "Old Man Emu". I had to perform it three times that first night, 'cause they just went berserk. I knew I had a hit straightaway; I wasn't that surprised when it went so well on *New Faces*, 'cause I had actually tested it. But then it got hard. It was thirteen years before I sold any records after that. That was number one for five weeks; I left the farm, and then discovered how hard showbiz really is.

Did the success of "Old Man Emu" spur you on to write more songs immediately?
I wrote a whole album of songs then, and I wouldn't sing any of them now; they're all bloody awful. Even though I did write a follow-up to "Old Man Emu", I didn't want to be regarded as a comedy writer. And today I still don't want to be pigeonholed in that. There are still a lot of people that think of "Old Man Emu", "Crocodile Roll", "Budgie Song",

and that's what I'm best at. But to me they're like a cheap calling card. They're fun and they might even be regarded as clever, but I hope I don't go down being remembered for that. I'd much rather be remembered for "Cootamundra Wattle" and "Raining on the Rock" and things like that.

Not that I knock "Old Man Emu", 'cause if it hadn't been for that song I would still be battling in a drought, out driving tractors for sure. But that was a real shortcut, and I wasn't ready for it. It wasn't really until the late seventies that I got into writing songs properly.

You told me in Tamworth a few years ago that the idea usually comes first, with an opening line that then suggests a melody to you. And then more words will come.
That's generally it, but I don't stick by any formula.

Has it ever been the other way around, where you've come up with a series of chords or a little refrain, and built a song around that?
Out of 260 songs or something, I've probably written twenty where I've gone into a feel. It often happens backstage where you're pretty keyed up before a show and you're getting into a bit of a feel with a guitar rhythm or chord structure, and I'll put words to that. I might have had half a song, or an idea of a song, and they get married that way. Sometimes that'll work. But I don't think I've ever written a song that I'll be remembered for doing it that way. My best songs are where I've been inspired by a story and wrote something that was quite strong to start with. With my kind of stuff, the music and the rhythm's got to support the words, not the other way around. When I'm writing stories about certain subjects, the lyrics have an atmosphere, and you've got to feel what that atmosphere is so the music describes that. For instance with "Raining on the Rock", I had a John Denver-ish type of melody originally. It just didn't work. Eventually I found that droney thing that gives you that shimmering heat, by tuning the E string down to a D, which is quite common. So I found a melody that suited the lyrics, and that's important for me.

And once again it comes back to being an entertainer. I might purposely write a song to a certain rhythm because that's the time in the show when you can no longer be sentimental and it's time for singalongs and foot tappers. In a two-and-a-half-hour show you've got to have all those elements.

Some of your songs are really strong melodically; others have that basic singsong tune. Do you restrain the melody deliberately in some of your story songs?
It's an unconscious thing, it's just natural. If it's a happy song I'm not going to put it in a minor key, 'cause it wouldn't work. I learned a fair while back that it's a bit of a waste of time being clever. If a melody came to me naturally—it just naturally flowed that it wanted to go there, with the lyrics already in my head—I don't think I'd stop it. It's the lyrics telling me to do that. In other words I don't really let the melody become separate.

I was doing a masterclass the other day, and I mentioned that the lyric is first, and the second most important thing is rhythm. The melody comes after that. Quite often in a story song I write in a kind of a conversation. I don't ever try to use a language that doesn't seem like a conversation, 'cause I want to communicate to people just like I'm talking to you now. So I often listen to myself, speak the lyric and then hear it as a suggestion of a melody in the voice. Because what people don't realise is there's no such thing as a non-melody. If I come up with melodies they're fairly Aussie melodies, because Aussies have a melody in their voice that's ours. That's why Irish tunes are beautiful, because of their lilt. And that's what annoys me when I hear Nashville licks in an Australian song, because that comes from the way they speak in the South of the US. They go, "Goddamn man!" And that's how they play the guitars. Ours is fairly sleepy.

So when you're writing lyrics, are you always conscious of the way you're going to be pronouncing the words, how that will affect rhyme and the stressing of certain notes?
Yeah, to me it's just so obvious, observing successful people in folk and country, they've all done it in their own voices. Willie Nelson, Johnny Cash. If Willie Nelson tried to sound like an Aussie we'd laugh at him. It seems amazing to me that anyone thinks that they can communicate at all by not using their own accent. Even though I did suffer from that in the seventies. I didn't think I could sing in my own accent, because I was embarrassed. If you do a lot of covers as a youngster I think you tend to get into that habit. But thankfully the first song I ever recorded, "Old Man Emu", was my full-on accent. And after thirteen years I realised that was still my biggest hit. What's wrong with me? Go back to my real accent and the real me.

Does each of your songs reflect back specifically on a time and place, or do you strive to make them immediately universal and timeless?
I think ballads about people living in the bush are timeless. Just like "Waltzing Matilda". I don't think you have to worry about that. Unless you're writing about tractors and trucks, those things change. But people don't. And people are still suffering the same things in droughts now as they did in the old days. There are things that certainly do have a date. Like "The Vasectomy Song". That was when the blowing in the bag thing first came in, breathalysers. Now breathalysers aren't any big deal, but when they first brought it out it was on everyone's lips.

But are they signposts for you for your life? Do you remember where you were when you wrote songs?
Yeah, in that way they are. "Galleries of Pink Galahs" for instance, I think that's timeless, because there's always going to be droughts, there's always going to be young people leaving the land, but that was very much about the drought our family went through. There's only one boy left on the land now, and that was mainly because of droughts. And "Cootamundra Wattle". They all have a date to them, but still they are timeless. That's the great thing about this genre that I'm in. They do live on. And once you win fans with this kind of music you don't lose them. They don't go away. It's not trendy, in other words. Whilst your recording facilities get better and you might have learned to record more efficiently, the acoustic guitars still basically sound the same and there's a drum or a foot tap, there's nothing too electronic

about it all. You wouldn't want to be a trend, because it means you're gone tomorrow. Whereas this just keeps building. It's wonderful how you just keep building your audience.

Is there a particular reason why you've re-recorded "True Blue" a number of times?
The first time I recorded it, it was a very raw form, recorded on a four-track. And then when we were putting down *Mallee Boy* in 1986, John Singleton, who I wrote "True Blue" for in the first place, for his TV program, rang up and said, "I've got the 'Buy Australian' campaign as my client, and I want to use 'True Blue'." So I thought, well, bugger this, I'm going to re-record it and do it properly this time. So that's the version that everyone knows, and that really became a hit because of the "Buy Australian" campaign, and all the wonderful true blue Aussie pictures they put with it. I couldn't have asked for anything better.

We put out a *True Blue* album eventually, which was a compilation of *Mallee Boy* and *Warragul* and all my hit albums. So I came up with the idea recently, now that there's been a few albums since, to put out *True Blue Two*. And Phil, my manager, said, "Well, we'll have to have 'True Blue' on it." So I said, "Well, not the old one. Let's do it with an orchestra, so it gives it another dimension." So that's the only reason. I did change the words, but now I actually sing both lots; I put "Vegemite" in the first chorus and not in the second two.

I wondered why you had "Vegemite" in one version and not in another.
I didn't really want a commercial product in the song. I was a bit annoyed that I'd put it in there, so when I re-recorded it, I put in "or will she be right", which is about the Aussie apathy. I wish I'd put it in there in the first place. But then, I sang it with Steve Waugh's team the other day, and there's no way you can change them. It's "Vegemite" as far as they're concerned.

You wrote on the *True Blue Two* album that the song "True Blue" is still the undercurrent to everything you write. What do you mean by that?
All the things that "True Blue" means. First of all, in the Australian context it means very Australian. So all the things I write are just true in the roots. I write about fair dinkum people who are true blue. I write about bush people and good people that are out there struggling all the time. "True Blue" is used at a huge amount of funerals. Especially for dads. Kids write in and say, "We used 'True Blue', there wasn't a dry eye in the house." They use it for their mums as well. That to me is such a nice accolade because if someone plays your song at their funeral, there can't be any better pat on the back for a song than that.

And as I said, if I write about the nature of the country, that's true blue. "Is it a cockatoo?" The reason I mention the cockatoo in the song is because it is the nature of the country that we're losing. Everything I'm writing I really try hard to make sure it is true blue.

Did you have any idea when you first wrote it in 1982 that it could end up being the landmark song it is?
Oh, of course not. No. But it was working for me really well in the live shows before it became

a hit, so it was a sleeper. By the time it was released the second time, I knew it was a strong song. Of course no-one could ever buy the kind of publicity the "Buy Australian" campaign gave it. I think "Cootamundra Wattle" and "Galleries of Pink Galahs" are just as good, but I've never had anything like that promotion. "Raining on the Rock" got further promoted once I recorded it with Warren H Williams, my Aboriginal mate from Hermannsburg. "A Bushman Can't Survive" was sleeping for years on my album and then Tania Kernaghan recorded it and got a huge amount of airplay, and then that became a hit. So airplay's pretty important.

When you've sat down to write a song like "A Flag of Our Own" or "The Land of the Truly Free" or "Keep Australia Beautiful", is it your intention to consciously write an "anthem"?
Oh, sure. Patriotic songs. I really have seen that as part of my job as a writer. I realised a long time ago that we had seemed to be taking all the American shortcuts and in the seventies especially we were still going through this period of feeling inferior to England. The fact that we've still got the bloody Union Jack on the flag still says to me that we really haven't come to terms with who we really are. It makes absolutely no sense to me at all, having someone else's flag on the corner of our flag. Any more than it would make sense having a kangaroo in the middle of the Union Jack in England. It's just crazy.

I get passionate about things. In "Rip Rip Woodchip" I was obviously passionate about our forests being sold off to the Japanese as woodchip. In "True Blue" there's a line there where Joh Bjelke-Petersen was flogging off the coast to foreign bidders at one stage, where I said, "Now be fair dinkum ... they sell us out like sponge cake." That's where that came from. "It's a Way of Life" is passionate about all our bush being turned into a billiard table. I don't purposely go out to stir people up; I feel passionate about these things.

There was a real backlash against you from "Rip Rip Woodchip".
Oh yeah, yeah. I still can't perform in Eden. There's only one venue, the Eden RSL, and their clients are all woodchippers. And there was a bomb threat in Taree at a concert. I visited the timber people in Eden; they thought they were going to win me across, but I said, "When you've been around the country like I have and you know how much of our habitat has been destroyed, you'd feel the same way as me." I've never had a go at people who cut timber for timber—if they selectively log and take the good logs out—but this clear felling for bloody woodchip ...

You have many signature songs, but I guess "Mallee Boy" is the simple statement on who you are and where you're from.
It's a real statement about being a country boy, that's what that is.

Do you remember where you were when that song came to you? Were you in the country when you wrote it? Or were you sitting in an office thinking about the country?
That's a good question. I was probably here, but my past as a farmer is all very clear in the lines. I've recently written one about my dad, which goes back to all that, called "It Goes Without Saying". All my childhood memory is clear as a bell.

So you can conjure up those memories and that feel of being back there chasing rabbits wherever you are?

Yeah, 'cause I know what the atmosphere was. Whereas if I'm in a new place, something like "A Thousand Feet" for instance, when I was out at Hermannsburg, it was important that I wrote it on the spot there. 'Cause there was a feeling that I mightn't have been able to take with me, whereas I was a Mallee boy till I was nineteen, so it's not hard to remember everything about it.

In "Galleries of Pink Galahs" did you come up with the opening line, which is the title, first? The alliterative and colourful quality might suggest something sunny, but it's an incredibly sad song.

I wrote that in a motel in Gunnedah. There was a big dead gum tree, completely covered in pink blossoms, all galahs of course. It was like they were all sitting around looking at something, like they were sitting in a gallery. And I went up to Ashford, which is up in the hilly country in the New England, and they were suffering from a drought, the town was dying, all the blinds were down and so I got the lines from that. A huge amount of things influenced "Galleries". Most of the time I'm thinking about the drought that we went through as a family. But there's "Sunburnt country wisely named"; Dorothea Mackellar wrote that in Gunnedah, so that was on my mind at the time, that's where she wrote "The wide brown land" and all that. You never know where an idea is going to come from.

That whole verse struck me the most as pure poetry: "Tortured red gums—unashamed/ Sunburnt country wisely named/ Chisel-ploughed and wire-claimed/ But never, never, never tamed." Do you ever write something like that and look upon it with awe?

Yeah, there are times when you think you're getting help. I don't know whether that's true or it's just that you get better at your craft. But they're all part of things that I've thought about. Like "tortured red gums", that was all part of this inferiority complex that Aussies had about themselves. When the early Poms came over here, the way they described this country was shocking. To them everything looked half dead because it wasn't green, the gum leaves were blue and all the twisted trunks with hollows in them, that was in my mind for years, I've had it in other songs. But the hollows are there for a reason; we've got parrots. The bloody Poms haven't got any parrots because they haven't got any hollow logs. There's all these things that you came to realise what is beautiful about this country, and it's not lush green, that's all boring. Even our native grasses have got a blue tinge to them. Up in the mountains where I've got some land in Queensland it's all kikuyu, the real Aussie colours. I call myself a bluey rather than a greenie, put it that way.

But that was where that line came from: "Tortured red gums—unashamed". In other words it was saying, very proud to be Australian. And the tortured red gums, a lot of people think they're dead, but there's only this much on the outside of any tree alive anyway. The centres of all trees are dead. You can have a dirty great big old gum that's still got his skin wrapped around, and he's still as much alive as the young one growing next to it.

Was "Cootamundra Wattle" a love song for your mother?
No, mainly Mary Kay, my wife. She was the one going through the camphor box. There's both; all songs are complex, your mind's thinking about several things at once. The biggest influence of the song was the smell of the blossom of the wattle that was in our backyard over here. We had a Cootamundra wattle with a huge blossom and that smell immediately took me back to when my mum used to take us out to show us the wildflowers at certain times of the year. Mum's a real gardener and that's where my love of the native bush came from originally. The chorus, where it goes back to my childhood, I think more of my mother there, but the rest of it is about Mary Kay being sad about the kids growing up. And I knew while I was writing that that every mum's going to relate to this one. But of course there's things about if time didn't pass, wounds wouldn't heal. In every relationship, or people who've lost their kids, there's a huge amount of things that people want to forget in their life. So it makes some people cry desperately. Other people it makes them happy. That's probably a sign of a good song when it can mean different things to different people.

When you write a song like that, do you play it to Mary Kay first?
Yeah. Especially a song like that. I'll know straightaway if it's a song she wouldn't want to hear.

How did she respond when you played it the first time? Did she cry?
She loved it, I guess. I don't know. I'm usually the one who cries. A good sentimental song will make me cry first, and then I know I've got something.

You've admitted that you cried when you wrote "Forty Years Ago", where you're lamenting the passing of a time when the world was safer.
It is very much about the fact that we've lost our innocence; in bush towns you have to lock your car now. A woman can't walk down the street without being worried at night. When we were kids, the only reason we came home at night from walking around the streets was 'cause it was teatime. No-one was worried about it. Dad would go to the dance and play the banjo and we'd all sleep in the back of the car. The only reason you'd wind the window up was 'cause of the mozzies. I'm not silly enough not to think that the world is improving, because we're not so ignorant about so many things now and the way pregnant teenagers were treated at that stage was terrible and all this narrow-mindedness was shocking. So I don't always agree exactly with what that song might indicate. It's just that we have lost our innocence. And it's about all these fellas that gave their lives for our freedom and you wonder how much freedom have you really got?

War and diggers feature throughout your work. What is the main connection for you?
I realised that we've got a very young history and we haven't got many heroes. I think the masculinity of the country needs somebody that they can fall back on and think we've got proof that we're brave. Ned Kelly stands up because of that; if nothing else he was brave. And the diggers, of course, that tradition of the diggers and Gallipoli, even though it was a shocking thing, at least it left us with a legacy that we weren't shirkers, and I think that's

very important for our psyche. If we ever had in the future to defend our country well and truly, I'm sure it's the spirit of the ANZAC that would carry us through, just like it does with the Wallabies and the World Cup cricket team and anything else. I don't think it's just about being patriotic. It's about feeling proud of your humanity.

Are there certain songs you've written that bring tears to your eyes when you perform them?
For a while, yeah. There was one called "Old Pancho" about Mary Kay's father. Even though she knew the song, as soon as she came into the audience I cracked up, I could hardly get through it. 'Cause her dad meant so much to her. Same with "Salisbury Street", I found it very hard to get through the song about my brother. And "Wrinkles", that was a big tearjerker. That was about my grandparents. But it's not necessarily that I was sad about my grandparents; I guess it's kind of an acting thing where you get so much into the lyric, you go along with it. And sometimes you've got to back off a bit. Back off from getting too involved.

Most of your songs are emotional, whether they're about love for a woman, your country or the environment. "River Crying Out" is one of your most despairing songs. When you wrote it, did you figure in the piano to underscore the sadness or did the arrangement come later when you recorded it?
I fought hard to get that whole feeling. It's probably not a very commercial song because the subject rubs some people up the wrong way and protest songs came and went. I am desperate for our rivers; I had the Hawkesbury in mind a lot of the time. And I think the melody did have to be a bit discordant and ugly.

You suggested in your latest book that being best known for proud Aussie songs, maybe you should leave pure love songs to other songwriters. Yet you have a significant output of love songs, and they're often about the reality of a man who has lived, loving a woman who has lived. I think the most romantic line you've written in a love song is in "Purple Roses", where you say, "So you wear your clothes more easily for comfort/ You used to be too skinny anyway." That's so real. How could you for a minute think that you should leave writing love songs to more commercial songwriters?
Probably because I've never really had a hit love song. I guess that's what shits me. "Cootamundra Wattle", to me, isn't really a love song. Just pure straight-out love songs. In the old days it was a lot easier for songwriters because they didn't actually have to perform their own songs. If I was an anonymous writer and I wasn't on stage, I would probably be even more honest. I would write some really scary lyrics. But I've got to hold back to a degree, because I'm wearing my heart on my sleeve on stage, and I don't really want my private life that exposed.

Talking about having hits, don't you see your whole career as a hit?
You mean my life as a song? [*Laughs*] When I say a "hit" I suppose it all comes back to the entertainer thing. One of my strongest love songs is "You and My Guitar" because it's a love

song with rhythm so it has all those elements that make it work for a show. "The Boomerang Cafe" works well for me. I've heard some women don't like "Purple Roses" because it's too confronting, so that's one reason I hardly ever do it. There are some very true lines there, about looking in the mirror; I think we all look in the mirror at times and see our father or mother and think, oh God! But you don't see yourself as other people see you.

There's also the knack you have for putting the romantic and the ordinary side by side, such as in "The Boomerang Cafe", in the line "With lipstick on your lips and vinegar on your chips." Do you think commercial love songwriters miss the romance that exists in the ordinary?
That's just honesty. I see people like Sting, for instance, who are so careful to be beautifully poetic all the time. I'm prepared to write of very ordinary things because that's real life. Life isn't always poetic. Life is everyday, and I don't worry about what people might think about lines. You can be too polished. Romance really isn't about floating on the moon. The things that I remember about, say, the first time I sat with a girl in a romantic way was probably in the Boomerang Cafe, where your legs are touching, just that incredible sexy feeling of the two legs touching. How do you put that in a song? I should.

On the other side there is your comedy writing. Do songs like "The Budgie Song" come from your own day-to-day experiences or stories people tell you?
Our youngest daughter had a little blue budgie called Blue Bum. And it dropped dead on us one day, so I bought another one, and the second one wouldn't talk. She said, "Blue Bum doesn't talk any more." She didn't realise it was a different budgie. So I felt really sad about that. But it was the money we spent trying to fix the damn budgie in the first place, and we did go through all that, putting that stuff on it. It's just a tongue-in-cheek thing really.

I love how the budgie got his very early on in "Bill the Cat."
Well, that's a protest song for the cat.

After hearing "Bill the Cat" and "The Vasectomy Song", I am of a mind that nothing is really taboo with you in songwriting. You've said, "There is nothing like a funny song to make people listen to a serious message." What other songs are funny that came from a serious issue?
"I'm Fair Dinkum" was just a rollicking kind of a folk song and then one night, I must have been feeling pretty jolly, I started putting on all these silly accents, and I realised, oh, it's about all the different nationalities that have come to this country. I mean, no-one apart from the Aborigines can say they are from here. So there was a message there really, and I'm sure the Indians and the Poms and all the accents I put on didn't mind at all. That's an example off the top of my head of a serious message—that everybody's welcome. In a way "Crocodile Roll", even though there was a pang of guilt about that because obviously there was a family that suffered by it. People have suffered from crocodiles, but I was annoyed that they were always blaming the crocodiles, wiping out

crocodiles, when all these signs are about. People are stupid; crocodiles shouldn't suffer for their stupidity.

Are there any subjects that you haven't been able to write about?
I haven't written much about the ocean, because I'm a bit of a land lover. People often say, "When are you going to write songs about fishing?" I haven't written a song about fishing. Anything I write about, I do get a certain amount from the horse's mouth. So it's a matter of experiencing things. I'm not mad keen about going out in the ocean, anyway. It doesn't thrill me at all.

I haven't written about the nuclear thing because I find that all a bit hard. I sweep it under the carpet and leave it to Peter Garrett. I figure if you feel strongly about something it's almost your duty to speak up because everybody can't feel strongly about everything. So if you're into the nature of the country —and I know a lot of people don't have it in their heart like I do, it doesn't get to them like me—when I'm walking in any pristine bush, whether it was out in the Mallee or the Mulga or Gidgee or rainforests, I don't care what it is, there's something spiritual about it. It just grabs me. This is what it's been like before even Aborigines were here. And it's all uniquely belonging to this country; everything you see is worth a hundred bloody Sydney Harbour Bridges as far as I'm concerned. But I'm probably part of only a small percentage that really feel that strongly about it, so it's my duty to put how I feel across, and it might make other people appreciate what's there that don't see it themselves.

When "This Ancient Land" was a success a few years ago, you said you'd long felt Aboriginal in your love for the land, even though you would never be arrogant enough to say you could possibly understand what it is truly like to be an Aborigine. Was "Raining on the Rock" inspired by the handing back of Uluru?
No, it was inspired by going out to Uluru more than anything. Actually, my new song, "Keeper of the Stones", is by far my strongest statement on that issue. Because Warren H Williams has recently been given the stones. He can't tell me how old they are, I don't think anyone can, but there's seven stones and each one of them has got traditions and messages and secrets about them. They've been handed down for God knows how many thousands of years. Warren has been a petrol sniffer and an alcoholic, and he would have gone through all those things of lacking identity. Because even though they do occupy their land now, there was a time when of course they were all brought into the mission, so his family would have been dispossessed. 'Cause the agriculturists moved into that area. But now they've got it back again. "You take me from the land, you leave me with no soul." The whole song is about how he's come out of that now. My dream is that thousands more Aborigines will come out of that whole thing and become proud of themselves. I can see over the years that I've known him how he's coming more and more out of himself. And I've encouraged him not just to try to write a good country song, but to write about his country. He's finding now, as soon as he does, they love him all over the land.

Do you keep a notebook or are place names, plants and trees, birds, animals and people crammed in your mind at all times?
No, I don't keep a notebook. I was a 100 per cent bushie for a long time so there's a lot of things there that have been ingrained. When I'm in an area it's amazing how a lot of locals don't even know the names of their own trees; they think, "Oh, it's just a bloody gum tree." Well, it's not a gum tree, mate. So I do go out of my way to find out the names of local things. I like to describe. Generally, if you hear a song of mine, if you know Australia, you'll know where I'm talking about just by the landscape I'm describing.

If you're not in a position to write a song on the spot, how do you remember?
I usually write on the back of my itinerary. I'm good at recycling paper. By the end of a tour, the other side of the itinerary has been written on completely.

At least you know when you wrote the song, as well. Or when the idea came to you.
When I first write, I actually date the first scraps of paper and put them in a drawer. I think one day someone might want to work out how I wrote or what the initial things were and how I changed things around.

Do you ever have writer's block?
No. I actually purposely stop myself writing songs, so I write better ones and be a bit fresh. I can write a lot of crap. But I don't have writer's block. I could sit down right now and write a song if I wanted to. Just about talking to you, or something. It's just the way I am. It's never easy to write a good song but it's not hard to write a song.

GLENN SHORROCK

SYDNEY, AUSTRALIA, MAY 2003

"I've always been a sailor in my psyche, in my own imagination," said Glenn Shorrock, sitting in the dining room of his home on the edge of Sydney Harbour. He is never far from water—he loves to sail and scuba dive—and it seems appropriate for someone for whom fluidity is so essential. He doesn't want to be stuck. If a song isn't working out, he would drop it altogether and do something else rather than persevere. In the best of life's ironies, he ended up having his greatest successes with a band whose other key members were perfectionists. But the band's name, Little River Band, had the water reference. Which could be a reason why he kept returning to it.

Glenn Shorrock was born in Chatham, England, on 30 June 1944 and landed in South Australia in the 1950s as part of the assisted passage migrant scheme, which brought many soon-to-be-successful musicians by boat to the Antipodes, and particularly to Elizabeth, the planned "City of Tomorrow" outside Adelaide. By his mid-teens he was singing along with a group of friends who called themselves The Checkmates. They went on to become The

Twilights, one of the country's biggest pop groups of the mid-1960s, a force in young Australian music alongside The Easybeats, Billy Thorpe and the Aztecs, and The Groop. Shorrock's distinctive lead vocal led The Twilights and his next group, Axiom, to major success in Australia, but each attempt to break into the overseas market—always by way of the home country, England—was a failure.

It wasn't until Shorrock found himself without a group that he began seriously writing songs, staying in London for several years in the early 1970s, "finding himself". He spent a formative period with Esperanto, an experimental rock orchestra comprised of people of various nationalities who recorded some of his early compositions such as "Statue of Liberty" and "Emma". By the time he returned to Australia and the newly formed Little River Band in 1975, he was ready for a creatively equitable scenario where his input was valued along with the other writers in the band.

However, it wasn't such smooth sailing. Little River Band was the first Australian musical act to break into the mainstream North American market in a sustainable way, and that breakthrough was triggered by the Shorrock-penned hit single "Help Is on Its Way". But musical and personality differences countered the phenomenal international success, and for most of his time with the band, Shorrock was looking for help in every corner. Songwriting provided an outlet for his frustrations, and gave the band some of its greatest melodies, but ultimately he and Little River Band were destined to part. And reunite. And part again. And reunite again, more lately under the moniker of Birtles Shorrock Goble.

Shorrock is both a comic and a romantic, bluntly honest and laconic at the best of times. "Glenn's not a person of many words," said his band mate and former nemesis Graeham Goble, who admitted it took twenty-seven years to get comfortable around him. Shorrock's songs are almost all personal, or at least from personal experience, and being that he will often take the path of least resistance, that could account for his lesser songwriting output than his contemporaries. That and the fact that he enjoys vacationing and relaxing at home with his wife, Jo. He has contributed to the music industry in many ways behind the scenes, including establishing a scholarship for new talent in his name, and still performs regularly. He loves to sing, and is driven by a desire to entertain, regardless of whose songs he's singing. Some would argue that one song like "Cool Change" surpasses twenty songs by a lesser writer. But one gets the sense that Shorrock would like to write one or two more truly memorable songs some day.

You were one of the many immigrant families who settled in Elizabeth. Do you think something was in the water there that nurtured all that musical talent?
There isn't much water in Elizabeth, unfortunately. There's something in the dust. But pro rata I guess it did pretty well. The earliest recollection of a musician I had was Doug Ashdown, who lived in Elizabeth. And the Tarney brothers—Alan and Frank. We met them because we started singing—The Twilights—and we obviously got the ear of some local musicians. When I say musicians, we were all sixteen, seventeen, younger some of us. So we weren't really musicians. We were just kids who were fans who copied our heroes, in whatever fashion we could.

But I didn't really notice much about songwriting to begin with. I just noticed the songs. And then when I bought the records, because I was a fan, I'd read everything that was on the label and eventually you'd look at the credits of these names underneath and then realise, oh, they're the ones that wrote it.

When you were starting in The Twilights and sounding every bit like Australia's Beatles, did you have any thoughts about wanting to write the songs yourself or was it all about the performance and the style?
Well, that's significant, because it wasn't until the Beatles came along that we really took any notice of songwriting at all. We just wanted to do the songs. The first time I noticed it was The Everly Brothers, it said "Phil and Don Everly" underneath and I realised, "Oh, they wrote those songs." And Buddy Holly. But it didn't matter that much until the Beatles came along, and that was a big part of what they were, their whole persona was the fact that they wrote their own material and recorded it but were a group as well. It appealed to your democratic sense in a way. It was all home grown, a little cottage industry. And that appealed to the guys that I was knocking around with, because we were close friends. "Hey, you know, we can do this as well. Let's start writing some songs as well." This is once the transition had been made from Snotty and the Nosepickers or Tirk, Thrust and the Y-Fronts. They were all silly names that we used to call ourselves.

How much in the early Twilights days were you sitting down and writing songs?
I was the first one to write, actually. I wrote our first record. Which was recorded and released locally through EMI. "I Don't Know Where the Wind Will Blow Me." And it had my name underneath it. But I didn't suddenly see myself as a songwriter. I just thought, oh well, I've written a song.

Was that the first song you wrote?
Yep. I can't remember how I wrote it, because I couldn't play anything. Well, I could play piano, and I can't remember if I did plunk it out on a piano. But I think I just went— [*Sings*] "Da da da da da di di di doo", that sort of thing—and one of the guys in the band helped me with it. But we didn't know anything about crediting each other in those days. They just thought, "Well, you thought of it, it's your words, it's your song." And then Terry Britten started writing and Peter Brideoake started writing and I wrote a couple more tunes with Peter. But Terry was obviously the more talented one and we thought, oh bugger it, we'll just sing his songs. Plus of course we were totally obsessed by the Beatles and we'd rather sing a Lennon and McCartney song than write our own.

Did you have piano lessons?
Briefly, nothing serious. Nine months of plunking away. I didn't like it because I wanted to go out and boogie. It wasn't called boogie in those days. Be a bodgie.

Having moved from England and grown up in an English enclave in Australia, what was so important about getting back to England to work musically?
We didn't want to get back to England at all. We just wanted to be like an English beat band and do it from Australia. We didn't think much of Australian talent at that time. The snotty little nosepickers that we were. We liked American music first; it was Elvis and Little Richard and the Everlys. Exactly the same as John Lennon and Paul McCartney and everybody else. They were the songs that they really loved, that was rock 'n' roll. We didn't like Johnny O'Keefe. We thought he was an impostor. Col Joye, very nice, but didn't really get you up and dancing.

Were you frustrated that you were recording other people's songs, whether it was your bandmates' songs or songs from overseas writers? Terry was obviously moving forward and having hits.
I felt he was a much better songwriter than anything I could do, and also I was restricted because I didn't play an instrument. He had much more ammunition than I had. He could play bar chords and he could change key and do all that sort of stuff.

Being quite a witty, conversant man, though, did you find yourself coming up with lyrical ideas?
Not really, because as I say I handed the cap over quickly to Terry and just got on with the business of promoting the group, of being the frontman. I thought Terry was terrific. I still do. It's just a pity he left Australia. Had he stayed in Australia I think he would have been a real force in Australian songwriting. But of course he wouldn't have probably won Grammys and written for Cliff and Tina and Lenny Kravitz. Swings and roundabouts. I was a real fan of Terry as a musician.

So songwriting wasn't compelling to you back then?
No. "I need something to come out of myself. I need some release. I have to get this out!" No, I never felt like that. The only thing I did feel was that I'd think up a catchy phrase or something and I'd think, "That sounds like a song." And I'd sometimes follow it and sometimes I'd forget it. I had no technique whatsoever. I didn't even have a notebook. I'd just write a story in my head. But I wasn't thinking about writing songs. I was thinking about making whichever band I was in better and enjoying myself. When The Twilights split up and I was left on my own, then I fell in with Brian Cadd and Don Mudie and they played me their material and that really gave me another avenue into how important good songs were. Because they'd already written and had hits with "Woman You're Breaking Me" and "Such a Lovely Way", both records I liked a lot. And it wasn't until Axiom split up that I started to write songs seriously. That I felt I needed to do this as well if I wanted to really get the best out of myself.

What did you admire about Brian and Don's writing? Were you conscious that songs like "Arkansas Grass" and "Little Ray of Sunshine" were destined to be standards?
I never thought "Little Ray of Sunshine" would be a standard. I thought that was just a silly,

sentimental, soppy little song that would come and go. I didn't think it would stay around. But "Arkansas Grass" was right down the pocket of what we were into. Brian, myself, Don and Chris Stockley and Doug Lavery. We loved The Band. The Band were the hot thing. And we wanted to get that sort of feeling but with an Australian connection. "Arkansas Grass" was not it, of course, because it was totally American. But an album we did called *Fool's Gold* had a lot of Australiana in it, and they really tried to incorporate Australiana the way The Band incorporated Americana into their material, so it became very viable, believable. Then we went to England and it all fell over. But I'd already started to write then. When I got to England I started to write. Because there was a piano there and I'd plunk away.

I saw *Planet of the Apes* and that last scene where it's realised by Charlton Heston [that he has been on planet Earth the whole time], that was very powerful to me. And went along with my love of Armageddon-type science-fiction movies, the warning movies. I've always liked those and still do, because I think we can draw a lot of parallels from them and learn a lot. So "Statue of Liberty" was basically using that emotion. I came out of the theatre going, "Wow, what a great idea, what a concept!" [*Sings*] "Statue of Liberty sinking in the harbour ... da da da da ... try a little harder." I couldn't quite remember the verse that is on the bottom of the Statue of Liberty. So I just paraphrased it. I was too lazy to go and research it anyway, so I just made it up myself. It sounded something like "Give me your hungry, give me your tired. Give me your homeless, give me your wanderers." But really it's "Give me your tired, your poor, your huddled masses."

It was also a reflection of what was happening with Vietnam and Nixon. Especially being in England at the time, Nixon was pilloried from hell to high water. He was a very unlikeable man. And being the armchair philosopher that I am, I waggled my finger through writing "Statue of Liberty". It's really weird; subsequently, everything that comes up about "Statue of Liberty" is "Oh, it was a great American song!" Sometimes they don't listen to what it's all about. "Oh, but now it's crumbling, shaking, quaking, trembling on its own foundation." That's the way it looked to me living in England, on the newsreels. But as I say, inspired by that last scene in *Planet of the Apes*. It worked out well, too. It was a really rocky sort of thing, and the people I was hanging around with liked it. Axiom had been and gone, they'd left.

Do you think Axiom would have lasted longer if you'd gone to America rather than to England?
Oh, absolutely. But none of us thought about America. We thought that was unreachable, that was just a utopia that we couldn't exist in. We thought England was a lot more user-friendly to us. A lot of us had British passports, which helped.

Did you recognise an interesting irony that the English immigrant whose first band styled itself musically and visually on the Beatles and the whole British pop scene ended up writing a series of songs infused with the spirit of the American West? Writing "Gunslinger" and "Man in Black", sitting there in cold, bleak England.
I grew up with cowboy movies as well.

And that was all around the time the Eagles were writing and recording *Desperado* in London.
Yeah, with Glyn Johns. That was strange as well.

Don Henley and Glenn Frey had the concept of rock 'n' roll musicians as outlaws, and that's where you were coming from, certainly with "Gunslinger".
It's not hard for a young rock 'n' roll musician in the seventies to feel like a desperado. It's quite easy to relate to that. But it wasn't just the Eagles. We'd already discovered Stephen Stills and David Crosby and Jackson Browne. There was always a strong country influence anyway.

You hadn't actually been to America at that stage, had you?
No, but you still felt part of it in a way. The Joni Mitchells, James Taylors. By now it was totally song-related, song-driven. It had to be in the song. It didn't matter if it was a country style song or a jazz-type song à la "Chicago", or whatever. It just had to be a really good song.

Why did writing become a deeply personal experience for you, that you did now need this outlet?
I was left by myself. My band had split up, my wife of four years, we'd split up, and I found myself a desperado, an outlaw.

Why did you stay in the UK?
Oh, I enjoyed it. I liked that feeling.

The misery?
No, I got to like the freedom, the independent feeling. I didn't really think about it too much at the time. I was too busy missing everybody. But gradually I got stronger from it, emotionally and everything else. 'Cause I really relied a lot on what was around me all the time, through The Twilights, through Axiom and through my marriage. And there was that four- or five-year period where I was not so much on my own but I was certainly going home every night to my upstairs garret, dressed in denims and with an acoustic guitar.

So you did start writing with a guitar at this point.
Yeah, I plunked away there. But I bought a piano. 'Cause I'd had that little bit of grounding on a piano anyway. And because I've got a good ear, I can pick things out. So I didn't feel I needed to become a better musician. I'd just make it work for me in a simple fashion. I still do. Most of my best songs are simple songs.

Would the melody come to you, or was it the idea, the concept?
Well, for instance, "Sanity's Side" is a song that was from that period, when I thought I was going nuts. Up in the middle of the night, with that independence that I now had. If I wanted to stay up all night I would, and I'd sleep all day.

Was it the lyric that would first come to you, then?

Mainly it was a lyric. And then I would go to the piano and I would sing that. That still happens now, I still join together. I have a collection of melodies or chord progressions or feels, and then I have a collection of lyrical ideas. And I'll take one and see, will that fit with that?

Were you working with structure a lot back then? Or were you more flexible with yourself and just let it flow?

The first verse, chorus, verse, second chorus was a way of writing songs, with a bridge in the middle to link it. I didn't restrict myself to that. "Help Is on Its Way" was a product of two separate songs played together. "Hang on"—that change there—that's a whole different idea to the first part. They weren't meant to be together.

Was "Help Is on Its Way" written during that London period, too?

Yes. All the songs of those early albums of LRB were written in London. Probably two or three years before I got to do them with LRB. "Statue of Liberty" and "Emma" were first recorded by Esperanto. That was another learning curve for me as well, being in that band for a year and a half. Being mixed up with some very clever trained musicians from a classical background. That was a bit of an eye opener. I found out I could be a force in that group as a songwriter, as a creative person, bringing something to the table. 'Cause they were looking for a commercial edge anyway. So I was pleased to provide it.

[*Shows a CD of demos written in the London period.*] See look, here's "Hang On"— that's "Help Is on Its Way". And there's "Emma". There's "Gunslinger". These are with Terry Britten, Kevin Peek, Alan Tarney and Trevor Spencer. Also known as Quartet. They were my friends and I used to attend their recording sessions and they would play on my demos for me. "Seine City", "Statue of Liberty". These are the songs I came to Beeb and Graeham with.

When you wrote those early songs, did you hear them laden with harmonies? When Beeb Birtles and Graeham Goble approached you to join them in what would become Little River Band, did you instantly hear their voices on your songs?

I wanted to work with them 'cause they could do harmonies properly. That demo was Terry and myself; that was a Twilights sound in a way. But you put Beeb there and it was the same thing. And then you add a third part to that, which is where Graeham comes in. Graeham always likes to sing above everything else, he likes to sing in that strong falsetto voice of his. Normally, I would put his part underneath, I would make it a lower part. That gives it a much more mellow sound, à la Glenn Shorrock "Seine City". I sang all the harmonies on that, that's why it's got that warmer sound to it.

Did you go to Paris and write it there or were you thinking about wanting to go to Paris?

Well, I went to Paris 'cause I wrote about being there.

People can write about being somewhere when they're not there.
No, most of my songs are from personal experience, definitely.

Was that just a weekend sojourn?
Yeah, over a couple of weekends. She wasn't that interested in me. Or maybe it was vice versa. She was on a career path of her own, an up-and-coming young model. And I lived in London; I couldn't really have a relationship with a girl that lived in Paris.

What were some of the songs that Beeb and Graeham played for you that convinced you that you wanted to join forces with them?
I'd already heard "Will I" and there was "Early Morning" and "Kings of the World". And then they played me "It's a Long Way There" and I liked the feel of that, that was just Graeham really. And "My Lady and Me", those sort of things.

It took some time for these songs to turn up on albums. "Sanity's Side" didn't happen until the fourth LRB album. Was being a prolific songwriter as important to you as it obviously was to Graeham?
No. It still isn't. It's not my driving force. I don't wake up in the morning and start working on songs. Graeham does. I'm not motivated that way, never have been.

But there were a lot of songs on those London demos. Were you attached to your songs and wanted to get them recorded?
I felt the others were attached to their songs more than I was to mine. I still do, I still think that you shouldn't hang on to them. You've got to let them go, like children. But then there's the other philosophy that Graeham puts forward, that every song has its time and you should represent it. Whereas I'm the one who says, "If you didn't like it then, you're not going to like it now." I didn't really have a lot of trouble myself, only because I didn't want to behave that way. And they lobbied hard. Graeham especially lobbied really hard. I didn't think that was kosher. I come from a different thing—if you don't like it, you don't like it. I'm not going to browbeat you, I'm not going to make you like it. And that's why I resent some of the songs I've had to sing of Graeham's and Beeb's. 'Cause I was browbeaten into it. And the trade-off was, "Well, if you don't do that, we're not going to do one of yours." Very political. The only one that really disappointed me was "Cool Change". They didn't want to do that. Beeb and Graeham did not want to sing that song because they felt it was too personal. They thought it was about me and not about them.

Graeham said he kept pushing for "Reminiscing" and no-one wanted that song.
I don't believe that. I liked it when I heard it. He says that he pushed hard for it, but I never felt that was the case. I mean, sure, it was a little bit off the wall. It talked about Glen Miller and stuff like that. But I thought it was terrific. I think there were some other songs that he really went to town on. A song I remember, "Light of Day", was on one album

and I just can't play it any more, it's got terrible memories for me. It was too hard to do. I had to sing it for them 150 times before they were happy with what I did. And that ain't my way of doing things.

Some of your early songs, like "Meanwhile ...", "Seine City" and "Sweet Old Fashioned Man" didn't seem geared towards commercial single releases.
Yeah, they were warm, toasty fireside songs.

At what point did you put the two songs together to make "Help Is on Its Way"? It didn't show up until _Diamantina Cocktail_, the third album.
I don't remember the other one, the "Why are you in so much hurry" one ... it's lost. But I think I pieced the two parts together while I was still in England. I don't know why it didn't get on the first album.

It's definitely a more commercial sounding song.
Yeah, well, we turned it into one, didn't we? I thought "Emma" was a commercial song, a radio kind of song. I thought "Statue of Liberty" had a commerciality to it, too. I thought "Man in Black" did. But no, "Seine City" and "Sweet Old Fashioned Man" were real personal things and were approached as such. That was my Stephen Stills part of the Birtles Shorrock Goble thing.

What was the inspiration behind "Sweet Old Fashioned Man"?
I was just feeling comfortable with a relationship again, once Jo and I got together. That was during the first album with LRB. A lot of those early songs went onto the first two or three or four albums that we had, and gradually you could hear the B and C songs coming in. Like "Sanity's Side" for myself; I didn't put that up as a number A song. I put that up for the fourth album. I knew it wasn't as good as some of the others, I was much more interested in pushing my other songs first.

Did you actually write "Home on Monday" in Las Vegas?
I started it in Vegas, yeah. I was calling Jo and we were both a bit tetchy on the phone, and basically I said, "Well, hang on, I'll be home on a Monday, somewhere around noon, I don't quite know when." And David Briggs was lying on the bed, and he said, "That sounds like a song." I said, "Does it, David?" So we started writing it out. I think I have the original lyrics somewhere. "Can you guess where I'm calling from? The Las Vegas Hilton. I know it's hard to hear, it's just the echo on the line." That was definitely verbatim. But it didn't really come into shape until later. When we did get home, Beeb and I went up to Healesville, his girlfriend Megan had a place up there, Ron Tudor's daughter, and we finished it off up there, we wrote the middle-eight. [_Sings_] "You looked so lovely when I left I nearly didn't go/ 12,000 miles is such a long way, help me get to grips with Hollywood/ you're getting through to me ..." It's basically Beeb's melody and my lyric.

It was on *Diamantina Cocktail* and had to have been written before Elvis Presley's death, so what was your original meaning of the line about the man from Memphis having gone, "never leaving a trace"?
He'd been there forty-eight hours before. He'd just finished his season at the Hilton and I was annoyed that I'd missed it by that much. I'd been out on the road with a rock 'n' roll band. I missed it by two days. It was just the way the itinerary ran. And I was looking for some trace of him. Some poster, or something, but everything had gone, replacing it with Little River Band. Which was boring. I wanted to see some trace of Elvis.

To this day I can't go to LA without singing to myself, "All the palm trees on the skyline/ have a good day have a good time." Was "LA in the Sunshine" instigated by you or by David Briggs?
David. I just helped him with it. We were smoking a lot of marijuana at the time.

What were your feelings about LA and the California experience at that stage, before the band had actually broken big over there?
We hardly went to LA in those early days. We stayed out in the provinces, in the colleges. We were still just an under-bubbling band in a way and we hadn't really made it in those big markets. But after "Help Is on Its Way" crashed through the AM barrier from the FM and became a big wide hit, then LA became a lot more appealing. We spent a lot more time there and the record company feted us because they realised that we were big time now, we weren't just a college band. We were mainstream.

Was there any influence coming to you from the exposure you then had to the major rock acts of the day, touring with the mega bands like Eagles, Fleetwood Mac, the Doobie Brothers et al?
They'd already influenced; I'd already noticed what they'd done and liked most of it. Still do. But I've never gone away and said, "Oh, I've got to write something like that!" I can't. I'm not good enough. I can only write to my own naivety in a way and I like that. I don't want to become a major "composer".

You weren't doing a lot of collaborating back then. When you did co-write with a band member, was it a pleasurable experience?
Yep, I didn't have any problems. Mostly somebody had got something almost finished and you would help out.

Did you and Graeham ever entertain the idea of writing something together?
I don't think so. I think Graeham was quite happy going along by himself.

He wrote with Beeb but not with you.
Socially, we didn't get on. We didn't mix. We'd just turn up for the sessions and the rehearsals and did what we had to do together and got on with it. But I wouldn't call Graeham and say, "Hey, let's go out to dinner".

And you need to have that kind of rapport with somebody in order to write together?
Oh, yeah. I use the old line I've used about Cadd. I like working with him 'cause we think at the same speed.

Which of Graeham's songs did or do you like?
"Reminiscing" obviously, I really love it a lot. And "Mistress of Mine" is a wonderful song.

He said he felt that was your best vocal.
Well, it was probably his best song. You know, a song is only as good as your singer and your singer is only as good as your song. "Long Way There" is a great piece.

Did you really hate "Lady"?
[*Laughs*] No, I didn't hate it. I just felt it was a bit of schmaltz, that's all.

Why do you think it was such a big hit in America?
Because most of them are klutzes anyway. [*Laughs*] There are naive people over there. But it works. I used to enjoy its reaction more than anything. 'Cause people loved it so much.

"Cool Change" seemed to be a kind of follow-up to "Sanity's Side", something even more introspective and longing.
Oh, yeah, it was certainly a cry for help.

Were you sailing when the idea came to you?
I've always been a sailor in my psyche, in my own imagination, even before I got on a boat. I was ten years old when I came on a boat to Australia; that changed my whole life and made me realise how big and wonderful this planet was. I had no real grasp of it, growing up as a geography student looking at the maps, until I spent six weeks on a boat. That wasn't sailing as such, but it was still a similar feeling to me.

I saw "Cool Change" about the image of the solitary man on the boat. Were you on a yacht when it came to you?
No, I was reflecting on my love of the white sand-blue water philosophy, lifestyle. I've always loved that. I just translated it into a metaphor for a release from the pressures of LRB. I wrote it about 1977–78 and then it got recorded in 1979 on *First under the Wire*. By that stage I had three or four years under my belt of hard work and touring and politicking and compromising and all the other things. I was a bit older than everybody else and I'd had the group experience several times before.

What is the story behind "The Rumour"?
I was just saying, beware of gossip, beware of rumour; sometimes it can become larger than it should be. It's one of those songs that I'd done and forgotten about. In fact, that came on the radio while I was driving to work one day when I was doing the *One for the Money* show

in Perth, and by then noises had been made about me rejoining LRB. I was driving along thinking, "Well, what if I did rejoin them? Should we try and recapture the songs or should we try and do something new?" And this song came on the radio and I said, "This sounds like what we should be doing!" And it was "The Rumour". Which I'd never heard on radio. I was really embarrassed, I thought, "Shit, I don't even know my own songs!" But I couldn't even sing it to you right now. I just don't know it.

Graeham said he had a bad reaction to that song; he didn't like what it was saying.
Yeah, well I sang a lot of Graeham's lyrics that I didn't really feel comfortable with. À la "Lady" and "Fall from Paradise". Quasi sort of religious things. But then I was doing the same thing with "So Many Paths". That was a bit of Shorrock preaching. That was actually a quote from a guru: "There are so many paths up the mountain, but the view from the top is the same."

Who was the guru?
One of the Indian ones. Sitting Bull, I think it was.

Was "Long Jumping Jeweller" a deliberate move to get back to a more Australian subject matter?
Not deliberate. I just enjoyed the story. I liked the message behind the song. "Everybody can't be heroes but some can still try to make their lives a little different, it's the time that goes by." I just like the story. I got in a bit of trouble because the people that wrote that said I was plagiarising their story. It was a short story in a high-school English curriculum book evidently from the sixties. And the story was told to me by Rhonda Schepisi, Fred Schepisi's wife. I think someone made a short film out of it as well. I just got sucked in a bit and started thinking about it and the [*Sings*] "Long jumping jeweller of Lavender Bay", it just scanned. It's an off the wall kind of idea anyway, which appealed to me.

Were the songs on *Villain of the Peace* written specifically for that album or were they songs you had lying around that had never made it onto LRB albums?
Some were, some weren't. "Rock 'n' Roll Soldier" was definitely part of the plan to record a solo album.

And you very much felt like a "Rock 'n' Roll Soldier" by that stage.
Yes. But I didn't try to make it specifically about me, I tried to dedicate it to all the people and especially I did dedicate it to a roadie colleague who subsequently committed suicide after having injured himself on one of our tours. And that was an inspiration to use it as a lead-off track. But it's a bit about me, a bit about everybody. Colleagues.

"Will You Stand with Me" was definitely written for that album. One of the only songs that I've written wham bam thank you ma'am in a long session. Most of them I come back to and come back to. I don't really spend months refining songs like Graeham would do, but sometimes they take a good couple of weeks to get them right. And then of course you get them to the band and that changes a few things as well. But basically I know what I want with them. "Cry in a Jungle Bar" was inspired by a novel by Robert Drewe. It's nothing really to do with his book, I just had this vision of stumbling through the jungle in the future on a safari and hearing this familiar voice and familiar sound and parting the trees and there's a jungle bar ... And Cadd's in there playing.

I didn't really think about what my solo album should be. I just thought I'd put it out and it'd do okay. I should have taken a year off before the album. I might have written more decent songs than I had there. But I didn't. There wasn't a "Help Is on It's Way" on there or a "Cool Change". And there should have been. I felt the ones that were there were good enough. And that's not good enough.

When you came back to LRB with "Soul Searching", it sounded like the third in the trilogy following "Sanity's Side" and "Cool Change".
Oh, yeah. Sure. I wrote that with Peter Beckett at his house in the canyons in LA. I'd gone over there at the encouragement of Paul Palmer to do a writing sojourn. Paul Palmer managed Player; Peter Beckett and Ron Moss and Crowley were all in Player. Peter and I got on well and we wrote it together, but it was mainly my spirit.

Being that "Sanity's Side" and "Cool Change" were written on your own, and "Soul Searching" was written with someone else who hadn't been through the wars with you, how did you manage to retain that personal edge?
I just insisted that we use all my lyric. [*Laughs*] But that thought is with me all the time. It manifests itself often. It's called style. It's an important motivation and catalyst for me, for getting my juices going. Anger and frustration. I haven't written many happy songs. I didn't write "Happy anniversary baby".

That wasn't a happy song. Haven't you heard Beeb's lyrics?
[*Laughs*] But everybody thinks it is.

It's a miserable song.
It's a cynical song. He's saying, "I'm so happy for you baby—NOT." I think it's bitchy.

After the *Monsoon* album, you contributed very little to the remaining LRB albums writing-wise. Was it because all the old tensions were still there between you and Graeham or because you were no longer inspired?
I think a bit of both. It was certainly clear that we weren't going to regain the glory that we had before. I didn't feel that the songs were near as good as what we used to do. 'Cause we had that purple patch of A grade songs that lasted us into five albums, and then after that the standard of writing decreased. I'm as much to blame for that as anybody else, but I kind of stopped writing. Well, I didn't stop writing, but I didn't accelerate or try to do better. Graeham's always trying to do better but I think he struggled through those years as well. And I've heard such good things that he's written

and they're very Graeham. This new batch of stuff that he's working on now is just classic LRB material.

What made you and Brian Cadd decide to actually sit and write several songs together?
We wrote about nine or ten songs. It was all part of my setting up a home in Fiji in that idyllic "Cool Change" atmosphere. I always thought it would be an inspiring place to write something. We wrote the whole *Blazing Salads* thing in Fiji. We certainly made the foundation there. Then we came back here and refined it and then we went to his place in Nashville. You're always tweaking things, especially with Brian. When you've got somebody else that you can bounce off, and you're actually doing it at his house, you never really stop the creative process. The thing about Brian is that you can suggest something and he's with you right away. That's what I mean about "think at the same speed".

Are you writing now?
I'm writing. I've got a whole potpourri of crap and ideas and moods, and a couple of songs that are almost finished. I go through bursts. I go in there and I spend two or three weeks, but by and large the real nuts and bolts is done at the piano just tinkling away as I used to do thirty years ago. And as I probably will do all my life. The new gizmos are fun to go up those paths that you couldn't go up before because you couldn't make the noises that you wanted to make. Now you can make the noises by just being a klutz on the piano, you can become an orchestra all of a sudden. That takes you off in a whole other direction.

What inspires you to go in there and have a play around?
Just to find out what's going to happen today. But I have to be in the right frame of mind, otherwise I'll pick up a book or go and see a movie or something. And also right now we're trying to get this new incarnation of our music, Birtles Shorrock Goble, up and running, and that's proving very difficult. That's pushing shit up hill. But we're all waist-deep in it now so we're going to follow it through, and if the water gets any higher it'll drown us or it'll float us again.

Sounds like a good start to a song.
Doesn't it?

GRAEHAM GOBLE

MELBOURNE, AUSTRALIA, DECEMBER 2000

It's all in the spelling. At the age of fifty-three, the previously named Graham decided that the addition of an unusually positioned letter "e" was numerologically more advantageous. He tried Grahame briefly, but then opted for the more unusual Graeham. The change was part of a new approach to his life—he was consulting a feng shui expert on the layout of his new house and studio—but it also coincided with a flurry of media coverage when his song "Reminiscing" notched up over four million airplays in the United States, earning him a coveted BMI Four Million-Air award in early 2001. To play the song that many times back-to-back would take over twenty-one years. There was much confusion among reporters over just how Goble did spell his first name, but he was resolute.

This meticulous and pedantic temperament characterised Goble during his long tenure with Little River Band and, by his own admission, often drove his bandmates—particularly Glenn Shorrock—crazy. As with many other international bands renowned for sumptuous harmonies (think Eagles, Crosby Stills Nash & Young), behind the scenes there was internal disharmony. Goble knew his analytical nature was less than endearing, but he believes that his tenacity helped LRB to succeed on such a huge scale—the first Australian group to consistently hit the high spots on the US charts. "I'm very clear on the fact that I ended up being resented by virtually everybody in the band," he said. "But if I wasn't there, it wouldn't have happened."

Nevertheless, Goble's memories of his time with the band are mostly fond and his views on his bandmates reverent, if opinionated. None of the negative views Goble, Birtles or Shorrock had previously held of each other was evident when, in 2002, the three decided to perform and record together again, and this interview, it should be noted, was conducted months before such a reunion was even contemplated.

Graeham Goble was born in Adelaide on 15 May 1947, and eventually moved to Melbourne. His first major band was Mississippi, and his composition, "Kings of the World", their biggest hit. Mississippi ended and Little River Band began almost simultaneously in 1975, with a song Goble had written back in 1972, "It's a Long Way There", opening LRB's eponymous debut album.

From there through a string of albums in the 1970s—*After Hours*, *Diamantina Cocktail*, *Sleeper Catcher*, *First under the Wire*—Goble shared the songwriting duties with Shorrock, Birtles and at times other band members, but it was often Goble's songs that made the charts in the US. "Reminiscing", "Lady", "The Night Owls", "Take It Easy on Me" and "The Other Guy" notched up massive airplay and drove album sales, right into the 1980s phase of LRB with John Farnham as lead vocalist on the albums *The Net, Playing to Win* and *No Reins*. Goble was a mainstay throughout LRB's various incarnations, although he has little time for the current line-up that tours regularly around the States. "It's a joke. It's an absolute travesty," he said about the Little River Band that plays his songs yet has not one original member in the line-up.

While Goble enjoys taking a trip down the memory lane of his vast songwriting repertoire, he's not stuck in the past. After LRB, he put together a group called Broken Voices to record one album, and then released two solo albums, *Stop* and *Nautilus*. Using session singer Steve Wade, both albums were showcases for Goble's post-LRB songwriting output, but kept him in relative obscurity. Then he moved one step beyond, and began singing lead vocal on the solo material he was recording.

All through our lengthy conversation he was itching to get into the studio to play some of his latest compositions. The new work he was most excited about was "Initiation Suite", a fifteen-minute opus that he hoped would form the basis for a film. It was nearly thirty years on from "It's A Long Way There", and a lifetime of experiences and songs separated the two, yet the similarities were striking. Lengthy works breaking new ground. His new songs reflected the long spiritual journey he had taken, as well as more earthly concerns—the break-up of his twenty-four-year first marriage, and his subsequent remarriage. Facing the new millennium with relish, Goble said, "I'm always pushing the music in a different direction".

What does the BMI Four Million-Air award for "Reminiscing" mean to you?
I'm reclusive by nature and I don't often go to anything, so I'm largely forgotten about. But I'm actually doing the best work I've ever done in my life. I've got many wonderful new

songs. I'm just trying to work out a way to advertise what I can do. Maybe the Four Million-Air award might help to bring a bit of focus.

I've also had a Two Million-Air award for "Lady" and One Million-Air awards for both "Take It Easy on Me" and "The Other Guy." I've had over ten million airplays in the States. The thing about it is that it's all rested on the LRB catalogue; there's been no significant covers anywhere else. So it's quite astounding the performances that my work keeps achieving.

You once said that often other artists perceive Little River Band songs as definitive versions of the songs.
I think it's the same with people like Cat Stevens. He's had few covers. And Abba is another example.

And of course in 1978 you never would have been thinking, gee, people are going to be playing this song on radio in twenty-two years time.
It's quite staggering; you don't realise you've written something like that until it happens, until it's history.

Your early influences were bands like The Hollies, CSNY, the Beatles and Bread. What about other songwriting influences?
Bread particularly. I would have to say just clearly David Gates, miles out; he's one of the great songwriters of all time. And equal to that would be Stephen Bishop. I think that he's written two or three of the greatest songs ever written. Clearly Irving Berlin is like up there and everyone else is down here. And Cole Porter. To me, they're still the yardstick of everybody. And the thing is, to be honest, I'm a real fan of my own writing. I just really enjoy my own songwriting and what I do.

At what age did you know music was your vocation?
Very early. I really knew very clearly by about the age of fifteen or sixteen. There was never any doubt that I would do what I've done.

You were learning piano from about eleven?
Something like that. I didn't like piano, I wasn't very good at it anyway. Then I played drums in a forties-type thing, and we used to do weddings and birthday parties. But then, it was about sixteen, I left school and went to work, and I saw on TV one night a guy playing a banjo. I thought, gee I really like that. So I went the next day and bought a banjo in the music shop, and then I looked for a teacher. A banjo has four strings. I started to learn banjo and I wasn't any good at that either, but within the first week I wrote seven songs. As soon as I had a stringed instrument in my hands, I suddenly had all these melodies. The banjo's tuned differently to guitar, so I just found my own chords. Then eventually I made myself a guitar with four strings on it and tuned it like a banjo. All my early songs were written on four-string guitar tuned to banjo.

What was the first song you completed?
When I was very young I played at this teenage dance and there were twins there, their names were Kay and Chris. I think that I wrote my first song about them.

Do you remember what it was called?
Probably "Kay and Chris".

Was it any good?
Shocking. But it was a start.

What were the mechanics of songwriting for you in the early days, and how do you write now?
What it's always been, and it still happens today, is that I hear everything at once—melody, lyrics, it just comes in. But that's refined and developed a lot over my life. I can give you a very recent example of what I've learned. There's a feeling comes over me and I know that there's a song trying to come through. It's almost like wanting to eat something or wanting to go to the toilet. You get the feeling, a sense of something. And it's like I'm taken over or someone's trying to contact me, because I really believe very much that I'm in some ways channelling this thing. Because when I write a song it's always done very quickly, completed in twenty minutes or maybe half an hour. I never labour anything, or very rarely; the only labouring I've ever done in songwriting might be when I've completed a song, there might be a couple of lyrics I don't like and sometimes I might sit with those and really put some brain power into how to fix up the lines. But for the most part it comes to me and I can hear the whole thing finished with harmonies and everything.

Recently there was a new song I've written called "Praise". I was driving home one night on the freeway and there was a car went past me that had a number plate "BLESSED" written on it. And I thought, that's an interesting number plate, I wouldn't mind having a number plate that gives some sort of message to somebody. Not necessarily religious, but a message. Then this feeling started to come to me and I thought, I need to write a song called "Praise"; this is what I've been asked to do. Two days later I woke up in the morning and had this complete song called "Praise".

Do you have an idea where it comes from?
I believe very much in spiritual realms. I've done a lot of spiritual study—not religious study, but spiritual study, I think there's a big difference—and I believe in things like guardian angels and the angelic realm. My studies have taught me that when we sleep our soul leaves our body and we go up and have interaction with the spiritual realms. I think that's where it comes from.

And your soul is sent back with these songs.
Yes. And also I think that you're overshadowed. Great people like Beethoven were certainly overshadowed by higher entities. Any artist is just a channel for the expression of the higher

realms. That's what I believe. I'm well aware that when I'm in the writing experience, I feel completely different than when I'm in a normal experience.

Do you ever come out of the experience with a song and not have a clue how it actually came to be because you've lost yourself for those twenty minutes?
No, I'm always very conscious in the moment. But there is certainly a very deep connection going on. Almost like a meditation. And many times I would go to sleep needing an answer to a particular song. I'd just ask, "I just want the answer with where I'm trying to go with this song, I haven't got the chorus worked out, I need the answer to that." And nine times out of ten I wake up in the morning and it's there. So it's like the email from the spiritual realm.

Your songwriting angels up there.
That's what I think. Because we're mere mortals, and when you realise songwriting's so powerful, it's so amazing the things that I write and other people write, I just get amazed at some of the things that I come up with. Because I know that I'm not coming up with it. It's too marvellous. I'm a real fan of songs and songwriters, but I'm very clear on the fact that it's not all my work. It's too wonderful. Often, no matter where you are, a song can help you to celebrate all sorts of amazing things and if you took all the music out of the world, and all the songs, what sort of world would we have?

If songs come to you from a higher plane, how would collaborations work, say with Beeb Birtles? Beeb has said that he would usually start a song and you would then finish it. How does that fit in with the way that you write, being that something is sent down to you?
The answers are sent. Someone can play me something but it's still the same process. I immerse myself in that—what's the answer here? And in it comes, that's where the chorus needs to be, and there it is. Beeb would have wonderful starts to songs, and what I can do really well is work out where a song needs to be. I can see where it can go. And more than once there was a situation where Beeb would have a really nice start to a song and he would be sitting with it for sometimes months, trying to get an answer to a very nice verse, or it needed something he couldn't work out. And then he would eventually say to me, "Look, I've got this piece of song, what do you think?" And not always but a lot of the times I could respond within a half an hour and say, "Here's a chorus", or something. And I think—and why wouldn't it be?—it would be very frustrating for some people who had tried to work something out themselves. There were problems with Little River Band because of my prolificness; there was a lot of friction around that.

How did the vocal arrangements come together for LRB songs? Did the composer of the song usually sketch out the arrangements?
I did all the vocal arrangements. Back in those days I didn't write anything out, we would sit around together and I would just give the parts. There were good contributions, particularly from Beeb, but in terms of vocal harmony ideas it would be fair to say that I did

the vocal arrangements for the band, and you'll be able to hear that with my new work. I've got a lot more complex and more adventurous with it now, because I'm doing all the vocals myself now, lead and harmonies and everything. But that was my thing, and that's what I brought to the band, because my previous band Mississippi had all those harmonies as well.

Were the vocal harmonies in LRB four-part?
They were three-part. It was essentially like Crosby Stills & Nash, The Hollies, that sort of approach. Built around triads. The four-part harmonies are people like Manhattan Transfer, where you get more of that jazzy sound. I'm doing a lot of four-part stuff now; to get the four parts you need to bring in the first, third and fifth, which is your triad, but then you want to bring in the sevens and the nines and that's where the fourth part comes in, and you get more of the Manhattan Transfer and Beach Boys, that thicker sound. We did a little bit of it but not very much.

So, for instance, Glenn would write "Help Is on Its Way," and then you would embellish it with the harmonies.
That's right. Really, I produced a lot of songs. I virtually produced "The Night Owls"; I've always taken an active role in the production of all my songs. For instance, we recorded *Time Exposure* at Air Studios in the Caribbean, and because we were away from home, we had two shifts. George Martin would record from nine in the morning until six at night, with Glenn, David Briggs and Derek Pellici, and then Wayne Nelson and myself and maybe Beeb would work all night from seven, and we had our own recording engineer, Ern Rose. So for a lot of the recordings of my own songs I would be in there working and mainly in charge. And that's how we got through it a lot quicker. I never got any credit for my production contributions with LRB at all. But it was certainly there in a big way.

Was that frustrating at the time?
Yes. Because there were a lot of egos involved with all of that, and I think that they thought I was already getting plenty through my songwriting royalties. When we started, the first album that came out, "Curiosity (Killed the Cat)", written by Beeb, and "Emma", written by Glenn, were the first two singles in Australia. I never saw myself as the writer of hit songs. Beeb and Glenn were the big stars, from Zoot and Axiom; they were very much the marketable thing. Beeb was fantastic-looking and Glenn had a great frontman thing. I was not a great live performer; I didn't have the personality that they had, and hung back. Then we recorded the second album, *After Hours*, by which time we got the American deal to release the first album in America. And, surprise surprise, they picked "It's a Long Way There", which was a nine-minute track when we recorded it, and I couldn't even imagine how they could do that. They cut it down, very badly may I say. Suddenly the focus shifts and then I end up writing the first hit in America.

Then the *After Hours* album wasn't accepted in America, and so they put that together with *Diamantina Cocktail*, and out of that came "Help Is on Its Way", which Glenn wrote. That was a really big hit, and that established Glenn over there. And I think "Happy

Anniversary" might have been there as well, which Beeb co-wrote with David Briggs, so that was fine, they were once again back in charge, so to speak.

It was like a seesaw.
It was, and they were the things that broke us. But then 1978 rolls around and we were recording the next album. The way it's worked out is that the producer comes in, we all sit around and play our songs, and he says, "I think these are the ten songs we should record." So we recorded the ten songs for *Sleeper Catcher*, and I had "Lady" and "Reminiscing" on that album. Glenn didn't like "Lady" at all. I put it forward for the first album, the second album, the third album. He hated it; he never liked it. And the fourth album, finally the producer said, "I think we should record 'Lady'." And Glenn, when he went up to do the lead vocal, said, "I've gotta tell you, I hate this song." I said, "I know you hate it, Glenn, but I'm not in charge, the producer says we're gonna do this." And he gave, may I say, a half-arsed effort. I don't think it's a great vocal, not as good as he's done on some other things. Because if he doesn't like the song he doesn't like the song, it's not any detriment to him. I don't like every song there's ever been; there have been a couple of his songs that I've hated. But I didn't have to sing the lead vocal, fortunately.

"Reminiscing" wasn't a band favourite either. I wanted Peter Jones to play piano on it, but he was out of town. They said, "We're not messing about with this, it's not that important, we'll get some other musician in." So we got one keyboard player in and we played it and it just didn't happen, and they said, "Oh well, we'll forget about it." Of course I don't forget about things, I push, and I said, "No, I want to recut it with another keyboard player." And so I got the complete "here we go again" reaction with the band. Under sufferance they recut it again with a second keyboard player. That didn't work out either. And then my original choice of Peter Jones, who's a wonderful player, came back. I went into the studio again and I said, "I want to cut it, because Peter Jones is back in town." Well, I nearly got killed in the studio, they just didn't want to know at all, and the band was very dark on me, wasting all this time on this crap song "Reminiscing"—I mean, why bother! I forced the issue and this is where I got a lot of resentment, but I really felt that the song was special. And we got it recorded. Luckily it was the producer John Boylan who could see the potential in the song.

Then *Sleeper Catcher* went to Capitol Records and they said, "We really like the album but there are no singles here, we can't hear anything." They waited five weeks before picking a single, and it went to some guy in the New York office, who said, "Look, you guys are crazy, 'Reminiscing' is a smash." So of course it went to number three and it was just incredible. After that it broke the band right across America, and then "Lady" came out after and went to number six.

And then came things like "The Night Owls" and "Take It Easy on Me". My songs kept getting picked as singles. And everybody knew what revenue that meant for me. It was tough. But as I said, "Look, where are we without these hit songs? We're putting our heart and soul into every song, but some songs are being picked as singles and they're our ticket to somewhere." So even though everybody could agree with that, it was still a problem because there was not an equal earn happening with the band. Glenn and I have had our battles over the years. We really didn't get on professionally very well.

He was a great writer, too.
He was a very good writer. He wasn't very prolific. But his best works were very good. But I don't think he had the will that I had.

Which were the Shorrock songs you hated?
"The Rumour"—we had a big thing about that, I was quite open that I didn't like what it was saying. I'd rather talk about the songs that I really liked of Glenn's, and I thought that "Cool Change" was obviously a fantastic song, even though I didn't enjoy performing it. It was a difficult song to perform because I'd sing the high harmony and the chorus wasn't an easy thing. In Glenn's songs they weren't enjoyable for me to perform because the harmony parts were demanding. "Help Is on Its Way" was quite up there all the way, "Cool Change" had long notes to hold. But I loved the content of what they were saying; I can see why they were so good.

There were a couple of other songs that I liked; one of them was on *Monsoon*, "Soul Searching". And "The Great Unknown", which was not very well known. I think Glenn could have been a much greater songwriter and even a greater artist. Glenn never wanted to rehearse; he said, "We do too much talking in this band." He just wanted to count it in and play. And we'd get one bar and then I would stop, and I would say, "Okay, this is not happening." My analytical nature drove him completely mental.

Some of the best bands in the world have had internal disharmony.
We had incredible disharmony. But you don't become that good without doing a lot of work. And Glenn, possibly even to this day, never appreciated what he had in terms of the people dotting the 'i's and crossing the 't's. The thing that disappointed me with him is that he would never take the trouble to really learn the melodies properly, he would never do any homework. Even in "Reminiscing", he changed the first verse, which is on the record.

How was it supposed to go?
The lyric is: [*Sings*] "Friday night it was late I was walking you home we got down to the gate/ and I was dreaming of the night/ would it turn out right?/ How to tell you girl/ I want to build my world around you/ Tell you that it's true." But then he says, "I wanna make you understand." And mine was "To make you understand." And I think there's a difference. To me, the "I *wanna* make you understand", that's really Glenn, because that's more forceful, but to me the gentler way was, it's all because to *make* you understand how I really feel. It had a whole different meaning to it. But, negotiation. "You want me to sing the song? That's the way it is." Every word in my song had thought put into it. And it was "to make you understand" because that's what it needed.

I think that the band was somewhere between Glenn's lack of attention to detail and my over-attention to detail. The band ended up somewhere in the middle. His freeness was paramount and a wonderful counterpoint to my own nature. I could always see where we could get to; Glenn was happy with where we were. And I could never get the band to where I wanted it to be. But if it had been all my way, I don't think it would have been as exciting and as good as it was. I think that Glenn's contribution was the fact that he wasn't like me. I see that now. But when you're young, you don't see that.

"It's a Long Way There" was an amazing opening statement from a new band, to say, "Here we are and here's nine minutes of us. Digest it."
Actually, I wrote it three years before it came out. When Little River Band formed I had sixty songs to play to them, when we started. [*He looks through his meticulously indexed folder of songs.*] June 2, 1972.

Did you think Mississippi might record it?
We used to play it live. But we never got to record a second album. "Kings of the World" and all that Mississippi stuff was recorded in 1972, and then after the album was finished I wrote "It's a Long Way There". It came out of the touring thing; we were on the road a lot. But I realise now it was about reincarnation, it wasn't about a career at all. I wrote it about a career. I wrote it consciously about the journey that I was very clear about what I was going on, and it was like I could see where I could possibly get to, and felt that I would get to. But then later when I did my spiritual studies, I could see that if we replaced a career journey with a journey of reincarnation through lifetimes, the lyric fits beautifully as well. So it can sit whichever way you want it to sit.

Did you plan the long instrumental passage in the middle?
When we were playing live with Mississippi we would sometimes jam through a section and there would be a guitar solo, but then when we were playing on stage I would think of other sections that could go over these chords that we were jamming on, so it grew out of that. Each night I'd add a bit here and there and suddenly it just went on and on. A lot of people have really liked that song. It's amazing that it got picked as an opening. I think because it was so unusual.

Going back to how "Lady" had been rejected for every album prior to *Sleeper Catcher*, I think perhaps some things turn out for the best and *Sleeper Catcher* was the best album for it to be on. I always heard it as a companion piece for "Reminiscing", a lovely sentimental piece, but also this perfect counterpoint to "Red Headed Wild Flower". Two different kinds of ladies, basically.
Very interesting insight, that. There are no mistakes in the world. You can talk about your disappointments at the time, but I don't regret one episode or one event in my whole life, and it's all turned out fine.

I used to walk along long beaches playing the first five LRB albums sequentially on my Walkman. There was no other way to listen to those albums. I had to start with the opening

track on the first album, "It's a Long Way There", and finish with "Mistress of Mine", the last track on *First under the Wire*.

If I had any disappointment, "Mistress of Mine" was a disappointment for me, because that was the best vocal Glenn ever did, and I thought it should have been released as a single.

That's my favourite Little River Band song. It's one of the most sensual songs I've ever heard.

I'll tell you how I wrote that. We went into a hotel in Germany, and there was a movie playing on the television, it was Humphrey Bogart and someone else, a black and white movie. I was unpacking my suitcase and got taken by this movie. Set in South America, a very hot steamy night, someone like Ingrid Bergman and Humphrey Bogart, that sort of situation. She says something like, "I love you, I want to be with you." And he says something like, "Don't be silly, it's just the heat of the night and the dance of the fireflies that's making you feel that way."

So I thought, what a great line. And immediately, I turned it around in my head, "She's there like the heat, she dances like the fireflies." That was my opening line. But that came out of Humphrey Bogart saying it the other way around. And then I forgot about unpacking, I picked up my guitar, and I was playing [*Picks up guitar and plays chords*] ... As soon as you do that you've got the Spanish chord. So I was just playing and watching the dialogue while it was on TV. And in an hour and a half when the movie was finished I had the song. I wrote the whole song while I was watching the movie.

After "Reminiscing" and "Lady", when we came out with *First under the Wire*, I thought the stage was set for us to get to where Fleetwood Mac were. We had "Cool Change" and "Lonesome Loser"—which is a song I didn't like—and I thought, they've got to go with "Mistress of Mine". I was very disappointed that they never went to a third single.

I think some songs are so precious. It doesn't benefit you, necessarily, as the songwriter, to not have had it heard by more people. But it's always going to be there.

It's a bit like Stephen Bishop's "Madge". He's written a couple of songs similar that may never be well known but they're just magnificent songs. "Madge" is just unbelievable.

The inspiration for "Reminiscing" was the Hollywood cinema of the thirties and forties, the white picket fences, a safe and secure romance, as opposed to the more tenuous romance of "Mistress of Mine". Any thoughts on why that tapped into the consciousness of music listeners more than any other LRB song and more than any other song you've written?

It's an absolute mystery to me, because to me it's nowhere near what "Mistress of Mine" is. A lot of musicians love "Reminiscing" because of the chords, the way they seem to work, they say it's a brilliantly written song. People like John Lennon and Frank Sinatra have gone on record as saying it was among their favourite songs at the time. There's a book by May Pang with a whole page where John Lennon and May made love to "Reminiscing". Sinatra said it was the best song written in the seventies.

But he never recorded it.
I got close on that one; that would have been a great thing if he had recorded it, because I love Sinatra, just amazing. You need to be a fairly good singer to be able to sing the melody.

In 1985 you said "We Two" was your "favourite" song and you said your "best" composition was "Please Don't Ask Me". What is the difference between your best and your favourite?
"Please Don't Ask Me" is one of the songs that I've written that really could become a world standard. I just really like what "We Two" had to say, and I just love the lyric of it, to me it was like "Reminiscing" but better. I loved John Farnham's vocal on it; I loved everything about it. I've written some new songs now, I've progressed a lot further, but it certainly would be up there.

There's one lyric in "We Two" that's just about my favourite. I wrote that while watching a movie, too. It was in Europe, he was a racing car driver and this girl was dying of cancer. He loved her, but she wouldn't tell him that she was dying. One time she left and went on a balloon ride. So—"To fly away on a big balloon is what she talked of"—that's all she ever wanted to do. The lyric is all about the script of the movie. So when you see the movie it all makes sense. "We are fools, we make all these rules/ we make it so hard to find love to feel free to be fresh out of school." I just love that particular lyric. All of the rules that we put around ourselves, often we don't feel free enough to do what we really want to do in life.

You've talked about spiritual not necessarily being religious. But there was the religious side, too, wasn't there?
No, not for me. Beeb, totally Beeb, and I got roped into it and I didn't like it, I hated it.

The whole theme for "Fall From Paradise" was Beeb's, then, and you finished it off musically?
Yes.

I heard "Fall from Paradise", again, as an incredibly sensual song. Not lyrically or thematically, but the music is so seductive.
Well, it's humanity, isn't it. The difference between the spiritual and religious is humanity. That's where my writing has always come from, not any denomination. The Christ energy to me is the main thing, but it's not a religion thing. I just look upon it in a whole different way; I've studied it from a philosophical point of view.

My view has always been that no-one's got the dibs on truth, and I've moved through lots of different beliefs and actually arrived, fifteen years ago, at Rudolf Steiner, who was a philosopher who started the Anthroposophical Society. He died in 1924. He gave a great deal about the truth about the life of Christ, huge studies about stuff that exists in no religions. Talking about the reality of the existence of these angelic realms, and the reality of dark beings and light beings. It's a lifetime study to even scratch the surface of what he's given.

I've always found the life of Christ very interesting, and I believe very much in that energy. But not in the way any religion sees it. So I can't fit into any fundamental, born-again Christian thing. But I got roped into it because of my association with the songs that I wrote with Beeb. "Fall from Paradise" and things like that. But when you study esoterically, everything, even the Bible, there's a whole different understanding of everything. It's not simple. The truth of the matter is very deep and it changes as you evolve with your knowledge. So it's very difficult because the general public use the words, "Are you religious?" Well, what does that mean?

Glenn was once asked about the spirituality that you and Beeb brought into the group. His response was to quote his own lyric: "There are so many paths up the mountain." I thought it was apt, the perfect response.
Our philosophical raves used to annoy Glenn. But Beeb and I got to a point, because he was Fundamental in his beliefs, and I was interested in all sorts of other things, where there were certain taboo subjects that we couldn't talk about, because his beliefs wouldn't allow him to talk about reincarnation, for instance. Two-thirds of humanity believe in reincarnation before you even start. Beeb would often just walk out because his beliefs wouldn't allow him to be talking about those things. But Glenn would not engage in any of that. Glenn has his own private spiritual beliefs, I know that, but he was never one to ever talk about it.

When John Farnham joined LRB, did your songwriting change to accommodate a different lead vocal, or did John immediately fit in with your style of writing? He sang the older LRB songs quite beautifully.
"Cool Change" he sang fantastic, we did it in a different key. I thought that he didn't sing "Reminiscing" as well as Glenn. He's a Cancer, the same as Glenn, and they've got a lot of similar energies around them. John had this amazing voice, and it was wonderful to have a singer that could sing anything that I could write. He was such a fantastic team player. He would be very much involved.

So you didn't have to change the way you were writing for the band.
Only that John made it possible to do far more things. I'm always pushing the music in a different direction.

What do you think the direction was that you were pushing it in the eighties?
I just think I was sick of the same thing. If you look at David Hirschfelder on keyboards and Stephen Housden on guitar, we had Stephen Prestwich on drums, and then the vocal ability with Farnham, it's hard to imagine a more talented band. The power, the amount of talent standing in that line-up, we could play and sing anything. I thought that we could go towards where Yes were at, we could be more musical and adventurous as far as vocals and music, and I think that we did. Songs like "Blind Eyes". To me, that was the most exciting band to be in. It was very challenging and wonderful and we got on really well, it was great. It was disappointing that it didn't happen for us.

Isn't it so interesting that it's those times of friction and disharmony that produce the success? It happened with all the great bands. When they iron out all the rough spots and they have the internal harmony, they're all happy chappies but it might not be as interesting to people listening.

You know why, though? It's never about the success; it's only ever about the journey. It's never about the destination; it's only ever about the ride. So it's not necessarily that that was the best music and the other one wasn't successful because it wasn't the best music. The point is that that band was a complete band with Farnham and all those people in it, for my taste everything in that band was fantastic, but the journey was completed. The soul journey had taken place. And that's all we're doing. We're not making hit records; we're only having a soul experience.

So although Shorrock didn't want to take the journey with you—he was happy to be where he was, as you said—that actual struggle with him *was* the journey. Which created all that wonderful work.

Well, the struggle is the only thing that's important. It's not where you get to; it's totally irrelevant how many records you sell or where your song ends up on the charts.

GARTH PORTER

SYDNEY, AUSTRALIA, JUNE 2003

On the day I visited Garth Porter, he was surrounded by old music magazines from the 1960s, photographs from his childhood and piles of paperwork related to the numerous projects he was currently involved in. The creative spirit in Porter that fuses his profound respect for past history and joyful devotion to exposing fresh talent was laid out on his dining table. He would assert that the present and future had more appeal for him than times gone by, but Porter is a deeply nostalgic person, and it is no wonder country music, its poetry and its sentiment, has such a strong appeal for him.

In our conversation it was almost like Porter was viewing his life as a series of sepia-toned scenes in a film. His recollections of riding to piano lessons as a boy, leather music bag strapped onto the back of his bicycle, were as vivid as the memories of driving in a van from Perth to Melbourne in his pre-Sherbet days, supporting himself through early bands by working for the railways around Australia, and his tales, in turn hilarious and poignant, of the roller-coaster life as a bona fide pop star in the 1970s, when the notion of being a top-flight country music producer was as remote as a day without screaming girls on the lawn behind his house.

We sat down to do this interview the day after Sherbet had reunited to play at a wake for a music industry figure, Wane Jarvis. Back in 1996, when I first interviewed Porter for *The Australian*, the thought of ever singing a Sherbet song again was repellent to him. But since 1999 Sherbet had reconvened, in one formation or another, a handful of times for special events, such as a benefit for the late Ted Mulry or a TV special for the band's thirtieth anniversary. By 2003 he was very positive about being back on stage doing "Cassandra" and "Summer Love". He told me the next day, "It felt quite momentous to me that we were going back to such an old version of the band." For someone who had spent many years rejecting outright any attachment to the band and music that had made him such a big star, it was momentous to hear him speak so fondly of them now.

Born on 24 September 1948 in Hamilton, New Zealand, Porter had a conservative farm upbringing, which instilled in him a love of family values and rural life that only caught up with him professionally when he moved into country songwriting in the mid-1980s. As a boy, apart from absorbing everything he heard on the radio, his greatest influences were The Shadows and the Beatles. By the time he joined Sherbet his influences, and those of his bandmates—vocalist Daryl Braithwaite, bassist Tony Mitchell, drummer Alan Sandow and guitarist Clive Shakespeare—were as diverse as the musical styles they employed. But it hardly mattered what they wrote and played; Sherbet's audiences screamed so loud the music was barely audible in concert. And Porter can still be dismissive of much of his output from that era, arguing that the heady lifestyle they led was hardly conducive to writing creatively. But time has smiled fondly on Sherbet and there are few of Porter's contemporaries who will deny that songs like "Child's Play", "Howzat" or "(Feels Like It's) Slippin' Away" are mini-masterpieces.

Sherbet benefited greatly at home from having Australia's first truly entrepreneurial band manager, Roger Davies. He made every attempt to break the band overseas, but other than its brief sojourn to the top of the UK charts with "Howzat", despite a record deal in the US and a temporary name change to Highway, the big breakthrough was not to be. Davies moved to Los Angeles to manage Olivia Newton-John (and, later, Tina Turner, Janet Jackson and Cher), while Sherbet—multiple winners at the King of Pop Awards—fell unceremoniously from their throne as Australia's most royal pop band. They metamorphosed into The Sherbs in 1980 and worked hard to achieve credibility, playing tiny pub gigs and struggling for recognition. In 1984 they quit, each member going his separate way. Porter's way, it turned out, was a newly paved road through country music, where he established himself as a multiple Golden Guitar-winning producer and songwriter for artists such as James Blundell, Lee Kernaghan, Tania Kernaghan, Gina Jeffreys and Sara Storer.

In recent years, Porter was also working with a number of younger, developing artists. He asserted repeatedly that reflection was not his bag. Looking back over his life and focussing on past achievements did not come naturally, he said. On this day, though, the memories flowed thick and fast.

When did you start playing the piano?

I went to piano lessons for about six months. I really hated it. I guess I might have been twelve. Mrs McNeil was her name, and she seriously and literally used to whack my fingers with a ruler. If I played something wrong she'd be sitting there, right there, I can still picture the very busy living room. She's an elderly woman. My brother had a guitar, and I taught myself to play his guitar. So I didn't start out in bands as a keyboard player, I started out as a guitarist, then I played bass for two years. And then "House of the Rising Sun" came out by The Animals, and everybody in the band desperately wanted to play "House of the Rising Sun" but it had this wonderful Vox Continental organ. So we decided, "Let's find an organ player." And we couldn't find one. But we could find another bass player. So I said, "Well, I'll sell my bass and get an organ. And I'll play the organ."

Did you learn to read music?

Not really. I know notes on the manuscript, where they are on a piano or a guitar, but in terms of playing music just put in front of me, I couldn't play it, no.

What made you move to Australia?

It was all to do with music, totally. It was about the time of "Whiter Shade of Pale", there was this new organ sound and it was a Hammond. There were quite a few bands using Hammonds in those days—Emerson Lake and Palmer, Spencer Davis Group, Crazy World of Arthur Brown. But particularly Procol Harum on "Whiter Shade of Pale". The sound of that organ was nothing like the Vox Continental, and I desperately wanted a Hammond organ. In New Zealand at the time, the only way you could buy a Hammond organ was if you were a church or if you had overseas funds. And I was absolutely neither of those. But I read that you could buy them just out of the shop in Australia. So that was it. "I'm going to Australia."

Had you been writing yet?

I started as soon as I fiddled around on a piano. I think I might even have an old music book with a song in really juvenile printing.

Do you remember what it was called?

It would have been a silly crappy little love song of some sort. Later on I had an old tape recorder that I'd record lots of attempts at writing a song as an early teenager.

On the Sherbet *Greatest Hits* album the liner notes said that "Back Home" was the first song you wrote.

That's the first song I ever wrote that the band did. I'd written a couple in the early Sherbet days that we used to play back in Jonathon's nightclub as well. One was called "One Man Team"—"I'm a one man team in a one man scene"—something like that. But I started dicking around writing tunes very early. I think it was an instinctive thing. You know, you just made up songs. As early as I can remember, I was into doing that.

When did you first become conscious of the structure and form of a song?
A song is a song. I didn't really think too much about structure at all.

When Sherbet was honing its performance skills as house band at Jonathon's, were you also honing your writing skills? Were you thinking this was a viable band that could be a vehicle for songwriting?
None of us really took the band that seriously in the early stages. We never discussed it, verbalised it. We were young, we were playing in a club, we were getting $60 a week for doing five nights, about eight hours a night, not constant, but off and on, and there were no big plans. All of our first hits were covers. A lot of bands of that era, even the Beatles, their first album is full of covers. And then Clive and I started writing together, and our first hit was "You've Got the Gun".

Once Sherbet became a commercial act, did you make conscious decisions about how the band should sound, so that you and Clive were writing to a particular idea of the Sherbet sound?
No, it was only song by song. The song would be conceived in a certain style, inspired by something that Clive had heard or I'd heard. Clive was the major songwriter in the very early days. He was the boss of the songwriting. I was just kicking along. And he was a great songwriter, really good. He's still a good fella. He'd been in an advertising agency, so he was conscious of the marketing side of it. I didn't have a clue; I just wanted to play. But in terms of direction, it was just song by song. I'm not likening it to the Beatles at all, but they would take a song as it suited, as diverse as "Revolution" to "Yellow Submarine". The Beatles did not have a direction. They had every direction. "The Long and Winding Road" and mellow as you like, as edgy as you like. They were all of these different animals.

Did you and Clive recognise that you had something special as a songwriting team?
I don't think we did, really. I never thought too much about that. We just did what we could in the time available to knock some songs together before we made an album.

Do you remember writing "You've Got The Gun"?
It came together off a riff that Tony Mitchell had. I can't remember whether it was Clive or I who tabled "You've Got the Gun" as a title. I don't think it was in the newspapers or anything like that. It was just something that came out of the air. We were listening to Yes, with the harmony things happening. And Daryl loved Crosby Stills Nash & Young. So we started getting more into the harmony side of things at that point. We'd always done vocal things like Jackson 5 covers back at Jonathon's, so we all were used to singing. Daryl was the only good singer; I was pretty amateur.

You did some lead vocal on the early stuff.
I did. I think that was just bravado. It was probably Clive and I had written a song that Daryl didn't want to sing. So it was like, "Bugger it, I'll sing it."

"Do It" sounds like it was written specifically for live performance.
Clive was the strategist, more than any of us. If it would have been up to me, we would have been doing less commercial things. Sherbet was the first commercial-oriented band that I'd ever been in. Back in New Zealand we would do Hendrix, Cream, John Mayall, Yardbirds, that British blues type of stuff. Also a smattering of Wilson Pickett, Otis Redding. Sherbet was the first with a commercial sensibility, and that really was Clive. He would think, "We've got to do 'Hound Dog' especially for the Melbourne audiences."

"Cassandra" was a standout track not only on the *On with the Show* album but in your repertoire up to then, and even afterwards. At the time did you know you had written something exceptional?
I liked it. That's all I knew. I'd just gotten the Mellotron and I really loved it because it had [*Sings chord progression in musical bridge*] "dah, dah, dah, dah"—I wrote all of that shit. I wrote most of "Cassandra".

Were you reading about Greek mythology at the time?
It was something in the newspaper. A story about Cassandra being the goddess or the Greek someone or other. I hadn't heard the name before. I thought, "Oh, that's a really cool name." So I just started writing a song on the piano.

How important was the Mellotron in those days for your writing? Did it open up opportunities for you?
"Cassandra" wouldn't have had that melody part in it if not for the fact that there was a Mellotron that you could imitate strings with. 'Cause that line wouldn't work on a piano. It'd be okay on an organ, but it needs that kind of timbre of strings. Piano is a percussive instrument. You need more that sustained timbre of the note, the graininess of strings that makes that line work. It isn't a Mellotron on the recording, though. It's strings through a phaser.

What other keyboard apparatus actually influenced the songs you were writing?
Clavinet. That was the mainstay of "Howzat", the riff.

Did you feel the *Slipstream* album signalled a major step in your writing development?
I think in general it's my favourite album of any that we did. That was our first step into 24-track. Sister Janet Mead had had this huge worldwide hit and Festival bought the 24-track recorder and Neve desk in Sydney.

On the basis of "The Lord's Prayer"?
Yeah. They made a fortune out of it. We'd done most of our recording prior to that in Melbourne, because they had 16-track recorders down there. Then came *Slipstream* and Festival had the 24-track in Sydney, so we booked in there to do it.

You're putting the sophistication of *Slipstream* down to the production more than the actual songwriting?
I was getting more interesting keyboards happening. That was the first full album that I had the Mellotron on. And prior to that, it was always pretty much, run into the studio, run out of the studio. *Slipstream* was a far more indulgent album. We worked twenty hours a day on that. And at the same time I suppose that our songwriting might have been coming a bit better as well.

Was it you or Clive who came up with the idea of a slipstream?
It was me who suggested the title. I got it reading one of Alan Sandow's motorbike books. Because a slipstream is the draught of air that an aeroplane leaves behind, or a car or a motorbike, when they're travelling fast. So it just sounded good. I wrote most of that song on one of those really crummy, shitty, I can't even remember the brand, a little keyboard about that big. About two hand spans of notes on it. More so me than Clive, but we used to write these incredibly whacky chord sequences into songs. Not every song, we'd do our straight three-chord rocky things. But, for example, you'd have to say that "Cassandra" is reasonably sophisticated chordally. "Summer Love" is extraordinarily complex chordally. Just absurd. That's whacky where I went with that. That's not Clive's thing at all. And the same thing with "Howzat". "Howzat" is a very out-of-the-box chordal structure in a song. And it wasn't deliberate; it was just sitting down at the piano going, "That's kind of good, okay." And then you start to find something and you sing along to it a bit, and you think, "Oh okay, that's kind of working." But they're whacky chord sequences in all of those three songs.

I remember writing in a country town motel somewhere where the song "Slipstream" was born. It would have been somewhere like Griffith or Dubbo. Just a little country town with the keyboard set up there on the bench and I was dicking around with this thing which just went "chink chink chink", a terrible noise. So maybe that's why it's got such a complex chordal structure, because these things just sound so bad you had to do something to make it interesting.

Do you remember writing "Silvery Moon"?
That was essentially a Clive song. He was trying to write a song similar to a Beach Boys song at the time. I wrote that thing that's built around the organ for the verses, then just polished it up a bit. Apparently that's one of our most popular songs. It's really weird because it's just a little bit, I don't know, cheesy.

It's schmaltzy.
Schmaltzy, that's the word.

But that's why songs like "Little Ray of Sunshine" have been so enduring. They touch all generations and endure. "Summer Love" is another of the more enduring Sherbet songs.
I wrote most of the music of that song. This is when I started dabbling in the saxophone, too. That's me playing the saxophone on that thing. As I said, it's really complex, where the chords go. I'll play it for you just to show you what I mean. [*Sits at the keyboard and plays*

some chords] After the intro chorus you expect it to rock and then it doesn't. [*Plays chord progression from chorus to verse*] That movement changes the key of the song from C, so now we're in E flat. [*Plays more of the melody*] Okay, now try A flat. [*Continues playing*] So now we're still in E flat. Da da da da da da da. Back to C. And then it changes again for the bridge part.

Where it suddenly becomes very R&B.
Yeah, I'd just gotten the clavinet, so the clavinet's into that Stevie Wonder R&B kind of thing. And I put a bit of sax in there as well. So it sits on A chords till the end, then da da da da da da da [*Plays melody back to chorus*]. It's just really out of the square.

Did you know it at the time?
Only in recent years I've had a little bit of a look back and said, "What the hell was going on in these songs? Where was my brain at?" You know, you would not do that. If you're trying to write a popular song you would not do that.

Was "Summer Love" written to order because you were between albums and it was, "Let's have a hit this summer"?
Yeah, that was Clive's strategy coming in. We were heading into summer, we were writing about August, September. That was written when I lived at Double Bay in a terrible unit with a view of a brick wall. It was like a real dungeon. I was hiring a piano from Hutchings, an upright piano was in there. And Clive came around. "We're gonna knock together a song, we need a new single." And so that's what happened. "Summer's coming up, yeah, let's write a song about summer."

With the *Life ... Is for Living* album, did you and Clive talk about the idea of a concept album with a song cycle, or did it evolve as you were writing individual songs and you realised that they all could link together quite well?
I think it was a bit of both. I often wonder why we've never had any covers for the song called "Arrival". [*Laughs*] It's just a montage of sound effects. I mean, who would put that as track one on an album? It was just like, "What?"

Why not? Considering some of the bands you've referred to that had influenced you, like Yes.
Yeah, but nobody went that far. Nobody went a sound effect montage of the evolution of man on earth. Never in the history of recorded music has a popular band put such an incredibly left-field concept as the first track!
    We kept the thread going as long as we could. But then it became too impossible to keep it. We dabbled with it on *Slipstream*, the first three tracks all tie in—"Slipstream", "Endless Place", "Wild Love". Those were all interconnected songs.

Life was far more overt.
We just extended that a little bit further.

"Only One You" was a really classy ballad. Did Daryl's vocal range guide the direction of some of the melodies and the keys that songs were set in?
Yes, it did. That's the reason "You've Got the Gun" was in a falsetto. 'Cause as I said, we'd been doing all this Michael Jackson stuff. And Daryl had this incredible falsetto. Unbelievable. One of the best you'll ever hear anywhere, and that goes for his normal voice, too. So that would allow us to do things like "You've Got the Gun", like "Free the People", like "Only One You".

Was "Only One You" written mainly by you or Clive? It was in that "Silvery Moon" vein.
Mainly Clive. Minnie Riperton was around at that time. So that might have been where the idea for that came from.

I think the *Life* album was ahead of its time and highly ambitious.
That was a pretty heady time. We shifted from one studio to another, Clive was starting to get really pretty out there ... It was tough going, that album.

"Child's Play" was your last hurrah with Clive. Do you remember writing it?
"Child's Play" had been sitting around for a while. That was written for a supposed TV show that never came about. It was a TV series that children were going to write the scripts and the adults were going to act and the series was going to be called *Child's Play*. And they wanted some music for it. So we wrote a chorus and Clive and I were that close to writing a whole song, that we said, "Let's just write the whole song and then we'll cut out the bits for the series."

Best film clip that you guys ever made.
That was Larry Larstedt. I think that was his name. He got right into The Monkees.

"Howzat" and the love-is-a-cricket-match-metaphor—you wrote that to a title, didn't you?
Yes.

It's never been one of your favourites.
Oh, it's a crap lyric.

"You told me I was the one, the only one who got your head undone, and for a while I believed the line that you spun." What's wrong with that?
The best line in that song—I remember that Tony and I wrote that downstairs here—and we got to the chorus—"Ha-a-howzat, you messed about I caught you out, Howzat. Now that I found where you're at—"What do we do now? What will we say? Where will we go? And then—yes! Zingo! "It's goodbye." It's strange, when people listen to songs, they never know the struggle that you went through to get a certain part.

That "It's goodbye" is what carries the song off.
When I hit that, those chords and that word, I just felt like, "Now this chorus is nailed." Until you get to that point it's just the start of something.

Somebody told me that the lyrics were in fact inspired by a real event in your life.
I guess it's a reflection of something that might have happened at some time. It's like, okay, we've got a title "Howzat"—what do you write about? There's not a lot.

It came up when we were driving back from doing a gig in Wollongong. It was Roger, myself, Tony and Daryl in one of the cars. We were talking about the next album, and Daryl and Roger were seriously into cricket at the time. So we're just, "Yeah, write a song about cricket." At the time I wasn't that interested. I am now. Actually, I've bought Dickie Bird's memoirs. I'd read the whole book and then I was flicking through it, having one more look at the photographs, and there's Dennis Lillee in one of the photographs with a Sherbet T-shirt. Which gave me a bit of a blast.

As you've never felt it's one of your best works, how do you feel about it being your best known work?
I don't think that way too much.

You don't cringe about it now at least. You went through a phase of really cringing about that work.
I think that was a by-product of the tall poppy thing, just feeling like the world was almost turning against you and nothing you could do would save you. It's just like I'd had enough of the chapter in my life. But I'm like that anyway. I'm not one for looking over *my* shoulder at *my* life. I look over my shoulder at other people's lives, for sure. But I don't do it for myself too much.

"If I Had My Way" was a killer ballad. Do you agree?
I don't think anything I do is particularly killer.

It was one of the few songs on a Sherbet album with the solo Porter credit. Did you, and do you, still prefer collaborating?
Whatever the song needs. I write quite a few songs on my own still. There is a degree of a little bit of extra satisfaction when you do it all on your own. But more often I'm working with an artist. On Travis Sinclair's album I wrote two or three songs on my own. But that was only because he was living in Springhurst and I was living in Sydney and we intended to write these particular songs, and I thought, "Well, I'll get them started," and before I knew it I'd actually finished them. So it's not by design.

How was the transition for you from writing with Clive to writing with Tony?
A lot more responsibility. Tony's not a lyricist so I found myself for the first time having to write all the words. I'd never had to ever do that in my life before. Clive was really good with words. A really talented guy in many ways.

And was the *Howzat* album important because you had to establish yourself without Clive as a band that could still come up with all the catchy melodies and lyrics?

I don't know that it ever felt like that kind of pressure. Just write the songs, we'll go in and record them. In that regard it was work as usual. But I think the impact of always co-writing lyrics with Clive was a missing element of the *Howzat* album.

Were you more adjusted when you sat down to write *Photoplay*?

That one felt a bit tougher because we'd had the big success in the UK and all around the world with "Howzat". But we didn't quite come to grips with it. We'd been over there, we'd been touring, we'd just come back, need a new album ... Jesus! What I should have said to Roger was, "I'm not going to record for six months. I need a break, I need to recharge my batteries, re-energise my creativity, my inspirations have got to be sought and identified again."

"Magazine Madonna" was a pretty good piece considering what you'd come out of.

It wasn't a bad effort but I don't think it was good enough. As a song? No. The chorus is a bit crappy. I rewrote that chorus many times. The verses are good but the chorus is a bit piss-weak, really. That was just not enough time to really get it together. Even when we'd recorded that song we were still editing and taking pieces out and putting pieces in, even off the two-inch, trying to fix it up.

Was there any particular story behind that song?

It was about us, actually. What happens when you get a bit older. It was autobiographical. I felt that the whole business was really disposable.

How did the change of scene in Canada and California help the writing process for the *Sherbet* album?

We wrote some of it here before we went. "Another Night on the Road", we had this riff and we jammed it and it felt really good, and then it was like, "Okay, we'll write a song about it." I have a lot of young artists come to me, country acts, even not so young, and they've got road songs. And I say, "It's a real sad thing, and it happens to everybody, but your life has become so narrow now that all you can write about is what you're doing in your career. You don't have a life outside of it. Come to me with something fresh, or in principle I don't want to know."

Do you feel that "Another Night on the Road" was that song for Sherbet?

For me it was. We'd become so busy and so full on, not necessarily by desire, but by circumstance and necessity, that we were constantly on the go. We were travelling all around the world. We were touring or we were recording. That was it. And so a song about the boring side or the monotony, the routine, the continuity of it all. At that time I would have had nothing else in my head that registered.

Do you remember writing "(Feels Like It's) Slippin' Away"?
Pig Morgan and I wrote it here, downstairs. And we demoed it when we were touring
South Africa, in a little studio in Johannesburg. I thought that was a pretty good song
but unfortunately the media took it as prophetic about us. They'd play it and make their
smart-arse comments.

You did write things like "Winnipeg Sidestep" over there.
I like that song. I thought I'd found something, an angle. That was a true story. Just about
all of that is what happened to us in Winnipeg. I felt that song was a bit of a turning point
for me in particular because I don't think I'd ever written that sort of a geographically
specific song about a particular experience.

It had an interesting flow to it. "(If I) Breakdown" was also interesting structurally.
That was written with a guy called Tom Seufert in LA.

What was it like having an outside writer working on Sherbet material?
I felt overall that we were getting pushed somewhere where we really didn't quite belong. It
was this stylistic thing happening. We'd just gotten this big deal with Robert Stigwood, and
working with this engineer who'd engineered Gary Wright's "Dreamweaver". We were
recording our first album overseas and all of that stuff. And we were living out of motels and
writing and touring, and it was the same old story.

**So even though you had a change of environment, it really wasn't changing the writing
environment for you. It was still this crazy living-in-a-bubble lifestyle.**
It was. We would have gone any way the wind blew us at the time. Even to changing our
name. Not quite grasping at straws—I felt as determined and as ambitious as ever—but it all
seemed to be going wrong. Not disastrously wrong like train wrecks, but it lost its sense of
direction and purpose. It's probably a good record. We were dabbling in all kinds of things. But
I'd be very surprised if we ever do a tour with a forty-five-minute show, if we did any of that.

**Were any of the songs in your Sherbet catalogue inspired from personal experience or were
they all generic or hypothetical situations on relationships?**
"The Swap".

That was famously about the Bondi Lifesaver.
"If I Had My Way" was about [wife] Mary when we temporarily split up. "The Way I Am"
was personal experience, written here. This back lawn here used to be covered with girls.
They used to be out the front and out the back. And they'd stay all night. They'd pitch a
tent out there and if you'd walk anywhere near a window you'd hear this screaming going
on. It was just driving me nuts. The neighbours eventually did something about it. The
neighbour over there put the hose on them. "Magazine Madonna" was about us. And so on.
If I look back and were honest about, it there's quite an amount that was autobiographical.

All that touring Sherbet did, all the small regional towns you played, the characters you must have come across, why didn't more of that get into your songwriting?

I suppose it was just different times and different moods that you were in when you were somewhere. I would say that there was nothing that happened that I felt motivated to write a song about. And maybe my perspective was, "I'm not going to find anything to write about in this place, anyway." Touring was actually, strange to say this, but that was the easy thing. It was physically tiring but mentally the biggest demands were the songwriting parts. Playing gigs was easy. That was fun. I loved every minute of every gig, just about. All of those years I can't really remember hating a gig or not wanting to be there playing. I loved it in The Sherbs, even when there were only thirty people in the crowd.

Were there ever subjects that you wanted to write about, or lyrics that you had which you couldn't use, because they didn't fit Sherbet's image?

Not that I can immediately recall. There were things that I wanted to do that I didn't get a chance to do until The Sherbs, though. I could get more serious with lyrics. When Sherbet finally finished and then there was that break that I needed, I actually didn't go back to the way I wanted to write, I went further than that. Because I was in such a hurry to get there, I overran the mark and I went more extreme than ideally I should have gone. I'd go down to the New Edition bookshop and go through all of the poets and flick through books. I started firing up my enthusiasm for lyric writing by reading a whole lot of things totally divorced from music. Because that's more than anything what I wanted to get better, to express things, say things and write songs about things that I felt had a little bit more merit than pop songs.

There was some good stuff in The Sherbs that we did. I think a lot of it was better than what we did in Sherbet. *The Skill* album immediately got an American deal. But we never went to America and toured it over there. I don't know why. So while this great news was happening for us in America, we were playing to twenty and thirty people on door deals here. We charted really high in a lot of regions in America but we weren't there. There was no video. There was no promotion happening for it. I think if we'd gone, it could have completely turned everything around. I remember Anthony O'Grady gave *The Skill* a sensational review at the time. He said, "This probably won't get any attention or recognised, because of what's gone down before." Tall poppies, all of that thing. Outworn your welcome. I remember reading it and I thought, "Wow, that is one hell of a great review. That's the review for an album that we've yearned for all of those years."

We had another hit-out with *Defying Gravity*, and there were some really nifty things happening on that. At that point we were writing really long songs. We just kept pushing further the way that *The Skill* album had.

Did you start listening to other artists seriously at this stage and take in some new influences in a conscious way?

You probably can't hear it but I got really seriously into Bruce Springsteen. *Darkness on the Edge of Town* was an album I absolutely adored. I was seriously into his highway songs, and cars, and romance with vehicles behind him and romance with the road. "Born to Run", that era. The Sherbs used to do "Born to Run" and we used to do "Badlands". So I had a very hot romance with Bruce. He doesn't know about it. Lyrically set me on fire and musically as well. So a song like "Cindy Is Waiting", that was my Springsteen-ish kind of thing. And we got a little bit into the Brit pop era. Bands like The Vapors, Tears for Fears, that kind of thing. Songs like "I'm OK" on *The Skill* album had that contemporary pop keyboard sensibility and melody thing about it.

I was definitely writing songs in that period still about myself and us as a band. "I'm OK" was a reaction against that indifference. We were living in a void of indifference. We could be self-assertive, and songs like "I Have the Skill", "I'm OK", "Never Surrender", you can hear it all in the song titles. That's probably some of our most passionate work. In fact it would be the most passionate stuff we've ever done. Way more passionate than Sherbet ever was. That emotional thing was always on a high with Sherbet so you never had to assert yourself and tell yourself that you were okay. That you won't surrender. "Never Surrender" is absolutely about saying to those that control the lives of bands—and I guess we're talking media people here, and to a degree record company people—that we weren't going to surrender. It took us a long time to lose that fighting spirit. Probably a year and a half in the void of indifference, and finally it just seemed like, "It's all too hard now. It's just getting too hard, becoming a bit too negative, too much of a slog."

Was it hard for you to say goodbye to it?
Once I'd decided, no.

Was it an easy move for you into country songwriting?
I fell seriously, deeply for Henry Lawson's writing and that gave me a gravitation towards Australian culture.

You'd read all the contemporary poetry so you wanted to go further back?
It wasn't overly conscious.

One doesn't come across Henry Lawson's writing by chance. You go looking for it, like you do for any poetry, really. Poetry is not in your face in our culture.
I remember what happened. My mum was over from New Zealand and we were walking around The Rocks and there was a Henry Lawson songbook there. And my mum said, "I want to buy you something, so if you see anything during the day that you might like …" It was there, and I thought, "Okay, I'll check this out." And then I just went, "Wow! Wow, wow, wow!" See, country's always been a little bit a part of me. Always. We even did "Can't Buy True Love" on the *Howzat* album, which is absolutely country. The Beatles were very country as well. George Harrison was purely a country guitarist. His idols were all of the American country electric guitar players. He just put it all over the Beatles, the fingerpicking stuff they did. People don't like to admit it but country music

is in so much of our music. In the Stones you can hear the country influence, it's in everything.

And I guess because I was brought up on a farm, that suddenly it seemed like this was meant to be. Because I did and I still do have an instinctive feeling for what songs should be about and what they should say. I write an awful lot of songs and co-write an awful lot of songs, and I'm not saying every one is right on the money, life is not like that, but I do feel that I have an instinct. It's my instincts that put Lee Kernaghan where he is. He came to me with the broadest American accent you've ever heard, and not one word of Australian in anything of his songs. And I said, "You've got to be Australian." That was the era of writing "Boys from the Bush". He resisted it unbelievably; he didn't want to know about it. He said, "No, that's old hat, that's hokey, I don't want to be like Slim, I want to be new and modern." I said, "Let the music speak that modern language but let the tradition live in the lyric." And that was the chemistry really. The essence of Lawson in the lyrics with contemporary subjects and themes—not always, I'm generalising very broadly here—and the music modern and contemporary.

You'd already worked with James Blundell by then.
I hadn't formulated this Australian thing quite clearly at that point. He was writing country stuff but at that point the penny hadn't dropped into that Henry Lawson Australian bush tradition. Not that Henry Lawson was purely bush; he writes a lot of "city" kind of songs as well. "Faces in the Street", it's about hookers in Sydney. I think the essence of Australian culture is most emphatically in the bush. It's where it began; it was the birthplace of our character.

Artists you've worked with, like Lee Kernaghan, Gina Jeffreys and Rod McCormack, have talked about how you brought a pop sensibility into country music, how the hook in the song was what was making the material so successful. Was there a conscious connection between the songwriter you'd been with Sherbet and the songwriter you were becoming?
No, not even a little bit. What Rod and Gina and those people actually missed was that it wasn't just the hook. I wanted to get some of that cultural value into my writing, which I'd experimented and developed through The Sherbs. Coming out of the end of that, I thought, "Okay, the Sherbs stuff didn't work as well as it should because I wasn't attentive enough to the commerciality of the song." But what I had learned to do was put stronger feelings, more real story value, not just dumb love songs.

And so what I was doing in country at that point was putting in the hooks, yeah, but that's not why "Boys from the Bush" is such a huge success. It's only a part of it. It's what it's about and what it says that is the reason. If it wasn't "Boys from the Bush" and it was "Boys from the Beach", nothing would have happened. It wasn't "Boys from the bush and we treat our women mean." Looking back on that song, what it did was legitimise the value of the lifestyles and the lives of blokes who were flung far and wide, separated geographically from each other, with no real interconnect other than sporting fixtures. No longer were they nobodies out here in the bush that nobody's heard of. Suddenly it was, "Here's your identity." And the song said, "You're cool."

Was it you or Lee who came up with that phrase, "The boys from the bush"?

I did. At the time I had no idea that that's what it was doing. But on reflection that's exactly why it made such a big impression. And still does. I think it's still his biggest song. And not because it was a hit song or a pop song. It was because of what it said. Even "Girls Night Out" for Gina, that was almost a role reversal from "Boys from the Bush", it was girls legitimising their social needs and behaviour and attitudes and freedoms. So it wasn't just a song with a hook. The theme and the way that language was used to describe the theme and the person in the song is the difference that I see. It's like the hooks of Sherbet, the meaning of Sherbs, combined together in a different genre, country.

You spend time getting to know an artist and finding out what moves them before sitting down to write songs. Is it more comfortable for you to write for someone else's personality rather than your own?

Yeah. Totally. I find it much easier. I would struggle writing about me now. There is no call for it, so I don't have to, I don't have to even think about it. There's me and my sensibilities in every song that I co-write whether I'm the artist or not.

How do you connect with the emotions and motivations of a young woman like Sara Storer?

Sara's a really strong writer. And she very much has her perspective on life. The challenge with Sara is to get her songs up without any trace of me being there. I don't want to dilute Sara; I just want to make Sara better. I don't want to change her, either. So when she has some songs with some boring parts, some below-par lyrics, structures, melodies, whatever it is, it's just, "This is not quite up to speed; this really should be better." And she does a lot of her own song repair work once I point it out. Which is the ideal way to go, but then there's always bits and pieces where in the throes of pressure, I'll actually do some writing with her or for her. As a producer, songwriting is a tool. It's not the reason I'm there. After all the songs I've written there's no ego involved in getting a publishing credit. I just want to make a great album.

Do you think songwriters are born? Is somebody a songwriter inherently or can anyone can be a songwriter?

Anyone can write a song, that's true. But not anyone can write a really good song. There's so many levels and styles and types. Few people are good lyricists and even rarer are great lyricists. Most musicians think musically about everything. Very few think lyrically about it. Relatively speaking. So it's almost the better guitarist you are, the more likely than not the worst lyricist you are because you're not thinking that way. There's a different part of your mind and your brain required to write words than it is to write music.

Do you have a favourite song you've written?

I don't think so.

Songs that you're particularly proud of?

I'd have to look through them. How many songs have I written or co-written? There's more than 500 songs. And if you ask me to name them I'd probably be lucky enough to name twenty.

They're not like children, then.

There's too many. What mother can keep track of 500 kids? Fair go!

Some have obviously done better for you.

Yeah, some stand out, like "Howzat" stands out because of its success.

"Cassandra"?

There's some pretty crummy lyrics in that one. And the bridge part's a bit crappy, too. But the essence of the song I like. As a song there's parts in it that I really look forward to playing, but there's certain parts—"Oooh, you make the stars shine, through the darkest night" ...

Are you criticising the lyric there or the melody?

Probably both. If I was to start that song again I'd keep all the verses, I love the verses— "One day I met a girl who never said a word"—that kind of does it to me. But the things that I value and regard the highest are things that I've written that I look back and think, "How did I write that? Where did that come from?"

Can you name one of them?

There's bits in "Cobar Line" that I really like:

> Going back to Ruby the last of her kind
> In better days she was the queen of the mine
> There's a room out the back she's an old miner's friend
> There'll be food on the table, a roof over my head.

That's a verse or more of that song I wrote one night and I went to bed, got up in the morning, and I looked at it and I thought, "Where the fuck did that come from?"

RICHARD CLAPTON

SYDNEY, AUSTRALIA, NOVEMBER 2003

My head was spinning as I left Richard Clapton's home. I felt like I had been on a wild trip, which might seem appropriate, given the Clapton saga—deep, dark folk poet turned pop star turned introspective balladeer turned rebel rock star with friends in high places and expensive habits turned family man in upmarket suburbia. Exhausting to hear about, it must have been exhausting to live through. But the story of Richard Clapton's glory road to inner peace, in all its joy and despair, was an essential factor in getting to the heart of his muse. To many, Clapton is one of the great iconic Australian songwriters—a genius. That genius was born of a painful childhood, an angry and sometimes reckless young adulthood and a fearless yearning to explore humanity.

He was born in Sydney on 18 May 1949. "My whole childhood till my early teens is very murky, very complicated. My parents separated before I was born and divorced by the time I was two. I don't really talk about my childhood," he said, settling into an armchair. The normalness of Clapton's life in the present day is very important to him, being a devoted husband and father the antidote to those uneasy early years when his mother died and his aloof, scientifically oriented father sent him off to boarding school. For much of his life Clapton made families out of the friends and fellow musicians he worked and played with in the different homes he created for himself in Sydney, Melbourne, London, Berlin and Los Angeles. While described as one of the most quintessentially Australian songwriters, Clapton led an itinerant existence during the periods he created his most famously Australian songs, such as "Deep Water" and "Down in the Lucky Country". Writing songs about places far away, inspired by different and distant perspectives, was often how he worked best.

Of all Clapton's early influences, Bob Dylan had the most profound impact. "I was hooked," he said, remembering the night a friend played him five Dylan albums back to back. "The sky opened up." While his 1972 debut album, *Prussian Blue,* exemplified the Dylan influence, his first major hit, in 1974, was a piece of pure joyful pop, "Girls on the Avenue". It went against Clapton's introspective grain, so he ran off to Europe and wrote the defining album of his career, *Goodbye Tiger.* By this time his guiding light had become Jackson Browne. The songs that were so Australian in subject matter and musical flavour had "LA introspective singer-songwriter" stamped all over them. After pursuing his dream to be a part of the Los Angeles musical scene, he returned to Australia in the early 1980s, cemented friendships and working relationships with rising star band INXS, and settled into the hard-living Australian pub rock scene. His songs then became more international in focus, and increasingly nostalgic.

Clapton loves to tell a story; he told me many. "Glory Road" was about flatmate Jon Farriss being petrified to tour Europe with INXS only days after the bombing of a venue in Amsterdam that they were booked to play in. "Oceans of the Heart" wasn't just a song written about his family's sea change in the nineties. It was the song he wrote after the man who lived next door to their Sydney home turned out to be a member of the underworld, had his house go down in a fiery inferno, and Clapton's wife Susie insisted they leave Sydney for a better, safer life. Clapton's stories are full of colourful characters like the beat poets from Melbourne in the 1970s, the German students he lived with in Berlin, and the various musicians he worked with, especially Sydney bass player Michael Hegerty, who played an unwittingly pivotal role in certain classic Clapton songs.

There were also vividly remembered episodes, like when Dylan was touring Australia, and was expected to turn up at a Clapton gig at Sydney venue Selina's. The excited Australian rock legend performed his set charged with eager anticipation, waiting for the American songwriting legend to show up. But by the end of the night, no Dylan. Clapton only found out weeks later that Dylan had in fact arrived, with a large entourage, only to be turned away by brusque bouncers who didn't recognise him.

Notorious for difficult relationships with record companies, Clapton referred to six potential overseas record deals that all fell through because of problems with his Australian label, which held worldwide rights. He had the support of people like Elton John, Lowell George and Jackson Browne, and aspired to be in their league, but eventually contented himself with the esteem with which he was held at home. "Had I been more entrepreneurial, more enterprising and cleverer than I am, I could have made a lot more of my life. I could have been a contender, but I didn't even get in the ring as it turns out," he said wryly and with a laugh.

With a new album, *Diamond Mine*, in the final mixing stages, Richard Clapton was buoyant when we met, and not taking anything for granted. "I think this cathartic thing of songwriting, it's got to be the most wonderful gift," he said before I left. "I know it sounds elitist and snobbish and all the rest of it, but I'm saying that in gratitude for the Almighty. Whoever God is, I've just been so blessed."

Do you remember writing your first song? How old were you?
About seventeen. From day one I've always had Richard Clapton bands. Bands that played my songs. I've never actually played anybody else's songs. I didn't know how to play other people's songs. That's what's pertinent. I never really figured that out. So I came from the literary side of things, because my real gift, maybe more than music, has been English.

Did you write poetry as a teenager?
Yeah, reams and reams of poetry. All throughout my teenage years. I just had heaps of it. So, don't laugh, but there was this shirt shop in London called Mr Fysh, and there was this whole homosexual thing going on around the guy that owned it. There was a murder and it was very mysterious and there was a lot of intrigue going on, and the first song I ever wrote was called "Mr Fysh". It's got nothing to do with sexuality or anything like that; it was just a really interesting story.

Do you remember the song?
No. All I can tell you is I went in and demoed it, once again with the very first band that I ever had in London, and I wish I had it somewhere.

Of course you didn't know at the time, this is the first song of a mighty songwriting career.
Oh, it was already preordained for me as soon as I heard Bob Dylan. Bob Dylan became my whole universe in those early years, in the first ten years. It wasn't just Bob Dylan, it was a whole way of life and a whole revelation to me. Dylan came out of left field and started releasing these records, these songs, where he was just saying the most remarkable things. Saying things that were in my head but I wouldn't have had the bravado to be going around saying and arguing points with people. He articulated everything that was going on in the heads of his generation.

And so the principle of that, thirty-five years later, still remains with me. Like this new album, people who've heard it are immediately jumping up and rejoicing because it seems to be a lost art of somebody trying to articulate the very profound feelings and emotions of their own generation.

You didn't have such a happy childhood. If you had, do you think you could have been as effective and insightful a songwriter as you turned out?
Damn good question. And a very challenging question. Because I'd have to say in an

abstract and obtuse way, without giving you any specific reasons, I don't know that you can become a good artist without suffering.

When I read about your youth it made sense to me, because you weren't parented effectively.
Well, because of this pretty miserable situation, my father didn't know what to do, so because he was already reasonably well-off he just booked me into boarding school. It was a very unhappy life. But the housemaster at boarding school was Richard Wherrett, and he was also my English master. He probably was a more forceful influence on everything I've done ever since more than anything else in life. What it is about Richard Wherrett and myself is the intellectual sparring that went on for five or six years. I was just this cheeky little bastard, but I had a lot of natural ability with English, and anything to do with linguistics. And I suppose I was his most challenging student.

Did you keep all the poetry that you were writing back then? Did any of it find its way into your earlier songs?
No, I didn't start keeping lyrics or poetry until London. And I've still got a folder somewhere under the house with a lot of that stuff. Don Walker or Greg Macainsh said something in an interview, which I thought was very true, that a songwriter really should be a hoarder. So since the early seventies I've tried to keep everything. It's good to sometimes go back and just have a browse through it. And I think there's even a song on this album that I derived from a really, really old piece of crap that I'd written. There were just a couple of lyric lines, and they've been sitting around for about twenty or thirty years, and I went, "That's pretty cool." And built a song from that.

You have always demonstrated an eye for detail in your songs. Is that a talent that stems from originally working as a graphic designer?
No. But this album I've just done comes the closest to my years as a graphic designer. What I used to do, doing magazine layouts and all that sort of stuff, was throw all this shit at the wall and look at it, and then you ponder on things, and you think, well, if I move this here and I move this here … And then finally using that process you come up with a final design you're happy with. I've written this album in exactly that way. Which is why Pro Tools is just the best thing that ever happened in our lives. In other words, I started out just writing slabs of music. But with Pro Tools it means you don't really have to immediately write a chorus. I've written everything straight from my very soul on this, without having to think about structure or anything. I come back and I do the structure later. So I get it all gushing out stream-of-consciousness.

When you started writing songs full-time, was it just you and the guitar?
Yeah. Just writing like Bob Dylan. I first became a serious songwriter in Berlin, which is where I lived for two and a half years. I was a totally penniless bum, which was great, I'm really grateful for these days, I actually found being penniless to be arguably a couple of the

happiest years in my life. You're totally free—I mean, what are you going to worry about? You haven't got anything to lose. I was befriended by these German university students, mainly architecture students, they picked me up off a park bench, literally, that's where I was sleeping on top of my guitar. And they took me home. So six of us lived in this commune and the whole deal was—that was really a bizarre part that I don't think people nowadays would get at all—they demanded [*In German accent*]: "You're a songwriter. A songwriter writes songs." 'Cause I was going to go and mow the lawns at the British Embassy. But I was told, "Well, if you want to go and mow lawns, you can leave the commune, because you're a songwriter. And songwriters write songs; they don't mow lawns. And we're not having you here to mow the lawns every day and come home too tired to write songs." So that's what I did for two and a half years. I sat there and I wrote the whole *Prussian Blue* album.

What was the process for you back then? Would the lyrics come first or the melody?
A bit of both. I loved music, so music could inspire me to come up with some lyrics, but that first album, *Prussian Blue,* was very lyric-based, and the song "Prussian Blue" is obviously poetry and I came up with the music as an afterthought to the poetry.

With such a deep store of lyrical riches, was it a challenge for you to give the melody equal attention, or did melodies come easily to you?
I guess melody came easily to me by a natural gift because I was very slack and unconscientious about melody. Don't forget I was still a Bob Dylan disciple. Bob was God and that was it. Melody? Who's into melody, man? I think there's some good melody on *Prussian Blue*. I thought it was great that I got a record deal so easily and did a first album, and then all the reviews came out and because I was the only one of my kind, the reviews for my first album were spectacular. It was like the second coming, being a Messiah and all that. But despite that, on release *Prussian Blue* sold about 2,000 copies. Australian albums didn't sell all that much in those days, but it wasn't good. And in their ultimate wisdom Festival Records threatened to drop me from the label. And demanded I come up with a hit single, which was quite abhorrent to me.

So when I wrote "Girls on the Avenue", I was living with a mate who was the A&R guy at Festival Publishing. He was really supportive and he coaxed me around, coerced me, "Go on, just give the bastards what they want. There's ten songs on an album, so you can still do what you want." So "Girls on the Avenue" was a deliberate attempt to write a strong melody, also very simple lyrics. To this day they're the simplest lyrics I've ever written. Maybe there's a message in there for me, seeing as I'm still getting so many royalties from "Girls on the Avenue". And that changed my life a lot.

I developed on from there, I kept running away and going back to Europe. And then there were so many trials and tribulations with Festival, and in the mid-seventies I had a big falling out with a girlfriend and I'd just had enough, so I ran away back to Berlin and just sat there and I thought, bugger this, I'm going to start all over again in Europe. 'Cause the Australian music industry in the seventies was just too frustrating. It was very parochial and very naive.

It was all about pop hit singles and *Countdown* and that's how you were judged. But Phil Matthews, who in the mid-seventies had signed me to Festival Publishing, kept sending me these telegrams, saying, "Look, you've got one album to go, I promise you I'll set everything up for you. It's all about you. You record anything you want to and nobody's going to stand over you and tell you to do this or do that." So I came back and did *Goodbye Tiger*. Hence that's the reason there's only eight songs on *Goodbye Tiger*, 'cause they're all so bloody long. I suppose from *Goodbye Tiger* onwards I had got very strongly into melody.

What about song structure? Was that a natural talent you had?
No, what I like about my songwriting is that I haven't got a clue what I'm doing. I think it's had a lot to do with my relationship to INXS, because in many ways INXS have always been naive painters in a similar way. It's all written from the heart. Half the time I'm playing chords that nobody's ever heard of, stuff like that, just like INXS do. Structure wasn't really a major consideration. It was what the song could do for the writer and for the listener.

You still had a pretty good nous for the commerciality of a song's structure.
"Girls on the Avenue", now I look back on it, is probably quite an impressively structured song and an impressively arranged song. So I think all along I'd always been able to do it if I wanted to. But I just didn't have the desire to get into that side, I suppose the Brill Building side of music. Which, by the way, I've always had a very healthy respect for. I love pop music as much as the next man. It's great. But it's like McDonalds. It doesn't have much longevity. It's not very fulfilling. It tastes great when you're first eating it but then you feel like shit afterwards.

We know that the song wasn't written about prostitutes; it was about these beautiful girls that were living in this house in Rose Bay.
In The Avenue. Do you know The Avenue in Rose Bay?

Did the title come first?
It may well have, because it was literally a song about the girls on The Avenue. I was quite drunk at the time. Knowing me, just to get a start, I would have just grabbed a hold of something to hang my hat on and it would have been "Girls on the Avenue". And then you sit there and think, how do you elaborate on that?

The prostitute side of it only came about because it was number one in Adelaide, so I went down with the band. And all these fairly slutty-looking girls came into the dressing room. I was pretty drunk—I was drunk all the way through the seventies [*Laughs*]—and these girls are going, "We love you, man. About time somebody wrote an anthem for us!"

I'm going, "What are you talking about?" And the guys in the band are going, "They're hookers." "They're what? What do you mean?" I said. "Write an anthem for *you*?"

No-one had mentioned that to you prior to that?
No, it was just this one fateful night. And for some reason it just stuck. And in the good John Lennon tradition, I believe in that. Once you've written a song and you've released it,

it doesn't so much belong to you any more; it's open to anyone's interpretation. So I never really tried to fight it.

The song also projected an image of you as a bright, sunny, poppy tunesmith, which was quite incongruous as you were really a dark folk poet. After the intimacy of *Prussian Blue*, was it hard to get inspired to then write a whole album to go with a hit single?
It was and I still have great regrets about that *Girls on the Avenue* album. That was my first experience of having to write an album in a hurry, and this explains a lot of my problems with Festival Records, and the music industry in general, this pressure, you've got to deliver this album and you've got six weeks to do it. I'm not that sort of person. I'm very fastidious about my work and I don't want to put this half-baked album out there. I think "Blue Bay Blues" was a finished song I had. But there's songs on that album I really regret. God, half the album's just full of fillers.

Do you remember writing "Blue Bay Blues"? Were you in Byron Bay?
No, I wasn't. The first guitar player I had in Australia was this guy, Roy Geiger, who'd run away from New York City with his girlfriend, Linda. When he was playing with me he was in Leichhardt, and it started to get all heavy duty in Leichhardt with crime and stuff. So they moved to Byron Bay and I was missing them, and that's literally what "Blue Bay Blues" was all about. Because they were just really beautiful hippy people. In the song I'm addressing Linda, but Linda didn't fit so I changed it to Janie.

Had you been there?
No, I'd never been to Byron Bay at that point. All I knew was what they were telling me. Ironically, after having written that song, I would have spent a good twenty years working in Byron Bay.

How keen was your sense of production and arrangements? Did you write with the intention of giving your songs a full, glossy sound? Did you envisage certain arrangements for your songs?
No. "Girls on the Avenue" was the first song ever recorded on Festival's brand spanking new 24-track console. I had a very dramatic love–hate relationship with Richard Batchens, the house producer. I played seventeen guitar tracks on "Girls on the Avenue". It went on for days, because everything had to be perfect. And there were no guitar tuners; you had to do it on a piano. Richard wanted to be Phil Spector. I'd hate him and go, "Man, this is so self-indulgent, this is ridiculous." Having said that, now in hindsight, we both have to admit Richard is responsible for my early sound, and it's to do with Richard Batchens, it's not to do with Richard Clapton. I was his candidate for him pursuing excellence on par. He wanted his records to sound as good as records out of LA or London.

Whereas was your demo for the song just you and an acoustic guitar?
Yeah. I think that was done on a 2-track tape recorder. I got this old rickety 2-track recorder

through the *Trading Post* or something, really cheap off a guy in Rose Bay. All of that stuff, until *The Great Escape*, I never had any other tools for writing.

Do you remember writing "Capricorn Dancer"?
Yeah. [*Laughs*] That was for this movie, *Highway One*, and that was really fun. Michael Hegerty gave me a marijuana joint, I remember that. I got really stoned and sat around ... Once again, I had to do that in a hurry. That was during those big dramas with Festival and the music industry here and I really wanted to go running back to Germany. I wrote the song one night, went into the studio to record it the next day, then I was out of here.

Were you much of a beach-going guy?
I was. In my youth, I was. No laughter from the galleries, please. I was.

You looked more like a night owl than a surfing boy, so I wondered how you captured the essence of that golden sand, shimmering sea summer. It wasn't just in the lyrics; it was in the chords that so graphically gave a picture of the ocean rolling in.
They were real watery, ocean chords, I know.

How did you find chords that gave a tangible sense of the ocean?
Made them up. That's been one of the best parts of my life. 'Cause I always work with absolutely the best musicians. I've worked with the best musicians all over the world, and they go, "What the hell is that?" "Well, you put your finger here, and a finger here ..." [*Laughs*]

Are you making up your own tunings as well?
Not really. I stole some tunings off David Crosby. One of my best chords I actually stole off a really obscure David Crosby solo album in the hippy days, *If I Could Only Remember My Name* ... I'll never forget, getting back to Berlin and this guy Ziggy and I sat down. "That chord is just the best, what is it?" It's one of the rare moments of my life where I've actually tried to work out what somebody's playing. You'd have to put the needle back on and go, "Hang on, where was it? Where was it?" It turns out it's a really cool E minor 9th. It's a variation. But it's good. They call it the Ralph chord.

But it's a Croz chord?
Yeah, it's really a Croz chord. I love that chord; I've been using it for thirty years now.

So all the evocative lyrical references to the coast came mainly from your childhood?
Even simpler than that. It's what we all love about being Australian, really. Just a very Australian thing. We've got it and no-one else has. There's nowhere else like the east coast of Australia, not that I'm aware of. Three or four of us lived in LA for a couple of years as well, we went to Zuma and all that sort of stuff, but it's nothing like here. It's just in our blood. All Australians who are born and brought up here have the same affinity. I've just bottled it, that's all.

Goodbye Tiger has been called "the definitive east coast surfing album". But you weren't in Sydney or Australia at all when you wrote it. You were holed up in Denmark overlooking a frozen beach. Is that why you thought about Palm Beach in "Deep Water"?

Goodbye Tiger was written in a really manic period of my life, very manic. The first two verses of "Deep Water" I had before I left Australia to go back to Berlin. And "sweet Christine" is actually Michael Hegerty's sister. We were all living in Bondi, just soaking up Bondi culture, so I had this half scrap of a song about Bondi Beach.

And then I was hanging out with all these beat poets and journos from Melbourne before I left and I really had to get out of here, this was after these experiences, battles with Festival, me storming out of sessions, I'd simply just had enough. So four of them came up from Melbourne to see Hunter S Thompson. This is when Dr Pepper and Keith Glass owned Archie'n'Jugheads Records in Melbourne. They were these young coke-snorting millionaires from Melbourne driving Jaguars, and it was beautiful. We went back to this wild party, and I was poured into a taxi, I get to Sydney Airport, I'm drunk as a skunk, and I haven't been to bed for two days, get on a jumbo, sick as a dog, walk into the apartment in Berlin, sling my bags and guitar down, and everybody was out, it was like the key under the mat sort of deal. I literally sat down and wrote "Goodbye Tiger" in probably two or three hours, very first night I arrived in Berlin.

Shortly after that we took off for Norre Nebel in Denmark. It was a really fierce winter and you had to dig yourself out of the front door, the snow was piled up. I'll never forget the beach being frozen; I'd never seen that before. Ice all over the beach, that's how cold it was. So all these guys, being bloody Marxists and everything, bloody intellectuals, they'd sit downstairs, and I had this little loft room, and when I'd get bored with their conversations I'd go up. I had some sort of portable recorder, so I spent a lot of that few weeks sitting up in my little loft room writing and writing, while they were all downstairs going on about Karl Marx. This is the northernmost tip of Denmark, and I'm writing about Bondi Beach, it's bizarre.

And Palm Beach.

Well, Palm Beach comes much later. The first half of "Deep Water" is about Bondi Beach, just about Michael and his sister and I going down to the beach at night, along the promenade there, with a six-pack of beer, hooning around on the sand having little private parties for three. Down at Bondi, not Palm Beach.

I wrote the bulk of *Goodbye Tiger* in that little room in Norre Nebel, and then Festival paid for me to come back and I had to go straight into the studio. But I'd left this girl in Melbourne behind, and as soon as I got back she came up. I had to split up with her 'cause she was an alcoholic and it just wasn't working out; I had my own problems with alcohol, let alone sleeping with someone who's got a bad alcohol problem. [*Laughs*]

Anyway, through the *Highway One* "Capricorn Dancer" episode, I befriended David Elphick and he's got Palm Beach Studios. Now for months I'd had this half-song about Bondi Beach and Michael Hegerty's sister. I'd played the stuff to Batchens and he was going, "Yeah, but if you can come up with another bit for 'Deep Water', this song could be great." So what happened was, this girl and I had this one- or two-day drinking session up at Palm Beach

Studios, and it got to Sunday morning and it was time to leave, so we got in her brand new sports coupé, went around that bend from Palm Beach Studios, and picture this—it's a beautiful perfect sunny day, all the suburban families are out there, we just get around to the bend where the fish and chip shop is, and the car broke down. And because we're both drunk, she's screaming at me, "You fucking arsehole!" "Well, you'd better phone the NRMA then!" I was totally conked out. And I was quite bemused by the whole thing, 'cause people are looking around going, "Look at these two loonies." So she went off to phone the NRMA and I got out and there's a scrap of paper on the floor of the car. Now you think about this—sitting out on the Palm Beach Road, I'm so drunk and the car won't go. My crazy eyes keep looking out to sea. Sunday drivers are cruising round, wish they'd piss off back to town! I wrote it down like a journalist, really. I just wrote down what was going on.

The reviewers all refer to this "sense of alienation and bewilderment" in the song. Which I guess is how you were feeling.
[*Laughs*] Yeah, I was. That's true.

And when did it occur to you that that could fit into "Deep Water"?
I don't think it ever has. Even to this day, even when I'm playing it on stage, every time I do it on stage, I go, how bizarre is this? I don't think these two bits even fit together! It's really weird. I had been trying to be a bit too clever. I can't even remember how I would have come up with such an impressive chord progression. I never could figure a way to really bridge those two bits together, now the verse chorus verse chorus, going into the "Sitting out on the Palm Beach Road". It's just been linked together by Kirk Lorange doing this flamenco-picking bit in the middle. But it's amazing, isn't it? Because people love it to death. And I go, "Thank you. I wish I'd finished it properly."

What sparked the idea for "Down in the Lucky Country"?
It was a very nostalgic song; there was a lot of vitriol in there about my father. There's a double entendre, which to me really sticks out but nobody else ever gets it. "People building up impossible walls, and they call it home sweet home." "Lucky Country" is about the romantic memories that I have of Bondi. Trams really did run down to the sea when I was a kid; it was such a special part of Sydney's character. It's actually a very complex song, which has been interpreted by the Australian public as a very simple patriotic song. They wanted that for the Olympic Games! And I'm going, "Whatever, how much money are you paying? It's got nothing to do with Australian patriotism but you can have it!" It's a song for my father, trying to explain why I couldn't fit into his lifestyle. I just wasn't into this house, car and family. You know, in the middle-eight, "They buy up false security and force it on their sons."

Can you explain some of the mystery of the lyrics in the song "Goodbye Tiger"? Who or what was the tiger?
The beat poets, the intellectuals from Melbourne, had a profound pride in Australian culture

and were trying to nurture it instead of this globalised culture. Too much Americanisation and all that kind of stuff. So we all called each other "Tiger". Like, "G'day Tiger. How ya goin'?" "How's it goin', Tiger?" In my youth, that's what Australian males called each other. And then it became "Mate". Tiger is a bit of an anachronism. Just this ocker thing that stuck.

The song is very simple as well. It's about the closure of the Station Hotel in Prahran. The Station Hotel is where all my most worthwhile bands from Australia came out. The Dingoes, Spectrum, Daddy Cool. I lived in Melbourne round about the mid-seventies for a year or two, and very much got caught up in that whole culture. "Goodbye Tiger" is about the end of an era, what we feared was going to be the end of Australian music. Because around the time I was writing, that was when the Australian music industry first started showing signs of sophistication and marketing, all that sort of stuff. To us the closure of the Station Hotel was symbolic of the closure of a really important chapter in Australian music. In many ways I think it is the essence of true Australian rock music, and I'm really happy to have been a part of it. I don't think any of us were making this blatant effort to be overtly Australian, it was just a matter of writing about your own environment, your own friends and your own experience, instead of trying to write about America and things like that.

And yet that came to you as you arrived in a jetlagged, hung-over state in an empty apartment in Berlin.
But I was like pining for the fields, you know. Not literally pining for Australia, I wasn't homesick, I was just very emotionally overwhelmed and profoundly concerned that Australian music had had this very brief burst of energy and it was going to be over and overtaken.

Had you been listening to Jackson Browne around that time? I wondered if *The Pretender* album, and particularly its title track, had influenced you.
Yeah, I'm catching up to Jackson. Jackson is my life; he's my raison d'être. I've got to be better than Jackson Browne.

You're absolutely correct about *Goodbye Tiger*. There were influences, and I wouldn't deny it, but I've got to get back to this thing about me being a naive painter. What's interesting about my songwriting technique is I don't have a clue what I'm doing and I'm incapable of stealing other people's ideas because I don't know how. Except for the one instance that I told you where I had to sit down for hours trying to figure out this David Crosby chord. I'm too lazy. Prior and leading up to *Goodbye Tiger*, I would have been influenced by Bob Dylan, Jackson Browne, Little Feat, Steely Dan, Joni Mitchell, Randy Newman, etcetera. All those influences probably go into a big pot. But when I say they're influences, they're very obscure and very remote influences because I'm just too naive. Unless I really sat down there and really fastidiously went, "What chord is that Randy Newman is playing?"

Did you see Australia through different eyes when you were living in LA?
Very different eyes. There's a lot more affinity between Australia and LA, as opposed to

Australia and Europe. Germany's very remote from Australia; their culture has very little in common with Australia, whereas LA does. By that stage I was enamoured with that whole cultural thing in LA. I felt musically I'd finally come home and this was where I wanted to be. But then, unfortunately, when everything went wrong and I'd run out of money, I had to come back.

What inspired "Get Back to the Shelter"?
I had these numerous occasions where I really needed to escape, and Berlin was a shelter. When I wrote "Get Back to the Shelter" I already had a public profile and I was well known here, but I had all the baggage that comes with that and there were a lot of aspects that I just didn't really enjoy, the Australian music industry, convoluted personal relationships and a lot of stuff. And it was great being still young enough and single and not attached to anybody. I usually had enough money in the bank to buy myself an economy seat to Europe and I'd regularly jump on a plane.

Where were you when you wrote that song?
In Sydney. When Andy Durant first moved into my flat in Vaucluse, I didn't know he was sick. We were going to try and write together and we probably could have really done a good project together, and then I discovered that Andy was sick. That was when issues like mortality and everything started to hit me. It freaked me out really badly, because it all just seemed so unfair how such a gifted twenty-five-year-old could have this horrible disease and it was going to be terminal. There was a lot of baggage like that, and "Get Back to the Shelter" is me just needing to get out.

But getting back to interpretation of songs, this guy who's a fairly wealthy businessman, who's financing this new album, how I met him was I played at his fortieth birthday about three or four years ago. And he and his mates were obsessed with "Get Back to the Shelter"; he was making me play it five times. I just told you what I wrote the song about, about my own experience, but this wealthy businessman, it meant something else entirely to him and his close circle of friends. I must ask one day what it really means to him. A song about Schiphol [the main airport in the Netherlands] and stuff like that.

Then you recorded *Hearts on the Nightline*, which was a culmination of your period of looking at that southern Californian rock genre.
I'd always been the darling of the critics, never had a bad review, and when I came out with that album, I remember the main review, I think Stuart Coupe wrote it, with this blazing headline—"The Americanisation of Richard Clapton". To which my response was pretty much, "Well, yeah, whatever. Screw you." He was inferring that I was just doing it to sell out, and I would like to explain to Stuart one day—in fact I think I have drunkenly tried to explain it to him once—no, I just loved it there. It wasn't about fame and money, it wasn't because I wanted to suck up to them, I just really loved it there and like the sponge that I am, I landed in LA and soaked it all up and ended up writing all these songs about LA. Is that some sort of crime? And by the way, "Hearts on the Nightline" is actually about Father Jim McLaren.

What made you think of him all the way over there in LA?

I had a very special respect for Father Jim. I got to know him; he interviewed me a bit because he liked my music. I just thought what a wonderful, good man, and I wanted to write a song about this guy. No other reason. There's not enough good men. "Hearts on the Nightline" is about his talkback radio show. See, I can blow out all your myths about my romantic song titles.

You're someone who has always had a lot to say about life and social issues, what you see around you. Do you think you've said things as effectively as you wanted to in your songs? Did you always nail it?

I feel yes. Richard Wherrett instilled in me what I think is really good and very healthy. I was very well read as a teenager and young man. I'd like to think of myself as sort of an Orwellian socialist. Richard got me into not just George Orwell and JB Priestley and that whole faction, but Sylvia Plath and a lot of really good healthy stuff. I developed a lot of my socio-political values from those early books, and then that was compounded a lot in Europe by the people I was hanging out with. And I suppose that makes me a left-winger by nature, it's not a pretentious thing with me.

However, the one thing about my socio-political leanings is that if you really do want to say something that is important politically, it's also important to candy-coat it, not just to get up on a soap box and bash people over the head with these messages. I've written some very savage songs, like "High Society", but I also tried to make "High Society" very pop and very palatable. A really good pop song to listen to with this barbed lyric in it about fucked establishment. God, I'm living with that to this day, the taxman trying to rip me off even when I'm broke. [*Laughs*]

After *Hearts On The Nightline* you seemed to settle back into an Australian lifestyle, and through the 1980s you found a perfect musical niche for yourself in the Australian rock fraternity, with the guys from INXS, Cold Chisel, Dragon et al. Was that important for the direction your songwriting was heading?

Absolutely. INXS reignited a lot of my enthusiasm for adventure and pushing the envelope. We clicked immediately, then I produced "The Loved One" for them and we had a hit with it. So they very quickly asked me to do their album. And then for me to jump into bed with these six guys who were considerably younger than me—Michael and Andrew were really out there musically—at first I was a bit worried, can I really produce a band like this? I remember right at the specific time they were so into Byrne and Eno's *My Life in the Bush of Ghosts*, barely listened to anything else. Michael was just into bands that made white noise. And Jon was into funk; he was into what came before rap, black ghetto bands.

INXS are the greatest bunch of guys, and par for the course I had to research what they were into, because my belief is that the record producer should best represent what the act wants. It's not what *I* want; it's what *they* want from their music. The point being, it lured me out of this very LA school of music that I'd been so absorbed in, which had culminated in me actually living there, and made me look at other stuff that was around, that was coming from all different corners of the world.

Can you give me an example of how this affected your own writing?

I was doing *The Great Escape* and I'd already started writing. I'd thrown off LA, and instead of having this blinkered "life is Jackson Browne and Randy Newman", I discovered there was other stuff out there. I really had to force myself to write "I Am an Island", that was so hard. I find it very difficult to write hard rock songs, 'cause I'm much more of a balladeer, as is obvious, but this being the heyday of Australian pub rock, I never really had anything to end the set with, I needed my live set to build. I know that it sounds a bit contrived, even though it's not, the lyrics are definitely not contrived.

The Great Escape is such a funny album, because I've got "Spellbound", where I'm literally writing about Van Nuys, it's so LA, that song, and on the other side you've got "Best Years of Our Lives", which was originally called "Bondondo Rondo", after this block of flats in Bondi that I didn't buy. I had all the chords for "Best Years of Our Lives" and I couldn't think of anything, and the phone rings, and it's Michael Hegerty in LA, getting all maudlin. "I wanna come home, man. Man, I'm so freaked out, I've got to come home." Michael is freaked out and pining for the fields. We used to live together around Bondi and he wanted to come home. It's similar to "Goodbye Tiger" really, you just want everything to be back the way it was before.

Did you take the audience for your songs into account when you were writing or were your songs purely outlets for your own ruminations?

My songs have always been from within and not from without, but I have critics who claim that from INXS onwards I was continually trying to chase trends and looking around at what was going on around me. I've accidentally written songs that have embedded themselves in the Australian psyche, and "Best Years of Our Lives" would probably be the best example of that. I reckon I get maybe 200 requests a year to play weddings, funerals, birthday parties, anything, and they all want "Best Years of Our Lives". But no, it's always been about me. I couldn't understand why people thought INXS would have influenced me to the point where I was looking outwards and writing. I lived with Jon Farriss for a lot of the eighties going into the nineties, and without me trying, Jon's influences rubbed off on me a lot. The rhythm of music and the feel of music did start to come to the fore. But it was not something I forced, it wasn't a deliberate thing, I guess living with the greatest white drummer in the world today, just he and I writing a lot of songs together, that came out in my music.

But anyway, everyone's raving about this new album and saying, "It's about time, it's so long, you haven't written an album just from deep within your soul since *Goodbye Tiger*." Everybody's an expert. Everybody can tell me what it was I was thinking. As a songwriter, that is one thing that really does bug you. People trying to tell you what it is you were thinking.

You went from using mainly Australian references to focusing on international concerns on *Solidarity* and *Glory Road*. Then on the song "Distant Thunder", you wrote "But now is the time to set things right/ Right here at home." You turned your focus back to Australia. What needed to be set right?

"Distant Thunder" was written about the Gulf War in 1991 and it's just a statement from me when I was getting to that age, forty-something. It's a bit of a world-weary song. Why can't we just all be happy together? Why can't we just get along? If you remember the Gulf War, once again it was like, oh, here we go again, it's the end of the world again for the tenth time in my short life.

But it's about Australia; it's about this country as a nation. I'm saying, "We've got to get ourselves together." It's just like what's happening now. John Howard wants us to be the sheriff of South-East Asia, as George Bush said. But we've got to have our own shit together first.

Did your periods of alcohol or substance use enhance your songwriting?

Yes, it definitely used to, but for the last several years, whatever chemical changes go on inside your body, now drugs or alcohol are something I prefer to avoid. I don't know whether it's old age, or the length of time I've dabbled in getting wasted, but I've found in recent times it's more of a joke. Even for this album, a couple of times I'd have a party for one, and I do vocals or write lyrics and I wake up the next morning and I go, "My God, what do you think you sound like? Simply awful. If I were you I'd stay sober."

Why is it when you're younger you can be more creative through putting chemicals into your body and when you're older you can be mostly creative when you're clean and open and honest?

I can't answer that 'cause I'm not a doctor or an expert in that area. But I think it's best summed up by Joni Mitchell. She was asked by a journalist if she had any regrets about her cocaine abuse and she said, "Yeah, who wouldn't?" And he said, "So do you still take cocaine?" And she said, "Yeah." And he had this look of horror and said, "But why would you do that if you can see the evil?" And she said, "I didn't say that." She said, when she *abused* the drug, she wouldn't want to do *that* again. Her answer was perfect. "Because of the chaos it creates in my mind." If you're a songwriter or you appreciate songwriters, you understand the answer. The chaos it creates in your mind, without which you can't really write a really great song.

And to answer the second part of the question, maybe it's just better being straight nowadays because I'm still living the other twenty years from before.

So what creates chaos in your mind now?

I think because I learned to do it with assistance over a long period of time, now I don't really need to have that sort of assistance to write any more. I just know how to do it. I've found for the last ten or fifteen years that alcohol and substances have been far more of a hindrance than a help. This album is probably markedly the most profound set of songs I ever wrote. But all of it written and created and recorded and produced without any alcohol. No booze and no drugs.

If you don't need the assistance because you know how to do it, does that mean songwriting is easier for you now?

No. No, it never will be, and I think that's the wonderful thing about it. The anecdote there is on German TV, seeing Andre Segovia being interviewed and another pretentious young journalist saying, "So how does it feel to have mastered the guitar?" And Andre Segovia said, "Sorry? Mastered the guitar? No, I would need to live for another 200 years to master the guitar." And I would need to live for another 200 years to master songwriting.

TIM FINN

SYDNEY, AUSTRALIA, DECEMBER 2003
AUCKLAND, NEW ZEALAND, FEBRUARY 2004

"I loved stories about the sea," Tim Finn said dreamily, recounting his boyhood. "I remember this one book I read over and over again about buried treasure. I guess there's an image there in the subconscious. That image of aquamarine waters and buried treasure, it haunted me for years."

He talked in fluid, sinuous streams of consciousness that were so lucidly organised in his mind, he rarely faltered. Relaxed, frank and funny, Finn shared his thoughts on writing and music on a breezy summer morning in Sydney while he was on a pre-Christmas family holiday. As it became clear we were running out of time, he happily suggested we reconvene when I came to Auckland to interview his brother, Neil, six weeks later. And there, in his serene home, the conversation continued to flow. Water was a recurring theme in our interview, just as it has been in his songs. Tim is an island boy through and through, and being near water, in water, under water, crossing water, is intrinsic. Oceans, rivers, swimming pools are his domain. And New Zealand is his home.

Aotearoa, rugged individual
Glisten like a pearl
At the bottom of the world
The tyranny of distance
Didn't stop the cavalier
So why should it stop me
I'll conquer and stay free

From "Six Months in a Leaky Boat"

They're not Australian, the fabulous Finns, but the mark they have made on Australian music is profound, and they spent most of their time on the pop charts from Sydney or Melbourne bases. Tim's years away from New Zealand also included stints in England and Europe. He only returned home in the late 1990s, and perhaps it's only that he can pick up and travel as he desires—to make an album with Neil in London, New York, Los Angeles and Seattle, to visit friends in Ireland or back in Australia—that he's content with a simpler life in Auckland. Notwithstanding that it's now the simple life that gives him the most inspiration for his work; after years of well-documented angst as a younger man, fluency is what characterises his existence today.

Brian Timothy Finn was born on 25 June 1952 in Te Awamutu, near Hamilton, on New Zealand's North Island. His childhood was idyllic—adventures roaming the surrounding countryside and coast; a large, warm and joyful musical family led by a spirited Irish mother; books, theatre and the guiding force of religion. He learned piano from a nun who taught him a bit of jazz on the side of the usual pianoforte, and he started improvising and writing songs as a teenager at boarding school, where he met Mike Chunn and the first seeds of what would become Split Enz were sown.

Bursting at the seams with creativity and songwriting talent, Split Enz was always destined to move beyond New Zealand's shores. Setting up base in Australia, the "arty" orientation of the band raised eyebrows at first but the hits came relentlessly. The theatricality of Split Enz was natural given the personalities and predilections of its members. Tim's songs were almost inseparable from the make-up and garb that he wore to perform them, "My Mistake" and "I See Red" as visually thrilling as they were aurally. "We looked like we sounded and we sounded like we looked, and the costumes were an expression of the music," Finn said.

There were also theatrics behind the scenes, tense relationships, members coming and going. It all affected Finn deeply, as did a tumultuous personal life, but there were great times in Split Enz, particularly when Neil joined, and embarking on a solo career was not a decision he made lightly. His first solo album, *Escapade*, and its hit single "Fraction Too Much Friction", were such major commercial and critical triumphs that he went with the flow, so to speak, and created a series of albums bearing the Tim Finn name.

The pull of brotherhood reunited Tim with Neil musically when he joined Crowded House during the *Woodface* period. They co-wrote gems like "Weather with You" and "It's Only Natural", but the older Finn knew that his destiny was to continue charting a solo course.

Fortunately for fans who enjoyed the fruits of the brothers' work together, there were more collaborative projects to come—the ENZSO album and concert tour, which saw the New Zealand Symphony Orchestra perform classical arrangements of Split Enz songs, and two Finn Brothers albums, in 1996 and 2004. The latter, *Everyone Is Here*, was still in production when I spoke to the brothers.

Tim's other projects have included film soundtracks and ALT, a trio with Irish singer-songwriters Andy White and Hothouse Flowers frontman Liam O'Maonlai. Commercial success is seldom the motivating factor in what he does, although his moves are watched with fascination by fans and media alike.

Well-read and a lover of language and words, the elder Finn is fond of quoting other writers, from Gertrude Stein to Lou Reed, and even the anonymous author of truisms on a packet of tobacco. Quotes are stored in his memory like memories of his youth. And if someone were to reference Tim Finn, they might quote from "Songline" on his last solo album, *Feeding the Gods*:

> Out across the open spaces where the music sets you free.
> Help me spread the message that's inside of you and me.
> We come from a long line, part of a songline ...

How do you think your homeland has infused your music through the years?
It's a very broad question because it starts right in childhood and songwriting begins in childhood. I think the very earliest years remain the reservoir you draw from for the rest of your life. We grew up in a small New Zealand town, the countryside was only three minutes on a bike away, we had uncles and relatives who were on farms, we were often out in the country. There's a pastoral quality, I think, to New Zealand songwriting generally. I've mentioned Te Awamutu in "Haul Away" as a place where I was born; I mention Aotearoa in "Six Months in a Leaky Boat". I sing about Te Whiti and Rouhotu in the song "Parihaka"— which was a song I did that was suggested to me by my sister, who read the book about Parihaka and the non-violent protests that went on over land issues and land claims, land seizures and confiscations, and subject matter that I don't usually go into. I had a Maori friend when I was a child and went fishing with his family and the different ways that they used to catch eels in the river and things like that were just fascinating and different to me; there was an otherness to it, and yet it was very much of my country. Te Awamutu means something like "impassable river"; it's a place on the river where the canoes couldn't get through because there were always trees and things blocking the river upstream. So you grow up with some sort of awareness of the language and the feeling.

Gertrude Stein said a great quote, which is "People are the way their land and air is." It really clicked for me; I think with songwriters and certainly painters, artists of any kind, they are what their land and air is, the place they grew up, the colour, the smell, the textures, the kind of people, the feeling in the air, all the tensions, things that are going on, family life, it's all there. So you can't escape it, it would be pointless to try. And I don't know if I'm any more that way than any other songwriter, it's just the fact that I've signposted it or labelled it occasionally makes people think, "Oh right, he's a very New Zealand songwriter." Am I? I don't know.

Is geography—where you are—important to you when you are writing?
It can be. Sometimes it's a very internal journey, the waiting for songs, or following the lead, following the little bits that come first, whether it's the tune or the chords or the lyric idea. Sometimes it's purely to do with the way you're feeling and what you've just been through or are about to go through. But sometimes, yeah, you're sitting in a landscape—I've always found the Australian landscape and the Australian bush very mysterious and somewhat dark and threatening in a way that New Zealand has never felt to me—and I remember being up at Byron Bay once at the Music Farm studios, writing a couple of songs up there, and the sound of the cane toads as the night came down, it was a very strange feeling, and the songs came out rather strangely, too. So definitely, you can be influenced by your surroundings. When I think of rivers and oceans, there's a lot of that in my work, a lot of ocean, a lot of water.

I wondered if that's because New Zealand is an island country, tiny islands in a huge ocean, and if you want to leave the country you have to cross a vast expanse of ocean. A lot of your imagery is about that challenge of trying to get somewhere or trying to overcome an impasse.
I read another quote somewhere, that the key to any artist's work is ask yourself what does he or she fear, and I thought that was quite interesting. Obviously there's going to be repetition of themes, and perhaps only one theme in anyone's work, but little offshoots and tributaries coming off that main theme. I'm not sure what my theme is. I think of songs like "I See Red", which is very much a visceral response, an angry response, a sort of frustration, and then I think of something like "Dirty Creature", which has quite a lot of fear in it, and "Six Months in a Leaky Boat", which is about coming through a dark time, but very positive. Even the key of that song, the key of D, which is always a very hopeful, positive key for me. And then "I Hope I Never" or "Poor Boy" or "Charlie"—is there a link between all those songs? I don't know.

But yeah, New Zealand. It was like a spring that was wound up very tightly in childhood of wanting to travel and get out of here, and it gradually unravelled and unsprung itself, and now that's over and I don't have any desire to go anywhere particularly, if it happens it happens. But I was very compelled to travel as a child. New Zealand is a small skinny little place, the water's never far away and we were always going to the beach, and the beach was always the place of excitement and sensuality and sexual discovery or just immersion in nature, the water, the sea, the ocean, it's all there. It's all there in my work, I'm sure.

Has coming home to live affected your songwriting?
I've gone through a major change in my life, which is to be married and have a family. It's a stage of life that a lot of people go through much earlier. Certainly Neil went through it much earlier. I've done all this other stuff and I think I was almost getting myself ready,

because I've embraced the role of parenthood with great enthusiasm, great love and it's
quietened me down in some ways and allowed me more moments of inspiration than
I've ever had. I think my writing has really crystallised and my last two albums more
consistently have focus than anything I've done. And also the fact that our mum was very
ill and died three years ago; that I was home for the last year and a half of her life was very
important for me. So it felt like it was the right time, and having children makes it harder
in some ways, but it's more exciting. When you get into your music room and you have two
hours off, it's very exciting and there's much more focus. Whereas years and years of
wandering and travelling and having all the time in the world to write songs, months would
go by and I'd do nothing. So it's much better now.

Can you tell me about your early musical influences?
Yeah. In the earliest stuff there would have been church music. Like hymns. I used to play
the organ in church and I'd be up with Mum in the choir in this funny, rickety old wooden
church, the Catholic Church in Te Awamutu, and because of the time lapse between the
congregation and me, I couldn't tell if I was in time or not, so she'd be watching and
listening to them and conducting me. It's a lovely image of mother and church and young
boy. I think that was pretty important for me, that experience. And then early rock 'n' roll
songs. We had an old record player; we played 45s, Dion "The Wanderer", a little bit of
Elvis. The Beatles—major, major epiphany. And a constant for many years, all through pre-
pubescence and then boarding school, the Beatles were the main thing. But also the Bee
Gees were very important. "Massachusetts", "To Love Somebody", "Words", early Bee Gees
were probably almost as important as the Beatles.

The sense of harmony; because your music is so harmony laden.
I don't think as much as theirs, but yeah. Mike Chunn and I—you meet somebody and they
are the perfect catalyst for your discovery of yourself—I think for both of us we allowed each
other to discover our passion for music fully. We were very close from the moment we met
at boarding school, so we'd follow the Beatles and The Bee Gees, they were the twin axes.
I wouldn't look at the whole body of work of the Kinks and say the same thing as I would
say about the Beatles, but I'd say exactly the same thing about "Waterloo Sunset" as I
would about "In My Life".

"Waterloo Sunset" was your favourite song?
Yeah, it remains to this day. And I read an interesting quote from Ray Davies recently where
he was saying that when people say that—because he gets that a lot and it is uncanny how
many people say that's their favourite song or one of their favourite songs—what they're
really saying is they love the record. Because he's really proud of the production of that
song. And he's right in a way, if you play "Waterloo Sunset" on acoustic guitar I'm sure
you'd still be blown away and think, what an amazing song, but it's the record that had
the magic, the total enchantment about it. Something that you continually discover as a
songwriter is that you can write a song, but then you have to make a record.

At what point did you distinguish Ray Davies, the songwriter, from the Kinks, performing rock group?

Much later. I wasn't even aware of how much I loved the Kinks or Ray Davies until after his first big run. Way after "Lola" and those songs that were around in the late sixties, early seventies. When Split Enz started, Phil Judd and I would have both said, Beatles, the Kinks, The Move, Small Faces. They were probably the four main bands that influenced us. And there were other things, too, like this odd record by two guys called McDonald and Giles from England. And some Led Zeppelin, and some classical music, but seen through the eyes of very naive listeners; we'd never studied music or anything.

You referred to playing organ in the choir and obviously the hymn melodies affected you.

Yeah, the minor chords. The melancholy.

Do you think your religious upbringing played a part in shaping your musical character for your life?

Oh, definitely. I was very spiritually inclined and spiritually aware at a very young age. It meant a lot to me. I didn't go under sufferance; I didn't hate it. Going to Mass, going to Holy Communion, receiving the Host, having that ten or fifteen minutes of communion with God, were amazing things for me. It was an access to another world. An internal world where it was very quiet and very still. It's in some ways trained my mind in the same way meditation does to just quieten down. And when you think about it, that's where true inspiration always comes from. The harder you try to write a song the less you're going to get. You've just got to be open and quiet and they come. So in many ways I think there's a link there.

Has writing on piano always been your preferred way, do you find guitar more flexible, or do you like to write away from an instrument altogether?

I've hardly ever written away from instruments. There was a song recently I wrote, about a year after Mum died, I was just walking around with my family feeling happy for no particular reason and a song popped through my head. All I had to do was go home and work out the chords, because I had the melody and I had the words all in one. That has happened a few times but hardly ever. Mostly the piano to start with, and then the guitar more so as the years went by. Now it's about fifty-fifty. The guitar is more rhythmic, in your body, your physicality is very much a part of that rhythm as you're strumming away, it somehow lifts you into a different kind of area. Like "Weather with You". The chorus of "Weather with You" I couldn't have written on piano, it had to be guitar. But the piano is wonderful for the chords.

The chords are laid out in front of you.

Yeah, it's an easy instrument. I think children should always learn piano and never guitar. 'Cause the guitar's quite tricky. The piano you just hit it like a percussion instrument.

Being that you've always been a closet drummer, how would you say the rhythmic essence of you takes part in your songwriting?

It's crucial. The phrasing. People say there's only twelve notes, and how many melodies can there be, but it's all about the spacing of the notes. I'm sure no-one's worked it out, but there must be millions and millions of varieties of ways that you can phrase those twelve notes. So rhythm is a crucial part of it. I've got to get a groove going somewhere. There's a great quote on the inside of a Drum packet—I used to smoke Drum—they always have these little homilies, truisms, and I read one which said, "Rhythm is the only thing in common with all the arts." That's a wonderful thing to think about, because with painting you could think of perhaps the rhythm of the way the colours are spaced or the forms and the shapes.

Do you remember the first song you ever wrote? Was it before you started playing around with Mike Chunn?

No. I'd written poems but I'd never written a song on my own, and Mike and I started writing songs when we were about fourteen or fifteen. Mike's got a tape of some of the first ones. There was one called "Near Hosts". I don't know why it was called "Near Hosts". A bit Catholic. That was certainly one of the first.

Did songwriting come naturally to you or was it a struggle at first to articulate your ideas in a cohesive musical form?

It started as a collaborative thing with Mike and then later with Phil Judd. For me it always felt good and natural to be collaborative in songwriting. It was only around 1977 when I emerged as a songwriter in my own right and wrote songs like "Charlie" for the *Dyzrythmia* album. That was a turning point. Up till then I'd collaborated with Mike and Phil, and enjoyed that process. I suppose I quietly stepped out from behind that and moved forward. I wasn't in any rush. And didn't trust myself in the process particularly; it took quite a while to get confident about it.

What did you most admire about Phil Judd's writing?

I loved his lyrics, the way that he was able to get very abstract. He also had the torment and the anguish from his childhood that he used so well in a song like "Under the Wheel". He obviously felt, on some level, betrayed by people and by life. And I suppose I really like being around that darker side and listening to it and learning from it. But also his open tunings, I'd never heard of anybody using an open tuning and he just started doing it. All of a sudden the chords were much richer and stranger. He was adventurous and believed in himself as an artist. Him, Noel Crombie, Rob Gillies, they all had gone to art school and they really believed in themselves as artists, and it was a really big thing for me to be around that.

How do you relate to songs like "Stranger than Fiction" or "129" now, nearly thirty years down the track?

I love "129", I still play it on stage. It's a funny song lyrically because it was so cynical. We were dying to be the biggest band in the world and yet we were singing, "The whole thing reeks of cheap striptease, there's nothing more dull than a curtain call." And yet we were longing for a curtain call. I love that. I love that play on opposites. So I still do that song now from a perspective thirty years on.

"Stranger than Fiction" is a much more unwieldy beast. I haven't played it except in ENZSO. Because it was always our attempt at orchestration in a way, and it was very clumsily done and has a certain charm because of that. I'm glad we didn't have access to orchestras back then. There's something nice about that naivety of the way we tried to orchestrate. But it was sophisticated and I love some of the lyrics there, too, of putting down hippies. We hated hippies long before the punks came out with all their anti-hippy stuff. We hated them for a different reason; we felt that they were perhaps a bit serious. We missed a lot of the humour of the real hippies from San Francisco; we just saw the antipodean version and they were always rather earnest. There was a lot of contradiction in Split Enz, and in me and in Phil, all of us. On the one hand we loathed the over-earnest tarot card reading hippy ethic, and yet we had friends who read cards for us and we wanted to grow our hair long and all the rest of it. So we were full of bullshit, really. But that was all part of it.

Did Phil's departure free up your writing or make you feel pressured that you had to take on more responsibility?
It freed me up. It was a real liberation. As much as I missed him and wanted still for that to continue, when I wrote "Charlie", that was a major turning point for me. I knew I'd written something pretty good, and I'd done it all on my own, and so from that moment on, from around '77, I really started moving fast as a songwriter. It was 1978 when I was writing "I See Red" and "Semi Detached" and "Stuff and Nonsense". So I was starting to really come into my own.

There were other line-up changes going on, a passing parade of people coming and going for a few years there. Did that affect your songwriting, having new personnel coming in that you had to cater to?
No, you don't cater, really, as a songwriter. You just write and hope for the best, try and get people to play them. It had an effect obviously on the underlying stability or instability of the band, but I was very much living in my own world then, in my own head, and just writing and writing and really in full flight. It was fantastic.

"My Mistake" is dizzy and at times dissonant, vaudevillian and a little sinister. "Bold as Brass" on the other hand is almost Beatles-esque in its merry melodic flow. How much of that difference was the dark and light in you, and how much of it was the different co-writers involved?
Obviously Eddie Rayner had a part in "My Mistake". It was mainly my song, and he'd be the first one to say that, too, but he gave me the confidence to finish it and suggested a couple of chord changes. The lyric element and the whole bouncy, slightly off-kilter music-hall quality was very much me, and it goes back to when I first started writing, even with Phil,

I did a lot of those songs on piano, where I'd be playing the bouncy sort of piano figures and the slightly dissonant or odd changes.

"Bold as Brass" I wrote with Rob Gillies. I'd written the tune and the whole recurring motif thing and the flow of the song was done, and then I literally gave the tape of it to Rob and he came back with a complete set of lyrics that seemed to fit exactly.

It's an upbeat, boppy melody compared to "My Mistake". So it's just the two sides of you?
Yeah. I think there are other sides, too.

One critic has referred to the "discordant tinge" in your music. Do dissonant chords come naturally to you or do you strive to find them?
We do love dissonance. But it was our kind of dissonance. It might be just for a few bars. Or there'd be a section of the song that was dissonant. But mostly we're very harmonically organised and sophisticated. Some of the chord changes are certainly outside the normal chords that happen in pop music, and one of the things I hate about pop these days, although there's always the odd great thing that comes along, but generally speaking there's just the repetition of the same old chords. Especially in R&B music and hip hop. They're always using the same kind of chord change, that one that drops down. I don't know if it's a minor third or whatever it is, but they use it over and over. You can write a tune and then you can subtly change chords under it and suddenly it becomes a whole other thing. There's so much you can do with chords.

There was an onomatopoeic aspect to some songs that often exemplified the nature of the band and its music. "Give It A Whirl" seemed to reel. "I See Red" was every bit as frenzied as if it had been called "Frenzy". "Shark Attack" was as panicky as such an incident would be. How much of the tempo and arrangements were conceived in the writing stage?
I always had arrangement ideas, counter-melodies and structural ideas for the songs, so it wasn't like I'd come with just a skeleton of an idea and the band would turn it into a song. We were never like that; we were a songwriter's band, so I would write a song and it would be pretty much finished and bring it to the band. And whilst I had ideas, so did they. Tempo, arrangement ideas. There often were too many ideas, but that was Split Enz.

Did you know "I See Red" would be as frenetic as it was?
No. I wrote that as a mid-tempo piano song. It's a bit hard to believe now, even I can't believe that, but I did. It wasn't a ballad, but it was definitely in the mid-tempo area. We started rehearsing it and it wasn't happening, and I said to the guys, "Let's play it really, really fast." And as soon as we played it fast, that was the song.

You said that "I See Red" was written in anger; it was quite a personal one for you?
Yeah. It wasn't written in anger but it tapped into a long-running frustration that I was having with a particular relationship. With songwriting, it's a mistake to think that you write it in the heat of the moment. Often you're actually feeling really good one day for no

particular reason, you just wake up and you feel actually pretty happy. And that's often the day when you'll get some good writing done. I never write when I'm in the midst of something.

It's too intense.
Yeah. It's the last thing you can do. You just feel paralysed and stuck. But when you begin to move through it or past it, even just temporarily, that's when you can suddenly tap into it. And you might be writing an angry song but you're actually feeling quite happy.

Of all the images in your Split Enz songs, the one I have never been able to get out of my head is "Squeeze me out of your life/ Down the drain like molten toothpaste/ I feel used and spat out."
[*Laughs*] I wrote the music first and only had a few lines and then I pieced it together, which is often the way I work.

Do you remember writing "Stuff and Nonsense"?
I was living in an upstairs flat in Palmers Green, North London, with a Turkish couple downstairs. And everybody was broke. I had a girlfriend who used to go out to work, she often did night shifts, so I used to write while she wasn't there. That was a difficult time, and yet the writing was really coming on. I had the strong internal life going on, as much as my external life was a bit up and down. So that was one of those songs that came through, one of the evenings there.

Do you need to have a melancholic disposition to write songs of melancholy?
I think so, otherwise you wouldn't really know what you were writing about. You might try, I suppose. Is anybody upbeat all the time? Songwriters allow themselves perhaps to feel it more. It's not sadness, it's just the melancholy of things passing and changing. As I said before about being stuck, if you're truly depressed—and I've known people who have been truly depressive—you can just tell the torment and the hell of it. There's nothing going on. There's no creativity going on.

But weren't you also truly depressed? You spoke in a documentary about clinical depression.
Yeah. I've been cursed by this. I've never suffered from what I would call true depression at all. But I agreed to do an interview with a woman who was making a documentary for SBS about the link between creativity and depression. I should never have agreed to do it. It's amazing how powerful that kind of thing is. It pisses me off to this very day. In fact I wrote a letter to the paper afterwards, saying it's an insult to anybody who's ever suffered from depression to call me a depressive. Because I know the difference.

But there's a melancholy, there's an Irish dark mood thing that can happen. Life is sad sometimes and there is suffering. I'm not one of these people that goes, "Right, come on, you'll be right, let's go, no worries!" I can slow myself down and just go through it.

256

Did "I Hope I Never" strike you as something quite grand at the time you wrote it?
I don't know about grand. I loved the music of it. I wrote the verses on a piano and the chorus on the guitar. I can't think of any other songs I've ever written where I've done that and on different days as well. It had an odd structural evolution for me. And the lyrics came easily and directly from the relationship I had with Phil and how it had fallen apart.

Oh, it was about Phil. "I hope I never have to see you again."
Because when I did see him, it was just too sad and difficult. The song's got an elliptical quality in a way, because there's a yearning and a sort of loss balancing all the way through it. That made me sound a bit pretentious for me to talk about it that way. But it was written after I'd rung him up; I was back in Auckland, he'd left the band, Split Enz were touring through New Zealand, I'd rung him up to try and reconnect, as I always did, and his wife said, "He doesn't want to talk to you." And it was devastating to me.

Do you sing it these days?
Yeah, I do.

Do you tap into the pain from that time when you sing it?
Yeah, it's funny with songs like that; it's a good question because you don't literally go back to that time or that situation or that person, but there's something in the song itself that works on you and is the thing that's alive and comes through. You don't have to consciously put yourself there. Or even consciously be there. It has its own life.

During the dark period in your life that led you to write the songs for *Time and Tide,* did you ever doubt your ability to create again?
It was a tough time for me; I think it is for a lot of people when they reach the end of their twenties. It's a strange time; you're letting go of a lot of stuff and being a bit afraid, because you really are an adult now, and what have you done and where are you going, all the rest of it, combined with a major relationship breakdown, once and for all finally letting go of a certain thing that had been quite difficult, there was all that. And the band—are we going to make it after all, are we really the best band in the world? At the same time really enjoying songwriting and feeling like I was writing some of my best work, luxuriating in and enjoying that. So there were two things going on. It wasn't all pain by any means. The band was on fire, we were at our best almost. I didn't doubt it. No. In fact I was feeling stronger and stronger.

Was "Six Months in a Leaky Boat" about your first marriage and the aftermath of that, or was it just about the early colonists of Aotearoa?
Oh, you know, just using that idea, it could apply to any stage of where you come through a really tough time but you've got this goal ahead of you, or there's a quest, and "Six Months" is very much about that. It's acknowledging the struggle but also the fact that there is an end in sight, there is something leading you on, some momentum. That's

perhaps one of the things I fear, being stuck. I love momentum, it seems natural, that's what life is. And sometimes you just don't feel it. So that song is using the idea of the early pioneers and the terrible journeys they had to get out here, but at least they were journeying, at least they were travelling and moving away from the old world.

"Haul Away" was your life story to that point. Did you intend for it to be recorded by the band? It's so stark and candid, almost like you just jotted it down unconsciously. "Now I'm having a nervous breakdown/ But my mates will see that I don't go down." Like a little diary entry.
Yeah. It was. I was completely influenced by folk songs and travelling songs. It was an extension piece, a companion piece to "Six Months", and I was reading a bit about the pioneer days, and a lot of those sort of songs—"I left Glasgow", "I left Liverpool and travelled out … struggled to set up a new life"—and mentioning towns and the names of horses and dogs and friends and people that died. It was a piece of whimsy almost; I was just entering into that and seeing it as a new idea for a song structure. Let's write a song that has chapters and is a travelling, journeying song, see what I can do with that. It was always for the band.

Does it matter to you what the vehicle is for your songs? You wrote songs for Split Enz that ended up on your first solo album, *Escapade*. You wrote songs with Neil for a duo album that ended up, along with yourself, on Crowded House's *Woodface*.
It's like what Ray Davies said about how people fall in love with a record more than they fall in love with a song. I think as long as you feel you're making a good record of that song then it doesn't matter, but if you feel that there are limitations … Like a simple example would be "Fraction Too Much Friction", which Split Enz had tried and because we didn't have a drummer who could play that reggae feel, it never felt right, it never felt good, even though I wouldn't have been able to say, "I want this to sound like a reggae pop song." I didn't even have that language. But there was something that the rhythm and the groove demanded that we couldn't do in the band. And suddenly I did it with Ricky Fataar on the drums and it just exploded for me. It was a revelation. So it's finding the right group of people and the right sounds and arrangements for a song, and if you can't find that one way you find it another way. And sometimes you realise that you've blown it, you've done it in the wrong situation.

Has that happened with any of your songs?
Yeah, it has. More with the solo work really. 'Cause with Split Enz, whether it was conscious or unconscious, the band impacted on the writing and vice versa, there was a two-way thing going on. You're writing for that band and that band was demanding certain things of you. It fed itself. And that limitation is good sometimes; limitations are very useful really. But as a solo artist you have no limitations, you can try anything. Play with this person, that person, a bit of an orchestra on here, a brass section there. And sometimes it gets lost in all those choices. Freedom is absence of choice, that's a good quote, too. It wasn't on the Drum packet.

How much was "Fraction Too Much Friction" about the relationships in the band?

It must have been. I don't remember being conscious of that, but I think it definitely had some of that in it. I tried to weave it more into the male–female area. But there was a lot of friction in the band towards the end, yeah.

Was "Made My Day" written with the band in mind or by that time did you know it would be for a solo work?

That was when I'd decided to take a few months off and make a solo album, so I was just writing in my house in Caulfield in Melbourne for that album.

It's one of your more exuberant songs from that time.

That's definitely a straight-ahead blast of optimism. I don't play it any more; I don't even like it that much. But people seem to like it.

You don't like it? Why?

A lot of the songs that I end up not liking much over the years, often it's because the verses don't live up to the chorus. That's just a personal thing. The perfect song is when the verse is as good as the chorus, but a lot of the time I knew I had a great chorus, and I'd cobble a verse together, and those are the ones I don't like as much.

Did you find you worked harder on lyrics when you became a solo artist, because you were the only one representing them?

I don't think it made much difference. I was always writing very personally in a sense. In fact "Parihaka" was the first time I'd written a song that wasn't so much about me or the things I had seen or felt or heard or was experiencing; it was very much looking at a situation outside myself. But generally, I've come to realise more and more that lyrics are the key. I don't know about other songwriters, but with me I write lots of bits of music all the time, fragments of melodies, chords, whatever, but unless the lyrics come there's nothing, there's not a song. When a certain theme enters your life, you're not even conscious of it, but you start to feel a certain way or you notice something that is a way of explaining what you're feeling, then a theme emerges and the lyrics come. I've written songs recently where I've had bits of music that are perhaps twenty years old, and I've suddenly worked out what the lyrics are supposed to be. So it doesn't worry me, I don't feel that music ages. It's the lyric that just makes it and puts it in the now.

So when you start from scratch on a song, do you usually find your way through the lyrics or the melody?

The first thing is often some sort of idea or fragment of a tune, even a fully evolved tune, and then the lyric starts to come. If no lyric comes at all, then it's very tough. That has happened to me where I've had great bits of music. I've still got them lying around. And I might sing a certain line where the chorus is going to go, but I don't like the line, I'm just singing it. It's like McCartney's story about scrambled eggs [In which Paul McCartney used "scrambled eggs" as a working lyric for "Yesterday"]. "Waterloo Sunset" was "Liverpool Sunset" initially. It's when the words are right that you've got it.

Does the opening line come easily to you, or do you come up with a hook line first?
It varies so much. "Weather with You", Neil played a big part in writing eventually, but it started out with me. I had "Walking round the room singing 'Stormy Weather'" and the chords that followed. I didn't have any more words. And then I had the chorus, "Everywhere you go, you always take the weather with you." And in fact they had separate lives as well. I'd sing that first bit about "Stormy Weather" and then on a different day I might sing the "always take the weather with you" part. And then with Neil it all started to come together.

It does vary a lot from song to song. Usually it's great to have a good opening line and it's great to have a chorus, and then you're pretty ripe. If you don't have an opening line but you have a chorus you can usually find an opening line. But if you don't have a chorus, that's really a struggle.

The chorus in "Weather with You" came to you in Lisbon, in Portugal?
Yeah, I was doing a TV show. It was one of those days when I was feeling happy for no particular reason, and you're often not when you're doing promotional tours, they can be really hard. Lisbon was wonderful. They made me feel like a star. I don't know why, but I was on the front page of the daily newspaper and I hadn't sold any records in Portugal at all. Put me on this big TV show and I was in between a magician and an exotic dancer. I was waiting to go on stage, and it was so absurd and yet so funny and lovely that I just started strumming and playing that song. It's often not when you're going, "I'm going to write a song today."

You've worn your heart on your sleeve a lot, and I suppose nowhere more than on the self-titled album. Was "How'm I Gonna Sleep" your ultimate post-love affair song?
I suppose it has that about it. On that album I prefer "Not Even Close". I think it goes to a much darker place. "How'm I Gonna Sleep" is, I guess, an easy song for people to relate to, the whole absence and longing and restlessness of that feeling of not being with the person you want to be with. But "Not Even Close" is both more personal and more abstract in a way. I wanted to write a song, and I felt a song in me that was pretty dark, but I was almost afraid to write it. I remember talking to Jane Campion, who had become a mate, she was living in London at the same time, and she said, "Why don't you read Flannery O'Connor?" She'd written a book called *Mystery and Manners*. I'd read some of Flannery O'Connor's short stories and I loved her work. *Mystery and Manners* is her book about writing and other things. She talks about how people would say to her, "How come your stories never have any redemption? There's no redemption, there's no salvation, they're just dark, they end darkly." And she would say, "But that's how life is." And having read that gave me the courage to just write about being desperate and utterly lost.

Is songwriting cathartic for you? Do you feel relieved, unburdened, after you write and record a batch of songs like on the *Tim Finn* album?
Yeah, definitely. For the songwriter there is a catharsis, there is a letting go, let's say. You can restore momentum and just move on. I don't think it's true that songwriting is therapy. Because it's not. Tom Waits once said a great thing: "Just because it's true, doesn't mean it's interesting." And I think that's right. You can search for truth and say, "Everything I write has got to be true." But it may not be interesting. He fictionalises a lot, and that's the way he gets to the truth. But I do tend to write from my life. I suppose I was very influenced by John Lennon and the whole confessional style of songwriting that he was so brilliant at. And Ray Davies to some extent, too, when I think about it. Also, I think when you get very specific, then you get very universal. Whereas when you start broad, then it just floats off into nothingness. So I do try and get down to the nitty gritty of what I'm going through. Actually I don't even try. Those are the ones that come and I know they're worth following. And afterwards, like with say "Dirty Creature", I know that that helped me; every time I had a panic attack after that I knew what it was, and I could say, "Well, here's the dirty creature." Just giving it a name really helped me. So it can be very specific like that. Or it can just be more general, you know, passages of time and stages of your life and you just move through and leave the songs behind.

You went through an exploration of Buddhist philosophy and did a retreat around the time of *Before & After*. Did you look back on some of your past intensity with a new calmness?
Yeah. I learnt about that without fully experiencing it. I learned about letting things go, and the idea of detachment. It doesn't mean that you can't have passion or emotion or feeling; a songwriter will always be afraid of being too calm or passive in a sense. I don't meditate but I find that swimming is very meditative for me, and having a good steam bath afterwards. I get into a really good zone. Swimming pools are like temples to me. When I tour, every town I find the pool. And some of them are very beautiful spaces and some not, but when they're beautiful it's really time out.

How did you come to write with Richard Thompson on "Persuasion"?
He'd written for a film, this piece of music on guitar, this beautiful melody, and I straightaway thought, "God, that would make a great song." So I contacted him by fax and phone and I said, "Can I have a go?" and he said "Sure." I sent him some lyrics and we went from there.

Did you feel daunted by his legacy? He's a pretty renowned songwriter.
And guitarist. Guitarists would say that he's one of the best guitarists in the world. He is an amazing guitar player and he's a great songwriter. But no, I wasn't daunted. There's a common language between songwriters. You can meet your heroes, as I did with Ray Davies, and be quite overwhelmed by that initially, but it's not hard to slip into the same deal with another songwriter usually. It was more that he's a very impressive man. He's somebody who practises a particular spiritual discipline, and it's funny because

they sometimes say you write what you're not, so a lot of Richard's songs are very, very dark. And yet when you meet him he's very happy, calm, content; in the midst of chaos he'd be the one smiling. And sometimes, if I critique my own work, some of my songs can sound too happy or too positive almost. They're the ones that I grow tired of and they're not all like that, obviously, I write a whole range of stuff, but some of the ones that are the happiest, that was probably because I was so bloody miserable, and I was trying to use the song to get myself out of it. But you can't use songs like that.

What inspired "In Your Sway"?
The lyrics I wrote for that were very much about that retreat I was on, where that phrase actually came into my head while I was up there. I've used it in some senses incorrectly, because when you say you're in someone's sway it means it's almost like they've hypnotised you, you're in their power. And it wasn't really like that. It was more like the idea of swaying to and fro, that lovely feeling when you're in water.

To me, it's only a semi-successful lyric, really, but it was definitely influenced by the feelings that I had on that retreat, and how difficult it was, but then you reach a point where everything just drops away and you feel pretty good; you feel better than you've felt for a long time.

What I found when I first listened to the *Say It Is So* album is that it shimmers. Marriage, fatherhood, happy experiences doing ALT and *Finn* ... is that what brought you to those songs?
That's right. There was a sequence of wonderful things and a feeling of freedom when I finally met Marie. I was forty-four when Harper was born, and I think at that stage of a man's life, it was certainly true of me, you can really embrace it fully. A lot of the ego and narcissism had dropped away, and I was just ready to love and be loved. And the songs were coming out. The lyrics were much stronger, themes that I was finding were pretty clear. Again I suppose about my life and what I was feeling about things, but I was more open to it and just embracing it and felt pretty good, pretty confident, it was almost a bit of a swagger in the way that I felt about it. I wasn't feeling intimidated or beaten down by showbusiness. All that had just dropped away and I was ready to write whatever the hell I wanted to write. It was a great feeling.

Reviewers termed it Americana and alt rock because it was recorded in Nashville, but to me it sounded like a coastal album. Songs like "Underwater Mountain", "Roadtrip", "Currents" and "Rest".
I wrote a lot of those songs in Sydney and we were doing a lot of trips down the south coast and yeah, there's a lot of coastal associations and water associations. It doesn't sound Americana to me at all, I agree with you. There's an influence of Wilco, I was very influenced by Wilco's album *Being There*, and especially a song called "Lonely 1". It's so beautiful it actually made me cry, it was the first time I cried listening to a song for years. It had a big effect on me. Because they're very ramshackle, they don't really try and tailor it and make everything neat and tidy. And so some of that influence was there, too.

In "Some Dumb Reason" you open with the line "I know together we can feed the gods", suggesting the title of the next album. Do you see both records as companion pieces?

I do very much so. *Feeding the Gods* was a title that was suggested to me. I'd been working on an idea with Dorothy Porter, the poet. She gave me loads of lyrics; we actually wrote some really good songs together. Maybe one day they'll see the light of day. But one of the titles of one of the songs was "Feeding the Gods", so I should acknowledge that, because it didn't end up being her words, that project didn't come to light, but that title was definitely from her.

Thematically I was getting more and more confident. *Feeding the Gods* crystallised everything that began in that process, and I think—I don't know if songwriters should say this—arguably, that's my best record. Years from that it will probably be much easier to tell. But those two albums belong together, and *Feeding the Gods* was very well received here in New Zealand. I think people didn't expect it from me. I've been inconsistent and I've been quite eclectic, but I think I'm moving much more towards classicism, recurrence. Instead of, "What am I going to do this time? It's time for another record, I've got to be different to last time." I don't actually believe that any more.

You've talked in recent years about being a classicist. What does that mean for you in songwriting terms?

It's got different layers to it; it's the opposite of romanticism. A romanticist would revel in the chaos of the world, perhaps. Whereas a classicist would turn their back on the world. It's finally a way of working and writing and creating where you're not responding to what's around you, you're going inside and finding the true inspiration there. You do a bit of both, 'cause I'm a romantic as a person. Although I think less so than I used to be. I'm not even sure what it means exactly to be a romantic. I think Lou Reed said it really well, he said it's like you draw the same circle a thousand times but you just hope that maybe you're drawing it slightly better. It's a much different attitude to the eclectic sort of attitude of, "I'll try a bit of this, this time, or I'll go way off into some other area." I used to do that all the time, influenced very much by the Beatles. Every record was very different.

Let's talk about your writing with Neil. How would you describe the differences in the way you write, separately and together?

We've talked about it quite a bit because we're making this record now, but I've found that there are quite clear differences in songwriters and there's also a lot of crossover. The differences mainly are that Neil writes through using tapes and demoing ideas, listening back and developing songs that way, going backwards and forwards between playing and listening. Whereas I just write. I don't demo, I just write a song and keep working on it for maybe weeks or months around the house, playing the same thing until the lyrics come. And when the lyrics come that song is done. But Neil might give it a little bit of this, a little bit of that, then he'll just listen back and leave it for a while. It's a subtle difference but it is a difference.

I usually wait for that lyric. The theme is really what I'm looking for, what is the song about, what is the mood, where's the lyric? Whereas Neil perhaps is a bit more unconscious in that area and he'll wait until some words just fall out of his mouth. When we write together, I might be the one who's more focusing on what the song's about, or looking for that theme, and Neil will be more working on the chords and making it more subtle and interesting, throwing a few abstract lines out there. But it's not true to say that he's abstract and I'm literal either, because there's a crossover. And we don't work together; we've hardly ever just sat in a room and come up with something. We've always got something that we bring, I might have a phrase, or an idea for a song.

Like "Stormy Weather".
Yeah, the opening line of "Weather with You". Or "Where Is My Soul" or "Angels Heap". I'll have an idea going that I'll throw out and Neil will pick up on it and it becomes something better than I could have done with it on my own for sure. It's an amazing thing to write with somebody, I've done it with quite a few other people. Neil's done it with a couple but I don't think he's collaborated as often as I have. It's something perhaps that I find easier to do.

Tell me about writing the songs for the *Finn* album. Were you in the Cook Islands for much of that writing process?
We weren't writing there. We just all went there for a holiday. But a few little themes came up, a few ideas.

Like falling off a bike.
Yeah, "Kiss the Road to Rarotonga". That's what one of the nurses said to me after it had happened, a beautiful Cook Island nurse with bare feet and it was a lovely third world hospital, which if you were seriously ill you wouldn't have thought of in that romantic way, but because it was just a graze it had this charm about it, the whole situation. And she said, "Oh, you kissed the road to Rarotonga." I'm sure it happens all the time, pissed white people falling off motorbikes.

The album had a very Islander, Polynesian feel to it.
Well, it was clear in a song like "Paradise". Neil played a lot of tea-chest bass, which gives it that flavour. Yeah, it was two guys in a room; it's got a lovely, appealing quality about it. It's homemade sounding and of this place. Sure.

Which of those *Finn* songs would you say most closely reflect your own style and personality? Is it too simple to attribute "Eyes of the World" and "Mood Swinging Man" and "Bullets in My Hairdo" to you and "Only Talking Sense" and "Where Is My Soul" to Neil?
Yeah, that would be too easy. It's just that I happened to sing lead on those tracks that you mentioned.

But one would think, Tim Finn, mood swinging man. That'd be Tim.
Yeah, I think I had a lot of input into that song, but they're Neil's chords. And in "Where Is My Soul", I had that chorus. We started singing it together one day out at Bethells Beach, but it was something that I'd been playing around with on the piano. "Only Talking Sense", the chorus of that Neil had already, but the verse was my idea. I had, "There's a wild thing in the woolshed and it's keeping me awake at night." The "wild thing in the woolshed" is an idea that I'd been working on using that A minor chord. So there's combinations that are quite slippery on that album.

I've read about your so-called "rocky" musical relationship with Neil over the years, with words like "jealousy" and "guilt" bandied about. It seems to me as an outsider that the relationship has always been fruitful and something quite wondrous.
Yeah, I think that's true. People put their expectations onto us because we're visible siblings. Everyone's got their own story. If you have your own brother or sister it's an intense relationship usually and a lot of people just give up on it in their lives, and only see their brothers or sisters at Christmas or whenever. Other people are incredibly close to their brothers and sisters and they go through all the ups and downs that that brings with it. You can get on each other's nerves more than anybody else on the earth, 'cause you've shared all this common history and yet you don't necessarily have any real natural chemistry. It's a weird thing; you're thrown together in this world.

With Neil and I, because we're creative together, that takes care of everything. Yes, we can fight and have arguments and get a bit shirty and rub each other up the wrong way, and then we just step back for a while, but there's an underlying love of songs between us, and it never goes away. We just have to look at each other and there's something there. We're interested in each other because we're artists. The brother thing almost drops away sometimes. We're just songwriters who really like each other's work and want each other to be doing our best work, and we get frustrated sometimes when you don't know that the other person's doing their best work. Then they do suddenly.

Do you argue in the middle of songwriting about the direction a song's going?
Yeah, we have done. It's really hard to be completely honest. True honesty is very rare, as John Osborne once said. Songwriters have to be pretty honest, because you're showing your feelings and your vulnerability. You might come up with a bad idea but you still have to try it, throw it out there. Yeah, we've had a few. This time more than any other time. With *Woodface* we only spent two weeks writing, and the same for the *Finn* album. This time around it's been nearly a year. And so there's been a lot of ups and downs, like one of us would believe in something, the other one won't.

Do you have an idea about where songs come from? Some people believe they are just a channel for songs.
Yeah, I know that idea, and I've thought it sounds good at times, 'cause sometimes you write a song and you think, "Wow, where did that come from?" Because it's so quick,

whoosh. But I don't think that any more. I think they come from within. I think you're really inspired, you look within. Inspiration is around you, it can be in the external, you can see something, feel something, do something, and that's where it suddenly clicks in. But then I think you find a way of creating that and presenting that and embodying that from within you. And from all your experiences and all your emotions and feelings. That's why I think it's good to be clear-headed and vaguely happy.

DON WALKER

SYDNEY, AUSTRALIA, AUGUST 2003

Amid the hell-raising, sweaty rampage that was a Cold Chisel concert in the 1970s and early 1980s sat the cool, calm, collected keyboard player and chief songwriter of the band, Don Walker. His face was expressionless, or perhaps dark and moody, just occasionally raising a sardonic smile. Walker cut a picture of rock 'n' roll cool that persists to this day.

Mistaking that demeanour for aloofness, I expected Walker to be diffident and guarded. In fact he was exceedingly friendly and open, not to mention stylish and decorous. Pouring tea in the kitchen of his elegant home, it seemed worlds away from the seediness of Kings Cross just around the corner, and certainly light years from the rural upbringing that infuses his work to this day.

Don Walker was born in Ayr, North Queensland, on 29 November 1951 to a farmer father and schoolteacher mother, his character shaped by the mix of respect for the land and fascination with intellectual pursuits. The family moved to Grafton in New South Wales when he was four years old and he remained there through his university years, until his work in the science field took him to South Australia, where Cold Chisel formed.

The big band and jazz music his father loved, plus the Presbyterian and Methodist hymns he learned as a child at church, were part of a melting pot of influences that included Johnny Cash, Roy Orbison and late-sixties rock like Cream and Jimi Hendrix. In his twenties, Walker developed an ear for rural and Chicago-based blues, enjoying Howlin' Wolf and Muddy Waters. Inspired by the work of Stevie Winwood and the Doors' Ray Manzarek and revering jazz keyboardists Jimmy Smith and Brian Auger, Walker ultimately developed his own piano-based rock style of playing that underpinned Cold Chisel's sound.

The band's repertoire offered a broad sweep of Australian life, often delivered with a sneer or at least a sigh. A discussion with Walker about his music is invariably also a discussion about race and culture, politics and religion, and his insights are unfailingly pertinent and usually wry. But it's erroneous to assume all of Walker's comments on any subject are tinged with sarcasm, and those who know him well attest to his sincerity and amiability. It was my own scepticism that made me go back after our interview and question him over a comment he had made about his admiration for Sherbet's song "Child's Play". Walker a Sherbet fan? "Yes, I thought 'Child's Play' was a good pop song," he assured me, adding, "I also used to like David Gates."

It's his pop sensibility that, above all, made Walker's songs such memorable anthems. A great admirer of the work of Harry Vanda and George Young—he prefers "Love Is in the Air" to "Friday on My Mind"—Walker fashioned a sound for Cold Chisel that was melodically distinctive and always perfect for commercial radio. Sometimes listeners were so carried away by the tunes that they weren't really sure what they were singing along to. Is that a plane or a train that the protagonist of "Khe Sanh" takes out of Sydney? And how many to this day are aware that "Choir Girl" is a song about abortion?

When Walker has strayed from writing for Cold Chisel or commercial writing for country artists like Slim Dusty, his work has been more personally satisfying but heard by few. During Cold Chisel's heyday he composed a film soundtrack, inspired by the music from *Pat Garrett and Billy the Kid* and *Midnight Express*. His music for *Freedom*, the first film for director Scott Hicks, was notable for featuring most of the Cold Chisel players as well as some vocal work from a young Michael Hutchence, but the film had little success. Walker's post-Chisel recording output has similarly been limited to a cult following, but the songs on those albums—two under the Catfish moniker, one with Tex Perkins and Charlie Owen, and one in his own name—are more telling about the person Don Walker is. "By and large, the songs that I love most and that mean the most to me have found the smallest audience," he said.

Has your music been influenced by where you were born and where you grew up?
It's been influenced hugely. And probably the influence of North Queensland and Grafton is stronger on what I do now than where I live now.

How important is location to you when you are in the actual act of writing?
The location and the ambience leaks in, even when you're not consciously trying to do that.

For me and I suspect for everybody. I don't think I ever go to a place with a view of, "Now I'm going to write a song about this place." But I can trace back and see how having been through somewhere, the ambience of it has leaked into what I'm doing. In the mid-eighties I did a certain amount of travel in Asia, the Soviet Union and Eastern Europe and wrote a set of songs during and following that, and everything about those songs is a little bit to one side of everything else. It's quite Eastern European in flavour.

You've been compared with Chuck Berry, who often used place names in his songs. But he said he used place names not because he wanted to evoke a sense of place, but because he wanted his songs to sell in those towns. I didn't think there was anything so mercenary in your work, but then I read that you had in fact written lyrics in early Cold Chisel songs that related to the places you were playing so your audiences could relate.
Yes, that's true, but it wasn't so I could sell records. We were still quite a few years short of being able to make records. And it wasn't so that we could sell tickets to gigs, because the people who were listening to us were coming and seeing us, so listening to us anyway. So it wasn't mercenary. It's just because it was fun. A lot of motivation in music, especially when you're young, before things get serious, a lot of the great philosophical explanations of why this happened and why you did that, all of it can be crossed out with a pencil and just write in, "Because it was fun." It's that shallow. But that's not shallow at all. It's the best reason to do it.

What appealed to you about piano as a child, and what appealed to you about it when you started writing?
It's the only thing I've ever been able to play. I was sent to a teacher who lived two farms away; this was pre-Beatles, so it never occurred to anybody to play guitar. So my mum bought a piano and my brother and I started to take lessons, and did it purely out of duty. My piano teacher was a smart lady called Dot Morris, who took one look at us and decided that classical music wasn't going to go too far. Apart from a little bit of Chopin, she took me through a lot of Fats Waller repertoire, and also Winifred Atwell.

Did she teach you theory at the same time?
Yeah, she taught me a lot of theory. She took me a lot further with the theory side of things than the practical.

Was it useful for you to know notation?
Yeah, I like the theory side of it because it's all so logical and fits together and it's easy. At the time, in another life, I was doing mathematics at school and uni, and there is a crossover there between musical theory and the theoretical end of science and mathematics, so all of that fitted quite easily.

Rock 'n' roll is traditionally played on guitar, whereas piano is a classical instrument. How do you bring rock 'n' roll to the piano?
The first writing that I was trying to do was for Cold Chisel, and Cold Chisel were a rock

band, and you can't really in the end write really plausible rock on a piano unless you're Jerry Lee Lewis. But he doesn't play piano like a piano player anyway. He plays piano like a criminal or something. It's like assault and battery what he does and it's got all sorts of attitude mixed into it that's not normal piano-playing attitude. So he's an exception. Put him to one side and maybe put Thelonious Monk to one side, who is probably my other greatest adult love as a piano player. Great rock 'n' roll is written by guitar players. Rock 'n' roll is a guitar-playing medium. I don't play guitar.

And then I figured out that the purest way to write songs is to avoid the influence of an instrument and to not write songs actually sitting with an instrument either on your knee or under your fingers, but to write them away from the instrument. Then if you get to something that makes sense like that, it's going to make sense on all instruments. But not many people do that. Very early in the piece, Elton John would write a rock song that to me, I could hear that it was written on a piano and it was never convincing. So to write a rock song you either write it on guitar or if you can't play it on guitar, you write it in your head.

Do you remember the first song you ever wrote?
It would be one of two. I wrote an instrumental thing for a music class at school, which was a sort of faux jazzy Brian Auger thing. And then the first one that I wrote with words was with a band that I was in at school. We were entered in the Hoadleys Battle of the Sounds, so I wrote a song for them. At the time it wasn't so much whether it was a good song or not; the amazing thing about it was that there was a song at all that hadn't been got off a record for all of us.

Having a cult hit like "Khe Sanh" so early in your career could be a blessing or a curse. Are you as attached to the song as Australian music fans are?
Yeah. Probably for different reasons. I'm attached to it because it's just the kind of song that I would write, or a young songwriter would write before they knew any rules of songwriting. Or any of the craft. It doesn't follow any of those rules, it has no chorus. The punch line of it is a line out of a verse, it has nothing to do with the title.

"The last plane out of Sydney"?
Exactly.

Which some people still think is "The last train out of Sydney".
Most people. And yet people love it out there to the extent that it's kind of untouchable, that no craftsperson in a publishing company or anything like that can really say anything. The kind of people who are normally saying, "Well, how can you expect anybody to like this? It doesn't have a rising bit into the chorus." These are the kind of things that are said to young songwriters to try and put them on the right path towards crafting great songs. But "Khe Sanh" is not alone in that. I sit down and play the first three Beatles albums and none of those hits, which are timeless and loved all over the world and always will be, follow any of the principles of American Midwestern songwriting, the accepted wisdom for song

craft. They don't have choruses either. They say the punch line and then they move on. They don't hang around and have a whole chorus selling you the punch line. They don't have time for that.

Some people have a big hit song early in their career and it almost becomes an albatross. But you obviously still love playing it.
I don't play it. When I get back together with Cold Chisel, yes, we play it. But that's so rare that it's not a problem. And as far as in my solo work, for some reason it's never requested. Maybe on one of the earlier tours somebody requested it and they heard me sing it. Whereas I know from mates who are songwriters or people who are just doing gigs out there, they hate the song. Because they cannot get up and play anywhere in Australia and New Zealand, South-East Asia or parts of London without some pissed idiot coming up and harassing them to play "Khe Sanh". So "Khe Sanh" is anathema to a lot of performers out there. But I think that's great.

I heard you say once that you wrote it on a napkin at a cafe in Kings Cross. Was that at the Sweethearts Cafe?
I don't know if it was on a napkin but it was definitely on some scraps of paper or a pad or something. At the old Sweethearts as it was in the seventies.

Did you know a particular Vietnam vet who inspired it?
I knew a bloke that I had gone to school with in younger years, but then he dropped out of school and he was rabbit shooting. He volunteered and went to Vietnam. The guy from the next farm went to Vietnam and came back. I don't know what happened to the rabbit shooter and I've forgotten his name. The other guy's name I remember but I won't say it here. He came back and was severely changed for the worst, which was a shame because he was a wonderful bloke. He died in a car crash quite young. The main bloke that I knew was Rick Morris, a guitar player in Adelaide. Who died only recently. And that's all.

Do you usually find your way to a song through the lyrics?
Yes.

Do you keep a note pad, write down bits?
Yep.

Does the opening line come easily to you, or do you come up with a hook line first?
The punch line of the song is the most important thing that I would be looking for. And then if you can have an arresting opening line, that's good.

But with "Khe Sanh", which was albeit an early song, as you said, the punch line had very little to do with the rest of the song.
At that stage I had no craft. I was just having fun. I didn't even think about the importance

of punch lines until the first time Cold Chisel started touring America and I started really listening to what was going on with American popular music.

On the *East* album the songs were clearly very well crafted with more of a pop sensibility.
After the *East* album. The *East* album was already out before we ever went to America.

But *Circus Animals* was like a reaction to *East*. It had an anti-pop sensibility and a whole different energy.
No, I think up until the *East* album I was writing on instinct. And then that all got knocked sideways by travelling overseas, along with severe self-questioning and insecurity about whether what I'm doing is valid and stuff like that. It took me a long time, then, to figure out how things work consciously. To figure out how to do things where it's not just instinct. And then get back to where you can do things with instinct with confidence again.

It's that balance between inspiration and perspiration, which a lot of songwriters talk about.
Yes. And the correct balance is an evolving thing. It changes as you get older.

Where would that be for you now, percentage-wise?
I try and do as little perspiration as possible. If you find that you're a songwriter it's because you're probably a bit work-shy in general, and I don't see that as being necessarily a bad thing. It's definitely a thing to try and keep a hold of and keep focused on.

Do you use resource material to find lyrics and phrases, or is your head constantly full of them?
Neither. I don't get good ideas often, but I don't go out seeking source material. There's various things that I'm interested in, not because they're source material for songs, but because I'm just naturally interested in them. And then inevitably that leaks into what I'm doing. Somewhere ten years ago I was reading a lot of Jewish religious work, and at the same time a certain amount of the Bible and Masonic work and stuff like that. Not because of inspiration for songs; that has absolutely no application for getting a hit song on Triple M. But just out of interest. And on subsequent albums that I did towards the mid-nineties, you could see that interest starting to leak through. A lot of things on *We're All Gunna Die*.

Some songwriters read poetry, and they use a thesaurus when they write. Your vocabulary is immense and your access to words and phrases is prolific. One can read your lyrics almost as poetry.
I've got a thesaurus downstairs and I almost never use it. I also bought a rhyming dictionary about ten years ago and I started to use that and then I realised it was screwing me up, that I wasn't actually getting any songwriting done. Instead, you spend all your time making lists of rhyming words and crap like that. It's the antithesis of writing the perfect, seamless song, which is usually done quickly. So I avoid that, too. Also when you hear stuff that other people have done, you can tell if they've had the rhyming dictionary on the lap. I think it's

not so much is it a perfect rhyme—some rough rhymes are bad, some perfect rhymes are bad, too—it's down to whether it's musical to the ear. A songwriter that I admire greatly and work with a lot is Red Rivers. And one of the characteristics of Red is that his lyrics really do look like poetry on the page. They're very simple, but you often hear in his work where he could have put in a word which would be a perfect rhyme but instead he puts in something else that might not be a rhyme at all but it's the perfect poetic word. And then he'll make it sing. It's something that always struck me and attracted me to what he does. 'Cause he's not from a literate background at all. But somehow instinctively he goes for the poetry rather than the craft.

As you're working on the lyrics first and writing away from an instrument, at what point do you then sit and work on a melody?
In the perfect situation, if you get the lyrics right and perfect so that they sing beautifully, they'll sing the melody at you.

Do you start humming it first?
No, it's all in my head.

At what point will you sit down at the piano and try to articulate what's in your head?
When it's all finished.

How do you remember it?
I've got the lyrics written out and if I can't remember how it goes musically, then it probably wasn't the right way to do it.

Aren't you ever in a situation where you're working on a few songs at once?
Oh, I'm always working on about twenty songs at once.

Does the melody ever come to you first?
Yes.

Can you name a song that was particularly melody-driven?
"Flame Trees", Steve Prestwich wrote all the music first. And so the words are written on top of quite an exact existing melody. A lot of the stuff that I wrote with Ian Moss for his hit albums in the late eighties, early nineties were songs where he presented me with completed music and melodies.

What about your own melody coming first?
"Carless in Isa" is a case where the music was there first. It was a case of trying to write lyrics afterwards and then realising very quickly that to actually sing something to this is inappropriate. It actually needs something that's spoken softly. And there's a lot, like "I Just Wanna Have a Party", where they both come together, and it's happening quite quickly.

"In the End" is definitely a melody first. Often, if the melody comes first, it's demanding a certain kind of flavour or story. The melody pulls the story out a bit. I guess it's the reverse of the words singing the melody at you.

What suggests to you that a song should have a frenetic pace, such as "Ghost Town" or "Hold Me Tight"?
With both those songs it was the music first. With "Ghost Town" I was at a very pissed-off, cynical stage of life. Sydney and the whole environment with the band, with the late night clubs, which is all very interesting when you first do it, but it's like any scene, it gets stale after a while. So it was a cynical set of lyrics about a scene after it had gone stale.

Whereas "Hold Me Tight" is jut a wild set of lyrics about totally unrelated people all doing this one wonderful thing.
That's right.

I love the line, "Ayatollahs always do it." How do you know that?
"Ayatollah" was just a topical word at the time. Someone pointed out a long time ago that in the Islamic world and in the Jewish world and in Eastern Christianity, clerics marry and have children, whereas in Western Christianity for more than 1,500 years anyone with the intelligence to study scripture has been forbidden to breed. Great eugenics.

How often do you have a song come to you at once in its entirety and survive intact, just a flood of inspiration?
It's happened from time to time over the years. It's the very best thing, and often they're the very best songs. So long as you're smart enough not to then go home and tool around, tinker with them. And so long as you have some sort of artefact where you can remember.

Do you feel inclined to rush home and get to the piano?
No, not to the piano. I've got a dictaphone.

Can you name a few songs that have come that way?
"Empty Beach" was like that. "Empty Beach" happened walking the two blocks between Darlinghurst Road and my house in Roslyn Street. "I Just Wanna Have a Party" happened quite quickly. "My Girl" happened very quickly while driving, as did "Charleville". "Carless in Isa" happened quite quickly while I was driving back in the middle of the night from the Tex, Don & Charlie sessions in Melbourne, back to Sydney. By and large, no, I work on it for a long time.

Have you ever been carless in Isa?
No. I've been in Isa quite a few times but never without a means of escape.

Where did the idea come from of being carless in Mt Isa?
I've got this book downstairs called *Eyeless in Gaza*. Which is an Aldous Huxley book. That title refers to Samson having his eyes put out.

Do you see yourself as a storyteller or a painter of pictures?
It's an interesting distinction that I've never thought about before, but I guess you can classify people like that. There's been a couple of times where I've been writing something and I'm quite involved in it, realised that all I've done is painted a picture and that I must make something happen. And gone back and taken the thing apart and actually made something happen. I would be a natural picture painter a lot of the time. Unless I'm writing a specific story song.

Do you stay out of the picture or are you more emotionally involved? I wondered, particularly in the Cold Chisel stuff, whether detachment was an important tool for you in telling those stories.
It varies from song to song. The first Cold Chisel album is about somebody that I was involved with and split up with long before we ever recorded. But those songs were held over. So they're not that detached. I'm involved there, sometimes to the detriment of the song. 'Cause those songs were not great. You can't be too detached if you're writing about a character that's not you. The test for me is I'm always careful of a certain amount of arrogance, and arrogance is not the right word, but you're really going out on a limb if you're there, a songwriter living in Kings Cross, and you write a song where the first person is driving a truck. You're halfway to being a bullshit artist. And the test is, does a guy who drives a truck like this song and relate to it? Many people when I was young, their test was, will the record company like this? Will all the other people out there, the other 98 per cent of the market who are not driving trucks, like this? To me it's pretty important—the truck driver had to like this. And the same with situations like writing about Vietnam. You're really a long way towards being a bullshit artist if you try and write about war experience and you've never been in a war. Rick liked that song. I won't say that it had his seal of approval or anything like that, but he didn't disapprove of it, or me for writing it.

Your characters are definitely not basking in the sunshine of Australian life.
Oh, I don't know about that.

Were you already fascinated by shadowy figures before you left Grafton, or did that come once you got to Adelaide, started touring, and then settled in Kings Cross?
I'm not consciously interested in shadowy figures. I just think the world is a lot more shadowy out there than is normally painted and I don't think that's such a bad thing.

Australia likes to look at itself as a happy, sunshiny place full of happy, sunshiny people.
Well, it is.

Not according to many of your songs.
I disagree. "Khe Sanh", yeah, there's a certain amount of discontent there. A certain amount of discontent is just a part of the condition of life.

I wasn't actually thinking of "Khe Sanh" because I think that man is troubled and justifiably so. I don't think of him as a dark, sinister, corrupt kind of character.
No, okay, name some dark, sinister, corrupt ones.

You're known for writing songs with characters who have lived a hard life, who have lived the dark side. You write about nighttime a lot, about seediness, like "Saturday Night". Even a song like "Showtime", which is about your own disillusionment, is just full of nasties.
Yes. Well, "Showtime" wasn't written on an inspiring night.

"Painted Doll"—is that about a heroin addict, a prostitute?
Yes.

"Barlow and Chambers"—about a couple of drug traffickers.
Yes.

And "Four Walls". What gave you a fascination for incarceration? There are a few songs where your characters are either imprisoned or have just come out of prison or are thinking about the possibility that they could go to prison.
There's always been a connection between real music and jail experiences. All great songwriters have dealt with this. Johnny Cash, Bob Dylan, Hank Williams. And there's always been a connection between rock 'n' roll. And on a personal level, we had guys that we were working with and that were very close to us who had a certain amount of jail experience, some of them quite a lot of jail experience.

You conveyed a sense of Australia as part of Asia, particularly in your Cold Chisel work. You were really the first songwriter to do that. Other songwriters were either writing material that could have been American or British, or they were interested in the urban Australian experience.
I had an uncle who spent three years in Singapore during the war against his will. My father had done a couple of stints in New Guinea during the war. Ian's grandfather was a trader who'd worked all his life, everything from pearling luggers to trading goods, everywhere from Broome and Carnarvon round to Darwin, with Indonesian islands. I think there were Chinese here within the first ten years of white settlement. And a lot of interaction with Asia before white settlement. So there's a lot of things, the way this country is seen, which are really the conceit of my hippy generation about the identity of this country. Things I could list, like, "There was never any good food here until somebody brought spaghetti". "This has only just become a cosmopolitan place since me and my friends became cosmopolitan", which is a favourite conceit of people of my generation. Baby boomers. And "We only started

to become engaged with Asia since our favourite politician, Paul Keating of the sharp suits, engaged us." The fact is we've been engaged with Asia for 150 years. In a hundred years we will look Asian. And to me it's a damn good thing.

When you were writing songs for Cold Chisel, did the prospect of the band performing the songs live guide you in their creation?
Yes. But there wasn't much that the band couldn't do. There wasn't much constraint in that. The only constraint there is that I tried to keep things so that it could be done with five people.

How much did you tailor the choice of keys around the vocals of Jimmy Barnes or Ian Moss?
There's guitar keys and there's keyboard keys. And I guess Cold Chisel finished up about fifty-fifty between them. The natural guitar keys if you're landing round E, you land at a point where Jim can go with a lot of power and very few singers can follow. Which is the natural guitar key. Or D if it's D tuning. I do a lot of things around there. And for things that are more piano-based like "Four Walls", of course it's more like piano keys.

With "The Things I Love in You" it's hard to imagine it without that ripping, throaty, Barnesy screaming vocal. Was that song written as a comeback Chisel song or did you already have that one floating around?
The song was floating around. At one stage I was mucking around with some songs with Spencer Jones and I showed him the idea because I thought he might be able to finish it off. He didn't get involved with it. And then when this 1998 Cold Chisel reunion came up I finished it off. I didn't think it was anything special, but the other people in the band jumped on it immediately, in particular Jim. Jim said, "That to me is a Cold Chisel song." And that was probably the first one I presented. Because for the 1998 reunion everybody else had a lot of material to throw in the pot, particularly Steve, but I didn't.

After "The Things I Love in You", you had to write more specifically for the project?
Yeah, in the initial meetings when everybody was bringing in their songs I didn't have much to bring in at all. I'd just done in quick succession the Tex, Don & Charlie album, my solo album *We're All Gunna Die*, and then I'd finished up writing a few things for Ian Moss's *Petrolhead* album. I didn't have much around. So a lot of that is written from a standing start. I assumed that the reunion album was going to be largely written by the other guys and I was quite relaxed about that.

What I like about "The Things I Love in You" is what I don't get. I always listen to it thinking, I want the full story here. What is it that he needs to tell them that I'm not hearing?
It's a guy in a situation where his girlfriend's in a room with somebody else. Which is about the most intense part of a life that a young bloke can go through.

When the other members of Cold Chisel started contributing on *East* and *Circus Animals*, was that a relief for you or did you then have a surplus of songs that had nowhere to go?
It was a relief for me. Writing a whole album was a bit hard. It was nice when *East* came along. I enjoyed *Breakfast at Sweethearts* because as a whole set of songs, it painted a picture of a certain time and a certain place which is very close to my heart. And in many ways that set of songs is quite personal to me rather than any of the other guys, because they all moved out of the Cross within three weeks. It was a good time of my life. But when the next album came along and they started writing, to me it was like, "Oh beauty, I only have to come up with four or five songs, and I can come up with some real killers."

So you weren't always writing, the kind of writer who would wake up each day and write a song; it was more writing for a purpose, a project, an album?
Neither. Songs with me kind of accumulate. I don't write every day. I don't have a set routine. I'd like to, but it doesn't work out that way. I'm a bit more disciplined about it now. In those days, songs just occurred when they occurred. And when album time came round it was a case of looking at what's there, and what we'd been playing live.

Did you ever present a song to the band that they didn't like or understand?
Yeah, "Showtime". They didn't like it from the start. Neither did the producer, neither did the record company, neither did the manager. It was a case of me saying, "Well, look, for me this song's really important, how about you give me this one?" And they were quite happy to do it under that rationale. But it's very much a pieced-together recording where everybody's just playing and singing their parts. Because it's not a song that anybody had any great passion for.

You were still in the early stages of the success of the band. Were you already that disillusioned with it?
There were definitely long periods of time pre-Cold Chisel having a recording contract where it looked like there was nothing happening at all and the dream that you had in your head of how it could be was so divorced from reality. So relentlessly that you wonder if you're some kind of lunatic to carry on. Because not only is the dream in your head not your reality, it's not anybody else's reality either. It's not like you can look round at any successful bands and say, "I wish we could be like them." We despised the kind of success that Little River Band and Sherbet were having. The dream that we had in our head was nothing like where they were.

Which is why you smashed up the Countdown Awards set?
No, we smashed up the Countdown set because it was fun.

***Breakfast at Sweethearts* is my second favourite Cold Chisel album after *Twentieth Century*. And I know *Twentieth Century* is not the favourite album of you guys. But I think musically**

it's stunning and I think the sequencing on the album is stunning, too. And vital, because of the mood shifts. From those frenetic songs to "Saturday Night" or "Sing to Me".
It's got some great things that happened and it's got some real disasters. I can't listen to "Sing to Me" or "Janelle" as they appeared on that album; to me it's the worst production choices, because I was trying my hand at production at the time. The harmonies that I made Ian sing in the background and choices with arrangements, it's just unlistenable to me. "Saturday Night", which is pretty much produced by me, is a great production.

When I heard the Tex, Don & Charlie album I realised that "Janelle" was in fact "Danielle". You wrote it as "Danielle" initially, for your daughter. Why did you change it?
I had a complicated personal life at the time and having a song called "Danielle" at that stage was intensely upsetting for somebody. So I changed the title. I don't even think about whether that was the right thing or the wrong thing to do. It's a pretty personal song. But everything works out in the end.

Was "Saturday Night" literally written after a Saturday night roaming around the Cross?
Not that I remember. The band I'd been in for ten years was breaking up. I think it's just a "kissing all that goodbye and moving on into the unknown" song.

After Cold Chisel first disbanded, did you feel that songwriting would still be an important part of your life?
No. I thought at that stage, "Well, that was interesting. That was a great way to spend ten years or so. But I'm really young and fortunately I've kind of reached a retirement in what I'm doing and have plenty of time to do two or three other things. And I shouldn't rush into anything, but I should get out there and really do some interesting things, some things that you don't get to do when you're in a touring band. Like really see a town." So I thought I'd travel for a little while and see what occurs. "And I've done that songwriting, and that's been good, and I've shown I can do that, but really only a loser would keep doing it to the point where you can show yourself that you can't do it." So I was going to leave it behind. But then it became clear that songs come out anyway.

I was interested in the work with Ian Moss for his solo career and then, later on, having Tex Perkins singing your words as well. Is it always important that the person singing your songs can be genuine about them?
Oh, absolutely.

Does that then guide you when writing something specifically for someone like Slim Dusty or Adam Brand?
If I'm writing songs for a commercial purpose that's different. That's craft for money, and I do a certain amount of that. And I wouldn't single out artists that I put in that category. From time to time there's been a song of mine lying around that a singer out there will come across through publishing or something like that, and do it.

Like "Big Old Car".
I like what Adam does.

That would be one of your more simple, ingenuous, warm and fuzzy songs; it's not one of the dark, complex numbers.
Yes. He and his manager, Graham Thompson, came across that song before Cold Chisel recorded it, and they were very keen on it from the word go. They wanted that song. And I said, "No, because Cold Chisel might be doing it." They found that frustrating, but that's the way it was. Then Cold Chisel did record it but didn't release it. That was even more frustrating for them, so the next opportunity they got, the next time they recorded, they did it. And did a completely different version. But there are songs that I write out there where people come across stuff in the commercial world and do it, and there are songs that I write commercially for people who are looking. It's a little bit different from the stuff that I necessarily write for myself or for Tex and Charlie or enterprises like that. Which don't sell nearly as many records.

Did you write "Good Friends" for Adam Brand?
"Good Friends" was a 60 or 70 per cent completed idea that was brought to me by my nephew Myles, in a raft of song ideas that he was showing me, because at that stage he was quite a keen guitar player and songwriter, and I recognised it immediately—amongst all the other stuff he had, which was quite heavy and dark—as being this sunny, commercial, instant hit pop song. I said, "We've got to finish this off." Which was very easy and enjoyable to do. And next thing Adam was onto it and recorded it.

There is that part of you that responds to the sunny side, and it's also quite guileless. What brings that out?
It's usually a stack of bills on the corner of the desk and a set of dismal sales figures for albums like *We're All Gunna Die*.

Not sitting down and looking at your little girl and thinking, "Awww …"?
[*Laughs*] The songs that I write for people that I care about are all there, but they tend to have a little bit more bite in them than just sunny, jingly sort of stuff.

"Little Girl" sounds intensely personal. Adam told me that he had been called in to sing the demo and then desperately wanted to sing it on his own album.
I've never known whether that song was a ballad: is it over-maudlin, or syrupy or what? I do know it's about a situation of shared custody, where you've got little girls who are spending part of their time with their mum and part of their time with their dad. And it's true. But when I wrote it I looked at the punchline and I thought, "This is like something Bobby Goldsboro would sing; I can't really show this to anybody." Even though it's about real life.

How is it for another singer to do something of yours that is so personal?
It can be great. When I did "Danielle" with Tex and Charlie, there could be no more

personal song for me. I sang the first half of the song and then Tex was to take over and sing the second half where it goes up. Now I had completely the wrong mental attitude as I went in; even though it's a personal song to me, I didn't have that in my mind when I was singing it. I was singing it with the attitude of this is a blues song and it's got one of those rare melodies where I can sing it in a bluesy way. That's the kind of thing that was going through my head as I'm singing it. So my vocal is quite artificial. Tex had a little girl at the time, and still does, who is not much younger than the girl that this song was about, my daughter. He swung in with no ego in his vocal and he just sang it like a dad singing a lullaby to a little girl. That was all that was in his voice. There's nothing in his voice of "Hey, I'm a singer" or anything like that. He just sang it softly as a man sings to a little girl when she's going to sleep. And it was a big lesson for me that he's singing the most personal song to me, as it should be sung. And had not been sung up until that stage. Because Jim and Ian, who had sung the song as "Janelle", they weren't singing it as a personal song at all, they were singing it as a live showstopper.

What is the appeal of minor chords? They are used to great effect on much of your work, especially songs like "Star Hotel" and "Saturday Night"—almost jarring but quite exquisitely melodic.
I like minor chords but I don't stick exclusively to them. Some writers that I really love do, like Louis Tillet, who pretty much writes in cycles of minor chords. It produces a real kind of effect. Louis is not the only one. And it produces a certain sound. I like to switch between.

It's those switches that make it so effective.
Yes.

What does a minor chord say to you?
I can't put it into words in a general principle. It's just a case of when you're working on a song it announces itself where it should go next and to get the effect to pull you into where the song wants to pull you.

There is a particular Don Walker sound that I hear; it's distinctive chord progressions and a bluesy pop piano. I hear it on songs as diverse as "Showtime", "Taipan", "Letter to Alan", "Build This Love", "Jericho Road", "He Can't Believe It's Over with You", as well as the obvious hits. Do you have your own ideas of what the Don Walker sound is?
No, absolutely not. From time to time I've had guys in the band say, "Oh, that's a Don progression." I'm always interested and surprised because I don't see that I've got a set of progressions or not. I'm not talking about Cold Chisel, I'm talking about other musicians, and they go, "Oh yeah! Yeah, there's a couple of things that you do all the time, over and over again." I'm not aware of it, so maybe I'm repeating myself and I haven't got onto it.

Is it important that your audiences understand your songs? Something like "My Backyard" on the first Catfish album, _Unlimited Address_, is evocative, moody and musically flows in a catchy way, but lyrically it's a mystery.

By and large the songs that I love most and that mean the most to me have found the smallest audience. Obviously, I would like a lot more people to hear that material. However, that's not the case in the real world. Ultimately with that stuff, what I'm trying to do is scratch an itch of my own, and these are songs that come out of me and that I can listen to and say, "Yeah, that's a little bit of me." If that little bit of me doesn't interest too many people or it's not marketable, that's regrettable but there are far worse things in life. The most important thing is not that a million people cheer and applaud, the most important thing is to be able to actually nail it. It's unbelievably pleasing to be able to get down something like "Carless in Isa", which has no marketable application whatsoever. I can die a few degrees happier knowing that I've done that song. Because it just nails something that's me. And that may be of no interest to any other human being on the planet. That's okay. But I'm ahead. I'm happier having done it.

Which isn't to say that some of the material you wrote for Cold Chisel, which was hugely popular, wasn't also representing a little bit of you?

Well, some of it possibly, too.

What about something like "Choir Girl", about abortion? It sounds like it had some meaning for you, whether it was personal or observation.

Two things with that. Things can be intensely personal when you write them, but then that gets graded away as you play it 200 times a year over the subsequent five years, and then it gets played on radio fifteen times a day right across the country for the next twenty years. It's like saying the same phrase over and over again, it becomes meaningless. And the second thing is that when somebody else sings something that's quite personal to you, by and large the result is not as personal as it could be. There are rare situations like I described with Tex, and certainly there have been situations where Jim and Ian have on occasion just really nailed something. But it's never going to be as personal as when you sing it yourself.

On the first Catfish album you seemed to be pushing the envelope structurally. Was it difficult, particularly after Chisel, to break away from a conventional linear musical structure? "Subway" sounds like it's closing in on itself, but it also has a driving force that propels it along so the structural innovation isn't necessarily obvious on first listening.

Yes to all of the above. That's probably one of my top five favourite lyrics and songs. Every few years on tour I ask the band to play it and it's a nightmare for musicians to have to play live because each succeeding verse is different. Jazz players would have a lot of fun with that; they could probably go through the changes. There's just three and a half minutes of changes straight there that don't repeat. It cycles and goes up a tone or a semi-tone each verse and cycles through the same pattern, but just when you think the pattern is there it goes somewhere else musically. The thing is that even though musically it's enormously complicated, I don't think it sounds complicated.

There was a lot of experimentation on that album.
Yes, and there's quite a lot of those Eastern European melodies which, when you talk about balancing major and minor, it's what the pop music from there is all about. And getting that exquisite sort of yearning and loss thing that's in Russian popular music.

Have you ever written a lyric that you haven't been able to find the melody for?
Yes.

Is there anything you've tried to write about and been unable to?
Yeah. But I know it will happen. I've got a couple of songs downstairs that have defied me for a long time.

Because of the subject matter?
No, not because of the subject matter. I very rarely consciously decide I'm going to write a song about *that* situation. It's happened once or twice. It happened with "Star Hotel", where somebody sent me the newspaper clipping and said, "Why don't you write about this?" But it very rarely happens.

After the European flavour of *Unlimited Address*, what made you look back to the Australian rural picture that you had grown up with on *Ruby*?
Following the travels I was doing overseas that the songs on *Unlimited Address* came out of, I found myself back here in Australia dealing not only with a range of personal problems but responsibilities and so by and large I could go a-roving no more. Apart from that I was doing quite a few driving trips where I'd just get in the car when I had a week and drive up to western New South Wales, western Queensland, I did a couple of trips up there. There was also a period in the late eighties where I spent a year or so in a little country town fighting a custody battle. And I think over the long term that kind of regional Australia thing has leaked into everything I've done since.

And is that the point where your birthplace and where you'd grown up came back to you?
Yes. I wasn't stuck in the same regional town where I'd come from, but nevertheless, regional Australia got me back to that.

"Three Blackbirds", on *We're All Gunna Die*, with its Banjo Paterson long narrative kind of verse, is about as far as you could get from "Cheap Wine". And Broome is literally as far as you can get from Kings Cross without crossing an ocean. It exemplifies the vast stretch in your work.
I'd never thought how far away from "Cheap Wine" it is, but I'm pretty pleased with "Three Blackbirds". I think it's eighteen minutes long. It's not even the kind of thing that you can

present on stage. But I should sooner or later. You'd only need two other songs and you'd have a set.

Is the religious or spiritual side of you part of your experience as a songwriter?
I think so. But I have very seldom written my spiritual beliefs into songs overtly. Recently, Troy Cassar-Daley sent me an idea for a gospel song that he wanted to pitch to Jimmy Little. I took that and finished it and took to the piano and there was no question where the music was going to go, 'cause I know where that stuff goes and how it goes. It was very enjoyable and easy to do.

You're best known for your snapshots of Australian life, but occasionally you'll come out with something so tender it breaks your heart. Was "This Is the Truth" written especially for Jimmy Little's *Resonate* album or had you planned to record it yourself?
There's a couple of songs that I've written in the last few years that are very positive, but I don't feel in a shallow way, that express deep happiness or contentment. That's one of them. There's another one that hasn't seen the light of day yet.

Is part of your spirituality that contentment now?
I think any songwriter is getting some sort of spirituality in what they do. Otherwise you're writing jingles.

I'd like to mention some of your songs that we haven't discussed in detail and get a response from you on each one. "Goodbye (Astrid Goodbye)".
We needed a set finisher.

There was no Astrid in either your life or Jimmy's?
No.

"Shipping Steel".
One of the important hitchhiking trips that I did in my life was when the band made the move from Melbourne to Sydney, with no money, and we basically hitchhiked up. I got picked up in a semitrailer. And halfway along the journey he stopped and bought some speed in tablet form. I had never tried it in tablet form at that stage. So me and the truck driver got into the pills and then he dropped me off in Sydney and I came into town with my suitcases, just flying. That was a very memorable truck-driving journey as a hitchhiker. And that particular journey fed into "Shipping Steel", but the subject matter shifted somewhere else.

"Ita". Did you ever get any feedback from Ita Buttrose on that?
Not specifically. No. For various reasons, occasionally once or twice over the years, we've had a chat on the phone. But not for any length of time. I think she thinks it's funny. She's a good girl. Somebody else told me that Greg Macainsh had a fantasy about Ita but I've never actually asked him about that directly. I have an idea that that's where this all came from.

For a generation of kids who were between twenty and twenty-five, I was a fair bit older, but she was an example of the hot middle-aged woman. That song was just a bit of fun.

"Houndog".
Musically, it's just like a battering ram of a song to show that we could do a Who or a Led Zeppelin. 'Cause that's where we were coming from after we'd done our pop album, to kind of re-establish who the governors are. I think on that whole album I was really scratching to find a handle on what I could write about that would have any meaning.

Your imagery is always pertinent. Like many people who know that song, the line "Through Nambucca, up the coast" is particularly resonant for me because it is so evocative of place, especially for someone who has travelled a lot on the north coast of New South Wales. You have a tendency to do that, to bring in a place name and completely change the atmosphere mid-song, such as the "Townsville sugar sunsets" in "Showtime" or "Lookin' down on Sydney Harbour in the rain" in "Painted Doll". Is that a deliberate device?
No, it's not deliberate, and now that you point it out, I'll keep a watch out for it.

In "Showtime" I thought it was maybe a stream-of-consciousness thing. I don't know about the ghost of Jimmie Rodgers, what that story is.
Jimmie Rodgers was the bloke who owned the next farm when we had a sugar cane farm when I was a kid.

In "Flame Trees" the lyric is about Grafton?
Yes.

Why did you reprise the phrase "set fire to the town" from "Merry-Go-Round"?
That moment in the middle of "Merry-Go-Round" had become one of the signature points in the live shows. I can't remember why I did that in "Flame Trees", apart from making that reference. The point is that nothing exciting is going to happen here.

"Tucker's Daughter".
Like a lot of those songs for Ian's thing, he had a piece of music. He sometimes had snatches of phrases, or syllables that he wanted to be singing on a certain note. So I would do a kind of a Rubik's Cube on them, shoehorning lyrics and lyrical rhythms and having the right syllable on the right note and stuff like that. And for it to come out to have a sensible lyric. Ian sent "Tucker's Daughter" over to me on a cassette express airmail from Los Angeles where he was, and he had the melody but the only lyric he had was "Hey there mother fucker." Right through the rest of the song. I couldn't use that, but I recognised that it had a certain percussive force.

I used to do some cotton chipping when I was young at Wee Waa, so I set it there and changed the name of the boss to Mr Tucker. And there was never any daughter in the picture when I was young, unfortunately.

"Mr Crown Prosecutor".

I had that line which is from the Bible; it might have been when Joseph went into Egypt, that the vine that's planted by the well can go over any wall. The message I take it to be, you stay close to God, which is the source—a well is a symbol of the source I guess— and there is no temporal wall that can withstand your grace. The simple situation is somebody's standing there in the dock who has done something wrong but goes through some of the hypocrisies of the environment.

"Bal-A-Versailles".

It's a love song for my wife and it's the perfume that she occasionally wears.

"Charleville".

I was in Charleville, I had stayed there the night previously in one of those condemned pubs. I'd made it a rule on those trips that I wasn't going to stay in motels, that I wanted to stay in pubs upstairs. I was in one of those places and I was the only guest and it's haunted. But it was an uneventful night. And the next day I was about ten miles out of Charleville driving south and this song just happened. Except I didn't know the street names. So I had to turn around and drive back into town and get the local street names right.

You love Slim's version of "Charleville", don't you?

I do. I love his version of anything that he's done of mine.

Including "Looking Forward Looking Back" which you wrote specifically for him. Was there anything of you in that song?

No, it was for Slim and that album. Not me. Slim's got another song that I've sent over there in the last year that's the best thing that I've written in the last five years. It's called "Get Along". It's a truck-driving song. It's not like other songs, and I hesitated to send it off to [Dusty's producer] Rod Coe, thinking, "I don't know what he's going to make of this." Because Slim is in some ways quite conservative. It's quite specifically for a truck-driving album. And truck-driving songs as a genre, it's like writing Mills & Boon novels. There's a real template for what's a truck-driving song or not. This song is like I've sent in a Xavier Herbert manuscript to Mills & Boon.

You prefer writing alone to collaborating, don't you?

Absolutely, yeah. But I do enjoy with certain people. If I'm writing with Micheal Smotherman in America, we do a lot of eating, a lot of drinking, a lot of walking around, a lot of laughing. And the writing of the song is about 3 per cent of it. With Troy Cassar-Daley, who I write with all the time, it's just so easy. There's something about the stuff that he sends me, it's very easy, there's no work involved.

You don't sit in a room together and write?
We have done that but lately, the last two or three things that we've written, we've done it over the phone and emailing each other lyrics. There's a thing we're working on at the moment where he's sent a punch line down. It's a particularly good punch line for a truck-driving song. "I've been down that road before." When you're young you do every stupid thing, because it's there. Whether it's drugs or women or whatever. But then there's a certain stage of maturity where you do and you don't do things as an act of will. And often the best people are people who don't do the wrong thing not because they figure it's the wrong thing, but because they've *done* the wrong thing. So that's the essence of "I've been down that road before." You can trust me not to do a stupid thing, darling, not because I haven't been stupid, but because in the past I've been stupid.

Do you have an idea of where songs come from?
I don't think they come from anywhere. I don't think I have a muse up there or anything like that.

So do you think it's more cerebral?
Oh no, you can't write much of any depth out of pure intellect.

So it comes from inside of you.
Yes. But sometimes you get the feeling it comes through you. From the other side of you, through you.

If you couldn't write songs any more, would you still play music?
I don't play music that much, aside from mine. I don't actually go and tinker at the piano for pleasure.

But you play with bands.
Yes, that's pretty important, and I would continue to do that even if I lost the capacity to write any new songs. Because I love the songs that are written for that certain thing that I do solo. I really love getting up on stage and doing that.

STEPHEN CUMMINGS

MELBOURNE, AUSTRALIA, FEBRUARY 2004

The exercise of dissecting the creative process is anathema to Stephen Cummings. Talking about his work is discomforting for him, and not too easy for the interviewer, as many journalists will attest. But Cummings has always been feted by the music press, who admire his resolve, in a commercialised and youth-focused music industry, to stick to his guns, regularly recording new albums of original material and avoiding the pressure many of his contemporaries succumb to of trading on a successful pop past.

In fact, talking about his earliest songwriting ventures with The Sports was the most difficult part of a difficult interview. While he was about to go into the studio to re-record some of his best known songs in a pared-back acoustic style, including a handful from the Sports repertoire, it was not as a concession to the rampant nostalgia market. The *Close Ups* album, released six months after our meeting, was more a gentle nod to the path that had led him to the present day, a sigh of acquiescence that what he had done so far was okay. Hitherto

Cummings had played no Sports songs at his concerts. Now he was prepared to do so again, just for a while. "I've kept doing all new work and haven't looked back at all," he told me. "I've kept moving on and on and gone forward. Otherwise you're always at the mercy of someone else."

I placed myself at Cummings' mercy on a typical Melbourne day when the warm summer sun gave way to bleak, chilly skies and rain forced us from his backyard to his garage-studio. "I don't know, I don't know," was a frequent response to just about any question, but after he had squirmed and resisted, he would surrender to the occasion and offer an insight into what drives him. If there was little by way of explanation of the mechanics of putting songs together, there was much about love, melancholy and some forthright admissions that he is the centre of his world and therefore all of his songs are about him or what interests him. Yet, in a frequent carp about having to answer yet another question about his songwriting, he would say, "I hate thinking about myself." And then he would discuss the benefits of undergoing ten years of psychoanalysis. He never used his friends as subjects for his writing, he said. And then described how one of his saddest songs, "Why Doesn't She Want Me", was directly inspired by a couple he knew. Welcome to the contrary world of Stephen Cummings.

He was born on 13 September 1954 in Melbourne, and has never lived anywhere else. "I'm almost pathetic, why am I still living in the same place I was born in?" he said with only a hint of irony. Cummings is quintessentially Melbourne, just like Paul Kelly, and it's not surprising that the two songwriters have often shared musicians. There is something appealing about working with someone, characterised as "perceptive and passionate", whose songs have been described as "adult", "suave" and "intelligent". Cummings has worked almost exclusively with Melbourne music identities, from Joe Camilleri, who produced The Sports' debut album, *Reckless*, to early co-writers Andrew Pendlebury and Martin Armiger, both of whom continued to work with Cummings on his solo albums after The Sports folded, and regular accompanists, guitarist Shane O'Mara and vocalist Rebecca Barnard.

After studying film at Swinburne College, Cummings switched to music; his first band, The Pelaco Brothers, also included Camilleri and Ed Bates, the latter moving with him into The Sports. While The Sports, who enjoyed chart success in the late 1970s with songs like "Who Listens to the Radio" and "Don't Throw Stones", were celebrated for fusing R&B and rockabilly with a pop sensibility, the eleven solo albums Cummings has since recorded (discounting three compilations) are distinctly non-commercial, and while the musical styles cover a broad spectrum from soul and R&B to country, blues, languid balladry and rockabilly again, it's his lyrics that earn him the critical accolades. The storytelling and minute detail of suburban life, the turn of phrase, all attest to an enthusiasm Cummings has for wordplay. He has also written three novels; he was working on revisions for the third, *Kitchen Man*, when we met.

For such a "serious artist", as Cummings has undoubtedly seen himself, it's interesting that his biggest commercial success has been in jingle writing, something he only dabbled in briefly. The Medibank Private ad ("I feel better now"), which he co-wrote and sang, is probably more entrenched in the minds and ears of Australians than any of his songs, but Cummings doesn't mind.

"The thing is, I've been able to keep on making records," he said philosophically. "I've always maintained my following really well and I've kept on moving on to new things, new things, new things all the time."

When did you start playing guitar?
I had a drum kit first, when I was about fourteen. I probably got a guitar at a similar time, but I didn't really learn how to play it properly. Just to play riffs on. I didn't end up doing any music until after I went to film school.

Were you writing as a kid? Short stories maybe?
No, not at all. I was always writing songs, though, in my head. I had a cassette player and I would sing my own songs, my own takes on songs.

Before you were even playing the guitar?
Yeah. I was walking around singing into a tape recorder in the bathroom, the toilet.

What were they about?
Just anything that I was listening to at the time.

Did you keep the tapes?
No. I throw everything away.

You don't keep demos?
No. I wish I had. I made three short 16mm films and I threw them away in the garbage. I only regret it because my friends were in them and I wish I had them now to have.

What about your reading as a young person?
Basically what I started reading was Girls' Own Annuals. They were the only books we had in the house, because I had an older sister. I became a huge reader through reading these annuals.

Where do you think the lyrical quality of your songs comes from?
I became as interested in films as music, and when I went to Swinburne, three times a week they'd have film nights with incredible history of cinema, all sorts of obscure films, so I really got sucked into films. And then got sucked into Jack Kerouac books and then more into other sorts of books. I always liked reading. When I was a teenager I used to get really bad migraines and to will it to go away, I'd read and get myself into this other state. I lived in the outer eastern suburbs then, so there weren't that many kids around, and to amuse myself I had to read. I retreated off into my own world. Strangely my two children are like that too. Boys don't usually read that much these days, but my older son is incredibly into reading.

Did you start using the guitar for writing before The Sports?
No. I always wanted to get into a group but didn't really meet anyone else that could play anything. I was very shy and didn't know many people. After art school, I went and lived in Fitzroy and then I met people who played and I started up in music. I knew what I wanted but I didn't know how you did it. Just about everything I've done is like that, my musical knowledge is much faster than my ability to do something. I couldn't play guitar that well.

How did your collaborations work with the other members of The Sports?
I was always the instigator.

Did songs happen during rehearsals or did you set aside songwriting time?
It was just something I always did. I'd get them to come over some other time and do it. You played all the time then so you had to have heaps of songs. You get really bored with the songs, you have to come up with more all the time to keep yourself interested and keep the audience interested. So I just had to get songs together. That was the most interesting part of it all.

Did you usually come up with a lyrical idea first or would the melody and the words come simultaneously?
Either or. I always had notebooks and I'd write phrases and things down all the time. A real magpie. Just things that would amuse me. Words or things taken out of context, I'd always write them down. I still do it, but having a computer's much better. I will have a list of song titles; there will be a list of fifty things that I'll get around to. I've always wanted to do a self-help book of songs. I've written a few lately like, "This is how a new life can open up for you." I try and think of things like that to amuse myself now. Because basically my life's great and stable.

Happy?
I wouldn't say happy. But stable. So there's more things like that interesting me. I set myself tasks. For my most recent record, I sat down for a month and said I'm going to write a rockabilly song every day. And that really turned me around now and sent me off, because I thought, I just like this so much, this is more fun than trying to be clever. Or trying to be ironic or pithy. The whole thing is I'm just trying to amuse myself. That is totally what I'm doing. Because you can be successful but successful doesn't last very long, so you have to work to your own agenda. And if you keep doing it for a long time, usually people in any art form go back to what got them into it in the first place. That initial enthusiasm. Because you know everything's fucked and stupid, and there's no logic to it all, and then you go back and get interested again.

When you come up with an idea, a phrase, a group of words, do they suggest a melody to you?
Yeah. Now I can play guitar better so I just sit down and play guitar. I make tapes all the time. The worst thing is I forget what I've done. Because I can play for two hours. I play

into the machine and then go back and say, "Oh, that sounds great. But what did I do?" So now I have to say what I did after I've done it. Like, "I did C 7th and I had a capo on the 5th." I'm like an idiot savant, I don't quite know what I'm doing. I wish I'd learned to play guitar better when I was younger and I wish I learned punctuation and grammar better. Because it's so frustrating, it's taken me so long to get where I am because I've had to learn everything backwards.

Are punctuation and grammar important in songwriting?
Not in songwriting, but in writing books. They're both similar, 'cause I've come to both arse around. I would have been happier and would be able to express myself so much better in both ways. But the other way of looking at it is, it has a unique thing to it, which I wouldn't have had.

How did you come up with the idea for "Boys! (What Did the Detective Say?)"? It was an unusual title.
Back then I was really interested in detective books. I used to go to community op shops and get all those old detective books, and records, and clothes. So it would have just come from something like that. I had hundreds. I've given them all away now. I can't read them in fact; I find violence upsetting.

I grew up watching all the Crawford Productions shows like *Homicide* and *Division 4*, very Melbourne cop shows. The song reminded me of those.
Well, there was Russell Street and stuff like that, yeah.

Do you remember actually writing the song?
No, I've written so many. The whole thing can be explained simply that we played five or six nights a week, we had to have songs, and so we just came up with songs all the time. But I've got no idea. Sometimes I hear some songs that I can't even remember writing them at all.

What about writing "Reckless" with Ed Bates and Andrew Pendlebury?
It would have been probably two of us and then one chipped in at rehearsal. That would be typical of one that I just walked around singing and then I would have gotten one of them over and nutted through it. I'm not being egotistical, I'm just saying I was more musically sophisticated than I could practically do.

"Reckless" had a really interesting pace to it; it was a very sophisticated song.
Yeah, a lot of them are based around the rhythm of the singing. I'm a good singer and you can get away with a lot; you don't have to actually do that much. Like John Lee Hooker, it becomes the singer or the song. John Lee Hooker's lyrics, some of them are quite good but a lot of the time he can just moan and it sounds more exciting and more interesting than most other people's lyrics and it comes loaded with more power and

overlays of meaning. I was trying to work in that more soul, R&B genre, and probably trying to show off as well.

What about "Don't Throw Stones"? Taking a maxim or platitude to base a song on can be a risky thing but it worked really well.
With "Reckless" and that one, I lived above a shop in Malvern by the railway line, I looked out the window of my bedroom and there was a laundromat. Most of the songs I just filled with little bits of things that were around me. I've always dealt with the miniature of my life. Both those songs, I would have been in my kitchen; I'd usually write the songs at the kitchen table. It was a thirties kind of flat above a shop and The Sports practised in the horse stables at the back. Andrew Pendlebury, who I did most of the songwriting with, and Ed Bates were really great guitar players as well, so they could translate it really well. I'm not just saying it was me; they were both incredibly good musicians so I was lucky to be working with them. I'm just saying I was the more pushy one that would drive things along.

Where did the idea of "Who Listens to the Radio?" come from?
I listened to radio and I still listen to radio. I go to bed every night listening to BBC news radio. And I listen to the radio all day. All the songs in The Sports were written in the same place in Malvern. I had a laminex breakfast table, and my partner was teaching, she would go out and I'd just be there all day and write heaps of songs.

The word that comes to mind to describe the early Sports songs is "punchy". A lot of that has to do with your vocal, but it's also in the rhythm and the timings. Was there any conscious discussion about how the songs should sound in that regard?
Not really. When we got Martin Armiger in the group—'cause Martin was a really good songwriter in his own right—to me the group became much more whole, like how I wanted it to be. It started out being more like a retro sound and then I realised if we were going to keep going, we'd have to be a pop group to survive. Then I had someone with equal vision that wanted to take the group somewhere. Martin was really sophisticated musically. He had his own tape machine and had his own studio set up when he was eighteen, so he knew how to get the sounds and he was really great that way.

Were you precious about how your songs had to sound when you'd written them?
Yeah, I was a very manipulative sort of person. I had a pretty strong vision of how it would go. But Martin added a real lot to the songs.

Have your collaborations worked differently since The Sports?
It's like Miles Davis; he'd have a vision of what he wanted to do and he'd get other people in who could accommodate his vision. He was very mercenary. I did two records with Steve Kilby because he had something that intrigued me that I couldn't do myself. That thing was part of me, but I didn't know how to do it myself, so that's why I did two records with him. One would have been enough.

When I did things with Martin, it was just like two friends getting together and it was quite good. And the same with Bill McDonald now, I'm friends with Bill now as I was with Martin then. With Martin I was probably more thinking in commercial terms, this is going somewhere. Now I'm just doing it for the hell of it; when I'm with Bill we're just doing it for the pleasure. Also, I'm so much better musically now than I was then. Talking to me about The Sports, I can't even think about it. It's not that I don't like it or can't remember the time or have an aversion to it; it's just that it doesn't register in my brain at all, in my consciousness. I'm not a looking-back person. I never think about how I did anything. Writing with all these different people has all been good, and it's all been exactly the same. When you're a songwriter you keep doing it because you haven't been satisfied, and you're looking to that special thing. It's like if you wrote a really good song, you feel invincible for about ten minutes. "I can't believe I did that. How did I do that? I'm so clever."

What are some songs that made you feel that way when you wrote them?
Lots of them. "I Fell from a Great Height", I think that's a really good song. Good songs seem to happen really quickly and you don't know how. "Love Is Mighty Close to You", Jimmy Little's covered it and Vika and Linda [Bull]. I was just playing guitar and that was a really good song straightaway. I would have thought that then. I can't even think what I thought then. It's too long ago.

Do you consider your songs as components of albums, to be heard in a context, or can you appraise them individually?
I like to think of them as part of albums.

How do you look back now on songs like "Gymnasium" and "Stuck on Love" from *Senso*?
I should have taken more care. My partner always says I'm so lazy and slack. She says, "Your things could be really good but you're just so slack that you won't follow through. The lyrics are three-quarters really good but you don't pay enough attention to them and finish them properly."

Do you agree?
Yeah, I think she's probably right. I am really slack.

The intimacy in your songs belies the shy personality you're known for. What is it like writing a song like "Love Streams" with someone else?
In that case Andrew wrote the music and I just wrote the lyrics and melody. Quite often that would happen, that he'd make a cassette and give me a set of chords and I would just sing over it and then we'd get together in person and we'd modify it together by me singing.

You've been known for "sad songs". Do you have to be in a melancholy mood to write melancholy songs?
[*Very long pause*] I went and saw a psychoanalyst for ten years so I have a lot of things

floating around. To tell you the truth, until I was about thirty I didn't have a thought in my head. And then it all came at once.

So where were all the songs coming from?
I have no idea. I was just doing them. In some ways they were a bit stupid. I wasn't thinking about anything. Then it all came in a rush and I thought, "Oh my God!" I went through all these things that a normal person would have gone through when they were twenty. Because being in a group is like delayed adolescence anyway, and so all through those times I was playing so much and working and doing crap, I didn't have a thought in my head and then all of a sudden I woke up and I was thirty and I thought, "Oh fucking hell. What's happening? I'm going to die!" Then I was depressed for all that time, and I broke up with someone who I'd lived with for a long time, that's how I went and saw a psychoanalyst, and I did that for ten years, twice a week.

You kept writing sad songs after you got happy again, though.
Yeah, I know, just getting it all out, dumping it all.

If you have a subject, a phrase on your list of titles, and you know that's got to be a sad song, do you have to wait until a day you feel sad to write it?
No. I'm happy most of the time. I'm really quite a happy person.

Do you remember when and how you came up with the idea for Lovetown, which exists as a mythical location and a state of mind in at least three of your albums?
Yeah. No. Yeah. I do. I can't really remember. I thought of it as a whole concept. That's when I started to chronicle the failings of mature life.

I'm sure there are critics who have written that about you and you're just quoting them now.
[*Laughs*] I was just trying to look for a place where I could come in, make my own. Ed Kuepper was too good a guitar player, I couldn't compete with him. Paul Kelly was writing meaningful songs about deaths in custody and things like that. There was nowhere else for me to go. I thought I'd stick with love songs because it's universal and it's all I've ever been interested in. Just getting a girlfriend was all I've ever been interested in. It was just that I explored the miniature, the everyday dullness. The thing of "You're famous, I can't go on, I'll go on." I don't know, I haven't questioned it. Some of the titles just amused me.

But then again, some of the songs just happened out of exploring your own conscious. I've had an incredibly stable life but there have been times when I've been really unstable. I've been with just two people, one I lived with for thirteen years and one I've lived with for about thirteen years now. But all that changes, too, and things go up and down. I've just kept everything around myself, 'cause I'm really self-centred. Things to do with my life or what interests me at the time. Musically it's the same, too. Like the chords or styles that I've explored have been what interested me at the time. I'm probably happiest now because

I've been writing much more by myself, which is what I always wanted to do, but at the same time I really love collaborating with other people, especially with friends.

Do you remember anything about "Some Prayers Are Answered" on *Lovetown*?
It was good working with Andrew again and I like working more with acoustic guitars, because when I was growing up I had John Prine records and I liked all acoustic, folk, I had heaps of records like that. So I felt like I was expressing a part of me that I really loved from when I was younger and now I could do it.

What about "She Set Fire to the House"?
I once played a show with Dave Mason from The Reels, and he said to me, "Man, someone really did a number on you, didn't they?" For someone who's grown up with no religion—I've never been to a church in my life—I had an incredible amount of guilt. For a long time. There's a line in that song, "For all the guilt in this world, seven years is enough for any boy or girl." I look back on a lot of my life and I'm amazed that I'm alive. The number of times I was driving and drinking.

Reckless.
Yeah.

What inspired the Jane songs? A trilogy of songs about one character, not just in one album, but stretched out for years.
That's just me playing a little game with myself. That doesn't mean it has no meaning.

When you wrote the first, "You Jane", did you know that you were going to write a couple more songs and bring her back?
No, I didn't. I just liked the idea of a story song and it became another song, "Melancholy Hour", and then it became another one, "Walk Softly But Carry a Big Stick", so I thought I could take that on further. I was living in Ripponlea then, and I used to look down at the lights from this pizza place. That was sort of a movie thing. I liked the idea of people meeting again later and then getting back together again. I like all those romantic clichés. The main thing is that I am interested in love.

The second time Jane appears, she says, "Don't ever use this against me in some dumb song." Was Jane and that situation real rather than fiction?
Always fiction.

Do your friends say that to you?
No.

Because they know you won't, or because they know it's futile to protest?
They just never have. I've never used any of them.

Paul Kelly said that there is one character that keeps popping up in his songs. It's one of a number of interesting similarities between you both, including your sharing of musicians.
He works all the time and can offer them more money; he's richer than I am.

Paul is a frequent collaborator. Have you ever discussed the idea of writing together?
No, but when I was writing all those Sports songs, one day I had a knock on my door and it was Paul Kelly, he'd just come from Adelaide, he'd moved to Melbourne. He came out to our rehearsal and said, "I've got to play some songs." He gives an illusion of being very shy, but he's really ambitious and really together in a business way. He came and played about fifteen songs in a row. I couldn't stop him. I wasn't overwhelmed but I was quite impressed. He had a lot of really good songs to start off with. But I don't feel like I'm jealous of Paul or anything like that because I don't feel we're competing. We're going at two different things. I can't write songs about the nation or anything like that because I'm too self-centred.

Once where you were talking about acting being not so easy for you, you said, "I have a strong sense of self. It's hard for me to get out of being me." Does that also apply to your songs?
Well, they're about me. They're not about me literally. I can remember being dumped by a girl in art school or things like that, or someone being mean, or being mean yourself to other people. I wouldn't literally write about that incident, but I can remember the emotion and feeling, so I would write a song like that. I could see a phrase, "Please stay". Okay, I'll write a song called "Please Stay". I was talking about psychoanalysis. Basically I was very shy when I started doing it, but once you go in there you're just talking off your head. It was very freeing in that I'd just bang on about anything. It's like people who go on twelve-step programs, quite a lot of them are really good speakers because they have to get up and share and come really out of themselves. I've come out of myself more by going to see a psychoanalyst. I was scared of the idea of a psychoanalyst, that I was feeling so fucked that I had to go and see someone. I don't mind mentioning that, because I think lots of people are too scared to go and do things like that, and it actually can be a really big help to them.

Was it a result of all the therapy that brought on a more optimistic mood when you wrote the songs for *Spiritual Bum*?
Yeah, I was in a really good mood. I hit a strong patch and I wrote the *Wonderboy* book and I was really full of joy. But then it went. [*Laughs*] And I moved on to another phase. I just love that title, *Spiritual Bum*. That was a found phrase. I was reading an essay by Henry Miller and he was talking about people in the twenties in Paris, and he said, "They were all getting into gurus and I wasn't and I was regarded as a real spiritual bum." I thought, oh that's a great phrase.

Right until your last album, *Firecracker*, you were writing exceedingly heart-wrenching songs, like "One Kiss" and "Why Doesn't She Want Me".
A couple I knew were staying together for the children. They hadn't had a root for about four and a half years. He loved her but he wouldn't have sex with her. He didn't find her

attractive, but he loved her. I found that to be really depressing. If I was her I would leave. So I wrote that song. I was thinking of it for her; this person was a singer, too. I thought they could do it as "Why doesn't he want me", and then I thought she might be offended. And I thought, I wonder if I give it to them, if they'll recognise it.

Did they?
I don't know if they did or not. But things like that happen all the time. A lot of the things I write are about things like that. It's not that they're about me, it's just if you write songs in the first person they become immediately more powerful.

Heartbreaking.
I stopped doing that a bit because I just found that I was bringing me down too much. So that's why I did the last record more upbeat.

But the lyrics on *Firecracker* are similar to what you were doing on *Spiritual Bum*. You still had all those morose lyrics; they were just residing in a more sprightly and exuberant form.
A guy at the ABC in program music said, "Some of the songs are so depressing. They really make people uncomfortable." And I thought, oh yeah? Well, I'll put really upbeat melodies and keep the same lyrics and see what happens. And so people think it's really happy and really up vibe. But it's not. There was one review of it and the guy said, musically it's really great but it has the most obscure lyrics I've ever written. And I thought, man, they're the most straightforward lyrics I've ever written in my life.

They were more sparse.
Yes, they were sparse and hammering home that sort of thing. What I try and do now is make them really simple but more powerful. Even to say "Can't pin her down, she's not a butterfly" in "The Keys to Her Heart", that's quite a clever lyric, quite poetic actually. Or [*Sings*] "I'm sitting here feeling sorry for myself/ Treading water in the maelstrom of life" in "The Popular One". That's quite a sophisticated lyric but to a really basic Bo Diddley beat. I like the juxtaposition of things like that.

Which do you think is a braver thing to do—writing songs or writing novels?
You've got to have more to say if you're writing novels. It's probably why songs are better to me, 'cause I don't have enough to say.

But you obviously do, because you've written novels.
But I've only got really that one thing to say.

What is that one thing?
I can't go on, I'll go on. It's hard but it's fun. Life's hard but it's good. And people who are capable of being really horrible and really nice. Just that contradiction, that's what that's all about.

How did you get into writing jingles?
I've actually only written about three or four in my life. I only did it if someone rang me up.
I always need money. It's like the John Cassavetes thing, he did all these crap Hollywood
movies and he used the money to make his own movies. That was my philosophy about it.
I'm a musician and a craftsman, I was plying my craft.

Do you have a daily songwriting routine?
Yeah. I come out here, my computer's on; I'm fixing up my new novel. I'll be doing that and
I'll get bored, and then I'll pick up the guitar and I'll start playing and messing around with
chords and I have a digital recorder and I start playing around there. Then I'll get bored
with doing that and I'll go back and keep working on my book.

**Do you ever go between documents and suddenly start typing lyrics for a song while you're
working on your book?**
I find I'll be writing—I'm correcting it at the moment, going through and fixing it up—and
see a phrase and I'll highlight it and cut it out and shove it in my titles list. Also in the
book I drop my own lyrics into it all the time. So I reference myself.

Are there still infinitely more ways to write about love?
Yeah, there's millions of ways. It's relationships and people that I'm interested in. My mum,
for Christmas, what do I buy her every year 'cause I know it's the thing that makes her
happiest? I buy her a slab of romance books. Those Mills & Boon-type romance books. She's
eighty and she just loves them and devours them. And she didn't even like my father that
much. She said to me, "I could have walked all around the world and never found someone
less suitable." But she says it in a nice way; she said he was a really hard worker.

How much has being a Melbourne person guided your songwriting?
Well, I've only been here so I don't know. But I think of myself more as a Melbourne person
than an Australian.

What is being a Melbourne person?
It's like a state of mind. Come early to enjoy disappointment. It's like a Jewish thing—"Oh
well, it won't be any good anyway." I do think of myself that way. I'm almost pathetic, why
am I still living in the same place I was born in? Thank God I'm not still living in the same
suburb; that would be really depressing.

ROB HIRST

JIM MOGINIE

Midnight Oil:
ROB HIRST & JIM MOGINIE

SYDNEY, AUSTRALIA, OCTOBER 2003

It seemed like a true Midnight Oil moment. Rob Hirst was talking earnestly and then cut himself off mid-sentence.

"There's a whale out there," he said, pointing out the window. "It's just surfaced. Just have a look between the Norfolk Island pine and that lamppost. There! See?"

I felt like I'd landed in the middle of a song.

> So farewell to the Norfolk Island pines
> No amount of make believe can help this heart of mine
> > from "Dreamworld"

We paused to observe the whale from the window of the Manly cafe we were in, across the road from the cerulean Pacific.

"Midnight Oil should be seeing white pointers, not whales," Jim Moginie quipped.

"There's a few out there, too," Hirst rejoined.

He might have been referring to creatures of the sea, but equally he could have been alluding to the various individual and corporate reprobates that fed his creativity for the two decades that Midnight Oil reigned as the most powerful, politically outspoken force in Australian rock music. Moginie, with whom Hirst started writing songs at the age of fifteen, has long shared a compatible world view that much in modern society needs changing. But for all their cogent beliefs and righteous indignation, Hirst and Moginie's chief concern has always been to make great music. So when we sat down to talk about songwriting, politics was not the central topic of conversation. It was there, unavoidably—for much of Midnight Oil's career their provocative reputation preceded them—but they certainly didn't harangue about Aboriginal issues, military imperialism, ecological degradation or any of the other topics which were as pertinent today as they had been in the early 1980s when the Oils began to attract widespread attention for their stance.

We met less than a year after the band's lead singer, Peter Garrett, had announced his departure from the fold, and for all their loyalty and affection for the charismatic frontman who had abandoned music to pursue a political career, Hirst and Moginie surprised me with their frankness about internal band politics. They discussed the tension between their love for the band, its history and achievements, the camaraderie with fellow members, and their growing frustrations at being limited and confined as songwriters, having ideas and songs changed or rejected, and living with the public's perception that Garrett had written all of Midnight Oil's songs. "In a way we became successful ghostwriters," said Hirst without a trace of irony.

The composer credits in Midnight Oil were never clear-cut, as all members, including Garrett, guitarist Martin Rotsey and the succession of bass players—Andrew "Bear" James, Peter Gifford and Bones Hillman—contributed in tangible ways to the creation of a song. But the songwriting backbone of Midnight Oil was Hirst and Moginie, men for whom making music is so intrinsic that they are very much the poets and slaves Moginie wrote of in the final song on the final Oils album, *Capricornia*.

Rob Hirst was born in Sydney on 18 May 1956. "I always wanted to play the drums, just like Ringo," he said. "Or Dave Clark or Charlie Watts, the British echelon of bands from the early sixties was what got me hooked on music." He joined his school band and learnt the rudiments of drumming on a drum majors course.

Jim Moginie was born in Camden, near Sydney, on 3 September 1955. The musician known as "Mogenius" amongst his peers had no formal music lessons and taught himself piano and guitar as a teenager. "I'd say I'm Irish in a way about music. Playing around without being too skilled at it," he said modestly. "I always liked a good idea played badly, that's what Irish music's all about."

Growing up in Sydney's upper North Shore, they met as teenagers; Moginie was already jamming with James, and Hirst joined in, brimming with lyrical and melodic ideas. Despite forming one of the most intrinsically Australian rock bands, neither Hirst nor Moginie were influenced by Australian music growing up. Hirst moved from a love for British music to American, while Moginie was transfixed first by the Beatles and then by progressive rock.

When Midnight Oil formed, a "potpourri of discordant styles", as Hirst put it, fused with the surf music of northern beaches pubs and the punk music of inner-city bars. "All this experimental surfy, long-winded, beautifully constructed stuff arrives with the energy of punk, and that describes where we were when we made the first album in '78."

Their music developed into singable, danceable, potent rock with weighty themes. National pride, world politics and environmental concerns were already present on the Oils' first few albums, but it was 1982's breakthrough *10,9,8,7,6,5,4,3,2,1* that brought, literally, their power and passion to the fore. Through their considerable catalogue of fourteen albums and two EPs, including the masterpiece *Diesel and Dust* and its inspired follow-up, *Blue Sky Mining*, to later works like *Earth and Sun and Moon*, *Redneck Wonderland* and *Capricornia*, Hirst and Moginie wrote songs that swept across Australia's landscape from the ocean to the dead heart, almost always looking outside of themselves. The words "I" and "me" were rare indeed in a Midnight Oil song, although the sensibilities of the band's writers were central to everything they delivered.

Eventually, Midnight Oil's status as a message band hindered them. Both Hirst and Moginie wanted to express more personal issues and tried, but felt constrained. "Psychedelic melancholy never had much place in the Oils," said Moginie, who has found satisfaction working with the likes of Neil Finn, Silverchair and Neil Murray. Hirst has found different projects to absorb his prolific output. He has written, performed and recorded with his band, Ghostwriters (irony fully intended), with blues outfit the Backsliders, and in duos with Paul Greene and Dom Turner.

But both know that their greatest legacy will always be with the band that created classics such as "US Forces", "The Power and the Passion", "Beds Are Burning", "The Dead Heart", "Blue Sky Mine" and "Forgotten Years", that donned outfits emblazoned with the word SORRY to perform at the 2000 Olympic Games closing ceremony, and that, according to author Tim Winton, expressed so uniquely the "restless energy, the hope, the dismay, the paranoia" of modern life in Australia.

When Peter Garrett left Midnight Oil, there was a flurry of media attention and letters flooded in to the major newspapers. One such letter read: "Nothing has taught me more about the virtuous responsibility, humour, pride, sadness, passion and spirit of being an Australian than the music and lyrics of Midnight Oil. Their collective work ... the constant worldwide touring and politicising have reflected the heartbeat of my Australia."

As I talked with Rob Hirst and Jim Moginie, the perpetrators of that heartbeat, there was an overwhelming sense that even without the captivating Garrett, the Oils would live on. "It's a common aesthetic that you get, when people have been playing together in such a long-term band," said Moginie. "There's no sense of it being tired or old hat or old school. It's just really good. And so the question is, what to do with it now? That's the question."

When did you both realise that you wanted to write original songs?
HIRST: Right from the word go. In fact I think one of the very first times Jim and I met at Jim's place, we embarked upon a couple of early songs that might have ended up on or

were rejects for the first album quite a few years later. Pretty much from the word go, when we were fifteen.

Do you remember the first complete song that you wrote together?
HIRST: There were a couple. One was called "Gettin' Gone". There was one called "Blue December", there was one called "Missy". There were bits and pieces that we had which were then pilfered.

MOGINIE: Initially the songs were instrumental pieces that we played. "Oh that's a good bit", "That's a good bit" and then just put it together. "That bit goes with this bit." You just intuitively go slot, slot, slot. And then Rob would usually bring in a melody or a lyric to put over the top. That's how it started. I don't think there was a real songwriterly, Dylanesque thing about it at all. It was more garage rock, what can someone bring to the table? Our early album was probably, dare I say it, a conglomeration of all these parts played really fast, like a prog rock band, but a lot faster and played in pubs. With this surfer guy, Pete, as he was in those days, screaming over the top. There was no grand plan. It was an intuitive process of being drawn towards something that was kind of Australian and kind of something that would work in a pub, something that you wouldn't get glasses thrown at you.

Rob, where did the idea of chords and melody come to you as a drummer?
HIRST: I don't think it really matters what your instrument is, because the songwriting thing comes from somewhere else. You have great instrumentalists that aren't songwriters; you have singers that aren't songwriters. So for many years when Jim and I used to get together, all I could bring was gifts that were already there. They were gifts of melody, of rhythm, and a way with words, which is not something you can teach people or study. It's there.

Would that have come in part from what you were listening to as a teenager?
HIRST: Instinctively you gravitate to a kind of music when you're young which excites you. We were lucky to grow up at a time when there was a hell of a lot of exciting music on the radio, whether it be the American school, originally the folk from Bob Dylan onwards and then people like The Band and Creedence Clearwater Revival, and then the English school. The Beatles, the Stones, The Who, The Hollies, the Animals, all of those people that I listened to. Hardly any Australian bands.

Very few Australian songwriters that I speak to have Australian influences.
HIRST: Australian influences later, definitely. I think part of the problem was, even our great artists of the time, O'Keefe and others, were heavily borrowing American genre and singing about overseas places and people, so it wasn't really until people like Greg Macainsh [from Skyhooks] made it possible for you to write about, in his case, Carlton or Balwyn or something. And then we've got this whole palette of Australian places that we can use without a cringe factor.

MOGINIE: I was obsessed with the Beatles like everybody else. I had a picture of them in my suitcase when I was seven years old at school. Then I went through this phase of prog rock, which was inevitable being an adolescent guitar player. I was obsessed with Jan Akkerman for about five years, from Focus. The desire for instrumental prowess took over for a while, learning how to understand to play an instrument. I still don't really understand how to play guitar, but it's always the journey isn't it, not the destination.

And then there was this awareness in the mid-seventies with bands like Chisel and Skyhooks, and even Rolf Harris. I remember Rolf Harris talking on Donnie Sutherland's show.

Yes, Rolf used to do *Sound Unlimited* forums and he'd be going, "Why are you all singing in American accents?"
MOGINIE: That made complete sense to me. I mean, LRB, I'm sorry, there was that saturation of the airwaves. "Can you guess where I'm calling from? The Las Vegas Hilton." So what? What about the Narrabeen Arms?

Well, he wouldn't call his wife from the Narrabeen Arms. He was homesick, give him a break.
MOGINIE: I know. But there was a lot of cultural space being taken up by Americana. It's still happening to a certain extent, it's always going to happen. But to make a music that is purely Australian, that certainly did call out to me and the band as well.

What does the perspective of the drummer bring to the songwriting table?
HIRST: As I was saying, your main instrument didn't really make that much difference; the songwriting thing was already there. In the end I went from cheesy keyboards to strumming a guitar. In fact Martin used to come up to me and say, "Look, playing the guitar is great, and I derive enormous enjoyment from it, but in actual fact like many guitar players you just fall into the same clichés." It may actually be an impediment. It was better off when you were on the Casio and you were fumbling your way around.

I don't think that playing the guitar or keys or any instrument is necessarily an advantage to your songwriting. It can be a vehicle. And I think the reason why Jim and I have worked so successfully is that in a way we cover each other's butts. I bring in stuff, which is just melody, rhythm and a lyrical idea. As does Jim. Jim has for years, right from the very beginning actually, delivered entire demos, some of which are remarkably unchanged after Midnight Oil has a go at them. Jim could fill out instrumentally the stuff that I heard in my head. If we'd both just been from the singer-songwriter Bob Dylan three-chord sort of thing, it wouldn't have been as intriguing.

Did you sometimes find the best way to convey your idea to Jim was to sing it?
HIRST: Quite so. In fact, sitting in the car in traffic with the windows up and just bellowing it out, I'm sure that's where all the best songs are written. Whichever instrument, you fall into clichés, which in a way might be an advantage for a drummer. It is a melodic instrument if you tune it properly, but it's not an instrument where you sit down like the piano or the guitar.

MOGINIE: A lot of drummers are really good singers. Part of the thing from being behind a kit, you don't have that pitch thing as much. You can hear it all going on; you're not involved with it. It's just there, so you can sing over this thing.

HIRST: Levon Helm is a classic example of that, one of my favourite singers, and his ability to play such great drums and sing, it's really quite difficult, it's a bit like tapping your head and rubbing your tummy, but over a course of a night. And even the much-maligned Phil Collins. I would urge people that think that Phil is untalented to actually try to play "In the Air Tonight" and sing it at the same time. To play that drum pattern and sing it, it's definitely a right brain left brain thing. It's like an axe down the middle of your head to do it, very difficult.

Nevertheless, Jim, you would tend to write on guitar?
MOGINIE: Well, I got this old German upright piano for my seventeenth birthday, which I've still got. As soon as I got that, you could almost see songs, on the keyboard. The way the chords looked. Suddenly you had this movement in the left hand and the right hand, rhythm, chords, and it all became really interesting then, because before then I'd just fiddle around on Woolworths organs and cheap guitars. Getting the piano was really a powerful thing. You could find melody and chords and bass, and the movement of bass against chords. Everything was freed up.

HIRST: We went to see the great American songwriter Jimmy Webb; he was doing a round of seminars. We'd seen him in the Green Room in London and we loved all those amazing songs, and the one bit of advice that he was able to impart was if you get stuck with a melody and an obvious chord progression, try changing the chords around underneath the melody for something a bit more intriguing. Which I think is good advice.

Can you give me an example of where you did that?
HIRST: The Midnight Oil song "My Country". You start playing it in an A minor and then you actually change it to a G underneath it, and it gives this lift to it. I'm particularly fond of that lift that you get.

You didn't start out as activists who wanted to get messages out through music, but as musicians who wanted to make good music. At what point did the penny drop that you could do both and be successful?
HIRST: I don't think it was a case of whether we could do this or be successful. Our concerns as a young band were just, like any other garage band, to try to get a gig, to try to hear each other on stage. They were much more day-to-day prosaic concerns than the big picture stuff attributed to us later on. Some people over the years almost thought that Midnight Oil were activists that devised a career with a slide rule. It was as though we had cynically devised its twenty-five-year career, with a nice beginning and end. If people knew the truth, it was just getting from album to album, from gig to gig intact.

MOGINIE: I remember being interviewed at one stage and I ended up getting frustrated at all the questions about politics. I'd say, "It's just a band, it's just a bloody band!" I got into all sorts of trouble from management and certain members. "It's more than a band, it's not just a band." And I said, "Well, if it doesn't work as a band, it just doesn't work. It doesn't matter how many messages you want to whack on top, if the band part of it is no good and the songs are no good, no-one's going to want to listen to it.

Midnight Oil had a real job. Everyone's got a role in the band, and if you try to cover all bases yourself, it's not going to work. There was always the pressure on Rob and I to bring the songs in, or the expectation of pressure. And Martin would also be called on for great musical parts and inspired playing and lots of input into what he thought was good or bad. The various bass players would chip away and chip in. And then Pete would come in with his incredible ability to articulate something. He would always be a fan of a certain song or a certain idea. Probably to the detriment of other things that could have got through. But he had to find himself in those songs, and he had to make them sound like it was about something. That was his job. Often you might bring in a song, it might be a slightly psychedelic thing about a feeling or a mood, and he just isn't that kind of guy. He's more like a shark; he just goes straight for the jugular. "This has to be about this or about that. And I have to be able to sing it with some sort of conviction." You can't make a singer sing what he doesn't want to sing. It's unconvincing.

HIRST: But as it turned out, particularly in the first fifteen years, with a few hiccups, the lyrics I was writing and the majority of the lyrics Jim was writing, and our interests, and my particular interest in history, and political history and world events, actually dovetailed very closely the majority of the time with the kind of stuff that Pete could and would sing. And in a way we became successful ghostwriters. So much so that a line like Jim would write, "US Forces give the nod", 99 per cent of the people would hear that and say, "That's a Pete Garrett line." But it was actually written by Jim. Etcetera. Right down the track.

I think that later on, as you get older, a natural process comes in where you like to substitute the directness of an anthem with the subtlety of something a bit more intriguing. And that's increasingly where we had problems as writers for our lead vocalist.

MOGINIE: On early albums, Pete sang lines like "God is hiding in this teacup" without any problem. But towards the end that kind of line wouldn't have worked with Pete. "What's this? God is hiding in a teacup? God isn't in a teacup." Quite literal. But on the other hand there were songs that we did later on, like "Surf's Up", which was just about having a surf. And of course all the reviews were, "Oh, they're going on about water pollution." So the image of the band took over and came back to bite us a little bit. You just couldn't write a song about something whimsical. It was always, "Oh, you're talking about something important. You must be. It's Midnight Oil."

There's nothing too cryptic in many of those best known message songs, going back to "Armistice Day" and "Short Memory", no ambiguity. The poetry is in their clarity. In the

same way that in "Beds Are Burning" there's no doubt about your message: "Let's give it back." How hard was it to edit your ideas down to such simple lines?

MOGINIE: Rob as a lyricist has always had the ability to deliver something very cogent and very clear, unequivocal, simple and direct. And it's not about bringing a whole lot of choices in; it usually was right. In most cases it would arrive pretty much in its form. "Beds Are Burning" is a case in point. It always felt right. "Short Memory" was a song that Rob had the words for. There was a musical backing but we decided to completely change the chords underneath it, and it became quite a hypnotic, simple song. Very moody. Pete chipped in some lyrics as well. There was always clarity.

Did the lyrics pour out of you in that concise form or was there a lot of perspiration to get there?

HIRST: It was a lot more than I would even admit. I'd like to say, "Yeah, man, twenty minutes I wrote this fucking great song." But in actual fact in the majority of cases I would spend ages on them, until I found something that in some way seemed to me something just beautifully put. That was the only time I could relax and go to sleep at night. I've actually crystallised something.

So it was hard work for you?

HIRST: Mainly really hard. And I would do it in the way probably most songwriters do, and that is you just keep lists of stuff. So for example if you're on a roll with an idea, rather than looking at a blank page or blank napkin, you go through these pages of ideas and you draw links to them. It's a much better way usually of finding something whereby the central idea holds together but you're coming at it tangentially because all of these lyrics come from a different mood, a different place, a different time. But almost always held together by a central chorus idea, which was simply put.

Would the lyrics come first for you?

HIRST: No, often the melody. I'd come up with a melody and then I'd look through all the lyrics, saying, well—[*Sings*] "Oh the power and the passion"—that actually fits that melody really well. The rhythm is right, the melody is right, I just go through, try to bring these two things together.

How significant was song structure? "Beds Are Burning" had no bridge, and several of your hits like "Short Memory" or "Forgotten Years" just had an instrumental break, even just a percussive break as in "Power and the Passion". Was this so as not to detract from the simple verse/chorus formula of getting the message across with as little fuss as possible?

HIRST: In the case of "Beds" I had the chorus already, that was the foundation point. Then we had some dummy lyrics for a while, until we went to the desert, and I rewrote the lyrics travelling around with Charlie McMahon in his four-wheel drive, with Charlie talking at me. Then Jim had the riff, and we had a basic song.

And then Pete came in and said, "We've actually got to make a statement." As is Pete's wont. He said, "Something like, 'The time has come!' You know, 'Give it back!'" I said, "Right, okay." So that became a kind of bridge.

It's like a pre-chorus.
HIRST: Yeah. And then Jim said, "We need something to wake people up at the beginning of the song." So three big chords, like a wake-up call. And then Warne Livsey, who produced quite a bit of our stuff, had the idea of throwing the drum kit down the stairs, that big percussive break.

"Blue Sky Mine" was very similar; everyone was throwing in different things. It started off as a Jim song, then the lyrics were changed, I brought in the "blue sky" idea, Pete rewrote a whole lot of lyrics to that idea, then harmonica became a big figure. Warne actually came up with the initial riff, which was on a keyboard originally. Those songs illustrate the power of being in a band as opposed to being a solo artiste.

"Blue Sky Mine" seemed to find a structure all of its own; it starts in the chorus, but you don't know it's the chorus until the chorus comes back at you after the first verse, which I find is a really interesting dramatic device.
MOGINIE: It sounds really good. You've sold me on it. [*Laughs*]

And "One Country" never seemed to quite get to a chorus; instead it just built up to a climax. I get the impression that you worked on your songs in an organic way and weren't conscious in those cases of ignoring conventional song structure.
HIRST: Yeah, it wasn't calculating. I wish we could have written some of them in the way you've described. But those two songs you've mentioned came up in diametrically different ways. "One Country" was a song that Jim had written entirely, and came to the band ironically saying, "I think I've written a fucking anthem!" That's what he told me. And it turned out to be a fucking anthem. But that was entirely a Jim demo from beginning to end. Whereas "Blue Sky" was one that we toyed with for eighteen months at least.

MOGINIE: It nearly collapsed under its own weight, the amount of work we did to it. It just went around and round in circles. And the arrangement was very basic. It was based on an idea I'd written when I was about fifteen.

Obviously you weren't thinking about asbestos mining when you were fifteen.
MOGINIE: No, that was from reading a book by Ben Hills about the Wittenoom situation, where the mining company was, pulling out the asbestos and all the mesothelioma victims. But the arrangement of that song was completely thrown to the wall, it was like plasticine and we moved it around to something it ended up being, that would work for the song and was interesting. I've always delighted in the fact that the arrangements are kind of wrong. There's something about them being wrong that makes you prick up your ears and notice.

"One Country" was a dictaphone demo written in hotel rooms in America, and then I got back home and realised the first half wasn't enough; that works, but stick a bit on the end, take it higher. Rather than trying to make the first thing any bigger than what it really was, rather than put a chorus in the middle of it or something conventional.

The vocal arrangement at the end, did you hear that when you were writing or did that come in later?
MOGINIE: I heard that, I actually heard a woman's voice originally. But then seeing Bones had just joined the band and his voice was like a woman's voice [*Laughs*]—well, he could sing high—it was the perfect vehicle to introduce Bones to the public.

What was that original idea for "Blue Sky Mine" when you were fifteen?
MOGINIE: It was called "Doubt", and it just had two parts in it, the verse and the bridge. Then we shoved the chorus in there, which had dummy lyrics, which weren't very good. And then we had a whiteboard in the studio where we kept writing lyrics on it. I became so obsessed with it. We were all really sick of it, but we thought, we've got to get this across the line, there's something good about it.

HIRST: Jim handed on the Ben Hills book to me, and it was harrowing. And then the "Blue Sky Mine" idea came from something that our accountant said at one of our business meetings. "Oh, you don't want to invest in those companies, they're blue sky companies." Which means, you might make a million dollars, but you'll most likely take a giant bath. I'd just read the Ben Hills book, and I thought, this is blue asbestos. I put the two things together and then that became the chorus.

MOGINIE: Wasn't it originally "A walk up and down on the hungry mile"?

HIRST: That's right, and "Hungry Mile" actually ended up being a Ghostwriters song.

MOGINIE: But it was a matter of drawing it all together, and in a way, the political agenda of the band really helped with that song, because we could actually complain about something in song, as was our wont.

HIRST: Being an established complaint rock 'n' roll band. But only because, as Jim said, we felt that as long as we had the strong songs first then it would be credible. If you start to become just mind-numbing sloganeering with a couple of chords, then the game would have been up very shortly. "Blue Sky Mine" came up during the recording of the album and although we thought we had a pretty strong album, we were still looking for this lead track to hold the whole thing together.

Would opening lines come easily?
HIRST: Well, mostly nothing came easy, but certainly a good opening line is something to be cherished.

Who wrote, "The godforsaken rifleman stands rigid at the bar" in "Written in the Heart"?
HIRST: Yeah, that was me. But I live with those lyrics now; I think that's so fuckin' undergrad.

What about "The rich get richer/ The poor get the picture" in "Read about It"? That's a brilliant opening line.
HIRST: Yeah, I'll take credit for that one. [*Laughs*]

And "Like a heat wave breaking as you smell warm rain" in "Tone Poem"?
HIRST: That's a very Pete line.

MOGINIE: I remember my original line, which was replaced. Peter always replaced all my good lines.

What was the line?
MOGINIE: "Nothing's sadder than a dream that's lost, nothing's sadder than a dream that's got." That was the original line.

HIRST: I must say, there's a couple of Jim lines which for one reason or another didn't make it to the final cut, which I still weep over openly. Lines which although I understand, because I know Pete so well, why he wouldn't/couldn't sing it, but lovely stuff that Jim would write which had a psychedelic, tangential quality which really should have been there as part of the Midnight Oil palette.

MOGINIE: Psychedelic melancholy never had much place in the Oils.

HIRST: Occasionally you'd get through. Like the lyrics of "I'm the Cure", going way back. That managed to get through the quorum.

MOGINIE: Yeah, some things that didn't mean anything, I always liked the sound of that. If it sounds good and it sings well, just go with it. Like working with Neil Finn, which I've done, just whatever falls in his mouth. It was fascinating getting involved with that because it was so opposite to what the Oils thing was all about. Working with Peter, it's got to be about something, it's got to be clear and unequivocal.

HIRST: As you get older you realise, most people realise, that nothing is clear and unequivocal. So as a songwriter you find it harder and harder to slug an ear, I think. That's why I cringe with "the godforsaken rifleman". It sounds like someone's read an edition of *Time* magazine or something. It was of the time. Angry young men with guitars, five against the world, that whole period, I understand where it comes from. But you've got to be able to disown some of your stuff, haven't you.

Generally Peter's contribution was lyrical?
MOGINIE: There's only one song, I think, that made it through that was musically Pete's. That was "In the Rain" from *Breathe*. Which I really like. Often he would come in with a

verse lyric if a song was already established and it would sound good. "Beds Are Burning" was a case in point, where there was a verse about a lizard man, and that was the version that he sang in the outback. Rob's original lyric was with the "forty-five degrees". It came to a point where we had to decide which one, and I think the band came back to Rob's because it felt more about what we'd experienced out there.

HIRST: I was taking more the John Fogerty approach. I felt a little bit of empathy because there is the lead singer/guitarist/songwriter for Creedence, a genius I think, it was incredible what he'd done, but he was basically just a middle-class boy from Berkeley in the same way that we were white guys from the North Shore. But he wrote as if he grew up in the bayou. So I thought, when we go to the desert, it's my job to try to translate this, what I'm seeing. Albeit through white Sydney suburban eyes, but to try to get some form, get it with those lyrics, which describe a place and a feeling. Which was what Fogerty was so good at.

MOGINIE: We had the idea of making music that would sound good in a car driving. It was quite a thing for me, that hypnotic thing of pumping on the road somewhere.

Jim, you've written a number of songs with Peter, "US Forces" and songs like that. But Rob, you didn't collaborate just with Peter. Was that about personal dynamics?
MOGINIE: Pete's contribution to the band in terms of writing I think was pretty big. Because he would bring a certain Australianness to it or a certain Peteness to it or a certain Midnight Oil thing to it, which made it make sense as a band thing. Putting his particular world view into the music. Pete wanted to assert himself more as a songwriter. So it was tricky. Because often Pete would judge, especially on the last album, "This isn't going to work, but this is." He'd quite often choose my things towards the end more than Rob's.

HIRST: In the case of "US Forces", Jim would bring in the song, pretty much as you hear it, arrangement, idea and everything, and sometimes on the actual day of recording it, Pete would, with all his own lyrical ideas on the floor of the studio, pick ideas out and throw it at the band. Out of the blue. I should add, this isn't at demo stage, this is at hit red, we're going to record it. Often these ideas were great, sometimes they missed the mark. There was brinkmanship, because often we'd got used to a song, thought they were a pretty cohesive, compelling set of lyrics, and suddenly there was this new idea. And we had to make a decision on it immediately because today was the day we were recording it. This actually made some of the recordings incredibly stressful for the writers. And so the credit there would be the lyrics that Pete added on that day.

And "Power and the Passion", once again, Jim and I worked up the basic idea, started with a chorus, with Jim's riff underneath, and then I had the basic verse idea—"People wasting away in paradise"—good opening line, I thought it could lead anywhere. And then the lyrics that Pete added, the "Big Mac" lyrics, which were pure Pete, made the song fantastic. But almost always delivered at the nth hour. I would sometimes dread coming into the studio because it was just so fraught.

On "US Forces", the opening motif that lures the listener is then countered by a vocal in a different key. Was that jarring quality part of the point?

MOGINIE: [*Laughs*] No, actually, what happened was we recorded in the wrong key for Pete's voice, but we kept the introduction. It works, and Pete comes in with that weird key. At the time, we thought, "God, we've got to save this recording 'cause it's all in the wrong key." And then we kept the drums and we redid all the guitars, because we realised the chorus was three semitones too high for Pete. The original demo went up to a C. The introduction was in the old key, a C chord tuned down to a B.

So it wasn't part of the meaning of the song?

MOGINIE: We're not real ones for analysis about this sort of stuff.

HIRST: Often you find that the accidents are the best bits.

What about the key change in "Power and the Passion?

MOGINIE: It's weird having a song which is in B minor and then the chorus is in E flat minor. But we love that; the contrariness of it, that it wasn't musically correct. We embraced this quirkiness. And part of the quirkiness of those original records was just from ignorance.

Rob, when you're writing, are you already hearing how the drums will underscore the song? "Kosciusko" sounds steered by the drums.

HIRST: [*Laughs*] That was the moment in the band where the drums managed to obliterate almost everything else. You had to be there; it was the eighties. In retrospect the obvious thing was it was like a fucking drum solo with vocals over the top and studded with a nice acoustic thing and everything else was blown out of the water. But the thing about it is, if you played that song the original way we played it, it's just like a country rock song. It would have been really unimpressive. It was originally much slower.

So when you're writing you don't consider how the drums will sound? Is that more an arrangement thing for later?

HIRST: Sometimes Jim would have the best drum ideas. It's almost like I already know how the drums will be, so I dismiss it really early on. And so often it's been Jim or Martin who'd say, "Try this drum idea." The idea's really simple, but it's the last thing I would think of.

Right through the Midnight Oil repertoire, harmony vocals were prevalent. Was it important to write as many songs as possible that employed harmonies? Was that part of your wanting to be a pop band as well?

HIRST: Yeah, we love pop. It's just that pure pop never worked with us. It had to be always power pop or pop with an edge. When we tried to do pure pop it always sounded like a bit of a joke for some reason. But by the time we did *Blue Sky Mining* we were layering harmonies on top of each other, Bones would sing higher and then I'd sing higher again, and then there'd be a counter-melody. Listen to the "King of the Mountain" dub mix, for example, it's just harmony on harmony. If we're going to have Pete's character vocal on the verses, which tended to be more didactic and less melodic, but entirely Midnight Oil and compelling, we wanted real big singalong choruses as a counterpoint to it.

MOGINIE: It was based on this realisation that you should actually have a three-dimensional quality to your music and not just the song is enough. Production, performance and the writing were all one. I never really felt that there was a formula with Midnight Oil, even though there probably was.

Was it important that each collection of songs that formed an album subscribed to a particular theme at the time—the arms race, nuclear disarmament, Aboriginal welfare and land rights, the environment—or was it just important that any issues of concern to you were represented on each album?
HIRST: None of the above. It's just that the men in Midnight Oil, the men we became from a boy band in a garage, actually shared all these concerns, genuinely. So if Jim and I would confine our "politics" to some lyrics, Pete transcended it and he would go out and do the media and the ACF and Greenpeace and confront it directly. We had different vehicles for roughly the same thing. And this was the crazy thing, when frictions arose in the band it always seemed quite remarkable to me, because we were so close in what we believed, in the wider picture. We might have disagreed on minutiae but in actual fact in what we thought about our country and what we thought about the basic moral issues of the day, we were fairly close.

Were you writing complete songs during the Blackfella/Whitefella tour or did the songs for the *Diesel and Dust* album come after you got home?
HIRST: "The Dead Heart", the early version of "Beds Are Burning" and another song of Jim's called "You May Not Be Released" were written around about the time that we got the request from the Anangu people, round the Rock, to have a song to commemorate the handing back of Uluru to them. We sent three songs off. "The Dead Heart" was actually finished before that Blackfella/Whitefella tour. So they played "Dead Heart" through the loudspeakers out there in the desert.

MOGINIE: Whereas "Warakurna" was written after visiting.

HIRST: "Bullroarer" was also written afterwards, and we filled in the lyrics for "Beds Are Burning" afterwards.

Were you furiously taking down notes?
MOGINIE: Always. Got to have notebooks.

HIRST: Nothing sadder for a songwriter than to be looking at a blank page. Andrew McMillan was chronicling the whole trip, which became that book *Strict Rules*. Andrew would sit in the spinifex, with his Williams boots on, covered in this red dust with his little portable typewriter and get it all down. Meanwhile, there was this really cranky film crew following us around, complaining bitterly about their cook. There was all these dynamics happening. And in Jim's case it was just a simple notebook of impressions.

MOGINIE: It was seeing Australia for the first time. Being from here and then seeing that, you really felt like a European. They call white people Europeans out there. So it pulled us up very short in terms of what our cultural assumptions were.

One reviewer described *Diesel and Dust* as "a true diary of the Australian experience". Being that most people living in Australia will never have that experience of being confronted by indigenous issues and culture—as you'd said in "Power and the Passion", "no-one goes out back, that's that"—did you see that album as an absolute cry for attention at a time when the band was able to elicit that kind of attention?
HIRST: It's like action–reaction. We'd make one album like *Red Sails* and it had taken four months and cost a mint, because we were living in Tokyo, the most expensive city in the world, and it had blown out the budget and had every sound including the kitchen sink on it. And then the reaction was, "How about some campfire songs in E minor, C and G? How about that for an idea?" So even before we went out back, we'd already decided we wanted to make a totally different album than the one that had gone before, we didn't want to spend more than five weeks in the studio, we wanted all the songs to be written before we went in, rather than do songwriting in the studio.

But were you also inviting Australia to go out back? If not literally, then metaphorically through your music?
MOGINIE: We just wanted to share our experience. Selfishly in a way. We were certainly trying to get a point across about what we'd seen. But from a perspective of being Australians, and being an Australian band. This is the most Australian experience. It's a part of Australia that's essentially hidden. No other people knew about it in those days, it just wasn't a topic. There was a feeling about the issue coming forward, the land rights issue, and we were a part of it, we didn't cause it. With *Blue Sky* there was a different feeling, that's when the environmental thing started to come forward as well. I don't think we heralded it, I don't think we brought it forward as a subject; there was something in the air. But certainly music is an amazing thing with a political message; it makes it go down a bit easier. If you can sing about something important then it's great. The trick is not being too preachy about it.

While most Australians live in cities and on the coast, you were depicting Australia's internal landscape with your imagery. Many of your songs make strong visual statements. Tim Winton mentioned you in the same breath as Arthur Boyd and Henry Lawson. How did that analogy resonate for you? Can you see yourselves as poets of that style?
HIRST: I think a song like "Warakurna", in its message and construction, its origin, and the version we managed to put down, is a pivotal song for us and for the album. Whether it

314

stands up with the kind of people you're talking about I don't know, but that whole thing that Jim was getting at—"This land must change, this land must burn"—it's just a great metaphor. Obviously the land burns, but this whole idea of, what's going to happen to these people? Are they going to be swallowed up in this bushfire of change? Little did they know that Hansonism was just around the corner and that the gains during the Whitlam years and the long-awaited compact Hawke was talking about with Aboriginal people, which never happened, was all going to be swept away by the Howard government. It was quite prophetic. And from a songwriting point, it's one of the most unusual arrangements. It took us ages to learn it.

Did you see yourselves as painting pictures through your songs as well, in the way that Boyd literally did and Lawson lyrically did?
HIRST: I was really satisfied that we'd reached a point where we'd been able to take our own landscapes, our own colours, our own people, our own experiences, put them in a musical form and have them accepted everywhere in the world, because that album was the first real international success. To have that heard internationally was a very satisfying thing. Because for years it was "Wichita Lineman", it was "By the Time I Get to Phoenix", it was Glen Campbell singing, and that was fine, but we actually felt that we managed to reverse that tide for a while and sell Australia back.

But responsibility came with it. Because at the same time, nagging at the back of our minds as writers was, where's the Aboriginal band who was doing this? As it turned out it was another four or five years before Yothu Yindi managed to do it, and we were already touring with a band that was much better known in the desert than us. The Warumpi Band were the headline act in the desert; we were the support. So at the back of our mind was, have we actually done justice to what we've seen and the people that we've met?

Were you surprised that they chose "The Dead Heart", which was more about the rich heritage and pride of indigenous people and therefore a more subtle reference to the handing back, over "Beds Are Burning", which had the direct "let's give it back" message?
HIRST: Maybe in the version that we gave of "Beds Are Burning", it was still a bit ill conceived. It was that much stronger later. The gaps were filled in.

MOGINIE: We really weren't ready to let go at that stage. It was a bit embryonic still.

HIRST: With "The Dead Heart", I said to [producer] Nick Launay, "I want this song to be driven like the sound of the axle of a four-wheel drive battering its way across a Gunbarrel Highway. Okay?" The song had been much slower. Jim had said, "Why don't you try it twice as fast? It still works, in fact it works better, and then we can add this great pulse of the desert thing." Even though we hadn't been there yet. To this day when that song comes on the radio, there's nothing else sounds like that song. I guess there's a lot of Midnight Oil songs that could come under the umbrella of "international rock songs". But there were some songs that could not have come from any other place or band.

That song is like a chant, as well.
MOGINIE: Rob had the lyric first and just to break it up, the "Do doo doo"s seemed to work really well.

And it has that minor to major chord shift, which seems to represent optimism.
HIRST: I've actually learned the expression, it's called *tierce de picardie*. It's the correct classical term for when the minor goes to a major and gives you that great lift. The song starts in B minor and then goes into B major.

With "Beds Are Burning", how did the concept for the title and hook line "How do we sleep when our beds are burning" come about?
HIRST: I came across the expression "beds are burning" whilst viewing a son et lumiére exhibition by Denis del Favoro in Paddington. It related to the impact of Mussolini's Fascists upon the lives of ordinary Italians: "How can we sleep when our beds are burning?" I thought the idea could equally relate to the European impact on the lives of Australian Aborigines. Hence, "How can we dance when our earth is turning?". I came up with a melody for the lines, and a rough idea for the beat. It sounded like a good chorus for something that we could flesh out later.

"Dreamworld" could be about anywhere in Australia that's targeted for development. It also has the connection to the Aborigines and their dreaming. Were layers of meaning part of the plan in a lot of your songs?
MOGINIE: We'd be happy to leave things slightly ambiguous. That song was inspired by the theme park that was being built, that's the initial thought. It was more about these things outside, Norfolk Island pines.

HIRST: They've actually replanted the Manly beachfront with Norfolk Island pines. There used to be an outfall here at North Head, and they discovered in certain winds the blowback of chemicals was dissolving the little wax coating on the needles of these Norfolk Island pines, and they were all dying as a result. As soon as they stopped that outfall they started to recover. But in the meantime a lot continued to die. That's what that line came from. Once again it was a case of getting a good opening line, so it was either going to be that line or it was going to be "The Breakfast Creek hotel is up for sale." The Breakfast Creek in Brisbane was and still is this iconic pub that Joh's henchmen were going to destroy. They'd already destroyed Cloudlands and then they were looking around for any other beautiful old building to wreck.

MOGINIE: That was a long time coming, that song. The verse was from an instrumental part of another song and I had the chorus lying around from somewhere, and we just knocked it together in about half an hour.

HIRST: I remember "Dreamworld" coming together on one of those afternoon songwriting sessions at Giffo's place, with bits and pieces thrown together, and eventually I sat down with Pete and we nutted out which lyrics he liked best from the ones on offer, and in what order.

The title track of *Earth Sun and Moon* has a personal and spiritual sentiment. Did it come from a particular moment or event?
MOGINIE: That was from this NASA thing, a documentary called *Blue Planet.* This idea of being in space and looking back at the Earth, which caused the astronauts to have this revelation when they got on the Moon. I thought that idea seemed kind of cosmic, the fact that there's this ball sitting there that's got water and land and earth and air and stuff on it which doesn't exist anywhere else. It's pretty unique. All around is dark; there's nothing. One night I was with the family, when the kids were really young, and getting a musical idea, just looking at the full moon coming up out of the water. Probably Byron Bay or somewhere new age like that. And then going home and fleshing it out with some other bits and pieces.

But spiritual, yeah, possibly spiritual. Because the name of the track was appropriated for the album title, the song assumed all this importance, which I really didn't want it to assume. We made a record about a whole lot of different things but because of using the song as an album title, it all became about the environment again. I have complicated feelings towards it because it wasn't really what the album was about. There were all sorts of songs on the album. "Truganini" was about the last Aboriginal woman in Tasmania and "Bushfire" was about bushfires.

What about "Outbreak of Love"? That sounded really different for the band, not just sonically but in its mood. The word "love" is rarely used in a Midnight Oil song, and the love for Australia to that point was usually a tough love.
HIRST: It came from Churchill, "This is not the end. It is not even the beginning of the end. But it is, perhaps, the end of the beginning." So I just added "the end of the beginning of the outbreak of love." And "the outbreak" can mean a threat. Love could work, I thought, as long as it was threatening. It would bring it more into the Midnight Oil thing. It had to be a dangerous love, not a mushy love. Maybe the song was a portent of things to come, because the dark, brooding thing that I also used a lot on my other band, the Ghostwriters, particularly the *Second Skin* album, was something I grew to love. I love Leonard Cohen, I love Nick Cave, I love that threat in the darkness of that music. It was never going to work as well in the Midnight Oil context, and increasingly it didn't.

Was it always clear to you when you were writing on your own, which was something for Midnight Oil and which was something for an outside project?
HIRST: I always at least played the rough versions of all the songs to the band. And if someone jumped up and said, "We've got to have that song!", then the priority was always Midnight Oil. Unfortunately, often there'd be no feedback at all. I would have preferred people to say, "Well, that's a heap of shit, Rob." But a lot of time I was just left in limbo. It was neither good nor bad nor commented on.

MOGINIE: For me, I was getting a little bit sick of what Midnight Oil was, which was this very politically correct right-on articulation of something. I think there's a lot of other things you can express apart from eco-passion in music. We were caught in a thing where the character of the band overtook the band and it was a struggle towards the end to actually make it feel like it was new.

Rob, were there songs that as soon as you wrote them, you knew were just for your own project?

HIRST: Yeah, quite. There's a lot of stuff on the three Ghostwriters albums that were entirely personal and I couldn't really expect Pete or any other vocalist to tackle them. In the same way that Jim perhaps increasingly felt constrained by Midnight Oil, I felt constrained by having to write with Pete in mind. Because songwriting is also a very cathartic personal experience. Unless you're just a Brill Building formula-driven songwriter and you work eight hours and you deliver them. But we don't work that way; they actually mean a lot to the writers and then often eventually to the band and maybe even to our audience in the end. To be frank, I think the rot set in around about the *Breathe* album. I understood that there was a curiosity to find different songwriting partnerships and chemistries, and that was also something that was being put forward by Malcolm Burn, our producer on *Breathe*. He basically didn't give a rat's arse about the band's history, what we did live, wasn't interested. He wanted us to take this giant left turn and go into the area of atmospherics and mystery and the kind of stuff that you might expect to hear from a band recording in New Orleans.

So you wrote songs to the concept?

HIRST: We were a bit song-light at the beginning of that album. Malcolm's approach to recording was to walk in, have it all set up and press record. Anything that went down that day might become a song. Never before had we written so much in the studio and with an idea of reinvention of the band.

MOGINIE: It was an experimental phase. We wanted to throw away some of the misconceptions about the Oils. We were almost sick of ourselves. We were sick of what we were on about. And we just wanted to break out. I'd been working with Neil Finn a fair bit; he works so much in the moment, and a lot of *Breathe* was like that. The brief was very much just what happened on the day. I like it for that, for its shambolic, dark, brooding rumblingness. And I'm proud we did it. But then again, when we went to *Redneck*, the next album, we completely abandoned that ship and we got on the other one, which was, let's get back to structure, let's get back to some songiness about it.

HIRST: I actually do enjoy the *Breathe* album a lot. I think we learned a lot. We learned how to suggest rather than to state. We learned how to even groove, for a bunch of white guys from Australia. But I still think that our greatest forte was when we were incredibly pissed off. We make a very good angry band. We were up there with Rage Against The Machine and all those that can really spit it out. This wasn't faked anger. We walked every morning past the sign "Redneck Wonderland", which had been scrawled on the banks of the Yarra River, and we were all of one mind. Just so pissed off with what was going on with the country at the moment, particularly the way the media had embraced it. *Redneck Wonderland* was a really angry album. The band was angry about Pauline Hanson and angry about this homophobia that was going on.

Given the significant output of songs in the last decade, does it frustrate you that your best known songs are from earlier in the Midnight Oil catalogue, or are you simply glad that they have endured as classics?
MOGINIE: Bands have their era, they have their time, and part of growing up is understanding that it doesn't matter how long you go on for, you're not going to be able to change perceptions. If they grew up at a certain time and you were fresh to the public and there was a serendipity happening with the film clips and your records are being played on the radio and the gigs were great, no matter what you did, you couldn't make a mistake. It was all happening. And then at certain times you can't get arrested in your career, you can't get your thing on the radio. But there's nothing you can do about it; it shouldn't stop you from being creative. So I'm glad people love that stuff. I wish they could have heard more of *Capricornia* or even *Redneck* or bits of *Breathe*. But the people that wanted to seek it out did.

You both obviously still want to write.
MOGINIE: I never stop. I can't stop. I don't want to stop writing.

HIRST: It's part of who you are. Whatever anyone else is doing, including Pete, there is still going to be this desire to make music, write songs, to play. I'm still hoping that Jim and Martin and myself will get together and do something, but at the moment the songs are going towards a Ghostwriters album or an album I want to do with Paul Greene, maybe a folk pop album. Or something I want to do with Backsliders. They all get written and at the moment there's different vehicles for their expression. But regardless of what we do, all of us are acutely aware that the most potent chemistry is, was and will be Midnight Oil.

Mental as Anything:
MARTIN PLAZA & GREEDY SMITH

SYDNEY, AUSTRALIA, APRIL AND MAY 2004

There's something quite sane about a rock group that stays contentedly together for three decades, its members spreading their talents across music and visual art. Characterised by their easygoing natures, self-deprecating humorous outlook and notable lack of internal conflict, Mental as Anything is one of Australian music's unassuming success stories, with a catalogue of songs that have indelibly marked the nation's cultural consciousness and the pop charts. Hits poured from the pens of the band's writers like beer on tap.

Drinking was a main focus of Mentals' songs, along with partying, cars and girls. But despite taking their rightful place in the pub rock movement of the late 1970s and 1980s, despite having played their first official gig on the same day that both INXS (then known as the Farriss Brothers) and The Boys Next Door debuted in August 1977, the Mentals were boys you could take home to meet your mother. They were lovable drunks rather than riotous louts; they made it cool to be daggy. At all times intelligence pervaded their creativity, but these art school graduates from Sydney wanted to be smart, not pretentious. They wanted to be mental as anything.

Names were telling. All of the band's members changed or embellished their names. Chris O'Doherty became Reg Mombassa. His brother Peter added "Yoga Dog" to his moniker. David Twohill became Wayne "Bird" Delisle. They all wrote songs, but the two members who composed the bulk of the Mentals' chart hits, such as "The Nips Are Getting Bigger", "If You Leave Me Can I Come Too" and "Live It Up", were Martin Plaza and Greedy Smith.

Plaza took his name from the Sydney pedestrian precinct also known as Martin Place, but was born Martin Murphy on 23 December 1955 in Sydney. His parents were decidedly unmusical and what he knew of music was gleaned from listening to the radio while in the shower. He picked up the guitar at twelve wanting to play Monkees' songs, and having mastered that, he began sketching out song ideas in his late teens. He was also sketching ideas for paintings, and his love of art led him to Alexander Mackie College of Advanced Education, where he met his future bandmates. "I'd seen Martin around, I thought he looked a bit stuck up," Greedy Smith remembered. "But then I heard him play with this band, The Capsicums." It was surely a date with destiny.

Andrew "Greedy" Smith was born on 16 January 1956, also in Sydney. His early listening was folk and country music—Patsy Cline made him cry as a child—and his first instrument was the harmonica, which then guided him to blues music. Early songwriting ventures as a teenager were with his friend Keith Welsh (later to form Flowers with Iva Davies), with whom he played in two different bands. He joined the Mentals progressively, first playing a few harmonica licks, and then, after accidentally breaking Plaza's amplifier, he was recruited on a more regular basis to pay off the debt. When the songs started taking shape and it was clear an organ was needed to fill out the sound, Smith was assigned keyboard duties. Having never had piano lessons, it was on-the-job training. "One finger, really simple stuff," he said, recalling the early performances. "I've been learning on the job ever since."

The hits came in quick succession. As the four chief writers usually preferred to write individually rather than together, it made for an abundance of material. And while there was never a conscious decision to adhere to a particular style, musically or thematically, the songs always reflected the band's collectively quirky personality.

The Mentals toured overseas several times and had international chart success, particularly with Smith's "Live It Up", which was used in the original *Crocodile Dundee* movie. But the quintessentially Australian group was happy to live it up at home, where their humour was easily understood, where they could focus on family life and continue to paint and exhibit their art.

When Mombassa and Doherty left the band in the late 1990s to pursue art full-time, it was the first line-up change in over twenty years. Plaza and Smith were happy to keep working on art and music simultaneously. When I met them, individually and then together, at Plaza's home by the sea in Sydney's east, each was talking about paintings and exhibitions in the same breath as a new CD they were working on, an album of covers called *Songs the Lord Tortoise*.

They each revealed different methods of writing but their songs seamlessly sit side by side on albums and in concert. The force of Mental as Anything is more potent than any individual element, as both found when they embarked on outside projects, solo or with other musicians. They always came back. "The whole solo experience is a nightmare because you're not with the band, you've got nobody to blame but yourself," Smith said. "To get songs to their full fruition is a lot scarier."

"Mentals are more fun, really," Plaza said, which said it all.

PART I: Martin Plaza

Do you remember the first complete song you wrote?
I think it might have even been "Nips Are Getting Bigger". I had a couple of other ones that weren't really complete; that was the first one that was really in some sort of form with a chorus and structure.

There hadn't been the impetus to write seriously before the Mentals?
No, because I thought I was good at it, but I'd never really had any real encouragement apart from a couple of times at parties, people would give me a few drinks and say, "Come on Marty, play us a song." I could tell there was something there, but it wasn't till I started getting up on stage and people started to come and see the band that I realised I had something that was working for me.

How do you think your music and art have influenced each other from those very earliest days through to now?
I see them as fairly separate things. I show pictures still, and if I'm working on an exhibition—I'm working on an exhibition at the minute—if I get stuck on a painting and I'm not making any progress, I might go and do some work on a song. But I can't articulate any real connection, apart from its composition in a way. You work a painting till it looks right and you work a song till it sounds right.

So if you take a break from working on a painting to go and work on a song, it doesn't necessarily fire up something in you to go back to the painting with?
No, no, no.

When the band started looking at doing original material, did you all consciously sit down and discuss what kinds of subjects you'd write about and want to play in the band? Like, "Let's write about romance, surfing, drinking, and keep it quirky too!"
No. They just all seemed to be about drinking for the first few years, all of our songs. Although Reg had some pretty strange songs. He wrote a song called "Talk to Baby Jesus" about growing up in Papakura, which is just outside Auckland. Baby Jesus was a Maori guy who was a real local sort of pop star. "He's got his own Falcon and he drives it like a tank." So a lot of Reg's stuff was more anecdotal, about growing up, some of it to this day

I'm still not sure what it was about. He's got a very interesting lyrical approach, and he reads a lot of occult and stuff. A lot of it's quite spiritually based, although he's not really religious. My songs tend to be more about traditional boy–girl or partying or drinking. And things like "If You Leave Me Can I Come Too", I like to avoid lyrical clichés, I guess that's one of my motivations, too, if I want to do a song, like a romantic song, I want it to have a fresh lyrical approach that hasn't been addressed before.

When Reg and I first got together it was just the two of us, and my background was just sixties pop music. He's a bit older than me and he'd already been living out the bohemian Kings Cross Darlinghurst lifestyle. And got influenced by all these great musicians, like Peter Doyle, slide player, and they introduced him to a lot of—which I listen to a lot too now—vintage Hawaiian music and hillbilly music from the Appalachians. Reg was playing all this weird slide stuff that I'd never heard, with different open tunings. So that plus my pop music might have something to do with the way our sound developed.

Were you writing because of a compulsion or because everyone else was?
I must have been doing it compulsively but I wasn't that prolific. I started writing more later on, but that was because I thought I probably should, because I'd accepted that this was my job now and that I should be a bit more professional about it. Still, the songs that popped into my head almost complete were always the best ones. Whenever I tried to sit down and be professional—you read Elvis Costello writes a song a day and think, well, I should try and do that—but I can't work like that. I work in spurts. I might do a batch of two or three songs over a few weeks, then I don't do anything for a while.

Is the desire to receive those spurts of inspiration still there now?
Yeah. In fact it's more fun because of the technology that's available; you can realise your ideas immediately now. I've got a little digital workstation up in the studio out the back that's almost the equivalent to a studio twenty years ago. It's amazing. So I might get an idea at night, I can just go down there and slam it down and have a listen in the morning. And if it's good I'll work on it and if it's not I'll forget it. When we started, if I had an idea I could put it into a dictaphone or something, and at least you'd have the melody there, but the technology that's available makes songwriting more fun than it ever was.

So are you writing on a keyboard now rather than a guitar?
No. But I use keyboards to dress things up. I write on guitar most of the time. Sometimes I just write in my head, I'll have a melody, I might just be in bed, and if I think it's good enough to do something with it I'll pop up and figure out the chords and put a little drum pattern together, and just put it down, maybe a little bit of bass, and then go back to bed and have a listen in the morning and see if it's working or not. In that sense I don't actually *write* on guitar, but that's the way I put the chords together. Because when you hear a melody you don't actually hear the chords, you just hear the notes and it's not till you pick the guitar up that you figure out what the chords are.

When "The Nips Are Getting Bigger" came out I was in my final year of high school, and not that my friends weren't party people who liked a beer, but we also saw a double meaning in the title referring to Japanese immigrants at a time when Asian immigration was becoming more noticeable. Was that at all intentional?
I was being a devil's advocate in a way, because it's basically about pouring bigger nips. But I had a feeling it would be misconstrued. A lot of people thought it was about nipples, too. So it's been misconstrued many ways. Which I thought was great. I wasn't talking about Japanese people, but I had a feeling that might come out. Although, "nips" was at that point more in the American vernacular than Australian vernacular. If you saw *McHale's Navy* and shows like that, they talked about nips. Australians called them Japs more than nips.

The melody popped into my head when I was driving across the Harbour Bridge one day in my '63 V-Dub. I kept singing it all the way, I was living at Chippendale at the time and I got on my guitar, I put the chords around it, and I just threw the words together really quickly. I was actually having a drink while I was doing it.

So the title didn't come to you first?
No, it was the melody of the chorus that came first. In a sense the words are just a vehicle for the melody that I put together very spontaneously. I just wanted a vehicle for the melody 'cause I thought it was good and strong. It's such a simple song.

Where did the idea come from for "Possible Theme for a Future TV Drama Series"?
I guess you could say surf music was another one of our influences, The Shadows and that sort of stuff. We'd already done "Instrumental as Anything", which has got that surfy twang, and we were constantly coming up with riffy little things. That one was almost another instrumental, but I thought, no, it would have been probably a bit too close on the heels of "Instrumental as Anything", so I made the riff like the chorus but I put some words and a couple of verses as well. I mention a few options of what it could be used for, in the song. "Use it in your new cop show, commercial or even the news/ Or how about Bill Collins' movie reviews."

How do you view that first collection of your songs on *Get Wet* now?
It's kind of very naive and unprofessional, but that's part of its charm. I went through a phase when I couldn't even listen to "Nips"; I'd be in a supermarket or something and it would come on, and I'd think it sounds so dinky. But I'm coming back to liking it again, now. It's really in your face, it's very brittle-sounding.

"Come Around" is driving and pacey, a very catchy pop song. Do you remember writing that?
That was a bit of a "Dada" exercise. I'd had the chorus in my head, and I wrote a few chords out on little bits of paper and chucked them in a box or a hat, and just picked them out at random. I said, "Okay, that's going to be the verse, no matter how it turns out." So that's why the verse is a bit weird.

It turned out quite well, considering.
Yeah. It was difficult putting a melody around those chords, it took a while. And it still sounds a little bit sort of pitchy to me when I listen to it. That's one song that we actually play really well now. But when we recorded it, it was still really fresh and I hadn't really got my head around the melody properly. When I hear it I cringe badly.

What about the lyric? Did you write that after you had the melody completely written?
Yeah. That was just another case of a silly romantic idea to use as a vehicle for the melody. I normally have the melody first and the words have to be put together to fit the melody.

"Cannibal" is beautifully warped. Was being slightly twisted something that came naturally?
The lyrical hook in that song actually came from my wife, Kate. 'Cause we'd just started dating, and she quipped at one point, "If I were a cannibal you'd be first to go." I thought that was pretty funny and put the rest of the music and lyrics around that line. So she should have got a credit on that.

"If You Leave Me Can I Come Too?" is possibly my all-time favourite song title.
That little gag had been flying around for a while, and I just thought it had to be committed to a pop song.

It's amazing it wasn't a country song already.
I think Barbra Streisand and Richard Marx wrote a song with a very similar title a few years afterwards, a really schlocky one. But yeah, it was one of those things that just had to be done, really. And musically it was inspired by John Lennon's song "Oh Yoko". Although it didn't end up sounding like that. That happens to me a bit, too. I'll think, "Gee, I love that song, I'll try and write something like that." And it often finishes up sounding nothing like what inspired the idea but it turns out okay anyway. Which is good. Because you don't want to plagiarise other people's work.

"I Didn't Mean To Be Mean" was another nifty title. My dad used to say that. I'd say, "You're mean!" And he'd say, "I didn't mean to be mean."
Before the song came out?

Oh yeah. When I was a kid.
Well, I'm sure it's been said a million times. It's a bit of a cheap trick, but as I said, I liked to avoid clichés and if it's there and you can put a good three-minute pop song around it, go for it. That was produced by Elvis Costello. So that was a lot of fun working with him. He's a great guy, really good guy. Got to know him and The Attractions quite well when they came.

"Bus Ride" is one of the finest examples of making something magical out of the mundane.
I like public transport to this day. It's a circus. It's always a circus to hop on a bus. When I wrote that song I wasn't doing a lot of bus travel but it's a true story. Our office at the time

was up at Bondi Junction, and I lived around the corner and I had an old Renault at that point and it wouldn't start. So I hopped on a bus and I hadn't been on one for quite a while. And I just enjoyed the ride up to the Junction. Because it was like a freak show, really. Very interesting.

Each time you had a major commercial hit, did you feel pressured to come up with another one, or were you happy for one of the other members to have the next chart success?
I felt under pressure, yeah. In fact I prefer the way things are now, 'cause it was a bit too much pressure, really. I didn't really like it. In a way I was relieved when Greedy started writing. I guess you're asking was I put out, but I was relieved that someone else could take the ball. I was a bit concerned that maybe I wouldn't do it again, but "Mr Natural" went quite well and a couple of the other songs I wrote later on.

You've usually written Mentals' songs alone, but occasionally in the past you'd write with Reg or even more occasionally with all the members. What would be the impetus for collaborating on a song?
There's not too many. There was "Apocalypso". Reg had that song for quite a long time; it was more like a Jimmy Reed sort of thing. [*Strums blues chords on guitar.*] A real rootsy R&B thing. And I'd just heard ZZ Top's 12-inch of "Legs". So I changed the key of it by myself, played around with it for a while and I took it to Reg, and I said, "I reckon this would sound really cool to do it like this." And Reg, he's just such a sweetheart, he probably just didn't want to hurt my feelings, but he said, "Oh, cool." So I turned it arse-about so it was very different. I reinterpreted it rather than sitting down together and collaborating.

And there are a few songs where all the band members have a credit. Was that just because something got worked on in the rehearsal situation?
Yeah. Usually the bones would come in and then everybody would put their two bob's worth in, and depending on how, what proportion of stuff finished up being contributed by various members, then we figured out whether we should say it was a collaboration or not. But it was never really us all sitting around.

Do new melodies still come quite easily to you?
Yeah. I'm working on this song at the moment that I did yesterday. Very simple but it's coming together very nicely.

When an idea comes to you, do you think of that as a magical mysterious thing, or is it quite pragmatic for you?
No, it's a really nice thing to happen. And it can be a situation where like what happened to people like George Harrison and "My Sweet Lord", and the remarkable thing about that episode is that it got recorded and it went to number one, and it's still regarded as his song, even though he got sued and he happily paid. But nobody twigged that it's identical to

"He's So Fine", the Shirelles. Even the bridge, it's exactly the same, almost the whole arrangement. Inadvertent plagiarism.

So when a melody comes, you have to be a bit mistrustful?
Sometimes I twig, oh no, that's something else. And if I like it enough I'll continue and then I'll run it by a few other people and say, "Does that remind you of anything?" If they say straightaway, if they nominate the song that I think it might be a knock-off of, then I'll have second thoughts, but if nobody picks it up then I'll continue.

Have you had that happen where you've unconsciously taken a melody from somewhere else?
Yeah. The song that I'm working on at the minute actually, it's a little bit like that great Stones song "Paint It Black". Which I didn't realise until this morning when I listened to it again. I was thinking, oh shit it's exactly the same, but then I figured out the melody, I played them both back to back, and it's actually quite different. It's not litigious. Sometimes it's just the mood of the melody. I just think it's mathematically incredible that people still come up with original melodies, when you've only got mathematically a certain combination.

So where do you think they come from?
There must be something spiritual about it. I don't know. It's a good thing that it still happens, but that's another mystery to me that it can still be happening. Although, you do hear some very close knock-offs. Some of them are just shameless regurgitations, like a lot of the hip hop stuff. That's like doing a sculpture out of found objects. That's always been a part of music, too, you know. The Beatles borrowed a lot of riffs and bits and pieces, and so did the people before them.

What are a few of your favourite songs written by other members of the band?
One of my favourite songs of Greedy's is "The World Seems Difficult", that's a really pretty song. All of Reg's songs were great, for different reasons. I think one of my favourites is a song called "Psychedelic Peace Lamp". And Pete's "Beserk Warriors", we still play that quite a lot, that's a great song. "Brain Brain" is a lovely one of Pete's, too. And "Live It Up" is just a classic, undeniably great pop song.

PART II: Greedy Smith

What does harmonica playing teach you about melody and chords?
It teaches you a lot. I used to play the little harmonicas you can only really play in one or two keys, and I would learn by playing along to the radio, lots of pet food commercials and things like that. It taught me to realise when things didn't work and when they did, and when they did they really must have struck. The thing was, it was mainly faking and

cheating the whole time. And that's how I got into songwriting, too. Because we were playing to art students and they were really critical, so that's why we clowned around. We wanted to be self-effacing at best. Just so that people wouldn't think, "Oh, they're really stuck up." That's why we thought it was a really good idea if you wrote the songs, nobody could tell you how to play them, because you wrote them, didn't you. Martin and Reg were writing a few songs, I thought, I used to write songs, I'll do this. So I started writing songs, too.

Do you remember the first complete song you wrote?
I think it was called "I'm Coming Back". I wrote that with Keith, though. The first song that I wrote completely by myself was called "Another Man Sitting in My Kitchen", that's on the first album. And there was another song called "I Can Hardly Believe It's a Radio". Which is really silly. "Another Man Sitting in My Kitchen" was just a jealousy song. I went through a period of that. It was a big issue for me for a while. It's a really good thing to write about, at that time particularly, in terms of tone. Because you can have the romantic angle but you can also be a bit annoyed.

You follow the same theme in "Insurance Man"—a droll look at jealousy in love. Were these hypothetical or real scenarios?
Probably were real at the time. I was very old-fashioned. I'm a Capricorn, so very loyal, and I think I did have my first experiences of jealousy at the time, and I didn't realise what a powerful feeling it was. You had to be cool, though. In our circle you didn't fall to bits and pieces. There was another one along those lines, too, from a different point of view. "Fiona" is like a confession of unfaithfulness. And I wasn't. It went:

> Fiona if you plan an inquisition
> we'd better get over with right now
> I'd better tell you about my new position
> You're gonna find out about it anyhow
> I'm not a heretic as far as true love goes
> But I've changed denomination
> and I guess it shows

INXS played their first gig on the day Elvis died, as did The Boys Next Door, and I understand you guys did, too. Do you think timing is crucial in creative endeavours or is everything arbitrary?
I think if you look at it statistically in terms of songs that came out, you have to have an idea, you have to have music, but also you have to have an audience, and you have to have a receptive audience that's receptive to an idea. At the time everybody was very excited because they'd had years and years of music getting, we thought, very turgid and planned. The rise of progressive rock, where it was getting very musically tricky, almost little bits of jazz mixed up and calling it pop music. Emerson Lake and Palmer, Yes, Genesis, it seemed to lack spontaneity. That's why the punk movement started. And the thing is that the people liked

the idea of seeing their peers playing songs, so they were receptive. I think the time was right.

I look back now and I think, what a bloody cheek you'd have to have to write a song when nobody knows you. You write a song and you expect people to actually listen to it? I watch those shows on TV and they're singing other people's songs and I have a great deal of trouble listening to them. I know they're trying very hard and it's well meaning, all that sort of television eisteddfod. And they've got a reason to be there! We had no reason to be there, we were at art school, but we had the gall to do it.

Talking about art school, do you think music and visual art infuse each other?
No. I think they're both leisure activities to a certain extent. I love art and I love music but I'm not sure that I like music more than art. I think that the idea of art rock and stuff like that is like the anathema to where we came from as a band and as songwriters. We wanted to avoid that at all costs, because it wasn't right for us and it wasn't right for the people that we would have wanted to impress or not be pilloried by.

When I think about art rock I think of Split Enz or Queen. I was thinking more about as a painter, somebody who loves working in the visual art side of things, when you're then writing a song are there influences that go across both art forms?
I think there is a bit of the can-do that you need. You need the flash of inspiration followed by a lot of patience to realise it. That's what it's all about. And the optimism to think you can give it a go. To create something from scratch. And as in painting, with songwriting the first thing that you find out is that you feel that you're copying everything. You really think once you write a song, you're copying everything. You're not really. You're flattering yourself if you think you can copy a proper song when you're writing a song. But it takes a certain amount of nerve, and I think it's the nerve of creativity coupled with the patience to see it through. Here we are at Martin's place, he's got paintings everywhere, he's irrepressible.

Art school really is just a halfway house for teenagers avoiding having proper jobs, that's all it is. That's why so many bands start there.

Did you feel you had to write within the confines of a set style for the band, or was it just that you were all like-minded musically?
As far as writing songs that have a certain vein, I think musically I can always stand up and say, "Well, I actually learned to play music on the job while I was in the band." My music writing has come out of being in Mental as Anything. Before that it was very limited. So that's probably why it's very hard to get out of it.

But thematically you were all writing quirky songs.
I've never understood the "quirky". "Spirit Got Lost" was a song that was quirked up by Reg. It was a song that I wrote and the lyrics were a bit too straightforward romantic, so Reg brought in the cargo cult thing. "Your letter got lost? How about your spirit got lost?" Then we were able to go into the New Guinean rituals, and that's about that.

329

That's got the great line, "All the people round here are too bony for kissing". One of those classic Mentals' lines, ingeniously simple and clever and evoking a funny image. Which of you came up with that?
I think it was Reg in the toilet writing his bit; he was sitting on the throne in the recording studio. We never used to write in the studio, so that was probably one of the few that was ever done that way. I wrote the music and I'm not sure who wrote, "The spirit got lost now something is missing". I could claim credit on finishing off the line but it's one of those things that's lost. That was very collaborative.

Was there a competitive edge in the band?
Yeah, always has been. Everybody would put forward songs and everybody wanted the best for their songs. If you're a songwriter you have to think your songs are best, otherwise you wouldn't bother, it's part of the thing. And after a while, usually over the course of an album, things sort themselves out, some songs work in that environment and others don't. And you just have to live with it. There was a tendency to try and balance it up, but it didn't always work out that way. I quite often didn't have as many songs on there. I'm not as prolific as the other guys. I could never keep up with any of them. I never submitted more than one other song per album that didn't make it on.

So you don't have drawers full of rejected songs.
No, not many. Martin and Reg write like they paint. They paint and they write songs all the time, and I can't do that. They're actually a lot better musicians than me for a start. And I see songwriting like doing cryptic crosswords, in terms of the actual getting it to work in the end. I spend a lot of time, I waste great chunks of my life, trying to write songs, always have. [Laughs] And not getting anywhere and being really anal and perverse. I might like part of an idea of a song and despite nothing else working, I'll persevere with it for years. [Laughs]

Do you ever give up on a song?
I really hate it when I have to give up but I've had to give up a bit more lately and I want to force myself to write a lot of songs, but I often find I can only write if I've got the inspiration. If I'm writing to be like a songwriter it just comes out very stiff and unbearably mediocre.

So can writing be compelling for you?
If I have an idea I feel that compulsion, but I don't have that many ideas, to be honest. [Laughs] "Live It Up" is a case in point where I wrote all of the words and the melody in my head on a bus in Canada. Then it took two years and I'd nearly given up on it and then I bought a drum machine off Vanda and Young, through Bruce Brown. It was the first LinnDrum Machine that was ever in Australia.

Are you sure Iva Davies didn't have the first LinnDrum Machine?
That's what Bruce reckoned it was. But probably Iva had it first. I went to Iva's house and

he had TVs in every room! That was back when he lived in Lindfield. I was working at the Charles Hotel in Chatswood, and Martin used to work at the KFC in Artarmon. Iva used to clean the Kings Cinema and I remember going to his house and there were TVs in every room, I guess he was in a Roxy Music kind of mode at the time.

But the song was originally a swing song and then I was able to turn that round. I wrote all of "You're So Strong" and fixed up "Live It Up" in one night, the first night with a LinnDrum.

But "Live It Up" started its life on a bus.
Yeah, I had all of the music in my head, and then we'd do it with the band, we'd done all of these versions of it and it wasn't really working at all. It was like a rejected song, we weren't even considering it for the album. And I thought, gee, I hate to give up on this song, and I worked it out. I wrote "You're So Strong" first and I thought, this is great, this drum machine, it's so liberating. And then I thought, gee, maybe that similar idea could do it with "Live It Up". And it all fell into place.

What was the original inspiration for it?
As far as the lyrics go, I really identified with it. We'd spent a lot of time in nightclubs and I just hated them. 'Cause you can't talk to anybody. It's always about talking to girls and I've always felt awkward about that. So I wrote about a girl who felt like that in a nightclub instead of being me. It's a wallflower song. But also great because it makes me, the singer, sound really good, because it's me actually talking to them and taking them out and giving them a good time. So in a way it's probably the most presumptuous song I've ever written. I'm made out to be the hero.

The chorus in "You're So Strong" is in fact really strong. Did you write to the title?
No, it happened at exactly the same time. The idea of that is a bit of a feminist fellow-traveller idea. "You mightn't think so but I know, you're so strong." It's like supporting a woman. Sometimes, particularly when they're hanging around the blokes, they quite often seemed to be voices lowered, there's not the same sort of braggadocio that you get with blokes. Maybe it was just me, but I used to end up with really strong women. In fact I've gone from strength to strength as far as women go now. Now I'm just scared of my wife.

Does she know this?
Oh yes. I think it's how she runs me. But I've always been attracted to strong women.

Where did the idea for the intro to the song come from?
The DX7. You get inspired by the instrument you're playing and Elton John's keyboard roadie had said, "You should branch out, get a DX7. I live with the guy who invented them!" And we went up to his room at the Sebel and he showed me how they go, and so I started with that. So the two pieces of equipment. There's no talent, it was just getting the right boxes. [*Laughs*]

So sometimes the equipment guides the writing.
Oh, it does! Going back to "Spirit Got Lost", I wrote that all on the Casio, and I sequenced it within the Casio. Of course we didn't do it like that when we took it to Dunlop and Brown, who were producing; they had a Fairlight in the studio and they really wanted to learn it. And I said, "Go to town with it. I've sequenced it, you'll be able to do it better." So they sequenced the whole thing, playing bones and things like that on the Fairlight.

Occasionally I write songs on guitar, not very often, but one that I did was "He's Just No Good For You", I worked out the lines for it and everything. I'm a hopeless guitarist. I've been playing guitar now for thirty-five years and I'm just shocking! I'm a left-hander but that's still no excuse. But I still occasionally write songs on it, and that's a totally different thing. I think the difference between keyboard-based writers and guitar-based is the sound of the way the music goes together. A lot of the original ideas I have are usually in buses, cars or planes.

How do you capture them?
You've just got to remember them.

Do you use a notebook or tape recorder?
No, I used to try that but they'd all break on me. I had a dictaphone that broke, I bought one in Singapore and it broke as soon as I got on the plane and I just thought it's not meant to be. You have the 4-track at home, you do that. But the actual inspiration and main ideas of songs usually never come up when you're in front of anything you can actually record it on. No, that'd be too easy! [*Laughs*]

But also, I had two theories of songwriting at the time. The first was that if you couldn't remember it then the song isn't any good, it's not very catchy. I see myself as mainly trying to write popular songs, and I think of them as being catchy. And so that would be the test, if you didn't remember it. And now I'm getting closer to fifty and my short-term memory is shot, it's getting harder to write songs. [*Laughs*]

My other rule is the real test is writing with a hangover, which we used to do a lot. The first example of that was "Too Many Times", a song I wrote after a night drinking whisky with John Swan in Macy's in South Yarra. A lot of bands used to stay at Macy's in Toorak Road, it's a pub. We had a big night of it, met up after a gig and drank. Or maybe we even played together that night. And I had a shocking hangover the next day. "Too many times I've seen the sun come up through bloodshot eyes this week." It was like confessional and it stuck to me. And the words are really quite tricky in terms of construction, to get the right emphasis and make them sound normal but make it work. And I did that through the most shocking hangover. I had the wrong rhythm and it was terrible, and it was Peter, our bass player, who gave it the swing feel and made it work.

It's quite leading in the lyric, because when it starts off, "Too many times, too many times" it could be about anything. Too many times I've had my heart broken, too many times I've taken a wrong turn. But it's too many times I've woken up with bloodshot eyes. It's

something quite mundane and droll in the end.
It's actually a very depressing song, it's incredibly depressing. "What is there left to do, but to drink and watch the view/ I think that it might rain this afternoon."

"Date with Destiny" has a great relentless minor chord progression all the way through it. "My Door Is Always Open" and "Mouth to Mouth" also have that spooky feel that "Spirit Got Lost" had. Do you have a preference for the black over the white keys?
Ahh! Well it's funny, they were all white key songs, no black keys. But I remember the first music I wrote at home when I was about ten or eleven and that was all black keys. And I do love it. And I like fifths. Now I try and steer away a bit from the minor stuff 'cause it's just so sad.

But what was the appeal of that minor shuffle spooky kind of sound?
I like Eastern European music, and I always loved "Those Were the Days", that Mary Hopkin one produced by Paul McCartney. And I'm addicted to *Fiddler on the Roof.* It's like Russian Jewish gypsy music. I'm not Jewish but I love all that stuff. People used to say we had sad lyrics with happy music or happy lyrics with sad music. And that's probably about as arty as we ever really get in music, getting that juxtaposition of things.

"The World Seems Difficult" signified a change in tone for you. A little more gentle and wistful even, both lyrically and musically. What was going on around that time?
Martin and I were mixing or remixing the *Mouth to Mouth* album in England, and that's when "Live It Up" went up the charts there, was going really well, and we had to come back for three weeks tour and then go back to England, which is ridiculous. And on the first night of the tour I was really jetlagged and I wrote it in the motel room in Gulgong, the town on the ten dollar note. I wrote it on the Casio and had it all programmed up and then took it away. Unfortunately, it bears a resemblance to another song; I didn't realise until an interviewer told me that it's very much like the bridge to "The Logical Song" by Supertramp, and once you hear that you can't get it out of your head.

How did you feel when that was pointed out to you?
Horrified. Devastated. It never occurred to me.

What made you write a more gentle song, though?
I think it was the Casio. It was the instrument again. It was just whingeing. I'm embarrassed about it now, I don't like whingeing songs. I call it "complaint music".

What are a few of your favourite songs written by other members of the band?
I like "Catalina's Reward" from Martin, I think that's such a great idea and so beautiful. I've always loved "Berserk Warriors" because it's so crazy, that allegory of Bjorn and Anna's break-up. Reg has got quite a few, I really like "L'Amour No More". That's got a sort of Marlene Dietrich thing. "Apocalypso", of course, 'cause that's got a great idea of Santa being upset about things. "Brain Brain" is quite good, too, because it paints a picture.

Do you agree with Ian McFarlane's summation that Mental as Anything "made its greatest mark by elevating the ordinary in life to the extraordinary in life"?
Very nice of him to say that. We did write about ordinary things. We did want to write about stuff that we knew about because we used to make fun of bands who took themselves at all seriously. How we fitted into the world was that we were the ones who didn't.

JAMES REYNE

MORNINGTON PENINSULA, AUSTRALIA, MARCH 2003

It's an irony not lost on James Reyne—a master of irony—that his most successful and best remembered songs are ones that emerged in almost throwaway fashion when he was young and, well, reckless, while the work he has been writing and recording in recent years is more ingenious, yet largely ignored. He prefers to discuss the songs he writes today than talk yet again about "Beautiful People" and "Reckless". According to Reyne, those and other early songs from his career were written quickly and unselfconsciously and sometimes he had no idea what his lyrics even meant.

But Reyne understands his place in music history. As lead singer and key songwriter for Australian Crawl, his songs and distinctive vocal were prevalent across the airwaves through most of the 1980s. His early solo career, which directly followed the band's split in 1986, was also hit-making, but Reyne only recently became wholly satisfied with his work. "I'm very, very self-critical. If something's crap of mine, I'm the first to think it is. And there's a lot of stuff that's got through that shouldn't have."

We talked about his career and songwriting achievements one morning, sitting at his large kitchen table while Reyne slowly came out of a self-confessed hangover. His family were at the Red Hill Show; in the rural heart of Victoria's Mornington Peninsula, the annual agricultural show is a must-attend event. If there was an irony about bringing up his family back on the Peninsula, whose inhabitants had been the focus of mockery in early Australian Crawl songs, and whose cushy, upper middle-class enclave Reyne had forsaken for the metropolitan lure of Melbourne, Los Angeles and London, it was shrugged off. His English wife, Tina, liked the area because it reminded her of the south of France. And the pastoral district in which they set up their acreage home was miles away from the lifestyle in Mt Eliza, where Reyne and his friends had grown up. Even if it was just a few miles up the road.

Born on 19 May 1957 in Lagos, Nigeria, to English parents, Reyne was four years old when the family moved to Australia. The path to showbusiness for James and his younger brother David began in a home filled with the witty and stylish songs of Michael Flanders and Donald Swann, Gilbert and Sullivan, and Fats Waller. When James discovered rock and pop, it was in a singularly American direction, with Creedence Clearwater Revival his band of choice, along with Dan Hicks and the Hotlicks, Canned Heat, Little Feat, JJ Cale and various blues artists.

Reyne took up guitar in his mid-teens but was more interested in singing than crafting music. When he did start writing in a cognisant way, it was initially for his own amusement. After dropping out of Law and Arts degrees at Melbourne University, he was accepted into the Victorian College of the Arts Drama School, but was disillusioned with the earnestness of its teaching. Pragmatic and devilishly cynical, Reyne quit drama school in third year and focused on music. Australian Crawl was formed with mates who also hailed from the Mt Eliza area. Their image was of a sunny surf band with beach ditties, but blonde hair and tanned good looks notwithstanding, their style owed more to the punchy urban sound that Melbourne bands such as The Sports had fostered. "It was power pop for modern people kind of vibe," Reyne said, looking back. "We all lived in the city. We were night-time guys."

It was hard to shake off the "spoiled brats from the beach" tag, however. "We were trying to fight back, trying to be taken seriously. I know I was constantly as a young guy going, 'I want to be taken seriously.' I laugh now when I hear people say it. I mean, who cares!"

Reyne can't shed his conservative Mt Eliza upbringing—to this day he worries that his mother might read something that too explicitly describes the meaning of "The Boys Light Up" and its notorious second verse about fellatio—but he hasn't exactly mellowed. Still acerbic, biting and critical, he likes to have a dig, whether it's at the latest hotshot Australian actor in Hollywood who takes himself too seriously, Australian Crawl's first record producer, or FM radio announcers. He does a wicked impersonation of the generic radio guy. "If you've got some jock going, 'Hey mate, bloody 'Beautiful People', what's it all about?', what I want to say is, 'Mate, you're a fucking idiot. Shut up.'"

He was recording a new album when we met. *Speedboats for Breakfast,* released in 2004, was even more witty and challenging than the shamefully under-promoted 1999 album, *Design For Living*, and Reyne believed, as is customary for many artists, that it was his best work to date. Should a radio station invite him in to chat, he knew they would end up playing "Reckless" or "Errol" instead of something new. But he'd stick to his guns (rather than throw them down) and make music that satisfied his own standards.

"I've matured, I'm a grown man, and I write grown-up music. Any craft you do for twenty years or more, if you're self-critical and you maintain some focus on that craft, then you can only get better. I'm a much better songwriter, I'm more attuned with my strengths and weaknesses, I'm more attuned with the world, I'm more in tune with life, I'm more attuned with taking the piss. After all, it's pretty much for me about taking the piss. And the pressure's off. I'm enjoying it, I really enjoy it."

Where did your penchant for lyrics come from? Had you been writing poetry at school?
No, I always liked reading and writing stories and I used to write little plays when I was at primary school. They put them on at open day. One was called *Dr Surgeon and the Vampire*. And we used to do episodes of *Superman*. I'd be Superman and Clark Kent, of course; I had to be everything. So I was always interested in that and always did okay in English literature. But in our house our parents played a lot of music and my mum sang light opera. One always reads this about musicians, but it really was in our house a lot. We'd always be going to see my mum in a play. She'd be in either amateur light operatic or half-professional. And my father was always playing music.

How old were you when you wrote your first song?
Probably thirteen or fourteen. I can't remember what it was called. It would have been shithouse. It was just an exercise in wow, I can put three chords together, and just sing over the top of it. It was more about singing to me. I was always into singing.

So you didn't start off wanting to be a songwriter?
No. It was just something I did. And then, always wanted to be in a band, and we always had funny little bands. Usually blues bands, because you could do a whole lot of songs, 12-bar songs, and just change the key and the tempo. First year of university I lived in a house in South Yarra with a guy called Mark Hudson. And because I didn't go to uni a lot, we just used to sit around this house and write lots of songs; we just did it for something to play. It wasn't a conscious "Wow, let's write a song." We wrote "Beautiful People". And I remember I wrote a song called "Man Crazy" when I was still living at my parents' house.

When you wrote "Beautiful People" were you thinking about who might hear it?
We were just having fun. We'd make up these funny songs. We had a little band and we never played anywhere except in our lounge room, 'cause we had a little set-up, and Archie would come over with his bass, Archie Slamet. We were going to call it Archie Slamet and the Doors. But we never played to anyone. A couple of friends of ours might come around and we'd just have a bit of a jam, but we never thought we'd play anywhere.

Did you also write "The Boys Light Up" before Australian Crawl or was that once you had the band?
I think it was really early, very early in Australian Crawl, where we were probably just playing in a lounge room as well. We certainly always had that one.

How did your mother and her friends react to that song? Did they get it?
I don't know.

Nobody ever made a comment to you?
No. Even now I don't know if people get it. It's not about anyone in particular. I always wonder if people get the second verse. "About the hummers she's been giving and the money that they save", the lyric is. "To her it is skin lotion." I'm surprised no-one's ever gone, "What are you talking about? Are you kidding?!" All I know is, it was banned, which was a blessing—thank you for banning it—because it meant everyone would go, "Oh, I've got to go and get it." It was banned by *Countdown*, I don't know why, because maybe they thought it's about a vibrator. It's not necessarily about a vibrator; it could be about anything that's in the drawer. But I thought the filthy bit was about the hummer and the skin lotion. To her it's skin lotion, to him it's promotion. And I don't even know if people know what the hell I'm talking about, if they actually realise.

Do you want them to?
It would be funny if they did, but it doesn't worry me. It's an old, old song that will be sitting on my shoulder for the rest of my life. I think lyrically it stands up, it's sort of funny. I just like the idea that it's quite soft pornographic in what it's talking about. But then again by explaining it, it ruins it. I'd be amazed if people knew what "Oh No Not You Again" is about. I didn't write it, but I know what it's about. People think, "Oh what a lovely song" and they sing it at gigs. It's a song about heroin.

Some people don't know that "Hammerhead" was about drugs either.
"Hammerhead" is about heroin. And people go, "What a lovely song."

The beauty of some songs is that people can interpret them as they want.
That's right, and that's why explaining it sometimes ruins it. I probably shouldn't say this, because anyone who's even vaguely interested in reading about me might go, "Oh, what a shame." So it's nicer to have your own image of what it's about.

Do you remember writing "Lakeside"?
I don't remember specifically where and when, but that's a very Peninsula song; about all the people that came down and go to Rosebud and Dromana, which they still do, in their panel vans. Before they built the highway, they used to drive through Mt Eliza and we'd stand there watching all the panel vans going by. Rubbernecks. [*Imitates*] "It's so nice down here!"

Would you say that as a group of performers and songwriters, Australian Crawl was quite impressionable and reflecting other sounds that were going on in that era?
Yes. We certainly were musically.

I want to throw a couple of comparisons at you. The lyrics in "Indisposed" made me think of the B52s' "Rock Lobster". Their "He was in a jam, met a giant clam" and your "He got hit by a car, now he's lying on the tar."
Well, I only had a tiny bit to do with that song. Brad Robinson wrote it with his father. Unfortunately, both of them are not with us any more, but his father was the president of the Arbitration Commission. He was the guy that would decide in the National Wage Case. So he had a fairly significant job and we had this funny little band. And Brad started writing this song, because I got hit by a car and broke both my wrists. Plastered from here to here. [*Indicates length of his arms*]

So it was about you.
Yeah, it was about me. And boy, was I indisposed. It used to be a joke. Because the only thing I got together was going to the toilet, I made sure of that. But I couldn't do anything else. We were working five or six nights a week and it was very sweaty. So the band would have to dress me, undress me, I had to go back and live at my parents. My mother had to bathe me at twenty-three! It was terrible. You can't do up buttons, you can't eat. You can't do anything. People would have to cut your food up for you. And we were on the road. We had a residency at Bombay Rock and the big joke was, they used to undress me down to my underpants and just leave me, and go, "See ya!" And I'd be standing there, I couldn't open doors, couldn't do anything.

So Brad started writing this song as a joke. Because we always had our tongue firmly in our cheek. He played it to his father and he thought it was hilarious and he wrote some lines as well. And then it got to the third verse, and we always used to take the absolute piss out of Peninsula Grammar, because we went to Peninsula Grammar, and we used to joke about the "ra ra ra" of all-male private schools, just the whole attitude. So the only line I probably had was "Peninsula ra ra".

It reminded me of "Rock Lobster" because of that simple rhyme that paints the picture really clearly.
It's very childish rhyming but also it's not easy to do. You start with "Tell you about my friend-a, he got hit by a fender." Then you go, well, where am I going to go with that? What rhymes? Gender? Mender? And then once you've established that as your MO, lyrically, you've got to do a couple of verses.

The other song from then that really sounds like someone else was "Love Beats Me Up". Was that deliberately a Police influence à la "Walking on the Moon"?
It probably was. Certainly they were huge at the time. We weren't very good musicians at all then, there were other bands that were much better musicians, so we probably worked out

early on that doing that white reggae thing is an easy way to get a song together, it's an easy way to get a feel and an arrangement, because if you can think of a good solid bass line against everything you can turn almost any song into an okay-sounding, white reggae song. It was probably me sitting in my bedroom having listened to a Police record that was around on the airwaves. Not nearly as good as a Police song.

Was it you or Guy McDonough who came up with the original idea for "Errol"?
Guy had the original musical idea. He and I were sharing a house at the time and there was a biography that had just come out. Because I was reading the biography, I think I went and got *Gentleman Jim* and a few of the films, so Errol Flynn was around at the time.

I gave the book to him and said, "Have a read of this. How wild is this guy?" Because we thought of ourselves a bit as lads about town, early twenties, a bit of stardom thrust on you. We got into the idea of Errol. And then he certainly had the musical idea and started a bit of something, and I started coming out with lyrics and then together we came up with lyrics. It was his instigation, that song.

Was it written quickly?
Yeah. And again it's just silly rhymes. Just playing with funny rhymes. Getting "swashbuckling" into a song. And how to sing it when you sing it. If we were conscious about anything, it was trying to play with the words in a song lyrically. So we could never write a love song. If someone came with a love song, you'd just go, "Love song? What are you doing?" We were far too cynical for that. Even now, I think, how do you write a love song? I don't think I could write one. Unless it was so removed. I think "Love Beats Me Up" is about the closest thing.

Tell me about "Hoochie Gucci Fiorucci Mama".
Oh. I hate it. I think it's rubbish.

Was it you or David Briggs who came up with the idea of a soft, plaintive piano melody belying a nasty, vindictive lyric?
I have a bit of a problem with David Briggs having his name on the song, because I wrote the song. I wrote it on piano, and that's about the extent of my piano playing. I had the song completely written and I think it was one of those things of, "What other songs have you got?" when we were recording the first album. I said, "Oh, I've got this." "What is that? That's great! Play it again!" One of those. He as the producer. And he said, "That's great, but it needs a middle-eight." And so that crap on the end of it—"Inside her empty castle her lonely heart will dwell"—that's him saying, "Here are some chords, you've got to have a middle-eight." And I was resisting, going, "I don't want a middle-eight. I think it's nice, it goes verse chorus verse chorus, finish, thank you, bye. That's the essence of it, the simplicity of it." And he said, "No, you've got to round it out." And he was just fresh from the success of [Little River Band's] "Lonesome Loser". Great song. Great lyrics. "Beaten by the Queen of Hearts every time." That's just happening, that one.

Normally back then, your songs with scathing lyrics had sharp, punchy melodies. This melody could have been a love song ballad.

Didn't think about it. I don't mind the tune, it's okay, but a lot of the lyrics are really twee and ignorant and awkward. And kind of naive. It's probably me trying to be like Greg Macainsh or something, trying to write those songs about Melbourne. "I'd better get Toorak Road or something into it." That's probably where it came from, if anything.

What was the original flash of inspiration for "Reckless"?

"Reckless" honestly took about as long to write as it takes to sing it. It just came out. And I still don't know what the big deal is about it; I never thought it was any good. I did this miniseries once called *Return To Eden* and a lot of it was filmed around Sydney. I wrote it when I was sitting around waiting for a set-up. I had it for ages and I never thought it was any good.

It was one of those things where we were going to record and Bob Starkey, who used to be in Skyhooks, was living in a motel on Canterbury Road in Middle Park, and he had this little studio set-up. I wanted to do some demos, so I put a few songs down and he said, "What else have you got?" And I said, "I've got this thing." So we put down a very rough version of it. I don't think I even played it to the band; I didn't think it was any good. And then we got to the point where we're going, we've got eight songs, we need two more, is there anything else anybody's got? I said, "Well, I've got this thing I did with Bob ..." And played it to the band and they went, "Crikey, we should do that."

Is it about the landscape of a relationship?

I think so. I was going out with a girl, we'd been together for quite a few years, and I hadn't seen her for ages. I was always on the road and then I did this film thing, and I don't think we'd seen each other for a while. I was sitting on the grass of one of the houses they were filming in and a ferry went by. That's all it was. There was one of those pontoon jetty things, and because they don't anchor them, because of the waves, it was bouncing around. I've never thought of this before, but I think that's what it was. I remember it now. Probably I was hung-over.

What about the geographical spread from the harbour to the Antarctic and then back across to the Australian bush?

It just fell out, honestly. Images of alone people. Lone figures, stuck. I think recently at that stage one of those Russian subs had been stuck underneath the ice in Antarctica, couldn't find a way up or something like that. And there's always that great John Longstaff painting of Burke and Wills with that thing on the tree saying "DIG". And just Scott of the Antarctic, you know, and Captain Oates saying, "I am just going outside and may be some time." Off he goes and dies. It was just those lonely figure images.

Because you were feeling a bit lonely? Missing your girlfriend?

Probably. I don't think I was lonely.

Missing your early morning wrestle?

That was just a line that fell out. I never even thought about it. I think if they're good ones, they probably do fall out. If you think about those things too hard you probably won't ever find it.

So when lines like this fall out, you're not deliberately trying to be cryptic.

Well, see, talking about "Reckless", you've got that line about the Manly ferry, and then you've got "She don't like that kind of behaviour." I mean, what the hell does that mean? And then "Throw down your guns, don't be so reckless." What the hell does that mean? I don't know, it just came out. That's why I always thought it was shithouse. I thought, it just doesn't mean anything. You can probably read something into the verses a bit. But that bridge and chorus don't mean anything. I thought, well, it's one of those songs that I'll fix up one day. I'll change those lyrics and fix them up. And then suddenly people are telling me what they think it means. I go, okay, fine. "It's an anti-war song, man." Okay, good.

When I lived in London at one stage, when Jacques Chirac was testing the bombs at the atoll in the South Pacific, there was a huge demonstration outside the French embassy in London. I went along and there were lots of Australians, obviously. An Australian was on a microphone up on the stage, and some busker had a guitar. And honestly, I was standing there just as part of the crowd, and the guy spotted me and in the mike went, "James Reyne! James Reyne's here." And all these people turned and looked at me and said, "You've got to come up here and sing 'Reckless'." And they were singing along and I was just going, "Fuck!" That was a good moment.

What did you think of Paul Kelly's version of "Reckless"?

Oh, that's another moment that was really amazing. I was in a pub in Sydney, didn't know anything about him doing it, just went out with some friends one night. Oh, Paul's playing just acoustically, we'll go along. We were having a drink, and suddenly he said, "Here's an old Blind Jimmy Reyne song." And he sang that. That's what he said, just like an old blues singer.

You've heard the recorded version as well?

I didn't until a long time after that, had no idea he'd done it. I think someone sent it to me. And that was another moment. You think, now that's really cool, that's good.

When you wrote it did you originally conceive of the rhythm section driving it?

No, when we recorded it we were between drummers, and Buzz Bidstrup came and played drums on that. He had one of the very first commercially viable drum machines. And we'd never used a drum machine.

By *Sons of Beaches* your songs had a grittier and more jaded edge to them. You sounded over it.

Well, I was pretty sick of it. 'Cause we were really well known by then. We actually were arguably one of the bigger bands in this country. And I was just going, "Oh, this is a bit of a drag." I think I was still on my "no-one's taking me seriously" rubbish.

Was Red Symons spot on when he wrote of you, "underneath these matinee idol good looks there lurked a truly evil bastard"?
But see, Red saying that is Red and me being truly evil bastards. We'd sit and have a drink and just take the piss. It's not being horrible, it's just having fun. People would say, "You're so cynical" and I'd say, "No, we're realistic." Calling it like it is. I always thought that quite a lot of the lyric content was quite okay, quite good compared to my so-called peers at the time. At least I thought them out and I had taken some time to make them interesting, something you could read. If you read it on paper you'd go, "Oh, that hangs together fairly well." But now I think about it, I think, what a laugh. What a joke.

Were there conscious changes to your songwriting when you started writing for James Reyne rather than for Australian Crawl?
No, I don't think so. Probably the only shift I made is when the band finally finished and we're all going, "Oh, thank God". When the band split, *The Age* did the split of Australian Crawl. They'd interviewed everybody else in the band and I think except for Brad everybody else had really paid out on me. That I was a megalomaniac, how I intimidated other people out of having any songs on the albums.

But everyone was writing.
That's right. Because you had to pay lip service to band democracy. But I just remember it because it was a big article, and Spooner, the cartoonist, had done this cartoon of this really low slinking dog with my face on it. I got nothing but that sort of stuff all the time. *Juke* would always make these things up. "We hear that James Reyne's joined the cast of *Holiday Island* or one of those terrible soaps. We hope he drowns." All the time. That's all I'd ever read about myself. I'm going, what have I done? Fuck off! So by the end of Australian Crawl, God I was glad it was finished. It took about a year to finish, too.

But I had to make a conscious decision, the band's finished, thank God, what do I do? I love writing songs, I've got a lot of songs I've written, I've demoed a lot of songs with a friend of mine, and I want to be a singer, but I'm going to get out of this country, it just gives me the shits at the moment. That's why I went to America with these new songs.

Where did the idea for "Fall of Rome" come from?
There was a film made in 1986, *Pandemonium*, and funnily enough only yesterday after how many years is that now, seventeen years, purely for some other reason I actually saw the guy that made the film, Haydn Keenan. Haydn had made a film called *Going Down* and an old girlfriend of mine, who unfortunately died, is in the film. She died before he'd finished shooting it, and he had to do some mock up shots of another girl walking away from camera. And he rang me just out of the blue and said, "I've got this particular scene that Vera was in, and I really want a song for it. Would it be too much for you to come and

have a look at the scene? It would be quite poignant if you wrote the song." So I did that, it was called "What's It Like", just an obscure little song. That's how I got to know Haydn.

And then he was making this film called *Pandemonium* and he had the script and he said to me, "Have you got any songs?" I read the script and I wrote "Fall of Rome". But the song didn't get in the film. The intro to "Fall of Rome"—"I want no part of this despair"—is from something that was in the script. I think he didn't have the money or he had a falling out with somebody and in the end he got one of his mates to do the music. So it didn't actually get in the film. And I was laughing yesterday saying, "Well, it was a top ten smash, Haydn."

Is that a song that you like?
Yeah, I quite like that song.

Is "Hammerhead" one of your favourites?
I don't mind it, it's okay, I can take it or leave it. I think it's a good song, it's a well-constructed song.

It's such a beautiful tune with a smooth melodic flow, and yet it's about something quite sinister and desperate. Was the inspiration from someone close to you? Or was it about you?
Not necessarily about me, but let's say I thought I knew what I was talking about. I wrote it with Simon Hussey; the music Simon and I wrote together and I wrote the lyrics. From memory it seemed to come quite easily.

Was it important to have a melody that would lure the listener in the way that drugs lured the subject of the song?
That was accidental. And I shouldn't make too much about the fact that it's about drugs. It can be taken many ways. It was an exercise in trying to write a song about that subject but to also make it that it could be about a relationship. It's a song about a relationship. And whether that relationship is with a substance or a person, it's an obsessive relationship.

How large a part has personal experience played in your lyric writing, and how much more is just observation, wry, witty or otherwise?
Probably the latter more than anything.

What was "Slave" about?
I don't know. I went to Vancouver to write with a guy called Jim Vallance, and it was set up, it was very preconceived. We were making a record, we should do some writing, we need to get some singles. Jim had a track record in writing good early-nineties pop rock singles. And he was contacted and sent some stuff of mine and would he be interested? He said, "Yep, I like the sound of this stuff." So I went to Vancouver for a week or two, and just went around to his house every day. He'd be playing the piano, and I'd play the guitar and we'd be plugged in, we had headphones on, both had a microphone, and it's just, "What have you got?" So you just start playing and record everything for two days.

You came in with lyrics?

No, I came in with a couple of ideas but I think maybe he had the coda to that song. And then the third day we go back and we listen to absolutely everything we've recorded, and going, "That's crap, that's crap ... ooh, what's that bit? What's that bit? What's that bit? Oh, that sounds alright." Then an hour later, "Oh, that bit. Well maybe we'll put that bit with that bit ... that could be a verse, that could be a chorus." Songwriting by numbers.

Did you enjoy that?

Not really. Jim's a lovely guy and we got some good songs out of it, and I think he's very talented obviously. And then it was a matter of writing lyrics on the spot. "You know the path is deep and wide", that's from [*Sings*] "Oh, the path was deep and wide/ From footsteps leading to our cabin/ Above the door there burned a scarlet lamp..." You know that song "Hickory Holler's Tramp"? I'd heard that on the car radio driving to Jim's place the day I had to come up with some lyrics. And I had a list of titles I'd often look through; I've got one of those books, the top ten singles since 1955 in America and England. Sometimes you'll get inspiration from anywhere or steal from anywhere. And I think I saw "Slave". Everyone does it. It's how well you hide it, really.

On *Design for Living* "After You've Gone" sounded like a fairly intimate relationship song.

No, of all the songs on *Design for Living* that song was me and another guy sitting down, let's write a song. The words to the chorus in "After You've Gone", the guy I wrote it with, Dan Knight, I think that's his.

So you've never seen yourself as a sensitive lyricist.

Oh, no, shit no. In fact if I accidentally strayed they'd go, "Oh no, no, no." I don't even think in those terms.

What were the noticeable LA influences that crept into your writing as you spent more time there?

I can tell the songs I've written in LA, because often they're writing to order. I was sent on a lot of those, as many others were, like go and write with Holly Knight for two weeks. And I go into Holly's place, a lovely person, but they're nine-to-five songwriters. It's like that Diane Warren thing. You know, she's made a fortune. And Holly's the same, had a lot of big hits, got a real talent for that, but I find it very difficult, coming from where I was coming from lyrically. Holly would say something like, "I've got this great idea, James. 'Stuck on the edge of the night, on the outside looking in'." And I'd think, that's so clichéd, I can't live with this. It almost became an exercise in me gently trying to turn them around to my way of thinking. So you'd ultimately meet, not even half way, it would be more in their corner lyrically than mine.

Were there any hits from your late-eighties solo days that you just didn't like?

Yeah, "Some People", I think that's crap. I wrote that with Jim Vallance. He probably thinks it's crap, too. Just very standard pub rock, you know. And I think 'cause it was up tempo and had a beginning, middle and end, the record company decided it had to be a single. "House of Cards" I think is crap.

You wrote that with Simon Hussey. Did he bring a more formulaic method to the songwriting you were doing in the late 1980s? "House of Cards" and "Motor's Too Fast" were quite formulaic songs.

Oh, absolutely. We weren't so much writing to order; it was one of those things where Simon and I would go, "Righto, next January 18 to February 15, let's just put aside those four weeks to write some songs, because I've got to make an album, I need some songs." Simon had a little studio in his house, and he's a very shy person, he's very happy at home with the door closed in his studio. I'd go down there sometimes and he'd have a whole piece of music done. He'd have an idea for a melody if not the complete melody, and all these interesting changes. Or it would be a rough melody that could go either way, and I'd sit with it for a while and come up with something. And then it would be writing words, often, to a done piece of music. "House of Cards", he had that sort of chorus thing, and then it was just written on a bit of paper as fast as you could. It doesn't mean anything.

I think "Motor's Too Fast" is good lyrically; I'd read an article about a kid who had silver-top sneakers and he robbed his mother's jewellery. So I wrote about that. Musically, it's just that classic chord progression: C to A minor, D minor, F, G. A million songs are written in that. "Every Breath You Take", same chords. "Stand by Me", same chords. It's classic, to the point where, when in doubt, you can always play those chords. There's a million melodies you can do over those chords.

The album *Design for Living* was a bold piece of work.

I thought it was the best thing I'd ever done at that point.

The title track is musically an incredible pastiche of styles, from sixties lounge to nineties Beastie Boys rap to swing. And lyrically it's an obvious throwback to "Beautiful People".

Well, Michael Flanders wrote the lyrics. There's this beautiful, great song they've got, called "Design For Living", that Michael Flanders and Donald Swann song, but it's on a piano, a very Noël Coward kind of song. I always loved the lyrics and I'd stolen the "Garden's full of furniture, house is full of plants" from that song in the first place. I just thought, for fun, I'll take those lyrics, because I love them, and they still stand up, and I've only used some of them, I haven't used them all, and if at the very least I turn some people onto Michael Flanders and Donald Swann, that would be great. I did the right thing, contacted their estates and tried to get the permission, and never heard back from them. So I thought, well, if they hear about this and they get upset, certainly whatever royalties there are, it would be a nice problem to have. Michael Flanders and Donald Swann in a rap song in Australia? I haven't heard.

While you were going in so many different musical directions on the album, your lyric writing seemed sharper than ever.

Yes. It's the first time I actually considered myself a songwriter. I can write good songs. Since making that, I've found this whole new confidence, I've written more and better songs than I've ever written in my life. I've got them coming out of my ears. There's no pressure on me. I've accepted the fact that okay, they can all go and get stuffed. I'm just doing it because I love it, I'm having a great deal of fun, there are no boundaries, and the stuff we've been doing now, this latest album, which I hope to finish next week, it's streets ahead of *Design for Living*. It's just interesting I've hit my straps when no-one's really going to hear it. [*Laughs*]

STEVE KIPNER

TOPANGA, CALIFORNIA, USA, SEPTEMBER 2002

He's excited. Always excited. Steve Kipner is the most ebullient and excited man you could ever meet. There is a humility about him, too, mixed with an endless wonderment at his songwriting successes, and when he lists his hits—what song was recorded by whom and, importantly, what number it reached on what chart and for how long—it's not that he's trying to show off; he's just genuinely amazed.

On the day I visited his Topanga home for this interview, Kipner was jumping with excitement because one of his songs, "Stole", had rocketed up the US Contemporary Hit Radio and Urban charts. Covered by Kelly Rowland of Destiny's Child, it was representative of Kipner's recent output—cleverly crafted international pop, written for breakthrough artists and tailored to the teen market. "It's all over the place!" Kipner claimed. "It got over 110 radio stations immediately. This is an exciting day for me."

It was the same twenty months later when we met again for a photo shoot at the Olympia Studios in London. His latest talent, Natasha Bedingfield, had hit number one on the UK airplay charts with another Kipner co-write, "Single". This was all the more exciting for him as Bedingfield was the first artist on his new label, Phonogenic.

Kipner's string of Top 20 international hits for more than two decades, for artists as diverse as Olivia Newton-John, Chicago, Wilson Phillips and Christina Aguilera, makes him one of Australia's most successful songwriting exports. There have also been huge hits in Japan, Europe, Canada and the rest of the world, often recorded in foreign languages. Most have been written and recorded in his tiny home studio. He bought the canyon house in 1981 following his success with "Physical", and while his rewards have been plentiful and he could no doubt afford to move to something far more opulent with a more spacious studio set up, Kipner prefers to stay put. "Even though it's small, this room is lucky for me."

Born on 14 December 1947 in Cincinnati, Ohio, to an American father and Australian mother, Kipner moved to Brisbane at an early age, when his father was stationed there as a member of the US Air Force. The family decided to make Australia their home and Steve's father, Nat, forged a career as a songwriter, producer and studio/label head of some distinction. Through his Spin Records, Nat Kipner signed the Brothers Gibb and recorded their first hit single, "Spicks and Specks". Later, Maurice Gibb returned the favour by producing "Toast and Marmalade for Tea" for the junior Kipner's duo Tin Tin. By that time Steve was in London forging his career and from there he moved to Los Angeles. His time in Australia, then, was relatively short but incredibly formative. Kipner still talks with a broad Australian accent and he chose the house in Topanga because of the eucalyptus trees growing all around. "My only recollection of childhood is Australia. I was technically born in America, but I never really related to being an American, because every childhood memory is Australian."

Do you do your co-writing here or do you tend to go to other people's studios?

Sort of fifty-fifty. Most of the people I write with have studios also. When I'm producing a record, it's sometimes easier to record the vocals in a studio that can accommodate larger amounts of people, like the artists and managers, camera crews. Last week we worked with the English group S Club 7 and as they have seven members, my place would have been way too crowded. I did four songs on Victoria Beckham's album, and she came here by herself and it was quiet, so the home thing worked perfectly. It's just a funky little studio. The best studios in the world might look a little nicer but they wouldn't actually be technically superior. This equipment is as up to date as it can be.

Do you think that nationality—or at least where one is brought up, spends one's formative years and is educated—affects what you write and create? Do you feel you have an Australian sensibility after all these years?

Seriously, I really do feel for me that's been an advantage. I recall being at an A&R meeting; some record company guys from different countries in Europe had come over looking for some songs for their particular artists. There were about twenty writers in a big boardroom;

all the American writers were playing demos that they thought were very pop. I could tell that all these songs weren't going to fly, because they were great songs but they were so R&B and American sounding, and sure enough the A&R team said, "I'm afraid most of these songs definitely won't work for us in Europe." Living in Australia, England and the US has given me a broader, diverse education in musical tastes. Maybe that's one of the reasons I've survived so long, because I don't feel I'm attached to just one style of music. Growing up in Australia there were both American and English influences. I'm lucky to have had hits in Europe and Asia that wouldn't have been successful in America and vice versa.

Initially you were writing with your father and other people. Do you remember the very first song you wrote?
One of the first songs was, [*Sings*] "You can twist to the beat of the windshield wipers/ dum de dum de da dum dum / I was driving along in my hot rod ..." All my beginning songs had the same melody. I was about twelve. The first record I ever had released was when I was around fourteen; it was sung by Vicky Simms, an Aboriginal boy, and I think it actually got in the Australian Top 20. It was called "I'm Counting Up My Love for You".

My first group was Steve and the Board. I was the singer and I didn't write the songs. I never imagined music would turn into a lifelong career; I was one of those guys just going along for the ride, having fun. Being in a group had its benefits. I loved the idea of music and all that, but I wasn't putting too much time into seriously trying to hone any real skills. As a kid my main interest was art. I liked to draw and paint so I assumed I'd be a commercial artist. But then when "The Giggle Eyed Goo" became a hit for my group, I thought, "This is what I want to do." We moved to Melbourne as there were TV shows and a lot of work for bands there at the time, so any thought of continuing with my commercial art studies was thrown out the window. Then I went on to different bands. I relocated to England and I was in a duet called Tin Tin. My partner, Steve Groves, and I wrote all the songs designed for us to sing; we never gave a thought of writing for other artists.

He wrote "Toast and Marmalade" on his own, didn't he?
Yeah. Maurice Gibb called up and said, "Barry's got the flu and it's too late to cancel the studio, so you guys go in and use the time." Well, we didn't have a song ready. Steve Groves had a new song started, had these two verses, but not the rest of the song completed. So, unprepared and with only five of six strings on a guitar, we reluctantly went in and recorded those two verses and then transposed those same verses up a key and then up again, very untraditional as there was no actual chorus or other sections that make up the average song, but somehow it worked.

Tell me about the move to Los Angeles and how you got established here as a songwriter.
After Tin Tin broke up, I moved to California to join a new group, Friends, and made an album for MGM, and after that I formed a trio called Skyband and released an album on RCA, then another duo, Think Out Loud, on A&M. Nothing really blew up big time, but

together they made just enough noise to keep me going. Then one day the whole group thing came to a dead end, and I thought, "Geez, what am I going to do now?" It was the first time reality struck me, how am I going to make a living, what do I want to do? I just started writing songs, thinking they could lead into a solo album. I tried these songs out on the public by playing in small coffee houses and music bars around Hollywood for free, but who would possibly even want to sign me? Do I even want to be a solo artist?

I understand you gave a tape of some of your demos to a record company executive while you were selling plants outside his building.
I sold a plant to the assistant of a hot-shot record guy, Al Corey, who was the boss of RSO Records. His secretary played my tape to him, he liked it and called me in and signed me to a singles deal. It was a small deal, but at least I had a chance to get my career back on track. Al Corey said we had to get the services of a good producer. And by pure luck I had a girlfriend who managed a health club where one of the trainers told me his brother was a famous session guitar player. He turned out to be Jay Graydon, who convinced me to use him as a producer; all his best friends were the best and highest paid musicians in LA. They made records with Steely Dan and Toto and all the biggest acts at the time and they would work harder for him because he was one of them. So Jay was hired by RSO to be my producer. We just started to work on my stuff when Jay said, "I'm afraid something has come up and we need to take a break for a while." Jay informs me that Alan Sorrenti, a singer from Italy, is on his way over. "And as we have to stop your project for a while, why don't you write some songs with him, and they'll be the songs we record." So I did write and record four songs with Alan. And almost immediately, one of those songs became one of the biggest Italian hits ever, sold 1.2 million singles.

What was that song called?
"Tu Sei L'Unica Donna Per Me." I wrote in English with him and then he translated the songs into Italian. This resulted in an Italian publishing company, Recordi, offering me $25,000 if I would sign the publishing of the songs to them. Then this guy's main competition, Miguel Bose, whose mother was an Italian opera singer and father was a famous Spanish bullfighter, contacted me, and I did four songs with him. And his album went to number one in Spain and Italy and all of a sudden I'm doing great and making all this money. Wow, you can actually make money from songwriting! I had no idea.

Until then I hadn't seen myself as being a full-time songwriter for other artists. Also, I started around that time getting into R&B, soul and black music, such as Stevie Wonder's *Songs in the Key of Life* and that *Amigos* album by Santana and the Brothers Johnson and the Jazz Crusaders. I used to go and hear Little Feat live at the Troubadour Club. In fact I got so into it all that I divorced myself from everything musically I had known before and did a musical left turn. Something hit me over the head and I really discovered a deeper love for music. Back in the sixties I was such a huge Beatles fan, I ignored a lot of other great music that I didn't discover until years later.

When you had moved from the UK to Los Angeles in 1973, were you conscious of the strong singer-songwriter movement?

One of the first singer-songwriters that ever floored me, and I was a huge fan, was early Randy Newman. He was a big influence on me starting when I was living in London. James Taylor also knocked me out. After living in LA for a few years, when I was no longer involved or connected with being in a group, I fell into a more open attitude to songwriting. I also started smoking a little pot back then and that moved me deeper into the music, and a new appreciation for well-written, meaningful and touching songs and the desire to try to write them. It all got much more interesting to me.

Did you ever learn to read and write notation?

No, not well. For some people that obviously can be the greatest advantage. But to others it can be a disadvantage. Because there's the correct way to speak but sometimes saying things the wrong way is what makes it interesting or unique. And some people that are musically illiterate will go to a chord that technically is wrong but has this sort of charm about it. Truth is that if I were a better musician, my answer would be different.

How did you and Terry Shaddick get together to write "Physical"?

Terry was an English friend of a friend of mine, and we started hanging out and jamming together. Then one day at Terry's we decided not to write a love song, nothing about the usual emotional side of love but to write a song about the physical side of love, about the physical side of sex. Not knowing at the time that it would end up being called "Physical". So we completed the verses and we had this little bit of chorus music, and then right out of the blue we started singing "Let's get physical" and it all just fell into place. There wasn't much sweating over it, it just came out. I remember us being excited about the song, thinking it would be perfect for someone like Rod Stewart or some male rock singer. I sang the original "Physical" demo so our impression was it was for a male to sing. What happened next was unplanned. By pure luck Olivia's manager, Lee Kramer, heard it through his office wall as I was playing it to Roger Davies in his office; turns out that Lee Kramer also managed Mr Universe and saw it as an opportunity to promote Mr Universe by having him pose on the cover with Olivia and call the album *Let's Get Physical*. One thing led to another and it worked out beautifully—without Mr Universe involved!

How did you collaborate on that? Was there a separation of music and lyrics between you?

No. We just got into it. I was playing guitar and Terry was playing his Rhodes electric piano. With an old drum machine keeping the groove.

How much do you think the success of that song can be attributed to Olivia's performance of it and her whole change of image?

The controversial side of it worked in our favour. You've got to remember that it was banned in one or two states here in America, it was banned in South Africa. It sounds so tame now, but it was very racy for the time. "Let's get horizontal." Which is the same type of borderline thing that "Genie in a Bottle" has—"You gotta rub me the right way." "Physical" was obviously not about exercising. It shocked everyone and it helped Olivia of course, but I think the song wouldn't have been so huge if anyone else had recorded it.

Roger told me there was a chance it wasn't going to make it. Just before it was to be released she panicked and didn't want it on her album. Her record company had another song scheduled to be the first single but it was the promotion men who said, "No, it has to be this one." So she said, "No, it can't be 'Physical' because everyone will think I'm a bit slutty." So the compromise was to come out with the video first to give the impression the song was about exercising.

Were you conscious after "Physical" that you had to live up to it?
Sure was. I remember stressing out thinking, "God, that was such a huge hit, how am I ever going to write another one?" But luckily not long after, "Heart Attack" went to number two for four weeks. That's when I started getting into the technology, too. All my recording is done these days into a Mac computer using Logic Audio or Pro Tools but my first introduction to sequencers was from my mate John Farrar; he showed me one of the first sequencers systems that recorded drums and keyboards, and I was so blown away by this new technology that I immediately ran out and bought myself a set-up. Paul Bliss was a writing partner of mine from London, and we started experimenting with the drum section of this machine and wrote our first two-bar drum loop and had it repeat throughout the whole song, and then the keyboard parts. The verse was seven bars long, which means that the two-bar drum beat would eventually come out of sync with the seven-bar verse music, causing it to move the beat around. The drums changed timing throughout the song. Our naivety caused a really interesting mistake; it wasn't like we were trying to be clever.

We finished the demo and took it over to John Farrar and he used our programmed parts, transferred into his system, then added some more parts to it. I'd say about 75 per cent of the finished record of "Heart Attack" was the original demo which he then recorded with Olivia. He put real guitar on there and other sounds and made it a lot better. But that was the first time that something I made at home, the demo, became the record. That recording has been written up as one of the first really sequenced records. People have said to me years later, "Oh, that was so clever how the drums turned around, how did you think of that?" And I'd say we were just brilliant, but really it was an accident with these two bars out of time with the odd-shaped verses.

You've always collaborated. Why?
I really like the ping-pong bouncing back and forth part of it. "What about this?" "No, what about this?" It gets things moving fast. I like the interaction where one thought leads to the other writer having a new idea or twist and that in turn takes you somewhere neither of us anticipated. My best collaborations are usually with better musicians than me. Somebody that will play something that I wouldn't have thought of. I usually start singing anything that comes into my head and that's the beginning of a chain reaction, a melody starts developing or some lyrics and then when you start to get an idea of what this song

could be about and what style would best suit it, R&B, rock, pop etcetera. It's almost like going out to play; you're just having fun.

What have been some of your best co-writing experiences?
Every song usually has its own story. This new Kelly Rowland song "Stole", for example, didn't start off with "Let's write a song about a school shooting." We first started writing a song about a runaway teenage girl who comes to Hollywood and then things go wrong for her. We had the chorus finished—"Mary's got the same size hands as Marilyn Monroe"—but then when we started to write the verses we couldn't come up with anything original and it started to sound a bit boring. We lost interest in the concept and then went off the idea altogether. So we scrapped that whole song and we started again writing different lyrics and melodies. We wanted to touch on a social consciousness theme, and got an idea about school shootings, like the Columbine tragedy. We liked the new verses but couldn't find a chorus to fit. We tried and tried, then I remember thinking that maybe we could use that other song's chorus. It wasn't lyrically related to these new verses but it sounded cool putting the two songs together. And all of a sudden we realised that that girl from the first unfinished song could be one of the victims in the second song. Really confusing, I know, but it worked. So each song is like an adventure. You don't know how it's going to turn out.

All the people I work with are like my best mates. Johnny Farrar is one of my best friends, no question about it. I could never be a writer like John Farrar. He's like the loneliness of the long-distance runner. He sits there and he's such a perfectionist and he works so hard day after day and he's all by himself. I'd just get so lonely. He's exactly the opposite. I remember when he was writing "Magic". I walked into his house when he was writing that on acoustic guitar and it was the strangest chords and it sounded so odd. I kept thinking, how can he turn that into a song? And he did. It's a fantastic song. It's so different. But I like the interaction and I don't like the solitary side of it.

What's the story of "Hard Habit to Break"? Did you know that you were writing that song for Chicago?
I'd had a good chunk of it written, the verses and the chorus, but I wasn't sure how to finish it. I knew it was potentially a good song. At around the same time I'd been working on making the record "Twist of Fate" for Olivia with producers David Foster and Umberto Gatica, who were also making the Chicago album. Umberto confided to me, "We're really having trouble finishing this Chicago album, we've got some good songs but we don't have that big killer hit one." And I thought about that song that I could never finish. I called this guy, John Parker, who I'd had some success with before with songs for Laura Brannigan, Dolly Parton and Sheena Easton. And his contribution was great. He took the verse and transposed it and so it jumped up to another key and it gave it some height and some life. Then we wrote a whole middle-eight, which wasn't on my version. And then the ending was all new. We hired a saxophone player to come in and play something Chicago-ish—in those days we really didn't have a lot of synths and ways to make big productions at home but we did the best we could—then we presented it to Umberto.

I had heard they liked it, but I didn't know that they were going to record it immediately. So I took a few days off, went up to Big Bear with my wife Lizzie. That night there was a big snowstorm and we were cosy in this funky rented mountain cabin that didn't have phones, when there was a knock on the door and an annoyed, cold manager said I had an urgent message to call someone. I asked him if I could use his phone in the office and he refused. So Lizzie and I got in the car and we went to the local grocery store and used the outdoor unsheltered call box with this blizzard in full swing. Lizzie got some coffee and sat in the car while I returned David Foster's call. And he said, "We've recorded your song but we need an extra verse, can you write one quickly?" And I said, "Great, I will be back tomorrow night." And he replied, "No, you don't understand, we're in the studio right now. They've sung the whole song and we need the new verse right now to complete it." So I would come up with a line, call John Parker, then call the studio and have Chicago sing it while I tried to come up with the next line. Time for a confession here—my wife Lizzie came up with "Two people together but living alone." Of course I never gave her any credit.

So you were prepared to serve the performance of the song, rather than your original concept of it.

I don't think I was that precious about it. I really wanted to get a Chicago cover and if writing another verse would help then I'd give it a shot. There have been other situations where someone has asked me to change something in a song that I felt would damage it and so I refused to change it, resulting in the song not being recorded.

***Chicago 17* was a huge-selling album.**

Yeah, and so was *Chicago 18* and the two different Greatest Hits CDs. It goes on forever. I love that. I had two songs on their eighteenth album; one was "Niagara Falls". That's a song I feel I failed to make as good as it could be; I tried really hard to come up with a better line to rhyme with "As long as Gibraltar stands" and we settled for "I'll always be your man."

"If She Would Have Been Faithful", that's the other song on *Chicago 18*. I really liked the song but wasn't in love with the record. It was the new Chicago and the big snare and everything just didn't sound too great to me. That's one of the few songs I've written that I can say is autobiographical; I was thinking of a specific girl, the girl I mentioned earlier that managed the health club. We lived together for three years and she ended up screwing this other guy, and if she hadn't done that I would never have met my wife, Lizzie. I wrote it with Randy Goodrum. He's a fantastic piano player. I actually dreamed that chorus; it came to me in the middle of the night, I woke up and there it was. We've made a new demo of that song; I wanted to give it another chance. And now the singer Brandy is planning to record it on her next CD. We rewrote it as a duet and all the verses are much more young and contemporary; some of those words in the original were too big, like "Reconstructing details with old photographs." That changed to "Going over how it used to be with old photographs."

When some of these younger artists get your songs and then come to meet you, are they surprised that you've been around for a while?
Not only that, but when I'm producing, say with 98 Degrees, LFO, O-Town, this Kelly Rowland one, these kids are basically the same age as my daughter. So I really am different. I don't think of myself as being this old fart. But I am actually old enough to be some of my collaborators' father. But I don't think of that until I look in the mirror. I forget about it and I feel like I'm just a kid. I swear on my life, I feel just as excited as when I was just starting. I really can't wait sometimes.

How easy is it to write about themes that an artist such as Christina Aguilera or Kelly Rowland or Jessica Simpson can perform? Do you actually have to get inside the head of a girl that age?
I try to imagine myself in these different emotional/heartbroken/heartbreaker teenage angst situations. I have to believe what I'm singing about because if I don't, how can I expect anyone else to?

Do ideas, bits of lyric, a melody, come to you while you're driving, or in a movie?
Yeah. I write a lot in the car, I put a CD of just the music-only track in the CD player and sing along to it. I used to get embarrassed when I'd pull up at a red light just singing away and I'd look over and someone's staring at me. I hike in Topanga State Park with headphones on, singing out loud like a madman. When I get a good idea I document it with a little digital dictaphone.

You're an incredibly happy person. Some songwriters seem to need misery to fuel their inspiration.
Writing sad songs is a big part of my gig. Storytelling that people can relate to. My songs aren't autobiographical, but I try to imagine sad situations to get in the right frame of mind. It's important to try to write these songs from new and fresh perspectives, so I'm afraid when any of my friends have a bad break-up in a relationship, I grill them to find out how they feel, to try to see it from a different perspective.

How did the Christina Aguilera song "Genie in a Bottle" happen? Were you asked to write a song for her?
No, the song was finished, I felt it was a hit, and we sent it to several A&R people at the same time. And got an immediate interest. RCA had a girl group from Florida called Innocence with an international release already planned, so we thought that was a good place for the song. At the same time Ron Fair, also from RCA records, the A&R person for Christina Aguilera, said, "She's here in LA, can I bring her up to the house and just put her voice on it? Please don't make a decision until you've heard her sing it." So she came up to my partner, David Frank's place, just a mile up the street from me, put her voice on the demo, and we were blown away at how she sang. We agreed to make the record with Christina on the condition it would be the first song released from her CD.

It's important to try to make the right decisions as to where your songs will end up, as chances are few and far between. An established famous artist is not necessarily the best home for your song; music styles can change so fast and a song that sounds hip today can sound dated within a few months, and that can cause a problem if your song is recorded but not planned to be released until later that year. An example was "He Loves U Not". Britney Spears' record company, Jive, wanted this song for her but wouldn't confirm if it would ever be a single or not, and its best case scenario was the third single, which would be at best six months away. Sean "Puffy" Combs, who has BadBoy Records, had said he also wanted that song for his new unknown girl group Dream and guaranteed us, "If you do it on Dream, I'll guarantee it will be the first single and we'll release it as soon as you finish recording the girls." So we took a chance on an unknown group as we felt the song was current and maybe wouldn't be in the future. It was the first single, and it was a huge hit.

Do you have any sense of where the songs really come from?
I still get surprised when one minute there's nothing and then somehow a little while later a song exists.

Do you have a standard method of writing, then?
A lot of songwriters sit down and they say, "Okay, what's a really good title?" I have no idea. In fact, if the music isn't playing I shut down, too. I just loop it around and the music will play, and I might have the eight bars of music going around and around and I'll literally start singing stuff. I'll sing anything and I don't know what it is. I'll sing until something feels good. And then when I get an idea—that's the hardest part, getting started—then it's easy for me because I know what it's supposed to be about. Then it becomes the technique.

There are little formats you do, like "don't bore us get to the chorus." You can't have too long till you get to the meat of the song. Something that I do a lot and—without bragging—somebody said today that they use "that Kipner thing". Usually I have a verse or two verses, then a thing called a "pre" or a "B section", the little bit before the chorus that sets up the chorus, then it usually all goes back to the verse, and then most people go back to that little bridge again, that little section into the chorus. But because I want to get to the chorus quicker I try and make it that it goes straight to the chorus. Then after that, when you need this big long bridge, you just go back to that "pre" section later on and it almost feels like a new bit of music. It really makes things concise. Editing is a really important thing; you don't want people's attention spans to wander. So I go out of my way to think about how to cut the fat. I calculate, I'm conscious of little hooks that will make people, even if they're not listening to the song, go, "What was that?" I try and use words that you're not used to hearing in a song, because then it sounds wrong and then you at least pay attention to it. If something sounds wrong it's better to jar people than to have it become bland. I am aware of those things and try and do things that are a little left-field.

These days, in addition to songwriting, I produce the finished records. We consider ourselves record writers rather than songwriters. The reason is a majority of A&R executives are so used to hearing demos that sound like records—"this song's a hit or it's not a hit"—

decisions are made that quickly, so the demo has to be as close to a finished hit record as possible. In the old days you could play a song on the guitar and someone says, "That's a great song", but when it's turned into a record with another producer, chances are that it can work out great or it can go terribly pear-shaped and waste the opportunity. So when you write a song now, it's not only the song and the concept and the style but it's also the musical parts and the whole package that counts, and that's what you have to deliver to carry on being successful. Not just emulating what's on the radio at the moment but taking a chance to do what isn't contemporary yet.

SHARON O'NEILL

SYDNEY, AUSTRALIA, MARCH 2004

When Sharon O'Neill arrived in Australia in 1980, there were no prominent female singer-songwriters on the scene. The seventies had been an era of interpretive women singers with powerful voices—queens of pop like Colleen Hewitt and Marcia Hines or soulful chanteuses like Renee Geyer—but if there were women writing songs, aspiring to be Australia's Joni Mitchell or Carole King, the record companies weren't finding them. When O'Neill crossed the Tasman to embark on a new phase of her already established career, the men were doing pub rock and the women were ... getting goosebumps. "There was Christie Allen, and I know for a fact that when I came over, every label wanted one of those," O'Neill remembered.

O'Neill had no intention of being a pop princess singing other writers' songs. Her record company imported her from New Zealand because of her strong songwriting skills, which had been acclaimed and awarded back home. Shy and unwaveringly heartfelt about her work, she only surrendered to pressure once, recording a cover song, "How Do You Talk to Boys", which gave her enough recognition to do a support on Boz Scaggs' 1980 Australian tour. Perhaps audiences had been craving an intelligent female artist performing original material. "The first couple of shows I thought, 'Oh my God, am I going to get through this? They don't know anything that I'm singing.' But the audiences seemed to enjoy the fact that they didn't know it and gave it a shot."

She shot to great heights in her new country, but Australia had never been in O'Neill's sights. Born on 23 November 1952 in Nelson, a small town on New Zealand's South Island, she grew up hearing music her Scottish mother and Irish-descended father played from their homelands. It led to a love of folk music, first Steeleye Span and Fairport Convention from Britain, and then Joan Baez, which directed her to other American music. She fell for the West Coast sounds of the Eagles, Linda Ronstadt and their extended musical families. As O'Neill tentatively started creating songs, it was that mix of influences that guided her. She played in folk clubs, joined various bands in Christchurch, and worked her way to the North Island and the big smoke of Auckland, which was the most she had aspired to.

Her first album, recorded in Auckland in 1979, was *This Heart This Song*, and contained songs with a strong Californian flavour. The essence of writers such as Karla Bonoff and Eric Kaz, whose songs were recorded by Ronstadt, reverberated through O'Neill's originals. "It was that whole era of music, and the Eagles, Jackson Browne and James Taylor, that was very inspirational, they were all my favourites. It was a natural influence to be writing what I liked to listen to," she reflected.

Only four years later, O'Neill was in Los Angeles recording her fourth album, the landmark *Foreign Affairs*, with Ronstadt's early producer John Boylan, who enlisted the likes of Bonoff and Don Henley to provide backing vocals. If the experience of working with such luminaries was heady, so too was the change in life that followed—a falling-out with her record company and a marriage breakdown—and once she left the limelight she never made a pronounced return. By the mid-eighties Australia had a new breed of female singer-songwriter—aggressive, sassy women like Chrissy Amphlett and Deborah Conway. O'Neill recorded two more albums containing fine, often intense songs, but mainly she contented herself with writing for other artists, either by herself (the title song from the ABC-TV series *Sweet and Sour* was written by O'Neill and sung by Conway) or with co-writers, including her new partner, Alan Mansfield, an American songwriter and keyboard player who had joined Dragon. Their songs together have included "Younger Years" for Dragon, and "True Love", a hit on Robert Palmer's last album.

I was beguiled by O'Neill's speaking accent, an interesting hybrid of New Zealand, Australia and the United States. The cross-cultural effect has always been prevalent in her life and work. But it was clear that New Zealand was still very much at her core. She had just returned from a visit home and had reconnected with her roots.

"I loved growing up in New Zealand and I do love New Zealand. I've just come back from Nelson and it was lovely, life is different, it's fantastic. It's really quite a musical little town. There's a lot of buskers and hippies and it's quite special. It's always been a folky little town, and that probably had quite an influence on me."

Are you writing songs these days?
I am. I've got a lot of unfinished work, actually, which sometimes for a songwriter is really frustrating, because I've got these ideas and am not completely happy with them and I've got to go back and reassess them. So I've got a lot of unfinished business with my songs at the moment. It's a strange place to be.

It's not the usual way for you to write?
Not really. When I used to be performing more, there was more necessity to try out new material live and see how it went over. And I would complete things a lot more quickly. Now I'm a little bit more anal about it and sort of picky picky. Because I have the time to do it.

There's been an impression that you disappeared off the radar. Did you continue to write all this time?
I've always written. And in fact it's probably because I started out as a songwriter more than a singer. Singing was almost a vehicle for the song. It's always been a passion, and it's sort of come full circle because now I'm back being more of a songwriter than I am a singer. I went through that whole pop star thing that happened, quite incredibly in front of me before I even thought about it, so now I'm back doing what I did in the first place. And that love is still there and I still get the enormous buzz out of creating something even if it's just at the piano here. Quite often that's the way it'll happen and that's the way it used to happen in the olden days. Or on the other hand I'll go up to the studio and put it down with more parts and a little bit more intensely. But either way, it's still a passion.

What gets you inspired to tap into the creative source?
A lot of different things. Sometimes it's other people's emotions, stories I hear around me. Sometimes it can quite simply be a song title, like a phrase that I think, oh, that would be so cool to write something about that. Or just being in a real good frame of mind and going to the piano and playing chords. And quite often just doing that purely and simply because I feel like doing it, some lyrics will come from out of the blue about something.

Has piano always been your favoured instrument for writing on?
Yeah, it has. I get more melodies from piano than from guitar. I still like playing guitar, but it's quite a different concept writing-wise. I'm not that comfortable with a guitar hanging around my neck. Unless I'm maybe sitting down. It's like a whole different feel of an instrument to me. I also like piano because I'm really comfortable with the black notes. So you can use a C sharp minor any day and I'm a real happy camper. I don't know why it is. I just gravitate to there. It can be a real bitch for musicians in the studio sometimes but I like it.

You wrote poetry as a teenager?
Yeah, I loved poetry. I still write poetry, quite apart from my songs.

361

So a lot of your poems don't turn out to be songs?
Yeah, a lot of them are just what they are. I'm gradually getting all my scraps of paper together and getting them into the computer so that I've got something tangible in front of me that I can print out and go through and actually see over the years what I've been writing about.

Do you think you might find some lyrics in there that could be songs?
I think so. Some are funny, some are completely rhyming, and some don't rhyme at all. Some are just thoughts, some are on the back of a book in the glove box of the car. But there could be something that might just trigger me once I've got it all together and I read through it, it might just stir up a song.

Have you taken a poem or a set of lyrics and decided that they're quite perfectly complete and you need to find music to fit them afterwards?
No, I've never actually done that. I've only done that when I've had lyrics given to me and music is needed.

Do you find that hard?
It is quite hard. Because it's like coming in after the show in a way; it's really strange. And I've only done that on a couple of occasions. Once for a film, when it's handed to you and you think, my God, where's the chorus going to be and what feel has it got to be? Has it got to be up, has it got to be down, has it got to be sad? I did the soundtrack to a New Zealand movie called *Smash Palace*, and that all happened together, that was really quite bizarre, and really fast. The lyrics had to be written about the movie so I had a plot to work on. Which is a better way to do it than just have somebody say, "Okay, write a song about that. Write a melody around that." That can be quite hard.

Don Walker explained to me that he'll usually write the lyrics first and the lyrics will sing a melody to him.
Yeah, I can understand that. And that works in reverse a little bit, too, because I find sometimes I start a song and I'll just spew out some working lyrics. I'll be thinking to myself, this is not what the song's going to be about but it'll do for now while I get it together. And they stick. They stay there. I try to take it somewhere else and it's like, no, I think I might be starting to like that, maybe that'll take the song somewhere. I really think that's a cool thing that happens. You end up with what you didn't want in the first place and you actually start to really enjoy it and it leads you on in the song.

Can you name a song that came that way?
An example is "Don't Let Yourself Drown", which rolled off the tongue fine as a working lyric in the metre of the song but when I went to really settle into the lyrics, I couldn't shake it. I tried to because it always struck me as a weird phrase, like where am I going to take this? But it ended up staying, with quite a few other lines, and developed into this weird scenario that

got quite colourful as it progressed and was not too far from something I knew about as a kid. Bizarre how these things happen. It wasn't on an album, just a B-side I think.

Did growing up in New Zealand and first having success there give you any kind of unique perspective on music and songwriting?
Possibly. It wasn't much of an industry when I started out. It was hard coming from a small town to get to the point where I did. It was quite mind-boggling to me because I always thought of myself as little Sharon O'Neill from Nelson. And by the time I got to Auckland it was like a big city and it was kind of freaky. I thought it was going to be really hard to make my mark. But I think the ingredients for songs was quite different. I felt I had a lot to write about, about Nelson itself, how I felt there, the size of the town, excursions that you go on and the scenery and family life and small town life. It has come out in some of my songs; there's a song called "Kids in Our Town" and that was very much about growing up in Nelson. So the influence was there, but that could be anywhere.

What was important for you about being recognised as a songwriter and not just a performer when you started out in New Zealand?
I was full throttle a songwriter and I did encounter a couple of barriers in that area. It got me the record contract in the first place, because the head of the record company appreciated my songwriting abilities, and that's the reason why he signed me, which was quite unusual because there weren't a lot of girls writing songs. I think there was only one other, Shona Lang, and then there was me. To have success in that area was really good because it kicked that whole generation of female songwriters out there who felt that they could do it. The New Zealand television industry was very restrictive so the only music shows that we had were shows that recruited people like myself to go on and sing what was number eight for Linda Ronstadt that week. They would redo the song and you would go on and perform it. It was no avenue for songwriters. So it was quite a hallmark to actually get to do an album of completely original songs.

But I wanted to play piano on stage and I always did, and it got to a point where there were visiting record executives out in New Zealand from the States, and they loved the show but they couldn't stand it that I didn't come out from behind the piano. And it really pissed me off, because it's part of writing to play an instrument.

Hadn't they heard of Carole King?
Well, they probably didn't think that it would go round again. So I tried that, I went out front, and I'm quite comfortable out front, actually, but I like to dart back and play an instrument if I can, it really depends on the venue. Sometimes it's not practical to have a piano set up, so the only alternative is a synthesiser, which is fine. I did it, but I also went back and played the piano again, and just fought for that.

Were you still in New Zealand when you wrote "Words"?
Yep, Wellington, actually.

What inspired it?

Definitely a piano-written song. I think at the time it was just a release for me. It sounds kind of arty-farty but it's like the words coming out of the keyboards, just getting out there, getting all this stuff out that I had going on inside. So it was a bit cathartic.

Do relationship songs have to be based on personal experience?

I don't think so, no. A lot of time I'll be speaking to someone who's going through something and I know what they're going through, because you get the feeling from the phone call or whatever it might be, and that can take it somewhere else. It might seem that you've been through all that, but my God, if I'd been through everything that I've written about ... [*Laughs*]

Many of your songs have been about bad relationships, let-downs, advising other women to get away from bad relationships, particularly in that early eighties period. "Maybe" sounds pretty heartfelt.

That's quite a general thing, but there have been moments that followed that, moments that ensued, where I probably wouldn't have been able to get through the video.

Life imitated art?

Yeah. That happened on "We're Only Human". That was a co-write so it wasn't like there was anything going on, it was just an observation of a relationship where you can't be perfect all the time. And then when it came to do the video shoot, I was splitting up with my husband. I actually broke down on camera. And I don't think it was relevant to the lyrics that I was miming at the time, it was just emotion.

"Maybe" sounded like the melody came first.

Yes, it did actually. It was quite ironical because we discovered later that my partner, Alan, wrote almost the same chords on the same piano at the same period of time at the CBS studios at the time. It was really spooky because when we got together and we talked about it, he played me this thing that he'd done. Because I went into the studios before rehearsal when I was rehearsing for the album, and wrote that song in about five minutes. At the old upright piano, with the new blue carpet, in the studio. It just wrote itself, and I have no idea why, because I wasn't going through anything like that. It was just one of those observations of what it must be like when the communication breaks down. Unless there was something subconsciously going on. But the chords at the beginning were definitely what carried the song along. And Alan had been on that same piano, just fiddling around, and had come up with something very similar around about the same time. He was doing stuff with Marc Hunter at the time.

And you didn't know each other?

No. It's a bit spooky.

Does that make you think that melodies have a life of their own and that they are sent to you sometimes from somewhere else?
I don't know about that, but I think sometimes things just flow. I'd like to think that it was something heaven sent, but I think maybe when you're in a real creative moment you're maybe not even aware of a spooky little moment that things happen, and it completes itself, the lyrics are there and it's done and you start rehearsing it a couple of hours later.

Could the instrument itself have had something to do with it?
Oh, I think the piano definitely would have, yeah. Because there's the old black notes coming out again.

Was recording "How Do You Talk to Boys" back in 1980, which you had not written, a difficult step for you to take?
It was actually, because at first I had a little bit of a run-in with the record company exec who gave me the tape and said, "This will be your first Australian number one." Those were his words. I just wanted to make a point of always doing my own stuff, and they just chipped away at me so long I thought, well screw it, I'll do it. And so I did. It's not to say I wouldn't have liked it to have gone to number one, but I was kind of glad that they were wrong.

It did have an impact.
It did get played and I have a lot of respect for Steve Kipner, he's such a great writer, but it wouldn't be the kind of thing that I would write, so it was hard to get behind lyric-wise.

You wrote with Steve Kipner much later down the track. How was that experience?
That was "We're Only Human". He came in after the fact, because I'd already written it with Richard Feldman. We had sat and written and mapped the idea of the song out and bandied around the lyrics and that sort of thing, and then we drew Steve in afterwards and he put his magic into it, and he was there when we recorded the demo. He's very hands-on demo-wise, which was great.

What do you think his magic was that he added to it?
I think he's got a sense of structure, where a song should go, and he knows what he's talking about. He'll drag it out of waffling, put it that way. He'll make it keep your attention.

Do you think that your songs have lacked that?
I think some do. There's one song, "Face in Rainbow", from my first album, that actually got the APRA Silver Scroll of the year in New Zealand and I was very flattered about that, but I never forget hearing it on the radio one day and the refrain at the end is going and going and going, and when the announcer came on he says, "Ah, is she ever gonna stop?" That's pretty much telling it like it is, isn't it? So I've grown as a writer, too, I tried to be aware of things like that, but I know in some of my earlier works I've waffled.

Did commercial pressures take your songwriting in directions it might not otherwise have gone?
In the *Foreign Affairs* period it did, because I finished the album and they didn't hear the single. It was disappointing because I was very happy with the album and they wanted a single after the fact. So then I had to think well, there's no single on the album, what am I supposed to write? It was the first time I was asked for something that I had to get together, and that was "Losing You". I wrote that purposefully to see if, would that be okay as a single? And they said, okay fine, and that was the first single.

They hadn't heard "Maxine" as a single?
No, they hadn't. So that would be the only time I can think really that I physically had to think commercial, because I didn't really know what they wanted, since it wasn't on the album.

You wrote "Maxine" in Sydney while on tour with Boz Scaggs?
It was after that. When he left we did our own little pub gigs in and around the place, the band that I had, which was a New Zealand band. We were staying in the Cross in a little pub, that was our base. We'd go up to Newcastle and we'd come home at three in the morning. And this particular girl was always in the same place and for me, coming from where I'd come from, I hadn't seen much of city nightlife before, I was really green. So I really felt sorry for her.

Was her name Maxine?
No. I didn't know her.

Where did you get that name?
Just out of the blue. Just things that have the right connotations. It seemed to sing right for her choice of business, really.

You've said it was lyric-driven and the music was "incidental".
Yeah.

That surprised me because it was a melodically hooky chorus. Do you remember how the music came to you?
Just a piano riff, basically. I just made an extra effort with the solo chords. But it was a very simple pattern on the piano, because I just needed to say what I had to say.

Were you happy with John Boylan's production? He made it very slick, especially with the vocals at the end.
That was all my arrangement with the vocals and I wanted that counter-melody, which I'd done in a few songs before. It had a walking feel to it. I guess it was an LA production. I didn't know what slick meant until I got back and they said, "Oh, you've just done it in LA and it's pretty slick." And I went, "Oh, I suppose it is, because it's a long way from previous

recordings." That was his style. I was happy with it, definitely. He was a good producer for that moment in time, where I was at.

Did you do vocal arrangements at the time you would write a song?
Yeah, I often had that as part of the overall songwriting.

Did you have a feeling you'd written your biggest hit when you wrote "Maxine"?
No. It was an unexpected hit. All the shit hit the fan about the lyric content and the way the video was done. It had to be re-edited, and then it wasn't allowed to be played until after eight at night and all that stuff. Trying to get it on radio for the record company was so difficult. So we almost gave up on it. Then one day I heard it on the radio on a major station and it just blew me away, because I thought, thank God somebody's actually going to play it. In hindsight it has been my biggest hit, but I didn't realise that was as far as it would go, because the next two albums I thought had really strong songs on them but no-one's ever really heard them.

I think some songs stand the test of time without having airplay. They stand up on their own two feet when you sing them and play them, no matter what. And it doesn't matter that people maybe haven't even heard it. They will enjoy it. So I think they do have a life of their own without radio and TV.

Loneliness and isolation seem to be ongoing themes, right through from "Maxine" to "Poster Girl" on your last album.
"Poster Girl" I can definitely relate to on a personal level. It was very much about looking back at what I had been through and being marketed. I didn't even know what marketing was when I first came to Australia. Just being marketed and getting lost in the shuffle with it all going round around you. So that was like me personal. But there's been a lot of times in my life when I've had to be on my own, like recording an album overseas on my own, maybe being in London in a dingy little flat, catching the tube and going to the studio on my own. There's been a lot of moments and a lot of travelling that I've done and I've had to live with my own company a lot. So it may have an influence on my writing.

With the *Foreign Affairs* album, recording in LA with John Boylan, having top session players on board and vocalists like Karla Bonoff, Timothy B Schmit and Don Henley, it must have been pretty thrilling given what you'd admired musically.
It was. It was gobsmacking really.

Did you get to know Karla at all and talk to her about songwriting?
We just chatted like you do when you hang out at studios. That's all. They were very quick. They came in and did what they did and they left. Probably to go to another session.

I can see the influence in your work of her songs like "Someone to Lay Down Beside Me". Again, the kind of isolation.
Oh yeah, beautiful songs. She was definitely, along with Linda, an inspiration. And I respect

her so much as a songwriter, when you hear Linda do one of her songs and do it exactly like Karla does it, it's so cool. She sticks to the pattern, to the structure, which goes a long way to say that it's a great song.

Were most of those songs written before you got to LA? Did you do any writing over there?
I did do some writing; I did "Hearts on the Run" over there. I stayed at John Boylan's house and he had his little studio, so I honed some of the songs in his studio. He needed that because he charted everything for musicians. But the ideas I took with me and some were completed. Like "Maxine" was completed. I probably re-demoed that over there for him in a better form. And of course "Losing You" wasn't written at that point. I wrote it there.

Does that produce different results? Does where you are when you write have an effect on what you write?
I think it does very much. There's one thing about writing in your own studio and being comfortable in that, and the phone goes and you can take the call or anything like that. But there's another thing if you're in somebody else's house and you've got a deadline, and money is being spent while you're there and you really have to get it together. So I found that most of my creative stuff was done late at night after the studio was finished and I could actually relax and not worry about any time frame.

The only other time I really wrote in LA, I did a songwriting trip, which had nothing to do with the record company, it was all to do with the publishing company who put me together with writers. It was my first attempt at co-writing, so it was quite a different experience. It was after *Foreign Affairs* and there was a two-year period when all the shit hit the fan with CBS, so I couldn't go into the studio and do anything. So it was like, well, I may as well write some songs and experience what that's like. I found that really weird because I was so used to writing on my own, and it was such a business over there and I didn't know these people. I said, "I'm here from Australia and my publishing company told me to hook up with you." And they were expecting a call. So I'd drive over and you sit there and say, "Hi, how are you?" and you have a cup of coffee and then have to be creative. In some cases the writers had ideas, like there's a couple I wrote "Trojan Horse" with, they already had that idea to write a song called "Trojan Horse", so that helped. We just sat around and nutted it out lyrically and musically. But it's not my choice to write that way. I like writing with Alan, because we don't just sit down and say, "Today we're going to write a song." It's a creative feeling. And he's really good with lyrics, he'll come out with some really cool things out of the blue and we relax with it.

Is the key to your songwriting partnership with Alan the personal relationship or was the collaborative chemistry there before the love chemistry?
We were together as a couple. And it was not something that we said, "Well, now we're together maybe we should write songs together." It's something that we never planned. Alan had been writing with Dragon, and that in a way introduced us to writing together, because Dragon were looking for songs. And we thought it would be really cool to write something for

Marc. We started to dabble in that area and it really worked. That was a nice way to begin, because it wasn't like, "Let's try and write some songs for me." It was this third thing, and we both knew Marc really well and we knew what he would sing and what he wouldn't sing. So the writing for Dragon kicked it off.

I think the first thing we wrote specifically for me was "Physical Favours". And the way we write together usually is Alan will be sitting at a keyboard mucking around and something will happen. He'll come up with a riff or something and I'll start singing something with it.

Are music and life very much intertwined for you both?
Yeah, they are very much. And it depends on who's doing work. At the moment we're not writing a lot together because Alan's out working, playing, so there's not a lot of energy left over at this point. But then when we have time off together, we usually come up with things.

How was working with Marc Hunter?
Marc was great, because he was stroppy about what he wanted to say and what he didn't want to say, and he had a really good sense of where to take a song. And he was a great singer. I thought he was an excellent singer. He used to give me chills. I love his solo stuff; we often play his solo albums. He generally liked what we presented and he would just bring it to life in the studio. He would muck around maybe with a vocal and take it somewhere that you go, well, that's really cool. He was very creative melodically.

Is there more satisfaction for you in recording and performing your own songs, or in having successful artists record your songs?
I love the process of recording; I love doing the vocal and finishing a song off and sitting back and thinking that was a real good experience. But it's such a buzz to hear somebody else singing it, too. We wrote Robert Palmer's last single, and the first time I heard him singing it I couldn't believe that somebody like that was actually singing one of our songs.

You wrote "True Love" with him, didn't you?
He basically copied our original demo and added bits to it. It's very much us, but with somebody like that, who loves the song and wants to do it, you give something away.

So it wasn't a true co-write between the three of you?
Not really. He kept everything musically and he kept most of my lyrics and he and I sat around the table and he tossed in different lyrics, things that he would sing that I wouldn't sing that are very much Robert Palmer things. We still have the demo and we still really like it and probably we'll re-record it and just leave it as it is. We won't be using his lyrics, because I wouldn't sing some of those things that he sang.

One of my favourite songs of yours is "Sweet and Sour". Was that song written to a brief for the ABC series, or was it something you'd already been working on?
It was written to a brief, to the title. The title was *Sweet and Sour*, the band was going to

be the Takeaways, and they wanted something upbeat to be a theme. There was another one on that album, too, "Glam to Wham", which was also a brief.

Were you detached enough from it that it didn't bother you that Deborah Conway was singing it rather than you?
No, not at all. I love her voice. It was one of those moments when you think, oh, how cool! Someone else is doing your song. It was great. Because at the time it wasn't the kind of thing I wanted to do.

***Danced in the Fire* was a tougher album, in terms of musical style and lyrics, than your earlier work. Was that what you'd been through personally, or was it more the advent of new technologies to write with?**
A little bit of both and also experiencing writing with Alan. That put more of an edge on it. He's a very funky, rhythmical player. Lyrically, *Danced in the Fire* was exactly what had gone down—marriage break-up, moving into a different point in my life—so it was quite an important album for me to get out. But I tried not to make it too dark.

Was the woman in the song "Edge of Winter" a real person?
No, that's just an observation, that's just a homeless person. Loneliness and dreaming of what could be. It's just supposed to be the black and white of it.

During the long hiatuses that you've had in your career, were there periods when you couldn't write, where it was just too hard?
It was quite difficult when I split up with Brent and I'd only just got through the CBS thing. It was quite hard to just clear my head. I had to resettle myself, if that makes any sense. I think sometimes you need to be really clear-headed and not emotionally torn one way or another. I mean, good songs can come out of that, but sometimes when your life's in a bit of an upheaval you've got to put your roots down again and it's hard to be creative.

But you can draw back on that. Which is what I did with *Danced in the Fire*. Because at the time I wouldn't have written it. I had to wait until I had moved out and got a flat in Bondi and was actually looking out at the water and feeling a bit stronger and then that settled in me lyrically.

How difficult is it to be writing constantly but not having your songs heard?
It's really tough. At first it's almost a bit of light relief, it's like that little mouse has jumped off the wheel and you can breathe a little bit. But then as time goes by it's really hard to get back on the wheel. There's a loss of profile that has fuelled you over the years, so it's like, is songwriting enough any more? To just feed yourself. So it's hard. And that's why I'm really anxious to get all this music together and put out an album regardless of what happens. If I have to sell it at a gig, I'll sell it at a gig, or whatever, but just to get it out there, because it's been a long time.

NEIL FINN

AUCKLAND, NEW ZEALAND, FEBRUARY 2004

In the huge, cavernous warehouse space behind his wife's chandelier design shop on a busy thoroughfare in Auckland, Neil Finn was setting up his new studio. The chandeliers received plaudits of their own when used in the stage sets of the Finn Brothers' concerts around the world following the release of *Everyone Is Here*, which Neil and Tim were still working on when we met. The album was a tribute to family, from the dedication to their late mother, Mary, in the credits, to the opening lines of "Disembodied Voices"—"Talking with my brother when the lights went out/ Down the hallway forty years ago ..."

Neil Finn is a family man. His wife and sons have made creative contributions to his career, both inspirational and tangible, and, more importantly, have grounded him during the roller-coaster ride of international fortune and fame. Then there's the strong Irish Catholic upbringing in rural New Zealand, memories of large Finn family gatherings full of music and song, and always the presence of his big brother, Tim, who paved the way.

For all Neil's triumphs as a uniquely gifted songwriter, envied and sometimes unconsciously emulated by his peers, the older he gets, the more he seems defined by kin. Even when he is not writing, recording or touring with his older brother, he is frequently subject to comparisons and scrutiny within the familial context. As a teenager recruited to Tim's band Split Enz, to fill the void left by co-founding guitarist and songwriter Phil Judd, Neil was the shy nascent talent who, with a defining number one hit, "I Got You", threw the perceived hierarchy into turmoil. He followed with a string of instantly accessible songs, such as "One Step Ahead" and "History Never Repeats". Then when Tim branched out on his solo ventures, Neil took the songwriting lead for Split Enz and with a flourish of almost naive panache, created the glorious "Message to My Girl".

It was a sign of what was to come. In Crowded House, which he formed with Paul Hester and Nick Seymour, the younger Finn relished creative control and unleashed a stream of joyful pop masterpieces, immediate classics like "World Where You Live", "Don't Dream It's Over" and "Better Be Home Soon". Tim came on board for the *Woodface* album and in 1995 the pair wrote and recorded the *Finn* album. After Crowded House ended in 1996, Neil recorded two solo albums, *Try Whistling This* and *One Nil*, laden with intricate melodies and mesmerising imagery, but less commercial in approach. Whereas *Everyone Is Here* was already creating excitement six months before its release. By the end of 2004, with sell-out concert tours and pleasing album sales, it seemed the Finns together had reached a new creative peak.

Neil Finn was born on 27 May 1958 in Te Awamutu, New Zealand. Influenced by the music Tim was listening to, he was particularly transfixed by the guitar-playing singer-songwriters of the early seventies such as Neil Young, Carole King, James Taylor and Donovan. He joined a local folk club to develop and showcase his burgeoning guitar and vocal skills. While the Beatles were more Tim's passion, their guitar pop sound echoes through Neil's work in an uncanny, almost spiritual way. He has been hailed around the world as the natural successor to John Lennon and Paul McCartney, and it makes him uncomfortable.

"You can't really process that sort of comparison at all, and it doesn't interest me to, particularly," he said frankly. "If there's things that are reminiscent of Lennon and McCartney perhaps they're too ingrained for me to do anything about anyway, and I certainly don't set out consciously to mimic them or anything like that. Also, it makes me feel pretty vulnerable because when you actually compare their output as songwriters to what I'm doing, I know whose I'd rather have."

Like Tim, he knows there is an inherent New Zealand sensibility in his work, but can't always characterise it. "I was born here and I grew up here and all my earliest memories and my sense of who I am and where I belong and the light and the land are all wrapped up in what comes out as music," he said. "A lot of songs I've written in the last twenty-five years have been written outside of New Zealand and they have probably as much to do with the house that I'm in as the town that I'm in as the country that I'm in."

Finn is often thought of as taciturn and intense. He has a meticulous, studied yet largely unconscious way of putting songs together, and as he himself isn't really sure where the magic comes from in songwriting, he is less prepared than his brother or some of his peers to delve into overly deep analysis of it. He likes to keep it mysterious. Or maybe mystique is something that other people like to attach to his work. As abstract as many of Finn's lyrics can be, the spark is often something as rudimentary as the behaviour of a besotted fan or his dog being hit by a car. But when he matches random lyrical images with melodies that soar to create inspired moments of whimsy, there is an undeniable musical beauty that is both genetic and distinctly Neil Finn.

Do you remember the first song you wrote and how old you were?
I wrote some music. On the back of a Donovan record there was a poem. I bought the record, what was it called? *Fairytale* was the record, and it had a poem on the back, which was something like "Precious little do we drink the sun kiss the rain ... We will find out if good can be bad and bad can be good." I think that was it. And I wrote a little tune for that. I was about twelve.

And what about your first complete song?
I was probably fourteen. Tim asked me to do a couple of supports for Split Enz back then and so I wrote a couple of songs in honour of that. One called "Late in Rome", but "Serge" it became known. Part of the lyrics were written by Roddy Murdoch, who I was playing with at the time. He and his family befriended me and I used to go there and listen to music and write a few songs with him. I wrote the music and he wrote some of the lyrics with me, and it was about an old dancer looking back on his life and it was a very odd song for a thirteen-year-old boy to be singing, but nevertheless. The idea of fantasy characters. And the chorus was: "Serge, he's a dancer, knows each dramatic pose/ Rolls the ladies they fall over, his future's in his toes."

Some of the lyrics were influenced by Roddy, too, 'cause he was an older guy. But I didn't have any of my own stories, really, so I was interested in other stories, inventing characters. And Split Enz at that stage was fairly fanciful, so I was probably being influenced by that as well.

What are the mechanics of you writing a song? Just you and acoustic guitar?
Or piano. I'd usually be playing the piano or the guitar and then have a notion. It's just like drifting away really, doodling on a piece of paper, virtually. And then something just strikes your ear as being attractive or hooky, and you work it and you work it and you change a couple of chords around and all of a sudden a kind of a pattern emerges. And then one little rhythmical thing will change and it'll suddenly start to sound like something, and then what I often do at that point is make a little demo of it. Ever since I got a 4-track recorder, that became the way that I would do it. I'd get an idea and very quickly try and make a quick demo of it where I didn't even really have the whole thing sorted out, I'd just have maybe a verse and a chorus and no structure, but just a couple of bits and a few lines and you'd throw them on, even sometimes without words, just make sounds that sounded like words, and invent melodies and fashion sounds to make them pretend that it's a real thing.

And then eventually it is a real thing. Then I'd just quickly overdub on it, put a harmony or a guitar part and it starts to develop an atmosphere.

And I'll go back and possibly do another demo of it straightaway again, now that I've listened to this vague little impressionistic thing. I'll listen to it and I'll go, "Well, it's really great there, where I did that, where that melody took that little turn, and that line I really like and those chords are great." I'll do another demo now where it's more honed and it's embellished upon. And at that point I get something that's a bit more formed, and I'll go, okay, now I'm going to write every line I've got already and I'm going to try and make up as many as I can that seem to fit in the phrasing, and I'll let that be fairly unselfconscious and just words come out and lines come out that don't necessarily mean anything but kind of follow a thread if you can, but that's not even that important.

So the next demo you've got is something that sounds like it's a song, because it's got words and it's got a core structure and probably still a few question marks about it. And then you play that one back, and if you get the chills and you go, "Wow, that sounds like something", then you know you've got a song.

And you've got lyrics and melody coming simultaneously?
Yeah, floating around, and some of them are cementing themselves and some of them are falling off the way. You'll attach yourself to certain things that just feel good to sing and have a certain image that's interesting, and I don't really think about what they mean generally until I've got the ones that I like already and then I'm like, why do I like them? I like them because they're suggesting something. And what are they suggesting? And then I'll write some other things down that seem to come off that idea. I find that as long as possible I can leave it in the domain of not being quite conscious about what I'm doing, the better. And eventually I'll have something which is melodically and chordally quite set but often I'll have a verse and a chorus and no second verse, and sometimes when you come back to those later to finish them, that's the hardest part of the lot, it takes days, sometimes weeks.

Can you elaborate on that "not being quite conscious" state?
Well it's useful to not be too conscious of what you're doing, because you can talk yourself out of it. You want to stay in that moment as long as you can before you freak yourself out. So I suppose you are in a different state of mind. But it goes in stages sometimes; you can get inspired for a couple of minutes and come up with a little thing, and then get distracted and then you can get back into it sometimes, too.

Would writing a bridge be something more conscious and deliberate?
Sometimes the bridge comes at the same time; you just find you've got the whole lot. You know, on the beautiful days when it all just falls out, and you get the lot. But a lot of the time the bridge comes from the process later down the track where you're playing it with a band, perhaps, and you're going, "Oh, something needs to happen here, maybe if we

just ..." You get an idea of where it might go because you've willed it into being and the band's rocking out on the chorus, and you get an inkling of what might happen, so we'll just try holding this chord for a while. And then hope that something drops into your head and then yell. Yell it out to the band.

Do you ever have a song come out all in one go where you don't have to do this two- or three-stage demo process?
Yeah, I've had songs like that before. And then before I had a 4-track recorder at home, I didn't used to do that. I'd put it on a cassette player to remember it but then you'd just be sitting in a room working like an old-fashioned guy, honing it and honing it.

At what point did you get the 4-track?
Just towards the end of Split Enz, I had a little cassette porta-studio, '83 or '84.

So the Split Enz songs were written more organically.
Yeah, just sitting with a guitar and working it around.

Do melodies ever come to you away from an instrument?
Sometimes. Occasionally when you're driving or sitting in a train or something. Not generally, though. I generally need to be with an instrument.

Do you carry a little tape recorder around with you?
No. I've had them before, I've had dictaphones before, but I've always lost them after about two days.

You sing something fabulous into one and then put it down and can't find it?
I'm not particularly organised in that regard, I don't carry a notebook with me half the time. I sometimes do. And I don't have a tape recorder always handy. So I may have lost a few here and there but, generally speaking, in recent times anyway, I have to mark out a period of time where I'm going to have nothing else going on and just settle in, and for a few days nothing happens, and then you find you're in the zone. You make a start on something and it doesn't seem like much and then all of a sudden it does turn out to be something good, and then you gather your thoughts and you start to be in the right frame of mind to approach it. But it's a deeply mysterious thing; it's just as mysterious now as it ever was.

Sibling rivalry was so often referred to about you and Tim; how real was it in the Split Enz years in terms of songwriting prowess?
I don't remember in Split Enz there ever being any, apart from a natural inclination, if Tim had written a good one, for me to go, "Oh shit, I really want to go and write something that's as good." There's that, and that's real positive, I think. I don't think there's any way that's a bad thing.

And that's not necessarily sibling-related.
Well, I suppose it's sibling in one sense. But we were a six-year difference; up to that point, till the end of Split Enz, he was clearly for me my older brother, and I was never a serious threat. Maybe towards the end of Split Enz we were more on an equal basis as songwriters, but it was later, probably, from a distance where there might have been things that were difficult to deal with. I probably felt guilty when I was successful with Crowded House, in a sense, that he wasn't there all of a sudden, after having been there for years and years. And he probably felt weird about it too. So we dealt with it a bit. I don't think the sibling rivalry is ever as major a factor in our everyday lives as it was for some people imagining and looking on.

It has its pressures, and when we work together, coming back from working separately, we have moments when it's difficult and awkward. We have different perspectives and aesthetics about what we like in music, so sometimes I'll find lyrics that he's written and think, I wouldn't have said it like that, or that sounds awkward to me, I just wouldn't do it like that. And similarly with him. We have our different approaches. So there's a bit of ego attached to that. We're not used to having to give way on those things, so there's some difficulties there. But I wouldn't say that our relationship is characterised by conflict at all. And a lot of people project their own experiences; they have their own difficulties with brothers and sisters. Some people can't believe that we even work together, they say, "I couldn't imagine working with my brother on something like that." So maybe people will just imagine it must be incredibly hard.

Why did you and Tim write songs separately for *True Colours* rather than together?
We hadn't ever co-written. Well, we had written in the same room once, I think, and they weren't particularly amazing songs that we came up with. So it wasn't comfortable. I don't know what it is. Sitting down and writing a song with somebody is a very difficult thing to do. Some people seem to be able to do it fine and no problems, but it involves allowing somebody to hear you at your most embarrassing in many ways, because sometimes before a song is an idea, it sounds like nothing, or sounds like a very exposed bleat or a grunt. So you've got to let your defences down and it's the same with a brother as with anybody. We got to a point finally where we were able to write together on the *Woodface* stuff, and I'm not quite sure why that suddenly seemed so easy. We just had a two-week period where we were between things and grabbed the opportunity, both hungry for it, and things just happened. We were more open about it. But in *True Colours* we weren't used to it. The nature of writing a song is generally speaking a solitary thing.

"I Got You" came from a title that Tim threw at you?
I think it was, yeah. I thought the verse was really strong; I always thought that the chorus was a bit weak and probably would have to be changed or find an alternative. Which is ironic when you think about it because it probably was the king hit of the song, really.

I thought the verse was what drew you in.
Yeah, that's why I liked the verse, because it had a sense of mystery about it and a bit more interesting chordally, but the chorus nevertheless is what everyone sang along with. And it only really became obvious that it was a good song when the band started to play it and it suddenly felt easy to play.

Did the success of that make you feel pressured or inspired as you wrote for subsequent Split Enz records?
I don't know if it did either, really. In some ways every time you sit down to write a song you're in the same boat as you were in last time. You only feel like you're worth something if the one you're working on turns out well. It maybe created a little bit of pressure in some ways. 'Cause you've suddenly got something to compare what you're doing to, and you forget the process and just think that the song was always that good and always sounded that complete and you don't remember when it was just a little bit of a fragile thing. So when you've got a song and it's in that fragile state, you could be forgiven for discounting it and going, "Oh, this is not as good." But sometimes you just work it through and it turns out to be just as good.

Do you remember writing "One Step Ahead"?
Yeah, I've got a tape of me writing that song, actually. So I remember that one better than most. I got the little guitar figure that goes with the melody and just sang it round and around and around until a few words popped up. I was at the South Yarra Hill Suites in Melbourne. Having just come back from playing in Perth.

What about "History Never Repeats"?
I was probably thinking about not repeating myself after "I Got You". We were in Perth when I wrote that one. In Cottesloe. And *True Colours* was going nuts at that time, going mad. So I was probably nobly thinking that I didn't want to repeat myself, and just write another one.

"Strait Old Line" was reminiscent of earlier Split Enz melodies, that almost dissonant sound. Were you thinking along those lines when you wrote that one?
No. I was thinking of just trying to write a song. And actually that song's quite different as a record than it was when I first wrote it. It was a much more sedate, almost gospelly song. When I say sedate, it was just slower and more measured. In my mind it didn't have that jazzy kind of feel at all. I was really happy with what Split Enz did with it, but it wasn't what I imagined.

Did that happen much?
It probably happened more with Split Enz than in subsequent years because I was more in control of the overall sound of Crowded House than I was with Split Enz.

Was "Message to My Girl" a simple love song to your wife, Sharon?

Yeah. In as much as I could. I've always been a bit guarded about writing very direct love songs, which is possibly a hang-up of mine, because there's nothing greater than a very simply expressed love song. But there's just so much, and there was so much out there that seemed crass, that my love songs always seemed to have some twist or a bittersweet quality to them. So it's not for me to say, "I want to say I love you." I'd say, "I *don't* want to say I love you."

Was it hard to write it?

No, it wasn't hard to write, and I'm proud of the song, but to some degree I listen to it and go, well what a cop out. You know, like, why couldn't you just say it? I spend the whole song trying to say how I really want to say it, and I really do, but I just can't bring myself to.

But you were very young, weren't you?

Yeah. But there's always some reservation or confusion or angst associated with it. Which is probably very real and true in some ways, because people are like that. It's not often that people express the joyful moment of absolute blissful love and it sounds convincing. There's been a few memorable ones, but generally speaking, it's the ones that are tinged with the trouble that have the more lasting effect somehow.

Did the players in Crowded House have any discernable influence on the way you wrote songs for that group?

I wouldn't say on the way I wrote songs. They certainly had influence on the way the songs ended up sounding as a band and in some cases I suppose in terms of the textures of things. But no, the songs were at least three-quarters formed when we played them at rehearsal, and at that point it was really only a case of defining the atmosphere of the songs and finding the way of presenting them.

I wondered if knowing their capabilities as players and singers might have guided you in a particular direction that was different to Split Enz.

I think I was developing along certain lines anyway. What affected me more as a songwriter was meeting Mitchell Froom and suddenly being opened up to another aesthetic that I'd been aware of but never been part of, which was an American tradition of traditional songwriting. His interest in things as diverse as Hank Williams to Aaron Copeland to R&B to soul music. I don't think any of it's overt, I didn't change into an R&B singer, but when you listen to the first Crowded House album, there's influences there and atmospheres that come more from an American style of music than anything I've done before. And that influenced my songwriting, the way he responded to the songs that I was playing with him when we were working them up as a first album.

He had a blaster box which he would record stuff on. He would have a keyboard that he'd play bass on and a right hand that he'd play Hammond organ parts and the sound of the Hammond organ and also the way he would approach the bass, a song like "Something

So Strong" was a classic case in point; it was originally a gentle, slow, ethereal kind of song and he suggested giving it a kind of R&B feel and really changed it quite dramatically to the point where I gave him a co-credit on that song, because he really pushed it in a particular direction. I was delighted by that because it wasn't something that was in my vocabulary at all in Split Enz. And that made me think differently about songs.

The only other thing I would say is the way Paul played brushes on a snare drum fitted with a style of song which I was attracted to at that time and probably drew me into it more and more, like in "Four Seasons in One Day", kind of very intimate quiet. Paul is a particularly good brush player and it's not an easy thing to do, so that was something that definitely attracted me to that style of songs.

The moodiness and darkness that's often referred to in relation to your work is usually attributed to your own mood at the time of writing, but do you have to always feel what you're creating?
The irony of that is that I don't often feel moody or dark when I'm writing songs at all. I'm attracted to those atmospheres, I always was; even when I was a teenager, the songs that I usually liked best on albums were the ones that had the sense of mystery and a melancholy to them. So it's just something that I personally liked. But hopefulness as well; I don't think any of them are bleak. I don't think it's that easy to write a song when you're in a depressed frame of mind. You can be feeling a little melancholy maybe, but to be able to be receptive you can't be too self-absorbed in some kind of deep mood anyway.

I hope that the music I'm playing is going to make me feel something. And so how I'm feeling to start off with in a way doesn't even really matter. It can make you feel sad or make you feel hopeful, it doesn't matter to me, as long as it makes me feel something. I get set off by a set of chords or a melody and then the rest follows that, but it's like trapping a mood and making that into its own independent being.

Was "Into Temptation" more a case scenario than something personal that you were confessing?
Yeah, that's a song which is quite complex. It certainly wasn't relating a story of something that actually happened to me in that you can read the lyrics and imagine me in this situation. The reality of the origin of some of the lines is actually quite comical in some ways. The beginning of that song is, "You opened up your door, I couldn't believe my luck." It was to do with staying in a motel in Timaru, and there was a rugby team and a netball team at the bar, getting really tanked, and they started pairing off as the night went on. I heard a knock on my door and went to the door and looked and there was no-one there. And then I looked up and there was a netball player knocking on the door of one of these rugby players as I was there, and they looked at me as they were standing at the door and I looked at them, and she disappeared in the room and they spent the night shagging till dawn. And I wrote those lines down that night in a notebook.

The choruses were to do with when I was in LA and there was an earthquake, and I was in a hotel, so, "Into temptation, knowing full well the earth will rebel." Somebody was describing the idea that whenever those natural disasters happen in LA, somebody is always saying, "Oh, they're paying for their sins." It was just an idea of natural disasters happening to punish people for their sins, that's where those lines came from. So I banged them together and they suddenly described some scenario. Which of course is the reason the song works, because it sounds like the guy singing it really lived it. And that has to be the case; you have to believe the singer.

Can you tell me the stories behind a few other Crowded House songs? First "Mean to Me".
Another hotel in New Zealand, in Palmerston North, this girl, an American fan of Split Enz, came up. I was doing a tour with Dave Dobbyn here, in between Crowded House and Split Enz actually, and she had written to my parents and said that she knew I was playing a gig in Palmerston North and she was going to come and see it, and she was a huge fan, and would she be able to meet me? And she wanted to write because she thought if she just rocked up and I was in any way mean to her, it would destroy her and that she couldn't bear it. She wanted to know that I would know she was coming and it would be okay. So she turned up at this gig and I actually had a very bad fever at the time and was really ratshit, actually. But I went and said hello to her after the gig briefly and then just went to bed, went back to my hotel room.

A bit later on, couldn't sleep so I went to see what was going on in the bar and she was dancing with this poet guy who happened to be there, a guy that we knew. And I had understood that they ended up spending the night together but I actually later found out from her that they hadn't, or she insisted they didn't. That was what the song was about, loosely speaking. But she came up to me a year or so later and was really put out by the fact that I'd told people that she'd spent the night with this poet guy, she insisted she didn't. I think she's completely fine about it now, she's actually chuffed that she's in a song.

"World Where You Live".
I wrote the verse of that in Tim's house in Melbourne and the chorus of it I wrote in my manager's condominium in Santa Monica. It was inspired by his neighbour; every morning I'd be woken at about six in the morning and this woman who lived next door to him was making very loud moaning and groaning noises. And I never heard any other guy, I don't know if there was a guy there, actually, but she sounded like she was having wild sex with somebody. It might have only been herself, I don't know.

You have a lot of these experiences of people having sex near you.
Well, it's a fascinating thing. It's the detachment of listening in on that. Being an observer is probably quite good for songwriting because you can take it in but you don't have to take part in it. And with "I don't know where you go, do you climb into space to the world where you live?" I was just kind of assuming; I didn't know what was going on. That's where those lines came from.

"Don't Dream It's Over". You've said that you wrote "There is freedom within, there is freedom without" just because it would be appealing in America.
I only put that together later. They love that kind of thing, yeah. "We won't let them win" is another thing that Americans really love, the idea that they will never, never let them win. That was a song that came pretty much in one go on my brother's piano in Melbourne. It was just a song about trying to reassure somebody in a way.

Did it strike you at the time as being any more remarkable than anything else you were writing?
Oh, I knew it was a good song. I had the 4-track at that point, and I'd written it on the piano but I went back and did a little demo of it the same day or maybe the day after, on guitar, and it was a really cracking little demo, actually.

"Four Seasons in One Day". A song about the weather in Melbourne?
It could equally apply to the weather here, actually. Yeah, that was inspiration for the title, but obviously it's about emotional weather and the changeability of everyday life. The spark was the crazy weather in Melbourne. One of my fondest memories of Melbourne is when the cool change would come in and the big black clouds would roll in over the Domain and the sun would hit them. You'd have had a beautiful sunny day and then all of a sudden these really big, menacing, really thick-looking dark clouds rolling in, but they'd be lit intensely by the sun. And then be this really bright green underneath them. We used to live right beside the Domain in Melbourne. That line was the spark for the whole song in a way.

"Better Be Home Soon".
I wrote that in Osborne Street in Melbourne and it was just me attempting to put myself in my wife's mind. Not that she ever did it to me, really, but the staunchness of being able to say to somebody, "Look, there's a limit. And don't assume I'm going to be here when you get home."

You've published a book of lyrics. Does that mean you think song lyrics can stand apart from the melodies that usually accompany them and be taken in separately, like poetry?
I think I made it clear in the foreword of that book that I don't make any claims that this is poetry at all and some of them stand looking at and some of them don't. But nevertheless, as a document for people that are interested, they are a record of a body of work. It's valid, but it's not poetry.

You have said that words should obey the rules of the song, rise and fall in the right places, and that you often like words for their sound rather than their meaning.
An ideal world would have it that they would mean amazing things and they're incredibly poetic at the same time and they sound great. But given that that's not always possible to be in the top 5 per cent of your best work all the time, the absolute bare minimum for me is that they sound good. And I would accept something that makes no sense if the words

sound magical, in some way they evoke something, and that seems like an incantation or something. Sometimes a foreign language can sound incredibly attractive but you don't know what they're saying. It takes you somewhere, anyway. It's always been about the sound of the words.

Do you hear and devise arrangements at the time of writing a song?
Sometimes. You get clues about what they're going to sound like and ideas for counter-melodies. I don't think it's quite the same as Brian Wilson, who seems to be able to imagine, or was at his peak imagining trumpets and French horns and backing singers and the whole bit, very specifically. But yeah, I get ideas for arrangements. The overall thing rocks through my head quite nicely, and sometimes if you try to analyse what it actually is, it's not always easy to pull it apart. But you kind of have an idea of an overall sound.

How was it collaborating with Jim Moginie?
There was a mutual appreciation of each other's work that was there for quite a few years. He's a guitar player I greatly admire and he's got a good melodic sensibility and he's pretty whacked-out in his ideas, so I had a feeling that it would be a good creative partnership. The first thing we did was go to the beach for a week and did a whole lot of playing. It was a very, very inspiring time.

What about Wendy Melvoin?
We'd had a day at Chad Black's house in LA and played guitars a bit. And jamming around, came up with the music of a song that was called "Secret God" in the end, and that was the spark for me wanting to work with her in the studio because it was a really enjoyable day and I felt quite a bit came out of that.

As you feel writing is a very solitary thing, what is the ideal situation for you to collaborate?
A lot of it has to do with just tricking yourself into doing it, and that's what's good about having another person in the room. It makes you think outward rather than inward and it sparks a different kind of experience. You write differently and you think about things differently. Because you've got somebody to impress, somebody to perform to or for. On your own it can get very moody and introspective.

Is it quite a different experience with other co-writers than writing with Tim, with whom you have such an intimate acquaintance?
Essentially it's not a lot different. He and I might well tend to just drift away. In recent times he'll get on the drums and maybe an acoustic and I'll be on piano or guitar and we'll just start playing a chord sequence. Sometimes he'll have a title or a little melody, and we'll start with that. Generally, the way we write, more often than not he comes with something but I make something up on the day. That seems to work together. I'll hear what he's got and then I'll make something up to go with it. It seems to be quite a good approach.

Are you more relaxed with him than you are with someone you're not related to?
Sometimes I am. Sometimes when we sit down to do that process I'm not relaxed at all
and nothing will happen. But every now and then we just get into the right spot. You get
a couple of days to relax with it and you just get into the zone, then it's really enjoyable.

**On the first _Finn_ album, that shone through, that felt like a really happy, unselfconscious
experience.**
Yeah, it was easy, because we didn't labour over anything on that record.

Tim said this new one is more laboured.
We've worked a lot more hard and in a more concentrated way on this record, and I
think it'll be an appreciably better record for it. Although I'm fond of the _Finn_ record.
Not a lot of people got it, but the people that did, really got it. And they might find this
record too involved. There's something about the half-baked nature of that record. It was
a pretty indulgent record in some ways, and not that easy to get into. When I listen to it
now it's almost got a weird sound about it, too, a muffled sort of sound about it. But
these things hit you afterwards. I'm fond of it, I don't mean to put it down, but I listen
to it and about four of the things on there are a bit outstanding and the rest of it sounds
a bit half-baked to me.

What do you think is outstanding?
I think "Only Talking Sense", "Suffer Never", "Angels Heap" and one other one that I liked.
"Mood Swinging Man", I think that's really good.

I like "Where Is My Soul".
And that one. They are probably the standout songs for me, yeah.

**I'd like to talk about a few of your solo songs. Where did "Don't Ask Why" come from? I love
the image of the Yellow Pages flying through the sky.**
That was a series of random images; I can't really explain where they came from. That came
from the jam, just Wendy and me in the studio. She was on drums and I was playing
Wurlitzer and it just all came.

Were you feeling acutely conscious of your mortality when you wrote "Anytime"?
Not particularly. These things come along and then you think about it. I don't often start off
with the idea that, oh God, I'm wondering about how long I've got to go and then I'm going
to write a song about it. It doesn't really come like that. You get a few lines and you go,
"Oh, okay, I'm writing about that today, am I?" It's more like that. And the first line of that
was, "See a dog upon the road", and that was to do with taking my dog Lester for a walk
and him getting hit by a bus, only very lightly as it turned out, just as well. He just got a
fright and was a bit bruised. And the line isn't actually describing that at all; it's describing
the idea that you're in a car and you see a dog run out in front of you and at that moment

when you decide what you're going to do to avoid the dog, there's a truck behind you and the whole thing's in the balance. It could go any way. I liked the idea of that instantaneous moment where suddenly you realise that it could just be all gone like that.

And then the rest of the song's an attempt to describe how valuable it is to feel like that all the time, if you can. To be continually aware of the fleeting nature of life. Not that you can be, you can't be, obviously. And I didn't regard that as being a negative song at all, I thought that it was, do good things and you make the right decisions when you know that you're going to die. You don't fuck around with stupid things so much.

Do you dream a lot and do your dreams influence your writing?
I do dream a fair bit and I'm sure they do influence my writing. I find them interesting, dreams, but I like the thought processes you have just before you go to sleep and they sometimes have dished up a few lines here or there. That's the kind of state that I'd like to be in when I'm writing lyrics, often just random, free-forming notions one after the other and they don't relate to each other necessarily but they come off the back of each other. Often the relationships between those sorts of lines for me describe deeper things when you get in underneath them. They're like little puzzles that you don't quite fully understand yourself, but for other people they trigger off a whole experience for the song and it's that possibility of multiple meaning that is always the most exciting for me. You get a few lines that run together and somebody might get it gloriously wrong and you don't want to spell it out to them too much. I like the words that don't seem too obvious.

Do you think there are an infinite number of melodies?
There's an infinite number of variations and how they can be presented. It's all to do with the rhythm of the melody. I'd say possibly every combination of notes has been written that would be pleasing to an ear. But it's the amount of time you linger on one note as opposed to the next. I don't know if anybody's worked out how many theoretical variations there are in the way you can string notes together, but it'd be in the millions, I suppose. There's an infinite variation and when you match that to somebody's personality and the way they sing, then I think there's still plenty out there. And people are recycling in their own way. It's continual recycling of the raw materials. But there's a lot of titles been taken now.

Is that a problem for you?
Well, there's a lot of words, a lot of phrases have been owned now in popular song, so that is a problem in a way. You find yourself singing something and go, "Oh, bugger. Dylan did that years ago." So there's the diminishing pool of stock phrases. But even then it's the way you tart it up, isn't it. There's still plenty of possibilities.

Do you have favourite keys that you work in?
Yeah, I've got keys that are quite recurrent. E flat is a popular key for me. And F I like. And C I've got an affinity for.

Any reason why you're drawn to E flat?

E flat is a very rich key. And I often work with a capo on three on a guitar, so that puts you in a sort of E flat mode. You play C and it's an E flat. I've written quite a lot of songs in that. "Fall at Your Feet" and "Pineapple Head". Actually, "Pineapple Head" is more like F. But the capo on three. It's in a block section.

Are you attached to your songs, like children?

I couldn't possibly imagine that they are in any way as precious as children but there's a lot of similarities in the sense that once they're written and they leave home, you can't control who they sleep with. I always thought that was always quite a good way to look at cover versions. You might not approve of what somebody does to your song but you've got no control over it. But I love the fact that they do have their own life and they have a journey that you can't predict. They're out there independent of you. They exist without you. And you never know where they're going to turn up. In somebody's lounge room, in somebody's bar. It's magical. And every song has its own story. Any songwriter will tell you that every little story you hear about a song being of value to somebody, whether as a comfort or an encouragement or an accompaniment to something important, is a total vindication and confirmation of the value of the whole thing and whether the struggle's worth it or not. Sometimes you think that being a songwriter is like a selfish occupation, and who needs another song in the world, there's enough already, and it's a vanity. But you only need to get a couple of people come up and say that something helped them through a difficult part of their life and you go, "Praise be!" Couldn't ask for more.

Of all the Australasian songwriters, you are one of maybe three—the others being Nick Cave and Paul Kelly—who are interviewed often and in depth about your songwriting. Does it belie the mystery of your art to have to discuss, dissect and analyse repeatedly?

It's a little bit disconcerting at times, because you realise you don't really have much of a handle on the moment of inspiration, you can't really say why and when that's going to come, and it's infuriating that there isn't a clear way. I still haven't figured out the smallest aspect of what brings inspiration, what you have to do to bring that along.

I would say in both of their cases, their lyrics both stand them apart from most people. And I would say, objectively speaking, and I'm not putting my own lyrics down, but I think I'm less of a natural lyricist than a natural melodist. So if I've got something that's mine and at its best what I feel most natural and intrinsic to me, it's the melodies rather than lyrics. I am envious of their ability to be able to tell a story. That's a great talent.

IVA DAVIES

SYDNEY, AUSTRALIA, NOVEMBER 2003

As I drove along Sydney's northern beaches peninsula to meet with Iva Davies on a bright, clear morning, it occurred to me that the vast expanse of ocean beneath his home and studio underscored in a way the musical grandeur that the composer and songwriter had found himself lately swept up in.

In the new millennium, the gentle family life Davies was living guided him through daily existence with the constancy that so many of the songwriters of his generation and before found only after creating some of their most passionate and personal work. The scope of his recent work was larger in scale—pivotal songs for spectacular world events and a major Hollywood film score—and far removed thematically from many of the trademark Flowers and Icehouse songs that were inspired by private angst and the minutiae of daily life as viewed from the windows of his bachelor abodes in the Sydney suburbs of Lindfield and Erskineville.

And yet the process was almost always the same, regardless of the subject matter or the equipment and view at his disposal. Davies builds music in layers, thoroughly reliant on electronic devices, and almost always via experimentation and through a state of meditation or a mindless task, like window gazing or vacuum cleaning. He would rarely just come up with a subject for a song, write a lyric and then hum a melody that fitted. He would be more likely to feed a sustained bass guitar note through a sampler and play that hum through a loop for hours on end until he saw a song emerge from the sound. Whether writing alone or in collaboration, hit pop songs such as "Love In Motion", "Hey Little Girl" and "Electric Blue" were made that way. So were his soundtracks for the ballets *Boxes* and *Berlin*, and the films *Razorback* and *Master and Commander: The Far Side of the World*.

Master and Commander, an evenly collaborative effort with Christopher Gordon and Richard Tognetti, followed from work Davies had done on his enduring song, "Great Southern Land", for the millennium New Year's Eve, and the new song "Circles in the Sky" for the 2000 Olympic Games. Projects of a grandeur that a little boy learning bagpipes in a country town, or even a teenager mesmerised by Pink Floyd, could scarcely have imagined.

Iva Davies was born on 22 May 1955 in Wauchope, New South Wales, and moved as a child to Wagga Wagga. His father was a singer and his mother a pianist, and in their close-knit country communities they were involved in forming choirs and creating a world of music for their children. At age six he started learning the bagpipes. By the time he started high school in Sydney, he was fairly accomplished, and when instruments were allocated in music class, he landed the dusty old oboe that nobody else wanted. He became, as he recalled, "a mini prodigy", won a scholarship and studied at the Conservatorium, but "never really engaged with the oboe". After abandoning his professional orchestral career, he kept his cor anglais (which showed up in occasional haunting solos on his Icehouse work later on) and turned to popular music.

Meanwhile, Davies had taught himself acoustic guitar and joined a folk trio. They played clubs, concerts and recorded an album that was never released. Davies' parallel life also included the defining moment of hearing *Dark Side of the Moon* for the first time, "the thing that made me form my view of the world, which hasn't changed since". Other mysterious and darkly playful influences such as early Roxy Music and Iggy Pop also worked their way into the Davies psyche. But he only wrote a few songs as a teenager, not yet aware of the career that was beckoning. When he dropped out of the classical arena, Davies wrote lead sheets for hit pop songs of the day, and transcribed artists' catalogues into songbooks for various music publishers. For better or worse, Richard Clapton, Little River Band, Dragon, Australian Crawl and Cold Chisel, among others, can thank Davies for the sheet music of their songs that came out in the 1970s and early 1980s.

By this time he had formed Flowers with friend Keith Welsh. It was Davies' first experience of playing music with amplifiers and drums, and his first exposure to the pub culture that cultivated the Australian bands of that era. Flowers played pristine covers of rock songs from The Easybeats to the Sex Pistols, with a special emphasis on the glam rock era of Lou Reed, David Bowie and T-Rex, before introducing some original songs and then recording them on the 1980 *Icehouse* album that catapulted Davies to instant stardom. When he disbanded

Flowers and decided to proceed alone, albeit behind the guise of a new "band" named Icehouse, his musical style was both embraced and snubbed. "One of the reviews of *Primitive Man* was 'Davies dehumanises music'," he recalled. "They were afraid of samplers and synths and machinery."

But Davies was at the vanguard of the new wave of electronic music in the 1980s, and by the end of that decade many of his songs were already deemed classic. From his classical origins to the classic pop he created is not such a vast expanse, he explained in a detailed conversation that covered his entire career.

Were there advantages in having classical training when you began to compose rock music?
Yes, and I would encourage anybody to learn the rules because the only way to effectively break them is to know them in the first place. It sounds like a simple thing to say, but all the originality that any of the composers managed to produce was the way in which they particularly broke the rules. You can't carve out that originality unless you know what they are in the first place. Otherwise, you're just as likely to be walking on some territory that's already been covered. Another great advantage of having that background was that I could coach people. The reason why Flowers ended up being able to do those perfect versions of things was that I could analyse what I was hearing. That's why we didn't get the chords wrong, and we did have the right sounds, and there was the right instrumentation. That was purely because I knew how to analyse music.

How did your songwriting start?
It comes back to *Dark Side of the Moon* and Pink Floyd, and hearing a studio-created picture. I wanted to make a picture in stereo. The tape recorder had a function called "sound on sound". There weren't many multi-track tape recorders then. But on mine you could record something, go back over that tape to get a level, and then add it to it. You could keep repeating this process to superimpose more layers. At that time there were no drum machines. I remember putting down drum patterns on this tape machine by using pieces of paper and cardboard boxes, and hitting them. Then I'd put a synth on, and guitar.

This is how a song like "Icehouse" was written. By then we had a drummer and I would get him to play the beat. I'd invent that beat and we would rehearse it. Then I'd turn the tape recorder on and I'd get him to play it for six minutes on his own. I'd bring the recorder back home, plug in the keyboard, and play over the top of it to build the song up. I spent all night doing that with this song, laying another layer of keyboards and another layer, until by seven in the morning I'd written the lyrics. I had to wait for everybody in the apartment upstairs and out the back to wake up so that I could finally sing it.

At what point would the melody come to you? It's one thing to start layering different sounds and getting a groove going, but at some stage you're going to go [Sings] "Hey little girl ..."
It's not always been exactly the same process but an awful lot of them were driven by putting down a groove first. That's where things like the LinnDrum Machine became really

important. The groove will dictate a whole lot of things. It will dictate the speed and it will dictate whether it's got energy or melancholy and so on. The next most important thing is the harmony. I guess that's because I think cinematically. I have to have a shape. I have to know there is going to be some drama and then there's going to be some relief. So that shape will manifest itself in the basic blocks, like verses and choruses and bridges. But those basic blocks must provide a harmonic journey. The most difficult thing for me to find is a set of chords that goes somewhere, and somewhere different. It must be a set of chords I haven't used before or that hasn't been used before. So that's the hard part. I labour just to find a progression that goes somewhere and I do that without even thinking about melody. But once I know that I've got a great movement, I'll just play it over and over again. Then, eventually, you start hearing lines.

So your lyrics come with the melody?
Generally speaking I'll do what Peter Gabriel and Bryan Ferry and a lot of songwriters do. That is to arrive at a melody with no lyrics and then fill it in syllabically. "Hey Little Girl" was right at the end of a whole process. The album was done and the Americans were saying they didn't have a single, and they didn't have quite enough songs for the album. I was put in a pressure cooker where I had to do something. All I had with me at that point were two harmonic sketches, two sets of chords that didn't actually go together. I had a title on that occasion and that's a bit of a rarity for me. I don't write things down but I do put them away. So I went back over the cassettes of those strange little harmonic ideas with grooves under them. I liked one particular progression, which was a chorus. But it hadn't come from anywhere and it wasn't going anywhere. So I had to go back to the harmonic building blocks again. I had to create harmony that would go to that chorus. Once I'd done that, and the only other thing I had in my mental suitcase was the title, it was just a case of making the title work on the piece of harmony. All that was done in a night in Georgio Moroder's home studio.

There was a strong pop sensibility in Flowers songs like "We Can Get Together", "Sister" and "Can't Help Myself". Did you recognise the potential of those songs immediately?
"Sister", no. "Sister" was always a phenomenon that outdid my expectations. I wouldn't have picked it in the way that it stuck. "We Can Get Together", yes. These songs were collected painfully over quite a period. I went from trying to write with the keyboard player and then eventually to doing things alone. But they were collected over a long period of time and they'd been added to the set. I'm not prolific. But by the time we got to the point where Regular Records were involved and we were going to make an album, I wrote a last-minute addition, "We Can Get Together". Then "Can't Help Myself" was written. So it was right at the end of the whole Flowers history of adding songs to the set. Maybe I was homing in. It seems odd to me that the ones that ended up being the singles were the very last ones I wrote.

Back then you were compared to David Bowie. When you later toured with Bowie, did you have any conversations about songwriting?
No, I had lots of conversations, but I don't think so. I don't think songwriters do. You

wouldn't. I still don't understand the process. I haven't got any better at making that big leap, because, for me, it's really hard. It's never become any easier.

Because it's a mysterious process?
Yes.

Even though it's quite methodical and mechanical for you in a way?
It is and it isn't. All I know how to do pertains to the whole process of getting the magical set of chords and the great melody that comes out of those chords. I know the mechanisms by which I have to start somewhere and start working. I don't know how to manufacture that moment when I go, "That's great! I know now I've got an idea". I can labour away at that whole process for a week and have nothing that excites me. I don't have failures; I don't write things and then throw them out. They either happen or they don't. Most of the time they don't. But I'll just keep working away until that nut cracks. And when it does, then I get excited.

I know for a fact that my method is really unlike a lot of people's methods, so I feel that I'm a freak. I know that Paul Kelly can sit down, pick up a guitar and write a song in an hour. That is such an impossible kind of idea for me. I'd love to be able to do that, but it just takes me weeks. I'll sit and listen to one sound. I wrote a song here when I was fooling around with a sampler and it was a peculiar sample, which was actually a bass guitar note put through a lot of processors. I made it into a keyboard sound. It had a really interesting texture. I made a loop of it, and played a B flat major chord, and I played it for three hours in this room. And I did the vacuum cleaning, just seemed like the thing to do. It had this amazing kind of Tibetan monk ommmy thing about it, it was fascinating to me, and after a while all the harmonics in it, because it was a loop, kept repeating. And then in the end the harmonic changes came, I could hear pitch and a line, and that became the basis of a song over one chord. Which I really rate as a song. That was the Olympic song, "Circles in the Sky". I've told a few people how that came about, but is that not a really weird thing to do, just listen to one chord for hours and hours and hours?

It's like putting yourself into a trance state so that you can lose yourself in it and see something, like those 3D drawings in magazines.
I'll do that over days, I'll just constantly repeat something, and when I go to sleep I'm hearing it; it's a tape loop. Then after a while the pictures start appearing in it. It will complete itself in my head.

You've always been fascinated by gizmos. Does the equipment inspire the creation of the music or is it there to serve your creations?
No, it inspires. I said before that I'm not very good at the songwriting part. If I make myself sit down to do it, probably something will happen. The hardest part is making myself sit down to do it. One of the easiest ways to make me sit down to do it, and to spend the time, is to have something new to play with. In the process of learning a new gadget I will start setting up those things that go round and round and out of that something will go, "oh

great, that's really good". It's almost become a cliché for me that, if I have to write a new album, I have to have a new toy. [*Laughs*]

So you're not the kind of guy who wakes up in the morning and you've dreamed this song and you'll grab the first piece of equipment that's there because you've got to get it out.
No. Not at all. There have been a handful of occasions where I felt as if the song had almost written itself. But there'd be perhaps five of those. It would feel as if I didn't do this, this just fell into my lap. One of those is "Great Southern Land". Another one would be "Man of Colours". At the time I lived with Bob Kretschmer, our guitarist, in Erskineville. We had a two-storey terrace, the bottom half of which was a 24-track recording studio. I had an idea about how I'd like to write a song in which the last word of each line of the lyrics became the first word of the next line. It would be just a kind of "device in meter". And before he'd got out of the shower in the morning, I had written the entire set of lyrics. Not too much longer after that I'd actually set them. Now that's a completely back to front process for me and I don't usually do that. "Great Southern Land" was lyrics first, too. Not all of the lyrics but the core. But that's not my usual method.

Having initially studied an instrument and played instrumentals, how easily did lyric writing come to you?
I put far more effort into the lyrics than the music. Once I've gone through that horrible process of trying to get the harmony and the melody, I sit down to craft the lyrics. I think it's lyrics that drew me to songwriting in the first place. It could never be said that The Velvet Underground was an absolutely slick band. They were not. Nor was T-Rex. They had attitude and I was fascinated by the fact that they projected, beyond their capabilities, an absolute and utter self-belief which, in turn, then actually produced works of art. They transcended their real abilities.

It was all aligned with the fact that those are works of art, and it will be these writers who we will look back on as the Beethovens and Mozarts of this era. Those people who got it right, who said something important really well in a song, will be the icons of the cultural generation. I've never come close, but that was what the aspiration was. So that's why I spend so long with the lyrics.

I grew up in Lindfield. Can you tell me the story behind the song "Icehouse"?
That was 18 Tryon Road. That was all dovetailed into this ABC orchestra that I was in, which used to rehearse in the Masonic Hall in Lindfield, and down the road in Tryon Road there was this beautiful big, old, two-storey mansion on the corner which had a tennis court behind it. The woman who owned it was a patron of the arts, and she had it turned into flats and it was rented out to members of this orchestra. We were all students as well, and the rent was very cheap. I first moved in with a French horn player and we had another French horn player upstairs, and a clarinettist and a violinist upstairs and out the back we had a trombone player and a cellist and a trumpeter. So it was mad. Completely. At the same time I had this other double life going on with the folk friends.

Anyway, as you know Lindfield is a beautiful, old, leafy, strangely Edwardian, conservative area. Eventually, I ended up living in that flat on my own and I went through a whole period there when Flowers were starting, where I had a very, very insulated life; I lived on my own very quietly. And had these weird hours, where we'd do a gig and I'd go down and clean this theatre in Chatswood at three o'clock in the morning on my own, and then come back and start to write lead lines. A very strange existence. I was up most of the night for years.

Across the road was another beautiful old house, but really dishevelled. I noticed over a period of time that the lights were always on all night; very weird in Lindfield. I'd see people coming out of there during the day and they'd wander up the street and then come back with some shopping. I'd see them for a couple of months, and then I wouldn't see them any more, I'd see somebody new. So it had a very strange vibe about it; I couldn't work out what was going on. It wasn't until after the song had been recorded that I found out that it was a psychiatric halfway house.

So I was looking at this house across the road, and that was my picture and that was where the song came from. It was an invented story, basically an amalgamation of the house that I lived in and the one across the road. And the house that I lived in was quite freaky. It was unbelievably cold. It was a beautiful place, but other people were really freaked out by it.

Do you remember writing "Love in Motion"? That sounded more like a mood piece, like a perpetuation of a groove.
Yes, exactly. It was. I wrote that in London. I've written very few away from my safety zone, but that was one. We were perforce on tour and needed an interim single; we were between London and America, and there was no going home, it just had to be done. I shared a flat with the one roadie that we had, and I had a porta-studio. Things were developing in my world of being able to multi-track stuff; I had four tracks then! And had a drum machine and a keyboard. I'd recorded a sketch and played it non-stop in this flat, much to, I'm sure, the frustration of that roadie. Just over and over, and I wrote the lyrics in the taxi to the studio.

I was fascinated by these people who can write songs by just using these ejaculations— you know, "Hey!" "Whoa!". Songs that use those sounds as a really key hook. If you go back to look at the catalogue of songs there are a whole load of them. Marc Bolan was absolutely fantastic at doing this, just writing songs with gibberish that sounded great. So I wanted to try and write a song with these "Aha"s. And part of the exercise with me, too, is to not repeat the territory that I've already been on. So I'm constantly looking for something I haven't done before. The meter device in "Man of Colours", I thought could be an interesting idea. I thought that it might sound good if I got to the end of a line, then the last word of that line began the next line. It didn't quite work out that way, but that's where "I, I am a man, a simple man, a man of colours" came from.

Where did the reverence for Australia's heritage come from in "Great Southern Land"? I think you've said you'd written it after coming back from an overseas trip.
There are a whole lot of things in there that I know could be directly related to my growing

up in the country. But there are also a whole lot of new things, too. "Great Southern Land" is one of those songs which fell in my lap to a large degree. So the process of writing it must have been so fast that I can't go back and remember where B came after A and C came after that. Whereas I can with other songs. I can certainly remember that whole image of getting on a plane to leave Australia, going to sleep over the desert, being asleep for two hours, and then waking up and still being over it. I remember it dawning on me how large it was. That made a real impression on me; I thought, "Wow, this is a big place." Then the whole experience of being overseas, having to deal with the English press, going to America and seeing the vast concrete sprawl and miles of freeway and shopping centres and parking lots; and then getting incredibly homesick. And then coming home.

It was the first song that I wrote from coming back. And I did have this new LinnDrum Machine. There was a certain thing going on in the back of my mind about how there had been songs written about Australia which were every cliché in the book and every postcard. I think it was certainly part of my mission to weigh the other side of the scales.

Thematically, it was one of the earliest pop songs to deal with the inequity between the indigenous Australians and those who arrived later.
Well, as soon as you're stupid enough to think, "I'm going to write a song about my homeland …" And seriously, I'm not very brave. I mean, Peter Garrett's very happy putting his politics completely on the line. I tend to need to include something weighty in a song. There are songs of mine, "Love in Motion" for example, which are pure exercises in whimsy or relationships. But there are others that are fairly loaded in a veiled sort of way. I don't soapbox though. I like to think that songs are there to make you ask questions rather than give you answers. So it was quite a stupid thing for me to do, really. I would normally have thought, "Write a song about your homeland? Ha, I don't think so!" I thought to myself, "You could go so very wrong with this. If you're going to do this it's got to be really good. Otherwise you're just going to be completely lampooned for it."

And so as soon as you've made that quantum leap of going, "That's the subject about which I'm going to write", then you have to encompass everything, and then it becomes impossible. It's only going to be four minutes long, how am I going to do this? How do you not leave stuff out? So the only way that I could do it was just to do it in a kind of involuntary cut up method. I decided to not complete a sentence but to just put a lot of fragments together that, chosen in such a way, would suggest a lot of things. So that one phrase might mean seven things. People have pulled the lyrics apart and said, "What were you thinking when you wrote 'Burnt you black'? What was that all about?" My response to that has always been, "That's why I only used the phrase, because I don't want to tell you."

It can mean many things. It can be about going to the beach and getting sunburnt.
Yes. And these are things that just came out of me. For example, my father was a forester for forty-two years and the management of this very unique landscape, in terms of fire, is quite bizarre. Anywhere else in the world, a forest fire has only one meaning and that is

disaster. But from a very early age my father said to me, "Half the natural species here cannot propagate unless they're burnt. That's the way they evolved." But that's only one meaning of that phrase. I just wanted to choose a whole lot of ideas that I knew wouldn't necessarily weigh the scales on one side. It became obvious, for example, that I'd have to write two verses and not three. Normally my songs at that time had three verses. This only has two; and that was simply because I couldn't see any way to do it other than to go "modern/ancient", "black/white". There have to be two sides of this scale. And if I'd thrown it out with any third component the scales would have been unbalanced. So, yes, it's a funny piece of work, isn't it? [*Laughs*]

On *Primitive Man* your lyrics had taken quite a leap. Were they more personal?
No, I don't think so. Some of them were. There are a lot of songs about a particular person.

Someone who didn't know that they were about her. Does she now?
Probably not. Right from the beginning I was so nervous about writing songs that I wanted them to have nothing to do with me. "Walls" and those songs. Of course when I look back at that first album now, it's just a picture of me alone in the flat in Lindfield, it was a very isolated existence. But I thought I was doing a really good job of writing songs about somebody else. Now I can see perfectly what a bad job I did of not including myself in those songs. I walked into the studio during *Sidewalk* with a new song and sang it. Bob Kretschmer, the guitarist with whom I ended up writing *Measure for Measure* and *Man of Colours*, was there. At that point we were not yet close friends but he said to me years later when we were living together at Erskineville, "As soon as you walked in and sang that song, I knew there was something horribly wrong with your relationship." That was "Don't Believe Anymore". It came as such a surprise to me. I said, "Oh really? Was it that obvious?" I thought I'd disguised it really well. I thought everyone would think it was a song about somebody else.

Can there be a paradox between heavily layered electronic music and lyrics of an intimate nature? Is there a risk that the style and sound can overwhelm the words?
I don't think they're mutually exclusive at all. Hopefully, a song like "Don't Believe Anymore" persists, even though it was very much a sampler-driven atmosphere, it's a very synthetic song, totally Fairlight-based. But so many people over the years, probably more than any other song, have come back to me and said, "This song prevented me from committing suicide." Or, "This song changed my life."

How much would your own vocal style influence your writing?
Good question. I hadn't had to grapple with that until recently. I didn't realise how much my voice does dictate what I do. I've realised that I have been trading on what I can do; my range and my attitude has dictated a lot of what I've done. But I didn't realise that at the time; I'd thought, "I'm writing a song, anybody can sing this." It was quite an interesting exercise, for example, to hear Tim Freedman singing "Don't Believe Anymore". He's a great

singer. But the treatment is so completely different. Tim Freedman has the most wonderfully pristine and accurate pitch. But his voice doesn't stray into areas where mine has, those which are more blatantly emotive. I've now listened to myself and thought, "Oh, I hope I didn't overdo it."

What inspired "Trojan Blue"?

The key thing for me was pottery. I was fascinated by archaeological digs when I was a boy. I had a number of books when I was very small, eight or whatever, and one of them was the discovery of Angkor Wat, the hidden city. Another one was the discovery of Troy, or what they believed to be Troy. And it was all about these broken pieces of clay, these bits of pots that told this story. Putting that puzzle together and this amazing story of this woman who was so powerful and had such an effect on that ancient world that there was a ten-year war. And that led then in turn to the whole idea of looking at what happened to Troy and going, "Well, that's my fault." It was to me the image of this fabulously beautiful person and all those devastating consequences, and how you put those elements together.

You've described the way the music happens, eventually suggesting a melody, which in turn hopefully suggests a lyric. But where do lyrics and ideas come from?

If I'm using that process, then a couple of survival techniques kick in. One is, don't go too much further with this and waste too much time unless you've got a hook. I focus on the part where I've created a block that I know will be the chorus. I know I have to pin that part down first. I won't go through the whole exercise. I'll home in on that. I must have that hook. And if I can find a melodic hook that I know is not going to be impossible to fill in with words, and if I'm happy with it, then I'll keep pursuing the whole process. But I must get to that point first. Otherwise I'll throw the whole sketch out. Then, once I've done that, I'm up and running and I know that every time I arrive at that point I've got the hook. From there it's down to that whole process of looking at a picture until you start seeing something. I'll keep working on it because once I've got the notes of the hook, I'll start hearing sounds. Sometimes that has given me a whole chorus, or the important part of the chorus; just hearing those sounds. I used to do something that lots of songwriters do; that is, once I've arrived at the point where I have the notes of the melody, I actually sing it with no lyrics. And that's fantastically helpful because quite accidental sounds will, later on, start to sound like something sensible.

But you wouldn't sit down and go, "I'm going to write a song about a street cafe."

No. Probably not.

The idea doesn't come to you unless it is specific, like "Great Southern Land"?

It has happened, certainly. There was the *Code Blue* set of songs. There was the discovery of my Uncle Charlie's crashed World War II bomber. I submerged myself in Australian histories and picked out all those stories about unknown heroes. But the main purpose of the exercise for me was to go one very important step further than that, to not limit the songs to being just about those particular stories. I would never do that. I always evaluate lyrics in terms of this rule: is this going to mean anything to anyone else? A number of times I've done songwriting workshops and I've always said, "Look, don't waste your time. The last thing I want to hear is your personal diary. I really don't want to hear about the fact that you had a bad time at the supermarket this morning, it's just not interesting to me."

So for the *Code Blue* songs, I did get ideas from newspaper articles and also a number of Australian histories. I also read *For The Term of His Natural Life* about the Tasmanian convicts. From that book I wrote "Mercy on the Boy", which is about the idea of being hemmed in. It has everything to do with that book and nothing to do with it at the same time. The song's about the underlying idea, whether it's being imprisoned in a relationship or a jail. So in that sense that exercise was slightly different. I had to go through the intellectual process of finding all the stories, and then working out which one I could actually turn into a universalism and finding a way in which I could do that.

Did you write the songs for the *Sidewalk* album at the same time or after writing the *Razorback* soundtrack? I wondered if your initial work on the Fairlight doing the soundtrack raised different possibilities for potential songs.
Yes, it was concurrent. The same thing happened with *Boxes* and *Measure for Measure*. What happened initially in the *Razorback* process was that Russell Mulcahy was filming and playing a whole lot of music out on the set. This included some Peter Gabriel songs from his fourth album, which featured a lot of drums. So I assumed, incorrectly as it turned out, that the reason I'd been asked to do the soundtrack was partly because they wanted some song-like material. It wasn't going to be an orchestral score. It was going to be driven by the sort of thing that Peter Gabriel does, which is generally atmospheric ambient music. I started going down that road and then very quickly ran into a brick wall, because that was not what the producer wanted. I spent a long time being completely lost as to what they did want until I produced something that sounded more like Stravinsky than anything else. That seemed to come home. But in the process of writing these earlier things I wrote a number of potential songs. And a number of those found their way onto *Sidewalk*. "Shot Down" and "The Mountain", for example. These were directly from sketches that I did for *Razorback*. So they were happening at the same time. Similarly, things from the ballet *Boxes* ended up in *Measure for Measure*. The projects cross-pollinated.

How influential was the experience of writing *Boxes* for the Sydney Dance Company?
This was the beginning of the period with Bob Kretschmer. That period was quite intense because we lived and worked together. I'd just moved out of that relationship and I was free. I was in a house with a brand 24-track tape recorder, and I'd never had one of them before. New toy, new life, none of the aggravation and a whole lot of bleeding still going on, but total twenty-four-hour concentration on the work. We just ate, drank, breathed and slept writing music through that whole period. The two things to write were *Measure for Measure* and *Boxes*. Bob was great because he had a very keen aesthetic sense. So I could depend

on his taste as a polished sounding board. But also he was very open to experimentation. In *Boxes* we were doing quite radical electronic experiments. Some pieces from *Boxes* are reasonably out there. We could indulge ourselves so that was what was great about it. It wasn't so much the fact that it was ballet. What was attractive was the fact that when you write a score for a contemporary ballet there are no rules. You can do anything, which is so liberating.

Some of the songs on *Measure for Measure* were just outright experiments. There's one quite strange song called "Lucky Me" on *Measure for Measure*. That was a radical piece of experimentation and I improvised most of the lyrics live to tape.

And yet some of that album is perfectly crafted pop. Which brings up the Roxy Music comparison. I really heard it on "Paradise" and "No Promises".
Really?

Oh yes, "No Promises" just reminded me so much of "Avalon".
Oh God, it's so Bowie, though.

You recorded that album partly in the studio that was owned by Ferry and Eno.
Ferry was somebody whose early work I'd really admired. It was funny, though, because it was the peripherals of the whole Roxy Music thing that I was attracted to, most notably Eno. But there were certain Roxy Music moments which I think are landmarks. I never got over "In Every Dream Home a Heartache". That's the kind of song I wanted to write; it's a cinemagraphic picture, which is quite sinister and dark. It's a fantastic song, very early and full of Eno doing his tape loop experimentation, but very sinister atmosphere all through it. It's Bryan Ferry being a character. You see, this is the difference. Paul Kelly writes a song and you always know it's Paul Kelly singing the song. But what I was doing, what Ferry was doing, and what Bowie did in *Hunky Dory* and others albums, was to "become somebody". In a lot of my songs I am somebody else, for just three minutes. In that particular Roxy Music song he's very quietly telling you that he's unwrapping a parcel. He's describing where he is, and he's obviously in a mansion. He's wealthy and it's quiet, and he has a deep affection for whatever it is he's just received in the parcel that he's ordered. The song is an ode to a blow-up doll. It's really very warped; it's quite scary. It's written by a rich deviant. It's a fantastic song; you have to hear it. That was the influence that he had on me. At his best he's a very clever lyricist and a lot of it is quite confronting.

Do you prefer to write alone?
Apart from that period with Bob, I don't think I've ever been very comfortable collaborating.

Did your collaborators have to surrender themselves and their contributions selflessly to your process?
That's the wrong way to describe it. Basically, I'm dysfunctional in that situation. Because my method is so weird, I literally am unable to contribute anything to the process in a

normal sort of way. Every manager that I've ever had has said, "Look, you work best when you're under pressure, otherwise you get lazy."

How was the experience of working with John Oates?
That was me being my most stressed. What was remarkable about him was that he initiated the whole thing and, sadly, I haven't really ever thanked him properly. He met me in an airport in Adelaide when we were touring *Primitive Man* in 1982, and they were on tour. He came up to me and said, "I saw you last night, we played in that same venue, and you were fantastic and I went and bought your album." He had a copy of *Primitive Man* in his hand. I, of course, knew who he was. That was that and it was a lovely exchange. Then we were touring *Measure for Measure* four or five years later, and I was in the bar of the Mayflower Hotel in New York City. The phone rang and the barman gave it to me and it was John Oates. He'd tracked me down. I don't even know how he knew that we were touring. He said, "We've got to write songs together." And I said, "Yes, okay, but I'm in the middle of a tour." And, being terrified by collaboration anyway, I was mentally trying to get out of it.

And you never write away from home if you can help it.
Exactly right. So I made every excuse in the book. He said, "I don't mind, I'll wait until you're finished the tour." So I said, "Well, I'm going back to Australia after that." "Well, I'll come out." And he did, he followed through the whole thing.

So he wrote with you out here?
Yes, in the funny little terrace in Erskineville. He packed up a whole load of flight cases, the guitars, his LinnDrum 9000, and an armadillo skin ukulele from Mexico. He put himself up for a week, and we started with a blank sheet. I was completely terrified. He, at that time, was fascinated by the new generation of LinnDrums. So he started creating a groove, not dissimilar to the way I would start, and got part of the way through that. Then I said, "Well, the next thing I do is to come up with a set of chords that go somewhere." So I played around and built some harmony with a chorus. And that was all good.

It then got to that very awkward moment of truth where you go, "Okay, well I guess you've got to sing something". I was so awkward in the situation that I said to him, "Well, if I was Daryl I would probably do that falsetto thing, like [*Sings*] 'All I can do.'" And he went, "Yeah, yeah! That's great! That's great!" And that was my impersonation of Daryl Hall! So I developed that further melodically, and I only had that piece of lyric for the chorus. Then it got even hotter because we needed a title. He had a notebook and he'd brought a whole lot of ideas with him, and for whatever reason, none of the things appealed to me. There wasn't enough that I could substantially get involved with to write a full set of lyrics. But I was absolutely desperate because I wasn't bringing anything; I couldn't offer any other titles. The only thing I had was a phrase from a really ancient Tyrannosaurus Rex song, a song called "Jewel", early when he was just an acoustic guitarist. "Her eyes are electric blue." I said, "What about 'Electric Blue'?" And he said, "That's great!" Well, it wouldn't fit anywhere into the melody that I'd created. I would have given up at that point. I would have said, "No, I've got to find something that actually fits better. Leave it with me and I'll work something out." But he said, "No, no, no, no, just tack it on the end." [*Sings*] "La la la la, electric blue."

He had an idea about a kind of Four Seasons, Four Tops falsetto thing. He comes from that whole school of Philadelphia soul anyway. I guess it makes sense because he sings that style of backing vocal for Hall & Oates. So we started with the backing vocals. We had almost nothing except a chorus with the one "All I can do" line in the middle of it and "Electric blue" stuck on the end. And that was the point at which he left Australia. That's all there was.

I filled in all the gaps later, gave it a subject and wrote all the verses and so on. But what's remarkable about the whole story and what I'll never forget, is even with it in this state he said to me, when he was about to leave, "Whatever you do, this has got to be a single, you've got to record this. If you don't record this, you make sure you tell me and give it to me, because Hall & Oates will put it out and it will be a single." He knew from just those few pieces that it was a hit. To this day I still don't understand why it was a hit. But he knew then.

Was that then the starting point for *Man of Colours*? Did the commercial feel of "Electric Blue" guide you in writing an album that, whether you'd intended it or not, was radio-friendly?
No, a great deal of *Man of Colours* had already been written and he turned up in the middle of the process. I'd already written "Crazy" and I must admit I had more affection for "Crazy" as a song. The problem with "Electric Blue" for me was that it wasn't a song to which I felt emotionally attached at all. That always made it feel to me like a calculated exercise.

The cor anglais on "Man of Colours" stands out for the arrangement and for its being a "real" instrument amid your usual assault of electronic instrumentation.
The cor anglais is a very melancholy instrument and so I always had it there in the demo. Of the lyrics, though, I'd always told the press the story about Andrew Wyeth, the artist.

But that was only a catalyst, wasn't it?
A whole lot of other things were going on there, too. My mother is an artist and she was starting to go blind. I lived upstairs in that funny terrace, watching people go past, a whole world. Really an awful lot of the songs on that album were to do with my physical surroundings. The other thing was that I was, once again, even at that point, freshly released from that relationship; the one in which I'd written—or painted—all my portraits of the one girl who never even knew they were about her. So Andrew Wyeth was an interesting story that reminded me of my own songwriting situation; the fact that he'd painted those 102 paintings of the woman and kept them secret.

The Helga paintings.
Yes. And I'd written all those songs for that girl and, even though they were public property, nobody knew who they were about.

I would be interested to hear some of your songs with an acoustic guitar or piano, à la Jimmy Webb's _Ten Easy Pieces_. Have you ever had a desire to expose your songs in that way?
No.

For you, composition and production are so tied up?
They are, yes. Any number of times I've been asked to do an in-store or something like that with an acoustic guitar, I've just had to say to them, "I'm sorry, it can't be done." They don't exist without all the production. But I don't apologise for that. It goes back to _Dark Side of the Moon_. How can you remove from "Run for Your Life" all those sound effects, the helicopters? Or how can you remove the cash registers from "Money"? But that doesn't diminish the value of the songs. Those elements are just too interconnected.

But don't you think a song is essentially a melody and a series of chord progressions and that certainly you could sing your hit songs with a guitar or a piano and they would work?
Yes, okay, I should probably qualify that a little. I always go back to the thing I learned way back when I was writing lead lines. That's when everything gets reduced to the melody, the words and the chord symbols. That's the song. I do reduce everything to that. The qualification that I should have made is that it's impossible to play my songs with just a guitar. The harmonies, the voicings of the suspensions, are not guitar-friendly things. The sort of harmony that interests me enough to put a melody on top has to be more complex than A, G, C on guitar. That's why I always write from the keyboard.

Do you find the song form restrictive and are lengthier works more likely to be your focus now?
No, I find the song form a good discipline. I feel like I've really achieved something if you can make it all work within that frame. That's always been the challenge for me, to get things to fit into the small box. I so admire the people who do that easily. All I've been trying to do is do it as well as the people I admire.

ANDREW FARRISS

SYDNEY, AUSTRALIA, SEPTEMBER 2001

They were among Australia's greatest songwriting duos. After the enduring team of Vanda and Young, it was INXS's Farriss and Hutchence whose international achievements forged new paths on which many Australians, including Savage Garden's Hayes and Jones, have since travelled.

The seemingly unstoppable partnership of Andrew Farriss and Michael Hutchence ended in November 1997, but by then Farriss had been simultaneously forging his own path as a songwriter collaborating with other artists, and as a producer. Hutchence was perhaps the most influential figure to come through Farriss's life, creatively speaking, and his premature departure quite naturally rocked the foundations of Farriss's and his INXS bandmates' existence. But life and songwriting go on.

Farriss's production and co-writing work with artists as diverse as Yothu Yindi and Tania Kernaghan reignited his creativity after a slow and sombre spell. To the point where in late

2001 he began writing songs for INXS again, but with the awareness that he was a changed person writing for a changed band.

Born in Perth on 27 March 1959, Andrew was the second of four Farriss children. He and brothers Tim and Jon started playing music as young teenagers. The family moved to Sydney and settled in the leafy northern suburbs, near the surf scene of Mona Vale, Newport, and Whale and Palm Beaches. It was at a party thrown by some surf filmmakers in 1977, on the very day Elvis Presley died, that the Farriss Brothers band made its debut, featuring all three Farriss boys, friends Garry Beers and Kirk Pengilly, and the quiet, poetic Michael Hutchence, whom Andrew had befriended at school. The line-up remained intact for twenty years, severed only by Hutchence's death.

As the INXS story unfolded, Farriss found himself writing, as he put it, "a soundtrack for whatever we wanted to be". He and Hutchence began writing together regularly and the band played the Australian pub circuit relentlessly. "Which was very good for us as people because it toughened us up", Farriss said. When they started playing in the United States, they made an instant impression. But while Hutchence revelled in the spotlight, Farriss was wide-eyed and somewhat amazed by their success and particularly the impact his songs had. From the breakthrough single "Original Sin" on, Farriss felt a huge responsibility to the band and to the public hearing his music. Although usually the lyrics were from Hutchence's pen, Farriss believed, and still does, that there are also messages in the melody. "That was more where my head was at … actually making it so that when the music was on, regardless of what the lyric was about, the music is speaking to you."

Farriss's music spoke to millions through songs such as "What You Need", "Need You Tonight", "Never Tear Us Apart" and "Suicide Blonde", and at times he countered Hutchence's darker mood by writing uplifting lyrics like "Baby Don't Cry" and "Beautiful Girl". The INXS catalogue is weighty and Farriss is conscious of the part he has played in the band's phenomenal worldwide success. But he stressed that in INXS's history, individual achievement was often secondary to the good of the group. "I'm very fortunate to have been involved with that group of people. You can achieve great things when you work together as a team. I suppose you can be the greatest songwriter in the world and you can hang 400,000 platinum albums on the wall and you can stare at them, but if you don't share it with anyone, what's the point of it?"

When we met, Farriss had just moved back to Sydney after a five-year stint in London. He was in the process of setting up an office and studio in a tranquil location near his family home in Sydney's north, a stone's thrown from Davidson High School, where it all began. Outside his office window was a forest of trees. "I wanted something that brings the environment into my head," he said. Andrew Farriss seems to have a lot going on in his head. Asking him specific questions didn't always get specific responses, but as he meandered through stories about life in INXS, writing with Hutchence and the art of songwriting, his pondering uncovered the complexities of his journey so far.

Are you writing yet in this new studio?
I've been starting to write a little bit here. I'm pretty portable when it comes to writing,

I write anywhere. But if I have to spend large amounts of time in a place, and I'm assuming that for as long as I live in Sydney I'll be coming to this space, then I'm very fortunate to have the choice to have nature as part of my environment. I spent many years living on the road and in hotel rooms and concrete buildings, buses, public transport, whatever. And you start to become very aware that your life is that.

If you woke up tomorrow morning and you had this germ of a song, would you sit at home and write it, or would you come here?
I probably would most like to write at home. But I have three young children, and their home is their home, as much as it's mine. They live there and so does my wife, Shelley. Out of respect for them, I'd come here. I find it very hard to differentiate between time with my family and time for me to work; I have to physically go somewhere else to do that.

When did you first start writing?
I started toying around with songwriting as a teenager without really realising I was doing it. I always have difficulty with straight music theory, the idea of just performing other people's written music. To me it always sounds particularly uninteresting and uninspiring.

Were you classically trained?
I started off that way, but I had no concentration for it. Which is probably more my fault than the people who wrote the music. I just didn't have the attention span or the intelligence to cope with hours of repetitive exercise. So I decided pretty early on in the piece that I'd find a piano teacher to teach me how to play chords, not just structured note exercises. I got interested in trying to play pop songs and whatever commercial songs were on the radio of the day. And then, more interestingly for me, trying to figure out how they were constructed. I'd get people's songbooks and I'd rearrange the chords. I didn't even know what I was doing, I was just messing around with it. I didn't think about it too much, that's the funny thing. I didn't ever set out going, "I'm going to be a songwriter."

So you didn't form a notion early on that songwriting could be a career as distinct from performing?
At that point in my life I was a fairly shy sort of character and fairly introspective, and I used to like the songwriting thing simply because it's inwards, you're only challenging yourself. It's a personal thing, unlike performance-based things—"Look at me! Look at me!" Songwriting's not about "look at me", it's only about what you can come up with, it doesn't matter whether anyone's looking at you or not. I think I was probably always conscious, though, especially in my mid-teens, that I had more of an interest in writing songs than most people I knew.

Do you remember what your first complete original song was?
My first song I can remember was a song called "River", which was a simple song—actually I was looking for those lyrics the other day—just a song about a river flowing. Gosh, I wish I could write songs that simple again. As adults we find it difficult to be simple, don't we?

Did you put it down on tape?

I think I did, but I don't know where it went. I only really started to recognise that the whole songwriting process was going to become useful quite a long way down the track. Whereas a lot of people recognise now from a very early age what it all means, and the dollar signs and everything. But I was preoccupied with normal teenager things. Girls, cars, you know. And music was just part of that culture. To me it was part of providing a soundtrack, especially in the pub days, as the Farriss Brothers in 1977 to about 1979, those two years. The only reason I probably wrote music was to have a soundtrack to go out at night and be with people our own age and party.

Being that you were relatively shy of the limelight, what drove you to be a part of the performing Farriss Brothers rather than just writing their songs and letting them go out and play?

I suppose that any songwriter wants ultimately their song to be performed. That's their ultimate dream. Even though performance-wise I mightn't have had a great desire to be on stage, I was realising that in order to create music someone's going to have to perform it. The band was probably a logical progression, to be involved with a group of people, to have a platform to have the music.

But I started writing songs when I was a singer in a band in high school, and at that point I was quite confident in my abilities as a performer. It was only when I started to take it all a bit more seriously, and then my friendship started to develop more with Michael Hutchence, and he and I started writing songs seriously as older teenagers together and started to fool around with what we thought were adult concepts and ideas and things, that I began to feel self-conscious.

More cerebral?

Yes. A lot more. Teenage angst kind of stuff. It was only when my older brother's band broke up, we decided to have a jam together one day. We thought, who should we get down? We thought, well, Michael and Kirk and Garry. And that six of us then played for the first time on the 16th of August 1977.

When Elvis died.

That's right. That whole thing was very strange. We played this show on the Northern Beaches, Whale Beach, a party, and we were received really well. We were a bit in shock, we didn't really realise that we just put something together that was important. And then I began to realise I was going to have to write songs for commercial purposes.

You realised that already?

Yes. I began to realise that I was starting to write a soundtrack for whatever we wanted to be. I'd try and think, where are we going, what are we doing, what are we? Rather than be too self-analysing.

Along with the Beatles, who were your early musical influences?
I liked the Rolling Stones, in particular that period of about 1968 to 1971. I was slightly scared of them when I was younger, I found the Rolling Stones a bit overwhelming. But I liked the Beatles right from a very early age. I liked Roy Orbison, I liked country music, I liked and I still like all sorts of things. I liked some classical music. I liked some variety performers. I really liked Rolf Harris when I was little; I used to think he was fantastic. We went to see him, in England. He knew my mother and my mother's sister when we lived in WA, because I guess Western Australia was a very small place in the sixties. I liked lots of things, I found the whole period really fascinating.

While you were getting into that Rolling Stones period, at the other end of the spectrum there was the introspective singer-songwriter period.
I remember listening to "Lay Lady Lay" on the radio when we were kids in the late sixties. I liked Bob Dylan's writing; his lyrics are like he's thinking. The great ability for any lyricist is to almost have lyrics just a wave of thoughts, rather than a carefully constructed essay.

Actually, I got a chance to meet Bob Dylan playing the Nara Festival in 1994 in Japan. I went to get an autograph for our manager's daughter. It was in this old Japanese temple and there were about a hundred monks all in purple robes with bald heads in front of Bob Dylan. And he was standing there with his black Ray-Ban sunglasses on. So we stood there and waited for all the monks, because they obviously see him as being someone reverent, that's the thing that I found fascinating. And it got to the end of all the monks, and Bob looks at Michael and me and he goes, "Oh, you guys are in INXS!" He was really funny and suddenly changed and became quite animated and quite light, whereas before he was quite dark and serious. Which completes a riddle for me about him, where I read once that Keith Richards said about Bob Dylan, he's quite a funny guy. I didn't quite understand what he meant. He's a real genius, a really amazing man.

I was also influenced not just by Americans and British people, but also by Australians. I genuinely liked Rolf Harris's songs when I was a kid. You know, "Two Little Boys" and "Tie Me Kangaroo Down, Sport". I like the animation of what he did. I like The Seekers; I like Bruce Woodley's writing. I like some of Billy Thorpe's early writing.

What was the first song you wrote with Michael?
Probably "Those Four Boys", a song we had about the Beatles, just saying they were a bunch of clever guys, something like that. I can't remember exactly how the song went.

And when did you first write with your brothers?
I've never really written much with my brothers.

There are several songs that have all your names on the credit. So I thought maybe you were playing around when you were all young, putting songs together?
Not really. No. The songwriting relationship that I developed with Michael, that was more my writing relationship.

So the songs that have all the names on it are more songs that came together in the studio?
What songs are you referring to?

"Don't Change", "Just Keep Walking", "Listen Like Thieves", "The Swing".
Oh, okay. "Don't Change" was a song that came together when we were jamming very much a straight-out rock pub thing. In those days, the first two albums, Michael and I were very insecure about standing up for whatever it was we were doing artistically. Everything was about the band. Individual achievement didn't seem terribly important. Which I suppose is the way it really should be. But it's not often the way it is in reality. We were always doing the bulk of the writing, and it was more a performance-based relationship that I had with the rest of the group. Being in a band's a strange thing, because you're really working as a group of people to achieve a common aim. And you all contribute certain things. You all play a part in the picture, so to a certain extent we all put in the ideas that were coming out from anyone. We'd all put in ideas and that makes the thing stronger. That's what helps to make something successful.

Do you remember how "Listen Like Thieves" was written?
Garry had an idea for a riff on that song, and we were rehearsing for the actual album, before we recorded. It just didn't feel right at all, so we changed that around.

I think it would be really good to see the guys in INXS as songwriters themselves develop more. The moment INXS started to try and be an international act, consciously decide to do that, in about 1982, those early pub years that we spent as a group and the way we originally wrote, it tried to linger on, but it never really worked for us internationally. It doesn't translate that well. The really big success we had came when, ironically enough, we became more conscious of how to marry simple phrases and simple ideas to simple pieces of music, which anyone around the world can relate to. It's good to try to keep your songs fairly simple so they can communicate with anyone in the world, anywhere.

At what point did you realise that the chemistry you and Michael had in your writing was so potent?
There was one point specifically where we'd written "Original Sin", Michael and I, and INXS recorded it with Nile Rodgers producing in the Power Station in New York in 1983. That turned out to be a number one hit for us in Australia, New Zealand, France and other places, and we were getting death threats from people in the United States because they didn't like the racial overtones of the song. So we realised, hang on, it's different from the Australian pub mentality. We're really operating on a different level here. And the next album, *Listen Like Thieves*, we had a number five hit in the US with "What You Need". Michael and I had written it. And I remember sitting at home and actually feeling a little bit overwhelmed. Everyone was calling me going, "Isn't this incredible? Isn't this amazing? It's fantastic!" And I remember hanging up the phone going, "What am I getting into here? What is this?" Realising that you're sending messages to people, it's all becoming bigger and bigger.

Then I realised on the next album we did, which was *Kick*, that I had to sit down very seriously and do nothing but focus on songwriting for a while. Everything else got excluded in my life. Probably to the detriment of my health, my personal life, everything. I literally didn't do anything, I just wrote music for a while. So that we wouldn't be yet another story of "Yes, you've had a couple of nice big hits overseas, now be good little boys and go home again." I thought, we can do a bit better than that. We can take this thing, this football straight through the goal posts. I said to Michael, "Let's really sit down and nail this thing." So we did. We sat down and designed a lot of the writing on that record. And I asked a big call on all the other guys in the group and it was really very mature of them, very open-minded of them. I said, "Look, if you can just trust Michael and I to just focus on this record and back us up, we will have a very big record. I'm absolutely sure of that." And so Michael and I were very much indulged, to be able to do that process. Which resulted in that particular record. *Kick* wasn't so much about the pub days of everybody feeling that you're kind of footy players. That record was a bit different, it was a record that we had to make. I remember ripping the phone out of the wall at home, literally, and just living in my pyjamas for two weeks, and writing for that record.

So you did a Brian Wilson.
Yeah. And many years later, actually, on the last record that we made with Michael, I was in Dublin, and the U2 guys invited us to go around to the studio. I'd never met them before. Michael said, "I really want you to come and meet Bono because he's a good friend of mine." I said, "I don't know, I'm a little bit overwhelmed, they're such a big group." He said, "Don't be stupid, they really want to talk to you." So I said, "Okay, fine." So I went around to this house and I walked through the door and Bono was treating me like royalty and at the same time making fun of me, because, he said, "Ah, you're just like Brian Wilson in your bloody sandpit, aren't you?"

You weren't that eccentric, obviously. But you were focused.
That's what it takes, though. Ultimately, you really can't be fooled by anyone's calm and cool exterior. Anyone that comes up with any music that really lasts a long time, they go through a lot to come out with that stuff. Some songs are like pulling teeth and some songs come out so naturally that you don't even understand what happened. But I think the magic of the songwriting is to be able to know when something is good and perhaps worth keeping, and when it's not.

How did you view your partnership with Michael?
I probably looked at myself as being a support structure for Michael. I didn't really think of us as being competition for centre stage. I didn't want to be on the front page of all the papers with all those supermodels, I didn't want that. But I understand if somebody else does. He was very much an enigmatic front man of what we were as a group, and I saw myself more as being able to design the right songs to help that.

How did your collaborative process work?

Michael never actually played a musical instrument. When I met him he was reading books by Herman Hesse like *Siddhartha*, Kahlil Gibran and philosophers, and I was playing footy and was interested in how to fix my dad's car. I realised that he had an ability with words, to understand how to reach in to grab philosophies and concepts and mess around with them. In fact he was far more interested in words than he was in singing, than anything else. Just words and poetry. He used to write poetry. I remember sitting there one day reading something that he'd written, and I said, "This is great, have you ever thought of singing any of this stuff?" And that's where that started. It had never entered his head before. So he started messing around with the poetry he'd written, trying to make it musical. I think one of the ironies for us, having come through the pubs, is that there might be a guy who's standing there who's worked a fourteen-hour day with a beer in his hand and a cigarette. The last thing he wants is to hear the meaning of life by Kahlil Gibran. He just wants to hear, "Rock out dude."

So all that philosophy had to go out the window for a few years, and it wasn't until we left Australia that we were able to get into the sophistication of being able to talk to a wider group of people with a wider range of philosophies. Not that Aussies aren't able to recognise that, it's just that the environment that we were performing in, in those early years, was very much a working class experience.

What about the actual mechanics of how you wrote a song together?

Michael just wrote the lyrics. I wrote lyrics and I like to sing a bit, and I played guitar. I started to write a lot on the guitar, more than the keyboard. The keyboard became secondary to me for a while. And the mechanics of how Michael and I used to work together were particularly based around that, in the very early years, where we'd sit down with an acoustic guitar or a piano and just put chords together and then try and marry them with different sets of lyrics he might have, or I might have had. Years later, when we started to play very big venues and big gigs around the world, it was very important that he'd written the lyrics. Because when he walked on stage, he'd have that absolutely magnetic electrifying look, just like some of the most famous singers of all time on stage who've written their own material. You know that the person is at one with what they're singing about. This is not a theatrical thing you're watching where someone else has written a song and they're doing a very clever rendition of it. It's not Barbra Streisand. This is something different altogether again. It's the artist married with the music. And that's right smack bang in the middle of what he wanted to be on stage.

You and Michael had such different personalities; if you had written all the lyrics as well, they would have been very different songs.

On the album we did after *Kick*, Michael wanted to write lyrics that were more self-analytical and not so commercial. He wanted to write lyrics that became perhaps even more confronting. He started wandering off onto lyrics like "Suicide Blonde". And I was like, where are we heading with this? But I think he felt he needed to do that. And so I went down that path. But on the following album we did, *Welcome to Wherever You Are*, I just had the birth of my first daughter, Grace, and life had changed for me dramatically. So I was writing lyrics like "Baby Don't Cry" and "Beautiful Girl", lyrics about how wonderful it is to have something else in your life besides yourself to worry about and think about. I began to have some interesting conversations with Michael, where he was still interested in writing fairly dark introspective lyrics, and I was trying to write very positive, happy songs. But I'm an artist as well, and I'm not alone, I was working in a partnership. So we did both. And I think commercially it was confusing for people listening to the record.

Interestingly enough, when we were working with Tim Rice, who of course from his work with Andrew Lloyd Webber is one of the most famous lyricists ever, I asked him what song he knew of INXS's and he said "Baby Don't Cry". Which was a set of lyrics he said he loved, which I think Michael couldn't have cared less about, because it was very much a personal thing. I was being selfish at that point, and writing lyrics that instead of suiting a lead singer on stage, were more about me and my life and the things that meant something to me. That whole period of songs around *Welcome to Wherever You Are* was probably the most involvement I ever had on all levels of writing, lyrics and everything.

Was that gratifying?

I was trying to send very positive messages through that album to people who were listening, not send negative, darker images. And I think Michael realised when Tiger was born, later on, what on earth I'd been doing four years before. He suddenly switched, and on that last record we did together, the two of us found a lot in common, we both had young children and we really enjoyed writing together. Also the last album, *Elegantly Wasted*, Michael wrote all the lyrics on that record. I didn't contribute anything lyrically. He was incredibly passionate about that, to the point where there was one night we had a very strange conversation when my mother had died and I said to him, "Look that's a matter for me, lyrically that's a very personal issue with me." And he was like, "I don't care, I just want to write, I've got to write this, got to get this out." It was all very intense.

He wrote about your mother's death?

No, he didn't in the end. I still want to record that song, which is personal for anyone in life who experiences those emotions. My younger brother Jon started writing a song about that which I'd like to finish with him. But I really enjoyed the writing experience of *Elegantly Wasted* with Michael. I'm glad that the two of us sat down together like we had done before and saw eye to eye on most of that record.

With most of your writing with Michael, would he bring you lyrics first, which you'd put to music? Would you bring him music first and he'd then write the lyrics? Or did your lyrics and his music magically fit together?

Sometimes they would. There were some pretty weird things that would happen. I remember with "Need You Tonight", I called a cab to go to Hong Kong; I was going to go write with him there. I had started working on the music; I'd written a riff and I'd written these other parts, I didn't think that much about it, and I put it on a tape. I got out at the other end and he said, "Have you got anything?" I said, "Yeah, I've got this." So he put it on and it was the music for "Need You Tonight". He goes, "I know what that is, it's this!" And he starts singing this thing. And I'm like, that's kind of weird. Because that only happened literally as I was getting into the cab, and then as soon as I get out of the cab, he finishes the song. That's a bit strange, isn't it? That album *Kick* was pretty bizarre, actually. All I can say is it was all meant to be. I don't know what you believe, I believe things don't just happen randomly; I think everything happens for a reason. And that was just one of those situations.

Do you have a concept of where songs come from?
I think they come from somewhere outside of yourself. I don't think that it's any coincidence that certain messages or sounds or influences get put out into the mass public. There's something slightly larger at work with all that. Talking about the Beatles, for example, I was reflecting the other day that I'm really happy that the world's most successful group made a conscious effort to put positive images into people's minds, that the larger majority of their work is actually very much about love and respect and peace and wanting good things for people. I think that's fantastic, and I think that that's the way it should be.

Do you think the songs, then, exist in their own right and are using you as a channel?
I subscribe to whatever does it for you as a songwriter is what you need to do. I personally think that whatever's going to happen is going to happen anyway, and that it's all been pre-organised for us. I don't believe that you should give up that easily either. Like when you were joking before about the Brian Wilson thing and the pyjamas and sandpits, I also believe that if you don't apply yourself to what you're doing, you won't find it anyway, even if it is or isn't where you think it is. In other words, when I said I literally lived in my pyjamas and pulled the phone out of the wall for two weeks, I did that because I wouldn't leave until I had what I wanted. I made that happen. Maybe that was meant to happen anyway, because it was predestined, but I thought, I had to do that in order to get what I wanted, I wasn't going to just give up and leave and say, "Ah well, it's just not happening now, I'll go out and do something else." No, I'd just stay there until I got it right, until I got it exactly the way it should be, and I figured it out.

Keith Richards said once that he imagines he has a little antenna, and when he's tuned into it he can pick up the vibrations. I think a lot of it has to do with your emotional state, too. How relaxed you are. I don't mean necessarily you can be happy or sad, but you need to be focused, and one of the interesting things about songwriting, I read it somewhere, is that a bit like meditation, writing or any kind of creative art form, it's very healthy for you. Because you're concentrating on a particular thing that's creative. And because you're concentrating on that creative thing, it's quite healing. Especially sad issues, issues which lyrically demand a fair amount of self-examination in the process of writing. It must be some form of therapy for people to get stuff out when they write, to release thoughts or perhaps negative concepts, and acknowledge to themselves that they're actually thinking that.

Music's a bit different to me. Musically, I've probably written the most successful things when I've been completely relaxed, undisturbed, just completely in a little world of my own. Lyrically, it's the opposite almost, you need to be quite connected to the real world, and this is the interesting duality for me, just me personally, it may work differently for other people, but for me music works best when I'm, in a sense, cut off from the world, and lyrically I work best when I'm open and quite engrossed in the world. It's the duality of that, the balance of that, that gets complicated.

So a song then might be written in two stages in that you'll come up with the music and then you'll get out there to find the lyrics?
If I'm writing a song by myself I usually do write it in two stages. Michael and I often wrote our most potent songs in that way, where we'd never write together in the same room. Ever. All the really big hits, I wrote the music in a separate space, even a separate country sometimes, and then him writing a lyric. And then we'd get together and work it out.

Do you think when people listen to INXS songs they are diverted by the lyrics first or the music?
I find it intriguing that a lot of people give songwriters accolades purely on the basis of lyrics. Because if you look very carefully at what's happened in the last ten, fifteen years, the most commercial thing in the world today is not the lyrics, it's the feels, it's the music. People are interested in dance and feeling good. They're not interested in somebody philosophising down a radio or on their CD, they're just interested in having a good time. And that for me was more where my head was at, just getting feels and getting into the music, and actually making it so that when the music was on, regardless of what the lyric was about, the music was speaking to you.

If I was to look at a broad cross-range of the most successful "songwriters", there's so many songs that really stand alone. The Bee Gees. What would "Stayin' Alive" by The Bee Gees be without that feel? You put "Stayin' Alive" into a nice little ballad song, no-one would care less. You put that big thumping disco feel into it, and everyone goes, "That is amazing." And that's what I'm talking about. You need the two to work together. Then when you combine the feels with the right lyric, and then you combine *that* with knowing the theatrical nature of what you're doing, then you've got it all. Then you've got all three parts of it—you've got the music, you've got the lyric and you've got the performer performing all that in sync, and then it's very powerful.

With "Original Sin", the watershed song, did you write that lyric together with Michael?
He wrote that lyric. We did two three-month tours of the United States in 1983 and on the first tour that we did, we were sitting on a bus, and Michael was looking at some kids playing in a poorer section of one of the US cities, and he started thinking of those lyrics. Great lyrics, really good lyrics. I most liked Michael's lyric writing when he used to think outside of what was worrying him in his life more, when he used to write lyrics about other people.

A lot of people say "Don't Change" is the best INXS song. It was so early in the band's life. How do you feel about it now?
It is a good song. I like that song. I like a lot of INXS's material, which sounds funny for me to say. There's some I'm not crazy about.

It's interesting that some writers or artists say, "I can't listen to my own work." "I can't read my own work." I like people who go back on their work and enjoy it.
Well, we've been around for so many years that some parts of INXS's career almost seem like other people, because it's so long ago, and events which formulated some of the ideas behind it, I can remember a lot of them, but a lot of them I can't remember. And then it starts to become interesting, because I'm listening to work that we did and I have no idea why we did what we were doing with some of it. Some of the other guys in the band probably could, but some of it I just can't remember.

What motivated you during INXS's first international boom period in the late eighties to move into co-writing and production with an outside artist like Jenny Morris?
Before producing the *Shiver* album I'd worked on her *Body and Soul* album, and I'd written a song for her called "You're Gonna Get Hurt". My friend Ian Moss helped out on that track, he played guitar and sang on it. My brother Jon played drums on it as well. That's a good recording. I think Jenny and I were both surprised at how that recording came out. So then she asked me to work on "Body and Soul", the title track from that record. So I produced that one, and it came out pretty good as well.

To write with her, as opposed to writing with Michael at that point, was it a different process?
Jenny and I tend to work from the ground up, and build ideas. She can play guitar, so we were able to talk music. Music for music's sake, as opposed to just marrying lyrics and music. Also, Jenny's lyrics and the way she approaches her writing is a little bit more like the way I prefer to write and approach lyrics. Most of her lyrics are pretty positive. Whereas Michael really liked and was always a big fan of Nick Cave, some of his favourite records were like The Birthday Party records; he liked the dark side of the force.

Did he like Jim Morrison as well? Because there's an obvious parallel there.
That's interesting. There was a time in the mid- to late eighties when there was some pretty strange stuff going on. The first time INXS went to America we were on MTV a lot, in 1983, in fact we were on high rotation for most of that year, and I can remember the keyboard player from the Doors, Ray Manzarek, came backstage to one of the gigs we were doing in Los Angeles and he said, "I just had to come and talk to you"—meaning Michael— "because I was sitting at home watching MTV and your band came on, and I was very disturbed by how much you reminded me of Jim Morrison. It actually disturbed me, it was something I had to come and see for myself." He was really impressed with Michael; there was something familiar for him. And in that regard a little bit spooky now in hindsight, thinking back on the characteristics of the two people.

What brought you together with Yothu Yindi and how did each of those projects you did with them help you to develop as an artist and a writer?
My relationship started off back on their *Freedom* album, working on a song called "Our Generation". I ended up playing the beginnings of that song to Mandawuy Yunupingu, he loved it and added some lyrics to it, and we moved part of it around a little bit and changed the lyrics of what I'd started and messed around with it, and that's the song that they recorded.

My next project I did with Yothu Yindi was on the *Wild Honey* album. When I was living in England I started working on a couple of songs with Mandawuy, one called "Super Highway" and the other one called "Matter of Choice", which is a song about unemployment in the Northern Territory. And I began to learn more about the people and their culture. I was intrigued with them as people more than anything, and the music as well, the way Mandawuy thinks as a writer, too, he's very poetic and he's very focused about what he wants to achieve, and that's good. He's very positive, a lot of his lyrics have always got positive messages or at least they're descriptive, and animated, too. And obviously knowing the man like I do, he's not big on fiction. He likes telling it how it is. So I began to develop more of a relationship with them as people and as a band.

And then on *Garma* I was involved very heavily. I produced that record and was involved with Stuart Kellaway, Jodie Creed and Mandawuy on the writing process. It was funny, because before we started that album, I said to them, "I really want you to have the songs written before I start producing, I don't want the pressure of it." And so when we finally got together, they all turned up literally at my door with their instruments going, "Well, we're ready to get started!"

Writing?
Yeah. And I had to just laugh and go, "Okay, well, they want me to be involved with the writing, which is really a compliment, so okay, I'll help write." I have immense respect for Yothu Yindi, I think they're a very important group of people. What they've attempted to do, to marry modern technology with their ancient culture and do it the way they've done it, is very interesting. And be open-minded when they're doing it.

And your foray into country music? Was that a really different experience?
Oh, definitely. For a start, I can guarantee you that coming from writing with someone like Michael for many years, who's not afraid to explore, let's say, the darker areas of life, then writing with country people, it's like visiting Mars. The country fraternity, and some of the characters involved in that particular area, are very cut and dry about what they will and won't sing. A bit like flower arrangements, they won't mix waratahs with roses.

Are you interested in doing solo projects?
I've been working for many years on an instrumental record, which is not really a pop record, although these days it probably would be considered a pop record. It's more of a textures album. It's just got sounds on it that I like, rather than pop structures, little pieces of music that are quite short and then other big, long stretches in there. I don't even know what to call it.

After Michael's death, how long was it before you were able to start writing?
I found it very difficult to start writing pop songs again. I actually started working fairly shortly afterwards on some instrumental pieces, which were part of my solo thing. As far as writing popular music again, thinking about commercial music, I just had no particular desire to do that for quite a long time. I didn't really feel like it.

Did you write something about Michael, or about how you were feeling in that time immediately after?
Not really. I sort of did and I sort of didn't. I think when you lose someone who's very close to you, you go through all these different emotional periods. You go through things from disbelief to shock to anger to sadness to being overly sensitive to then being insensitive. You go through all these different modes and I really didn't trust myself at that point to believe that I was stable enough to think about it objectively.

Did you have to redefine yourself in any way as a writer or performer after Michael's death?
Yes, I have actually. One thing he and I used to say to each other every so often was that we didn't really compete for the same things. I didn't want to be the lead singer of a band and be "Mr Fabulous". But he did. He really wanted that. But at the same time we were both writers. So when we were writing it was always for "Mr Fabulous". And I had absolutely no problem with that at all, and neither did he. I just wanted to be a writer and I liked what came of that. I was very lucky to have that. And he was very lucky to have someone like me helping to create who he wanted to be.

So when Michael died and for some time afterwards, I had to re-evaluate who I was in a sense and what my next thing was going to be all about. I'm still processing that even now. I suppose I spent the first part of my career trying to write for one very narrow conduit, to funnel all these ideas into this target point. I'm almost imagining the next part of my life could be about going in completely the opposite direction. Trying many different things with many different cultures and many different types of people. And whatever I can do. Whatever style of music.

COLIN HAY

TOPANGA, CALIFORNIA, USA, JUNE 2004

Colin Hay is very comfortable with his past. In live shows he weaves his chart-topping Men At Work songs into a set with his much vaster output of solo work, tells ripping yarns about his life and times in music and beyond, and calls the show "Man At Work".

"I feel like I'm in my own cover band," he said, sitting on the shady, eucalyptus-canopied terrace of his Topanga Canyon home. It's hidden away in one of the Los Angeles area's most creative enclaves, with an impressive full-scale recording studio in the basement and a funky timber, stone and glass love shack on top. Hay's recent marriage to salsa soul singer Cecilia Noël got a spread in the *Australian Women's Weekly*, which Cecilia proudly showed me. "They love him there," she said.

Hay didn't originally come from a land down under. He hailed from the far reaches of the Northern Hemisphere and is well ensconced in America now, but he and his music will always be connected with Australia. Not just because he taught the world about Vegemite sandwiches, or because he has family in Melbourne, but because the humour, irreverence and unpretentiousness of his work and his persona are so Australian in spirit. As he sang on his 2002 album, *Company of Strangers*, "I'm a stayer, not a sprinter; just call me a lucky bastard."

Hay was born on 29 June 1953 in Kilwinning, a small coastal town in Ayrshire, on the southwest coast of Scotland, and grew up nearby in Saltcoats, where his parents ran a music shop. It was a bucolic existence, idyllic scenes of dairy farms and bonny lasses, traditional Scottish and Irish folk music, and airwaves full of the Beatles. He started playing the guitar at twelve, taught by a teenage girl on whom he had a crush. Girls seemed to be everywhere in Hay's adolescence and with hormones raging and songs ready to burst forth, his family uprooted and took a ship to Australia in 1967. Almost as soon as he disembarked in Melbourne, the fourteen-year-old started playing at the Beaumaris Folk Club, singing Beatles, Bob Dylan, Cat Stevens and James Taylor covers. Not long after that he began playing original songs.

Hay knew early on that songwriting was key. After working his way through cover bands in school and university, in 1978 he met guitarist Ron Strykert and by the following year they had formed Men At Work. From its inception, Hay wanted it to be a song-based band. Having people hear and enjoy their songs was always the goal; success on a mega-global scale was beyond expectation, and the phenomenon that Men At Work became in some ways detracted from the essence of the music. "I think the songs were really good, they were memorable and they had depth, although it wasn't obvious at the time," said Hay. "People thought we were a light band because of the way the album sounded; it sounded very poppy."

The album, *Business As Usual*, was an immediate success in Australia, with "Who Can It Be Now?" and "Down Under" topping the local charts in 1981, and countries around the world following in a domino effect. CBS in America rejected the album twice before finally releasing it, and when the US did pick up on the Men At Work craze in 1982, the result was a number one album for fifteen consecutive weeks, sales of ten million records, and a Best New Artist Grammy. Neither Little River Band before them nor INXS after them—both songwriting-based bands who gave Australian music a place in the world's biggest market—had a Grammy or such an instantaneous rise to the top, but for Men At Work it was a short-lived reign. As Hay's song "Overkill" from their second album, *Cargo*, prophesied, it was too much too soon. *Cargo* was released a year after the first album in Australia, but only three months behind the band's US debut. By the time of the third album, *Two Hearts*, in 1985, declining sales and internal tensions ended the band.

Hay got a solo record deal and moved to New York first and then Los Angeles. The career that followed was unspectacular, but only by comparison with what had come before. There were failures, self-doubt and a drinking problem, but the music always flowed. Eight albums containing songs that celebrate life, examine human frailty, delight in the wonders of love and laugh at Hay himself have ensured constant interest from critics and fans alike. And although he dreads the presence of uncouth Australian fans at his overseas concerts—the ones that just come to get drunk and sing along to "Who Can It Be Now?" and "Down Under"—he seems to love them, too, or at least what they represent.

"I'm very, very grateful for those times because it enabled me to actually continue what I'm doing now. That's why I have such a great relationship with those songs. Because they look after me. And you have to respect that."

How did you deal with being uprooted and relocating to a place on the other side of the world as a teenager with your formative years lived out?
It gave me a double perspective on everything. There were things about Scotland that I dearly loved. I loved just the way the place felt; obviously it's my home.

Were you upset that you had to leave?
I don't think so. Being upset was overshadowed by the excitement of going somewhere else. There was a girl that I really liked in Scotland and her name was Janet Roos. And I had kissed her. I had kissed Janet Roos, and that was very exciting. And then I went to Australia.

So yes, it was tricky work going somewhere else, but—I've said this a few times—it was a little bit like going from a black and white world into a world of technicolour. Because Scotland's very grey and cold and rainy, but brilliant at the same time. But Australia was really vivid and there was big surf. Everything was big, everything was huge, as opposed to Scotland. And I started playing music quite quickly, and I met really good people as soon as I got there, so it was very exciting.

Did your migrant experience find its way into your music later on?
I think it did in ways that I don't really think about so much. Because for many years I used to dream about going back to Scotland and they were really hallucinogenic dreams. Very psychedelic. They were heavenly, like it was really like a heavenly place. It wasn't, it was just Scotland. But for me, it was somewhere where I grew up, and it became magical. I never went back there for sixteen years, and the first time I went back was with Men At Work. So consequently there was probably some imagery that got in there from that kind of experience.

But more about the dreaming back to home rather than the idea of migrating to a foreign land and starting again in a new place?
Yeah, it was more about where I'd come from as opposed to where I was. Obviously the "Down Under" song became very famous, which is interesting for me because it was pretty much seen as being a beer-drinking song and a song that people wave flags to and yacht races and things. But really that song lyrically was more about the fear and trepidation of Australia becoming over-developed in a very American kind of way, and in the process perhaps losing quite a lot of its uniqueness or its spirit if you like. And I don't really know anything about Aboriginal culture per se, but when I first went there everything was really foreign to me, it was like black man's land. It was like everything was hot and dry and arid and mysterious.

You went to Melbourne. It's grey and cold and rainy there.
Not if you're from Scotland. And not if you drive down the coast. But this was written in '77 or '78 when I'd seen more of it than Melbourne. The song tries to also convey the spirit of the place, which as you know is mysterious, and eternal. And the song in its original form was a bit drier as well. The verses were very Barry McKenzie-inspired. And the choruses were really about the idea of some kind of death involved, the death of Australia in a sense. The corporatisation, the Americanisation, the more the country becomes like everywhere else. The coastline of southern Queensland looks pretty much like Florida. In other words, selling off the country and its resources for short-term gains. That was really on a personal level, not really necessarily understood by that many people that actually listened to the song. Because by the time it became successful it was just one of those tunes, people either love it or hate it depending on where you were at a particular time. But it always had a different kind of feeling for me than it did for a lot of other people. It's also a good beer-drinking song.

I always saw it as a song about that rite of passage that Australians go on where they backpack around the world, and they're always recognised as being Australian. As a Scot who'd come to Australia to live, you probably hadn't even done that.
No. But the choruses and the verses were different in that sense. The verses were definitely about that thing of leaving and trying to figure out … Like a friend of mind went into a bread shop in Brussels and tried to speak French and the guy there is from Brunswick in Melbourne, you know. So as far as a people go, they are quite travelled, they get around, they move around the globe. Other people do it as well, but for Australians it seems to be, like you say, some kind of rite of passage or some strange breed of bird that all of a sudden feel like they have got to move in order to discover who they are. But the choruses were more interesting to me, just the fact that it seemed that the country was being sold in a kind of a cheap way.

Did you have to constantly explain to the Americans what chunder meant?
Yeah, and the Vegemite thing and all that kind of talk.

Well, you taught the world about Vegemite.
Yeah. But what's really interesting to me about the song is that it doesn't really matter where I go, it doesn't even really matter about the words so much. I play the song in Bolivia or Chile or Brazil, they have no idea, but they just like the tune. And then you discover that the song is just a song. That people like no matter where they're from. It's interesting to play the song somewhere like Argentina, and the whole crowd is singing along, because they're actually from down under as well if you think about it.

How do you feel about the term "novelty song", which some people view that song as?
Mmm. Well, people like to put different things in different bags. I don't really think it is particularly; I think it's one of those songs that people started to think of in that way

because it was so all-pervasive. You know, it was kind of like, oh, if there's a yacht race or if there's the Olympics or whatever, you drag that song out and play it. And so that's what happens to it. But it's not that for me. And I don't really care that much about what other people think of it, to be honest.

Were you happy to have "Down Under" associated with Australia's win in the America's Cup in 1983?
I was happy enough because of the reasons why it was. Because John Bertrand liked the song, and he used to play it on the yacht to scare the Americans, to intimidate them when they were down at the harbour. And it worked. And then from that point it became ridiculous. Because then everyone's going, "Oh, it's great that you wrote that song for the yacht race." So as far as Australia's concerned that's the association. I like the song. We've looked after each other very well over the years.

And that traveller motif has recurred throughout your work.
You think so? I don't know. Probably. But I think that's the case in many, many songwriters.

You travelled a long way from home and then started a career where you were travelling all the time.
I think that's true of a lot of people in New Zealand and Australia, not even if you're a songwriter, but just that whole notion of what a short time people have been there for, I think is interesting as well. The fact that people have just been there for a minute in the scheme of things. And the same can be said here as well in America. I get that feeling about people are wandering around, wondering where the fuck they're from, where they belong. I think Australia has that in common with America, in a microcosmic way, because it's just this attempt at having all these different kinds of people from different parts of the world trying to make sense of it.

What do you like about living and writing in Los Angeles?
I don't really care about that so much, I could be anywhere. I could be in Australia or here, and I don't consciously think, "Oh, I'm writing this because I'm living in LA." I never really consciously associate that.

Actually, that's not strictly true. I had an album called *Transcendental Highway* and that was written about being here. And there's a song called "Looking for Jack" on the first solo album that I had, about the experience of being in Los Angeles, but more about the fact that this is where people come to try and figure it out, to try and realise their dreams. When I first came to Los Angeles, everyone seemed to be looking for something but I couldn't figure out what it was they were looking for. You know, driving around the freeways, and when you first come here you can't find the centre of it. It's not like New York or any place that's got a centre. It was all spread out and I thought, well, where actually is Los Angeles? I couldn't really find it.

I had this song that I was working on, it was the last song for this album, and I didn't even know how to finish the tune because I was trying to figure out what it was that people were looking for. And then I saw Jack Nicholson at this concert and I walked up to him and I said, "Excuse me, Mr Nicholson, my name is Colin Hay, I used to sing with a band called Men At Work. I just want to say I'm a great big fan of yours." And he said, "I can't hear you." I got a bit embarrassed and I walked into the green room. I was standing there talking to this girl and then the door opened and he came in and he made a beeline for me, and he said, "I just wanna say I'm a great big fan of yours, too." So I felt immediately elated, because Jack had just paid me a compliment. And then he walked off. Then I was looking over the girl's shoulder, just looking to where he'd gone. She was still talking to me and I was distracted, and she said, "What are you doing, Colin?" And I said, "Sorry, you'll have to excuse me. I'm just looking for Jack." And she goes, "Yeah, everybody's always looking for Jack!"

But the thing that was really exciting for me about finishing that tune was that that is exactly what people are looking for. He was an incredible physical person to hang that thing on. Because if you say, "Well, who do you want to be like?" I want to be like Jack. Because Jack sums it up. He sums up Los Angeles.

What I like about being here particularly is that I'm strategically placed. I can go to Central America, which I do sometimes, I can go to South America to play, I can go up to Canada, I can go across to Europe, even down to Australia, wherever. Also there's great musicians I can call up and they can come up on a Tuesday. If I want somebody to play some bass or some keyboards or drums, it's a phone call away. It's an incredible place to record and to write in that sense, I really love that aspect.

I wondered also if the appeal was something to do with the heritage of so many great songwriters whose songs have been born in canyons like this.
Yeah, I really like that idea. I like the fact that you might run into Ry Cooder or you can still hear a little bit of slide guitar if you drive across the canyon. My closest friend here is a guy called Chad Fischer, who's a great songwriter and producer and engineer, he lives off Laurel Canyon, and we drive up there and he goes, "Oh, Frank Zappa used to live there." There's still people living there and making great music there, so it's actually still very vibrant.

Can you talk about the mechanics of writing songs?
Traditionally, I would sit around with a guitar or some kind of instrument and I would have a musical idea. Then I would put it on a little tape, it used to be cassette, then it became a DAT recorder, whatever I have at hand, and I would put down the musical idea. And then I would sing ideas to it. Sometimes they weren't even words, sometimes I would just mumble things. And then sometimes I'd listen back to it and think what those mumblings sounded like and put words down that way. Or sometimes I would have a very specific idea lyrically that would go with the music. But the music traditionally always tended to come first, and then the lyrics would follow. Lately, I've been trying to do it the other way around. Mainly because I have been a little bit immobile in the last week or two. I had an operation and it was a little difficult to get around, so I found myself finishing off ideas that I had lyrically. I've been trying to write sets of lyrics and then perhaps try and put them to music.

So a song like "Down Under" was a musical idea first for you?
It was actually a combination, because I had this "living in a land down under" line in my head. [*Sings*] "Living in a land down under ..." I would have this thing that would repeat in my head, but that was it. And then Ron Strykert, he used to do little tapes at home, which were really cool. They were percussive and guitar things and he had this one little piece that was just this repetitive trance-like idea, he was playing bottles, and then he had this bass riff that kept repeating. I was driving down Power Street in Hawthorne and that tape was playing, and I sang the line over his tape, "Living in a land down under." That was very exciting to me. Then I wrote the rest of the chorus and then two days later I wrote the verses to it. So it was a bit of a combination, that one.

Do melodies come to you away from your instrument?
Oh yeah, all the time. I'll just sing and I'll call my machine.

Darren Hayes calls his voicemail. I said, "Why don't you just carry a little recorder around with you?"
Sometimes I do, but sometimes you just don't have them. But you've got your cell phone, so I'll call home and just sing the melody. I had two mini discs full of stuff and I lost it. There was a lot of stuff on there, like maybe two years worth of stuff.

How disciplined are you in your writing?
Not very. I try to be more disciplined the older I get. I'm disciplined once I start doing it.

But you procrastinate?
Yeah, I put it off. I'll go down the street or I'll do all these other things before I go down there. But I know that when I get down to it, it'll be good, I'll enjoy it. I always forget that it is really enjoyable for the most part.

Has that changed from the early days? When you were in Men At Work did you have to find ways to motivate yourself?
I don't know what it's like for other people but when I was in my twenties, it's almost like how, when you're growing up, you have that period where you just seem to grow for a couple of years, whatever age you are you seem to get taller. "Oh, he's shot up, hasn't he, that young boy! He's so tall now!" There was a period of time at university when I started writing a lot of tunes. Then Men At Work was in existence, and there's something about having a vehicle for which to play your song. So you'd take a song in, which I was excited about, and all of a sudden, boom! We were playing it. That was inspiring to me, so I wrote a lot of songs during that first period of the band. There's something immediate about a band, because you just play it and all of a sudden there you go. Whereas now it's a bit more solitary. It's different. Sometimes I get friends to come up and we'll just play the tunes, which is a little more like it used to be.

Where does inspiration come from? Do you have to go in search of it or does it come to you effortlessly?

I don't necessarily think that you have to be inspired to write songs. People talk about being inspired a lot. I get excited when I'm writing a song, but it's not like I go, "Oh, I'm really inspired to write a song." Because I treat it more like it's my job. It's a job of work that I love to do. I treat it more like, "Oh, I'm going to go down to the studio, I'm going to go down and work."

I remember writing a song here once on a Sunday, I just decided that I wanted to write a song, 'cause it was Sunday, and I thought, "I have to write a song today. I haven't written a song for a while." Then I started to think about what to write a song about. And this was an example of a song that presented itself to me, because I remember thinking about this girl that I knew in Scotland. I was five and she was six, and she could beat me up. And she did. She was like a tomboy, she was really strong and she could always wrestle me to the ground and then pin my arms down and then she would lean down and kiss me and then get up.

What was her name?

Her name began with an N and it had three syllables. I can't think of it. But because it had three syllables it didn't really work, so the song became "Maggie". I thought, "Oh, I wonder what happened to her?" And then the song really just popped out and all the lyrics and everything came in half an hour. And while I was writing the song I was weeping uncontrollably. [*Laughs*] First time it's ever happened.

Can you write away from your studio? Can you write when you're on the road?

Yeah. I like that sometimes because when you do soundchecks and different things, sometimes when you least expect it is when you come up with really cool things. Like on stage you're just messing around. I like doing that. Look, there's no problem with finding ideas, having musical ideas, lyrical ideas, ideas for songs, they come all the time. But the thing to do is to finish them. That's the challenge. Often I get to a point where I can't finish something and I'll call up my friend Chad often, or sometimes Cecilia helps me as well.

How did you collaborate with Ron Strykert and Greg Ham, and what did you gain, if anything, from writing with them?

Ron was an important person for me to meet because I was writing songs before that and I was pretty happy with the way things were going, but he opened up a whole other aspect of guitar playing. He was a beautiful guitar player and he had great song ideas and so we complemented each other quite well, because I was quite stable in the sense that I could sing and play the guitar, and he would add an incredible amount of colour to what I was doing. And then if he had an idea for a song I could take it and give it some structure, so we brought different things to the relationship. But it wasn't like we wrote a lot of songs together. What would happen was he would be quite inspiring to play with so I would go off and write songs, but it was because of what we were doing together. Something would spark an idea.

And I didn't write much with Greg. He tended to write by himself sometimes. I only wrote, I think, one song, "Be Good Johnny", with Greg. That was just in a rehearsal one day, we were just messing around with a musical idea, and I just said, "That would be great to have this tune written from the standing point of a nine-year-old boy." Greg was a very funny man and he almost had a childlike quality to him, so we wrote that tune just about the fact, and everyone can relate to that in a sense, 'cause at some point when you're grown up everyone's expecting you to toe the line and be a good boy.

And the title was a take on Chuck Berry's "Johnny B Goode"?
Yeah, it obviously was. But I can't even remember at the time whether it was conscious. The thing that came first was "be good". [*Sings*] "Be good, be good, be good, be good, be good", that whole thing.

But you chose Johnny.
Yeah, absolutely. But I can't remember thinking, "Oh, that's like Chuck Berry's song."

How did you get the idea for "Who Can It Be Now?"
I was living in St Kilda, I was on the dole, and everyone that came knocking on the door seemed to want something. Whether it was the police or people looking for drugs or the rent man or the doorman. So we'd sneak up and see who it was before we opened the door, just to make sure it wasn't somebody we didn't want to see. And then I was in southern New South Wales; my girlfriend and I at the time had some land in Bermagui. And I wrote the song in about twenty minutes, sitting in the bush, with the frogs.

Are you generally a quick writer or do you labour over songs?
Sometimes the writing of a song is quite quick. I like those ones if they're quite fast. But sometimes you write a song and you have the bare bones of it. And then you go downstairs and start recording it and it's still in the process of being written, and then sometimes it changes and sometimes it morphs into something else. Often songs develop a life of their own and they demand to be played in a different way, or they just seem to speak to you and tell you about something maybe that you hadn't thought of.

Can you give me an example of a song that's done that to you, that's surprised you down the track?
There's a song called "My Brilliant Feet", which was about George Best, the football player. But then it was really about me, at the end of the day.

I saw that as a very reflective song. A recurring theme with Australian songwriters is the early success at epic heights, and then a life of songwriting that often surpasses it creatively but never lives up to the masses' expectations. Do you think you're writing far better work now than you were in Men At Work?
I don't really, actually, to be honest with you. I would put "Overkill" up there with anything

that I've done since then. And "Down Under". And "Who Can It Be Now?" I think that they're songs that stand up. I think I'm getting better as a songwriter and a musician and in every way, but I don't necessarily think that what I'm doing now is better than what I did then.

That's why I like playing live all the time, because people would come and see you play, they don't care about that mass expectation or record labels or anything to do with that. They just like your music and they come and see you play, and so your music grows.

Can you tell me about writing "Overkill"?
That was the song that I thought, maybe I've got a future as a songwriter. Because I liked that song and to me it had good melody and it went interesting places, chordally and stuff. It was also when I started to feel weird being in Men At Work with the other boys in the band because I would take songs to them, like I took "Overkill" to them, I played the song and nobody responded. And I got upset, because I thought it was great and I didn't get the response that I wanted. So I just recorded the whole thing myself. And I really liked it. And I thought to myself, "Well, if things don't work out with the band I can always just carry on by myself." And as it turns out, I think more than anything else, most of the problems in our band were the fact that nobody could really communicate very well. Maybe people were impressed by the tune but chose not to say so. I don't know about other bands, but in our band it was highly dysfunctional. Interesting if you're in it, or if you look back on it and think, "Oh, that's why that happened."

Do you remember coming up with the idea for "Overkill"?
Yeah. I remember being down at St Kilda Pier, where we ended up doing the video for it. And thinking to myself that it was like leaving behind everything you knew. Leaving behind all your comfort zones, everything that was familiar to you, people you knew and the gigs you played and backstage rooms. Everything that was very comfortable. And you'd now grown up, and you think, "Oh, actually, this is all going to change now." Because it was just getting huge. And so you're looking forward to that but it's like stepping into the unknown.

Was writing for a solo career liberating or did you feel more pressured?
Completely liberating. Completely. I was so excited. I mean, they all stiffed, you know. [*Laughs*] But I like the records.

What was going on for you prior to writing the songs for the album *Wayfaring Sons*?
Failure. Professional failure. I was living in New York, I think it was around '87, and *Looking for Jack* had come and gone, had done nothing, I couldn't even tour it because the record company was over. I could either go back to Australia or just live in New York. So I stayed in New York and wrote all these tunes for the next album. But constantly was the realisation that, "Oh! This is what a failed album feels like."

There seemed to be some magic at work in the title track of *Wayfaring Sons*.
I like that tune, I wrote that in Switzerland. I was doing a promotional tour and I was sitting

in a bar somewhere or other. And that was very much about going to Australia and that feeling of being homesick but not even being sure of for where.

It's that travel motif I was talking about.
It's like going to Australia, and thinking, "Oh, I really miss Scotland, it was great." And then you go back to Scotland and you think, "Oh, I really miss Australia." Because Australia gets in your blood very quickly, it really is a place that envelops you. It changes, there's an ambivalence, a love-hate thing with me as well, and I think it's got to do with being in a relationship where you feel like you've been rejected, and you leave, and you're never, ever really reconciled in any way, shape or form. That's the way I feel about Australia in many ways. I came back to Australia and I wanted to live there and I was excited about it, but I found that I couldn't really do anything, people weren't really interested any more. So I thought, "Fuck it, I'll come to LA where *nobody* gives a fuck about you." You get thirty seconds to say something to somebody and then they change the channel. I thought, I'll go somewhere where there's a lot of people like me and there's no support system. If you do anything at all it's off your own bat, you know you've done it.

Do you have to feel deeply the things you write in emotive songs like "Storm in My Heart" or "Into My Life" or "Waiting for My Real Life to Begin"? Can such emotions be written about hypothetically?
I think they can. Sometimes I have a close relationship with a tune, but I have varying feelings about different songs. Some songs I feel closer to than others. And it changes all the time. Sometimes I'll once have really had strong feelings for a song or what the song is about and then I just don't really care about it.

But do songs like those have to be based on real experience?
Sometimes they're based on real experience or sometimes they're based on someone else's experience that's been told to me. I used to feel like I had to feel personally involved in what I'm writing about, like it happened to me. But then I realised that my life experience was limited by what I'd done, how I'd lived, people I'd met, all kinds of things. So I thought, well, I'll just try and use more imagination, conjure up situations and just pretend that I know about something, or write about different situations that are going on. Because it's much more interesting than just what I've gone through. Sometimes investigating yourself all the time is boring.

And then sometimes you start off writing about something that has happened to you and it ends up being something else. It all just shifts. And sometimes it can shift just because you find something that rhymes with something else and you go, oh, that's interesting, because that's better, it takes us somewhere else.

"Waiting for My Real Life to Begin" was like another take on John Lennon's "Life is what happens when you're busy making other plans." Was that a personal song for you?
Yeah, "Waiting for My Real Life to Begin" is one of my favourite tunes that I've come up

with, and it's actually not my line. It was a drummer that I was working with at the time, a guy called Thom Mooney, he came around here with a lot of doughnuts, we used to have doughnuts and coffee. I said, "How are you doin', Thom?" And he says, "Oh, you know, Colin, I'm waiting for my real life to begin." So I thought, that's cool. And I wrote the tune right then. That just wrote itself. Sometimes a verse is about me and then sometimes the next verse is about something else and so forth, so it's broken up a bit like that. But that idea of being rejected, being dropped by a label, which was my case, giving up alcohol, which also I did, and feeling like everything will be fine next week, if I can get that new record deal or if I can win that hand at cards, or if I can, you know, I'll just have one, it'll be fine. Just chasing that thing that doesn't really exist. Not being here, not being present, not being really alive, all the time just waiting for something to appear that's going to make you happy, that's going to actually provide some kind of fulfilment. I think we all feel that from time to time. And one of the ways of me personally dealing with stuff like that was just playing live again. Because people are sitting in a room and you have to entertain them. It's very immediate, it's very real, it's very, "Oh, I have to actually give these people a good night out." Instead of sitting around just talking about it.

What inspired the song "Company of Strangers"?
Travelling around and doing what I do. Constantly night after night being with strangers that, for an hour and a half or two hours, you have quite an intimate relationship with. And then you move on. That was one aspect of it. But then the other aspect of it was that eventually we're all going to have to accept everyone else. And not live in fear.

Was there a moment that triggered the idea for "Beautiful World"?
I was driving across Topanga Canyon, and just sang the tune. Thinking, well, things are so chaotic and horrible in the world that I'm going to really enjoy the fact that I can drive across the canyon in this car, and take great pleasure in those simple things. It's also a way for me to enjoy my life, be much more simplified, because before, when I was drinking, everything was about highs and lows, everything was much more chaotic. And when you stop that, when you take that out of your life, you don't really have the chaos any more, or it's a different kind of chaos, but it's not as chaotic, so everything is always okay. Pretty good. So sometimes I would ritualise things in order for me to get greater enjoyment from them. Whether it's having a cup of tea or a cup of coffee, I'll ritualise it. Or I'll drive in the car and I'll make a ritual of it. Because then it becomes a little bit more heightened. So that's what that song is, really.

You wrote "Lucky Bastard" with Paul Kelly.
Yeah, on the Internet. By email.

So you never sat down together and worked on that?
No. I went around to his house one night, having dinner. And he says, [*Imitating Paul Kelly drawl*] "Ah, you know, you're a fuckin' lucky bastard."

A lot of people think Paul is a lucky bastard.
Well, he is as well. We're all lucky bastards. So anyway, I wrote the first verse and I sent it to him. And then he sent the second verse.

Just lyrically?
Just lyrics, yeah. Back and forward, back and forward, till we had too many verses. So that's how that worked. It was fun; I enjoyed doing that.

What do you think the purpose of a song is? Is it merely to entertain? Should it celebrate life? Should it offer comfort or connect the listener with some higher power?
I think it's about connecting. I don't know about the higher power business. I think for one thing, it should make you feel not necessarily good but it should make you feel something. It should transport you, it should take you somewhere. In the best way possible. There's something thrilling about when you first hear something that you've never heard before. I always go back to when I was in Scotland and I was sitting in my first cafe, and I had a Coca-Cola, and I was by myself, I think I was thirteen, and "Good Vibrations" was playing on the radio. I didn't know anything about the West Coast of America or the Beach Boys or anything like that. All I really knew was that I really wanted to go there. Or even in the music shop when my father played the Beatles. The sound of the guitars and the sound of the harmonies, it was like a mysterious world, a world that I wanted to belong to. It was all so very exciting. The first chords to the Kinks' "You Really Got Me", the way it makes you feel excited about being alive.

So your ultimate hope for your songs is that they transport people to their own special place?
Well, to me it's circular. Because if I write a song and I think, oh, this is a cool song, and I play it and I get the response, I know that it's affecting people, then that comes back to me. So it just keeps going. It's something which feeds on itself.

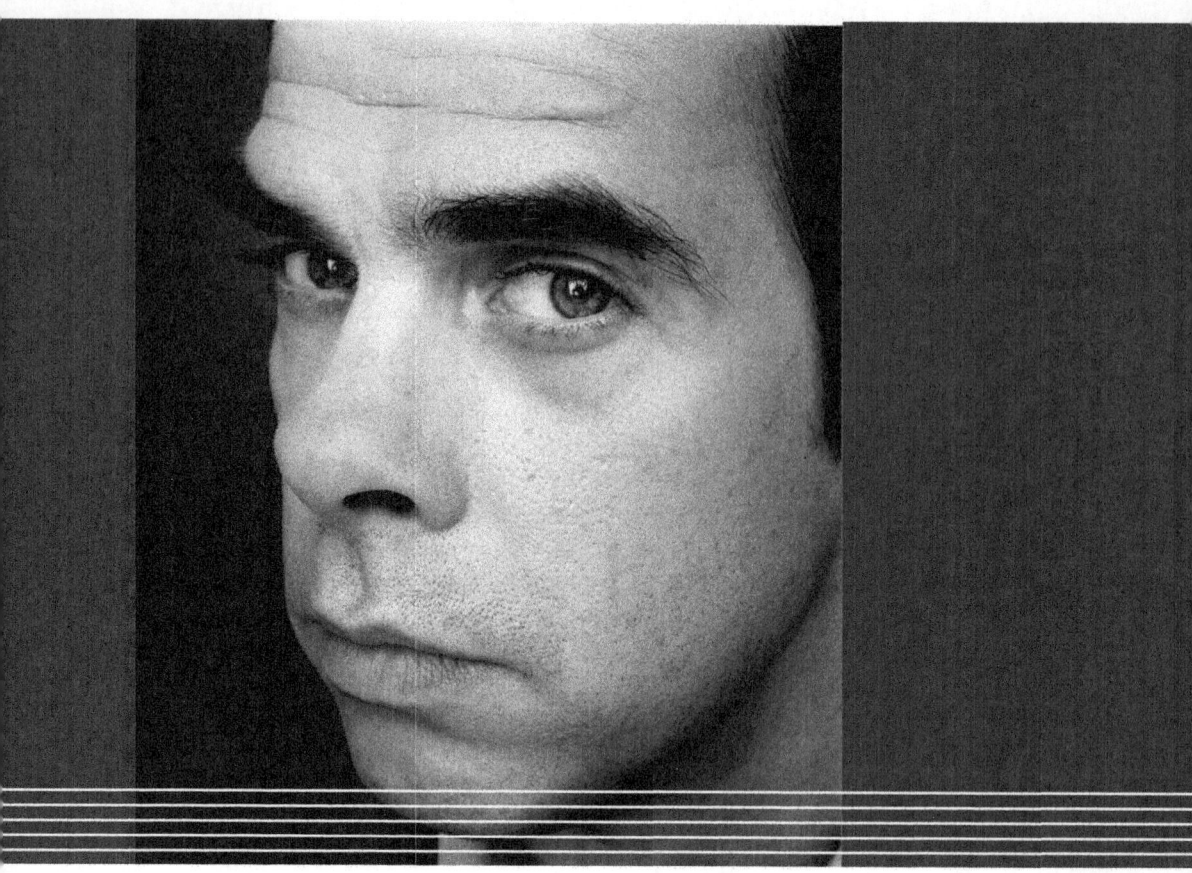

NICK CAVE

HOVE, ENGLAND, MAY 2004

Nick Cave is a spiritual man, so I decided the best way to start was with a confession.

"I was a complete Nick Cave virgin," I said boldly. "I'm not sitting here before you having spent twenty years falling at your feet. It was a real experience for me to learn your work. I went on a journey."

"Oh, good," he responded. "And why hadn't you listened to it before?"

"I never went in that direction," I admitted. "I think the kind of music that I was into might be the kind of music you would abhor."

"And you thought that I was a miserable bastard and you didn't want to know," Cave said, eyebrows raised.

"Something like that, yes."

He nodded. "Well, I know deep down that I will always be kind of marginal and that my music isn't going to be universally liked, that your average person, whatever that may be, is not going to really take to my view of things. But it's the only view I have; it's not something that I can do anything about. And I happen to be very fond of my view of things, so I don't have any desire to do anything differently. But I do understand that it's not for everybody."

"Would you want to be for everybody?"

"No. I guess I don't really want to be for everybody."

And so it was that after many years of withstanding interviews with avid journalists falling over themselves to impress Cave with their knowledge and ardour, of usually giving them twenty minutes tops either by phone or in a hotel room during the promotional round for a new album, resulting in stories that invariably begin with a reference to how "Nick Cave hates giving interviews", the "miserable bastard" of alternative rock spent three pleasurable hours talking about his songwriting. With the intermittent sounds of neighbourhood traffic and seagulls in the background, we sat together in his "office"—an unkempt one bedroom flat— after first meeting at his home around the corner.

During the interview the phone rang a few times; usually it was his personal assistant, checking that he was okay, wondering why I was still there. One call was from his elderly aunt from Melbourne, who was in England and visiting him that weekend. Cave was extremely relaxed. It was his first day off in months, having worked relentlessly in Paris and London on his new album, *Abattoir Blues/The Lyre of Orpheus*, and the flat-cum-office was in good need of airing and cleaning. But it was quiet, private and comfortable for Cave, who liked to take many long thoughtful pauses when answering questions, and who laughed and made me laugh a lot.

I particularly enjoyed his anecdotes about encounters with Rolf Harris and Barry Humphries. While feeling more Australian than ever, and visiting home regularly, Cave doubted he would feel comfortable enough to live back there in the foreseeable future. The journey, personal and creative, that Cave has taken since leaving Melbourne in 1980 has been long and arduous but is by no means over. It's not a happily-ever-after place that he's in. He might be living a less troubled life, but it's his ability to summon the dark side that keeps his journey evolving.

The journey I took to get to Cave, as I indicated to him, was more than a drive down an English motorway. To venture through Nick Cave's recorded output chronologically is to travel across the map of a songwriter's heart laid out bare, tortured and loving. It's a challenging journey, sometimes painful, always confronting, occasionally bright, sometimes funny and often luminous and magical. God, love—particularly the loss of it—and death are his main themes. Macabre violence is but one expression of it—certainly one that his followers have relished—but devotion, holy or secular, and a love of life are also paramount. Cave's belief system was always, in its own warped way, life-affirming, and it brought him to this point, living quietly in a genteel English seaside town that reminds him of his old stomping ground in Melbourne, and is not too far removed in character from his quiet beginnings in country Victoria.

He was born on 22 September 1957 in Warracknabeal, one of four children, to academic and religious parents, and grew up in Wangaratta before being sent to Caulfield Grammar School in Melbourne, where he met Mick Harvey, his lifelong musical collaborator. Their first band, The Boys Next Door, debuted in a suburban church hall in August 1977 (more than any other Australian band that began on the date of Elvis Presley's death, Cave's debut was perhaps the most portentous) and immediately created fear, loathing and fervour in the hearts of those fascinated by his wild antics. A self-destructive culture of alcohol and heroin permeated his creativity for most of two decades, but at no time has Cave been anything less than prolific. With his second band, The Birthday Party, and then Nick Cave & The Bad Seeds, which has survived with some personnel changes for more than twenty years and fourteen albums, through living in London, Berlin, São Paulo and now Hove, Cave's muse has stayed present. Plays, poetry, a novel, film scripts, film scores, acting roles, lectures—all were slotted in around addiction and rehabilitation, intense and sometimes public love affairs, raising children, loving God and writing songs.

Cave's influences have encompassed Elvis Presley, Johnny Cash, Lou Reed, Van Morrison, Bob Dylan and Leonard Cohen to name a handful. But from the dark southern gothic, biblical and savage musical turns in songs such as "Tupelo" and "The Mercy Seat" to grisly murder ballads, tender pieces of spiritual devotion like "The Ship Song" and "Into My Arms", and the bucolic imagery in newer songs like "There She Goes, My Beautiful World" and "Breathless", Cave has offered up a style that is unashamedly derivative yet completely, uniquely his own. He has never adhered to musical trends, existing solely in a Nick Cave world. And it's so vast and complex a world that even three hours with him is barely enough time to scratch the surface of it. Entranced by the journey I had taken so far, I was willing to try.

Has the way you write songs changed since the earliest days?
Yep. I've always worked hard at it, but these days, at least for the last five years, I work a very strict routine with songwriting. Which comes to a degree with a lifestyle change as well. Getting up early, coming into this room and staying here till about five o'clock. I do that every day that I'm not on tour or making records or doing other things. And I guess that's something to do with some notion that the muse is unreliable.

So you have to be on standby for it?
Yeah. To walk in and be prepared. And so this office, to me, represents periods of incredible frustration and also amazing periods.

Does it get easier, the process of connecting with the muse?
You have less doubts. The way that I write is, I have a project to do, and I come in and do it. I say, "Today I'm going to start writing songs for the new record." Invariably there's a three-week period of not being able to write anything, and it's a deeply frustrating period. But that becomes less and less so, simply because I know now after fourteen albums that eventually it comes. And I can see very clearly the way that it comes. With one song that's often about not being able to write anything, but a couple of lines suggesting something else for the next song, and this sort of thing grows until you can cut the front ones off, and then start, and you've got some substantial songs.

So the first one is just like warming up.
Yeah, and it's usually very tentative and frightened and conservative. Really not knowing what to write about. But I find that if I'm writing for a particular project, then the songs begin to feed off each other and they begin to suggest the next song.

You're never flooded with inspiration between projects? You might just be walking along with the kids and an idea for a song comes to you?
No. I'm taking everything in and my inspirations come from everywhere. They come from the good and the bad and the beautiful and the ugly and deeply flawed things and extraordinary things. They come from watching really bad movies, from watching really great movies, listening to really bad music, great music, I find everything is either telling me what not to do or what to do. So you absorb stuff without really realising it.

But you're not taking notes?
I'm not taking notes. And it's almost a rule of thumb that I don't work outside this office. I feel that I give a large amount of my time to this; I work it as a job. A job which I love. And it's also necessary not to be thinking about it. It's not as easy and as cut and dry as that, obviously. But I don't think creatively in the company of other people. I don't think creatively with my children. My mind doesn't work in the same way as it does when I'm alone here. I need solitude, I need the phone not to ring, I need friends not to visit.

You've said that you filled the void in your life left by your father's early death by writing. While you've written a novel, plays and film scripts, why have you focused most of your energy on writing songs? Is the song a more powerful form of art?
Yes. It's because music is right up there at the top of the ladder in regard to the effect that it can have on me. As opposed to the effect that a movie can or even a book can have on me. I love the immediacy of music, the reliability of a song, that you can play it again three weeks later and it still does the same thing to you, and the mystery of the whole thing. I don't know why one note alone is just this kind of idiot noise but you put another note next to it that suddenly can turn into something that can change your life.

I suppose there's something in the fact that my father always considered rock music to be right down the bottom. Like it was something not even really worth wiping your shoes on. My father drummed that literature and poetry were the great spiritual aspirations of mankind. I always felt like I was doing the wrong thing with music; I should have been doing something more worthwhile. Until it suddenly dawned on me that I was. That actually, music to me means a hell of a lot more, it reaches a deeper part of me than books that I've read.

But your work is poetic and literate.
Well, it is, yes. I try to combine the two. And I do hope that my father would be able to see what I did now and review his opinion.

How do you think your father would view your lyrical work now?
I think he'd be jealous.

Jealous of the quality or of your success?
Both. [*Laughs*]

Do you hold your body of work up as a worthy example of literary achievement?
On a good day, yes I do. On a bad day, definitely not. The whole thing with writing and making music is that when I'm in the moment with it, I feel like a different person, I feel like what I'm doing is the greatest thing not only that I have done but that has ever been done. It's this extraordinary feeling. I get the same feeling performing live on stage, that it feels like I'm exactly the kind of person that I always wanted to be. Unfortunately, when I go off stage or when I finish a record and it gets sent back to me and I have it in my hands, it's very anticlimactic. I realise I'm just this guy like everybody else. But the feeling that I get in here, when I feel like I'm really doing something that's great, is beyond any other feeling that I get.

So when I talk about coming in here and I do it as a job, I don't mean that in any demeaning way to what I'm actually doing. It's not a cynical activity. One of the reasons why I never listen to my music back or never listen to live recordings of what I do is because of this terrible fear I have that I won't be able to regain that feeling once I actually look at it.

When Johnny Cash died, you wrote in a tribute piece that you lost your innocence with him at the age of nine or ten, and previously you had no idea about rock 'n' roll. You said, "I watched him and, from that point, I saw that music could be an evil thing, a beautiful, evil thing." Why evil?
I think at the time, as a young kid, I suddenly realised that it could represent something other than the stuff that my mother and father were playing, which was not of any particular interest to me, it was classical music basically. Just in the same way as my kids relate to evil things. They want to dress up and they want to be the bad guy. That's pretty much what I was getting at, that music could be done by the bad guy. It could be great, much more exciting.

Was that then the beginning of your lifelong fascination with iniquity or had you already been aware of it through your relationship with the church?
[*Sighs*] I'm not sure if I have a lifelong fascination with iniquity. [*Laughs*] A lot of my songs, probably all of my songs, are dramatic in the sense that they have a beginning and they have an end and they have a narrative curve, and often a moral at the end and a verse that sums up what I've been talking about. I've been writing that way for a long time; it's just the way I think about things. In any movie or in any story there needs to be conflict, or else there isn't a story. And I think that works in my narrative songs.

But your subject matter has been on the nasty side as opposed to the happy, fluffy side.
I don't really relate to the happy, fluffy side. In the music that I like I relate to tragedy and to sadness and to violence, to aggressiveness. I find that exciting and I haven't ever thought

about that or questioned that. At the same time I find certain songs of praise very exciting as well, but a song of praise or a good uplifting song is usually suggesting an evilness by its absence. What I'm not interested in is songs that don't address that at all.

You've said, "All love songs must contain *duende*." Deep sorrow. If a love song, or any song, is never truly happy, how do you account for the heartfelt joy in the songs of, say, Stevie Wonder, some of the Motown songs, or a song like "Wonderful World"?
I think that "Wonderful World" is putting forward almost a polemic, that it is a wonderful world. It's saying we are all suffering, and we may see this world as a bad place, but I'm here to tell you that it's a wonderful world, the dark sacred night and the bright blessed day, and to look for these kinds of things. And I think that's a very beautiful thing, but in some way it's the springboard to the notion that it actually isn't a good world.

So a song like Stevie Wonder's "For Once in My Life" is suggesting the fact that the rest of his life isn't happy.
There you go, yeah. For me, music is a good thing. It's not a bad thing. In the world that we have today, which seems to me so destroyed and exhausted by the horror of it, to be able to get up and play music is a good thing, it doesn't matter what you're singing about. I really cling to that, that what I'm doing is a positive, life-affirming, God-driven thing to me. It doesn't matter what I'm writing about. It's a great thing to be a musician; it's a great thing to be a songwriter. And it's a very pure thing, and to somehow have a deep understanding of the purity of it and not do things to violate that.

How does a songwriter summon deep sorrow? Does one have to have experienced it?
Everyone's experienced sorrow. I don't think I've experienced it any more than anyone else. I don't ever consider myself to have been an unhappy person. I've had troubles like anyone else, so I don't know.

It's interesting that in the joy of your marriage, you wrote a song called "My Sorrowful Wife".
Well, you met her.

She looked pretty chirpy to me.
She is chirpy. But there is a sadness that lives in my wife, that I've noticed. That I noticed from the start and I found deeply attractive.

Do you think it's a brave thing to focus on that sadness, where an average songwriter might have written some glib, happy song about being newly wed?
I wouldn't want to demean our marriage. [*Laughs*] I'm reluctant to talk about this a lot, the sorrow thing, because I don't like the idea of putting myself as a miserable, sorrowful person who sits around and mopes. Because I'm absolutely not like that, I never have been like that. But I find that the basic words that can be used to express sadness, and also to express violence, are much more interesting than the words to describe happiness. It comes from there.

There is a fine line between despair and humour in much of your work. Have you felt misunderstood?

Yes. Humour is really important to me. Always has been, and I guess more and more so. In that it helps provide some kind of levity when you are writing quite a despairing lyric, and people don't just dismiss it as, "God, I really don't want to have to listen to that kind of thing!" Most of my comic songs, if you want to call them that, are pretty sorrowful states of affair underneath the whole thing. And I like that, that the first response is to laugh. It's laughter in the dark, inevitably. But I also just really enjoy it; it's entertaining for myself here alone to write stuff that I'm smiling about when I'm writing it.

Does it concern or bother you if people don't get your sense of humour?

It doesn't really. It does bother me that people dismiss what I do because they're under the impression that I'm just this ...

Lugubrious.

That it's just this miserable shit. "Oh, I don't listen to that kind of stuff." Because of what they've read about it. When in actual fact they could quite possibly enjoy it.

If you wake up and you're particularly happy, it's a beautiful day like today, and you walk down here, where does the sorrow come to you from?

It's irrelevant. My moods, such as they are, seem to have nothing to do with my circumstances whatsoever. It's really to do with the writing and the use of words, and rhyme. If I can sit down and write a line, then put another one next to it and it rhymes beautifully, it echoes back and forth in the right way, and it can be deeply sad, it can make me happier than anything, I can feel extraordinarily happy about that. It has nothing to do with my emotional state, what I write. I can be real happy and write a sad song. I only have to sit down and play an A minor chord. It just puts you in that kind of frame of mind; musically, that chord suggests all the sorrow in the world.

Do you intend the music to convey mood and atmosphere equally to the lyrics, or is music mainly there to serve the lyrics?

I think one of my problems recently, in the last three or four records, the music has taken a secondary place. This new record that I've made, I've had a completely different songwriting process than the last ones in order to rectify that. It was much more band-oriented, it allowed them to be involved in the writing of the music. They had some stake in it, as opposed to just doing the songs that I've brought along. And that's improved things immensely.

I found *And No More Shall We Part* a very musical album.

It's not that the songs were musically uninteresting; it's just that I felt that the band hadn't been able to flex their muscles in the music. In particular that record, actually. This new one, which is a double album, it's very different, in the sense that it's much more powerful and much more convincing musically. Within the playing. I'm not talking about the chordal structures or the songs themselves, but in the playing of it.

And that's an important component for your writing, the band's involvement? When you sit in here and you sketch out a song, just you and your piano, that's a complete song, is it not?
Yeah, it's important for me to be able to know that the song that I've just written works at its most basic level, which is sitting and playing it at the piano. That I can take it back home to my wife and say, "I wrote this." I don't say, "Well, when the drums come in here, it's going to be good." It's good, I could play it at a party—not that I would, not that I go to parties—but it works on that basic level. Which is a great thing. But going into the studio, some songs didn't get taken from that basic level.

Is that because they were so complete?
Yeah, because they sounded convincing in that state. So that the last record, I had three other members of the group and I went into a very small studio in Paris and said, "Right, we're going to write songs." I didn't have any lyrics, I didn't bring any chords, anything. It was just, "Alright, you're going to help write them as well."

When did you write the lyrics?
I went back and wrote the words for the music that we'd come up with.

Do you do a lot of rewriting?
This record I did. This record I kept coming back and working away at them. What tends to happen to me is that songs can often start off with untruths or things that are unauthentic, or you've read something and you like that, and you write it up and then you rhyme it and then you suggest something else. But you have these lines in here that aren't really your own. A song that's written quickly often can have that kind of stuff left in. You forget whether it's meaningful to you or not. It just sounds alright on the page. And those lines really come back to haunt you, when you're playing live and you're thinking, "Fuck, why didn't I get rid of that?"

Is there a line in a song that you perform regularly that you wish that you had changed?
Yeah. There's a song, "The Loom of the Land", which has, "The elms and the poplars were turning their backs." Which I thought was really nice. And then I was reading *Lolita*, and it said, "The elms and the poplars were turning their backs", and it's like, oh, right. I read that and wrote it down, stuck it in the song and didn't go back to sort that out.

But people borrow from each other all the time.
People do borrow all the time; people do steal all the time. And I don't really have any problem with that. But I don't like the idea of someone reading *Lolita* and going, "Oh. How often has he done that?"

Do you overwrite? Do verses get discarded?
Yeah. A lot gets discarded. I had to edit a lot on this new record, I was really pushing to get the songs shorter. I succeeded sometimes and didn't other times. You become very attached to stuff, and sometimes you write a lot of sprawling songs, it's obviously got three verses too many in it, but it's like, "Oh, I don't want to lose that one, and I don't want to lose that one ..." But I do try and edit stuff down to keep it.

What does the piano offer you as a songwriting tool?
The A minor chord. [*Laughs*] I love the piano. I wish I played guitar. I know I'd write totally differently. Each year I vow that I'm going to learn the guitar and I never do.
But the piano's a deeply soulful instrument, a sad-sounding instrument. It sounds really good on its own. And the piano certainly has an influence over the types of songs that I write. I've always written on the piano, or I've not written on anything at all, just sung the bits.

Was "The Mercy Seat" written at the piano or did that actually come to you away from the instrument?
That was written in the studio. That was just a bunch of words and I came up with that slowly descending chordal thing. Mick came up with the verse chords and we stuck them together. That is a really good song and it can be played in a thousand different ways and I don't think we've ever done a concert where we haven't played that song. It's like what I was saying before, that song works, if I just sat down and played it now and sang it, it works perfectly well on that level. And that's a testament to a good song, as far as I'm concerned.

Many have commented on the long repetition of the chorus at the end. Repetition has been a common structural device in your writing, through to and most notably in "Babe I'm on Fire" on *Nocturama*. What's the purpose of repetition within a song?
It's a musical thing as much as anything else, in that you can just keep shifting it up a notch each time and I have a band who can do that. It's like Spinal Tap, taking it to eleven. You can take it to twelve, thirteen, fourteen, it just keeps rolling on, and I love being able to do that. And having a basic structure within a song to be able to do that. Especially once you don't rely on a chorus to get in the way of that.

When did you start reading the Bible closely for your own gratification rather than because you were instructed to?
When I was about twenty-two.

Do you draw your biblical references off the top of your head, or are you constantly re-reading it and looking for new inspirations there?
I go through periods. And I'm not reading it to get stuff out of it for my lyrics; it's not like a thesaurus or lyrical tool. I read the thesaurus for that.

You read the thesaurus?
Yeah, it's sad, but I do sit and read the thesaurus. Because I love words. I just think, oh God, what is that? And look it up and it means this and I find that really exciting. About the most exciting thing in the world. [*Laughs*] And I've always been like that. I can remember being eleven or so and picking up an Edgar Rice Burroughs Tarzan book and reading something about "the lazy lion waving his tail spasmodically", and I thought, God! I've always been really turned on by that.

A thesaurus is like a map.
Yes. It's just such a wonderful idea and adventure.

And the Bible you read for pleasure?
The Bible I read for spiritual enlightenment, I would say. I read the Bible these days to be reminded that the words of Christ are actually to me the right message. And in this world the words of Christ have been so violated and hijacked and used for deeply unrighteous political purposes that it's important for me to go back to the Bible and remind myself that I'm not absolutely out of my mind to be thinking that Christ has something worthwhile to say. That's why I read the Bible these days. But it is an incredibly beautiful book.

Do you read the New Testament now more than the Old Testament?
I've always been more interested in the New Testament. Apart from very early on. The Old Testament to me really has been nothing more than an extraordinary kind of storybook with wonderful tales. But the New Testament spoke in a very different way to me.

I'm interested in your focus on antiquity, creating characters and stories from the past, in preference to contemporary settings.
I tried to create an alternate environment or arena in which these stories could play out, that was a kind of hybrid of different things that I was interested in. But I think it's become less that way over the last records. I've got the word "frappuccino" on the last album. [*Laughs*] "I woke up this morning with a frappuccino in my hand."

That's contemporary.
Yes, very. There is some sport in putting in a very contemporary thing. There's a rather pleasing jarring effect to have some of these elements suddenly come into a song that feels pastoral or timeless and adds a kind of ugly jerk into the times that we actually live in.

You described love songs as the idea of "the cry of one chained to the earth, to the ordinary and to the mundane, craving flight, a flight into inspiration and imagination and divinity". Did "Into My Arms" exemplify that?
I wrote that particular song under very difficult circumstances. I wrote a few songs like that, but that one I wrote about three days into some drug rehabilitation clinic. You were allowed out of the clinic if you went to church, and I had gone to church that day, it was a Sunday,

and I'd come back and I was feeling very ill, and sat down and wrote that very quickly, and I didn't have anything there to play it on, I had the melody in my head. So even though that particular sojourn into rehabilitation didn't work [*Laughs*], at least I got a good song out of it.

And had you taken that flight?
Well, I certainly felt that I'd done something worthwhile. Doing that meant more to me than why I was actually in there at the time, put it that way.

You said that through the use of language you wrote God into existence. Is writing always a link to divinity?
It's one of a million things you can do that's a link to divinity. Living is a divine act in some way, and I feel the idea of divinity is something that reflects the good in us and that can be claimed in all sorts of different ways. I don't think that you have to be involved in creative things to have a link to divinity, or that I'm doing something particularly special. I think you can get that same link sawing a piece of wood or looking after your children or being an accountant if it's something that you feel is rewarding to you and elevating.

Not all songwriters feel divinely inspired when they write songs.
Why I'm being hedgy about this is, "divinely inspired" seems to suggest that you sit at the piano and God comes down and it's not like that at all. It's just most of the time numbingly hard work.

Why is the love song "the truest and most distinctive human gift" for God? Does God need gifts from man?
I think it might be nice for Him, don't you?

Some songwriters believe songs are gifts *from* God. From the divine, from a higher power.
I think it's a bit of each. I think that in some respects if we didn't do things that in some way glorified God, God wouldn't exist to us. That it's these things that breathe life into Him.

What's your feeling now about "Mutiny in Heaven"? If you listened to it right now in this room, would you reconnect with the place you were at when you wrote it?
I know very well when I wrote that song. That was basically a bass line that the band played to and it sounded great in the studio, but I hadn't written anything for it. We had one day to go, and I was sent home to write the lyrics for it. And I stayed up all night and came back and sang all this stuff over the top of the bass line. And Rowland Howard, who was the guitarist at the time, said, "Well, where do I play in this? All it is, is just this fucking singing all the time!" Blixa Bargeld was in the studio at the time, visiting, and he goes, "Oh, I could put something in there." And he did these wonderful bell chords that he does through it.

I love that song. I couldn't write a song like that any more. I couldn't hold true to some of the viewpoints and I couldn't be bothered writing a song like that any more. But for when it was done and the age I was at, I thought it was really good.

How did "The Ship Song" come to you?
I think what happened was there was another song on a record that we made before that, which I didn't have all the lyrics for when it came time to do the vocal. I can't remember what song it was. So some of the lyrics I just pretended to sing stuff, ad-libbed, incomprehensible mumbo jumbo, not even words, just mumbled, meaningless nonsense. But then the *King Ink* book was being put together, a complete collection of my lyrics, so I had to come up with the words. I didn't want to write, "Woah yeah, come on, baby, get down, blah, blah blah," or whatever nonsense it was, so I wrote "Come sail your ships around me" instead. And then later on I was looking at the printed lyrics and thought, "God, that's good, you know, that's a nice image." It reminded me of *Gulliver Travels*, of a giant being circled and subdued by a fleet of tiny ships. I thought that that line deserved a better song. So I worked on it a bit and wrote "The Ship Song".

As your most covered song, does the fact that other artists want to sing it validate it for you in any way?
Yeah, very much so. I mean, depending on the artist, obviously. I'm always happy for people to cover my songs. Because it's enormously flattering.

By the stage of *Let Love In,* you were saying that you were drawing far less, if at all, on outside influences and relying on your own power to influence yourself. But I did find that "Nobody's Baby Now" was reminiscent of Bob Dylan. It could sit really nicely alongside "Just Like a Woman".
I wouldn't mind that.

It didn't surprise me that Paul Kelly had done a version of it.
Right. Way back I was asked to write a song for Johnny Cash. It was the beginning of these American Recordings where he was getting different people to write songs for him, and he asked me to write a song, and that was the one that I wrote. And after I thought, "Fuck it, I'm not handing that over. I really love that song, and I'm going to do that."

As you wrote it with the intention of Johnny Cash singing it, was it something different from what you would have ordinarily written for yourself?
Possibly. One of the things that I really enjoy and value and find to help enormously is when I'm asked to write music for people, or asked to write songs for films or whatever. A case in point is with Wim Wenders. He would literally ring me up and say, "I'm making a new movie, it's about this, I want a song about time." And I'd go, "Alright, I'll have it to you in a week." And would come in and write something. It's not for me, it's completely for him, so I feel a complete freedom to write whatever I want to write. I feel suddenly that it's not totally my responsibility. Because it becomes a craft thing. Purely craft.

Is that where the thesaurus comes into play more than ever?
The thesaurus is always in play. And it's the same with other sorts of writing. Scriptwriting.

I was asked by Johnny Hillcoat, "I want you to write a film about bushrangers". Which I have no particular understanding of or great love for, they're just Australian bushrangers, we all love 'em, but I didn't have any particular fascination with them. But I just found it very easy to do, to write things for other people. Very freeing, and you learn a lot by doing that. You go other places that you would not normally go.

Again, it's like this notion of a map; you're following paths.
It's also that Nick Cave and The Bad Seeds have always been a very insular set-up. I don't have much to do with other musicians, I don't hang out with other musicians, I don't talk about music much. It's always felt very much to me about coming into an office and working away on my own. And the times that I'm dragged out of that can be immensely rewarding. I did road songs for Marianne Faithfull for her new record, the music to three songs for her, and then went into the studio and recorded them with her. And certainly you learn enormous amounts of stuff doing that, watching the way someone else does something. You find yourself suddenly growing. That happened recording with Johnny Cash, and that's why it's interesting to read your book, because you find out the way other people go about things.

When you were with Johnny Cash, did you actually talk about songwriting?
He did. I was too busy polishing his shoes, you know. But he had his way of recording, which was actually quite similar to mine, in that I don't think he's the kind of guy who likes to do fifty takes of something, he just wants to get it done. And he was quite ill, so it had to be done now or not at all.

Are you often in awe like that or is that quite a rare thing for you?
Well, I'm not often in awe, but when I am in awe I'm in awe. We just did here in Brighton on the weekend this Leonard Cohen concert. That was really interesting because it was a lot of different singers singing Leonard Cohen songs. And Leonard Cohen songs are done in a particular way; you always know they're Leonard Cohen songs, even though the musicians change and the musical styles change. It was really interesting to see how brilliant these songs were in the sense that they could be done in any form. These songs are just extraordinary. And there's so many of them. But that was nerve-racking, because I ended up getting "Suzanne". It was the one song I really didn't want to have to do.

Why? Is it too great a song?
The pressure. The pressure's too much. [*Laughs*] It's so easy to fuck up; it's actually a really difficult song to sing.

You've also recorded the work of other writers, especially on *Kicking Against the Pricks*. Why has it been important through your career to perform and record covers?
It wasn't an important thing to do before we did that, but we certainly benefited so much from the *Kicking Against the Pricks* record musically that it turned out to be really

440

important. We just did it at the time for something to do. We felt that there were certain expectations about our music that it could benefit us if we destroyed those expectations. But it proved to be very valuable because we found out we could play all different kinds of music. And so that opened things up a lot.

It was a great selection of songs. I found the inclusion of "By the Time I Get to Phoenix" interesting. It's an unconventionally structured song for Jimmy Webb, being that it has no chorus. Is that what appealed about that song, were you paying tribute to Webb's overall mastery in pop songwriting, or was it more about that theme of a relationship ending, as all must do?
It was all of those things. There were certainly versions of it that were great, that influence that version possibly more than the original. Isaac Hayes did his twenty-minute version of it.

By which time he actually got to Phoenix.
Well, he does a long explanation about what women are actually like; it's very funny. How men have just got to go out.

So what did you take back with you into your own songwriting from the intense focus on other writers' work?
It was mostly that I learned how to sing in a different way on that record. I discovered a quality in my voice that I didn't realise was there, and it was to sing softly up close to the microphone. That there was something that was actually quite attractive about my voice, which I had absolutely no idea of before. And that consequently allowed me to write different sorts of songs, where they could be pulled back.

When describing the process of writing "Far from Me", you said, "I find quite often that the songs I write seem to know more about what is going on in my life than I do." What other songs depicted or foretold your life beyond your own awareness at that time?
There's a comical element to that whole conceit, that the songs are ruling my life.

I didn't think of it as songs ruling your life, more just life imitating art, maybe.
I don't know if I could think of another song like that. There are songs that I find quite difficult to extract from the events around the song and I find quite difficult to perform on occasions. I can just about perform that song now and see it as a song about a failed relationship without the actual relationship itself hijacking the song, and I'm kind of back there. Not that I have any particular bad feelings about that, but it's just that I'm singing it about a particular woman and situation that I don't have any particular feelings for any more. And in some respects I see that as the failing of that song. That I can't lift it out of that, because it is so specific. But I'm sure that for other people it's probably the beauty of that song.

Is it necessary for somebody listening to the earlier songs to have knowledge of your personal relationships, inner and external conflicts, your addictions, beliefs or literary influences at those times to fully understand them?

I would hope not. If it is, then it's what I'm saying, there's a certain failure in the songwriting. You don't need all that. And it has been something I've been very conscious of and that I've been trying to pull away as a character so that the songs can breathe a little bit more. That this character that I'm supposed to be suffocates a lot of these songs. It feels like that to me.

So I guess there's been, on some subconscious level, a certain amount of effort to make my life appear as uninteresting as possible. So that there's just nothing to talk about any more. I actually feel I lead an incredibly interesting life. It's not all about being in this office; I have so much more in my life. But it's stuff that no-one's really interested in talking about. So it's great.

Notwithstanding Kylie Minogue's considerable contribution, did you ever see "Where the Wild Roses Grow" as a commercial hit?

No.

It must have amused you to think about what all the people who bought the *Murder Ballads* album on the strength of that single would have made of it.

Yeah. I was on *Top of the Pops* two weeks running with Kylie, trying to fumble my way through the song. And then I remember being in a toy shop getting a toy for my son and this little kid coming up to me in a Power Rangers outfit, and he goes, "Are you that old guy that was on with Kylie Minogue the other night?" He was just this little kid but he really loved the song. And I'm just like, [*Under his breath*] "Oh, fuck off you little bastard." [*Laughs*] But it suddenly occurred to me that these people may even be buying the record, and it deeply troubled me.

"Are You The One That I've Been Waiting For?" on *The Boatman's Call* was so simple and guileless lyrically. Was it more difficult for you to write than your long, complex, literate story songs?

I think that's very beautiful, that song, and I was really pleased with the lyrics. I remember writing it in a taxicab on the way to Michael Hutchence's house, for some reason. It's easier for me to write a narrative than one that doesn't have a denouement or an end. I'm hardwired to write narrative type songs because there's a logic to that, in the whole structure of the song. You know when the song ends, it ends the way a story ends. I find those particular songs, the ones that are really narrative, like on *Murder Ballads*, really easy to write. All I do is get two characters, give them names, stick them in a song, and off they go.

And kill at least one of them.

And yeah, [*Laughs*] one kills the other, and you say it's not a good thing at the end and move on to the next one. But just on that point, a lot of these narrative songs, I don't know what the story's going to be. It's not like I've thought of the story and I'm going to put it in words, it's very much about inventing a character and the scenario and letting it play out. The songs write themselves in some kind of way. The other ones seem strange for me to write.

Because they're so exposed? Because you're the character?
It might have something to do with that. But I'm the character in a lot of them, even in the narrative ones. Not so much the *Murder Ballads* record, but a lot of the deeply personal ones are still narrative. "Far from Me", that's still a narrative song with a beginning and an end. They are harder to write because I don't really know how to end them, they're just this chunk of stuff and I don't know where they should stop. I suppose they should stop at four minutes, or something like that.

Is that what you do then? You let the structure guide you?
Yeah, I write three verses or four.

"Love Letter" on *No More Shall We Part* is something very grand, like the best of Webb or Newman or the grand popular music composers. Were you pleased with that song?
Yes. I like that, it took a very long time to write, and went through all different sorts of versions. I remember a friend of mine coming up, I'd been living at his house in Ireland, working out there, and he heard me play it live a year or so later, and he said, "God, that song turned out really well. 'Cause when you were playing it at my place it sounded like the worst fucking thing I've ever heard." So it did go through a lot of versions. But it had the basic chorus, "Go get her Go get her/ Love Letter Love Letter". I like that song.

Can I name some of your songs we haven't mentioned yet and get your responses to them? "From Her to Eternity".
I guess it's one of my favourite songs that I've written, as a piece of music, especially, and have great joy in playing live. We stopped playing it for a while and brought it back in on the last tour and lyrically and musically it propels forward. I remember writing that sitting up in bed with Anita Lane, she helped me write that. And conceiving this notion that the object of desire is being up on the next floor, and all of the connotations of that. I thought the recorded version of it was extraordinary; I'd never heard anything like Blixa's guitar in that song, and I've never heard anything like it since. From anywhere. It's just so out there. It's so powerful, but it's basically piano-driven. I heard an early Górecki piece or something like that, done on the piano, which sounded incredibly similar to it, years later. But it just has this magic about it.

"Deanna".
"Deanna" was written about Deanna, based on "Oh Happy Day", and I like that one too.

I was interested in the contrast between the melody and the lyric.
Yeah, it's got a jaunty rock 'n' roll piece of music but it's a dark lyric. At the same time it, to me, really sums up that relationship that I had with that particular girl, which was a really fun, youthful relationship where anything goes. Lyrically it talks about that excitement of young love

without any responsibilities, where you feel you could just do anything. That's not necessarily anything good, it's anything bad as well. [*Laughs*] Deanna on the one hand really likes it, but on the other hand every time she says her name's Deanna, they go, "Oh, are you *that* Deanna?"

"Tupelo".
"Tupelo" is based heavily on a John Lee Hooker song. It welds the mythic flood of Tupelo, which he talks about in his song, with the Elvis thing.

How do you feel about that song now?
Well, it used the John Lee Hooker song as a kind of springboard for something else so I'm very much aware of that, and I'm aware that I took full songwriting credit for it. [*Laughs*] I was talking about that earlier, that you kind of wish now that you had have been a bit more generous in that respect. It's a good song, some great lines in that. "The sandman's mud" and all that spooky stuff.

Do you have lines in different songs that you relish the opportunity to sing?
Well, there's verses. I'm particularly proud of the first verse of "Nobody's Baby Now", which takes so long to get to the point. I've read the holy books and I've searched through the books on human behaviour and I've searched the world round, trying to work out why you're nobody's baby now. I like the way that stretches for so long to get to that line. It reminds me of "Tupelo Honey", the Van Morrison song, about all the tea in China, talking about getting the ship and putting all the tea in it and taking it out into the sea and dumping it into the sea, and you realise he's working on that "You're worth all the tea in China" line. It's just such a beautiful idea to expand on this cliché.

"The Weeping Song".
"The Weeping Song" was written very quickly. I wrote that in Brazil, walking from the place that I was living down to the bar, and that came out of nowhere, with very little thought. And there's a narrative thing going on. "The Weeping Song" isn't actually one of my favourites.

I was interested on that album, *The Good Son*, in the whole notion of calling a song a song—"The Weeping Song", "The Ship Song", etc. Do titles come to you easily?
No. Obviously in some the title's already there. But I think that was a bit of both. It was that I didn't know what to call "The Ship Song". It was just these lyrics and everyone kept calling it "The Ship Song" and then, "Well, we can do that with a few of them" type of thing.

"Papa Won't Leave You Henry".
I like that song a lot. That was another one written in Brazil. It's this sprawling lyrical thing. We were playing that as a very slow ballad on a different chordal structure altogether, which then became "Darker with the Day". It had a different melody, but very slow and it made for a very haunting thing. That song was composed over a long period of time and something that I would sing to my little son, Luke. It was kind of a nasty fucked-up lullaby.

444

Whether you're in London or Hove, Berlin, Brazil or Melbourne, does your physical environment affect what you're writing?

I'd like to say that it didn't, but actually I think it really does have an enormous effect. Living in England, which was a place that I hated to be but have spent an enormous amount of time in, I found I looked outside. The world that I was creating was not English, it was something else. And through living down here, I started to understand England and started to love certain aspects of it, which have definitely crept into the writing. A lot of the songs I think are very English, especially the pastoral side, the vegetation, the kind of animals that are in it, and the flowers, all of that stuff to me is very English. But it's an England that I don't really know much about, it's an England that I know more about from reading poetry. I enjoy setting songs up in these English pastoral settings that all seem to be on the point of collapse in some way. I'm interested in that old notion of England as the fair England, being some kind of New Jerusalem, almost like heaven. The ancient notion of England and the rolling green hills. And to use that for a stage where other things happen within it. I like the tension that's set up with that.

So England finds its way into your work now more than Berlin and Brazil did at the time you were writing songs there?

Berlin had a huge influence over me simply because it was a lifestyle influence; it was a place where we got some kind of recognition. We lived in London for a long time and people just thought we were this whacked-out band from Australia and didn't take us particularly seriously. But when we went to Berlin they didn't have these prejudices; they just liked us. So we suddenly got some positive attention and became part of the Berlin arts scene. But I wasn't interested in my songs becoming German.

You can't live in Brazil and it not have an impact. I mean visually, everywhere you look. It's so different and so beautiful and so horrible and such incredible extremes. For the first year in Brazil I was just constantly looking around me. I was living in São Paulo, which is a big, nasty city. But within that there were both sides of the coin there all the time.

How Australian do you think your songwriting is?

I think in some respects it's very Australian, because many aspects of the kind of world I've created are just pilfered from other lands, so that I've created my own setting and world for my songs to play out in. I have enormous love for much about Australia. The countryside, the bush and all that stuff. But there's bits of America and bits of England, and I've created my own unique land. I think that's quite similar to a lot of Australian cinema, to Australian songwriting, Australian society. It's largely a kind of hybrid, mongrel society.

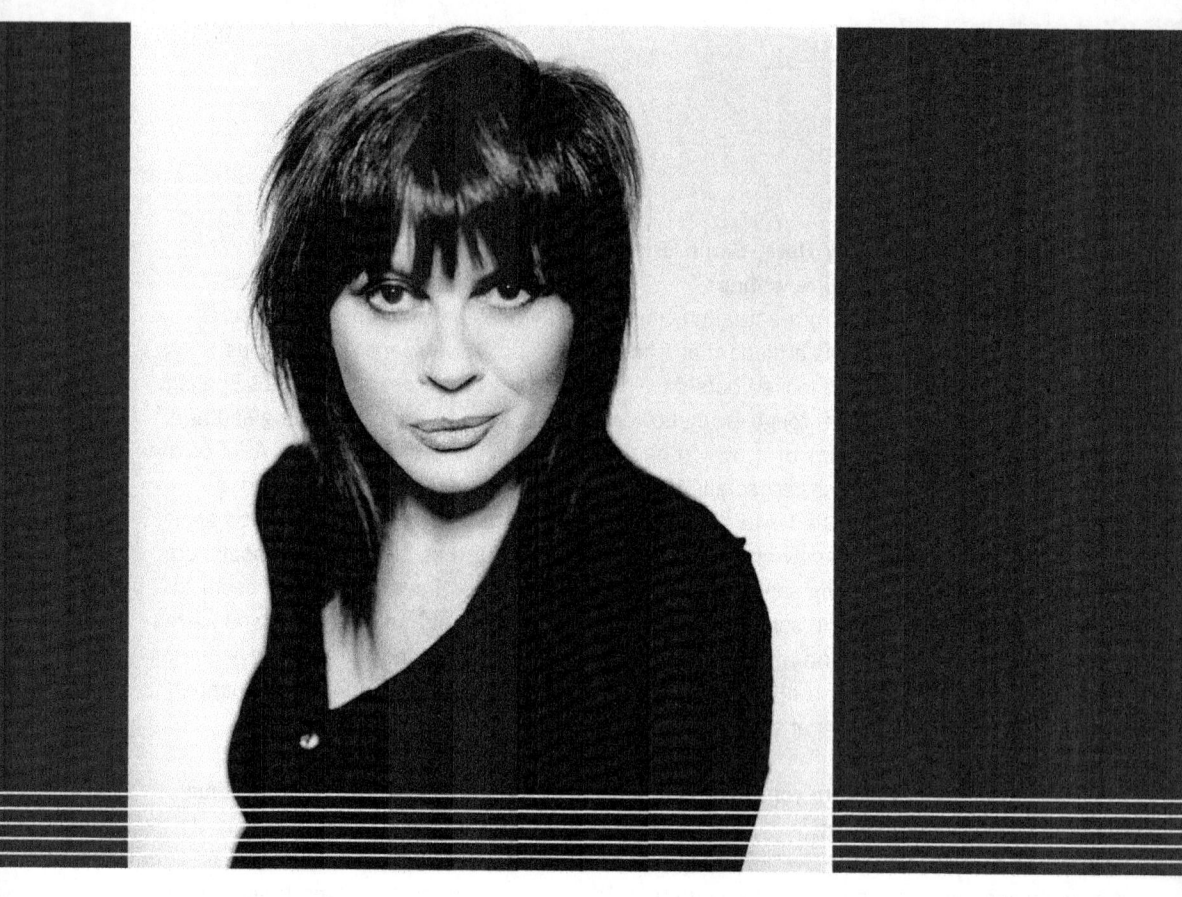

CHRISTINA AMPHLETT

SYDNEY, AUSTRALIA, MAY 2003

"I had my eighteenth birthday in prison."

It was early morning, and the curtains in Chrissie Amphlett's hotel room were drawn. Immaculately dressed and made up, Amphlett sat in a plush armchair in the faint light, drinking tea and telling me about her wild times as a busking gypsy, living out a version of James A Michener's *The Drifters*.

"I was travelling with two French people, we were in Torremolinos and I was singing in the streets. Franco was in power, and it was illegal to sing in the streets or eg or protest. We were all rounded up by the Guardia Civil, those little men with the Mickey Mouse hats and the machine guns. And we were put in a commissariat, the police station, for three days. Then we were taken out of there and put in the *penitenciaria*. I ended up spending six weeks in the Malaga Penitenciaria and then I was transported with about thirty men on a bus. I was in the cage at the front of the bus and I was taken from prison to prison every day, until we got to

Barcelona. I spent two weeks there in a beautiful prison run by nuns, in a huge dormitory full of French prostitutes. Then they put me on a little bus and drove me through the Pyrenees and dumped me on the French border. I got out and there was nothing in my passport."

A dark, disturbing life experience and no criminal record to show for it. Amphlett's retelling—and she has doubtless told the story numerous times—was romantic and almost tender. Life on tour with a rock band in Australia and America was much tougher, it seems. "When I was on the road with Simple Minds and Icehouse, at the beginning of Divinyls, all the road crew used to stand over me and carry on, and I thought, I've been there, I can cope with this."

For all her wild teenage years, indulging in sex, drugs and rock 'n' roll (not necessarily in that order) from the age of fourteen, Amphlett was actually very shy. She poured her heart out in confrontational lyrics—her first hit, "Boys in Town", was boldly autobiographical—and wore a school uniform with fishnet stockings, but inside she was insecure and often unable to assert herself within her own band. "I'm cream puff inside," said the woman who burst onto the popular music scene in 1981 with a torrent of attitude. Australian audiences had never experienced anything like her. She was, and to many still is, the country's foremost feisty, wild woman of rock.

Chrissy Amphlett was born in Geelong on 25 October; she preferred not to specify the year. "I'm a Scorpio," she said, indicating that had more significance than the date itself. Her parents had wide-ranging musical tastes, participating in musical theatre and opening their home to friends and relatives for parties filled with singing. An older cousin was Patricia Amphlett, aka Little Pattie. At the opposite end of the spectrum, Janis Joplin was the first major influence on Amphlett from the rock music world. "She was the wildest thing and I thought that she was it. I would try to get my voice to sound like her," she recalled, and then added that she cannot bear listening to Joplin today. "She's just too raucous," said the songwriter and performer whose breathy, shrill, uninflected vocal and sexually charged, often demonically possessed stage presence were the Divinyls' hallmarks.

When Amphlett met guitarist and budding songwriter Mark McEntee, their chemistry was instant. They began writing together immediately and formed the Divinyls as a vehicle for their music. Their songs had catchy pop hooks with a solid rock 'n' roll edge, and Amphlett's lyrics became more incendiary and ironic as the years went on. By 1991 the international hit "I Touch Myself" was superbly tongue in cheek.

The Divinyls toured and performed with many hard-rocking bands, from the Ramones and Aerosmith to U2 and INXS, but that kind of life had a time limit. Unlike Chrissie Hynde from The Pretenders, to whom Amphlett was often compared, pouting aggressively on stage in middle age was unappealing. As she matured, Amphlett spent time on her acting career, taking on memorable stage roles in *Blood Brothers* and *The Boy from Oz*. She also moved to New York, got married and started writing songs with a new collaborator for a planned solo album. The Divinyls, whose last album was recorded in 1996, were on indefinite hold. The passage of time seemed to have separated Amphlett and McEntee—for so long joined at the hip—more than geographically.

She was on a month-long visit with her mother in Geelong and on a very quick side-trip to Sydney when we met. She was busy but exuded tranquillity. There was a beautiful calm in

Amphlett's demeanour, yet enough of the cheeky spark remained in her eyes and her laugh to hint that while the wildness might have been subdued, it would never be gone for good. It was a reassuring thought.

As a teenager listening to the radio, were you at all focused on how pop songs were crafted?
Never even thought of that. No, never. Never studying the craft of pop songwriting. Listened to the Jackson 5, who I absolutely adored. And always loved the Supremes and Aretha Franklin. I had very varied taste.

Was there any influence from your musical cousin, Little Pattie?
Only the fact that she made it when she was fourteen, so I thought if I hadn't made it by the time I was fourteen it was all over. I thought it was possible. We used to watch her on the TV.

Was there anything happening musically in Australia that interested or inspired you when you were young?
Wendy Saddington was wild, I really liked her. I thought Renee Geyer was really good. But that's about all. Everything else was too showbizzy and the women were too nice. Women were nice girls in Australia that performed and sang. I always wanted to know what was really going on.

Did you have an idea of writing as a part of what you wanted to do in music?
No, I just used to do covers and it was not even about performance; I used to stand there and freak out. I was very shy; it was really hard. It wasn't until I put on the school uniform that I really freed myself up. Until then I was always in trouble with whatever band I was with, because I just used to stand there, I couldn't talk. But that really freed me up.

When did you first start writing songs?
When I was about five I was writing songs. It was funny, I used to get on the family piano and hammer them out and write songs, just repetitious things, line notes and riffs. But then I never pursued that.

Were you making up words as well to go with the melody?
Yeah.

Do you remember any of those songs from when you were five?
[*Sings*] "You do things to me, honey/ You do things to me, sugar/ You do things to me, and I like it." This was a five-year-old. Then the music was going bom, bom bom, bom.

It still could be a potential hit.
[*Laughs*]

Were you traumatised by the Spanish jail experience or creatively inspired?

Well, the coffee was really bad. Until I got used to it. I threw up but I got used to it. And I shared a cell with a gypsy who had her arm shot off. To get her off my back—because all the Arab girls, all the Moroccans were bisexual—I used to draw them. And that gave me power. I did a lot of portraits in there and that helped me survive. I had something that they wanted. I didn't really draw portraits before then, but when I was incarcerated—when you're incarcerated things come out, whether you find God or whatever you do to survive—I started drawing. I've got the drawings in storage down in Geelong. Dolores, who was the gypsy, on the night I was going to be deported, she took a lot of them. So I've got some. It's my only documentation. And the girls used to wail at night and put curses. It was only the Moroccan girls who really believed them. But they'd come out and they would have disfigured their faces themselves.

You didn't keep a journal or write down any prose at the time?

No, I just remember it. Around all that time I was a street singer, living that very sort of French romantic existence, and that's where it led me. But what I learned out of that was that my creativity was survival. It gave me power, to be actually creative for myself and help me survive. I didn't realise that then, but it was probably the first lesson in really expressing one's self in a form of survival.

When you did start writing, did you consciously draw on those experiences?

No, I was having a terrible relationship with this drummer and that's what "Boys in Town" came out of. I wrote it in the bath every day, sang it in the bath, "I am through with hanging 'round all the boys in town." I liked this guy and it was a hopeless relationship. But I'd been quite promiscuous, and because I was so wild when I was younger I had no sexual boundaries and I had no idea. My teens were quite troubled in that regard. So "Boys in Town" was a very freeing song for me in that when I wrote it, it cleared me to move on. Because it was the summing up of everything.

Did you write that before Divinyls formed?

Yes, I suppose. And then I met Mark and on the very first day we got together, he put the music to it. I'd written the lyrics and melody, but then Mark put all the guitar underneath.

Did you and Mark really meet at a choir performance?

I was singing in a 2CH choir. It was an eight-piece choir and I used to go there in my little punk ripped things. It was a way to develop the top range of my voice, which is all contributing to the way I sound. And by practising and singing in this choir I learned to sing with other people, because I was always a soloist and liked to be out the front. This gave me a discipline. It was so far away from what I wanted to be, but it was a sort of training for me. And Mark came to a performance because one of the persons in the choir said, "You should meet Chrissy." So that's how we met. I used to arrive to rehearse with the orchestra, little punky girl, black hair, totally not fitting in and it was crazy.

A little punky girl who clearly had an idea of furthering her career.
Oh, yeah, yeah, I was always very driven. That was my purpose and my focus and that was what kept me, that drive. Somehow that was my centre. Because I was very confused, but all ambition.

By this point you knew you wanted to write your own songs, then?
And to express and to also develop our own sound. It was also the punk days and I found that very inspirational because it was doing things differently, and it was honest. I saw Deborah Harry in a bathing suit, and I thought, okay, that's different. That changed things. Because up until then everything was quite conservative, to me anyway. It was Steely Dan and all that, which I hated. Slick stuff, which I just couldn't relate to and I couldn't work out how I was going to fit in. But the writing helped develop some sort of thing that was yours, and it was original.

Australia did have AC/DC and The Saints and a lot of those bands that weren't slick.
AC/DC I absolutely adored. I loved their spirit and they were so bad.

Who else from the punk genre inspired you?
Ian Dury, The Motels, everybody. Very freeing for the female.

When you started writing with Mark, was there a delineation of duties—him music, you lyrics? Or did you come to him with other melodies?
It sort of blended. Even though he had the instrument, so I always depended on the instrument. I couldn't put things in chords. Mark is very, very musical and he has an amazing knowledge of chords, and his slant on things was interesting. And together we had similar things that we wanted to achieve. We had similar taste. But yeah, I tended doing the words and melodies, and Mark did melodies, too. I would come up with a line or something in the music. But mostly it was because he was holding the instrument.

Was there a deliberate intention to be quirky in parts, musically? "Science Fiction" is quite quirky in the beat.
Yeah, but that's Mark. Even though that's my drum fill. Not that I always came up with things like that, but I was always into little hooks and things; I loved that sort of stuff.

You came up with that interesting phrasing? The vocal doesn't strictly follow the melody.
No, and it developed. I remember standing in the studio when we were at Paradise, and I started singing, and Mark Opitz said to me, "You're going to be around a long time." Because I was singing it straight and then I started bending the melody. I don't know what happened, it just occurred. I think that stuck in my head; saying a positive thing like that was very affirming.

Your performance style has always been very visual, very provocative. Did you write songs to fit that image?

No, never. By the time I put on the school uniform we had all those songs, "Boys in Town", "Science Fiction", "Only Lonely", all that *Monkey Grip* period. I used to wear anything and just stand there. We used to perform a lot in the Cross. We made it to the Piccadilly, that hotel on Victoria Street where we used to work every Friday night for this priest, Father Cyn. And then I started to wear the school uniform. 'Cause it was an AC/DC thing. Girl schoolgirl. I was singing lyrics like "Boys in Town" and all that and it was very exposing and embarrassing for me. I'm standing up there telling everybody I'm a slut, basically, but I'm sick of it. And so when I put the school uniform on, it once-removed me because I had a character and also the school uniform was very submissive. So then I had to juxtaposition myself against that and I became assertive, because I couldn't be submissive. So somehow wearing suspenders and stockings made me, "Don't fuck with me then." Because here I am standing there, looking like this, nobody laugh at me and nobody fuck with me, and I'm singing a song like "Boys in Town."

But that then didn't give you the confidence to go back to Mark and say, "Great, we can write more of these really out-there songs because I feel safe now in my school uniform"?

No. I never wrote songs in my school uniform. It was never contrived like that. We just wrote what we felt and so there's quite a disjointed body of work, really, because it's just whatever was going on.

You think it's a disjointed body of work?

Yeah, I think it's really weird. [*Laughs*]

When I listen back on those early hits, it evokes a whole era for me.

Well, the tempo, everything was fast, my voice and the guitar. So there was a sound.

Even "Only Lonely", which you could slow down and make quite a ballad out of, it's quite a tender song but it is still quite pacey. Was it important to always keep the pace going?

Just how we were. I think it's insecurity. Too fast, a little bit. Slow is harder. To fill in the space simply is much harder. Fast and frantic is easier. But you don't realise that when you're doing it. And it's fun. It's commanding. But slow, the groove's got to be great. Singing slow is much more difficult, more exposing. And of course I've always had a problem with my vibrato, and to stretch a note out slow, I had to use vibrato. I used to use very little vibrato. So it was all those sort of things that come into it.

While you say your songwriting wasn't contrived around image, did you realise your voice had a certain tonal quality that lent itself to songs based around certain themes? Did your voice influence your writing?

I suppose the keys and things like that. But I was always the last one considered in the group.

Even though you were writing?

Well, in regards to getting a key right and things like that, sometimes there were fights because the key sounded better with the guitar. There were always those dilemmas, which happen in a band. And the guitar player and the singer always have that in rock 'n' roll, this conflict. One's always trying to outdo the other. It all makes for wonderful explosiveness, well, for us anyway. It was dangerous and it was marvellous. It was explosive and it was unpredictable. And it added to what was going on.

Were you conscious of the dearth of successful female songwriters when you first started?

No, it was marvellous, because I was it. But even I wasn't considered. I don't think I've ever been really considered a songwriter until recently. I was a performer, I was a singer, I was a sex symbol. I was thought of as a monster, everything else but a songwriter. Until the Americans said, "You're a poet", I was never thought of like that here. Because my lyrics were very simple. And I remember guys used to say to me, "It's embarrassing what you do, your songs and things". I was always a bit on the outer in the scene. I used to turn up to benefits in my school uniform and they'd all go, "How could she?". In this country, how you look comes first. And your youth. If you're not attractive, it's everything here.

Over the years, did the way you and Mark write together change or did you usually stick to the same method?

We never had a formula. It was the inspiration, and we used to do things in different ways. We were always under a lot of pressure, because once we were signed to an American record deal we were touring, so we were writing wherever we could. We weren't always inspired, but we had each other to stress on, which was good. We really needed each other in that regard, because we were in this together. I don't think I could have done it under all the pressure of delivering. It was enormous, the job was huge. So we just wrote wherever we could and it was different. And sometimes we'd work with other people, we'd bring in somebody else if we were stuck. And then the record company had me going over to America to write with the Hollywood people.

How influential was a producer like Mike Chapman on your writing?

Not at all. He was just very supportive and into the band. I think he was the one who told the guy who signed us in Chrysalis to go and check us out, way back in the beginning. So he was a fan and then we eventually got to work with him. And the fact that he produced Blondie and all that before. But he was never really in the writing process. He just loved what we did.

He seemed very tapped into your mood with a song like "Pleasure and Pain"—was that tailor-written for Divinyls or did he already have that song?

Holly Knight and Mike Chapman wrote that. I don't know whether they wrote that especially for us.

Do you like that song?

It's okay.

You're very convincing with it.
I commit. If you're going to sing a song, you've got to commit. If you can't commit to the lyric and the vocal and the singing, it sounds like that. And I suppose it's just very committed.

The collaboration with Tom Kelly and Billy Steinberg interested me. They are ultimate pop craftsmen. You had already met them before you wrote "I Touch Myself", hadn't you?
In '85, I went over there, just me on my own, and we wrote a song called "Like a Cat", which Cyndi Lauper recorded eventually. Mike Chapman heard that song and he said, "Oh, it's too gimmicky for you." But that was the first song that we wrote.

Were you excited at having a cut by a well-known artist? Because that hadn't been your MO for writing.
I remember meeting her somewhere at a party or something, and she said, "Are you sure you don't want that song?" I said, "No, you can have it." And it felt really good. I appreciate it more now.

How comfortable were you writing explicit lyrics with guys you didn't know intimately? Were you detached from the content of that song?
It was just fun. Being silly and having fun. It was hilarious because we were throwing things back and forth. And Billy's really childish, in a great way, but very childlike. So you can be really silly with Billy and we always got on, he always could get in my head. I was speaking to him a few weeks ago, and we haven't written together for ages because he doesn't write with Tom Kelly any more, and he said, "Oh, I miss writing with you. What we did I really felt was credible, working with you." I thought, what a lovely thing to say. He was really nostalgic.

Do you see yourself still singing a song like "I Touch Myself" in another ten years?
I don't know. I haven't sung it for a while.

What did writing in places like Los Angeles and Paris do for you creatively?
It just was inspirational. It inspired us, gave us things to write about, a backdrop and an atmosphere. I always find it better writing in Paris than LA. Though, actually, I remember writing "The Good Die Young" in a hotel in LA. Which is not a very LA song. It's not a kind of obvious pop form structured song for its time. I've never liked working in LA, because I'm sure there's this huge radar screen up there, it's zapping everybody's energy because there's so many people there writing, trying to make it, and it's such a superficial showbiz sort of place. I was never totally comfortable. I need atmosphere, I need a subject, I need emotion. And I just don't just write on the drop of a hat.

Does the subject usually start the song? I want to write a song about masturbation, I want to write a song about feeling slutty, that kind of thing?
Or emotion. A feeling. A recent song that I wrote, I was on a train to Woodstock and it was snowing. I had just written twenty pages for a book and I was talking about myself, feeling

really exposed and dreadful. It was an aspect, a part of my life, and I was feeling really awful. I was sitting on the train with this emotion, the ground was covered in snow and I looked at the snow and I came up with the title "Painted White". Because I knew that I could just whitewash these feelings. I got off the train and we started writing this song called "Painted White". My songwriting partner in Woodstock is Kevin Salem. I've written a lot of songs with him now. So that came from a feeling and a scene, on a train trip of an hour and a half.

So you still like to write with other people?
I have to collaborate because I need instruments and I don't really play. And I just love collaborating, because it helps me be objective and it keeps making things potent for me.

Has your acting work made an imprint on your songwriting and vice versa?
No. Very different. It's been hard having an acting career because then I've always rushed off with the band and it's always been a commitment, so my acting career has suffered a bit.

Is it something you want to continue pursuing?
I think it's something I should continue. I enjoy it.

Do you find it irritating that you are best known for songs written as long as twenty years ago or do you have a comfortable relationship with those early hits?
It is hard, because people lock you into a certain thing, and you've got to constantly try and do something different. I've got this reputation, and being older, it's difficult to shake it off, for people to see you in a new light. That's what I'm attempting to do, but it's not easy. To spur my career into a new decade. To do it into a third decade and to think differently. I'm doing it, but it's hard to get other people to think differently about you.

TODD HUNTER & JOHANNA PIGOTT

CAMBEWARRA, AUSTRALIA, JULY 2003

Sovereignty. It's a key word for Johanna Pigott. Ask her to sidle up to her husband, Todd Hunter, for a photo, and she resists. "No, no, sovereignty." Talk about why they don't write songs together any more, and she gives a one-word explanation. "Sovereignty".

It's amusing and baffling, because after more than twenty years together, Hunter and Pigott have a disarming rapport, the kind that couples who live or work together over a long period of time develop. They don't just finish each other's sentences, they tell each other's stories. They talk about each other's lives before they met as though they were there, as active participants. They have different recollections of work they did together, and yet somehow find a way for both versions of a story to co-exist. "Rain" was written in Ultimo. No, Bondi. Never mind, it was written.

They try to disown any notion of romance being part of their creative mix, and yet there is a palpable sense of romance in their behaviour towards each other, in the home they have

455

established, and in the studio they have built behind their house, nestled between the New South Wales South Coast and the Southern Highlands. It's peaceful, private and spacious, the complete antithesis of their manic and intense existence in the 1980s when both were embroiled in the Dragon saga, as writers of some of the band's biggest hits and, for Hunter, as bass player alongside his volatile younger brother, Marc, the lead vocalist. Life, love and music in a country setting were the antidote to many years of being surrounded by decadence, just as finally leaving Dragon and composing music for television in the late 1990s set Todd free after more than twenty years of dysfunctional family and band relationships.

"I really wanted to find my way out of Alcatraz," he said, smiling. Todd Hunter always looks jovial. But his memories of Dragon, the hit-making group he formed in New Zealand in 1972, are imbued with tragedy. Drug abuse, violence and death were the legacies left behind, which countered the band's joyous pop of seventies hits like "This Time", "April Sun in Cuba", "Are You Old Enough?" and "Still in Love with You"—mostly written by the band's troubled keyboard player, Paul Hewson—and the power pop hits Todd wrote with Johanna in the eighties, including "Rain", "Cry" and "Speak No Evil".

Dragon lost a drummer, Neal Storey, to a drug overdose in 1975, Hewson died in 1985 after years of heroin addiction, and in 1998 Marc Hunter succumbed to throat cancer. The story of Todd Hunter's musical life and songwriting journey cannot be told without referencing that dark backdrop, and after many years of clamming up, he talks openly about it. "I've come around that whole thing," he said. "I'm sort of reconciled."

Hunter was born on 22 June 1951 in Waitara, beneath Mount Egmont, on New Zealand's North Island. His family had a strong Fijian heritage and were all musically inclined, forming groups and playing in local communities. Todd and Marc emulated the Beatles and other Mersey sounds in their early bands, but when Dragon began in Auckland, it was as a progressive art rock outfit. They made two unwieldy albums in New Zealand before moving to Sydney and morphing into a pop band. Songwriting duties fell primarily to Paul Hewson, Robert Taylor and Marc Hunter in the early years; when Todd contributed, it was always on a co-writing basis. But co-writing within the band was fraught at best; an outside co-writer was—at least in theory—a better bet. Enter Johanna Pigott.

Pigott was born in Sydney on 4 November 1954, the seventh and youngest child of an academic family. Her early musical influences were guided by her siblings' tastes, from Wagner to PJ Proby, Doris Day to the Beatles. She gravitated to the major female artists of the early 1970s—Joni Mitchell, Carole King, Dolly Parton and Linda Ronstadt—but rather than pursuing music initially, she studied architecture, met writer Tim Gooding and focused on acting and scriptwriting. After a few years of alternative theatre and *Restless Years* scripts, music beckoned, and Pigott and Gooding formed the art/punk rock outfit XL Capris. Hunter, looking for an escape from the chaos of Dragon, produced some songs for her band. Their partnership grew from there.

While Hunter struggled with the ongoing drama of Dragon, Pigott struggled with retaining her independence while being inexorably dragged into the mire of the Hunter brothers' tense relationship as she co-wrote songs for them. She continued scriptwriting, and with Gooding she conceived and wrote the landmark 1984 ABC TV series *Sweet and Sour*. She also made the *Pop Art* album under the moniker of Scribble in 1986; produced by Iva Davies, it was heavily electronic and distinctly uncommercial. Her greatest songwriting successes came with Hunter, and when they veered from Dragon and wrote "Age of Reason" for John Farnham. they were able to make the healthy life changes such a hit could afford them.

But the issue of sovereignty became pressing. Hunter writes musical tracks and Pigott is a melody and lyric writer, so they had often written in different rooms, but eventually they ceased writing together at all. Hunter worked on television scores and, more recently, was producing a new band in Sydney, while Pigott focused on scriptwriting and editing. They've talked about writing songs again, but just as "a vague desire".

Whatever the power play might be between Hunter and Pigott, they have survived many challenging years together, and have contributed memorable songs to the Australian songwriting canon. And that kind of fortitude earns them whatever sovereignty each desires.

Todd, was your early exposure to Maori culture a key to shaping your musical destiny?
HUNTER: No, I think more the Fijian harmonies were.

PIGOTT: One of the most stunning things when I first went to Fiji and we drove out of the city was people sitting in their villages with no electricity, singing. It was the first time I'd heard those Dragon harmonies, right there.

HUNTER: There are particular inversions of singing that you can't help but sing. Even now when my mum gets together with her sisters, they start singing, and these three-part harmonies happen.

PIGOTT: Of a particular sound. That thing is just in your family and you might not even have picked it as much had we not gone back there as adults and heard it in the darkness.

I was a huge Dragon fan when you first came to Australia; I wore out the grooves on my *Sunshine* album, and there was definitely a different sound, but as a teenager I couldn't put my finger on it.
HUNTER: There was a thing on that *Sunshine* record and in the early days of Dragon where everyone would sing and the combination of those voices would make that thing happen. As everybody died or left, it got less and less until in the end it was just Marc and me screeching up over the top because everyone in the middle had gone. But that early thing, they were South Pacific harmonies, basically.

"This Time" has all the band members credited as songwriters. I understand that you were basically told, "Sit in that room and you're not coming out until you all write a song." How did a band that had previously been deliberately non-commercial come up with such a catchy pop song on demand?
HUNTER: We went back and forth with stuff and around things. Our circumstances were so dire, we were really trying for something hopeful and up and happy.

Were the lyrics—"This time gonna head in the right direction"—literally a reference to where the band was, both in that room and in your career?
HUNTER: Yeah, it was. And then a couple of weeks before the record came out, Neal died. So it's a perfect Dragon thing, of course.

Paul Hewson had an extraordinary talent for pop craftsmanship. Did you find yourself taking note and being influenced by his writing?
HUNTER: No. Not at all.

PIGOTT: Todd can get very bossy and make them come up with something, which is quite awesome to watch. So I can imagine you might have done that a bit back then. You probably got no credit on a lot of things you did that for, actually motivating people to pull it together, to make something happen.

Do you remember any of the stories behind Paul and Marc's songs?
HUNTER: "Are You Old Enough" was written on Magnetic Island when Marc and Paul hired a dinghy. Paul went into wherever the hell that little township is and bought a twenty-dollar guitar. They were going out on the outboard, a couple of local girls went with them, and they wrote that song. Paul mainly wrote it and Marc helped, and then just smashed the guitar and came back in with a new song.

That guitar served the purpose of one song.
HUNTER: That's right. Lyrics like "Scratch my back go the coloured girls" and all that sort of stuff, is all about that day.
 "April Sun in Cuba" is about a chess game. Paul was always writing about chess or wrestling or whatever, but it always came out as this kind of pop love thing. But in those days I wasn't looking at him thinking, yes, this is the way to make a great pop song.

What was your impression when they first played you "April Sun in Cuba"?
HUNTER: It was just in a bunch of songs and it didn't seem like a killer song. What happened around then was that we were in Melbourne, we were supposed to be going out on a Sunday night and there was a car that everyone was getting into and going off to have dinner. I didn't get into it because alarm bells went off and I got a cab instead. Anyway, the girl who was driving the car drove under the wheels of a truck and everyone got incredibly hurt. Paul's spine was all wrecked. It didn't seem like it was going to be a great song or anything, it was just like another song that we had to do, but in the recording of it everyone was completely crippled and smashed up. We were depressed and shattered and the one thing I remember is looking around the studio as we were recording it thinking, "Jesus, what is this?"

When you were writing with Marc, was there a unique creative connection that you had as siblings?
HUNTER: It was difficult writing with Marc. I can't remember that it was ever unwrought.

It was always a fighting thing, he's so in your face, and you'd have to fight back. So no, there wasn't any feeling of, "God, we're on to something here!"

In your face with what?
HUNTER: We had a very different sensibility about music. He was into Lou Rawls and that smoother thing, and at that stage I was into more abrasive stuff. We came from different directions and then things would get added later. I can never remember sitting down with him and writing. We may have tried to, but I felt what we came up with was crap.

The whole writing thing for Dragon was very fragmented, which is part of the reason it didn't work in the end, because things were coming from all directions and there wasn't one person that had a really strong lyrical inkwell going. I think that's what added to its fuzziness.

There was such a contrast between the perfectly constructed melodic pop songs your partners were creating and the self-destructive lifestyles they were leading.
HUNTER: Both Marc and Paul were really dark guys. I used to say to them, "What about all this? Isn't this all fabulous?" They'd say, "Oh, get fucked, you fuckin' nancy." But maybe songs were their expression of it.

PIGOTT: There's a train of thinking that our worst addicts are our most fragile angels. I mean, they were shockers. But why were they shockers? What was it they were anaesthetising, what was it that they were trying to put to sleep? There was a fragility about those guys that they didn't want anyone to see, and I guess that might have come out in the songs.

I was a peculiar figure in this because I was a bit threatening. But Paul used to invite me to take heroin all the time because he thought that this made you a better artist. You know, come hither little girl and have some heroin 'cause you'll be a better songwriter. It didn't make much sense to me, a nice middle class girl and all. But being a TV soap scriptwriter at that stage of your artistic development probably was almost as crazy as guys on heroin writing pretty pop songs.

Do scriptwriting and songwriting feed off each other?
PIGOTT: They're different. But I'll tell you why they're similar. I have written a book, and long-form writing is quite difficult for me. Short-form is actually very easy for me. Songs and dialogue for me are short-form. They're not long great screeds of words that you have to organise into paragraphs and stuff. They are things that you can get out really fast and so they have an incredible similarity about them. There's an immediacy about both of them. But as far as feeding each other, no. I would say they occupy separate channels in my head. Dialogue is something that I just hear, when I'm writing it I hear it. Songs, I probably visualise them. It's two different mechanisms.

Did your romance spring from a creative connection or vice versa?
HUNTER: No, no, we've never had a romance.

PIGOTT: We're looking forward to that. [*Both laugh*] I'd say it was a creative collaboration.

HUNTER: We had a funny start where we just fought like crazy. We punched each other to pieces around Europe when we first met. It was very difficult for the first couple of years, we just argued and fought.

Todd, do you think in your relationships it was actually quite comfortable for you to be close to somebody that you were sparring with all the time?
HUNTER: Yes, I came out of a dysfunctional family where we recreated it in the band. But with Johanna, the relationship came first. We used to hang around together for a while.

There aren't that many husband–wife songwriting partners in Australia.
HUNTER: A husband–wife songwriter team is a very interesting story. It's not a fabulous little idyllic thing. We've not been able to do it for years, and then we do it again. It's incredibly complex.

PIGOTT: Songwriting is an intense creative process. It's as intense as anything you could ever create. To do it with another person is a very intense thing. And to do it with your partner is a *very* intense thing. People say how wonderful, but you know, after twenty years it can be quite problematic.

HUNTER: So we had to stop for years. We had kids and the whole thing just got too hard to do.

Johanna, as mainly a writer of words, did music come easily to you initially?
PIGOTT: Melody and lyrics have always gone together for me. I've never really written them separately. I can remember our first songwriting together. Honestly, we were so different. I was in this joke kind of band. He was like in the centre of the horrible old … From my point of view, I had no respect for those old boys.

But you wanted to be a punk, didn't you, Todd?
HUNTER: I was attracted to the whole punk thing. I just loved the irreverence of it, the deconstruction of it.

Teaming up obviously brought something out of both of you, because you became quite prolific from then on, after neither of you had been strong working songwriters.
PIGOTT: The XLs were not serious, we were not contending for an ARIA award or anything. We were just being facetious and having a good time. So when I met you, it was like, oh, this is a real musician and music is serious and you can actually write things and make records and people can hear them. It was quite different.

Was there any resistance to bringing an outside writer into Dragon?
PIGOTT: There was huge resistance there. I think there was a resistance to you being alive then, frankly.

HUNTER: We reformed in 1982, and did a bunch of Paul's songs like "Ramona" and some other things which didn't work. "Rain" turned things around. "Rain" was in a bunch of songs that we recorded at the same time and it was a signifier for what was going to come. I remember Kerry Jacobson saying as we were recording, "You know I don't like to play this sort of shit. What is it?" It was uncomfortable for everybody.

"Rain" was a completely new sound for Dragon. Alan Mansfield had joined and there was a whole new persona to the group. Where did the song idea come from?
PIGOTT: We used to have a lot of time in a studio in Ultimo; we were doing Scribble stuff. This was more like the model of our songwriting that wrote the big ones, where Todd would come in with a musical structure. It's the model for "Age of Reason", how that worked too. You'd come in with a track. I'd go, "I can't write anything to that." And he'd just push and he'd push. I remember originally over that track I sang, [*Sings*] "It's raining, it's pouring, the old man is snoring." Just to try and get something happening, because I couldn't think of anything. That's when it first came to me.

HUNTER: My memory is it was in Cecil, a crazy old apartment block in Bondi. You went out, I did this whole thing, sang these horrible lyrics over it, and then you came back and made it into an actual song. With a lot of things, I would do the whole track and then you would just make it into a song.

PIGOTT: I don't remember that. See, I struggled with that. I remember not connecting with it at all, and singing that, "It's raining, it's pouring." And then maybe that day happened.

HUNTER: I remember recording the song with a crapped-out old twelve-string.

PIGOTT: But there were also holes in it. It was this really patchy song. Marc would do things where you'd go, "Oh, no! No, you can't sing that, it's something you'd get sued for." And after a while he'd just make it, he'd weave it and he'd hammer it so that that's what the song would become. Just sheer nailing it with that great voice. We had the most hellish day.

You went into the studio with it still being, "It's raining, it's pouring, the old man is snoring"?
PIGOTT: No, that had gone. We had the chorus and Marc and I punched it out about the verses.

Was that a common way for songs to be written and recorded?
PIGOTT: For those guys, this thing was like a nightmare. They hated it. Marc didn't want to sing it. He was hammering these things that he contributed to eventually because that's what he could do.

HUNTER: Paul didn't want to play it. Kerry hated it.

PIGOTT: And old bossy boots here just made everyone do it.

Did you like it? Did you believe in it?
HUNTER: I thought it had something. Yeah, I did. I actually felt that it was something that the band had to do. The band re-formed to pay off debts and after a year or so we started recording and we went in doing the same old stuff and it was obviously just the wrong thing to do. I thought if we were ever going to get anywhere, it had to keep moving.

PIGOTT: It's like you have to come up with something because it's happening today. We're locked into this studio in East Sydney and Paul was pacing up and down. Eventually everyone got sucked into it. You know, songwriting ain't sitting around strumming guitars.

When you hear "Rain" now is that what you think of, the tension?
HUNTER: Not at all.

PIGOTT: No, when I hear it now I think of Marc's voice. I think Marc's voice is an incredible thing.

HUNTER: I think of when we played at the Entertainment Centre and the whole crowd was singing the song.

PIGOTT: Yes, standing up the back with ten thousand people singing along when they were playing it. Hair-raising, amazing. It's fantastic. Because your aim is to reach people, to communicate to people. And popular culture's the best way to do it. That was, I guess, one of those moments where you go, "Yeah. That's why I do this."

So at this stage had you realised that to have a commercial sensibility was fine even if your intellectual sensibility wasn't satisfied?
PIGOTT: Of course. That's exactly what it was about. The thing I had to give up was that artistic, precious, groovy thing and write a commercial song. And that was part of what the fight was about. There is absolute validity in writing commercial non-intellectual entertainment.

HUNTER: It's a hard thing to write something that will connect with people, it doesn't matter what it is.

PIGOTT: And the great thing about something like "Rain" is that people would come for years and years afterwards and say, "This is what it meant to me." Someone else would say, "And this is what it meant to me."

HUNTER: "And what about the hard rain? Isn't it terrible what they're doing with all the radiation?" Yeah, it's terrible.

Do you remember writing "Cry"?
HUNTER: I remember "Cry". We were on the Gold Coast.

PIGOTT: No, see, different memory.

HUNTER: There will always be completely different memories. I remember sitting in a car, outside the Broadbeach fucking shopping centre fruit barn, struggling to come up with lyrics for that song.

PIGOTT: The struggle for these song lyrics used to go on for weeks. I was a lyricist for these, and a melody writer. The structures were written. My memory is the morning it was recorded, we were sitting in that coffee bar at the top of the Cross writing it on a napkin. 'Cause you were saying, "Give it to me now!"

How did you come up with the idea of "Cry"? Was it because it was just making you cry?
PIGOTT: [*Laughs*] It probably was; that's probably the thing that was uppermost in my mind. But I did it, and I stayed away from the fight to get it, because we had to fight Marc to sing. He'd come along to our songs and just write another song over the top of it.

HUNTER: He'd say, "No, fuck you! This is the song."

Andrew Farriss said it was really important for Michael Hutchence to write the lyrics because the only way that Michael was going to communicate an INXS song with integrity was if he wrote it himself.
PIGOTT: That's exactly right, and in a way, I could understand that with Marc. But in some ways it wasn't right for Dragon, what Marc instinctively did, melodically particularly.

HUNTER: His lyric thing was like, "I'm lying under the tree with the panniers of wine." Whatever the fuck it was. I felt like fighting for certain things. And other things you just let go.

Do you remember writing "Speak No Evil"?
PIGOTT: "Speak No Evil" was a dream. It was a lovely song to write, and it was very easy.

HUNTER: It was mainly you and Alan, and I just had a small bit to do with it.

PIGOTT: Alan brought the structure in, and for some reason that melody and lyric just came out of the ether, like they do. And it got changed a lot. The original demo would have been more like "Papa Was a Rolling Stone"; it was less pop, much more blues, R&B.

HUNTER: Todd Rundgren wrote the middle-eight. It was my title, because I had "Speak No Evil", "Temptation", all these biblical titles at the time.

Was the "power pop" style a conscious direction you wanted your writing to go in or did that come more from the production of the songs?
HUNTER: We were always a pop band, that's all there was to it.

You got over your punkish phase pretty quickly, then?
HUNTER: Yes, I certainly did. I suppose it was that mid-eighties thing.

PIGOTT: It went with the long coats.

HUNTER: The long coats, yeah. But it was Todd Rundgren, too, with big harmonies and big choruses.

What was it like having Todd Rundgren produce the *Dreams of Ordinary Men* album?
HUNTER: I was in a pretty weird place then, so we used to have arguments about who was more uninterested in the whole thing.

PIGOTT: And I used to argue with him about lyrics.

HUNTER: We stayed up in this cottage in Bearsville, recorded in this studio, the snow would be six foot deep and we'd get out of the studio at night and muck around on the Fairlight. And Max, the tour manager, would ring and say, "Don't come back until morning because Marc's destroying the house." He'd just be shredding the whole place, it was really weird. So I had this whole thing where I couldn't play any bass or anything, it was just horrible. At that stage I was sick of it all. But that's what my life was.

PIGOTT: I can remember Todd Rundgren in this incredible drawl picking lyrics to bits and going, "It doesn't make sense." And me trying to explain that in Australia we pay tribute to stuff sometimes by just referring to it.

HUNTER: It's metaphorical.

PIGOTT: He couldn't understand that. He'd get you for semantics. "Well, you know, if the train's pulling out of the station, it's obviously going." He'd pick it apart like that. He won, of course, because he was putting it on tape. [*Laughs*]

HUNTER: He was a funny guy. He was so cynical it was fantastic. I don't think he wanted to do it in the first place. But apparently if you went bowling with him on Wednesdays then he was completely happy.

What did the inclusion of writers like Johanna, Sharon O'Neill and even Marc's wife, Wendy, bring to the mix?
HUNTER: Oh, complete destruction.

PIGOTT: [*Laughs*] The Yoko Ono effect. Times three.

HUNTER: I think it was really good. The band needed it.

PIGOTT: There's another contradiction for you, the naughty punk boys who end up giving their partners credits for bits on songs.

It's a really interesting kind of musical family that you all maybe unconsciously constructed. Sharon being a New Zealander as well, coming into the mix. I wondered if that female input

was an essential part of the maturing of Dragon's writing in the later years.

HUNTER: Yeah, sure. To decode the world.

Decode the world?

HUNTER: [*Laughs*] To mature, yeah. I've never really thought about that, but I guess that is unusual, isn't it. I guess you could say that it changed all those records. It's hard for me too, because in '95 I just bailed out and I didn't want to know any more. I had started doing TV scoring by then, so I was three years into *Heartbreak High* and Marc wanted to start the band again. It was incredibly hard for me, this thing that had been my life, to actually leave.

PIGOTT: Yeah, even for me, who was involved peripherally, when I decided to walk away, it was really hard. It's quite a compelling sort of nightmare to be in.

HUNTER: So you had to take your hands off and just forget about it really. They went on, they kept recording, they got all sorts of people through the band, last time I saw them there was some sort of revival thing on where they had 2,000 people screaming and yelling and singing. Had Marc not got sick and had Marc not been Marc, I guess, they could still have been doing it.

If you look at the geography of Dragon, beginning with the *Sunshine* album, when you started in Australia, there was a reference to Blacktown, then you flew off musically to places like Cuba and Zambezi, recorded and toured overseas, and ended up in Bondi Road physically, lyrically and thematically. What happened to New Zealand in all of that time?

HUNTER: Ahh. We had a very troubled relationship with New Zealand. We said to everyone, "We're moving to Australia." And they'd say, "Why on earth are you going to Australia? The guys are all big drunken footballers and the girls just have big tits and broken noses, and that's it." And we'd say, "Actually, we're going to Australia to get away from people like you."

So you abandoned New Zealand creatively as well?

HUNTER: Yes, we did.

Because unlike Tim and Neil Finn, it didn't turn up in your songs at all.

HUNTER: We really wanted to get out of New Zealand; it drove us crazy, it was so parochial.

What had inspired you and Robert Taylor to write "Blacktown Boogie"?

HUNTER: That's where we were playing. I felt much more at home; I felt like getting home when I got to Australia.

And so then Bondi was the natural completion of that musical journey.

HUNTER: Earlier on we didn't live in Bondi, because that's where the New Zealanders were, but then we ended up in Bondi Road. We actually wrote that song in England.

PIGOTT: Place is really interesting, you know. A lot of the Scribble stuff I wrote, and the early

Dragon stuff, I lived in places where I could see the sea at Bondi. And people used to say, "The reason I love your songs is because they are of this place." They weren't necessarily about it, but the people who knew it could sense it in the songs. It's interesting that you say that.

HUNTER: There is Fiji. Marc got the Fijian stuff in his solo albums.

Yes, and a song called "Island Nights". But when I asked you earlier about the Maori influence, I always had a sense of Dragon as warriors.
HUNTER: Mmm. Fijian warriors, though, rather than Maoris. We really got out of the whole Maori culture when every night when we would play in New Zealand there'd be a huge fight. People would get a bottle in their face and it was awful. It was really scarring, so we just got out of there.

PIGOTT: It's interesting, isn't it, that Neil and Tim's picture of New Zealand is quite benign, sort of lovely.

HUNTER: And ours was quite nightmarish. Ours was more like *Once Were Warriors*.

Todd, did the deaths of Paul and Marc, in turn, have a direct effect on your personal creativity?
HUNTER: It had a hell of an effect on it.

Did you stop writing or did you write prolifically? Did you write strange stuff?
HUNTER: After Paul's death, so many things happened that we thought, fuck it, we'll just keep on going. By the time Marc died I had been TV scoring for six years. It did get very dirty, very dark around that whole time. My producer used to say, "Oh God, what's happening here? It's so funereal." I kept working for six months on *Heartbreak High* after Marc died. There was fortunately a little two-week gap while he actually came down and died. And then I just went straight back to work. One whole year exactly after he died I had the most incredible breakdown, and so I didn't do any music for a year. All I did musically was play African drums. It completely changed my life around creatively, because I just stopped, I couldn't stand it any more. I did a massage course and didn't do any music.

What made you start again?
HUNTER: I got well and felt like I could do it, I could stand it. And in two years a job came along. So that's really the first time off in my life I had from music since primary school.

Did you write a song about Marc after he died?
HUNTER: Johanna did. It's called "No More Tears". Because I don't write lyrics, it's not like I'm a singer-songwriter that'll sit down and write about that.

PIGOTT: Lately I'd stay out of his studio. I'd do a Bernie Taupin, I just wrote lyrics. The music he'd written made me think of the brothers, the two of them growing up.

HUNTER: We've done that for years, where you would sit in the next room. In *Heartbreak High*, I'd be working along and we'd need a song. You'd be writing scripts in the next room and I'd write the whole track and you'd take it and bang, write a song, it'd be done in an hour. We actually got some great songs that way.

I'd like to talk about "Age of Reason", which you wrote while Dragon was still flourishing in the late eighties. It was another message song that followed strongly from "You're the Voice", ideal for John Farnham, but was that planned?
HUNTER: We were playing the Palais in Melbourne. John Farnham came in with Wheatley. Marc and Alan were standing, I was behind them, and Farnham said, "Why don't you write me a song?" So because I was sort of behind them, I went over to Johanna and said, "Farnham's asked us to write a song."

We went on tour with Tina Turner for six months so I did the track in Europe. You came over and actually made it into a song. This is my memory of it, it took ages.

PIGOTT: It took ages, yes. This is a great story because it's about persistence. Todd worked for months on this piece. And I'm just talking about the music; he worked on it and worked on it.

HUNTER: We were playing in ballrooms and I had this big case where I'd come home at night and pull the lid down and there was a keyboard and a Mac and all that sort of crap. And I'd just work away while everyone else was out getting shitfaced.

PIGOTT: I'd listen to it and listen to it and couldn't figure out how or what ... Similar to that "Rain" thing, but I was more respectful by this time.

And also feeling that if this is something that Farnham records, it's going to be listened to by a lot of people.
HUNTER: No. You know, what are your chances of getting a song done by somebody like that?

PIGOTT: We were sufficiently realistic to know that even if we did get one away to him the chances of it getting done would be very, very small. Whether it was good or not. It's all that random chook lotto stuff. But for me, as a lyric writer, it's a very different process when you're writing for someone. Because it's a whole discipline of keeping it to what that person might be interested in. It's not like the flow of writing what you feel. So it was a very difficult process. I was also pregnant with Harry, our first son. So I was probably stuck. Anyway, months and months, trying, trying, really nothing happened. And then the baby had to be born.

HUNTER: We got back from Europe.

PIGOTT: We lived in Bondi Road, the studio was upstairs, and there he was still working on this. This is months down the line. I finally listened to it, sat down on the stairs. Because when I'm listening to stuff and writing I go away from it a bit, I go to the next room, so I'm just hearing the shape of it instead of being embroiled in it. I sat in the stairs and that whole lyric came out—boom. And it was all about my son.

467

HUNTER: And your father dying.

PIGOTT: It was this moment of genuine inspiration that hadn't come to me for the seven months that I'd struggled with it. And that was written in probably about five minutes.

Did the title come as you wrote the lyric?
PIGOTT: It was one of those things that people describe where it was perfectly formed already and it just came through you onto the paper. "Age of Reason" might have been on one of my lists of titles. I probably picked up my book, looked at the list, seen that, and that just triggered it. It was one of those incredible things where the preparation had been done and the time was right and the child was there to inspire me and that came out. All that time, and during this whole dance with the devils of Dragon, I'd always been trying to get songs to be hopeful. I have this great longing for hope, and it was very distant to me for a very long time, but I felt like "Age of Reason" was my first true feeling of hope in a song. Properly felt. And I can attribute that to my son.

Does he know that?
PIGOTT: I've told him that, but he wouldn't get it yet.

HUNTER: So we got Marc in to sing it as a demo.

PIGOTT: He didn't hate it, but he wouldn't sing the third verse. So we had two people singing with him.

HUNTER: And then we mixed it up, sent it off, and that was it. We didn't hear anything. Ross Fraser, who's Farnham's producer, rang up maybe a year later and said, "Love the song. We're doing it." The tape had gone to them, got into their pile of 3,000 tapes.

PIGOTT: They'd listened to it and just thrown it on the reject pile.

HUNTER: And then they recorded the whole album and thought, "There's no single here. We should go back and listen to everything again."

PIGOTT: So after the album had been recorded they went back through the piles of stuff. This is the legend we got told; we don't know if it's true. But the whole story is a thing of a long period of time going by and persistence.

Is that a song that you're both proud of? By virtue of Farnham having recorded it, it's probably your most successful song.
PIGOTT: Our friends gave us a lot of flak.

Selling out?
PIGOTT: No, not selling out. Just lampooning us. [*Laughs*] Not our friends, but musical, little groovy snobs. That didn't bother me; expressing something that means something to me and having it go out in such a big way and being sung by such an incredible singer is an amazing thing. Is very satisfying.

HUNTER: And if you look at success, yes, that song enabled us to move down here, and it changed our lives.

PIGOTT: We could come and live here and work and slow down and actually become civilised human beings.

HUNTER: So on that level it's noteworthy. It's not the biggest thing that's ever happened to us because we've got TV earnings and stuff that became sustainable. But there's a funny shock of recognition when you hear it on the radio when you're driving. It is something; it's not just nothing.

PIGOTT: I get a thrill when I hear it in the supermarket.

Did you look for other opportunities to write for star singers?
PIGOTT: We were asked to write for Sir Cliff Richard at one stage. And we tried.

HUNTER: Well, you went to Melbourne and had an argument with him about Christianity.

PIGOTT: We tried but we failed, I guess. We couldn't figure that one out.

Do you feel personally involved with all of your songs?
PIGOTT: It's part of my Bernie Taupin policy where I don't get too involved any more. I just do it and walk away from it. Part of that is because I don't want to be overwhelmed by the creative process any more. I'm much more detached from it. It's so compelling, I think, being creative. I used to love the feeling of losing yourself in it, but now I hate losing myself in it. I actually want to stay on my feet and in the world. So I just do little bits of it and do it in moderation and forget about it when I've walked away from it.

Is that because there are other things that are compelling, such as parenthood?
PIGOTT: Yeah. It taught me that I actually don't like the feeling. It's a bit like an addiction or something. Someone else described it, Nick Cave, and I've been trying to articulate it for a long time. The interviewer said, "Do you take heroin to become more creative?" And he said, "No, I took it to become less. Because it's too hard." I find unless you can moderate it, it can be quite destructive. As I've seen around me.

I wonder if that was part of Paul Hewson's raison d'être. He was obviously an incredibly creative man.
PIGOTT: Yeah. And it's powerful stuff, you know. I think the happiest people have made writing a practice, and they do it each day. That's the way to go, just to make it your day job, you apply yourself and then walk away from it.

But inspiration still flows?
PIGOTT: There's no lack of inspiration. I think of ideas a thousand times a day. They just run off. It's all still operating.

So you could still sit and write like in the earliest days together?

PIGOTT: Technology's got a part to play in that, too. We used to play on an old piano and a guitar, or a bass, onto tape, and then when Pro Tools and computers happened, one person operated things, often, in our case. So I just got bored. I got further and further away, out on the steps, then downstairs, then across there. So technology's got something to do with it. But we don't write together now because it's bad for our marriage. We stopped writing together in order to get ourselves on an even keel.

What are the advantages and disadvantages of being husband and wife and co-writers?

PIGOTT: The advantages are that you can be creatively entwined and it's like you're heading in one direction very easily. The disadvantages are that that can be a very big problem, because you need some separation when you're in a long-term relationship.

HUNTER: We had to disengage. We were so fuzzy about everything, weren't we? It allowed us to do things but it stopped a whole lot of other things.

PIGOTT: Yeah, people think, wow, that's so great. But anyone who's been in it knows its downside. You don't go home at the end of the day and see somebody else and talk about what's on telly. It's just too intense.

HUNTER: At one in the morning when you should be going to sleep, you're sitting on the end of the bed with a guitar going, "Okay, what about if it just went ...?".

But now you can close the studio door.

PIGOTT: If he starts talking to me about a song in the kitchen, I just say, "No. Nine o'clock tomorrow morning."

HUNTER: But I don't any more. It's very compartmentalised now, so we're much healthier people. We're de-fuzzied. We've split everything up. We've got our own offices, we've got our own cars. It's a million times better.

MARK SEYMOUR

MELBOURNE, AUSTRALIA, FEBRUARY 2004

He's been referred to as enigmatic, brazen and earnest, his vigour and intensity always patent in live performance and in his lyrics. For a long time the intensity was about more than the content of the songs, though; the combined music and energy of Mark Seymour's band, Hunters & Collectors, was an all-out aural assault. It was a sound of rhythmic power, blistering horns and cacophonous synthesiser, and at the core was an impassioned voice and a heart full of expressive song.

To many, Seymour was and always will be the king of Australian rock angst. He wouldn't shy away from the notion, but separation from the Hunters was essential to put that angst in its correct context. To divorce himself from a sound that defined him even against his will. "I think the intensity of that bass/drum sound used to make me force the bottom note out so that there was this apparent sense of angst all the time even when I wasn't feeling particularly angst-ridden. I was reacting to the sounds around me," he said in a relaxed and markedly angst-free mood.

His third solo album, *Embedded,* had recently been recorded when we met in his manager's St Kilda office, across the road from the sea, on the top floor of an apartment block that one intuitively knew had been the scene for many intriguing incidents. There was something strange and mysterious about the place. Indeed, Seymour revealed, it was in this building that the inspiration for "Say Goodbye" had come to him some eighteen years earlier, the place where he had overheard a conversation that included one of the more memorable lines in Australian rock: "You don't make me feel like I'm a woman any more."

Relationships, politics (both partisan and sexual), social injustice, alienation, anguish, disillusionment and empathy were all present in Seymour's Hunters & Collectors repertoire, in songs like "Throw Your Arms around Me", "Do You See What I See?" and "When the River Runs Dry". Most of those themes have continued to be explored in his solo work, but since finding his own voice, the music has been more pop-oriented and certainly less raucous.

He was born on 26 July 1956 in Benalla, Victoria, to staunchly Catholic parents who were literary and musical, encouraging individuality and creative thinking. The tension between religious and secular teachings created an internal conflict in Seymour as a child and the resulting intensity and darkness for which he became known is still present, although tempered by age, experience and, after so many songs that chronicled relationship dilemmas, lasting love.

Seymour studied classical piano for seven years as a child and learned violin as a teenager, but it was picking up a guitar at the age of twelve that gave music a purpose in his life. Influenced by his older sister's record collection—Simon & Garfunkel and Bob Dylan especially—Seymour, with academic diligence, set about learning how their songs actually worked. "Those records were important to me because I physically sat down and learned to play a lot of them. I wanted to learn how," he recalled. "I think my consciousness of how songs were written vaguely started to gestate at that point in my life. But it took me a long time to start thinking, well, maybe I could do that. Many, many years later."

After starting out as an English schoolteacher, Seymour upset his parents by dedicating himself to a full-time music career. Hunters & Collectors, the quintessential pub rock band, offered music for the urban populace, anthems for a generation. The eloquent, intellectual bent of Seymour's subject matter might have been at odds with the working class persona he adopted for the stage, but the beauty of his work was how it subtly worked its way into the sweaty psyche of the audiences. "I knew there'd be people who'd be intrigued by it," Seymour said. "But I think we were more interested as a group to create an effect. We were more interested in just creating this mood in the room."

In the 1990s a growing frustration with band politics made Seymour restless. He had already recorded *King without a Clue* before the Hunters broke up in 1998, with assistance from the group's guitarist, Barry Palmer, but even that relationship fell by the wayside as Seymour spread his wings. "In those last few years of the band's life, the hardest thing to cope with was the fact that there was this inability for us to be able to talk to each other honestly about what we wanted out of life and music." Honesty is as fundamental to Seymour as the air that he breathes, and so is finding clarity in a chaotic and often difficult world. He might never again enjoy the adulation that he had as front man for Hunters & Collectors, but he still has stories to tell.

Does your lyrical gift come from reading and writing poetry as a teenager?
No, I think my consumption of literature was pretty much standard high school stuff. I just did what I was told to do. I studied at school, I studied quite hard. I was a good student. But there was nothing exceptionally imaginative about it all.

You've said that the lyrics for "Talking to a Stranger" were loosely based on Charles Baudelaire's "The Albatross". Because you were an English teacher, I wondered if poetry was an important focus.
Well, it did definitely become that, but much later. My interest in poetry didn't materialise when I was learning to play guitar. I think I really got interested in poetry at university. But by then I was starting to chew at the bit about where my career was going and what I wanted to do. So things came to a head. Even though I'd been interested in rock 'n' roll and learning the guitar for many, many years, it wasn't until then that I started to kind of go, okay, well there's something about poetry and literature that actually does fascinate me. But for me those decisions to leap into the creative world were all very cathartic and emotional. I had quite specific reasons; things were happening to me in my life at that time that made me want to go, "Fuck this, I'm not doing this any more. I want to try and do *this*." If you're making decisions to take a creative path in life, there's a leap of faith involved. You're stepping off into the unknown.

I didn't have a definite desire to be an English teacher. I basically drifted into it. And I was following a path that appeared to be preordained by my parents' expectations, much as they deny that vigorously. They'll be denying that on their deathbeds, probably. But that was the culture of the family. I could have chosen half a dozen different courses.

And you didn't have an idea at that stage that you could be a professional musician?
Oh, not at all. I believed that if I applied myself to it, if I worked hard enough at it, eventually it might bear fruit. But there was no plan, so to speak. In fact I was a constant source of frustration to the other guys in Hunters, who were much better organised in that way, much more professionally orientated people. I was basically flying by the seat of my pants, but I was creating things. I was driving the machine, but I didn't really think that it could ever bear large amounts of money.

Do you think the intellectual background puts undue pressure on you to be extra special in whatever it is you create? So much has been written about how intense you were all the time.
That had nothing to do with intellectualism. That had more to do with the fact I was just barking mad. I think there is a tyranny in intellectualism. Because it can block you. Melbourne Uni people stand out like dogs bods to me, anyone from my generation, you can pick them a mile off. They're incredibly self-critical, really rigorous and very sceptical. But at the same time it gives you a bit of an edge in language as well. I try to write hard or difficult words first. And then simplify them. I'm not satisfied with stating the obvious unless I am absolutely convinced that there is a fundamental emotional truth in it. I'm

genuinely searching around the issue, or if something strikes me as interesting, if it's something that I've observed in the world, my next step is that it will manifest itself in a song. If I can honestly say I have had an emotional reaction to that phenomenon that I'm looking at. But unless I believe that I can write it using language that actually has some form of beauty in itself, whether it's linguistically efficient or simple and punchy and it also has great metaphor, unless I can cover all of that, I won't go there. Even if I have reacted to it honestly.

Do those words generally come easily to you or do you have to search? Do you have thesauruses, dictionaries and tools with you?
No, no tools. I generally absorb words. I just read a lot; I absorb language all the time. But I have to say I find it incredibly difficult. Writing good lyrics is really hard to do. And writing naff, prosaic, dumb lyrics is really easy, and I just can't let myself … Well, I have written some pretty fucking dumb lyrics.

What do you think you've written that's dumb?
Oh, I could give you a list as long as your arm. I couldn't begin to tell you, we'd be sitting here for hours.

But that's just the Melbourne Uni self-critical part of you talking.
Maybe it is, yeah. I'm very reluctant to put pen to paper. I generally accumulate lyrics. I always have more than I need. But to make them sit comfortably within a musical form and also read well is a big challenge.

Do you remember writing your first song?
Yes I do. It was 1979 and it was a song called "Space Invader" and it was a song about those video games.

There was a hit song called "Space Invaders".
There was, but years later. I was the first. This was just this funny little pop song. I was listening to New York new wave music and it was like that era of glam punk and had that flavour.

What brought you to that point where you were ready to sit down and write a song?
There was definitely a sense of, "I have to do this now." I'd been going out to see The Models and The Boys Next Door, and in that era there were a lot of new wave bands happening that never really got anywhere, or surfaced and got to a point commercially and then disappeared. But in 1979–80 there were a lot of punk bands around, there was so much energy on such a very small scale in Melbourne. I became more and more obsessed with it and I kept saying to myself, "I can do this." I'd been playing in this cover band with some guys I met at uni who ended up being in Hunters, John Archer and Doug Falconer, and I convinced them to form an original band. We formed this

group called The Jetsonnes, and I think that was the first song that I wrote. It was a little bit like "Friday on My Mind". It started with just a two-string riff, E, A, E, A, very fast, very quick.

I used to bring ideas to the band, I might have two sections, like a verse and a chorus, and very skeletal lyrics, and the band would basically arrange it. How's this going to work, how are we going to get to this section? The song would take physical shape with the guys in the room.

And that's how it would work through the life of the Hunters?
It was far more egalitarian in the band. It kept changing all the time. I remember when I first started with Hunters I probably worked more like that than I subsequently did. In the band, personalities kept changing roles and it endured for so many years, and I think partly that had to do with the fact that the creative hat got passed around. But essentially what I did a lot of the time was I'd stand in the middle of the room and go, okay, musician B has come up with this set of chords, I can do something with that. And then just park my words there. And that might end up becoming a song. Then that guy might come up with a set of chords. It really was a moveable feast and it changed constantly. For many years it was an ideal situation for a band and it kept us alive because people felt motivated that they were having creative input. You think you've got something to say, and it's impacting on the way other people behave, and it does keep you interested musically, independently of the financial return. But I think my role was to give it form. To actually say, "This set of chords isn't a song until I've written the words and a melody."

When you wrote a Hunters & Collectors song, was the primary focus on how it would be played live rather than how it would sound recorded?
Yeah. I don't think we ever really lost that. There's a philosophical choice there that bands make, it was pretty much driven by performance. And every musical element then goes into making a song transparent and expressive and understandable, from production right through to arrangement and simplicity of words and all that shit. It's a huge palette. I don't tend to regard the studio process as being what makes the song fundamentally commercial. There are a lot of musicians who would argue with me on that. I think the attitude that studio production somehow gives the song a better chance in the marketplace is a really dubious one. Studios are there and the process of recording is important, it's the glue that keeps the process going. At any given time in history there is a particular sound that will define an era, and a lot of that has to do with technology. But ultimately the songs are what drive the business.

So in your solo work also, you would write a song thinking about how you were going to play it live as opposed to what it was going to sound like on record?
Yeah, essentially. And I don't stay attached to records for very long. I'll get a record finished and I'm thinking about the next one. It's all about self-expression; it's got very little to do with what the record sounds like. It's important to make records that sound great—I reckon

it's crucial—and I want to hear sounds that move me emotionally and that are connected with what the emotional truth of the song is. But I don't remain attached to sounds for very long; I tend to want to go and get on with the job of writing new material.

Do you remember writing "Talking to a Stranger"?
I had a little blue notebook that I wrote in. And I was reading Baudelaire. I was living in a house in Carlton with the keyboard player, Geoff Crosby, and we were really into the Talking Heads and Eno and we were experimenting. Having fun, basically. He was painting and I was writing. I was on the dole. And I bought a little drum machine and we both bought these MS-20 Korg synthesisers, which were hilarious machines, this tiny little keyboard, basically oscillators that made all these incredible, fantastic sounds. I had a drum beat, a very simple 120 beats per minute. I knew I wanted to write a dance track, something that had a very straight driven drumbeat, and I wrote the bass line. I was also really into Michael Jackson, and I wanted to write a really simple, funky guitar riff that just sat over the bass line. And you had these two intersecting melodies working.

Like "Billie Jean"?
Yeah. That's a good analogy. And I loved *Off the Wall*; that was my favourite record.

I remember being really enthralled by *Wake in Fright* by Kenneth Cook. It was a story about this young Australian teacher who gets posted to this country school; it's quite a famous early seventies Aussie film, which was extremely powerful. It's full of dread and anxiety and I really related to it, I really connected with it. And I wanted the song to have that deep sense of dread. I was also fascinated by that poem, because it alludes to the idea that the sailors killed the albatross, that tradition in early maritime history where the sailors would capture an albatross and that would keep them safe. But then the albatross dies and their luck runs out. I just love that idea, that imagery of a group of people who have gone off on this journey into the wilderness and something goes horribly wrong. The idea that human endeavour is basically flawed. I love that Homeric idea of the guy being strapped to the mast and having to take the wax out of his ears so he can hear the siren's song and he can't escape. All those legends speak powerfully about the human spirit and how we strive to discover, to venture into the unknown, and sometimes it bears fruit and sometimes it's horribly disastrous.

I really felt that at that moment, those two or three years in my life, I was stepping into a void. I was stepping off into a world that I had not been prepared for, that my mother and father couldn't possibly understand, that I'd come from a very sheltered middle-class existence and the idea of forming a band and trying to see whether we had success was an incredibly scary thing to do. I had all these very vague images and an overall feeling about what the song was about, but lyrically I never really tied it down too much to direct personal narrative style. Very few of the songs in that era were particularly direct. It was all about images and letting the music create a mood and just using the words to further define the mood.

Much has been chronicled about the energy of the Hunters' music, the atmosphere, the themes of alienation and sexual politics, the reflection of Australian culture. Were such themes planned out from the start?

I think all that's pretty true. Sexual alienation is definitely a theme that I have investigated at length. I've always been interested in the landscape and the world that I physically move through. But I do see my world as being populated by these characters that I never really understand. Human consciousness is just this weird, vague, dangerous place that we inhabit. You relate to people politely on a social level and you function as an individual in order to survive. But you can never possibly know anyone else fully, and it's that sense of the unknown and the way you're bumping up against it all the time, in the way you relate to other people, that keeps me going as a lyricist.

Did the other band members share those concerns?

I think people were interested in making it work orchestrally and to make the songs sound good and make them dynamic. Everybody put in. But what other people in the band's actual agenda was, I couldn't honestly say now that I could speak for them. I was motivated by my own personal needs and what I wanted to say artistically in a band. What other people were on about, it's probably a mystery to me even now. But that's the risk I took.

But did they discuss with you whether they felt connected to what you were writing about? And did they need to feel connected in order to play it?

You're talking about a bunch of really typical Aussie white blokes, you know, who don't talk about their feelings very much. So there was very little dialogue about that. It's not that I didn't need it, and more than anyone else in the band I valued the input of Robert Miles who in fact wasn't in the band, he was the front-of-house mixer. He was a person who could talk about art. He was very important to me and I still spend quite a bit of time with him. But no-one else, virtually. I mean, the odd person would come up and say, "Oh, I really like that. That's not bad." But there was more of a desire amongst the guys to try and make the whole thing work as a machine. It was like sailing a boat.

You'd chart the course?

Well, sometimes I didn't chart the course, sometimes I'd be at the top of the fucking wizard mast, hanging onto a rope. [*Laughs*] John Archer was on the tiller, the bass player. In all fairness to the band, I think the only way you can honestly claim to be fully in control of your artistic life and direction as a singer-songwriter is if you make it quite clear from the outset of your career, "I'm a singer-songwriter. And I do it all." Unless you do that, then history will determine how you're defined. There aren't many guys who've actually done that. Paul Kelly's probably one who's pretty undiluted, that's what he's done. But most of us who've been in bands have been profoundly influenced by the unknown motivation of the other individuals in the band.

As the lyricist, did you have carte blanche on the subject matter, then?
Pretty much, yeah. I was never comfortable with other people writing the words. Ever. I was very, very protective of my turf.

What if somebody else sings your lyrics? Does that feel comfortable to you?
I don't mind other people singing my words, but my general reaction is that they don't really get it right. There is an argument that you should try to get other people to cover your songs, but I think lyrics are too important to me personally.

Your brother Nick said that Crowded House tried to record "Throw Your Arms around Me" several times and the chemistry in the studio was never right. Pearl Jam and others have played it, too.
With a song like "Throw Your Arms around Me", a lot of people have tried to cover it because it's just so well known. But I think about the songs that have been covered by famous writers in America, the ones that have been successful have been songs that have matched the singer. Whereas with "Throw Your Arms around Me", maybe one day someone will come along and do a fantastic version of it. I think the key with that is that I don't really do a great deal with it. I just sing melody. And a lot of it just has to do with the inherent tone of my voice, which is a character voice, so it conveys a particular feeling when I sing the words, where someone else might convey something entirely different. But it is a song that's inextricably associated with my voice.

Do you remember when the idea for that song came to you, and was it a lyrical or a musical idea first?
It was a lyrical idea. It's a combination of Van Morrison—I discovered Van Morrison and Them around about that time, it was about '84, '85—and the idea of this story. I was in love with this girl. She lived in Carlton and I used to travel across town at night-time in the evening to see her, and I was acutely aware of the geography of that transition, crossing Melbourne. I became very physically aware of my environment for the first time, the real tactile sense of it, the real Melbourne experience. And I've never ever lost that. I think having that emotional commitment, that sense of opening up to somebody, and also still being at a fairly nascent stage as a writer, those two things emerged simultaneously in my life so I became very acutely aware of what my lyrics could convey, what tools that I had at my disposal, and I became, I think, a better writer as a consequence of that.

The setting of "Throw Your Arms around Me" in the future not only creates an atmosphere of great anticipation; it also seems to perpetuate the song as a timeless work. Did you use that as a conscious device?
You know, I think that that's partly why it's still really popular.

Because the story never happens; it's always what's going to happen. So you want to hear it again.
Yeah. I didn't think of it as an unusual device at the time, but in retrospect, I think you're

right. You don't hear it that often. I was trying to get across the idea that what was happening at that moment in time in my life and her life was going to keep happening. That what we were doing to each other was going to cause this chain of events to emerge, that we were going to have a profound effect on each other's lives, and we didn't really know what that was going to be, but there was a sense of an unfolding story. So that whole album, or a large part of it, was very much written about things that were actually happening, almost day by day. I don't do that much now. I very rarely do. I write lyrics, put them aside, just accumulate them. And then I look at them later. That's partly to do with how busy I am.

And also how experienced you now are at writing. Perhaps when you were still developing as a songwriter, everything was about what was immediate for you.
I think there's a certain thing that happens in pop music where young artists are coughed up by the business, and you look at them and go, "How the fuck did they arrive?" I have a firm belief that if they're good, young singer-songwriters, or singers in bands, there's a real sense that they're discovering how to do this, and in a way there is something quite difficult about becoming a master of your own skills. Once you've actually reached a point where you're really good at it or you're pretty bloody good at it, it becomes that much harder to be original. And at that time in my life, I think I was pretty typical of someone like that. Jeff Buckley for example, that album *Grace*, that's so radical, that record. He had a time and place in history. If he had have lived I'm sure he would have found it more difficult to do something as original as that again. Van Morrison with *Astral Weeks*, that's an incredibly unique album. It's so lateral and strange, and yet it has this incredible ambience. *Human Frailty* for Hunters & Collectors was probably the most interesting record we made. And it sounds really odd. But it does define it.

Was "Say Goodbye" about something you heard through a hotel room wall?
No, it was actually heard through a wall in this building. [*Laughs*] I happened to be on my own in the office, and this conversation transpired between the tenants that were here, which I thought was really, really funny. Because I'd been through something similar with my girlfriend, where I came home and she ground her finger in my breastbone. That all happened to me. A girl totally, literally nailing me to the floor and saying, "What the fuck are you doing?" But the line, "You don't make me feel like I'm a woman any more", that came through a wall. And I remember trying to analyse. "Okay, what's actually happening to me at the moment with this girl? I'm struggling with this, I don't understand how I can be in love with someone and they can be in love with me, but there's all this conflict." I couldn't grapple with that. And then I heard that, and I thought, "That's just fantastic." It suddenly gave it its humorous edge. I thought, "Ah, I know how I can get around this emotionally; I can actually make it funny."

So did you build the song around that line?
I had the lyrics written without a melody and I knew I had that line in the middle. It just basically told a story. And then I got together with the band in a studio in Prahran, and I

wrote the bass line and Doug played the drums, and that was the starting point. It was A minor. Until I was in there with them, I didn't actually have a set of chords. But a lot of the stuff Hunters wrote around the bass lines. Really tough, pushy bass lines. I remember at the time saying, "I want this one to be like 'The Slab'", another song on a previous album, which had a similar type of attitude, really jungly, tough bass line with a rumbling drumbeat. And I just started rapping the words over the top. It's like talking blues or something like that.

What was the story behind "Do You See What I See?"
I'd met another girl [*Laughs*] in New Zealand, who I eventually married—thank God. I remember being at the top of a hill in Auckland at the end of a tour we'd done in New Zealand. I'd been for a run and I was looking down on the house that she lived in, and I remember thinking, "I'm really just passing through here. I'm emotionally connected with the lives of people in that house, but at this moment I'm geographically separated from them and I could quite easily walk out of their lives and never see them again." I knew I had that choice, and that's a choice I didn't make. There was something in me that said, "I am inextricably bonded to those people." It had a huge effect on me in my life and it subsequently turned out to be true. I had an instinctive sense that there was a reason I wrote those words at that time. I probably wasn't as conscious of it as I am now. But I spied that little house with the backyard and the tea towels on the clothesline flowing in the wind and that was the touchstone for me, that image.

Was it important to you that listeners understood the true intent of your lyrics or were you happy for people to come up with their own interpretations? Both "Where Do You Go" and "True Tears of Joy" sound like very personal songs.
Later on I listened to a lot more traditional American country rock and traditional American songwriting, where they are very skilful at just making words resonate really beautifully within a very melodic environment. Like Tom Petty, Bob Dylan, getting back to that again. As I've gotten older I've become more and more interested in the kind of songwriting I was listening to in my early adolescence. And I've fully gone there now. When I started in the Hunters I was much more arty and conceptual. But "Tears of Joy" and "Where Do You Go?", I can see that I was heading in more and more of that direction of calling a spade a spade, but doing it in a way that sounded good.

With "Where Do You Go?" I was going out with someone then who had this obsession with thrift shops. She'd go out and look for deals in second-hand shops. She used to disappear for hours, be gone all day, I could never figure out where she'd gone. And eventually it dawned on me; she just had this network of second-hand shops that she went to. I made that construction in my mind; I imagined what she was doing.

As a mature solo artist, does the weight of songs like "Throw Your Arms around Me" and "Say Goodbye" hinder you in your progress?
I don't really think so. There are songs that I've released as singles as a solo artist which

I've dispensed with completely, because they were the wrong choices or I'm not interested in them any more and I just don't play them well any more. So I think I've probably got the same attitude to my material now as I had when I was in Hunters anyway. You write mediocre songs and you write slightly better ones and sometimes you write really, really good ones. And "Throw Your Arms around Me" happens to be one of those. I know there are times when I feel quietly frustrated by the notoriety of the Hunters repertoire and how much difficulty I've had getting my solo career going. But I've had to be philosophical about that because "Throw Your Arms around Me", if I wrote that tomorrow I'd be leaping out of my skin. It's a classic. And I don't really think it has much to do with Hunters & Collectors to be honest. I think it's got to do with I stumbled on a great idea and I was in Hunters & Collectors at the time. That's the way I would go with my writing, it's pretty reactive.

Were the songs for _King without a Clue_ written with the intention of being for a solo album, or had some of them started as potential Hunters & Collectors songs?
"Last Ditch Cabaret", which was the first single, I'd imagined that for Hunters at one point, shortly after I had the gig that caused me to write the lyric. And then decided not to because I really liked the words; the words really manifested something that was a completely unique Mark Seymour experience and I thought, no, I won't do that. But I was nurturing those ambitions. "You Don't Have to Cry Any More" was vaguely Hunteresque. This is all stuff that I've only realised in hindsight. At the time it was all a bit of a melting pot.

Was writing alone liberating or daunting initially?
I found it a lot harder than I expected to. But more because of the habit than anything else. I think it's taken me a few years to realise it was all meant to be.

Did you feel you had to keep making statements in your songs when the band was no longer involved in representing them?
I've always believed that each song is a discrete statement. You've got to be saying something.

Something important?
I think so, yeah. The lyric has to be underpinned by some fundamental point of view that needs to be made clear. Even if it's funny. It doesn't have to be earnest all the time. Sometimes I commit that ugly sin of being earnest. But I do try to be funny, too. So the point of delivery is always that it's got to be a statement. I don't think that's changed at all.

Without the full force of the group alongside you filling out your songs, have you found your songwriting is more guided by your voice, and what it can do?
That's probably the most important point that I'd want to make now in my life. Probably what was frustrating me most about Hunters & Collectors in the end was that the drums and bass were so loud on stage I couldn't hear myself. I was always struggling to rise above that.

And since that's gone, that actual sound, I've found that my knowledge of myself as a performer has become far more apparent. My voice can go there, I can say that in that way.

And that then guides you in writing a melody because you know where your voice can go?
It guides me in everything. Voice is paramount, absolutely paramount.

"Home Again" was like the antithesis of so much of the angst in your Hunters' songs. Do you remember how you and Barry Palmer wrote that?
I turned up at his house, this little wooden cottage in Northcote. I used to travel across town. I could hear him in the front room playing a riff. It had a beautiful chord shift, and before I'd even knocked on the door I was thinking, "I can do something with that." And the idea of returning home just came into my head. It wasn't my home, it was his. But just that image and that riff and then I went in there and pretty much wrote the words in the room. I did actually have quite a lot of stuff written about living in Melbourne in that time. Because it was in a period of dramatic political change, political upheaval, with the Kennett government and privatisation of government institutions. I was really, really upset about that guy and I wanted to nail him to the floor. [*Laughs*] So it's about Melbourne, that song.

You've referred to certain songs, like "Strange Little Town", as "Melbourne songs". What makes a "Melbourne song"?
"Strange Little Town" is about Brunswick Street, Fitzroy. It's a document of a particular environment, a room in a street, people in that room. Being in your own place, being in your own city, but realising you don't really want to be there. You want to move on and get to another place. "Strange Little Town" is a closely observed lyric about that little corner of Melbourne. It's so discrete. It's so different.

But does a Melbourne song have to reference a part of Melbourne, or is there something more intrinsic? And in fact, is there a distinct style that a Melbourne songwriter has that sets him apart from a Sydney songwriter or a songwriter from other parts of Australia?
[*Laughs*] Ooh, that's a tough one. I'm only speaking very broadly, but I've always associated Sydney with hard rock. And pubs. I think Melbourne's more intimate and discreet and I always feel that there's something really bracing about Melbourne. I come home here to work. It's a serious fucking place. Whereas Sydney I see as a kind of fun parlour. A song like "Ballad of the One Eyed Man", I had to come home to write that.

Can you tell me the story of how you came to write "Ballad of the One Eyed Man"? You were bashed and then went and wrote something tender with a very optimistic melody.
At the time it was a really scary thing to happen, I was in real trouble. I got out of it, I escaped. I was on tour with Hunters & Collectors, I think it was maybe the last tour or the second last tour and there was this real sense that we were all going along with this idea, well it's all ending, we're all basically just coping professionally, there was very little communication between band members, it was a very strange, disconnected time to be in,

really hard work. And my way of coping with that, which I think probably was the same for most of the other guys, was to stay detached and cool and just be very professional and do the job. Just get as much out of it as I could personally and don't really share too much emotionally with the others.

And then that happened. I remember being in the middle of it and I felt quite detached from it. Because I basically knew inside myself that I was going to survive it and I was going to escape and there was something quite strangely alienating about it. I didn't actually feel really strong emotions about it. And that weird sense of detachment, which appalled me because of the mental state I was in at that time anyway, enabled me to go, "This is just a guy, this is happening to me, but it also could be happening to anyone. Just a guy in the Cross who's run into the wrong people and these are just people on the street who need money." The fact that my consciousness was able to be in those two worlds at the same time gave me a burst of, oh, I can write about this.

Did you literally go home and write it?
I was writing it within a day, yeah. Or a couple of days. The idea is the walking where angels fear to tread. I just felt sorry for these people.

That's what came through. The compassion.
Yeah. And I quite liked the guy with the one eye. I did actually talk to him. He was the patsy, he was set up by this little bloke, this nasty little other guy who came up and slugged me behind my head with something heavy. But I took it to Hunters & Collectors and they went, "Uhhh, ballad. Fuckin' ballad." Beautiful. Just so bittersweet. And I thought, right, well, I've got to put it on my record. Daniel Denholm, who produced the record, just loved it. And the record company loved it. It's one of my best works. So I had a very perverse pleasure in getting that recorded.

One Eyed Man and Embedded seem to be albums of song cycles, if you like. Groups of songs that belong together. Maybe like a series of paintings on the same theme. Is that your intention?
I try to aspire to that, that each record is a chapter or a new stage and point of view in my life. But you never really know how realistic that ambition is at the time that you're writing. I always find that you write this song and then this song and then as you get into the guts of the record, you're seeing something emerging but it's still incredibly vague what that thing is. It's only really when you've finished it and you've lived with it for a while and even gone out and performed it for a few months, "Ah, that's that chapter in my life. That meant that. That was actually that image or that idea."

How different is it for you writing about the difficulty of human interaction now that you're a happy, settled family man?
Look, I don't think I'm particularly happy. I think I'm happy at times. And I'm certainly not settled within myself at all. We have this clichéd view of what marriage is all about and

parenthood. I think it's a stage in your life, people become parents, they have children and then that influences the way their lives are conducted. There's no question that it does change you, but it hasn't really changed my sense of the feeling of urgency about what I do as an artist.

So you're still grappling with the same questions?
Oh, yeah, shit yeah. Totally. And it's all internal dialogue. I'm looking unwell, I feel like this, I've got to write this down. If I stopped doing this I'd die.

Are you a disciplined songwriter? Do you have a daily routine?
No, not at all. I'm busy. I try to write when I can. Songs have a way of emerging one way or another. I'm not particularly precious about how I arrive at them, as long as I feel they have some grain of emotion, some fundamental statement. But how they arrive and when they arrive is a bit of a dog's breakfast, really.

Do they arrive from within you or do they come from somewhere else?
I think they come from inside. There's external stimulants, things that are happening that I'm seeing occur, and those are the stories that I construct in a lyric, things that are perceivable in the world. But what's pulling them together for me is an internal process.

PAUL KELLY

MELBOURNE, AUSTRALIA, NOVEMBER 2002

Paul Kelly is a man of few words—at least when it comes to talking about his songwriting. His songs overflow with lyrics that invite interpretation and analysis, his influences include great literary figures such as WB Yeats and Raymond Carver and his songs often carry literary references. He has published two books of lyrics and his website contains lyrics to dozens of his songs. Words are everywhere—except in conversations about them.

Referred to variously as a poet, a political commentator, a storyteller, "a mirror to the Australian spirit", Kelly sees himself largely as a music man, and resists intense focus on his lyrics at the expense of the music. The music, he insists, is what compels him. His forays into screen composing have included collaborating on the *Lantana* score and the soundtrack to *One Night the Moon*. He has also acted on stage and screen. But it's his large and outstanding catalogue of songs for which he is best known and revered.

Kelly was born in Adelaide on 13 January 1955 and like nearly all of the Adelaide musicians before him, he migrated to Melbourne to further his career. His first band was the High Rise Bombers, and after the departure of key original members it mutated into Paul Kelly and the Dots. After the Dots broke up, Kelly formed his own band and then moved temporarily to Sydney, where he recorded his third album—and his first solo—1985's *Post,* a watershed work showcasing his deeply personal acoustic style and featuring his best known early song, "From St Kilda to Kings Cross". Then came the band Paul Kelly and the Coloured Girls, later changed to the less contentious Paul Kelly and the Messengers before touring America. Five more albums followed, containing hits such as "Before Too Long", "Darling It Hurts", "To Her Door", "Dumb Things" and "Sweet Guy"—songs whose bright, catchy melodies often belied a dark, lyrical content.

He spent most of the 1990s recording solo albums and soundtracks as well as writing and producing for other artists. He has been drawn to work with indigenous artists such as Kev Carmody, Archie Roach, Ruby Hunter, Christine Anu and most memorably with the members of Yothu Yindi on "Treaty". The list of female songwriters whose work also bears his name is extensive—Vika and Linda Bull, Renee Geyer, Jenny Morris, Deborah Conway, Wendy Matthews, Debra Byrne, Monique Brumby, Kate Ceberano and more. And many other legendary songwriters have chosen to collaborate with Kelly, including Nick Cave, Tim Finn, Ross Wilson, Garth Porter, Colin Hay, Joe Camilleri, Peter Garrett and Mark Seymour. Then there are his recent band members, among them Shane O'Mara, Stephen Hadley, Peter Luscombe and his nephew, Dan Kelly, with whom he has also co-written.

"You often write songs with collaborators that you would never write by yourself," Kelly explained. "It's a way of dragging a song out of you that you wouldn't have come up with."

His songs are regularly covered, interestingly most often by women, yet Kelly sees himself primarily as a performer of his own work. He has occasionally recorded and performed other writers' songs—from the traditional folk song "Streets of Forbes" to Errol Brown's Hot Chocolate disco hit "It Started with a Kiss" (which in Kelly's hands sounds like it was always a gentle folk pop song)—but doubts he would want to continue performing if he couldn't write any more.

Interviewing Kelly at his St Kilda home on a cool, overcast day in late spring, it was obvious that talking about his work is like tooth extraction. Mostly it is shyness, but there is also a deliberate aloofness from a man who believes that the mystery of songwriting is what makes it so marvellous.

Most songwriters started playing in their early teens, but you came to music relatively late in the piece, didn't you? How old were you when you first picked up a guitar?
Guitar would have been eighteen or nineteen. But I had music through school; I played trumpet in high school for five years and a couple of years of piano before that.

Did any of that education help when you did start writing songs? Do you write notation?
No, the bands that I work with were all head arrangements, but having basic theory I think helps, knowing chords, how they work, what chords are related to each other.

When did you write your first song?
I would have been about nineteen. I was listening a lot to Van Morrison's *Astral Weeks* at the time.

What was it called?
"It's the Falling Apart that Makes You", something like that. I remember it. It was an open G tuning.

When did you start writing poetry?
About the age of fifteen, sixteen. Just like everyone; everyone writes poetry when they're fifteen, sixteen.

I didn't; I wrote prose. Were you writing any prose, any fiction at all?
Later on I wrote some prose, more like prose poems rather than short stories. That was after I left school.

You've said that the melody usually comes before the lyrics when you're writing. You strike me as coming from a lyrical background and your references are very literary.
There's been an imbalance of focus on my words, because it's a musical thing first. The words always serve the music, generally. I hardly ever write a lyric and try and put music to it. I know some people do, but it doesn't come to me that way. Focus on the lyrics is fine, because I think lyrics are important, but often it's at the expense of people focusing on the music. Which I think is just as important.

Do you ever have a title first and then think that's a theme, so what musically would fit that theme and then come back with the lyrics?
Yeah, it's a bit of a back and forth.

Do you think rhyme is important in lyrics?
I'm a bit of a rhymer but some of my favourite songwriters aren't. Iggy Pop's a great example of a songwriter that writes fairly standard verse-chorus things, but often doesn't worry about the rhyme. I tend to use rough rhymes a lot, because it feels more natural. Things are rhyming but they're not sounding too carefully rhymed, and that helps songs sound more conversational. But yeah, I have a natural tendency to rhyme. Even when I write letters to people I might rhyme in it.

Is the opening line the hardest thing for you lyrically?
No, I'd say the third verse is usually the hardest. I think the hardest part of a song is finishing it off. Often I have songs where I know the musical structure of it, I know where it should rise and fall in certain ways, and I've got most of the lyrics, and it's just getting the last few final lyrics, that's usually the slowest part.

Your opening lines often set the scene very quickly.
Yeah. I've got lots of opening lines.

So at the moment you've got opening lines wandering around in your mind waiting for the rest of the song to come along?
Not so much that I have opening lines stored up, but I find getting a start on a song is easier than finishing it.

Paul Simon said that after his earlier pop hits he became more interested in composing rhythms than melodies. I wondered if that rings true for you, given that much of your latest album, *Nothing but a Dream*, is very rhythmic and trance-like, dreamy.
I would probably say that's more the case with *Words and Music*, which is the record before that, which was very much made with the band. I thought *Nothing but a Dream* was much more of a folky, singer-songwriter record.

It is, but I wouldn't say that it has the soaring melodies that the earlier chart hits contained, the catchy tunes that you go away singing. I find *Nothing But A Dream* best experienced as an entity.
I think for a lot of songwriters that's a fairly natural evolution. When you first start off, you probably have your own thing that you do and then you get sick of your own template, and you want to find other ways to write. So I've done it more over the last five or six years where I write with a band and the way to write with a band is that you don't start with a melody, you start with a groove or a fairly simple chord structure and then you write over the top of the rhythm. I've always tended to do that with my bands, even with the Coloured Girls and the Messengers, we would sometimes get songs just by playing with the band. I always wanted to write that way. I've done it more over the last five or six years because the musicians I'm playing with are quite versatile and have had strong funk, soul and reggae roots.

I think it's a natural tendency of any writer to try and find new ways to write. No matter how wide-ranging your influences, we tend to fall into our own patterns. They'll always keep coming back; some songs I write now sound like songs I would have written twenty years ago, but there are other songs I write now that I could never have written then.

When you write a song that sounds like something you could have written twenty years ago, is that okay with you?
Yeah. Like that one just sort of popped out of the factory. I recognise those songs when they come, like that one just came out of an oven or something.

Do you ever come up with melodies away from the guitar? Do you hear melodies in your head when you're out shopping?
Hardly ever. It's piano or guitar.

I know you've eschewed the label of storyteller. I see you more as painting pictures, creating a sense of place and or character. I think of Jimmy Webb, whose pictures of Galveston and Wichita are etched on our minds, and of Randy Newman, whose characters took on lives of their own.
That's a pretty fair comparison. A lot of my songs are very situational; they come from imagining someone in a particular situation. So sometimes a sequence of events happens which makes it more a story, but other times it's just that situation. I guess most music theatre writes from that point of view.

Bob Dylan is an obvious influence; who else was influencing you when you were younger, and whose writing inspires you now?
Everything. When I was younger I listened to a lot of folk, blues, country music, Hank Williams and Stanley Brothers, lots of hillbilly music, Howlin' Wolf, Muddy Waters.

Were you ever listening from a songwriting point of view?
Yeah, you'd listen to something and try to figure it out, get the chords. All the time.

I wondered if Greg Macainsh's work with Skyhooks had resonated with you, being such a Melbourne songwriter and one of the first Australian songwriters to evoke a sense of inner city place, urban life.
I wasn't a big fan of Skyhooks; I got to Melbourne and they were winding up. The more Australian songwriters that influenced me were bands that came out in the late seventies and early eighties—The Triffids, The Go-Betweens, The Saints, Chris Bailey's solo records, the Hoodoo Gurus. I was probably affected more by a slightly later generation.

I mentioned the Greg Macainsh thing because when he wrote "When the sun sets over Carlton" and lines like that, no-one had ever really done that before; everyone before had tried to sound English or American or neutral. And suddenly there was a songwriter writing very much about where he lived.
Yeah. "Balwyn Calling" and all that.

You came along and took that a lot further. You probably didn't sit down and think, "I'm going to be the great urban songwriter and write about St Kilda and Kings Cross." It was probably just what you wanted to write about at the time.
I'm sure that's what Skyhooks were doing, I was aware that they were writing about places around them. Like Chuck Berry, I loved his songwriting, it had very specific details in them, they were songs you could see as well as hear; they were very cinematic. Lou Reed's a very cinematic songwriter, too. I like that kind of songwriting. Cold Chisel, Australian Crawl were all writing about where they come from.

When you toured with Dylan, did you get to sit down with him and rave about songwriting? Had you met him before then?
I'd done a show with him about twelve years ago, but hadn't met him that time. I met him

this last time just briefly at the start of the tour and a little bit at the end. We didn't really spend lots of time talking.

Would you have liked to? Were there questions you'd have loved to ask him about songwriting?
No, not really. I didn't have a great desire to meet him. It was nice to meet him; he was quite polite and shy. Friendly. But with someone like that, people are always wanting to meet him, so I'd rather just leave him alone.

Is that how you feel about yourself? That you would like people to also give you that distance?
I don't have a problem like Bob Dylan has. I don't have a problem at all, really. Sometimes on a Friday night in a bar, maybe, but I can choose not to go.

Dylan once said, "In my mind it's never really been seriously a profession—it's been more confessional than professional." Which is it for you?
I see it as playing. It's fun. Songwriting is a form of playing.

Playing as in playing music, or playing as in having fun?
Yeah, as in playing, as in trying things out, imagination.

How important is environment when you're writing? Do you write very different songs when you are at home in St Kilda to when you're recording in Sydney, or on the road, or hanging out in Los Angeles or New York?
No, it doesn't have much effect at all. It's just space and time. I don't really write many songs when I'm travelling or on tour, 'cause you don't get that much time. I tend to write more songs at home when I set time aside.

When you're on the road do you get ideas?
Yeah, I often get songs started. I always write things down, otherwise I forget.

I mentioned that I experienced the *Nothing but a Dream* album sequentially. Do you feel that your albums are song cycles and that the songs are deliberately sequenced and belong together? Or is it more random?
That one in particular, the sequence was very important to it. I like sequencing albums, that's fun. But it's more of a working backwards thing. So when I have enough songs I make a record. I'm not aware that I'm writing for a particular set of themes. But you know, if you write a song within a certain period of time, they probably hang together in some way that you're not even aware of.

Have you ever had the situation where you've got enough songs for an album but when you're recording you realise there's a song that just doesn't fit, it's not the right time for that song?
Yeah, I save songs up that I think might work somewhere else or later on.

I think you said that "Pretty Place" and "Would You Be My Friend" were written years before they were recorded. How do you know when it's the right time to bring a song out of the drawer and give it life?
The melody for "Pretty Place" was a really old one but the words came out fairly recently. "Would You Be My Friend" has been around for a while. And sometimes they go out to other people first, so you've got to give them time. "If I Could Start Today Again" went to the Bull sisters, so I just held back on doing that for a while. "Would You Be My Friend", Maurice Frawley did it on his record; I did a duet with him on it.

You've got a huge catalogue of songs. Are you in touch with them all the time?
No, some of them I've forgotten.

Even though they're taped somewhere or recorded by someone somewhere else, you've just forgotten that song exists for a while?
Sometimes, yeah.

Do people remind you, and go, hey, what about that song, and you go, "Oh, shit, I forgot I wrote that"?
Yeah, yeah. [*Laughs*]

And then you've got songs that actually took a long time to write. Do you know why "To Her Door" took about seven years to write?
I had a melody for it a long time before I got words. I sing little melodies into a tape recorder and every now and then I go through the tapes and have a listen. I heard that and I thought it would be good to put words to that. It's a good tune.

Do you think that song is one of your greatest, more deserving of attention than other songs you've written?
I just know it's a really popular song everywhere. I like it. It's one of those songs I can still sing, so that's alright. I like other songs better, probably because I've sung that one a lot.

Do you have many unfinished songs?
Yeah, lots.

You don't stress out about them?
No. They don't always get finished.

Is there ever a situation where you know a song is going to be important so you're more attached to it and more finicky with it, as opposed to other songs that you're prepared to let lie dormant? Or are you pretty laid back about all your work?
I'm usually thinking of more than one song at a time, so it's like, that's not working so I'll scratch around with that one. I have more music than I have lyrics, like I said before, so

there's always a pile of song ideas there, and if I'm not getting anywhere with one song I just have a crack at something else.

Do you ever write songs very quickly?
Sometimes. I might write most of a song very quickly and then it might take ages to finish it off.

You've said that "When I First Met Your Ma" only took an hour to write after seeing an old photograph. I found that one of your most personal songs, the one that could most likely have been autobiographical—before I read all your insistences that your work is not autobiographical. Even if you start a song that's triggered by something incidental, that isn't personal, do you find something you've been through or have felt finds its way into the work in spite of yourself?
Yeah, lots of things from your own life get into your songs.

When you write songs, do you try to consciously guide the meaning or do you try to follow subconscious directions?
The second one, yeah. I don't start off with a very clear idea in my mind of what the song is going to do, so it follows what words rhyme, other things come into it. It's a matter of having very light reins, I guess.

And yet in songs like "From Little Things Big Things Grow" or "Treaty", both of which were written of political intent with indigenous people, you must have had a more conscious idea of where you wanted such songs to go.
Yes, those songs are the exceptions. "Special Treatment" is another one like that, a specific situation and write to it. So there are always exceptions.

Have you ever formed an attachment to, or been so enthralled by a character that you've created in a song that you've wanted to take that character on a bigger journey, in another song or perhaps in a story?
Well, I'm sort of aware where certain songs are written a few years apart from each other. "To Her Door" then "Love Never Runs on Time" and "How To Make Gravy", I've got a feeling it's the same guy. He keeps coming back.

I hope he's in a happier place next time. Give him a break.
Yeah, he's a bit of a fuck-up, that guy.

***One Night the Moon* is very operatic in its style. Does opera interest you as an art form to get involved in, perhaps as a librettist?**
It's always been something in the back of my mind, again because I have said I write from inside a situation, which is what a lot of music theatre songwriting is. I love musicals, I like opera, and my grandparents sang opera. It's one of those things at the back of my mind that

it would be good to do. Probably where it hasn't matched is that the kind of songs and music that I write don't really suit music theatre voices. I've seen some of my songs sung in that context. "If I Could Start Today Again" was sung in a play called *Certified Male* by Glynn Nichols, and someone sings that song in there, but they sing it in a music theatre voice, which for me doesn't work for the song.

And you're not interested in just writing a libretto? There are issues you deal with in some of your songs that you've written with people like Kev Carmody and Yothu Yindi that deserve to be represented on an operatic stage.
It's hard for me to write words without music in my head. But a musical would be good to do.

Have you drawn anything from the experience of acting that you've taken with you back into songwriting?
No, I don't think so. I always thought the other way. I always thought being a singer, there were lots of correspondences between that and acting. Especially when you sing my songs. When I'm singing my songs at a concert I'm acting them out to a certain extent. 'Cause I'm not singing "me me me". So I'm often switching characters as I go from song to song, and genders and age and everything. I think there are a few similarities between singing and acting.

What kind of relationship do you have with your songs? Are they like children to you?
Yeah.

Can you pick favourites?
They change. The favourite ones are always the new ones. But there are some songs that last, that I've been able to sing over the years and still find them.

Other than "To Her Door", what do you really enjoy doing from your earlier catalogue?
I change the set list a fair bit night to night and from tour to tour, so even songs like "To Her Door" I've got to give a rest sometimes, so I don't always play that one. "Ma" has always been a good one. "Careless". Usually with every tour I go back and find some new old ones.

Are you satisfied with your body of work?
No.

What dissatisfies you?
I'm a writer, so I feel useless unless I'm writing.

But you've written a lot, and you've written memorable and powerful songs that have obviously influenced a lot of people and been recorded by a lot of people. Does that in itself satisfy you? Do you ever pat yourself on the back?
Oh, I guess so. But it's like, if a carpenter broke his hand or had an injury and couldn't work, he wouldn't be satisfied. So it's the same thing; you've got to be able to do new things.

So you don't like to rest on your laurels.
Well, who does? I mean, happiness comes from feeling useful.

Would you see yourself as a useful human being if you could not write songs?
I'd have to find something else.

Would you still sing other people's songs, if you couldn't write songs?
I don't know. I'm not sure about that. I became a performer because I had songs that I wanted to sing, so being a performer wasn't first and foremost in my mind.

Do you ever feel tempted to go back and rewrite older songs?
I do change words and melodies of old songs. Some are more pliable than others. In some songs the words that are written in front of me are the only words you can sing, you can't change them. Not necessarily because they're great, but because you get stuck with them.

Have you ever written something and been totally knocked out by it at the time?
Yeah. The best songs are the ones that surprise you. Astonish you.

You've probably co-written with more songwriters in Australia than any other songwriter. What is the appeal of collaborating?
Just again, finding new ways of writing. So you often write songs with collaborators that you would never write by yourself. It's a way of dragging a song out of you that you wouldn't have come up with yourself.

Someone like Renee Geyer is not really known as a songwriter as much as a performer. So obviously you assist in bringing creativity out of other people who might not have the confidence to write much on their own.
Renee's so inventive as a singer, therefore she obviously has the ability to write, because she's writing all the time when she sings. It just needs a little bit of harnessing.

When you are writing alone, do you have a daily routine when you put time in at certain hours, or do you wait for inspiration to strike?
No, just phones are off, and try to get a few hours out of it.

Each day?
No, it's never that routine. But the last couple of months have been like that. People ring and say, "Meet me for coffee", and I'm none of that. No, I'm not going out for coffee. No, I'm not going to go out for lunch.

Do you have an idea of where songs come from?
After they're finished, often there are a whole lot of little things where they come from.

John Updike said a great thing about writing, he said often you might have two different sentences on a page, completely unconnected, and if you look at them long enough you manage to connect them up. So often songwriting's a bit like that when you've got a line here and a phrase there and a vague idea there. Or you might have three or four lines that you think belong to different songs and they end up in the one song.

Do they come from within you or from somewhere outside of you?
It's very mundane and it's very mysterious at the same time. Often it's just things people say. I guess a lot of my songs come from just what people say.

Some writers believe that songs live in the instruments and they have to draw them out. And other writers believe that they're in the atmosphere.
I understand that feeling. A song is like something that you catch, so it feels like something that's outside of you. It's like catching a fish. The way Robert Hughes writes about a fish at the end of the line, you're connecting to a whole other source. That's the great feeling about it, that's the big charge.

You've been referred to in the press as "a mirror to the Australian spirit". Does that feel like a responsibility to you?
No, it feels like a nice turn of phrase.

How do you feel then about being a major influence for many songwriters today and do you ever recognise your influence in the work of other writers?
Oh, I can see it. But often you're both influenced by the same thing. So someone might assume we're influencing each other but we might both just be influenced by something further back. It's all just pick it up and pass it on. I was heavily influenced by lots of songwriters, and I steal from them all the time.

Who are you stealing from?
A lot of my lines come from other songs. "Sway my way" is a line in "Change Your Mind" that's from a Bic Runga song. "Change Your Mind" is nearly all borrowed lines. "Wild horses" are in there somewhere. "If I could make wild horses come and get their hay"— that's about three folk songs in there.

How important is acclaim from the industry and your peers compared to support from the public who buy your albums and pay to see you perform?
There's one even more important than that, songs that you think are good.

Yourself?
Yep. That's the most important one.

What you write to please yourself has integrity. As opposed to the pop music that's written specifically to chart.

I wish I could.

Do you? Is being on the charts important to you now, having done that?

I've always thought I was a pop songwriter, but obviously I'm not. In my head I am.

Why aren't you? You're popular.

Yes, I am. I am a pop songwriter. That's how I describe myself when people ask. People in taxis or strangers at parties. Pop for me, I have a much wider understanding of it. When you say pop these days people think of disposable pop, but pop music's a very wide river. Nirvana is pop music, Outkast is pop music. It's a big wide river and there's always a place to swim along in it; there's always a big channel up the side you can swim, just as long as you stay in the river.

DEBORAH CONWAY

MELBOURNE, AUSTRALIA, FEBRUARY 2004

It's a curious thing, the attitude to rock stars growing up. Authors, filmmakers, painters and classical musicians are allowed to age gracefully and it's acknowledged that they often make their greatest and certainly most thoughtful work in later years. Rock music is a different beast, the most ageist of businesses, and Australia's mature rock and pop artists face a constant battle with radio, record companies and the public's perception of who they are and what they should be doing. A recurring theme among songwriters from the baby boom generation, it's even more acute for women in the business.

Deborah Conway is most famed for the feminist and political angles of her early work in the mid-1980s with Do Re Mi. While she is justifiably proud of her first hit, "Man Overboard", with its provocative lyrics and unconventional song structure, the music she is making today is worlds away from the angst she revelled in for many years. Formerly the "angry young woman" of Australian rock, she has softened.

On a late summer evening in the large rambling house she and her family were sharing with film producer Bob Weis, Conway's three young daughters, with long, thick, dark curly hair cascading over matching hot pink dressing gowns, were giggling and doing their best to avoid bedtime. The adults were eating dinner—one can't talk about music and songwriting on an empty stomach—and Conway's reputed feisty nature was tempered by more familial concerns.

There's no escaping her luminous beauty, but in spite of glamorous album covers and videos, Conway has never really traded on her looks. She's too authentic for that, and the content was always more important than the packaging.

For someone so focused and mindful, it was both surprising and amusing to hear Conway repeatedly use the phrase, "it never occurred to me". With a voice so rich and distinctive, it's hard to believe a career as a singer wasn't always on the cards, but it was quite unplanned, as was the foray into songwriting, which has sustained her over two decades. There is a self-deprecating Jewish humour in her conversation, but overall, the career that never occurred to her has been satisfying.

Conway was born in Melbourne on 8 August 1959 and grew up listening to her father's albums of musical comedies, singing Barbra Streisand, Shirley Bassey and Judy Garland standards in the shower as a nine-year-old. Later she discovered Simon and Garfunkel, Carole King, Joni Mitchell and Bob Dylan, but their influences didn't show in her songwriting until her thirties. In between there were the punk and post-punk periods of music that she threw herself into. "It was deeply unfashionable to be able to sing in tune," Conway reflected. "And I ended up joining a band where all of their pedigrees were punk. I was listening to Barbra Streisand and Julie Andrews—what right did I have to be there?"

An avid *Countdown* viewer who loved to slate the show each week, it certainly never would have occurred to her that she might appear on it one day. Nor did it occur to her that a solo career was beckoning. After leaving the fierce Do Re Mi in the late 1980s, she continued to explore the darker, moody, more earnest side of her musical life. Initially with her Do Re Mi colleague Dorland Bray, and then with her husband and musical soul mate, Willy Zygier, Conway has collaborated on songs that have been confronting and, by her own admission, at times "bloody depressing". This is the artist who, after all, named one album *Bitch Epic*, and another—made with her first and only husband to date—*My Third Husband*.

Her first solo single, 1991's "Only the Beginning" from the *String of Pearls* album, became a huge hit; to this day it's the only Deborah Conway song commercial radio will play regularly. She finds herself limited by the "fossilising effect" such a hit has on her work, and has frequently taken on projects that are left of centre—from acting in Peter Greenaway's film, *Prospero's Books*, to getting inside the skin of another chanteuse in the stage musical *Always—Patsy Cline*. And her solo recordings since *String of Pearls* have, she concedes, been less than radio-friendly. "I can see that I haven't really made it easy for them. I've been difficult. I've put out difficult records."

But in 2004 the softening of Deborah Conway made it onto disc. Her new album, *Summertown*—significantly credited to Deborah Conway and Willy Zygier—was a shimmering collection of songs reflecting down-home harmony and grown-up love. Conway described the music as having gentleness and warmth. She was letting go of the angst, giving peace a chance.

When did you pick up the guitar?
Not until I was eighteen. And then I didn't think about singing in a band until someone suggested it to me at the age of twenty. It didn't really occur to me that I could, actually.

Did you try writing songs at all when you picked up the guitar?
No. I'd written poetry and things like that. I came to songwriting, I came to everything, fairly late.

You never had that epiphany as a teenager—"I have to be a songwriter?"
No. I didn't have an epiphany of "I have to be a musician" either. It simply hadn't occurred to me. I don't know what I was thinking I was going to be. I was quite relaxed about it. When I think about it now, it was like, shouldn't I have been more freaking out about what I was going to do with my life? But that didn't seem to occur to me either.

You've referred to Dorland Bray as your first mentor. How did he guide you musically?
He just knew what he wanted. He knew what he liked, he knew how to seek out new things, and he knew how to think about music in a way that I hadn't. He was very critical, and I guess I wasn't. I was never very critical.

Except of *Countdown*.
Except *Countdown*. That's right. And now the Eurovision Song Contest. That makes a songwriter feel really good. It's a really good thing to watch.

Dorland was really good for me. He taught me a different way to think about music and how to address it in a more semantic way, pulling it apart and working out how things worked. Ways of looking at it that I hadn't thought about before. And ways in which he constructed songs. It dispelled the mysteries of it. He made me realise how I could do it, that there was something I actually could do. And I loved everything he did. I was very uncritical of him.

You've almost always collaborated rather than writing alone.
I'm better at collaborating with people I know, rather than just anyone. I've tried the just anyone approach, but I need a history. I think I write better songs, because I'm not really a musician properly. I picked up the guitar too late. Dorland was a drummer, and he wasn't a great guitar player, he felt his way around stuff, but he was better than me. I was really woeful at that point. [*Laughs*] I'm only just slightly better than woeful now. It's just not natural for me. Singing feels very natural for me and I can just sing, but I can't just play guitar, and I've never been dedicated enough to spend the eight hours a day that you probably need to put in.

Being so moved by Joni Mitchell and Bob Dylan, the ultimate introspective singer-songwriters, it's interesting that you didn't try that.
I wasn't encouraged to do it.

To write on your own?
[*Nods*] Mmm.

Because it was a very democratic team mentality in the band?
Yes, that's right.

When you were writing with your Do Re Mi co-members, how would a song typically come together?
Dorland and I would generate it with a lyric, or Dorland would start it and then I would come in and then we'd finish it together. Then we'd take it to the other two and we'd hum them the melody and they'd jam. Dorland and I were the lyricists and they were the musical ones, they would put everything to it.

Was it a curse or a blessing for your first single to be such a defining and momentous hit?
It was a blessing. I couldn't imagine that would be a curse. It was fantastic. I mean, basically everything we'd done before that as well had been successful. I think "Man Overboard" is a fantastic song. It's lasted the test of time. We would never have picked it as a single; it was the record company's idea. The first EP that we released, before we'd even done a gig, all the alternative radio stations were playing it. That had the song "Standing on Wires". Then we made another EP, *The Waiting Room*, which had the first version of "Man Overboard" on it, and it was a really different, punk version of that song. These looked like long-play records but they were 45rpm, so people used to play it on the wrong speed all the time, of course. "Man Overboard" was slowed down and that gave us the idea that we could slow the song down. We tried that and it sounded really sexy and good, so that's how we recorded it for *Domestic Harmony*. But people were playing that on the radio, too. So for us it was like, "Yeah, of course they're playing it, because they play anything we do." It hadn't occurred to us that they wouldn't play it.

Do you remember writing "Man Overboard"?
I was sitting in a North Sydney flat and Dorland showed me this verse that he had and I really loved it I thought it was fantastic, and said, "Okay, well, what if I can do this next?" It was about an ex-girlfriend of his and an ex-boyfriend of mine.

So it was his lyrical idea, not yours? Everyone assumes that it was your lyric.
That's right, they assume that. But no, it was his. They were great words.

Do you remember if the lyrics flowed or whether you both had to labour over them?
It wasn't laboured at all. It was a beautiful thing; I remember it coming together very quickly.

It was structurally quite unconventional, having no chorus. Was song structure something you wanted to flout the rules of? Or did it not occur to you to put a chorus in?
It didn't, really. We hadn't had any choruses up to that point. "Standing on Wires" hadn't a

chorus either. We weren't much on choruses, Dorland and I. That was the most scandalous thing about it, apart from, you know, certain medical terms in the lyric. But I always thought, my God, they've made the song a top five hit, and it doesn't have a chorus. How incredible.

But the song is very propelled; it's not static at all, it's constantly pushing forward. So maybe when a song doesn't have a chorus, if you know it's going somewhere then you don't notice that there's no chorus.
I don't think it occurred to anyone. It just had a chant instead.

Much was made about the mention of pubic hair in a pop song. Did you think twice about putting in the line, "Your pubic hairs are on my pillow, your stubble rings the sink"?
No, we were very bolshy.

I guess every slighted woman would identify with the reference to "insincere 'I love you's". Ten years later when Alanis Morissette came out with "You Oughta Know", did it strike you as another valid way to make the point?
Somebody said to me something like, "Oh, she should have listened to Do Re Mi." When I heard Alanis Morissette, I thought, "God, why isn't anyone playing Liz Phair?" I thought she was a really sub Pat Benatar, and I thought Pat Benatar was pretty sub, too. It didn't do a thing for me. Liz Phair for me did the same thing, but just beautifully and with ironic wit and intelligence.

Was it part of your modus operandi to always have something vital to say in Do Re Mi songs?
Yeah. We didn't write love songs. They were all political, really. And I think I rebelled against that, too, when I left the band. I went the other way.

Your albums have had such clever and evocative titles, as have many of your songs. Do you ever come up with the title first and write to it?
Often.

So do you think lyrically first?
No, not always. But I find that it's better to have words floating around in the ether to start with. You might not necessarily know what the song's about, but if you've got a phrase then you can start cracking on a chord progression, and a melody might come from that. Certainly more recently that's how we've written; we've just written this last record. There's a phrase, then there's a chord progression, followed by a melody, and then the lyric last. But the phrase dictates how a chorus might work; you might have a line and the line will tell you something about the kind of thing that you're going to write. You might not know what it's about, but it's a mood.

Was London an inspiring place for you to write?

It was, because that was the time when I truly discovered that I could do it alone and that I really enjoyed it. I did enjoy writing with Dorland, and I'm proud of all the stuff we did, but it was like a coming of age for me, that period. The first time I started writing on my own was *String of Pearls*. Suddenly I found a voice; that was really a fantastically fertile time for me. Virgin wanted me to make a solo record. I hadn't really thought about it, it hadn't really occurred to me, once again, that I could leave Do Re Mi or would do something else, or that someone would be interested in a solo record of mine. So it was a kind of out-of-the-blue request. And then I just clutched at straws—what would they like? Oh, I know, they'd probably like a dance record in the style of the Eurythmics or something like that. I can't remember what the brief was. I was always very good at convincing people that I knew what I was doing, even though I didn't. So I managed to convince them, and we went to LA and spent ridiculous amounts of money. And came back with an effort that was so half-arsed, it was awful. I'm very glad now that it never came out. They just sat on this record for ages, and I just sat around in London waiting for them to put it out.

But in the meantime, as I was being dangled on this string, I started to write. And I found a voice. They weren't particularly sophisticated, but they were coming and they were mine, and it was really a fantastic feeling. I was living on my own in this little flat off Portobello Road and I'd get up in the morning and grab my guitar and it was really exciting, I wrote furiously. By the time Virgin said, "Look we think this is really not working," I went, okay. 'Cause I had an album full of songs. And I went to LA, which is where my boyfriend at the time was living, and I kept writing there. And then I went back to Melbourne and I kept writing there. And then Richard Pleasance and I made an album, and that was *String of Pearls*.

Did you recycle any of the discarded songs or did you just throw them all out?

Some of them appeared on B-sides. They were just stepping stones, I think, to other things. Bits of them have appeared in other songs.

You were then drawn back to London in the mid-nineties.

Yes. I really like it. The mid-nineties period, the two years we were there to write *My Third Husband*, was very difficult and very challenging, because we had a young baby and all of the ghosts of my past opportunities came flashing before my eyes as I was trying to knuckle down, staring at a blank piece of paper thinking, ahh, I can't do this. It was really hard. We put ourselves in the situation of being immigrants, I suppose. Immediately there was this barrier, because we're strangers in a strange land, plus you can't go out and enjoy all the fruits of this strange land because you've got this small baby that is preventing you from going to nightclubs or restaurants or music. You're at arm's length there and you don't have a network of family that you can rely on. So we were very isolated.

You did that deliberately, though.

I didn't realise—it hadn't occurred to me—that that would be the knock-on effect. I'd had this baby and I thought, "I'm not going to let this change my life, I'm just going to do what I'm going to do! And to prove it I'm going to go to London." I'm very stubborn that way and I refused to listen to the voices of reason, that said, "No, maybe you shouldn't do this ..." They probably were right. We made a bloody depressing record. But I really like *My Third Husband*.

You think it's depressing?
It's very moody. Depressing is not the right word. It's a very moody record. I was depressed.

Do you like your albums to be cohesive, with certain themes running through the songs?
I think that makes a better record, really. That's a part of putting the record together. I mean, there are some on *String of Pearls* that I'm deeply embarrassed about. I find them really amateurish.

Like what?
"For All the Wrong Reasons". I find that really embarrassing. It's just a very earnest piece. It feels very unsubtle and a bit clumsy.

Do you remember writing "It's only the Beginning"? Who was Scott Cutler?
He was an LA composer, actually the great-nephew of Irving Berlin. He was a nice fellow, a nice Jewish boy. Someone decided that we two should work together and we wrote a couple of songs. I'd written it with Scott a long time before *String of Pearls*. It was on the original for Virgin Records.

Did that start from a lyrical idea or did you have that melody already?
It came out of a conversation we were having. He was telling me about his woeful love life. He said something like, "Oh well, it's only the beginning." And I said, "That's it! That's the title." So we wrote the song.

It's catchy with a very hooky chorus.
It is very upbeat. And then I was embarrassed about that. I said, "Dorland, it's so happy, I can't cope, what am I doing?" He said, "Yeah, you're right. It's so happy." So we rewrote it and then I recorded that. And I went, "Oh no, I can't do this." I screwed it up; I tried to cloak it, disguise its happiness. The final recorded version is the original lyric without the de-happifying of it.

Does having written such a radio-friendly song get in your way at later stages of your career?
I guess it depends on the day. Look, it's fantastic that they like the song. It's great, and one would never want to decry the fact that one had a hit record and went on to win ARIA awards and whatever. People would put you in a cherished place on their record shelves and in their hearts with this one song, and people play it at their weddings and all that stuff. It was really important to some people. But at the same time it had a kind of fossilising effect on my work. It does tend to set you in jello. This is what Australian radio is, and there doesn't seem to be a place to play new things. It's hard, but I can see that I haven't really made it easy for them.

Why?
Because I've been difficult. I've put out difficult records. *My Third Husband* is a very challenging record. People get it after about seven listens. You can't put records out like that if you expect people to play them on the radio. I think there are some fantastic songs on *My Third Husband*. And I'm not embarrassed by any of them. I think the production is a little bit overwrought. Quite a bit overwrought, really.

How much do you conceive arrangements at the time of writing? With "White Roses", for instance, was that always going to be a piano song with trumpet?
No, I thought about the trumpet much later. We wrote it on guitar. Dorland and I wrote it in London. We'd been listening to Al Green in order to get inspiration. It's an Al Green song. You'd never recognise it, I can't remember which Al Green song it was, but we just took the chords and went, "Okay, let's write this." And started writing it. And Dorland said, "A classic, don't you think?"

Do you think now that it's a classic?
No, I think that's a bit generous. It's almost a classic.

It's a beautiful song.
It is a beautiful song, but in order to be a classic I think that other people have to record it.

There are some songs where the original version of it is so definitive that no-one dares touch it. But they're still classics.
Okay, maybe that's true, I'd have to think about that. But I still don't think that makes "White Roses" a classic. I think it's a good song, very accomplished. At that time it was the most accomplished thing we'd written, the most professional sounding. All of it's cornered. Everything fitted nicely together, slotted in beautifully, everything flowed beautifully on from what had just been, and that's a lovely thing, when it all fits together perfectly like a piece of IKEA furniture. I really think we did that very well on "White Roses".

And what about arrangements? Do you contemplate them at the time of writing?
Yes and no. For example, we've just written this last record that we're mixing at the moment, and we started out not wanting to be doing much touring this year because we've got three children and one parent has to stay at home. He's the guitar player, so let's write more songs that we can play with a piano. So we write this song called "Stay on Track" and I played the guitar but Willy was playing piano on it. And this was how it was going to be. Then we started recording it and Gerry Hale, who we play with, put mandolin, charango and cittern on it, and suddenly it sounds like a completely different thing than what I'd envisaged. It was light and whimsical and serendipitous and very beautiful. And it was very surprising for me.

Do you like being surprised by how your songs turn out?
I love to be surprised. I had to pick up the kids from school and I came back the next day

and my God, listen to that, that's not how I'd imagined it sounding at all, but it was a really fantastic surprise. It doesn't always happen that way. You might say, "Oh no, that's not what I wanted at all, that's not how I'd imagined it, I don't like it, I'd rather hear it how I imagined it." But in this particular instance, it was, "Well, that's not how I imagined it at all, but this just sounds fantastic, and of course it should be this way." And that has very little piano on the track.

"White Roses" was a far more tender end-of-relationship song than "Man Overboard". Is it more difficult to be straightforwardly sad in a song than to be angry?
I've written a lot more melancholy songs than really pissed-off ones. I suppose it's just more appealing for me to write about melancholy than it is to write about anger. I got that out of me. Everything that we did in Do Re Mi was pissed off. We made a living out of being pissed off. That was a question on Roy and HG, actually. "You were really angry about things! You were *really* angry about something, weren't you?"

What was the first song you and Willy wrote together?
I think it was "Now That We're Apart".

That's ironic.
Actually, that was an angry song.

Was it obvious immediately that there was a good writing spark there?
Yeah! That was really exciting, actually. He was just doodling around. I said, "Oh, that's really good." And then he gave it to me and said, "You write the lyric." And then I came to him and said, "No, no, this bit should repeat." "Oh, like a chorus, you mean?" "Yeah, like a chorus." "Oh, okay." So then I took it away and we wrote that bit and bingo, it's a chorus. Well, sort of.

Songs like "Alive and Brilliant" and "Today I'm a Daisy" have a wonderful buoyancy to them. Was that a reflection of your life at the time?
Yeah, I guess so. Newly in love, all that sort of stuff. You know, I haven't really had it tough. I'm reasonably buoyant anyway. I mean, apart from those odd moments of deep depression and melancholy.

Did you feel different as a writer when you became a mother? Did songs start to appear that you could never have written before?
I suppose you've got a whole new thing to write about. Becoming a parent opens up a whole new capacity to panic and worry that you never knew existed. And love of course. A whole new way of loving. A whole new definition of the word love and that concept of unconditional love that you probably have experienced either not at all or only in a very limited way. Where you just become much more open. So that gives you a new palette. It took a while for me. I can filter things for a long time before they actually come out in a creative way.

So it wasn't instant.
No, it wasn't instant. Although, interestingly, with the record that we've just written, things would happen and I'd be writing about them the next day, furiously, which I've never done before. It was a really beautiful, fantastic period, writing this record, that I haven't had since before I had children. When I had children I didn't really write about it till *My Third Husband*. Except *Ultrasound*, which is very good, very quirky and odd and more like a film soundtrack or something.

Did the new technology you were embracing when writing for the *My Third Husband* album create songs that could only have been written that way?
No, we only ever write on guitar. It was all written organically, and all those songs sound fantastic when they're stripped back to how we wrote them, too. Like "Bag of Sweets". That was the first song we wrote for the record. I had this idea while sitting on top of Primrose Hill, went home and just wrote the song all in one go. It all came flowing out, and I really thought it was great. I thought that was one of my finest songwriting moments.

You said in interviews at the time that you'd made "a circumference pop record as opposed to a diameter pop record." What did you mean?
What I meant was we went around the edges, instead of cutting through. We circled around the idea of what a pop record should be, as opposed to cutting straight to the heart of it. And therefore we made a very esoteric record, and a record that people didn't really quite get. Until they'd heard it a number of times. That's what I meant. And what a splendid way to talk about a really esoteric record.

Has your voice guided your songwriting, or do you write something and then find a way to tailor your voice to the song?
I write and sing it at the same time. So you're trying to push the boundaries of your voice as well. Depending on the kind of song that you've decided to write. I tend to write in batches. So that would dictate whether you were going to write a happy song or an up song or a black song. Or if this phrase has come to mind and you want to write the song that fits that phrase. That's going to dictate it. As far as the sound of my voice, it's interesting actually. Willy likes my voice when it's high, when I'm pushing. And I like my voice when it's low, 'cause I think I have a rich mezzo voice. He finds it more a thrill when I push it higher.

So he'll encourage the songwriting in that direction when he can?
That's right. That'll be like a key thing and I'll be going, "It sounds better when it's low." "No, no, I'm more excited when it's higher."

What are your favourite keys?
I like C, F, G, that kind of thing. He's higher, B flat. But it can be arranged within the song.

I'm interested in where a songwriter is a great singer, how much the voice is a part of the songwriting process.
I don't actually feel like a great singer. I used to think I was better than I was, than I do now. I think I'm quite a good singer. But I don't think I'm a great singer by a long shot. Not when I hear really great singers.

Who's a great singer?
John Lennon. Thom Yorke. Ella Fitzgerald. Judy Garland.

Do you think there are any great singers in Australia at the moment?
Kasey Chambers, she's a great singer. She's fantastic.

"Radio Loves This" was purposely ironic. Kasey had the same thing in mind when she wrote "Not Pretty Enough", but it actually became a huge hit.
Yeah.

Did you actually hope that your song would be a radio-friendly song?
Yes, it was obviously tongue in cheek, but it was the idea that radio obviously didn't love me. I was trying to write something dumb and obvious but with my own ironic twist to it.

And there you go, that ironic twist just made it too clever for them.
Well, possibly. But it wasn't a great song.

Did you hear Neil Finn's voice singing with you when you wrote "Exquisite Stereo"?
I didn't realise it was a duet as I was writing it. It only occurred to me afterwards. "Oh, it's a duet. I've written a duet. Okay, well obviously we have to get someone else to sing it. So I know who I'd like. Neil Finn. Let's get him." And he said yes, which was nice.

Has your acting work made an imprint on your songwriting and vice versa? I wondered if working with Peter Greenaway influenced your writing.
No, not especially. It was a very interesting experience, it was fantastic, but I didn't particularly get a song out of it. The Patsy Cline stuff was fun to sing, but I wouldn't have called it really an acting job.

Did you enjoy taking a break from your own music and interpreting someone else's?
Yes, it was really fun. I found it very relaxing. I had a bit of a freak-out, though. Because it was like, oh God, she was really great and I'm so sub. All that sort of stuff. But then I got over that and got into it and I just worked really hard at not necessarily sounding exactly like her because that would have been impossible. Interpreting her but also making a leap, not just singing it like myself. And I did really enjoy it. It was constantly challenging to me.

Did you take anything from singing Patsy Cline's songs back into your own writing?

I suppose in some way, there's a bit of a country influence in the stuff that I've been doing, just in the line-up of the band. It's hard to know if I would then have put a band together like I did without the Patsy Cline show. And so the songs that we've written have had that line-up in mind.

Does your Jewishness infuse your work?

I think that probably gives it its melancholy tinge, yes.

In America so many successful songwriters are Jewish—Bob Dylan, Paul Simon, Carole King, Randy Newman, Leonard Cohen, Janis Ian—to name a few. It's a common theme. The whole Jewish creative scene isn't as prevalent here as it is in the States, and there certainly aren't many famous Jewish songwriters. I wondered how much Jewishness plays a part in your creativity in general, and particularly in your writing. Willy's also Jewish and you're writing together.

It's not something that I've had to break down. My Jewishness is an absolutely integral part of me in ways that are quite hard to define. But as I get older and now that I have children also, it becomes more and more important in my life, and in a way that it's not important for my Christian friends because they'd laugh if you called them Christians. It's not equitable in any way. I'm not particularly religious, I don't believe in God, but I go to Shul on holidays, I'm observant, I fast, I have seders and first nights and I make an effort. I make chopped liver on Friday night. We do Shabbat every Friday night.

So it's about ritual?

That's part of it and I think it's also a proud heritage and it's rich, there are so many fantastic values that are contained within it that everyone aspires to, and that the Jews hold very dear. Whoever you are infuses your songwriting and whatever you're going through, but I think I would have ascribed my penchant for melancholy to being Jewish. It seems a bit mean to only ascribe melancholy.

What about spirituality, whether religious or not? Do you feel that being creative is a spiritual thing?

No. What is that? I think I am probably spiritual, but I'm going to deny it. I don't know, I really don't know.

Do you think songs come from within you or from an outside source?

It feels like they come from somewhere else, but I think that's crap. The best part about being a human being is that you're always constantly surprising yourself. It's wonderful to have this thing, this brain that works that way. And it's much more mysterious than thinking that it is a gift from somewhere else. It's nice, it is a romantic idea, but I'm firmly of the school that is not into outside forces at all.

Do you and Willy ever have to draw a line and put songwriting and music completely aside in order to function as a couple and a family?
No.

Are the two sides entwined for good or bad?
Yes.

You talk about songwriting while you're cooking dinner?
Yes. We talk about parenting while we're writing songs.

Can you imagine ever writing completely on your own again?
I can, but it's not as much fun. I like writing with Willy. He's surprising.

Do you ever argue when you're writing about songwriting?
No, we never argue about that. In order to write with someone you have to be able say, "Look, that's fucked." And not take it personally. That's why it has to be for me a close relationship in order to expose yourself in that way. Because it's like taking off your clothes. It's more intimate. You're exposing your deepest inner core. And you have to make sure the person you're exposing it to is going to take care of it and be gentle with it.

Are your songs like children to you? Do you have an individual relationship with each of them?
No, I have children. I don't need to have my songs like children. [*Laughs*] Songs you can leave, you don't need babysitters, you don't need to get them dinner or wipe their noses, clean up their vomit in the middle of the night. No, they're not like children.

GRAEME CONNORS

MACKAY, AUSTRALIA, OCTOBER 2003

In a place like Australia that likes to define its music strictly according to genre, Graeme Connors has never been an easy fit. Country artist, adult contemporary artist—the tags are there, but the only label that seems universally agreed upon is songwriting master. Connors is the songwriter that many songwriters want to write with, and it's always serious business when an emerging talent or established artist with a new album in the works boards the plane to Mackay.

The hub of Central Queensland, where mining, cattle, dairy and sugarcane industries converge, Mackay is also the gateway to the Whitsunday coast, a country town with few pretensions, a lackadaisical paradise where nothing seems too urgent. If you ever wondered what it was like growing up in such a place, Connors' songs serve as an accurate history lesson, albeit with a personal perspective. But while he is best known for singing about heading "a little further north each year", living life in the shade of a mango tree, burning cane fields and preparing for cyclone season, Connors' songs delve far deeper and wider into the Australian experience. City characters and outback characters sit side by side on his albums, where race and creed, politics and economics, tourist development and family values, along with numerous discourses on love, are explored with warmth, humour and pathos.

Connors was born on 29 April 1956, the third generation of his family born in Mackay, "the son of a son of a son of a railway man" as he titled one of his songs. Starting as a teenage singer for a local Mackay band that supported touring acts like Sherbet, Connors was plucked out as a solo act, taken south to the big city by a cluey entrepreneur, and was soon supporting overseas acts around Australia, from Del Shannon to Liza Minnelli and his hero, Kris Kristofferson. Kristofferson was impressed enough with Connors' talents to produce four songs on his debut album for Festival Records, *And When Morning Comes*.

While his solo career was floundering in the late 1970s and early 1980s, Connors was co-writing songs for other artists, such as "Hot Town" for Jon English and "I'm Married to My Bulldog Mack" for Slim Dusty. He then all but gave up on a performing and songwriting career of his own, and spent five years as the A&R man for Rondor Music Publishing in Australia, where on a particularly momentous occasion—or was it just another day at the office—he found a song called "You're the Voice" on a reel of tapes that had come in, and pitched it to John Farnham.

It was during the latter years of his publishing stint in Sydney that Connors would get up before light each morning and sit in his home study writing songs about his earlier life in North Queensland. These formed the basis of the *North* and *South of These Days* albums. The potent success of *North* in 1988 took him completely by surprise, but immediately found him an audience of listeners who appreciated thoughtful, well-crafted songs with tangible images and poignant storylines. Many of those audiences were country music lovers and Connors found himself unwittingly bundled into the country genre, something he had never expected, not least because of his Irish tenor-style voice. Through the years and albums that followed, he has enjoyed a strange relationship with the country music industry, which has bestowed many awards on him yet never fully empathised with him.

After fifteen years living away from Mackay, Connors and his wife Lyn took their young family back home in 1989 and are still there today, living outside the mainstream. Busy enough raising five children, Connors also runs his own music company, and it's a rare week that he's not breezing through the local airport; he flies regularly to Sydney for writing, recording and business expeditions, and still tours the country, pleasing the fans and storing up experiences for more writing. From an intimate piece like "Fireflies" to an all-embracing anthem like "Being Here", the song he wrote and sang at the Opening Ceremony of the Sydney 2000 Paralympic Games, Connors' songs have touched more Australians than Australians actually realise. "If you really know the intricate elements of community, then there's no community to which you are foreign," he said as he showed me, over a few balmy days, what he loved about being a child of his land.

Connors likes to drive. He likes to talk and drive, and he likes to write while he's driving. "It's the best place to write. When you draw a blank you get in the car and drive." This interview took place at different locations in and around Mackay, some of it in the car, touring the coast, the mangroves, the street on which he lived, the Pioneer Valley from the top of Eungella, and the tropical tranquility of the Connors' garden.

What did the years working in a publishing company teach you about songwriting?
The most important thing it taught me is about discipline. I'd see songwriters coming in day after day with half-finished tunes, with loads of dreams and ambition for their songs, but when you're in the battlefield of the business trying to present a song to an A&R guy, you know the floor as soon as it lands. If someone plays you a song and all of a sudden you go, "Uh oh, there's the weak spot", everyone's lost their attention immediately. So the discipline of rewriting, of actually being critical enough of your own work to face facts: this one ain't cutting it. The subject matter just isn't interesting enough or the approach I've taken is boring, or this has been done before in another guise. I would have a steady stream of hopeful writers coming in playing me material. When that wasn't happening I'd be sorting through the demos from overseas and eventually it becomes second nature—you hear a song and it's just perfect. The hair on the back of your neck stands up, the emotion is real, the craft is brilliant, they've nailed it. And you know that song is going to be a success one day.

There must be a skill in being able to recognise that in your own work. Were you able to go home from the office, listen back on what you'd written that morning and make the same judgement?
When I took on the job at Rondor, in my head and heart I had decided my career as a writer-performer was over. So for about the first year I didn't write a thing. It was like, my time is up, I had my shot, it didn't work, I'm now working on other people's songs. After that twelve-month period there were gaps in the repertoire. Slim Dusty via Rod Coe would always be looking for material, and a lot of the writers that we had signed to Rondor looked down their nose on the idea of writing a song for Slim. "We want a pop song, we want a hit song that's going to be on *Countdown*." So then to avoid the embarrassment of not being able to deliver songs, I started pitching my own. I already had records with Slim of "Married to My Bulldog Mack" and "Dieseline Dreams", so it was an opportunity for me to continue submitting songs that I'd written without the other writers feeling as if I was stealing attention away from them. That then lead to a situation where I'm thinking, "Okay, I can still write a song, Slim will record them, I obviously have a gift or a talent for what I do."

Then I went through this funny period of grieving that here are my kids growing up and I always wanted them to know me as a creative person, as I always saw myself. So I started writing songs that were stories of my life. They were genuine, and the analysis of those songs didn't happen at the level that was happening when I was in the office. I wasn't sitting here scrutinising my songs, saying, "Okay, who am I pitching this song to? Forget it, no-one's going to record that, throw it away and start again." These were personal outpourings that were really meant for my kids to go, "Hey, so that was what the old man was like. He worked in the music industry but on the side he wrote these little stories about his life." As it turned out, those little stories of my life overpowered the other work that I was doing. And I think the structure, the form, the craft that's shown in those was subconscious, rather than a conscious thing. It grew out of the analysis I did during the course of the day on songs; I'd get up in the morning and it had become second nature, without having to think.

When you were writing especially for Slim, what were the most important elements in crafting the song?

I was using generally personal emotions, as any writer would, and adapting them. "Dieseline Dreams" is a very poignant little tale about the truck driver with his son on a holiday, travelling with him, and he knows all the bends from Dad, he's looking out for roos, and in the end he falls asleep in the truck, and Dad of course is reflecting, thinking, "This is just like me with my dad, and I hope that he doesn't do this, what I'm doing." It's every father's wish that the children don't do what they do, because it's never good enough. I think that's directly out of tripping up this Pioneer Valley in the railroader with my father and how we used to be so proud of him. "My dad's a guard in the railway, we get to go in the railroader for free on a Saturday afternoon!" Of course they've taken it out now, it's only cane trucks. So that's my personal experience being translated into that particular story. That song's a little out of the ordinary, because Slim wouldn't normally do a descending interval base line. But Slim loved the story enough to go with it.

In "We've Done Us Proud" I kept changing the key to keep in the same three chords. Everyone thinks that Slim wrote "We've Done Us Proud". And that doesn't bother me at all. If anything, it's a tribute that I wrote a song so perfectly for Slim that everyone would think he wrote it himself. Slim was a joy and a challenge and a pleasure to write for because he was a man who knew his capabilities, and knew that you could push him, which I always tried to do, so he'd go, "Oh, that's a bit different." He was a fair enough man to take a challenge and have a go at it. But if it didn't work he'd iron it out. He'd slim it. He'd take what you'd done and turn it into his way of getting around that problem. There's no-one else I can think of who comes close, in terms of a songwriter wanting to write a simple, direct song. That's gone, it's over.

Whose music influenced you when you started writing songs?

I was in many ways just being buffeted around by the changes that were happening. Whoever was the hit of the day, I kept thinking, I'd better keep up with what's going on, where the changes are. Until I found people like John Prine, and later Jimmy Buffet, who were not successful artists in the sense of being household names. Randy Newman was another huge turning point for me. When I first heard Randy Newman, I just went, "Oh my God, this is just great work, and if this guy is not a household name, then who cares?" Those artists reinforced in me that it's alright to just be yourself, let yourself flow through.

Did Harry Chapin also resonate for you?

Very much. I always liked Harry Chapin, and I think *The Dance Band on the Titanic* is one of the greatest unappreciated CDs of mature songwriting. Brilliant writing. I was so filled with his music, the orchestral arrangement of his music.

What about the story aspect of his songwriting?

I loved it. "She Sings Songs without Words" and all those songs. They blew me away.

Your "Sicilian Born" always reminds me of "Mr Tanner", my favourite Chapin song, those songs that just make me cry.
Yes. Beautiful work.

Do you remember the first song you wrote?
"A Song of Your Own." I must have been thirteen or fourteen. It was a mushy little piece.

Do you still have it?
I didn't tape it. But I could sing it for you if I wasn't too embarrassed to do it. It was, strangely enough, written with the intentions of wooing a girl.

Did it succeed?
I think it maybe did.

"Mango Shade" was the first song you wrote for what would be the *North* album. Was there an occurrence that led you back mentally, emotionally, to this place?
It was wanting to leave something for the children. It was a story of my life in a sense, in the one art form that I understood well, and that was songwriting, lyrics. I can take you for a drive to Eimeo and there's a grove of mango trees that run down a beautiful road. And a little road up to a pub on the hill. That was always a beautiful place. In my recollection there's two contributing factors. In childhood, it was a beach with this grove of mangoes growing along the road. There used to be lots of them coming up the valley as well. People would just grow mango trees all along. The other one was, I used to mow the lawn for Mrs Diplock across the way, and she had a woman that lived with her that we think was her daughter, who hung herself on Christmas Eve from the lower branches of a mango tree. That's the line, "The mango trees in my home town grow strong and tall/ The leaves green and the ground below don't see the sun at all." If you go to any mango tree it's all dirt underneath, because the grass can't grow. It's thick foliage, it just blanks out anything. So that came from the childhood thing of the woman who'd hung herself underneath the mango tree that I had to mow around thinking of the ghost.

Every song on *North* in some way is a deeply personal story. "Sicilian Born" is a fellow that used to attend the church in Sutherland. Artistic licence is there, but both Lyn and the boys all know who we were talking about for "Sicilian Born". He was an Italian gentleman, hardly spoke any English, used to come and give the boys a Mintie after church and then disappear with his walking stick. And "The Metho Man" is a real tale. Like everyone, I take deeply personal experience, tangible experience, but I shape it and form it to make it a universal story for people to feel as if it's their own.

The French songwriter Gilles Vigneault said, "I describe people in my songs, and the more a song is local, the better are its chances of being universal."
I'll go another quote for you. Mark Twain, and I'm going to paraphrase it, said that the more deeply that he understands and knows the smells of the Mississippi, the corners, the bends,

the foliage, the people on the shores, then the more universal the Mississippi would become. If you really know your environment, that environment is the world. Because you know all the personality types that are likely to be popping up are going to be there somewhere. All the intrigues that happen in life are going to be there somewhere. The foliage, the buildings, the stories, the little things that happen. Fodder for the writer. If you really know the intricate elements of community, then there's no community to which you are foreign.

How did "A Little Further North" come to you?
It was winter, I was in the downstairs room, I had this Yamaha piano, and early morning I used to get up at five-thirty and I somehow started thinking about the tropics—it would be nice to be in the tropics, it wouldn't be so cold. And the idea of "A little further north", I reckon in retrospect, came from a live Jimmy Buffet record in which someone said to him, "Which direction is your music heading?" And he said, "South." Meaning down to Florida. Now that wasn't a conscious decision. But in retrospect, when I heard it after I'd written what I'd written, I thought maybe that was a seed that planted it.

You wrote in that song of an Australian experience that had been all but neglected in songwriting in favour of the urban life or the outback life. Nobody had really nailed the "going north" experience quite like that.
It was a happy coincidence that "A Little Further North" hooked into the collective psyche because people were doing that. People were starting, back in 1988, the whole shift. And I've since received so many letters from people saying it was their theme song as they packed up from Melbourne and moved to Brisbane. Or from Brisbane to Cairns. Or from Sydney to Brisbane. It was fortuitous, I have to say.

You didn't have a sense that you'd written a defining song?
No. I wish I could say that I was totally in control and that I knew what I was doing. But the thing is, it's a one-off, that song. People keep saying, "Is there another one of those?". And it's like, no. It was a time and a place and it was perfect for what it was.

There's a line in that song that's so exquisitely evocative in its poetry, "Salt breezes murmur through the coconut palm." It reminds me of Doug Ashdown's "The frangipani opens up to kiss the salty air." Do you have favourite lines you've written that you look forward to singing or hearing?
Yes, I do. In "Fireflies" that line, "I could take a shot of whisky to help me see it through/ Or lose myself completely making love to you." That is one hell of a line. There are others, too. I don't listen to my material a lot; I just let it float up when it happens. Once an album's finished, with me it's finished. I only listen to it again if I'm going to prepare it for live performance. Because I feel it's inhibiting to be going back over your old work.

A technique you use in "Let the Canefields Burn" and "Sicilian Born", and much later again in "Good Things in Life", is a dramatic unravelling of a story so that the chorus only reveals its full impact the third time you hear it. Each time it results in goosebumps, or even tears for me in the case of "Sicilian Born". Was that an obvious dramatic device that you understood from early on?

I must have a subconscious storyteller part of me that knows the trickery of telling a story well. Holding on, holding on, holding on, and then letting it happen. I've never studied literature. I'm widely read, but I've never studied the techniques of writing to get you to what you're talking about there.

In "Sicilian Born", when you learn he's gone home to die, it breaks your heart. And in "Let the Canefields Burn" the chorus is rousing each time, but only at the end does it have that dramatic effect because he's burnt his property down.

Well, he may have burnt himself as well. There's always that in it, too. Danced in the flames.

You've described your style as "quasi-journalistic". Where did your observant nature and talent for reportage come from?

It's just part of who I am. I've always been a very voyeur sort of person. I like to know what's going on behind everyone else's actions. That stems most probably from the relationship in the family. Observations about your parents' relationship and how you fit in. And always looking for the motivations behind the things we say or the things we do.

So one has to be careful around you.

You may just turn up in a song. I still find the human experience to be so fascinating, and every person is a different manifestation.

On *South of These Days*, "Child of This Land" sounds like a celebration of returning home to Mackay after many years away. Had you moved back by then?

No, all those songs were still written in Sydney. I was back here for *Tropicali*. "Before the Wet" and songs like that were directly instigated by being back in the tropics, there's a spirit of location.

Was Roy Rocket somebody you felt you could have been?

Roy Rocket was my interpretation of the mechanic who works for a company here called Carlyle Motors who was a great guitar player when we were kids, but never left town. There were a couple of them. Another guy who was a great keyboard player, but they had jobs, commitments, and they never ever went south to try and pursue it. I think Roy Rocket could have been me, definitely. It could have been me, geez. That close. Good at what you do, but never fulfil the promise.

But were you the "Prodigal Son"? Do you have a star tattoo?

[*Laughs*] I'm a bit of everything, really. I would love to be the prodigal son.

You left home at seventeen and went down south. It's obviously part-autobiographical.
There's a bit of me in everything, there's no doubt about that. Every single song, I can find where it's really me. And then I know where it diverges, and goes out into archetypes, or real people that I know of. I think "The Prodigal Son" is a lovely story, isn't it, to have someone waiting who never forgot. It's a beautiful story; whether it's true or not doesn't matter.

The *Tropicali* album had more catchy, sunny melodies than *South of These Days*. Do the melodies ever come first for you? Or do they come at the same time as the lyrics?
Most of the time they come at the same time. When you see a song written by Graeme Connors alone, you can be pretty sure that the first verse and chorus, melodies and lyrics, would have come together, and then I worked backwards with the lyrics to adjust them to the melody that I'd set on those first two. The most recent album, *This Is Life*, was a wonderful challenge for me, because most of those tracks were either written to musical beds, without any idea of what the melody was going to be, or strictly written melodies that Mark McDuff had come up with, and I set a lyric to it.

A lot of the songs on *South* were written at the time that I was doing *North*. So when I did face a new CD I was trying to use some of the Islander rhythms and their voices in the choirs. That was a childhood memory of music I heard in Mackay. The Islanders used to sing here at the corner of Sydney Street and Victoria Street under a big fig tree. They used to sing classic hymns with their Island harmonies. And those sounds really have stayed with me. I can still hear them, the rich, thick textures.

"Pacifica" talks about an aspect of Australia's history that hadn't really been dealt with in popular music.
It's the long overdue acknowledgement of the role the Islanders played in the development of North Queensland. And it pre-dates the legislation that came down by the Queensland Government, granting them full citizen rights, in 1994 or 1995. These people are in a bit of a netherworld in a sense because their forebears had been brought over here as indentured labourers at the turn of the century, they packed them all up and sent them home, all the ones they could catch, because they didn't want black people living in Australia. Good old white Australia policy. The descendants we still have here were the ones who escaped to the hills and grew sugarcane. But they didn't have citizenship rights. And a song that mentions Malaita and Guadalcanal, and "forty-four kanakas came recruited"—it was their song. They were loud and proud that they were invited to perform on it.

The song "Tropicali" brings in another of your preoccupations, which is the clash or blending of cultures, depending on one's point of view, and the sometimes uneasy, sometimes comical convergence of inhabitants and tourists in Australia. It's there again later in "The Great Australian Dream". When did you start to become fascinated with that theme?
"On the Edge of Paradise" from the *North* album started the ball rolling, where it's about all these southern tourists wanting to play. The realisation for me was that Queensland is a tourist state. You know how people constantly complain about the jungle that's become

the Gold Coast; they can't have it both ways. You've got to make decisions about which parts of your environment are interesting to tourists and should be made tourist-friendly. And I suppose it's a sideway snipe at the purists who keep saying, "Oh, we don't want the skyscrapers and all these bloody tourists!"

Some of the songs on *Homeland* are dated from an earlier time, in the early to mid-1980s, before *North*. Why hadn't you recorded those songs earlier?
They didn't belong on any previous projects. I try and conceptualise an album like a book. I always feel that my CDs have a flow that is in some way reminiscent of what you expect in a book, where the chapters lead one to another and at the end of it all you walk away with some sort of experience, some feeling of it. Even to the point where the most recent album, *This Is Life,* features a song called "All Hell Broke Loose", which dates back to '89 or '90. I found a home for a song that's been sitting in the bottom drawer all that period.

Some songwriters are very patient with their songs. Is that hard for you sometimes when you've written something that you're really fond of, to put it in the drawer?
Not really. We can use as an example "The Ringer and the Princess", which was lying around for ages. I thought it was too long a song, too wordy, and then *The Here and Now* was a bit of a clearing-house CD, where I was touring intensely and I had probably six or seven tracks, and thought, I've got an opportunity to go in the studio now, what else have I got? So went backwards, forwards and sideways. And to find out the true dates songs were written, that's usually a result of my writer's diaries. But I can go to those writer's diaries and find fragments that even pre-date that.

***Homeland* was full of songs relating that city/country tension that poet Les Murray has written of so beautifully. "Only a Cowboy Could" is an absolute heartbreaker.**
That's a really old song. That actually was written the same time as "Bailey", which was about 1981, '82, '83, something in that vicinity. And that was in collaboration with Peter Kenny, who happens to be my favourite orchestral arranger in the universe; he's just a brilliant Zen-focused musician friend. The results of everything I've done with Peter have led us to use small orchestras. And I don't know where the thought of that came through, but it just belonged on *Homeland*.

On *Homeland* the orchestrations often drive the songs rather than a rhythm track. When you leave the drums out, or keep them very soft and unobtrusive, is that decided in the writing process?
I think songs come with a certain arrangement tendency. Part of the biggest problem of contemporary music is it's driven by a drum machine. Transcribe my songs and you'll find unbalanced bar lengths. I'll have two-four bars snuck in here, there and everywhere. I'll have uneven length phrases. That has happened because I don't use drum machines, I don't build it around a measuring device. And so the length of my lyric will be dependent upon the melody that I'm working with, or the lyrical idea that I'm trying to get across.

"A Little Further North" is a classic example, where it goes, [*Sings*] "The sun sinks behind me in the west/ This is the time of da-ay I love be-est." Where it changes over there, it actually changes over halfway through a bar. [*Sings*] "Salt breezes murmur through the coconut palm/ As the colours change they set a scene of tropic calm." So that length of line, if I was doing it rigidly, I wouldn't have got those lines.

I believe that a true songwriter should stay away from those devices. I know when I'm working with McDuff—Mark's so proficient at computerised music, like drum machines and bass lines, he does it all, he's a one-man band—we still are always very careful not to allow the machinery to lead you somewhere, to actually allow the melody or the lyrical component to govern you as opposed to the musical element.

How did you get the idea for "Love Works"?

I was in Sydney and we were recording *Tropicali* and staying in these apartments down in the Darling Harbour side of King Street. There was an old lady used to come out of the apartment block opposite every morning with a bunch of flowers and a walking stick, and walk up King Street to York. I didn't think of it as a particularly significant work; I thought it was a bit religiousy-oriented, and I don't know why. And yet it has become a firm favourite in concert.

I think it's a profoundly moving study of the human condition embodied in one lonely old lady. It's also one of what I think of as your "truism" songs, philosophical songs like "A Blessing in Disguise", "We Can Change the World", "Love Is the Best Teacher of All" and of course "The Road Less Travelled". Lessons on humanity. Is there an art to making such lessons sound palatable and non-didactic in song?

In the writing of the lyric particularly, I am very conscious of not banging the drum, of not saying, "Hey! I've got some wisdom here for you." I try and find, if I can, a way in which it unfolds for us both, the listener and the artist. I feel really uncomfortable about even being seen as being on a platform, and saying, "Hey, I've got the answers." That is crying out to have the feet chopped down from underneath you. I have an in-built, you might want to call it humility, but it's not that, it's actually fear of being found to be a hypocrite. And that is something in "The Road Less Travelled" I'm very sensitive to, that I don't leave myself open for a shot. There have been attempts where people have tried to trip me up with a suggestion that I might consider myself a little wiser or a little holier than thou or a little something. And I'm very clearly not.

"The Road Less Travelled" grew out of the little quote at the back of Emmylou Harris's *Wrecking Ball,* where she thanked her producer for helping her take the road less travelled. I knew it had some significance in poetry, but I didn't even do the research to find out. Robert Frost I think it was, from the poem "The Road Not Taken".

And there was M Scott Peck's book.

I know this sounds really stupid, but I didn't know it until I got into the studio with Mark McDuff and he brought the book in and said, "Aha, I know where you get your titles from." I read the book; I wasn't overly blown away. I thought it was good, I thought we were both approaching the same idea. But I hadn't read the book before or the song wouldn't have happened. It's a fun song, too. It's got a bit of a message, but it's also the dilemma, isn't it. How do you live well? Taking chances and all that sort of stuff is really vital.

What was "The One That Got Away" for you? Was it the big John Farnham-style commercial career or was it something more personal?
[*Laughs*] That's just a whimsical little tune. I was going out on a boating trip to the reef with a bunch of people, including my son, and I thought it would be nice if I had a little song that I could do out on the reef that somehow belonged to what we were doing.

So it was about fishing!
No, it's far bigger than fishing. When I wrote it, it was really light-hearted. And then I came back and looked at it and thought, oh my God, what is it saying? Quite often you don't know what you're writing until it's finished. And then you live in a sense what you wrote.
It sounds absurd, but it is the truth. Sometimes you get on to something and you write a song and you're the whole time locked into it, it's like a little inspirational world, a cocoon that you're in, the song has a perfection all of its own, and then you finish the tune and you're going, "Oh well, how do I explain this? Oh yeah, it links with that experience I've had …" Or maybe twelve months to two years down the track something happens in your life and it's like, "Oh my God, I wrote it and it came." It's happened to me time and time again. And I think that's because I have been a really faithful writer. I have got up every day and done something. Every day I keep going.

Speaking of faith, how much has religion played a part in your life and in your songwriting?
I was raised in a Catholic environment and I believed it all. I was a true believer. I read the Bible several times as a younger person and it wasn't until later that I appreciated it for the literature that it was rather than necessarily the divine word. But my references are well and truly grounded in the Western tradition, which includes the Bible. And I find myself in lyrics a number of times popping up with something that's a play on a quotation that might be from the Old or New Testament, because it's part of my field of reference. When you're a child you need to be educated, and myths, legends, religion, are all part of a wonderful education for your imagination as much as your value system. I'm thankful for the poetry of religion. I'm thankful that I had an opportunity to have fear of God and all those sorts of things. I think that it's a good part of opening the human heart. It's sad if you never transcend it.

Why did you record a version of Rolf Harris and Harry Butler's "Sun Arise"?
In 1989 I was doing the *0-9* kids project for ABC, and I said, "We really need a sense of Aboriginality in something with white Australian connection as well." Something that says, "We too belong with you in this land." A sense of brotherhood. We can take and we can give. I feel strongly about that in songs like "You Me All the Same Brothers". Songs like "So Father Uluru Says", "Sun Arise", are again part of recurring themes that come forward.

"The Ringer And The Princess", he's Aboriginal and Asian. I have had positive feedback from people within the Aboriginal and indigenous community who feel comfortable with the reference that we're all part of one society. I don't see Aboriginal music or indigenous music as another language and another production value running parallel to what's happening with Australian music generally. It's got to be part. John Williamson's made inroads into that area as well. I always thought Slim would probably have a more concerted effort at that. But maybe time ran out before he did. Because he was such an idol of the indigenous community.

"The Ringer and the Princess" is a romantic, subtle way to talk about the subject of interracial relationships. Was it inspired by people you knew?
It was totally and absolutely fabricated. It was a way for me to address what I thought was a really important issue. I had heard, while I was doing a songwriting course in the Atherton Tablelands, of the concept of interracial marriage, and there were some negative comments made, particularly from the point of view of the woman. I thought, we need to redress this. So we put the woman as the heiress to a wealthy property and we put the fellow as a ringer with Aboriginal and Asian heritage. And we made them fall in love. They were still restricted by the convention that they never married, but their relationship was sound and strong and lasting. I received hate mail for that, from Victoria somewhere. He sent me a copy of the lyrics and emblazoned in red over it, "We know what you're up to and we're going to put a stop to it."

The melody in that song seems to be there purely to serve the story. Was that one where you had the lyrics first?
The whole thing was lyric. I wrestled with that lyric for ages, to try and tell the story as succinctly and in as short an amount of time possible. It was certainly very deliberately written and it had to be that off-handed narrative talk-sing. Even in the chorus—[*Sings*] "Oh the ringer and the princess, the dingo and the deer"—it's like you're talking through the whole thing. I was amazed when it took home Bush Ballad of the Year; I thought that was a huge step forward for Tamworth to actually say, "That's cool."

"So Father Uluru Says", on the other hand, has some interesting chord progressions. What was the purpose of your shifting of minor to major chords?
I've no idea. I wish I could tell you. That melody came with the lyric. [*Sings*] "White seeds, black soil, open the land and then buy the spoil ..." It's a very unusual chord to follow. It goes F to E minor, which is totally unrelated, a sharp jump. But then it skips back into B flat. That's an augmented fourth, which is another very strange jump to have between chords. But it just works. In the compositional stakes, I work with a lyric and a melody and then that leads you into an inevitable place musically for your changes. I wrote "So Father Uluru Says" at the piano and that would be a better explanation as to why those progressions have occurred. Because with a guitar, very rarely would you go a semitone movement to a minor chord, from an F to an E minor. Melodies and words come together on some songs, and they belong, that's it, it's finished.

"Boomerang in Paraguay" was about William Lane's "New Australia". Redgum had also done a song about it called "Virgin Ground". Had you heard that?
I hadn't heard it but afterwards people made me aware of it. But there's no comparison, I feel, between the two.

What interested you about putting that story in a song?
The whole concept of utopia, of perfection. The whole concept of starting again. I thought it was an amazing story, that someone could marshal the resources and the people to follow such a socialist dream, such an ideal. It didn't work, as utopias never do work, or can't work, because human nature doesn't allow it. But I thought it was a great tale of a man with vision and a dream, and that's how it starts off: "William Lane dreamed a dream about a new tomorrow where true freedom reigned ..." It's a really well-written song; it's a tough subject matter and I think we pulled it together really well. I know it's got a very good place in the hearts of a lot of people who support my music. It's regarded as a choice piece.

In "Big Jimmy and Felicidad" the upbeat style of the music is an interesting choice for a sad story.
I always heard it that way with the piano accordions thumping away and the zydeco vibe. It had to underscore it. It's yet another "Sicilian Born" sort of song where Big Jimmy develops. "Big Jimmy was a wild one, unpredictable as lightning, drinking and fighting." The next time it's "Big Jimmy was a wild one, unpredictable as lightning, isn't it amazing how a woman can change things." And then the end, it changes yet again. I didn't want to tell a sad story in a sad musical context; it just didn't belong together. Whereas by the juxtaposition of this up, busy music, the story unfolds for those who are really listening. It's like "Let the Canefields Burn", there are still people to this day who don't realise the song's about a suicide, and they sit there clapping, [*Sings*] "Let the canefields burn—ah yeah!"

"Hart Creek Debutant Ball" was written with Don Walker. You told me a few years ago that that song would give me a good indication of both your and Don's darker sides. Do you need someone like Don to draw that side out of you in music? I guess "Canefields" also shows your dark side, but you like to camouflage it, don't you.
You're probably right. It's all mirrors. But I had the first verse of that song completely in its entirety. "He was dead before he hit the floor there was nothing we could do/ Everyone just stood there stunned hoping he'd come to." And then Don and I started from there. I wouldn't have finished it without Don; it wouldn't have come out the way it did. It was a very even and wonderful experience writing that song together.

Do you prefer to write alone than to collaborate?
I really enjoy challenging collaborations. If that's not there, then yes, I'd prefer to write alone. And there will always be songs that I write alone. There are some new songs recently that I couldn't possibly have written with anyone else. They're too much my journey, whatever that happens to be, to bring someone else in on. The only way I could see that

522

happening would be if, musically, I was unhappy with something and I wanted someone to do an arrangement-cum-alteration musically.

What's important for you in a co-writing partner?
Someone who really pushes me, who challenges me to do better than I would possibly do on my own.

A lot of the co-writing you do isn't like that, because you've taken on a role as a kind of mentor to young songwriters, and you've gotten together with people like Adam Brand, to help him shape his songs, rather than to write songs that you would see yourself doing.
The primary reason that I'm writing with younger writers is the love of writing, and without sounding as if it's totally altruistic or anything like that, it's to see what they're capable of and maybe to give them a little prod along to think differently about things, or pass on a bit of my experience. I've been in that circumstance, with a stronger writer than me, and I have learnt enormously from that experience.

Who's a stronger writer than you?
I worked with Kent Robbins in America, and Kent was really good and really fast. I have a lot of regard for Don Walker. It's hard to say I view him as a stronger writer; I think he has strengths in areas I don't have, and I have strengths in areas that probably he doesn't have. I feel very honoured to be working with him and yet I also feel an equal friendship thing with him. We battle out line by line, and we're competitive enough to be trying to secure the next line. And the energy that's involved there is for the betterment of the song; it's actually just to write the best piece we can possibly write. I've worked with writers where you're in a circumstance where they're belting out lines, and you know they're not right. And so I generally take what's there and go away and spend time working on it and bring it back to the table.
    When I sit down with an experienced or inexperienced writer the energy is the same, about trying to create the best possible piece we can create. And if that means drawing out the other writer's story and altering it or changing it, whatever it is, I don't care what it takes; the whole purpose is that when we leave the table, the song is as good as it can ever be, and communicates something worthwhile.

"Good Things In Life" is probably the best example of that kind of collaborating, where you took Adam's story but gave it finesse.
That's a really good example of it. I really like Adam; when we get the opportunity, when it's not a business thing, we relate really easily together. We all have our little egos that come into play in a professional environment. But in a songwriting environment it really is a case of the ego's got to be left at the door for everyone concerned. That's an old cliché, but it is the truth and it's all got to be directed to the betterment of the song.

Tell me about "Paul Robeson on the Steps of the Sydney Opera House". What inspired you to write that, and why at that particular time did you write it?

It seems like I'd always known about Paul Robeson. They had those five minutes of Australian history on ABC radio. Something excited me about the idea of hearing his voice on this old, crackly mono recording singing an old labour song. Then I must have by coincidence seen the film footage somewhere in the black and white. It seemed there was a trail leading me towards this, I had to find out what the deal was with Paul Robeson, and why it was so important, apart from just the fact that he was a singer. I realised the political activism and how, in a sense, he was slightly misguided in some of the statements he made, which in turn alienated him during the McCarthyist period in America. He had all the right intentions in the world but he was the perfect person for them to destroy, because he was not only black, he was intelligent, he was famous, he had everything going for him, and what a way to destroy a man, to call him a traitor to his country. Because he came out and said basically what Sting said later, "I hope Russians love their children too." He just said, "Russians are like Americans; they don't want their children to die in a nuclear holocaust." And for that, in the times that he was in, he was completely ruined. They broke his health, they broke his mind, they were cruel, just damn cruel. It was racism gone mad. And the racism of ideas as much as anything else. They couldn't get Martin Luther King until later, so they got him. May as well have strung him up on a tree, as they would have in the old days.

So I wanted to remember his touch with Australia. I just felt he was a man of dignity and worth and value that never received the kudos he deserved at the time.

Did you speak the lyrics to make the point that Robeson had God's own voice so you couldn't compare?
Oh, there's no comparison, I couldn't, there was no way to sing that song. If God were a singer I know he'd sing like Paul Robeson. And then at the very end I sing, "I wish I could have seen him."

Has your voice usually guided you in your songwriting?
It would have because of the melodic leaps that I take. Because I have the capacity to do it, then of course you do it. It's one of those things that I have to be very careful of, and a lot of the reason I've been given by other artists and publishers as to why I don't get more covers, is because they can't sing the damn things. "The Simple Truth" is a two-octave song. Vince Gill is probably the only other guy who could cut "The Simple Truth" in the contemporary country area and do it justice. So the voice does play a part. On the last CD I was very conscious in particular songs of keeping smaller. Keeping it more in the centre. Songs like "You're Getting to Me", because there's a sensuality in not jumping sometimes. I'm learning just because I can do it, don't do it.

You said when you released *This Is Life* that you wanted to draw a line after many years of story songs, and concentrate on more personal, emotional and internal issues. You were already heading in that direction with *A Delicate Balance*. But listening to "When Lola Came to Town", it seems hard to believe you could stop writing stories like that.
I really loved writing that song, it was exciting to take it step by step. It's the mix of

freedom and control in those sorts of songs, just like "Good Things in Life". You know the outcome. As the writer, in most of these circumstances you know how the story ends. You know that the princess is going to almost drown, she's going to be saved by the ringer, and that they're going to live in some way happy ever after. You know that the Sicilian-born man dies, he's got to die. And you've got to find out which way it is he dies. Does he stay, does he go? So you're working towards something. "When Lola Came to Town", it had to be, he ran off 'cause he is just crazy in love with Lola.

And he just left the service station unattended.
I thought that was classic. Talking about nice lines that I'd be happy with, there's a couple in there that I thought were just gems. "Left the Caltex service station wide open". He couldn't wait; he just had to go. And of course that's a nod in the direction of Les Murray, that song. Because it opens with "an absolutely ordinary Saturday". Which is from Murray's poem, "An Absolutely Ordinary Rainbow". In Martin Place, where the man is crying, which I thought was an incredibly moving piece. I slipped that in, no-one's noticed it much. I often wonder if Les Murray even heard it.

So what about that decision that you no longer wanted to be identified with story songs?
Sometimes it's a trick you've got to play with yourself for your own creative health, where you have to go, okay, we're into a whole new ball game now. What was once is no longer applicable. We're moving on, we're going to explore new territory. That frame of mind can provide the energy for a growth, some sort of step ahead from which you can then regroup and put it all together again. But maybe it's also a statement of intent that you really don't want to hear any of those stories for a while.

Are love songs as easy for you to write as story songs?
I don't know. I know that there is nothing better. Story songs are fine, but I don't rate them as highly as a song that gets to the heart, that just goes, "That's me, that's how I feel, my God, you've written my song." In a relationship environment, the joy, the sadness, sweetness, delight, the bitterness, whatever it is that happens between two people, really is to me the top rung of the ladder as a writer. And I'm not depreciating the Australian stories or "The Ringer and the Princess" or all that sort of stuff. But I am saying that for me to create a song that breaks someone's heart whenever they hear it or makes them uplifted or feels great is top of the tree.

Are they harder to talk about?
It's really touchy territory. I can explain story songs very easily because they're different from you but once you get into love songs, songs that really are about connecting between people, I find it extremely difficult to get into the analysis of that. And also I think it's dangerous territory. Being the partner of a songwriter must be very difficult. Because there must be times when you go, "Hang on a minute, is that me in the song? Or is that someone else?"

Johnny Mercer said, "I think it takes more talent to write music, but it takes more courage to write lyrics."

I reckon that the biggest problem we have in Australia is we have an absolute dearth of serious lyricists. People who are prepared to go the distance, to write about things that matter, to write a clear, transparent lyric in a frame. And to stay with it. I don't see that sense of commitment coming through. It's hard work to write great lyrics—all the internal rhyme, all the rhythm, the energy of the changes, the vowel sounds. It's high craft. You give me a great lyric and I can make a hit song out of it with any music you want to add to it. You give me a great piece of music and it can still die in its tracks because the lyric says nothing and it means nothing to anybody.

Do you keep a notebook of lyrics?

No longer. Now I use a computer. In the past I used to have a songwriter's diary that lasted a year; every day I'd turn a page and do my work.

And write down lyric ideas?

Lyric ideas, melodic ideas. A melody to me is totally memorable when it's attached to a lyric. If I attach a lyric to any melody I can remember it in ten years' time, twenty years' time. It's burnt in my memory banks. But if you give me a melody without a lyric attached it's ephemeral.

Do opening lines come easily?

Sometimes. There's no rule. Sometimes the hook line or the last line of the chorus might come to you. I love songs where the opening line starts the song. Because at least you've got a beginning. If you get the hook line of the chorus, like say "A little further north each year", you then have to go backwards to find out why this exists. Whereas if I get "The sun sinks behind me in the west, this is the time of day I love best", the song is writing itself.

Is that how that came?

Yeah. Most of my really good songs just start and develop and the hook or the chorus makes itself known within the appropriate time. A lot of people advocate the concept of getting a song title and then writing backwards. A title generally makes itself apparent in the frame.

Do you tend to write more on guitar or piano?

Most of my better songs started on neither instrument. It just started in my head. Just floating, just the thoughts. And in many ways, anchoring it to an instrument is dangerous. We talked before about the lopsidedness of my phrasing. That exists because I don't have quite often an instrument in front of me, and I don't have the temptation of falling into accepted patterns, both rhythmically and musically. But I do love a piano.

What would draw you to a particular instrument when you're ready to give it its voice?

I just want to hear it sung, I want to hear it played and I want to feel the emotion of the song. It's how adept I am at either instrument to fulfil its role. If it's a strong up-tempo rhythmic song, the chances are I'll be playing it on a guitar. If it's mid-tempo with quite a bit of harmonic change, the chances are I'll be sitting at a piano; if it's a ballad the chances are I'll be at a piano. But quite often, even songs that are formed around the piano or the guitar after a period of time will swap instruments to see what it does, how it can be changed. Or if there are any little internal voices that I might wish to use that will give it some better depth.

You have a number of guitars. Do you write on all of them or one in particular?
No, I don't have any favourites.

Beth Nielsen Chapman told me that she tries to write on different guitars but she always goes back to the same one that she's written all her songs on.
That's most probably a mechanism for Beth Nielsen Chapman that works. We all have little belief systems that get us through. I think it's lovely and romantic, I think it's really sweet that the song is waiting in the guitar. But I'm sorry, I firmly believe the song is waiting in the heart and mind of the writer.

Your songs are lyrically very clear. Do you ever have the urge to write something completely abstract?
Yes, but I think if I want to do that, why don't I go and write poetry? Why would I? I love the form of popular song. And to me popular song is about understanding in time. You really should be able to grasp what's going on in one listen. It's like "Yesterday". Why is that a great pop song? Because you know exactly what it's saying and you walk away from it humming part of that song or grasping a few lines and attaching it to your life experience right there and then. I think obscurity for obscurity's sake is a joke. I know Bob Dylan is absolutely God for many people, but I think some of Bob's work can be a bit too esoteric. I think he's actually pulling our leg. He's going, "Come on you fools, see if you can make some sense out of this."

Do you have a favourite song you've written?
I honestly believe, and it's probably part of my mechanism like Beth Nielsen Chapman, that the best song, my favourite song, is still coming. And it is hopefully self-fulfilling. It keeps you writing. I know that there will come a time when I can sit back in my slippers and armchair, probably with a breathing apparatus, and a limited amount of time, and I'll listen to them all again and they will be warm and comfortable and wonderful, and it'll be revisiting my life's work. And that time, when it comes, will be good enough.

ARCHIE ROACH

SYDNEY, AUSTRALIA, OCTOBER 2004

It's all in his eyes. The pain and sorrow, struggle and redemption, hope and joy. Archie Roach's life and the lives of his people are played out in his deep, soulful eyes. He often keeps them shut when he is talking or singing. Sometimes it's too much to let everyone see inside.

Roach's songs have given form to the multitude of emotions behind his eyes. From his breakthrough 1988 song "Took the Children Away", through four albums of accessible, poignant and heartbreakingly honest material in a style best described as Australian blues, he has told the story of Australia's stolen generation with modesty, humility and a remarkable lack of blame.

Archie Roach was born in Mooroopna in northern Victoria on 8 January 1955 and spent his first three years at the Framlingham Mission near Warrnambool in the state's southwest before being forcibly removed from his family. After living in institutions and temporary foster homes, he found some semblance of normality with a white family who had settled in Melbourne from Scotland.

The young boy had never contemplated why his skin was a different colour to his friends'. "You can stick a room full of babies of all colours and they wouldn't worry about it, they'd all mingle and start doing what babies do with each other," Roach explained. "As we get older we tend to adopt other people's influences." So it was that walking home with a school friend one day he was confronted with the question, "Archie, how come your parents are white?"

"You know, they were just people, like me or anybody else. Until bang! Until that was spoken. And from then on I saw everything differently."

Receiving a letter from a sister he never knew existed, at fourteen he discovered his mother had died, and uncovered the truth of his tragic past and fragmented family. Confused and angry, he left his loving foster family and lived on the streets, looking for answers, taking to alcohol, living out every stereotype of the troubled urban Aborigine. He travelled and found other members of his family, piecing together the story of how he and his siblings were taken and separated. He met the young, plucky Ruby Hunter, who had also been taken from her family as a child and was living a similarly itinerant and alcohol-dependent life. They forged a close bond, and together faced their demons, battled to give up the drink, had their own children, took in countless more and individually and together developed their musical lives.

Roach's songs are full of children, mothers, dreaming, city streets and the words "took away". They are wistful, aching songs of something lost that can never be found, but also sanguine, joyous, celebratory and tender. Like the great Australian poet Les Murray, there is a contrast between the land and urban life, but through the eyes of one who has more right to the land than any white man, poet or not. Roach has had the support of musical poets such as Paul Kelly, who helped kick-start his career by producing his first album, *Charcoal Lane*, and David Bridie, who produced his second album. Roach has toured in America with Bob Dylan, and was once visited by Paul Simon.

He has picked up numerous Deadly awards, several ARIAs for Indigenous and Adult Contemporary releases, has worked with dance companies and orchestras, and has appeared in documentaries and on soundtracks, including the haunting vocals on Rolf de Heer's film, *The Tracker*. Roach has also won two Human Rights Achievement Awards. He and Hunter have been actively involved in educating, assisting and inspiring their people around Australia.

It was a humbling experience to meet Archie Roach. I spent some time with him on a park bench in Sydney, on a hot morning after the Deadly Awards where he had been honoured yet again, and shortly before he and Hunter were to fly back to South Australia, where they live in a rural community on the Murray River, near Hunter's own birthplace. They had recently worked together on *Ruby's Story*, a musical about her life, and it was clear that there were many stories still to tell, and new ways to tell the old stories. It wasn't so much about teaching us a lesson—although in listening to his work there are many sobering messages—but about sharing the journey.

Do you think the music you heard in those infant years with your Koori family and community stayed with you as you grew up, even subconsciously?

Ah yeah, I really believe in the power of the subconscious mind. I can explain it like this. I was in the city for a long time, Melbourne, and I left just to get away, trying to make some sense out of my life I suppose. I was about sixteen, I'd left my foster family, and I went up to North Queensland. And the strange thing there was that we were sitting around doing the usual thing, I thought they were just like city fellas basically, but one fella said something in his language, and I'd never heard the Aboriginal language spoken before, properly like that, not in fluent sentences. He said something and they all got up and danced. And it spun me out. It's something that touched me; it touched something deep down within me.

I really couldn't explain it at the time. 'Cause they wondered why, they said, "Oh, you don't do this down your way?" I said, "No, I've never seen it like this." It just all made sense. And I really believe that deep down within me, as an Aboriginal person, there's something that was there all the time that was so entrenched. It took something like that to open it up.

What music were you exposed to growing up in a white family and community? Was Hank Williams your first major revelation?
Oh, yeah, Hank Williams, of course. But what was really good, living with my foster father, Mr Cox, was he had a lot of variety, very eclectic in his music. He listened to Scottish ballads, he listened to Nat King Cole, Sam Cooke, Mahalia Jackson, all these black singers. So I was very lucky growing up and I suppose most kids just listen to the radio. I really enjoyed Dad Cox's old LPs. It was the only music that I ever heard at an early age and I thought it was the best.

And your foster sister was into gospel?
Yep, she played the organ in church, but she also got a Hammond organ when it was first introduced to Australia.

Were you more attracted to the keyboard than the guitar initially?
I was. It's strange, yeah. I first started playing the keyboard, an old electric one. It had the numbers on it, or letters or something, but really old stuff like, "If you were the only girl in the world and I was the only boy". I played old songs like that, "Danny Boy" and all them old classics.

When did you first get a guitar?
I was in high school. This friend kept on pestering me, he said, "Would you like to come along to this meeting?" I said, "What sort of meeting is it?" He said, "Oh, it's a church meeting." And I said, "Ah, no, I'm not really interested." But I went along anyway, after a while. I'd never seen anybody play guitar in church; it was just organ and very straight faces and all that. These people played with guitars. I saw somebody get up just with an acoustic guitar and sing a song. She put a country tune that I was familiar with to verses in the Bible. I thought, this tune is very familiar, but the way she sang it and the way she played, it was pretty moving. And I thought, that's what I want to do, I want to play the guitar.

At that stage did you think that you could make up your own songs?
Oh, no. I just loved a lot of music that was around at the time, and before then.

When you were living on the streets all those years, what role did music play in your life?
A big role. Even on the streets I always played. I suppose I played for my own pleasure, to keep me company sometimes. Music was a solace. If I didn't have music in those days I don't know what I would have done.

That was basically you accompanying yourself on guitar, playing other people's songs?
Yeah, but when me and Ruby got together and we tried to sober up one time—and we did for a little while, in this halfway house—during that time of not drinking I wrote a song.

Did alcohol help with your creativity or do you think it blocked it?
It's hard to say. It certainly influenced my writing, the early writing, and still does in a way. Not alcohol itself, as such, the substance, but what alcohol was to me and other people. Things like "Charcoal Lane" and "Down City Streets" and stuff like that. But I couldn't have created anything while I was drinking. I couldn't have sat down and thought. My main thought as an alcoholic was to get a drink, twenty-four hours a day. So there wasn't any call to write a song. [*Laughs*]

Having curtailed your formal education, how did you develop your use of language, your vocabulary and your awareness of history and culture?
I read a lot when I was young. I was lucky again that my foster family, the Coxes, bought me books. I read a lot of the *Encyclopaedia Britannica*. Growing up I read them all. Maybe not from page to page, but I read a lot of them and gathered a lot of information. My old foster dad was a crossword freak, and I used to be fascinated by what he was filling in these little squares in the newspaper for. I realised he was making words. It's funny, I have this relationship with the English language, I love the English language. Also, on the street I read a lot of newspapers, but that's just how I was taught or how I taught myself.

You valued education, obviously.
Yeah, especially the English language. And I do so hate it when people muck around with it today and don't pronounce it properly.

In songs or in general speaking?
In songs as well as in speaking. The pronunciation of a word. Like, if we're talking as Aussies we go along on the grass. If someone wants to sing they're walking on the graaass. [*With American accent*] "Green, green *graaass* of home." I don't speak like that so I don't sing like that. But I don't try to exaggerate the Australian accent either. Though a lot of folk singers do that. I don't put on a real heavy Australian accent.

While you were living on the streets, did you keep a notebook or journal and jot down thoughts?
No, a lot of things were just kept in my head.

Are you usually driven by the words and story of a song first rather than by a melody?
I'm of the belief that nobody, when they listen to a song, ever gets the rhythm, the melody and the lyrics all at once. I think that they either hear the rhythm first or hear the melody or maybe the lyrics. I've got an idea in my head what I want to write about, but then I find it on the guitar, the melody, the rhythm. But words in the English language have a rhythm of their own, so you can't force that rhythm. The rhythm comes naturally with the words that you use.

So with "Took the Children Away", was that an idea? Did you have that phrase and built a song around that?
My Uncle Banjo said, "You sing a lot of other people's songs. Why don't you write about that time when they come and took you away?" I said, "Why would I want to write about that? I don't remember much about it." He said, "Yeah, but I do, boy! I do!"

He said, "Your dad, the old dad come down, and he was gonna fight 'em all, and we all had to jump on him." I said, "You jumped on my dad?" He said, "Well, we had to stop him, they would've arrested him for fighting the police." So I wrote in there, "Dad shaped up and stood his ground." I got a bit of that from Uncle Banjo. I had the idea there, and then I went home and I sat down and started strumming a few chords. Three chords. Just a chord succession. And the words, "Took the children away ...", it just kept coming through my head. "Took the children away ..." So I worked mainly from that, off that and that rhythm. But the inspiration from Uncle Banjo.

Did the structure of songs come naturally to you?
Yeah, we performed a lot of country stuff, doing a lot of covers. Very basic song structure—verse chorus, verse chorus, maybe another verse, a bridge, if you can put a middle-eight in there somewhere it helps. But now I don't think of that. I think the song evolves itself somehow.

Do you remember writing your first song?
Yeah, "Open Up Your Eyes". I sang that at a country music talent quest, a songwriters' section. And I come third. Nearly a year up the track, a friend of mine, Clive Beeton, an Aboriginal fella from Tasmania, he said, "Archie, quick! Your song's on the radio! Who's singing it?" Got in touch with the radio station, we rang 'em up. "That song you played, 'Open Up Your Eyes', who sang that?" It was some lady called Valerie somebody recorded it. And I said, "Well that was my song." And they said, "How can it be your song?" [*Laughs*] And apparently the people that were there recorded some of the stuff that we'd done. So I just closed the door on that song, I didn't worry about it any more.

So the first song you wrote got covered by somebody else.
Yeah, but without permission.

When you wrote "Took the Children Away", was it initially painful or healing to write about your displacement?
When I first wrote it, put pen to paper and got up and sang it, I felt pretty emotional. But in 1988 it was in Sydney, we were at La Perouse camping with other Aboriginal people and they were having a little bit of an argument whether we were going to march from the city or from Mrs Macquarie's Chair. I said, "I don't know anything about this and there's no need to argue." And that's when I sang "Took the Children Away" first time in public. And old people come up and thanked me. I didn't know why. Thank me? Shouldn't be thanking anybody for that song.

The song is remarkably matter of fact and ultimately uplifting and hopeful at the end."Yes I came back" is perhaps the most powerful line in any song you've written. Do you feel that way?
Yeah, I do. Especially recently, we've done it with a twenty-two-piece orchestra with Paul Grabowsky, it was quite incredible. When that part comes up the orchestra builds up and up and you're so lifted up out of there, it's incredible. Out of that circumstance.

In the actual act of writing that song could you keep the anger at bay?
When Dad stood his ground, I wrote that down and I got up and walked around and started throwing punches in the air. And thought, I don't know if I can do this. Ruby was wondering what was going on. I said, "I'm just having a bit of a struggle with this song." I knew what I was going to write, see. "Dad shaped up and stood his ground." 'Cause he said, "If you touch my kids, over my dead body." And that's how I felt at the time when I was writing it. Funny, I feel a bit like that now. [*Laughs*]

Talking about it?
Yeah.

Given the accolades and awards you received for "Took the Children Away" was it ever difficult, as you continued to write songs, to retain the pure essence of what made you first start writing? Did you feel somehow bound to write according to what people then expected of you?
No. A lot of people come up and said that to me, people from all walks of life. A record executive at some sort of function said, "So do you see yourself as a crusader?" I just didn't know what to say. I said, "Don't be ridiculous." I'm writing from where I was, where I am at the moment, and where I was at the moment I was writing was back there, at the time I was taken away. And I was right there, you know, and Dad punching the air.

When you write a song that isn't necessarily based on an Aboriginal theme or a personal story—such as "Alien Invasion", which you said you wrote about the tagging of dolphins and whales in the ocean—do you understand that it might be difficult for your audiences to separate from the subject matter they know you for?
Oh, yeah, I've always been of the belief that I have no control over a person's interpretation of my songs. This may be my interpretation, but how someone else interprets it is entirely up to them.

Was there one particular case of death in custody that inspired "Beautiful Child"?
Yes. A man by the name of Lloyd Boney up in Brewarrina. I wrote that song, then years later I met his brother, Archie Boney. He said, "Thank you for writing the song". Not "for my brother" or anything. So whether or not he knew it, I don't know. It was kind of funny when I met his brother after writing the song. It was kind of freaky. I really didn't want to say, "I was inspired by what happened to your brother", because it seemed a bit too personal.

On a television interview recently, you described the pain of hearing the story of the bashed and killed teenager Louis St John Johnson, who you wrote a song for, and said, "I'm always getting my heart broken; I'm used to it." Is it possible to write authentically about pain without having your heart broken?
Yeah. To write about suffering you don't really have to be going through it, but if you have empathy, you can certainly write about it.

Did writing "Mother's Heartbeat" help you to reconcile the anguish of being separated from your mother and never seeing her again before she died?
Yeah, it's a big consolation, that song. It was very consoling.

Can you talk about your relationship with Paul Kelly?
Paul Kelly, I don't know whether sometimes to kiss him or punch him on the jaw. Nah, truly, if it wasn't for Paul Kelly I honestly don't think that I would have recorded anything, because it was the furthest thing from my mind. Just writing songs and singing to my family and community and friends.

Did he do anything to help you shape or structure those first songs?
The first album, *Charcoal Lane*, those songs were pretty much left the way they were.

What about David Bridie?
He writes a lot on piano and other instruments as well. When I used to write songs or when I wrote a song and sang it, I'd be listening for drums and the bass and the guitar. But after playing with David Bridie I found myself listening for a cello or a piano or a violin.

What have you and Ruby learned from each other musically?
What I've learned from Ruby is that sometimes you can just throw what you know about standard westernised music out the window. And work a lot more freer than that. I don't know what she's picked up from me.

Do you have different ways of writing songs?
Yeah. She'll just go with whatever comes out of her head straight there. Just spontaneous, whatever she thinks of, she'll write. Whereas mine takes a little bit more thinking about, oddly enough. Sometimes with English, and respecting it so much, sometimes you get a bit bogged down in it and you say, "I could probably say this a bit better than that."

How important has it been to have international recognition for your work?
I didn't even think of it, how important it would be. But I know that it is important if you want to continue in this line of work. I didn't like my first experience overseas at all, in America. But I know what to expect there now.

Is it true that Paul Simon visited you when he was in Australia? I read that Ruby was worried that all she had to offer him was Vegemite sandwiches.
Well, actually she had ham. And I made her feel worried because I know Paul Simon is of the Jewish faith. They don't eat pork or anything from the old swine. And she came out with ham sandwiches. And I go, "Mum! Mum!" And he goes, "It's alright, I'm not orthodox."

Did you know much about his work?
Oh yes! Our manager said, "Paul Simon really admires your work and he'd like to meet you." And I said, "Paul Simon? From where? What part of Australia?" "No. Paul Simon from Simon & Garfunkel." Oh, my God.

What did you talk about with him?
He's a very socially conscious man. He talked about his fleet of Bridge Over Troubled Waters vans in America, self-contained ambulances where they perform minor operations just for the street people. We talked about things that he thought might interest me and they did. And that interested him. We took him to the community and showed him the Aboriginal childcare agency and the health service and things like that.

He showed us a few things on the guitar. He showed us how he finds a melody. I can find melody on a guitar for a song, because of Paul Simon.

How does he find a melody?
He just showed us some finger placements and certain strings to hit. He'd do it in succession and keep on doing it, and change them round and you get a tune. It's finding a melody for a song when you're writing, if you haven't got a melody.

Does that happen much for you, when you can't find a melody?
No, it doesn't happen all that much, but it can enhance, if you remember those couple of strings or couple of notes that you played when you're singing. It's good to play when you're singing as well. It's effective.

The sensuality and universality of emotions on your last album, *Sensual Being*, were strong. I wondered if a song like "Will I See You Tonight" would have been as easy for you to write when you were still working through your anger in your early songwriting years.
Well, like you asked before if it was painful, but as well as healing, it was very cathartic. "Took The Children Away" was a hard song to write but in the end it became a release for me and very cathartic. But this was just something that I just felt ready to do. We are

sensual, physical beings. No matter how, I'm still flesh and blood and we still desire things and enjoy things in life.

It was quite a journey from "Took the Children Away" to "Move It On". Will there always be new ways to tell that story?
I suppose the good thing about writing and language—English is my language; my father's language is Bundjalung but I haven't spoken it, I grew up with English, and I love it—there's always many ways you can say something. You can express it in a different way where it's not so sorrowful and mournful as "Took the Children Away". It's more like, "Ah well, here we go again." That's "Move It On".

Do you wait for inspiration to come before you'll write songs, or do you enforce some discipline in your daily life for songwriting?
No, it's probably about 99 per cent mostly inspiration.

Do you trust the songs will always come to you?
Yeah, I always trust that. Even though there's nothing there, something will come.

Do you get as much pleasure from singing other people's songs as you do singing the songs you've written yourself?
I probably get more pleasure doing my own stuff because it's going around and round, it comes from somewhere else in me and then out. So it's a circle, mate. It goes round and round.

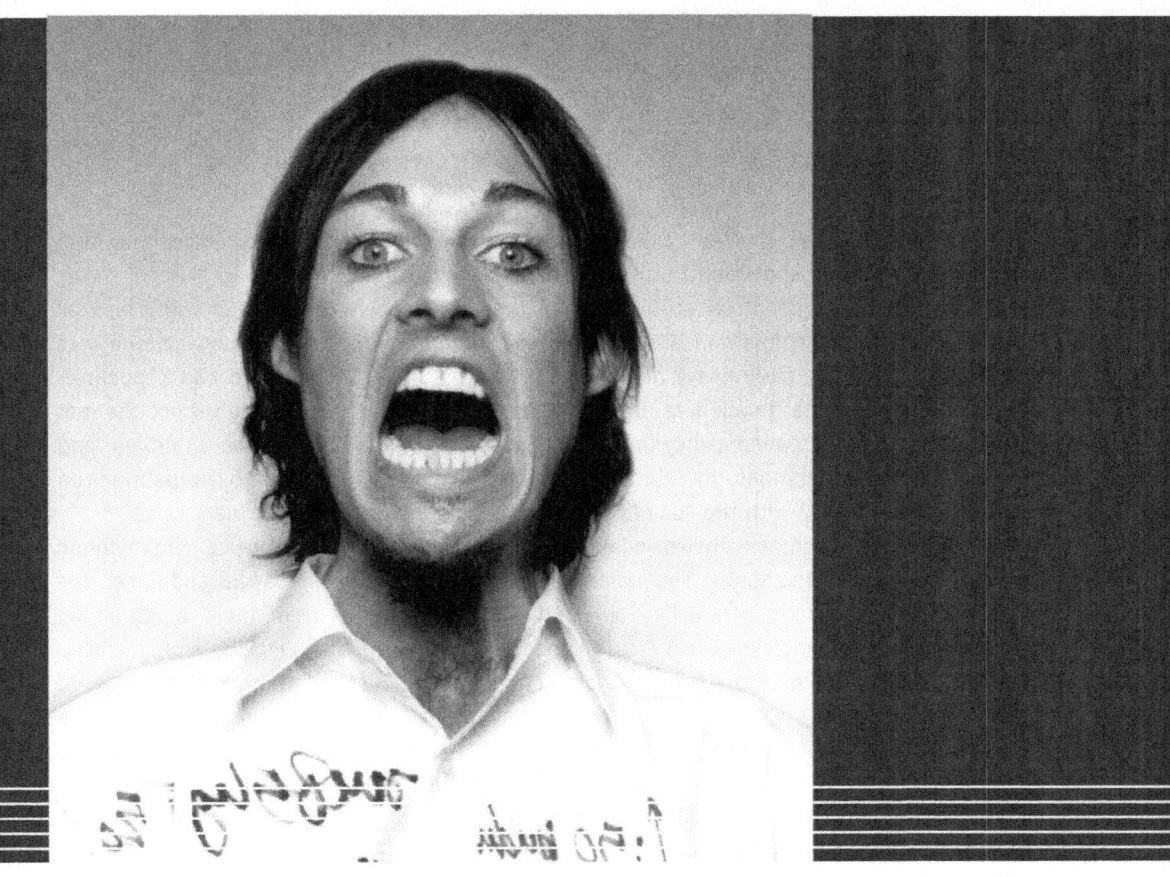

DANIEL JOHNS

SYDNEY, AUSTRALIA, FEBRUARY 2004

How do you get inside the head of someone like Daniel Johns? It's a head full of sound and colour, light and dark, rainbows and castles, with a gift of musical imagination that set him apart from most of his contemporaries in the 1990s and early 2000s. Johns is among the most exceptional songwriters Australia has ever produced, but like other creative geniuses through the ages, he has battled his demons and developed an idiom that serves him well but can often baffle those not in his closest circle.

It took some years for Johns to become truly happy. When life should have been trouble-free and full of possibility, he was living out the teenager's dream of rock stardom and suffering physically and emotionally as a result. When he first started feeling happy, it was a "crazy, psycho, manic happy". Serenity might be too far-fetched a notion for someone whose mind is as active as Johns', but in 2004 it appeared that a kind of peace had found his fragile soul.

Born on 22 April 1979 in Newcastle, New South Wales, he grew up on a musical diet that spanned the Muppets and Deep Purple. He learned violin as a child, played trumpet in his primary school band, and took up guitar from the age of twelve, beginning with classical lessons and then teaching himself to play more popular forms. As a teenager, he was influenced not only by early heavy metal—Deep Purple, Black Sabbath and Led Zeppelin—but by contemporary hard rock acts like Pearl Jam and Soundgarden. At high school he met Ben Gillies and Chris Joannou; they formed Innocent Criminals when they were thirteen, and two years later they burst onto the scene as Silverchair, after winning a demo competition run by SBS-TV and Triple J with the song "Tomorrow", a scathing attack on affluence.

Johns wrote all Silverchair's lyrics and melodies, while Gillies provided musical and rhythmic backbone to many of the songs. Thematically, their terrain was teenage anger and angst, the titles of "Pure Massacre", "Israel's Son" and "Suicidal Dream" from their debut album *Frogstomp* speaking for themselves. But the accessibility of the music and the craftsmanship that was way beyond their years ensured them not only Australian but international success. At the age of sixteen, they were touring America. At seventeen Johns was writing and recording a second Silverchair album, *Freak Show*, and battling a love–hate relationship with fame and its effect on how his music was heard. "Even back then I knew that I had musically developmental stages," he said. "I didn't want that many people to hear our first album 'cause I knew that was the case, so the second album I really tried to make it not do as well."

He failed in that intent, as the band's popularity continued to escalate. Johns' discomfort manifested itself in a struggle with anorexia nervosa; when that was past him and his musical career had reached a new peak as he turned 23, he was stricken with a rare form of arthritis, which rendered him unable to hold a guitar, let alone play it, for most of a year. And that left his music to work its own magic, something Johns had probably wanted anyway. Just as genius songwriters like the Beatles and Brian Wilson had made huge creative strides within a short time span, Johns' progress was astonishing. The *Neon Ballroom* album was a hint at things to come; by the time Silverchair's fourth album, *Diorama*, emerged in 2002, a transformation of epic proportions had occurred, and even Johns himself knew he had reached a creative place from which he could never turn back. The gut-wrenching, raw and tormented songs of the mid-1990s were all but renounced.

When he finally emerged from his illness in early 2003, it was to focus on love—he had put his relationship with songstress Natalie Imbruglia on hold for some time to be at one with his work—and on a new collaboration with dance music producer-composer Paul Mac. Their project, The Dissociatives, was hailed as a new coming by the enamoured music press, and their catchy, fanciful pop-infused pieces of delight inspired Johns to continue working in that vein. Nothing was ever officially said, but the prospect of Silverchair continuing was unlikely.

Less than two months after his marriage to Imbruglia, I met with Johns in the middle of a session with Mac. They were working on some new songs for a post-Dissociatives project. In a tiny studio filled with psychedelic colours, Johns sat—and often bounced—on a large exercise ball, speaking in a small, quiet voice about highly conceptual creative processes and gushing with childlike responses about people and things that made him happy. Daniel Johns was probably happier than he had ever been in his life; it was a good time to catch him.

Did the theory you learned from the early guitar lessons stick with you when it came time to start putting original songs together?

Not really, 'cause I could never read music. So every instrument I ever played, everyone was reading the music and I'd just quietly figure out how to play it in my head and make it look like I was reading. Had lots of instruments that I didn't want to play any more so I thought I'd better get one and stick at it.

When did you start playing piano?

Only three years ago or something. I got it 'cause I really wanted to play it on my demos at home, so I just started teaching myself how to play.

Did the creation of songs come easier to you once you understood the layout of the keyboard?

I find it harder because I'm not a very good piano player and it makes the songs boring. So I only write sections on piano. To write on the piano without knowing actually how to play it and just going off feel, you can write some really cool intros and outros and it's good for vocal melodies.

So you'll often shift between instruments in the same song?

Yeah, definitely. The piano I generally play when I want to think of vocal melodies and horn melodies and string melodies. The guitar's for laying out some kind of structure.

Do you remember the first song you ever wrote?

Not really. I remember when I was five or six I wrote a song and I couldn't play any instruments so I was just singing it out. Me and my brother were in a faux band called Goofy's Barbeque, and we wore one glove each. They were the first songs I wrote, they weren't very good.

So you've always been writing songs.

Yeah, definitely. I honestly believe I was writing songs when I was a baby. It's almost like every song you write is just a recall of what you wrote when you were a baby but you couldn't write it down.

A baby? Maybe even in the womb?

Yeah, maybe even in the womb, that's even cooler. Yeah, Mum was just chilling out listening to records. Yeah, let's go with that.

Were you writing poetry as a young kid?

Yeah, a little bit. Not much. I used to be highly conceptual on Thursday afternoons after Mrs Sheetram's class in Year 2. My best friends were the Year 3 students that loved to breakdance and were the cool cats and I used to think they were just God. Mrs Sheetram used to get us all to hold hands at the end of a Thursday afternoon and we all sung, [*Sings*]

"We are the world, we are the children ..." And I used to go, "Fuck, this is the most glorious moment of my life!" Thursday afternoon was hot! So I'd always write poetry on Thursday afternoons and hand it in to Mrs Sheetram. And she rang my mum up and said, "This kid's going to be a poet." [*Laughs*]

Do you think you had a good handle on language back then?
No. I still don't think I have a good handle on language. But I think I had a good handle of how certain vowels combined with certain consonants can sound musical. So I knew the words sounded rhythmical and I knew the words that sounded best when we sung them.

When you were listening to music in your teens, were you studying the way the songs were put together?
No. I only really got analytical about songwriting when I left school. Because prior to that, I think in high school any kind of outward declaration of knowledge or intelligence meant you were slapped over the head.

I did read that once Silverchair took off, high school was not happy for you. Rather than being admired, you were given a really hard time.
Yeah. High school was horrible; I hated it. But it made me more insular, which in turn made me a better songwriter, because there were no more obligations to be anything. If you feel like all these people don't like you anyway, you may as well be deliberately disliked and make sure that you're the best songwriter in the universe by the time you're forty, and they're all like, "Damn!"

Many successful songwriters wrote their first songs around the age of fourteen or fifteen, but those songs were rarely recorded let alone became hits. Looking back, are you glad that songs like "Tomorrow" and "Israel's Son" got such wide exposure? Are you proud of those songs now?
No. I'm not really proud of my stuff. Except for what I'm currently doing creatively. When I'm between projects, I don't have anything to look forward to, I'm just like, "Oh, it's all horrible, it's all horrible, wasting my time." And then I start writing again and it's like, "This one could be it! It's going to be the magic record."

Everything about my teenage musical career, I just see it as my musical developmental stages, but millions of people have actually got recorded documents of what those things were, which is not necessarily favourable. The last Silverchair tour that we did was when I kissed those songs goodbye from my life. That was a moment for me to swear to myself never to play anything from at least the first two albums ever again.

Back then, writing about war, death and suicide was probably a productive outlet for those thoughts. Do you ever wonder what you would have been doing, as a teenager in Newcastle, if you hadn't been writing about it and playing it out in music?
I think it was the beginning of looking into myself, exploring darker themes. Culturally,

that was what was influencing all of my generation. That inquisitive mind into other places where our thoughts are darker. All I've ever seen is a beach, and kids with bright swimmers on; now all of a sudden there's all this other stuff that I've been exposed to that I can write about that maybe will start some kind of fire inside of me and I'll get passionate about writing.

But at that early stage, you weren't feeling suicidal, were you?
No, I think there are a lot of autobiographical moments, but I was more culturally directed. Writing from seeing other people's things going on around me.

And watching television.
Yeah. I've always watched lots of television. TV's great. I haven't got a bad word to say about it.

Does television still inspire you now, or is life in your own world far more inspiring?
I think television still inspires me, even if it's subconsciously and I'm not aware of it, anything that you see that connects with a certain part of your memory has got to contribute to the way that you dream. And the way you dream is going to contribute to the way you create. And the way you create is, it's just a circle. It just keeps going like that. So anything you see or hear or smell, there's some kind of receptor in your brain that detects it, so now you can reproduce that smell and you don't even realise it's influenced your day.

Do you dream a lot?
All the time.

Do you wake up and write down what you dreamed?
No. Sometimes I get tapes going, 'cause I speak German in my sleep, apparently.

Did you learn German at school?
No. I know how to count to ten.

Do you dream vivid scenes?
Yeah, I love my dreams. They're my favourite thing in the universe. A lot of the time if I've had an amazing dream I instantly get up and start playing guitar and start playing piano, 'cause I know it's still fresh. I don't even know what it looks like any more, but I know if I get straight on a piano, music's another way to dream so somehow they will connect up and you'll reproduce whatever that dream was you had the night before that was so amazing. It doesn't always work, but sometimes it does.

What's your favourite TV show?
Probably dating shows. In America they have this show called *elimiDATE*. It's really cool. And I can't stop watching it. I don't want a plot, I just want to look at all the expensive

colours. Like you watch an old movie, and it's a good movie, but the colours are dodgy, so you don't feel like you're there. Some of the old movies that are shot, it all looks like plasticine and hazy smoky skies.

So it's a sensory experience for you.
Definitely. It's all about what it looks like. I don't remember any plot to any movie I've ever seen.

Having said that, your early songs were inspired by documentaries and news programs and current affairs, actual things that were happening in the world.
Well, that was new to me then. And now I know there's disaster all around and I don't want to contribute to more music influenced by that. I want to try and make things better.

How did songs come together in the early years?
It was just making up melodies and remembering it in my head. I started writing with Ben in Silverchair when we were about thirteen, 'cause we could play guitar together and two guitars always sounded better than one. We used to sit together playing in a room and then say, "What about this for a chorus?" It would take us half an hour to write a song and then we'd put it down and I'd write the lyrics and the vocal melody and then we'd play it and that'd be it. And it wasn't until I started writing by myself where I started actually contemplating what I was contributing.

And now is it a different process, less organic in a way?
Oh, now it's more organic. It's way more organic, 'cause back then the seed that grew into the fruit was small. Now it seems that the seeds are creating bigger things and the projects go for longer but it's not laboured over, it just feels like you're flowing as you're writing music. So you can write a song in seven days, but it's never been laboured over, it's just naturally growing and growing and growing until you find the point at which it can peak before it starts to wilt again.

When you're writing on your own, you just sit at the piano and move to the guitar?
Yeah, on the guitar there and the piano there and just play a part and then go, oh yeah, and then if I play that, I quickly run over to my guitar and write a guitar part for that particular section, and then sing into a dictaphone what I think the horn line will be and then press play and start playing so it's all going at the same time.

Do you use a multi-track at home?
No, I do it all on one little tape recorder, but I have a studio set-up which I don't use unless Paul's over. Because I don't know how to work it. [*Laughs*]

Do you prefer collaboration or writing alone?
They're different. I find the product from writing alone to be something which fills me with joy. Like when you have been slaving over something for a year and then you record it all and

it's exactly how you envisaged it. There is nothing that makes your body feel warmer or more tingly or special.

Collaborating is more instant. When you're writing by yourself you're going, okay, this is getting good, this is getting good, and it's more like a slow release. When it's writing together, it's like, "I've got this." "I've got that." Now that I'm writing with Paul it's a different dynamic; we've both got ideas flowing so you sit there peaking. "Oh yeah, that's great." "That's great!" "I'll do that, and I'll do that!" "And I'll do that!" Then the song's written and you go, "Yeah, your best song ever!" It's not as long slow burning.

You haven't had a lot of collaborators. Could you sit in a room with a stranger and just knock out a song?
No, I don't think so. It's about that energy with the person and even if you're completely different, if everyone's got a vibration, and if they're somehow in sync or rhythmic then you're going to write well together. Whereas a lot of the time when people go, "You'll really love this person, he's just like you", it's just so boring.

The reason I stopped writing with Ben is because I was going through a hard time and could no longer feel uninhibited with him. So now I've found Paul, who I just feel completely inspired by and uninhibited around. A lot of my best ideas come out when I'm sitting here with Paul.

Did Ben understand when you could no longer open yourself up in his presence?
I think so, yeah. We just stopped seeing each other, I was writing and then said, "I've written this album." It was never like, "I can't write with you any more." I was just sitting in my house and didn't want to leave and didn't want anyone to see me.

How did you and Ben complement each other?
I think we both made each other feel braver. 'Cause you didn't feel like you were doing it by yourself and everyone would laugh. I honestly think that's the main thing we both got out of it. Just the confidence to try something. 'Cause if I tried something and Ben saw it, it didn't bother me if it wasn't good.

Freak Show **was an album of more personal experiences. Did you write the songs on the road or in a space of quiet reflection after all the touring and adulation?**
Definitely quiet reflection. I had never written on the road at that point, I was going to never do it. I was just going to get home from tour, go to school, skip the last half of the day, go and smoke pot, and then sit in my bedroom and write songs. That was my therapy. I was going through all this stuff and didn't know who to talk to and didn't know what to do, so I was just exploring songwriting, but still trying to make it so that Ben and Chris liked it, 'cause that was important to me.

Was life as a teen rock star so bad that hate and suicide still had to have their place in your lyrics? Or were you just more closely observing other people around you?
I think it was a bit of both. The things that I said on the second record I definitely felt. That

was no longer a social commentary, that was actually stuff that I was going through that I was trying to make more universally accepted as a feeling instead of thinking people like that are absolutely crazy. So that was just a time to vent. Later on I learned to home in on that feeling and direct it in another way. If you've got anger and frustration all going through your head and then you pull it together and turn it into happiness, you're going to get this really exciting mental song that's born of hate and ends with a love child and it's the best song ever.

In "Freak" how did the opening lines—"No more maybes/ Your baby's got rabies/ Sitting on a ball/ In the middle of the Andes"—which I understand you'd seen on a documentary, relate to the concept of being a freak on stage in front of an audience?
That line was deliberately to alienate from the first statement. The whole thing about freaks being alienated from society and all of that was an important thing for me to try and reproduce lyrically. I wanted people to hate the first verse. [*Laughs*] I just wanted them to hate it. I knew it was completely stupid, made absolutely no sense, and I knew it was completely ambition over ability.

Do lyrics need to make sense?
Yes. They need to make sense in that it's obvious when someone's just writing drivel and it's obvious when someone's writing something with a deep sentiment. It's also the hardest thing to do to write something that seems to not make sense until you explore it and you see all of the parallels that it has with what is developing within the music. They don't need to make literal sense always, providing they're musical and they're somehow related to what's musically happening.

Conventional rhyming schemes don't seem prevalent in your songs. In fact, rhyming at all seems scarce.
Sometimes it happens. Like when I want to be pop, I'll put something that rhymes just for the kids. But most of the time, why would you? It takes all of the magic out of your stream of consciousness. Like if you're walking along this beautiful path, amazing lights, gigantic sandcastle in the distance, and you're walking along, you can get from here to there in one verse easily. If you have to rhyme, you'll take a step and then you've got to think of a line that rhymes with that, so that the development is so long and tedious and the song sucks. You don't rhyme and go to the castle. That's the theory.

There aren't many Australian songwriters whose lyrics don't rhyme.
It rhymes with the music. So you don't notice it doesn't rhyme. If you just don't rhyme, and put it over something like a cut and paste collage, it's just going to sound silly.

Nick Launay is one producer who pops up several times in my listening to the work of Australasian songwriters. He worked with Midnight Oil, Iva Davies, Tim Finn, Nick Cave. Did he have much influence on your writing or did you always present him with finished songs?
I always presented him with finished songs. Having said that, I think Nick had one of the

hugest influences on me in terms of where my music was heading, of everyone in the world. Because I had never met anyone that heard my comments about what I wanted to do musically and not felt patronised or judged or some older statesman looking down at this kid thinking, "Here's a bunch of stoned ideas." Nick was the first person, when I was going through the hard time, to go, "This is actually really cool. I like all this stuff you're saying. I'm going to make it happen." So I started really respecting him and then he started getting me into all this music, like Suicide and the first Peter Gabriel solo record, and Kate Bush *The Dreaming* and I was like, fuck! I hadn't heard anything even remotely like her until I met Nick. I was completely unaware of any music of that type in history. All I'd been exposed to was rock music.

And yet that kind of music would fit really well with your dreamlike state that you like to work with.
Exactly. So I started feeling the connection. Even *Diorama*, when he knew that he wasn't producing that album, he was still the first to hear all of the demos. He's amazing. He's undeniably amazing.

What changed so dramatically with your writing between *Freak Show* and *Neon Ballroom*?
I was writing lots of poetry and lots of music and not seeing them as things that are together. Just writing music and not knowing what to write the songs about because I didn't really want to talk about the stuff that I was going through. So I had all these dark musical pieces and this dark poetry. And I was like, I really can't be bothered writing the lyrics to these songs, so I'm going to see if somehow they can work together. I thought they were good. "Emotion Sickness" started as a really good poem. All the poems are compromised because I had to make them more musical and singable and fit it into a certain structure. Most of the poems from that album are better in their poetic form as opposed to the form they turned up in on the record. Because there was less going straight to the castle. More stops for photos and paparazzi. [*Laughs*]

When you were writing the poems, did the words ever suggest music to you?
Yeah, I knew that what I was writing was suggesting real cinematic soundscapes. I didn't quite have the ability to pull it off, but I had the ambition to at least do a variation on what I was getting inspired by, like film scores and classical music, on *Neon Ballroom*. And then took it further with *Diorama* because I had more ability and more to draw from and knew how to create it in a more spectacular way.

Did you write "Emotion Sickness" with the idea of the piano flourishes in it and how did you get David Helfgott to play on it?
That was definitely written with that intention. I was writing manic, discordant piano runs. I wasn't playing them, I was just singing melodies into a tape recorder and playing the guitar and having them come in as piano lines. And then I got together with Larry Muhoberac, who

wrote that piano part, and I was lying on the floor in his apartment singing the kind of melodies that I want running through it. He's going, "Yeah, that's great! It's really bent, but I really like it." And John Watson heard the kind of part that I wanted, and he said, "It sounds like something David Helfgott would be amazing at." And I was like, "Yeah, that's fuckin' cool. Do it." And then he wanted to do it. And he was the best. He's just the best person in the universe.

Did you think at the time that it was a bold thing for a young man to write a song about his eating disorder, as you did on "Ana's Song"? A line like "In my head, the flesh seems thicker" is pretty candid.
Yeah. I think the most shocking things have to be said in order to make a real artistic impact. At that point Nick had got me into John Lennon solo stuff and he really inspired me to just say it, just do it. It was something that hadn't really been written about and especially for a guy to write about that, I knew that it would freak people out and I knew that it would make people watch me like vultures. But I just thought, it has to be done and whatever happens after that is meant to happen, because it's important for me creatively to actually just say, "Fuck it, I'm doing it," and letting it go.

Did writing and recording that song help you get through and heal from that illness?
Writing the song did, but relentlessly touring it and it becoming a hit just made it harder. It made it a lot harder, because you're singing these lines, you've got to look the part. [*Laughs*] If people want to hear me sing these things I can't exactly look healthy. So I prolonged it.

Can you sing it now?
Yeah. It's still one of my favourite songs that I've ever written, because I'm proud of what I did with it and proud of who I helped with that. But now I can get up on stage and I look at it as that period of my life. Every songwriter, every artist has got certain periods in their life where they're expressing different things and exploring different outlets and options and I just see it as that period. It's no longer like I'm singing on behalf of myself; I'm looking at the pain and reading what's written next to it.

When you write such openly confessional songs, it comes with the territory that you then have to talk about the subject matter in interviews. Does that detract from the impact you want to make with the music, not letting it speak for itself?
Yeah. When I start doing interviews again, like for this Dissociatives record with Paul, I'm not going to discuss the lyrics. I'm not going to do it any more. Because you have to modify your answers; what you're saying in a song cannot possibly be articulated in a few sentences. You always have to water it down, you always have to bleach the green from all of the grass, and just give the details. All the magic's gone and you've stopped for paparazzi photos again and the castle's still awaiting.

You've talked quite a bit about visuals and colour. *Diorama* **sounded like a really colourful album to me. When you're writing, do you equate it with painting on a canvas?**

Yeah. Sometimes when I close my eyes and I'm playing a guitar, it's like as soon as you start the first chord is the first little dot of the painting and it slowly grows as you change chords. And different chords are turning the painting in different directions. So you close your eyes and the painting's there and all you want to do is just replicate whatever's painted on the back of your eyelids. And then sometimes that changes depending on what chords you go to and what melodies you're singing. Sound is the most potent colour, for sure.

What colours are you and Paul painting in at the moment?

The album is like completely mismatched, fashion-unconscious Muppet colours. Pastel dirty wool, but just millions of colours and crowd scenes and Miss Piggy.

What are the colours in "Across the Night"?

The colours in "Across the Night" were supposed to be just black with silver streaks. That's "Across the Night" completely. And then there's one little section in the middle where a rainbow grows and then disappears before section B, and then it just goes back to black with silver streaks. Just night.

Did you envisage *Diorama* **à la** *Pet Sounds* **or "Surf's Up" when you wrote it?**

Not when I was writing it, because I didn't really know much about the Beach Boys when I was writing it. It was only when Van Dyke Parks was suggested and I went, "Oh, cool, what's he done? Oh, right, that sounds cool, I'll have a listen to that." I think what I'm writing now is more influenced by *Pet Sounds* than what I was writing then.

When Van Dyke Parks was working with you, did you discuss songwriting with him?

He discussed it with me and now I see him all the time whenever I'm in LA, I call up and go and have dinner and hang out and he's become a friend and he's like my idol times a million, I just want to be like him when I'm that old. He's the coolest cat. He's just the best, weirdest, most gorgeous flower. And yeah, he just sat down and was telling me what he liked about my songs and what I was doing that no-one else was doing. I didn't know any of this because I'm not classically trained. He was saying it really inspired him to go and write again.

Did he talk to you about writing his own songs?

No. He talked to me about the way he was writing certain things around my vocal. Which is more helpful to me because I've had a million people talk about songs and I want my own perspective on that, anything that can contribute to my own perspective on songwriting.

Diorama **was a more positive set of songs. Were they all written in one go over a solid period of time?**

Yep. I think it's the most focused period of time I've ever had in my life. It was literally on my brain every second of every day for twelve months. No thoughts occurred outside of what I was writing.

And it was a happy, positive writing time?

Yeah, it was happy but it was manic. It was like crazy, psycho, manic happy. I wasn't comfortable in that happiness. It was like writing and trying to stay awake, drinking loads of coffee and then writing more and more and more and then you'd been up for two days and you're trying to sleep and you're lying in bed thinking of the horn parts and you have to quickly run out and get the tape recorder from the piano and then bring it back to the bed and then remember something that you should have played on piano. So you just don't rest. Mental.

What inspired the positive outlook finally?

It was firstly being in love, that's a pretty major thing to make you happy. But I wanted to write something positive because what I was writing was also heavily contributing to a mental state. Whatever was always enforcing upon me, everyone was always like, "You're depressed, you're sad, you've got an eating disorder." For years and years. So I needed to write something to pull me out of the hole and have people talk about good things to me.

If you were inspired because you were in love, how could you have spent twelve months thinking of nothing but the songwriting? You must have been thinking about your love as well.

Well, thinking about songwriting was a deliberate attempt to not think about the love.

Because you were scared of it?

Yeah. I was super scared of it. "My God, it's going to totally fuck my music forever." And I was going, "No, I'm not thinking about it, it's going to ruin everything and I have to do this album." That was when I broke up with my girlfriend, so every time I'd get sad I'd go, "No, write!" And there'd be all these kind of magic emotions and then when I finished the album we got back together, so that was cool. It was just on hold, otherwise we were entering dangerous territory.

How did "The Greatest View" come to you?

That was about having people watching over my every move, whether it's people that I was talking to when I had an eating disorder, and my parents watching to see if I'm good, and so and so making sure I'm not smoking too much pot and I felt like everyone was monitoring me the whole time. But they were all doing it on the quiet so it was a declaration of saying, "I know you're all watching me, I can see it happening. I can see your judging eyes." I could see it all happening, therefore the candid effect was gone.

Do you think marriage, or at least the security of being that marriage entails, will become a major theme in your writing, or is it important for you to keep it separate?

It's important for me to keep it in, 'cause it's cool. When cool things happen to you and everything's good, you've got to milk it and get everything you can out of it, because it's magic. Every song I've written since I've been in love was inspired to be a love song and then turned into something different or stayed the same depending on what I felt like the next day.

So you can write when you're in a state of pure bliss; you don't have to be suffering.
No, because I've got my suffering memory bank chock-a-block. It happens all the time, I'm deliriously happy and I'm like, "Yeah, yeah, this is the best day in the whole world and I'm writing a song and I love music and it's the best and it's so good and everything's cool. And remember that time you were walking home from school ..." And that's when the music starts. [*Laughs*]

So there's no fear that you're just going to write happy songs.
No, that won't happen. I like songs to be directed at the light from the dark, as opposed to the other way around.

What direction are the songs that you've been writing with Paul moving in?
It's more of a journey, like everything runs from one song into the next. We call it our conceptual album. We were trying to re-create something that alluded to the same magic that *Sgt Pepper's* was trying to create for that generation.

Do you have one particular guitar that you like to write on?
Yep. This one. This is the best guitar in the whole universe.

I wondered if the instrument you write on is significant to you and connected with the music.
Yes, definitely. Especially guitars which have history and really inspire you.

I've spoken to songwriters who believe the songs are in the instruments.
I don't think that actually. I think you connect with the instrument and the song's actually in the atmosphere and it's only attracted to certain vibrations that are created by the two of you.

Do you have favourite tunings? I read that one you like is what you call the "violin tuning".
Yeah. I loved that. I wrote a lot of *Diorama* on that tuning, but I'm over it at the moment. I like standard tuning, how the guitar is supposed to be tuned is really fun, I'm getting back into that, but I had a period where I hated playing guitar if it was in standard tuning. Now that I'm writing with Paul it's all gone real pop.

As you're such a strong melodist, how is it working with Paul, who's also a very strong melodist? Do you feel that you've both got equal contributions and equal control?
I do the vocal melodies, Paul will do a keyboard melody and if I have a backing vocal melody and it somehow doesn't work then I go, "What about you play the backing vocal

melody on the keyboard?" But for the most part we're aware of where our melodic positions are in the band, we know what holes we're filling.

If you couldn't sing any more, would you continue to write? Do you see yourself as a composer now?
Yeah, definitely. I see myself stopping performing for sure, there's no doubt that's going to happen, and just becoming a producer and writing people's songs. I'd love to do that. That's much more me.

DANIEL JONES

DARREN HAYES

Savage Garden:
DANIEL JONES & DARREN HAYES

BRISBANE, AUSTRALIA, APRIL 2004
LONDON, ENGLAND, MAY 2004

They were like a flash of love and light, once and beautiful, there and then gone. If that sounds dramatic, the tale of Savage Garden was just that, although in reality, it was a story several years in the making, and the musical reverberations will continue for ages to come. In a few short years a collection of sumptuous, unforgettable pieces of pop were conceived, created and unleashed on the world, and then it was over, leaving admirers and fans bereft.

"If I could rewrite it in many ways I would," Darren Hayes said when I met him three years after his split with Daniel Jones. "But at the time I guess I was naive about that, that people would also grieve the loss of this band, that as a nation Australians would be like, 'We don't want you to be over.'"

After news broke of Savage Garden's demise in 2001, Hayes released a solo album, talked to media and took the flak. Jones stayed silent, largely out of sight. Hayes: "I remember saying to Daniel, 'When I do my solo thing we have to be really united about this, we have to talk honestly about the fact that I want to go on and you didn't want to go on.' And it just didn't pan out that way."

Australia's most successful love song tunesmiths, who began composing together in Jones's bedroom, shared the same musical tastes, but were always opposites in character. Jones was the shrewd one who could see future success, particularly recognising the star potential of Hayes. But he craved privacy and shunned the spotlight, so after the duo he had masterminded sold 20 million albums and toured stadiums around the world, he withdrew to preserve his sanity. Hayes had no initial grand plan—as he described it, he came from the wrong side of the tracks and fame was a universe away—but once he tasted success, he would not return to obscurity. Their chemistry as songwriters and performers might never again occur in either's lives, but the only choice was to pursue separate paths. There is no animosity, although Jones reckons the song "Dirty", on Hayes' *Spin* album, was about him. Hayes, whose ingenuousness is disarming, told me, "I love him, he's beautiful, he's adorable."

They're both romantics, but Hayes is the more overt, understandable given that he is the natural melodist and lyricist. Born in Brisbane on 8 May 1972, he grew up in the underprivileged suburb of Woodridge. His records were hand-me-downs. He learned to harmonise listening to Fleetwood Mac's *Rumours* and *Tusk* and loved Michael Jackson, but couldn't afford to buy *Thriller* when it came out. INXS was the big indicator for him, though. "What I liked about them was that they didn't sound like they came from anywhere. They sounded global. Incredibly ambitious and excitable and wild and influenced by everything that was in the charts." Later listening included electronica acts Phoenix, Rhinoceros and Air. "They're influences that I might have brought to the table when I worked with Savage Garden but would end up getting buried in the mix because I'd be working with Daniel and a big pop producer and it would become something else."

Jones was born in London on 22 July 1973. His family moved to Brisbane a year later and settled in Logan City, across the freeway from Woodridge. He taught himself guitar, with some guidance from his older brother, and took piano lessons from a girl in the neighbourhood, but that was because he fancied her. Romance in Jones's life was always more guarded. As a burgeoning teenage songwriter, he used to fear dying in his sleep. "I was so in love with what was going on and what I was doing, that I used to freak out about not waking up tomorrow, so that it would be unfinished."

Thriller was his first album. He and boyhood friends even attempted to make their own version of the *Thriller* video. But his love for pop was supplemented by an attraction to ska, punk and Oi! music. "I could play you stuff that you'd go, 'Oh! Didn't know you did that!'" Jones said, sitting in the studio of his newly built mansion on the water's edge in an exclusive Brisbane suburb. "'Cause I'm more than a love song man."

With Jones's prodigious talent for mapping out and executing musical tracks, and Hayes' ability to articulate emotions in pertinent, often detailed lyrics, they believed they could transcend the covers band circuit that brought them together in 1994 and create something distinctive. After countless rejections, one astute manager, John Woodruff, was taken by their demos, and teamed them with producer Charles Fisher. The debut eponymous 1997 Savage

Garden album was laden with hits, including "I Want You", "To the Moon and Back" and, perhaps their greatest moment, "Truly Madly Deeply". Their second album, *Affirmation*, was also stacked with memorable songs. But within a year of its release, the plug was pulled.

Jones stayed in Brisbane, started a publishing company, wrote with the short-lived duo Aneiki, and more recently was developing new artists Julie Strickland and Wish. He made regular trips to London, writing with hitmakers like Pam Sheyne and Andreas Carlsson. And, importantly, he was enjoying the privacy of his beautiful new home with partner Kathleen.

Hayes went solo, with all the difficulties inherent after leaving a successful group. His second album, *The Tension and the Spark*, was an intensely personal work that he was about to start promoting when we met. He'd just relocated from San Francisco to London, in a house close to Notting Hill, a romantic location, I pondered, and a bold one. It was a long way from Woodridge, a long way from Jones, and further along the path from Savage Garden.

PART I: Daniel Jones

Did any Australian ballads move you as a teenager? Air Supply's songs perhaps?
Yeah, "Lost in Love". It's funny, as a kid you don't understand what's in a song that moves you. When you get older you understand why something could move you, and probably harden to it. I think the younger you are, the more vulnerable you are. I remember "Lost in Love" as a song that would nearly bring me to tears as a kid, because it would affect me somehow, musically, emotionally. But there were a few songs that did that. "Sandy" from *Grease*, there was something magical about that particular song. And songs have come and gone that I have chosen not to be a fan of probably because of society, but as a songwriter, I go, yeah, that's a good song. I think "How Am I Supposed to Live without You" by Michael Bolton is actually a great song, emotionally it's a beautiful song.

Some songs out there in the marketplace have the same effect on people now as what those songs had on you that you've stayed with your entire life. I still get people coming up saying, "'Truly Madly Deeply' was our song, we got married to it." It's going to be with them for the rest of their life. Even if they get divorced, they're going to remember. So even tomorrow music is going to get someone who is, again, emotionally vulnerable, tap into them and stay with them.

When did you start paying attention to the way songs were structured?
As a sixteen-year-old I had a friend who was a singer and he looked a lot like Michael Hutchence. So we put this INXS tribute band together and toured from Port Macquarie to Cairns. And learned every INXS song that was a hit. That was the best thing that could ever happen to me because I literally pulled apart every INXS song. I learned how to arrange a song and what combinations of instruments would work as a sound. So INXS was a big part.

Have you told Andrew Farriss that?
Yeah, I did. He came to our album launch in 1999. I learned from him, basically. You could

show me a note on a staff and I couldn't tell you what note it was; it would take me five minutes to try and work it out. I cannot read at all. Not even tablature, not even guitar tabs.

When you start composing a piece of music are you more drawn to the keyboard or the guitar?
For the melodic side of things, definitely piano. For the rhythmic side, guitar. Because your right hand dictates the groove that you're going to do. Your left hand can be playing any chords you like, but the right hand is the one that's actually doing what a percussionist would do.

Will you often work on both instruments together?
Both, yeah. Back and forth.

When did you first start putting original songs together on your own?
Probably around eleven or twelve. We had this Casio keyboard at home, and then my middle brother, Oliver, had bought a sequencer, which was like wow back then. I remember hooking up and discovering what MIDI was about, and sequencing up these bits of music that were coming out. It wasn't a song, it was more an instrumental thing, so it would have melodies in it with the piano. I'm not a great singer, but I can hear something. So you could literally replace every note with a word and you would have songs.

Do you remember your first complete song?
It was a track called "Blue Steel". It had no lyrical meaning whatsoever; I was about twelve or thirteen. It must have been like a glammy Bon Jovi type of song. I've got the lyrics written down somewhere in a folder.

Were you excited that you wrote a song?
Yeah. And have been ever since. I still get excited. I get more excited now because they actually make sense. It's not just a crayon drawing, it's a painting now.

Is that because of life experience?
Anything you do you get better at naturally. Maybe you find out who you are. I'm going through an interesting period now, because there are things that I've written that I would never have wanted to stand up and do myself. Various reasons—the cool factor of it or whether I thought it was credible or not, whether I believed in it. But give me a situation of being a songwriter and write for a particular artist, then lately I've had no problems being able to go, "Well, I wouldn't do that but Kelly Clarkson would say that." So I'm trying to work out, do I want to go there? Do I want to be adaptable to any personality?

Many songwriters who hit their commercial peak early say they are writing their best and most meaningful work now, years later, but they don't get the commercial recognition. Does that worry you?
Not at all. The beauty of being a songwriter—I've stepped out of a 20 million album-selling

band and gone, "I'm going to be a songwriter"—is that it actually doesn't discriminate. It doesn't matter how chubby I get in my thirties or how long my hair gets. I've chosen not to be a performer. no-one's going to tell me that I can't do a certain style of music now. Which is a lot of freedom. I totally believe in my ability in what I do.

What was the first song that you and Darren wrote together?
It was a song called "Trust in Me". It never made the album. It never made anything; I don't even think anyone's heard it. But it was a really pretty song. It was a bit of a Phil Collins-like song. It still had that Savage Garden sound about it, but it was just an over-sweet love song, which wasn't terribly cool. It had all the ingredients there of the chemistry that we were yet to find out. It had the good melodies, the good progressions, the good arrangements, the sounds, but it just wasn't a song that we were raving about.

Can we talk about that chemistry and the early signs of it? What were the qualities Darren had that made you feel there was something special there between you as songwriters?
You could tell straight away that he was an emotional-based person. He wasn't a logical person, he wasn't pragmatic. The moment we jumped in a room together, we knew where we were going. And because he had an opinion about something, I went, okay, he knows what he's looking for, he knows what he wants. He was questioning, he was challenging. I knew from day one that something was going to happen there, definitely.

How did your collaborations work? Was there a strict music/lyrics delineation with you both writing separately or did you work on songs simultaneously and equally?
Different every time. You cannot write a song the same way each time. I would do it every way possible.

Did you work out lyrics together?
I used to edit a lot of his lyrics and throw suggestions at words that he was stuck on. But they were totally conjured up from where he wanted to go. Predominantly he would do lyrics.

Did you ever come up with lyrical ideas on your own, before a melody?
Yeah, a few times. "Gunning Down Romance" was one of my titles, on the second album, in a little bit of a backlash to our two number one love song hits. But at the same time it was a musical thing that sounded very pretty and intense, about how even though you love being in love it can get the better of you, it can beat you. Which was the furthest song away from being a pop hit.

Did you both want relationships and love to be at the heart of all your songs?
I think that's probably pop music. The fact that it's relationship-driven. There's not a lot of songs that aren't about some form of emotional relationship.

Did you discuss issues of love and despair?
We definitely had a very open conversation relationship. When you're in creative mode the more you can talk about the better, because you're firing out inspirations all the time. We used to talk about what things meant. There might be a lyric that read one way—"Fly me to the moon and back"—obviously a metaphor, and then what you would do for that person and why you would do it, and you would elaborate on what you were trying to get at. Nine times out of ten we were on the same wavelength about what a song actually means to him or to us.

If Darren was singing a set of lyrics that were obviously very personal to him, did it matter to you if you couldn't relate to that issue he wanted to focus on?
No. There were songs that I had my opinion about and suggested changes. I think at one stage "Truly Madly Deeply" was called "Magical Kisses". And I went, "Not really cool, Darren." Prince could do it, but could we at that particular time? No. It was a bit naff. So we changed it and we scored a number one hit.

Has technology guided you in composing music or do you guide the technology?
Both. They work hand in hand. There are ways that I can use technology to inspire me to write something, and then there are ways where once I've written something, I can use technology to enhance that. But it's just a fact of songwriting now. When you need to have a melody there, you need to have a structure there, you need to think that someone could sing along with you, predominantly you'll use your guitar and piano so you'll actually write it organically. And then once you've written it you'll work out, well, it's a tempo about a hundred beats per minute here, so let's find a drum loop that's a hundred beats per minute, and it'll dictate the groove. And you'll source through fifty drum loops to see if there's one that's actually going in that direction. Once that fits then you're nearly there. Because you've already written your progressions and your melodies.

And then sometimes you haven't got any idea on what you're writing and you'll bring up a drum loop or a keyboard sound, and off you go. It's like something being born and you don't know what it looks like yet or what it sounds like yet. Some songs can take minutes, some songs can take years. It just depends.

How do you know when a song is finished?
The record company tells you.

That doesn't apply for you now, though.
No, it doesn't. I guess you're brave enough to play it to someone.

It's not necessarily finished when it's played to someone.
No. No song's ever finished. There's always a song that you could re-change or do this to or that to.

Do you think "Truly Madly Deeply" could be improved?

Oh, yeah, totally. Every song could be improved. Even other people's songs. I go, "I could do that or do this." I don't think there's been a perfect song written, and if anyone thinks they've written the perfect song, they should stop. Because ultimately it's the striving to get somewhere, trying to create a perfect thing. If you reached it, you'd have no more motivation to continue.

Do musical ideas come to you away from the instrument, just in your head?

[*Nods*] It's a combination of hearing one melody of a song and some girl speaking, or eating an ice-cream. It's there and you've just got to get it out. It could be anything; the sound of a doorbell may have a tone to it or a note that you hear or a truck driving past. It's just there.

Do you need to be inspired to write? Or will you just come into your studio and sit down and work regardless?

Mornings are the best for me; I can get really motivated from about seven o'clock in the morning. I get to about lunchtime and sometimes I don't come back in, because I get tired, so I'll go and do the business side of things, or something else. But sometimes I'll go through until ten o'clock that night and won't stop for lunch, and as gross as it sounds sometimes I won't have even showered in the morning, I'll just come straight in here with no shirt on, my hair's all messed up, just out of bed.

While a lot of the programming and mixing on Savage Garden songs was obviously done in the studio, would you have arrangements sketched out in advance?

We'd have full demos. Very rarely did our arrangements get changed. The production of our songs obviously got better as the songs got more developed and more focused. But arrangements were something that Darren and I were always quite in sync on. They're pop arrangements, and again it's come from INXS songs. It's come from an intro into a first verse into a pre-chorus, maybe an option into a second verse there or the first chorus, small segue or an instrumental, back into the second verse, back into a pre-chorus, second chorus, usually a middle-eight or some sort of transition, maybe a broken-down chorus, and then chorus to end, or come back in with another verse and then chorus to end. I can nearly see it structured before I even start.

What about embellishments around that structure?

Yeah, there's the foundation to a song, and then afterwards you can create illusions to make a transition better. So if you've got a verse that doesn't really go into a pre-chorus that well, you could enhance that transition or make it more fluent if you put in a nice string swell so it carries it over or a nice reverse cymbal or something that allows it to feel like it's going to go somewhere, so it slightly anticipates and then comes back in. And that helps the dynamics of your changes. But it's usually the bass note that dictates your actual foundation, it's what actually drives the song.

When you wrote a piece of music that Darren turned into a song, were you comfortable with how it might change its mood or direction in that process?
No, sometimes I would be brave enough to say, "I don't actually like what you've done to it" and be a bit precious about the music that I'd given him to put his stamp on. But not very often. I had a lot of respect for Darren and I think vice versa, so whatever I gave him, he would know where I was going with it. He would know that a piece of music says more than a page of lyrics. It can say whatever you want to interpret, metaphorically speaking. A piece of music can tap into your imagination and your imagination's unlimited.

What if you wrote a piece of music with an emotion attached to it for you, say it was sad for you, and Darren turned it into something that was anger?
Then we would miss each other, like any relationship. I would have to say something. And vice versa. He would sometimes say, "I don't like that change" or "I don't like this chord." It builds a little bit of tension in the room, but that's the chemistry. I'm sure husbands and wives have tension in their relationship at times, that's their chemistry, it's supposed to happen. And you get something from one another when that sparks up. If it was all smooth sailing the whole time as far as the creative process goes, I think our tracks would have been a bit boring.

Do you remember writing "I Want You"?
Darren got inspired from U2's "Numb" and Janet Jackson's "Rhythm Nation", very fast-syllabled lyrics. And even Billy Joel's "Start the Fire". The three of those songs helped create "I Want You", which I still think is one of the best pop songs we've ever written.

And really ambitious for a completely new act to put out a song where you can barely understand the lyrics because the singing's so fast.
Yeah, that's the fascination of it. It's a little quirky; it stands out amongst the rest of the songs. I knew it was a hit. I worked on the chorus with him, which was the most simple thing. He has this ability to write pages of stuff. And then it slowly gets edited.

There are a lot of Savage Garden lyrics. They're not sparse songs.
It's easier to write a song with less lyrics, obviously. It's like writing a song with one chord. Just keep hitting it till you're finished. So the less lyrics you've got, the easier it is to finish; the more lyrics you've got, the harder it is.

"Truly Madly Deeply" is considered to be the best Savage Garden song. Do you see it as a benchmark or have you long left it behind?
I see that song as freedom. I see that song as giving me freedom to be able to constantly create more. Because that made a whole bunch of money, it bought me a house and a studio and a lifestyle that enables me to continue doing what it is that I love. That was the one that sold 10 million albums for us throughout the world, on the first album. But see, songs and art, everything's subjective. I love music, but there are bands and music that I

don't like. They've been hits but I didn't like them. So there's no such thing as the perfect song that dominates the whole world.

But in terms of creativity, is that song still a benchmark for you?
Oh, definitely not. The song's got three or four chords in it, it's very simple, it's melodic, it's romantic, it's sweet, that's about it. It's got a magic about it. But it's just a nice, romantic song.

How did "I Knew I Loved You" come about?
We'd finished our album in San Francisco, and we'd put half of it on a CD and sent it over to Don Ienner, who was the CEO of Sony at the time. The first thing that we heard back, which we knew, was, "There's no 'Truly Madly Deeply' on it." I understand where they're coming from. There will never be another "Truly Madly Deeply"; "Truly Madly Deeply" is "Truly Madly Deeply". It's like having your first-born named Sarah; you're never going to have another Sarah even if you call it the same name. You'll never have the same thing twice and the same goes with songs.

So we got pissed off a little bit at that comment. We knew it was coming; we were smart enough to beat it. So we went, "Fuck you, here's a 'Truly Madly Deeply'." We sat down in a real cocky songwriting mentality, and went, "Well, if you want a number one hit, we can write a number one hit." And we wrote "I Knew I Loved You", which went to number one in America.

Are you saying that your hearts weren't in that song?
No. We love the creative process of putting something together. Our attitude going into it was, "Well, fuck you, we'll write a number one song." Then we naturally do what we naturally do. You can't put that much energy into something and not say it's come from somewhere.

It's still your child.
Of course it is. It was our backlash child. It was the child that we went, "Well, you think your kid's good-looking, look at this kid we've just made!" We don't have to like our own music; we just have to create it. And you naturally tend to like it because you've done it. It's excited you whilst you were doing it. Otherwise you would stop the idea as it was happening. 'Cause I've written stuff that I've gone, "Don't really like that." And just left it.

Was "The Animal Song" written specifically for the movie *The Other Sister* or was it a song you already had?
It was half an idea of a song we already had. It was actually inspired by the Hoodoo Gurus song "Like Wow Wipeout" with the drums. I wanted to have a song that had the biggest drums in it. It starts like it brings you straight up to this energy, and all it is is drums. Natives have been doing it for thousands of years. Actually, I still don't like the lyric content to this day, relative to the movie. I don't think they placed it very well.

Did you identify with all of Darren's affirmations in "Affirmation"?
Ninety per cent of them, yeah. I think there were one or two little contradictions in there that I went, well, that doesn't make sense, or I don't agree with that. It wasn't that long ago I actually read through that album cover, to see, there was one line that I still didn't know what Darren said and I'd done it a hundred times. "I believe that wedded bliss negates the need to be undressed." I'm still not exactly sure what that means. Perhaps to be married and to be completely giving of yourself to another one, you need to be metaphorically naked. You need to have stripped down every wall, every barrier or every guard that you've got. There was another one in there, "that trust is more important than monogamy." They kind of go hand in hand.

That's interesting that you didn't sit down and study the lyrics and discuss it with him.
You've got to allow a co-writer, and hopefully they allow you, and Darren does, to do what it is that you do. Sure, there's lyric ideas that I could have come up with, but the guy was good at what he did. He was going to be the one singing it, that's his part, his role. I'm the one that's doing the music. There was a lot of Darren in that record. And there's a lot of everyone in that record; there's a lot of human nature.

Do you remember writing "Crash and Burn"?
Yep. It reminded me a little bit of U2. I wanted a "With Or Without You" type song. It didn't quite have the emotion of "With Or Without You" but it was still a statement at the end of the day. But the record company didn't like the title because not that long beforehand there was a plane that had crashed. And we're like, "The plane crash didn't invent the term 'crash and burn' here, guys. Come on, where's your mentality?" And in the end we just said, "Let's call it 'Crash and Burn'." The song did well.

Was it a conscious decision to create a sound that was international, not directly connected to being Australian?
Don't even think we thought about it. For us, geography had nothing to do with how we sounded. Just because we were from Brisbane, it didn't mean we had to sound like Custard or Powderfinger. Even though we were from Brisbane, all of a sudden we were living in the Cross, recording at Charles's house in Rose Bay. John Woodruff was in Sydney, Roadshow was in Sydney, some of the people that helped make the record were from Sydney. And once we got success overseas, we were then moved to Los Angeles or New York or San Francisco.

In terms of where you would write your songs, then, it didn't matter where you were?
No. "To the Moon and Back" was written in a bedroom in Cornubia in the suburbs of Brisbane. And it was a number one hit. It didn't matter where it was written. You do what it is that you do, and you basically are who you are. So could I write a Paul Kelly song? I couldn't. Because I'm not like that. Where Paul Kelly probably is like that. Were we listening to all sorts of different pop music? Yeah. Does Paul Kelly listen to Duran Duran? I don't think so.

What do you think you learned primarily as a songwriter from the Savage Garden years?
I think I'm still learning from it. The biggest thing I learned was that I wanted to do more songwriting. I got such a kick out of it that I decided on the spot that this is what I want to do forever. Maybe it'll change one day but right at this particular moment I want to do it forever. My challenge or my question that I ask myself occasionally is, I wonder if I'll have anything more successful than Savage Garden. Because that's a huge thing. People don't sell all that many albums on a debut album. I think, will something else come along of that magnitude?

Do you want something else of that magnitude?
I think I do. I'll always want to reach for the top. I just want to push each time and try and go back for something better. It would be another learning curve; it would be another roller-coaster ride, if something was to go off that big.

PART II: Darren Hayes

What were the qualities in Daniel that made you trust him at the outset as a collaborator?
I didn't know anything about his songwriting ability. It was his ambition. He was the most confident person I'd ever met. He and his family taught me a lot about that. He didn't sway, he had this belief in himself, and in me. I guess he has the ability of finding the diamond in the rough. He definitely treated me like, "You will become something great one day." When we talk about Daniel and his tendency to step in the background, step in the shadows, I think that works very well for his ability to kind of be a puppeteer. I don't mean that in a negative way, but he definitely sees the big picture, and he saw that in me, even before I saw that in myself. So I think that's what got me in.

We did have a similar background in that we both liked pop at a time when pop music was not cool at all. When we were writing songs it was post-Nirvana, it was Pearl Jam, flannel shirts, Soundgarden, long hair. Pop was a filthy word. Whereas we'd put *Kick* up on the mantelpiece and say "Need You Tonight" is one of the most genius pop songs ever written. Not just from a songwriting point of view, from the production, from the sound of it, from the sound of the snare drum to the minimalism of the track. Because we both had similar taste in music, I think I knew that we were going to click.

It's a courtship and it really is a relationship. It's almost romantic. And it doesn't happen with everybody. Daniel had a way of understanding or anticipating what I was going to bring to a song. So he would write songs in a certain key or have certain arrangements. He would do his magic and he knew that I was going to bring something to it that would be the equal and opposite part of what he did. Whereas I think sometimes when you write with songwriters it is a total separate act. You can be in the same room with them writing chords and singing, but you might as well be doing that with a stranger, it's quite cold.

Also, if you're drawing analogies to relationships, it's not always perfect. It's quite turbulent. We were always aware that we were complete opposites. In the way that we presented ourselves to the world, the way that we did promo. Even the way that the band ended, it was almost two people in rooms side by side. Never in the same room really; sort of together but apart. All the intricacies, all the things that were great about the relationship and all the things that were really fucked up about it made for this incredible artistic union.

When did you first start putting songs together on your own?
I wrote songs when I was thirteen or fourteen. Now I write songs mostly on piano and I play very rudimentary guitar, but as a child I remember seeing instruments as being mathematics to me. When I sing, or if I move or dance, that's very natural to me, whereas I find playing an instrument is very cerebral and it can bog me down.

How did you convey your ideas to Daniel?
Daniel would write the music and I would write melodies and lyrics. And often I would write them a cappella. I'd be walking down the street and come up with melodies of songs in my head, and then sometimes I'd go to him and sit down and sing it and he'd try to work out what key it was. Sometimes I'd show him a bass note and say, "I think it's about there." It was extremely painful; it's almost like channelling psychic predictions or something, trying to write with me in that way. But Daniel was very, very patient about that and trying to find songs. I'm finding out now that while I know I'm a lyricist, I think I'm a melodist. That's what I do. A lot of these melodies and hooks come to me in the weirdest moments. Usually right before I go to sleep. It can drive me mad. You'd think that I'd have a tape recorder but I can't do that, so I ring and leave melodies on my voicemail.

Do you remember writing "I Want You"? Was it always the intention to cram such a fast-paced lyric in there?
It was, actually, I know that we toyed around with the idea of using the voice like another instrument in the song. I wanted the voice to be like the bass. So if you listen to what the voice does in that song, even though I have a high voice, it hums. It's just one tone and I wanted it to be like a percussive or a bass instrument.

That song had gone through so many other incarnations before it became "I Want You". They were just these throwaway lyrics that I was singing, like "Ooh, I want you ..." And he's like, "That's it!" And I'm like, "No, no, I'll eventually write better lyrics, these are just my basic lyrics." And he's like, "No, I'm telling you, that's a hit."

When you decided to write and record original songs together, was it understood that you both wanted relationships and love to be at the heart of the subject matter?
Daniel was always great about me and lyrics. I had a very free rein. I could sing whatever I wanted to over the top of the song or I could say whatever I wanted to say. He really encouraged me to be emotional. His music was very filmic and very emotive; it evoked a lot of visuals. And he got excited when what I did was as colourful as what he felt he was doing.

Did you feel you had enough life experience when you were writing the first album to plough the depths of love, hope and despair?

Yeah, I think of myself as being a bit of an old soul, really. I definitely had a very interesting/dramatic/traumatic childhood. I drew from a lot of those experiences. And when I really fell in love the first time, it was a massive shift in the universe. So it was not hard, I didn't have to fake any of that stuff or any of those emotions. When I wrote the lyrics to "Truly" actually, it used to be called "Magical Kisses". It was a very cheesy song. The verses were all the same as "Truly Madly Deeply", but the chorus was shocking. The night before we were supposed to record the song, I sat in the Bayswater Brasserie on my own drinking coffee and I rewrote this chorus with that melody and the lyric that you know today. And that's because I was just married and I was missing my wife so much and this was the last song that we had to record on the album, and once I recorded this song then I could go home to her. So in that song I still feel that innocence of young love and all the hope.

Had you seen the movie, *Truly Madly Deeply*?

Yes, and it moved me deeply.

Is that where the title came from?

Definitely. It was about a love that she had to let go of, love that was passing. The opening sequence of that movie just killed me because it opens with this woman in grief, she's just bawling her eyes out, and I thought that was amazing. In fact I thought that song was so personal that it was a B-side or a bonus track for the album. And then Charles went, "That's no hidden track. That is a hit."

How do you feel about that song today?

I think it's a very special song. "I Knew I Loved You" was the Nutra-Sweet version of "Truly Madly Deeply". They're both really classic songs but I think one of them will be around in twenty years and one of them maybe won't be. First of all I felt what I was feeling when I wrote "Truly", whereas "I Knew I Loved You" was a complete hypothesis. I was miserable and they wanted a love song, and it was like "Fine, you want a love song? I'll write you a love song." In the end I fell in love with the song as I was writing it and it became a piece of hope for me, actually. When I sing it I still smile. It was written as a "Fuck you", and it became this really innocent, charming, very sincere piece of music.

Do you think you have surpassed "Truly Madly Deeply"? Or does it go with you and serve as a comparison?

No, I certainly haven't surpassed it, and I don't think I will. It's like saying has U2 surpassed "With or Without You". I think "With or Without You" is the best song ever written. But I think if you've written one of those songs in your life, it's okay, it's enough. My favourite Madonna song was actually "Holiday" and that was off her first-ever album. She's made records for twenty years and I still love listening to what she's doing, and yet if I had to pick one song I'd probably pick "Holiday", which is weird. Maybe at the end of my life people will say that "Truly" is the best song I was ever involved in, and that wouldn't be a bad thing. But it's been written, it's been done, and to chase your tail or to chase glory or chase success the rest of your life, one, it would just be sad, and two, I think it wouldn't do service to the process of what songwriting is about, because it has to be reflective of where you are in your life at the moment.

Nick Cave believes that all love songs should contain deep sorrow. My first feeling when I listened to your songs was, oh no, Darren's just into joy. But hearing you talk and refer very obscurely to your past, I'm thinking you might tend to agree with him.
I don't ever focus on joy, isn't that interesting? I'm probably more focused on yearning and unrequited love, or love passed. I'm thirty-two now, and obviously I've had life experiences and have had therapy as most Americans have had, and analysed myself a lot, and I realised that the romantic in me actually yearns for the burn.

Do you think so? Or do you think it's just that you set up such high standards and expectations of what love can be that it's easy to be disappointed?
That's a great thing to say. I think that love should be all-encompassing. Love should be great. And you have one or two of those in your life if you're really lucky. I don't believe that great love happens to you all the time. I've certainly had relationships since my marriage ended and I haven't had a love like the love that I experienced in my marriage, but I know that I will possibly, because I'm young and I yearn for that. But having seen that, experienced that, and having written about that kind of love, I think it's God-like. If you'd know anything about spirituality, most religions will say that God is essentially love. So that feeling that you have when you connect with someone, you are being like God. We're meant to do that. Love exists on all different levels, not just romantic love, but true, great romantic union is what you're born for, we're meant to do that. And so it should be a struggle. I don't think it should come that easily. It's your birthright to be happy and to be loved, but I don't think that mindless, blissful joy is a subject I ever want to write about because it's very transparent. It's a quick fix to things, but lasting love and experiences that mean something, they involve some kind of sadness or sacrifice.

A lot of Eastern philosophy says that the reason we are mortal is that if you think of life or God as being this energy which is just pure love, when we take on a mortal form we're just little drops of God in flesh. But we're separate from God, and that's why coming together feels so good. When we come together it's that union, the coming together of God.

So do you feel that songwriting is a spiritual act?
I think that it is possibly the language of spirit. I imagine that when you go to heaven or wherever you think nirvana is, that that's the language. It's so universal, melody crosses all boundaries and all cultures, and it has a physical effect on me. I could be at a U2 show or I could be seeing *The Lion King* on Broadway and someone will hit a chord or a note and every hair on my body will stand on end and I feel like I could cry because something has touched me and reverberated in me. And it's not just musical; it's spiritual, definitely.

Do you have an idea about where songs come from?
I think they come from outside and it's like a radio station. I feel that I am an intuitive person or an empath or something. Most artists are; we pick up on what's out there in the ether or relate to things in a less literal way, and so for me writing a beautiful melody or a great song, I never truly feel it's my own.

What was the most signifying thing for you that confirmed you were a serious songwriter?
I think about a song called "Two Beds and a Coffee Machine", which Daniel and I wrote on the *Affirmation* record. That was one of the first times that I looked at myself as part of something profound and more than just a hit song on the radio. The first time you hear your song on the radio is an entirely different experience; it's just very surreal and, for want of a better phrase, you probably feel like you've made it. But the first time a song moves people, when you play a song like "Two Beds and a Coffee Machine", I remember both of us at certain times during writing that song would have to leave the room, because I'd have a lump in my throat or Daniel would have a lump in his throat. The first time I sang that song from beginning to end is the version you hear on the record. That moment when I walked back into the control room and no-one could really speak, because what had been said and what had been performed was so confronting and so emotional and so real. I think that was the moment; that's the song I would probably be most proud of.

Was it a conscious decision to create a sound that was international and not directly connected to being Australian?
Definitely. And I think Daniel had a lot to do with that. More than anything I think Daniel's a really great producer. His dream for us was more global, much bigger than that.

But can geography play a part in your creative energy? Are there different creative forces at work when you are writing in Brisbane or New York or London?
I just think that it was the education of growing up in a place that felt so ignored. That's what to me the catalyst was, coming from Brisbane. It's like a short man complex; it made me personally try harder. I felt like I was the furthest away from whatever the epicentre of the music industry was, and I wanted so badly to succeed. Like if you watch the movie *Star Wars* and Luke Skywalker is this farm boy on this remote planet, and he hears that far, far away there's this battle going on.

And then does it make a difference where you are when you write?
For me it really doesn't any more; writing is such an intimate thing. I've written with lots of different people since Savage Garden and I only truly click with one or two people. It's not about geography, it's about chemistry, it's a very personal, very intimate act. It's more about the mood and the time of day. I generally write songs in the evening. I write lyrics very separately to melodies and music. I'll have lyrics bouncing around in my head for ages and they don't have a song to go into and yet I'll have a song or a chord progression or a melody

and I won't want to commit to a lyric. It's not really about what part of the world I'm in, it's just about what my headspace is and what time of day it is.

What about when you were still writing with Daniel, when you wrote the *Affirmation* album but relocated yourself to the US? Did the geographical separation affect that partnership?
I think it did, actually, the geography had a lot to do with the tone of that record; that record was essentially a break-up record. It was the anatomy of my divorce, lyrically. I'd set up camp in another country, and not just another country but Manhattan, which is possibly the hardest place in the world, and I didn't know a soul, I was there alone. The whole record itself was quite an analytical record about standing on the other side of love and really coming down hard on yourself. Loneliness, really. Songs like "Crash and Burn"; I remember writing that song wishing that someone would say those things to me at that point in my life. Had I not been in such an isolated experience, I probably wouldn't have written that record. So maybe you're right, geography in that sense was a huge catalyst.

The song "Affirmation" treads the fine line of making a song not sound glib and clichéd, while getting worthy messages across.
It's difficult when you're a musician and you're being in any way political, because I always think of Bill Clinton with the saxophone and I just cringe. I think, "Oh, please don't do that." Worse so when you're from this romantic pop dynamic duo. It's like, "Who cares? You have an opinion? No-one wants to hear it. Sing us a love song." So I was aware of that. In fact I actually had to tone that song down; there were a lot of political messages in that song, there were some statements about oil and wars and things like that. I was definitely dissuaded from going that far. But I liked it. I thought the one great thing about me being the person that I am is that I have a podium and I can deliver sentiments or messages with a smile or a kiss or a wink and sometimes it sinks in without people realising.

You've said that the *Affirmation* album was your divorce album. Songs like "Hold Me", "The Best Thing", "Crash and Burn", "The Lover after Me" all sound overtly autobiographical if one knows you went through a marriage break-up and a move overseas. Do you want to put your heart on the line and expose yourself in songs or do you hope for some kind of disguise?
In theory I don't want anyone to know about my personal life. It's a very difficult line to walk, but as a songwriter you have to go there. I tried not to on *Spin*, my first solo record. I thought, you know what, I'm a good singer, I'm a really good songwriter, I'm going to write this pop record and I'm going to just perform it and polish it to perfection. The one thing I didn't figure was that people would know when I was disconnected. And I was disconnected. I had so much to say, and a lot of it was quite dark, and I didn't want to say that on a record, so I thought, well, I'll just make that choice, because they won't know, really.

I learned a big lesson with that record. I learned that that is a part of what I do that's integral to why it's successful. Whether people know about my personal life or not, there is this sense in the music that it is sincere. That the person has either been there or maybe they mean what they're singing. So it's a curse and a blessing, and there's a fine line that you can draw. Somebody like Alanis Morissette crosses it sometimes. I love her, but I think art should always be relatable to everybody. What we don't want to hear is when an artist is so self-referencing that it's like, "Poor me, I'm rich and I had a bad childhood and this is a song about me on my therapist's couch, and woe is me." The average person in the street doesn't relate to that. I try to take very personal experiences and then put them into the context of a song so that you might think this is your story, too.

How did "Insatiable" germinate?
I love that song. "Insatiable" was one of those songs that was very smooth and very sophisticated, and it was written in about twenty minutes.

Did you have the title and write to it? It's quite a potent word.
It is, isn't it? I think it just came. A lot of the time it's weird when I listen back to writing tapes, because it's like I'm speaking in tongues. Syllables will come out, then there'll be a word that will come out and that was the word, "insatiable". Then I'll flesh out much more complicated lyrics and poetry.

Do you labour when you're writing lyrics?
I totally labour over it and it's my least favourite thing to do. My favourite thing to do is to write free-form lyrics and some of my favourite songs are just prose, it might be two or three pages of a journal, of a beautiful story or a poem. It kills me to have to cut that down and put it into three and a half minutes. Some of my favourite songs happen when I say, "This is the lyrical structure and I am going to make the music fit this."

What songs happened that way?
"Santa Monica" is like that. "Hold Me" is a bit like that; I'm squeezing a lot of words into that verse, when I say things like, "tell me isn't happiness worth more than a golden diamond ring?" This was quite a long poem; it was almost a journal entry and then I forced that into a verse of a song. A lot of the songs on the new record were written like that because I find putting the lyric in afterwards, you end up writing words and piecing them in just because they rhyme or just because they fit a syllable or a phrase, and I always feel like that's a bit of a cop-out.

Do you write with a thesaurus or any tools?
I did on the first Savage Garden record; you can tell that a song like "A Thousand Words" is written with a thesaurus. But that's about it. Phrases just pop into my head nowadays. Sometimes I'll write little post-it notes on my laptop. I did a screenwriting course last year at San Francisco State, so I will have two or three screenplays going and a journal, and I'll have post-it notes and poetry. I'll steal from all of them. But I find it's more themes that I tend to write down now as opposed to actual words. On this new record I wanted to talk about falling off a pedestal. About being a hero and not wanting to be a hero. So if you look

at my laptop you'll find lots of references to falling from grace and shame and things like that.

Do you feel that that's what happened to you?

Oh God, on so many levels, not just professionally. There was a moment during the *Spin* promotion where I actually got locked out of a radio station in Australia. A big, high-profile radio station that I'd been involved with for years. That was the moment when I realised, wow, things have changed. There was a time when we could have driven past a radio station and thrown our single out the window and they would have added it to the playlist. But I loved that experience. My childhood and my upbringing, the odds were so stacked against me anyway that in some ways that period was almost like coming back to full circle and I liked it. I really did.

KASEY CHAMBERS

SYDNEY, AUSTRALIA, OCTOBER 2000 AND NOVEMBER 2003

I first interviewed Kasey Chambers for the US magazine *Performing Songwriter*. Her debut album, *The Captain*, was being released in America; a buzz was in the air. At twenty-four, she had already made the major leap in Australia from alt country to mainstream popular artist, with her growing collection of trophies topped off by her first Best Female Artist award at the 2000 ARIAs. But the "crossover" from country to pop was as unplanned and unselfconscious as everything else about Chambers.

She was writing for her second album, *Barricades and Brickwalls*, and talked about the dichotomy of her elation at success and her desire to also be out of the spotlight. Anonymity was becoming a far-fetched dream for her in Australia, where her image (facial piercings on a country music artist!) was the subject of much newspaper and magazine ink. Fortunately, the critics and the fans were less concerned with image than with her music, and particularly a voice that reportedly had Lucinda Williams in tears at first hearing. Respect was already growing in America, with encouragement from Williams, Buddy and Julie Miller and their ilk. Six months after our original interview, Chambers was touring around Australia with Emmylou Harris and widening her circle of admirers in the process.

On that tour with Harris, Chambers first performed a song called "Not Pretty Enough". Over the next year her world went crazy. The song became a huge hit on commercial rock and pop radio, *Barricades and Brickwalls* matched and surpassed the success of *The Captain*, she scooped awards left, right and centre, and she gave birth to her first child. "It sounds like a lot when you put it like that! You're exhausting me!" she laughed, when we caught up again in late 2003.

Family is at the heart of Chambers' life and career. Born in Mount Gambier, South Australia, on 4 June 1976, her formative years were spent in the harsh Australian Nullarbor desert, hunting for food and sleeping under the stars. Her less-than-conventional parents, Diane and Bill Chambers, brought up Kasey and her brother, Nash, listening to American country artists like Johnny Cash and Hank Williams while they wandered the land like gypsies. Until her solo success, Chambers sang with her family's acclaimed group, The Dead Ringer Band, who themselves have won a swag of Golden Guitar awards in Tamworth. The family stayed involved in Chambers' solo career, her brother producing, her father playing guitar in her band and her mother handling merchandise on the road.

While American success on the alt country circuit became a reality, it was her no-holds-barred Australian temperament that was behind such songs as "We're All Gonna Die Someday", with the lyrics: "Well they can kiss my ass lord/ they can all kiss my ass/ If they want to kiss my ass, well they better do it fast/ 'Cos we're all gonna die someday." Comments abound about her ability to "bottle the human condition" in her songs, but for Chambers it's far more artless. "I write about me and that's all it is," she said unapologetically.

Growing up personally and musically in the public eye, Kasey Chambers is a work in progress in every sense. While this interview is constructed from our two discussions over a three-year period, there was a strong sense, at the time of putting it together, that with a third album, *Wayward Angel*, and more awards on their way, the full story could not yet be told.

When *The Captain* came out the record company, people and media were really playing up your background—your family, living in the Nullarbor. Were you concerned that the story of your life to date was overshadowing the music, or do you think the two are completely interlinked?

I do. Because I think it's got a lot to do with why the music is like it is. I don't think it takes away from it, and I get the feeling, too, that people are so interested in the background because they're interested in the music in the first place. So I really think it does have a lot to do with how the songs come out and how we play them, and even how they're produced.

You've been living near Sydney for some time, you've won mainstream music awards, you've been touring the world, appearing on American television, and you've had a baby. Has it been difficult to keep the same flavour in your songwriting that was there so artlessly on

The Captain? **Have you had to be more self-conscious about what the songs were about and how authentic they would sound?**
No, I haven't, but I think they do sound a lot different than on *The Captain*. I think there is a different spin on a lot of my songs now. A lot between *The Captain* and *Barricades*, but I reckon even more now between the new songs that I'm writing and *Barricades* and *The Captain*. There is quite a shift in my songwriting, but it's not on purpose. The thing is, I don't sit down and go, "Oh, I have to keep this really authentic and rootsy and it has to reflect the Nullarbor." I never do that. I think it probably entered my head at one stage, just thinking, "I have to make sure I don't lose what I was doing before." And then I thought, thinking about it actually does that, actually loses it. So I just let the songs come out, and if they sound deeper than the last album then that's okay, and if they're not deeper then that's okay as well.

How have you changed as a songwriter as a result of all these major life changes?
It's hard to pick out specifically what's different. There's probably a little bit more of a positive vibe in my songwriting, just because I'm at a different place in my life where I don't feel quite as lost as I was then. And I'm probably a little bit more confident. Not so much about what I'm doing—because I'm not always confident about that any more either—but I don't care as much now about what people think of the songs. When I was writing *The Captain*, that was through my teenage years and I thought that I was being really completely 100 per cent honest with myself and didn't care what people thought of me. But now looking back I probably cared a lot more than I let myself admit.

When you had your baby I remember you saying, "I don't know how I'm going to write now, I'm so happy!" Was that an issue for you for a while?
It was for a little while until I stopped thinking about that. I thought about that when I first met Cori, because I was over the moon—you know what it's like when you're in love and everything's great—and I thought, "I can't write country songs, they have to be sad." And then I wrote "Falling Into You" and a few others like that. I guess having a baby and having a few months' sleepless nights certainly gives you the blues. But I haven't honestly been worried about it. And luckily I have the sort of albums that have quite a bit of life in them. It wasn't until *Barricades* had been out for over a year before people really started buying it. It gives me a lot of time in between albums to write a little bit, and when there's no pressure, it's easier to write.

If you had to describe what you write about in general terms, what would you say?
I write about me and that's all it is. Because even when I'm not writing a song about a subject that's about me, it's still the way that I see it. So every song that I write is through my eyes and how I see things and feel about things, and I guess that's generally the way for all songwriters, but I think some people can put themselves in a different position sometimes. Paul Kelly, who's one of my most favourite songwriters, has the knack of writing

story songs. "Everything's Turning to White" is one of my favourite songs, and he has a way of painting this picture, telling the story, and it wasn't even about him, it was the point of view of a woman. I just can't seem to do that. Actually, I just remembered I did write one that was kind of like that, where I made out I was somebody else, but it's a bit early to tell how that song will turn out.

What's that called?
Oh, none of them have names yet, I wouldn't have a clue.

So titles don't suggest themselves easily to you?
Sometimes they do. Just lately a lot of them don't, and I don't worry about that until I have to write it down on an album cover. Some people write songs around titles, but I never seem to do that. I just let them come out when they want to and I guess one day it will scream out to me what the title's supposed to be.

Was "Not Pretty Enough" an obvious title for you?
Yeah, that was the first line I wrote of the song. But in saying that, when I wrote it I still wasn't sitting down thinking, "That's going to be the title." But then sometimes it's different because when I wrote "The Captain" I knew from that moment on that it was going to be called "The Captain". I even knew that my debut album was going to be called The Captain; I wanted that song to be the gel of the whole album, and I knew the same when I wrote "Barricades and Brickwalls". I just knew that was going to be the name of the album and I knew that that's the song that I wanted that album to revolve around as well. I'm not sure if I'm going to have one of those for the next album. I'm not thinking about that yet.

Your earliest influences included Hank Williams and Gram Parsons. Do you think there's something incongruous about being reared in the harsh Australian outback while listening to distinctly American country music?
That's all I listened to. I didn't know that there was any other music out there; I thought everybody listened to Hank and Gram. But I know we did used to listen to Slim out on the Nullarbor along with all the American stuff, and a bit of Buddy Williams and that sort of stuff, which I haven't heard much of since then.

Lucinda Williams is one of your major influences, and she's become a friend and has sung with you. How has that been?
It's been really strange. She has been an idol of mine for a long, long time. It's been really interesting meeting the person behind the music. You put these people up on this big pedestal and you really do forget that there's a person there. It's really easy to do that, because you just think of them as this musician or this songwriter, and it's been good to understand why her songs sound like they do, why she writes the way she does, why that line's in there, and why she sings the way she does. You can really learn so much from that.

How does that then reverberate in the way you work and the way you perhaps relate to your fans? Because people did listen to *The Captain* and make assumptions about you.
Yeah. Which I think is a good and a bad thing in a way. I really like the fact that people can listen to my songs—well, anybody's songs—and get something out of it that relates to what's going on in their life, and yet it might be something completely different to what I put into the song in the first place. Most of my fans don't live a life anything like mine, and yet they still relate to my songs. I think that's the beauty of music, that's fantastic, we're very lucky to be able to do that. And also sometimes I think I would just die if people really knew what some of my songs were about.

So you quite like separation between the original intent and the interpretation?
Yeah. And yet sometimes it is just one line in a song. The rest of it's really in your face and they'll be able to figure it out exactly. But then there's just one line that I think, "Ooh, I hope they don't figure that one out."

Have you found it more difficult, with your success, to keep secrets?
No, not really. I've just gotten a bit more used to it. I have moments. There are certain things in my life that I'm always going to want to keep to myself. And I actually wrote a song about that just the other day.

Which doesn't have a title yet.
No, but I'm pretty sure it's going to make the album and I'm pretty sure it will be quite obvious what one I'm talking about. But mostly I am flattered that I get to share my life with so many people and that people are willing to be interested and actually pay money. There's not a part of me that would swap it. And the bottom line is that when I sit down and write a song the last thing I'm thinking about is that I actually have to play it to anybody else ever. I just write it and afterwards I'll worry about that.

With the title track of *The Captain*, I heard and read you talk about it as being for your father, your brother or a lover. Who was it about?
It was just about a friend at the time who ended up being a boyfriend. He was this guy who was supportive of what I do, and drove me down to Sydney all the time to do interviews and come to all my gigs. But a really shy guy and always in the background, and the song is about wanting to switch roles, saying one day, "I want you to be in the foreground and I want to just hang back and be no-one for a while."

I did want to ask you what was at the heart of this line, "You're the Captain and I am no-one." It's so stark in its humility.
I think everyone feels like that; it's not just me in the job that I'm in. Sometimes you just want to hang back and not have any attention and not have your heart out on your sleeve all the time, which being a songwriter, that's really what it's all about. They're your innermost feelings. Songwriting is as honest as I'll ever get with myself and that is really scary.

Everyone likes to think that they're really honest with themselves and I don't think people really are, and I'm not either, apart from my songwriting.

What inspired "A Million Tears"?
I was at a really lost point in my life where I was not sure about what I wanted to do and whether I was enjoying where I was going or the way my life was heading. But I think writing songs like that and "This Mountain" helped me to get to the next point of, "Yeah, this is what I want to do." And I'm so glad I did come to that point where I wanted to keep going. Not that I ever thought I wouldn't, but I was just feeling a little insecure about the whole thing.

But wasn't "A Million Tears" a relationship song?
Yeah, I guess it was, but it was more just about me. The relationship part of the song wasn't ever the part that I was scared about people knowing. It was more a lot of the other stuff that was just about me.

"Not Pretty Enough" was written about being unable to get airplay on radio and of course the irony was that it got a lot of airplay on both country and rock and pop radio. Are you able to have the same relationship with that song that you had when you wrote it?
Oh sure. I think I'm able to do that with all of my songs. When I get up on stage and play it, I am back at the place where I wrote it. Most of the time. It doesn't happen like that every time, every performer will tell you, you can't get lost in the song every single time, sometimes it's just not under the right circumstances. But when I'm doing gigs and I'm up there, there's such a difference between who I am when I'm singing "The Captain" and who I am when I'm singing "Not Pretty Enough" and who I am when I'm singing "Barricades and Brickwalls". That's why my live show is my life story. Because I don't sing "The Captain" as confident as I am a person now. I get up and I sing it as if it was ten years ago.

For me the reason that you write a song is because you want to say something, and you don't always want to say it to an audience, sometimes you just want to say it to yourself, but it's something you just have to say, and that's why a song comes out. And that's what I wanted to say back then. "The Captain" was who I was, what I was feeling at that point. So I just slip back into that every time I sing that song.

You've said you went through a "serious Fred Eaglesmith phase", which was reflected on *Barricades and Brickwalls*. In what way did Eaglesmith influence you before you met him?
I think probably as a songwriter more than anything, although I love his singing and I love his live show as well. Fred has this amazing way of making me laugh and cry in the one song. And sometimes back-to-back lines do that. It's a knack that not many people have. Matthew Ryan, for instance, just makes you cry the whole time. It's all very depressing. And I love that as well. But listening to Fred, it's not only his songs, he might tell a story before his songs and it'd just be the funniest thing you ever heard, and then he starts the first line and you just want to cry. I think listening to Fred is probably the biggest emotional roller-coaster you'll ever go on in your life.

Is that emotional roller-coaster and that balance between laughter and tears something that you want to strive for in your songwriting?
I don't think about that too much in as far as comparing myself. I sit back and go, "God, I'd love to write a song like Fred can." But it's just a passing comment; I don't really ever strive for that. I just want to write the best songs that I possibly can. Again, Paul Kelly, he's such a great songwriter that I know I will never be able to write great story songs like that. I'm not going to sit at home and try and do that, 'cause that would just be a waste of time. They'll come out when they want to.

Do you need to be listening to influential artists to feel inspired?
Oh, absolutely. I've heard a lot of great songwriters actually say they don't listen to a lot of music because it clouds them a little bit. I'm the exact opposite. When I fell pregnant with Talon, I was on holidays and I didn't want to have too much to do with music. I was really enjoying being home and just thinking about being pregnant. I went out on tour as well, but I found I didn't write one song the whole time I was pregnant with Talon because I just wasn't in music mode. But now I'm listening to a lot of music at home. When I get up in the morning, instead of putting the TV on I'll put a CD on.

So what are you listening to now?
At the moment I'm listening to Dido's latest album, I love that a lot. I'm really enjoying her songwriting a lot. I still listen to Matthew Ryan a heap.

What sparked the idea for "I Still Pray"?
It was going to a Paul Kelly concert. It was at The Basement and I went to see him when he was doing his Uncle Bill stuff. It's as simple as that, I just went away and wrote that song and then thought that would be unreal if I could actually get Paul Kelly to sing on it. And he said yes.

Does religion play an important part in your creativity? Was it meant to be a religious song?
I was brought up a Seventh Day Adventist in my really early years. We're non-practising now. I wouldn't say religious as much as spiritual. I believe in a whole lot of things now, but I'm certainly not a full-on religious person.

So the idea of the baby Jesus?
To be honest, sometimes you just put in a line because it sounds good. I remember seeing or hearing an interview with John Prine, who is one of my most favourite songwriters of all time—I've always said once I go to a John Prine concert and hear him live and meet him, I can die after that—and people ask him about his songwriting, and he says, "You know, sometimes lines don't make any sense to me but they rhyme so I put them in." If John Prine can do that then sometimes it's okay. There doesn't have to be something behind every single line. It's more about a song as a whole. There will probably be certain lines that aren't as great as other ones, and certain ones that don't make any sense, but that's okay.

Your voice might well have made you a star on its own. What is it that compels you to write and perform your own songs, as opposed to perhaps just interpreting other people's songs?

It's got a lot to do with everybody having their different way to express themselves, and you need something to express yourself or eventually it's just going to blow up inside you. And my thing is songwriting. Even if I wasn't singing my own songs, if they were absolutely crap and I would never make an album—I don't know, maybe they are!—I'd still write songs. It's therapy for me, instead of sitting down with a shrink, it's my therapy.

Can you have that therapy in a co-writing situation?

I find it really hard to songwrite with people. I always have. I've written a few songs with my friend Worm, who's my roadie. And I've written a little bit with my dad. But I mostly write by myself. I just find it really hard. Because it's as honest as I get with myself, it's really hard to do that while someone's in the room, especially a total stranger. I really don't know how people do it.

We've talked about some of your best known songs. Can you name another song that's particularly dear to you?

"Southern Kind of Life". I went through a pretty emotional time when I was writing that, it was when my mum and dad broke up and we sold our house down in South Australia and that was the end of that era, and that was really a hard thing to do. I didn't realise whilst I was writing the song how much it was going to mean to me afterwards. A lot of times, nearly all the times with songwriting, I don't even remember writing a song, it's just kind of written. Then I think, wow, I must have been in such a little trance, because I can't even remember writing that line.

So you'll sit down and write a song in one session?

Most of the time that's what it's like, maybe an hour or two and then the song's finished. And then a song like "The Captain", I wrote the chorus and then wrote the verses a month later. I just ran out of time that night to finish the song, and it came back later to me. But most of the time it's in one hit and it's like I get in this little trance and the song just writes itself. I think the ones that end up on the albums are the ones that write themselves, and I wish I did sometimes, but I don't think I have that much control over it. I think the songs are out there and they're just using me to surface. Sometimes I really feel like writing a song, that's all I want to do, I've taken a day off and I just want to write a song. And I sit down and not a thing comes out. And it's just got to be because there's just no songs around in that room at that time.

You think they're in the atmosphere, not so much in the instrument?

Maybe, because most of the time I write with a guitar, but sometimes I don't.

How else do you write? On a keyboard?

No, on nothing. In my head. But I don't do that if I've got a guitar there. It's only if there's a song there and there's just no way I can get to a guitar. I'd always rather have a guitar.

Do you write down music, or do you sing it into a tape recorder?

Neither. I just hope that I remember it. I've got this theory—it's probably not true—but if it's worth remembering then I will remember it. But there have been some times when I think, "Gee, I wish I could remember that song, I thought it was really good!"

Are the lyrics and the chords or melody coming at the same time for you?

Pretty much. Most of the time I'll sit down with the guitar and play a chord and hopefully something will come out. Sometimes I have a line and I think, "Oh, I'll sit down and grab a guitar and put that line into a song or something." But again there's no pattern. It just comes out the way it wants to. Sometimes I'll write a verse and go away and think about it for a while, and come back, and sometimes I'll sit down and write the whole song right there and then. I very rarely change a song after it's finished. Once it's done, that's it. Very rarely will I change a line or a melody or anything. That's probably me just being a bit stubborn, though. 'Cause sometimes Nash has said, "Are you sure that line shouldn't be different?" And I'm like, "No! That's the way it is!" But that's the beauty of working with your brother; I can go, "No!"

Has success made you feel pressured lately when you've sat down to write songs?

When I was named Songwriter of the Year at the APRA Awards, that was a week after I'd had Talon and I hadn't written a song for the whole time I was pregnant. That night I'm thinking, "Oh my God, I hope they don't know I haven't written a song for nine months!" And you know, I went home the next day and I wrote a song. I didn't try to, I just came home and it came out. So maybe that inspired me a little. Not that winning awards and things like that change the way you make your music or write your songs. It never has for me and it doesn't ever drive me to write songs or anything like that. But maybe that one time, because I'd been out of music for such a long time, I felt a little bit more faith in myself all of a sudden.

Credits

All interviews presented herein were conducted specifically for this book by the author and none of the material has been published previously, with the following exceptions:

The interviews with Andrew Farriss, Graeham Goble and Paul Kelly were originally conducted for the Australasian Performing Right Association (APRA) and excerpts were published as short narrative profiles by the author in the APRA members' journal *APrap*. They are used with permission.

The interviews with Deborah Conway and Nick Cave were originally conducted for this book with excerpts used for profiles by the author in the *Melbourne Weekly Bayside* magazine.

PHOTOS

Photos taken or provided especially for this book are as follows:

John Elliott took the photographs of Slim Dusty and Joy McKean, Johnny Young, Ross Wilson, Rob Hirst and Jim Moginie, and Graeme Connors.

Bob King took the photographs of Harry Vanda, Billy Thorpe, Glenn Shorrock, Garth Porter, Todd Hunter and Johanna Pigott and Archie Roach.

Henry Diltz took the photographs of John Farrar and Colin Hay.

Andrew Murray took the photographs of Terry Britten and Steve Kipner.

Keith Saunders took the photograph of Martin Plaza and Greedy Smith.

Other photo credits:

Bruce Woodley photograph by Paul West.

George Young photograph © J. Albert & Son Pty Ltd and used with permission.

Graeham Goble photograph by Leanne Temme.

Tim Finn photograph by Greg Semu.

Don Walker photograph by Sandy Edwards.

Sharon O'Neill photograph by Monty Adams.

Andrew Farriss photograph by Tony Mott © APRA and used with permission.

Nick Cave photograph by Polly Borland and is used with permission.

Paul Kelly photograph by Ben Saunders © APRA and used with permission.

Deborah Conway photograph by Erin Davis © *Melbourne Weekly Bayside* and used with permission.

Daniel Jones photograph by Dallas Kowald.

Kasey Chambers photograph by Ian Jennings.

All uncredited photographs have been supplied by the songwriters or their representatives.

REFERENCES

The chief inspiration for this book was *Songwriters on Songwriting* by Paul Zollo, now in its fourth edition (Da Capo Press, 2003), the definitive anthology of interviews with American songwriters.

Paul Zollo and I in turn were inspired in part by *Written in My Soul* by Bill Flanagan (Contemporary Books, 1986), the granddaddy of Q&A books on songwriters and, sadly, long out of print. I strongly recommend *Off the Record* by Graham Nash and Manuscripts Original (Andrews McNeel, 2002), for interviews with American songwriters in book and audio form along with some magnificent reproductions of handwritten lyric sheets. A nod also to Jimmy Webb's beautiful book *Tunesmith* (Hyperion, 1998), which offers an insight into the mind and magic of one of the world's greatest contemporary pop composers. Finally, a handy little pocket book to dip in and out of is *And Then I Wrote— The Songwriter Speaks* by Tom Russell and Sylvia Tyson (Arsenal Pulp Press, 1995), full of nifty quotes.

My bible for all things Australian in music is *The Encyclopaedia of Australian Rock and Pop* by Ian McFarlane (Allen & Unwin, 1999). Of the many websites I referenced for research material, the most valuable overall were Duncan Kimball's phenomenally detailed *Milesago* at www.milesago.com and Ed Nimmervol's *Howlspace* at www.howlspace.com.au.

LYRICS
Permissions to reprint song lyrics are as follows:

ROLF HARRIS
"Come to the Sydney Opera House" by Rolf Harris © Black Swan Music (London) Ltd. For Australia and New Zealand: EMI Music Publishing Australia Pty Limited.

"Back To WA" by Rolf Harris © 1978 Black Swan Music (London) Ltd. For Australia and New Zealand: EMI Music Publishing Australia Pty Limited.

"Back Home Clancy" by Rolf Harris © 1980 EMI Music Publishing Australia Pty Limited.

"Tie Me Kangaroo Down, Sport" by Rolf Harris © 1960 EMI Music Publishing Australia Pty Limited.

"Sun-A-Rise" by Rolf Harris and Harry Butler © 1960 EMI Music Publishing Australia Pty Limited.

"Fijian Girl" by Rolf Harris © 1967 Black Swan Music (London) Ltd. For Australia and New Zealand: EMI Music Publishing Australia Pty Limited.

"Po Kare Kare Ana" (aka "Hurry Home") by Rolf Harris © 1968 Black Swan Music (London) Ltd. For Australia and New Zealand: EMI Music Publishing Australia Pty Limited.

"Yarrabangee" by Rolf Harris © Black Swan Music (London) Ltd. For Australia and New Zealand: EMI Music Publishing Australia Pty Limited.

All titles: International copyright secured. All rights reserved. Used by permission.

BRUCE WOODLEY
"Sparrow Song" words and music by Bruce Woodley © Pocketful of Tunes/Universal Music Publishing Pty Ltd. Printed with permission. All rights reserved. International copyright secured.

TERRY BRITTEN
"I'll Be Where You Are" by Glenn Shorrock and Terry Britten © 1965 EMI Music Publishing Australia Pty Limited. International copyright secured. All rights reserved. Used by permission.

JOHNNY YOUNG
"The Real Thing" by John Young © Pisces Publishing Pty Ltd. For Australia and New Zealand: Warner/Chappell Music Australia Pty Ltd.

"Part 3 Into Paper Walls" by John Young and Russell Morris © Chappell-Morris Ltd. For Australia and New Zealand: Warner/Chappell Music Australia Pty Ltd.

"Smiley" by John Young © Pisces Publishing Pty Ltd. For Australia and New Zealand: Warner/Chappell Music Australia Pty Ltd.

"Here Comes the Star" by John Young © Chappell-Morris Ltd. For Australia and New Zealand: Warner/Chappell Music Australia Pty Ltd.

All titles: International copyright secured. All rights reserved. Unauthorised reproduction is illegal.

BRIAN CADD
"Arkansas Grass" words and music by Brian Cadd and Don Mudie © MCA/Universal Music Publishing Pty Ltd. Printed with permission. All rights reserved. International copyright secured.

JIM KEAYS
"Because I Love You" by Jim Keays and Doug Ford © 1970 EMI Music Publishing Australia Pty Limited. International copyright secured. All rights reserved. Used by permission.

RUSSELL MORRIS
"Wings of an Eagle" and "Sweet Sweet Love" © Russell Morris.

MIDNIGHT OIL
"Beds Are Burning", "Tone Poem", "Read About It", "Dreamworld", "Written in the Heart" all by Midnight Oil
© Sprint Music/Sony/ATV Music Publishing.

MENTAL AS ANYTHING
"Fiona" and "Too Many Times" words and music by Andrew Smith © Syray Music Pty Ltd/Universal Music
Publishing Pty Ltd.

"Spirit Got Lost" words and music by Andrew Smith and Chris O'Doherty © Syray Music Pty Ltd/Universal Music
Publishing Pty Ltd.

All titles printed with permission. All rights reserved. International copyright secured.

JAMES REYNE
"Boys Light Up" and "Reckless" by James Reyne

"Hoochie Gucci Fiorcucci Mama" by James Reyne and David Briggs

"Indisposed" by Brad Robinson/James Reyne/William McDonough/James Robinson

All titles © Warner/Chappell Music Australia Pty Ltd. International copyright secured. All rights reserved. Unauthorised
reproduction is illegal.

NEIL FINN
"Disembodied Voices" by Neil Finn and Tim Finn

"Late In Rome", "Into Temptation" and "World Where You Live" by Neil Finn

All titles © Mushroom Music Publishing.

IVA DAVIES
"Man of Colours" by Iva Davies © 1987 EMI Songs Australia Pty Limited. International copyright secured. All rights
reserved. Used by permission.

STEVE KIPNER
"Stole" composed by Dane Deviller, Sean Hosein and Steve Kipner © Little Engine Entertainment Inc/Big Caboose
Music Inc/Sonic Graffiti/BMG Songs Inc and used with permission by BMG Music Publishing Australia Pty Ltd.

"If She Would Have Been Faithful" by Steve Kipner and Randy Goodrum © 1993 Stephen A Kipner Music. For
Australia and New Zealand: EMI Songs Australia Pty Limited. International copyright secured. All rights reserved. Used
by permission.

COLIN HAY
"Down Under" by Colin Hay and Ron Strykert © 1981 EMI Songs Australia Pty Limited. International copyright
secured. All rights reserved. Used by permission.

NICK CAVE
"Abattoir Blues" by Nick Cave and Warren Ellis

"The Ship Song" and "Love Letter" by Nick Cave

All titles © Mute Song/Mushroom Music Publishing.

CHRISTINA AMPHLETT
"Boys in Town" by Christina Amphlett, Mark McEntee and Jeremy Paul © 1980 EMI Music Publishing Australia Pty
Limited. International copyright secured. All rights reserved. Used by permission.

Song Index

P

R

S

T

Z

Index

N

Printed by BoD in Norderstedt, Germany

9 780645 785906